Republic of Images

Republic of Images

A History of French Filmmaking

Alan Williams

Harvard University Press
Cambridge, Massachusetts
London, England
1992

Library of Congress Cataloging-in-Publication Data

Williams, Alan Larson.
Republic of images : a history of French filmmaking
/ Alan Williams.
p. cm.
Includes bibliographical references and index.
ISBN 0-674-76267-3.—ISBN 0-674-76268-1 (pbk.)
1. Motion pictures—France—History. I. Title.
PN1993.5.F7W55 1992
791.43'0944—dc20
91-25877
CIP

To the Memory of My Father,
Professor Harold Williams

Acknowledgments

Many people and institutions helped make this book possible. My greatest debt is to Rutgers University, which supported the project in a variety of ways. The Department of French allowed me to teach a two-semester sequence of courses in the history of French cinema, year after year, each term with different films until I had studied virtually every relevant work available in 16 millimeter in the United States. I also received a year's sabbatical leave, a summer research grant, and a one-year fellowship with the university's Center for the Critical Analysis of Contemporary Culture.

The initial impetus to undertake this large project came from the exhibition "Rediscovering French Film" at the Museum of Modern Art in New York City. Without the benefit of the Museum's comprehensive, multi-year retrospective, I might have written this book eventually, but it would certainly have taken far longer than the eight years it finally did. For the chance to view films which I did not have the occasion to see publicly at MOMA (or through the years at the Cinémathèque Française), I wish to thank Glenn Myrent and the Cinémathèque Française, Lutz Bacher, Chris Faulkner, and Tag Gallagher. For help with both film and print research, I thank Charles Silver and the Museum of Modern Art Film Study Center.

Many people have read and commented on the text at various stages of its composition. I am grateful to Dudley Andrew, Evelyn Ehrlich, Judith Mayne, and Elizabeth King Williams for their help. Richard Abel and Claudia Gorbman were particularly generous with their time and expertise. At Harvard University Press I received just the sort of support and occasional prodding an author needs from

Lindsay Waters. I am also grateful to Anita Safran for the editing and to Annamarie McMahon for the book design. For assistance with the illustrations, many thanks to Mary Corliss and the Museum of Modern Art Film Stills Archive and to Isabelle Delsus and the Cinémathèque Française.

Contents

A Note on Film Titles and Dates   *xiv*

Introduction   *1*

Part I: French Cinema Dominates the World Market

1. The Cinema Before Cinema   7
2. An Industry Begins   27
3. Growth and Diversification   *48*

Part II: The Golden Age of the Silent Film

4. Decline and Mutation   77
5. The Mental and the Physical   *101*
6. The Commercial and the Esoteric   *126*

Part III: The Golden Age of the Sound Cinema

7. An Unexpected Upheaval   *157*
8. Art and Entertainment in the Sound Film   *184*
9. Politics, Poetics, and the Cinema   *213*

Part IV: A New Kind of Cinema

10. War and Occupation   *245*
11. Liberation—Change and Continuity   *272*
12. An Alternative Film Culture   *299*

Part V: The Nouvelle Vague *and After*

13. Fourth Wave   *327*
14. Filmmaking at the Margins   *354*
15. Winds of Change   *379*

Notes   *407*

Bibliography   *431*

Index   *441*

Illustrations

Early moving-image technology: the Phénakistoscope. Museum of Modern Art Film Stills Archive.   12

Early moving-image technology: the Zoëtrope. Museum of Modern Art Film Stills Archive.   13

Marey's photographic gun. Museum of Modern Art Film Stills Archive.   19

Louis Lumière, *Repas de bébé* (1895). Museum of Modern Art Film Stills Archive.   29

Georges Méliès, *Le Voyage dans la lune* (1902). Museum of Modern Art Film Stills Archive.   39

Théâtre Vignard (fairground cinema), 1905. La Cinémathèque Française.   50

Max Linder in *Max Wants a Divorce* (1917). Museum of Modern Art Film Stills Archive.   62

Louis Feuillade, *La Nouvelle Mission de Judex* (1917). Museum of Modern Art Film Stills Archive.   70

Abel Gance, *La Roue* (1922). Museum of Modern Art Film Stills Archive.   90

Louis Delluc, *La Femme de nulle part* (1922). Museum of Modern Art Film Stills Archive.   99

Fernand Léger's set for Marcel L'Herbier, *L'Inhumaine* (1922). Museum of Modern Art Film Stills Archive.   106

André Antoine, *L'Hirondelle et la Mésange* (1920/83). Museum of Modern Art Film Stills Archive.   118

Jean Renoir, *Nana* (1926). Museum of Modern Art Film Stills Archive.   139

Fernand Léger, *Ballet mécanique* (1924). Museum of Modern Art Film Stills Archive.   *145*

René Clair and Francis Picabia, *Entr'acte* (1924). Museum of Modern Art Film Stills Archive.   *145*

Jean Renoir, *La Chienne* (1931). Museum of Modern Art Film Stills Archive.   *167*

René Clair, *Le Million* (1931). Museum of Modern Art Film Stills Archive.   *171*

Marie Epstein and Jean Benoît-Lévy, *La Maternelle* (1933). Museum of Modern Art Film Stills Archive.   *197*

Marcel Pagnol, *Regain* (1937). Museum of Modern Art Film Stills Archive.   *205*

Jean Vigo, *Zéro de conduite* (1933). Museum of Modern Art Film Stills Archive.   *219*

Marcel Carné and Jacques Prévert, *Quai des brumes* (1938). Museum of Modern Art Film Stills Archive.   *236*

Henri-Georges Clouzot, *Le Corbeau* (1943). Museum of Modern Art Film Stills Archive.   *261*

Marcel Carné and Jacques Prévert, *Les Visiteurs du soir* (1943). Museum of Modern Art Film Stills Archive.   *266*

Claude Autant-Lara, *Le Rouge et le Noir* (1954). Museum of Modern Art Film Stills Archive.   *282*

Max Ophuls, *La Ronde* (1950). The author's collection.   *297*

René Clément, *La Bataille du rail* (1946). Museum of Modern Art Film Stills Archive.   *305*

Jacques Tati, *Les Vacances de Monsieur Hulot* (1953). Museum of Modern Art Film Stills Archive.   *319*

Claude Chabrol, *Les Cousins* (1959). Museum of Modern Art Film Stills Archive.   *346*

Francois Truffaut, *Jules et Jim* (1961). Museum of Modern Art Film Stills Archive.   *351*

Agnès Varda, *La Pointe-Courte* (1956). Museum of Modern Art Film Stills Archive.   *357*

Alain Resnais, *Toute la mémoire du monde* (1956). La Cinémathèque Française.   *371*

Jean-Luc Godard, *La Chinoise* (1967). Museum of Modern Art Film Stills Archive.   *387*

Republic of Images

Note on Film Titles and Dates

Film titles are in French, with either a literal translation in English or the most common title for Anglo-American release given when the works are first cited. Reasonably literal translations are in parentheses; when the release title in English is much different from the French original, I use a slash rather than parentheses. Film dates are generally those of the works' first commercial release, but occasionally films are dated by festival presentation screenings. When general commercial release occurred more than a year or so after completion of the work, or when the lapse of time is significant for other reasons (for example, films made during the Occupation but released afterward), both dates are given, separated by a slash.

Introduction

The last, sad sequence of Max Ophuls's *Lola Montès* (1955) depicts the final attraction of a circus act: a long line of well-dressed, well-behaved men wait their turn to kiss, for the sum of one dollar, the hand of the aging, notorious courtesan whose love life once almost ignited a revolution. To encourage the crowd, the ringmaster murmurs *Payez-vous un peu de plaisir* ("Buy yourself a little pleasure"). The group quite deliberately resembles a queue of spectators waiting to enter a cinema, perhaps to buy a little pleasure watching one of the more conventional sex-and-spectacle epics in which the film's star, Martine Carol, routinely played during the 1950s.

Unfortunately, crowds like these did not flock to see *Lola Montès;* the work became one of the decade's most notorious commercial failures. The director's son Marcel later recalled in an interview that spectators leaving the Marignan cinema on the Champs Elysées would often walk around the block, sometimes in the pouring rain, to warn prospective customers against the film. This was, to say the least, not the reception that Max Ophuls had envisioned for his film. He had set out to make a big-budget historical "biopic" of the sort that postwar French cinema had excelled in producing. Ophuls thought of himself as an enlightened entertainer who could sell a little pleasure to cinema spectators while also expressing his own world view, as well as extending and exploring the artistic resources of the cinema. In films like *La Ronde* (*Rondelay*, 1950), he had shown that he could do this with great aplomb. But in *Lola Montès* he had pushed at the limits of mainstream commercial cinema a bit too hard, and something snapped.

1

Spectacular commercial failures of works that later become cinema landmarks are often seen as highly instructive by historians and critics of the cinema, though the lessons they are said to teach may vary. It is sometimes argued that such films demonstrate the terrible limitations of commercial cinema, in particular the general unwillingness of mass audiences to accept the demands and unwelcome messages of true Art. More specifically, and programatically, the young critics and aspiring filmmakers of *Cahiers du Cinéma* interpreted the hostile reception of Ophuls's work as a symptom of the decadence fostered by the hated *cinéma de papa* which they hoped to challenge and replace. One can also argue just the opposite: that *Lola Montès* demonstrated the enormous creative freedom available during the 1950s, and indeed throughout most of the history of French filmmaking, to those with the courage to exploit it. (Ironically, in the years since its restoration and rerelease, *Lola Montès* has become one of the few French films of the 1950s that contemporary audiences outside of France can easily see in revival houses, archive showings, and even from time to time on television.)

This history of French filmmaking, like most previous efforts to survey the field, will concentrate—though not exclusively—on works that have attempted to go beyond the purely commercial goal of selling a little pleasure to cinema audiences. Some of them, like Max Ophuls's last film, departed too radically from contemporary norms and became *films maudits*, "jinxed [or more literally, damned] films." But many others achieved at least in part the elusive goal of being both commercially viable entertainments and something more: works of personal expression, social commentary, aesthetic exploration, or various combinations of these (always overlapping) aspects of artistic creation. This focus on what is sometimes too facilely labeled "art cinema" is inevitably rather narrow and particular. It leads forward talking about filmmakers rather than film spectators, which in France means speaking mainly of the bourgeoisie (from which class the overwhelming majority of leading filmmakers have come) and treating the rest of society as shadowy receivers of a set of one-way communications. Such an orientation also inevitably deemphasizes important aspects of mainstream commercial film production such as the star system, the influence of audience taste as expressed at the box office, and so on. And so this book proposes simply to tell *one* history, among many possible ones, of French filmmaking.

The works which will receive the most attention in the pages that follow are, not at all by accident, those which spectators in nonfrancophone countries are most likely to have seen, or are able to see, or would like to see. To the rest of the world French filmmaking is not the mass-oriented *cinéma de sam'di soir,* but the works of personal expression, social commentary, and aesthetic exploration which the nation's film industry has produced so consistently (compared to other national cinemas) and exported so well. Internationally, French cinema has found its market niche with this kind of work, much as the nation's other export industries (clothing, food and drink, and so on) have traditionally been oriented toward socially upscale (often luxury) goods.

To tell the story of this small but highly visible and influential sector of French cinema requires also to tell the larger story of the industry which allowed—in fact, encouraged—its creation. And so this book includes a great deal of information on French film production in general, particularly at the moments of economic and moral crisis which seem to scan its history, like a strange rhyme scheme, every decade or decade and a half. However, these sections of the book do not pretend to give a continuous or comprehensive account of the French cinema's industrial history. To do it justice would require a separate, much larger book (one desperately needed), which would find space for thorough discussions of censorship, advertising and other publicity methods, generic trends, the activities of major producers, government regulation and taxation, and so on—all topics which surface from time to time in this book but about which so much more could and should be said.

Alongside this running, if partial, study of the evolution of an industry are accounts of the lives and professional careers of particular individuals, almost always film directors. These are not, however, to be taken as evidence given in support of the Great Men (and Women) theory of history. This book adopts the somewhat old-fashioned format of multiple creative biographies for a variety of reasons. In some cases—Jean Renoir, René Clair, and Jean-Luc Godard, for example—these accounts are indeed offered as chronicle and analysis of significant individual contributions to the evolution of French filmmaking. In other instances, these biographies are meant to serve more as examples of the problems and opportunities of a particular cohort (or generation) of French filmmakers, and in so doing to continue, from a slightly different angle of approach, the history of the larger evolution of the industry. In almost all cases this method also allows all too brief glimpses of a highly significant level of historical analysis, located between the individual filmmaker and his or her historical/ industrial context: the level of *networks* of individuals. The careers of selected film artists often disclosure how relatively small and socially coherent the French film industry has generally been. The phrase "film community," which will often be employed, is not simply a manner of speaking; it is meant to remind the reader that these people knew one another, helped or hindered one another, and formed alliances of varying degrees of coherence and durability.

Finally, this is also a critical history which offers analysis and commentaries on particular films, typically grouped together by filmmaker or by network or school of filmmakers. An attempt has been made to include commentary on as many films as possible generally held to be significant—in aesthetic, social, or moral terms—by the majority of critics and historians of French cinema. This is to say that this book accepts, at least provisionally, the notion—which for many modern critics is quite problematic—of an established *canon* of significant films. However, this accepted body of landmark works has on occasion been the object of a modest amount of tinkering (almost always in order to expand, rather than contract, the canon). Wherever possible, emphasis has been placed on films which can be seen without too much difficulty—in cinemas, on videocassette, or in public screenings at major archives throughout the world.

I

French Cinema Dominates the World Market

◪ 1 ◪

The Cinema Before Cinema

The nineteenth century, in France as elsewhere in the Western world, witnessed a striking increase in visual awareness. In several areas of cultural activity, appeals to vision (and to a lesser extent to the other senses) achieved something approaching parity with spoken and written language. This release and reevaluation of the sensory may be observed in all media, beginning sometime around the Revolution.[1] Two specific areas, both previously dominated by the Word, were the theatre and prose fiction. Classical theatre had been a drama of speech. Racine's plays, for example, did not depict events so much as talk about them. In the last act of *Phèdre*, the death of Hippolyte is recounted by Théramène, who enters the generic neutral Racinian decor and describes what has happened to those assembled on stage and to the audience. This description is by itself, of course, a kind of event, but not in as immediate a way as is the erratic progress of an orphan girl being pursued through a stage forest by a pack of baying, ravenous hounds—which is the sort of thing common enough on the nineteenth century stage in the postrevolutionary genre of melodrama.

Classical theatre staged its minimal actions in minimal stage settings, ideally unchanging throughout an entire play, whereas the nineteenth century popular stage gloried in extravagant and numerous sets. The other senses were not neglected either: melodrama included abundant music (often substituting for speech), striking sound effects, and even the occasional attempt at the *mise en scène* of smells. Classical theatre was orderly, hierarchical, and discreet; melodrama and related genres like the mime play were baroque, egalitar-

7

ian, and exhibitionistic, like the new audiences they appealed to. For this was, not coincidentally, the beginning of the mass marketing of spectacle, of which the cinema was to be one of the most notable later developments.

Vision and the other senses penetrated also to the very citadel of the verbal: the novel. In prerevolutionary works like *La Princesse de Clèves*, it sufficed to identify a character by social position and general psychological state, or a room by a phrase such as "richly appointed" or "unadorned." Suddenly, with Honoré de Balzac and his contemporaries, characters get complexions, eye color, shapes of noses; rooms get inventoried down to the type and texture of curtains. Balzac was fully aware of these innovations, arguing that it was not possible "to depict modern society by the methods of seventeenth- and eighteenth-century literature. I think pictures, images, descriptions, the use of dramatic elements of dialogue are indispensable to modern writers. Let us admit frankly that the form of [eighteenth century novels] is tiring and that there is something infertile in the piling up of events and ideas."[2] This distinction is revealing: according to Balzac, earlier novels suffered from *too much narrative*, which made them "infertile." His own writing, by implication, is more "living," capable of growth and reproduction, because of its sensory qualities.

Possibly the increasing density and diversity of the modern city accounted in part for such developments. This was the opinion of Walter Benjamin, who considered Paris, as much for its material as for its intellectual qualities, the "capital of the nineteenth century." In any event, Paris was the site of the exemplary visual consumer experience of the early modern period, the Diorama. Beginning in 1822, patrons of this attraction could enter a small theatre just off the so-called "Boulevard of Crime" and see "The Earthquake at Lima," "The Goldau Valley Before and After the Catastrophe [a huge landslide]," or the celebrated "Midnight Mass at St.-Etienne-du-Mont." These shows were produced by means borrowed largely from the melodrama; they made ample use of transparent fabrics printed on both sides (where a change of lighting produced a proto-"dissolve"), as well as sound effects, pyrotechnics, small moving models, multi-plane coordinated movement, and so on.

Many works on cinema history begin by citing the Diorama and its creator, Louis-Jacques-Mandé Daguerre, who (with the help of his partner) is said to have "invented" it. The truth is that they did something both less and more important. Like the cinema which it seems to foreshadow, the diorama was not a real invention. It was the assembly, perfection, and coordination of already existing techniques, some of which were once invented, but not, as it happens, by Daguerre. His originality is to be found in the domain of what Americans call "tinkering," and what the French, most prominently since Claude Lévi-Strauss, call *bricolage:* the bringing together of bits and pieces of already known techniques to produce a new capability. By contrast, invention means the creation of a new sort of productive process. To cite one example, the phonograph is a true nineteenth century invention. No apparatus like it existed as a model for its initial conception. The cinema, as we will see, was almost pure *bricolage*, though it did incorporate several inventions in the course of its elaboration.

But if Daguerre was not, in the strict sense of the word, an inventor, he was an inspired entrepreneur of the mechanically reproduced spectacle. In its modest way the Diorama was already a visual mass medium, in that it could offer the very same show to successive audiences. Though it could not travel in space, the Diorama show could deploy itself in time, via its crucial capability of mechanical replication of the spectacle. Because it was mechanically reproducible, the attraction had predictable, limited expenses, and these, after the initial investment, did not increase in proportion to the number of people who paid to consume it. A good Diorama show, capable of attracting large audiences, was quite a gold mine when compared to the artisanal spectacles with which it competed, such as theatre. But the age of mechanical reproduction was at hand, and Daguerre had the good commercial sense to move on to other projects before his creation was overwhelmed by the flood of competing mechanical or partly mechanical spectacles that were to characterize the mid to late nineteenth century—including the phonograph, do-it-yourself X-rays, Reynaud's Théâtre Optique, and the cinema.

The cinema, as *bricolage*, combined three nineteenth century technologies that had existed for well over fifty years as separate developments. These were the analysis of movement, the optical synthesis of movement, and photography. Once all three technologies were widely diffused, cinema was conceivable as a goal to almost anyone in the educated upper-middle classes, which explains why so many people in virtually all Western countries tried to "invent" the medium so desperately, long before the last necessary ingredient, flexible celluloid for film stock, was available. Photography came first. In 1826, or perhaps earlier, Joseph-Nicéphore Niepce succeeded in fixing on a metal plate an image of the view from a window of his house in Saint-Loup de Varenne, a small village in Burgundy. Like so many other inventors and *bricoleurs* of the day, Niepce, a retired army officer and veteran of the Napoleonic wars, tried his hand at many different problems before having one inspired episode of discovery. He came to photography via lithography, which he was attempting to improve technically and to liberate from the troublesome and costly intervention of the graphic artist. (Niepce could not draw.) His first photographs required exposures of many hours, and shadows cast by the moving sun made them blurred and confusing.

This was as far as Niepce got with the process, but it was enough to arouse the persistent interest of Daguerre, who wrote repeatedly to the inventor suggesting scientific collaboration and professional partnership. Niepce eventually agreed, apparently because he could not reduce his exposure times, and also perhaps because of his visit to the Diorama, with which he pronounced himself much impressed: "These representations are so real, even in their smallest detail, that one believes that he actually sees rural and primeval nature . . . The illusion is so great that one attempts to leave one's box in order to wander out into the open and climb to the summit of the mountain."[3] In 1829 the two men signed a partnership agreement and Daguerre learned the secret of what Niepce called heliography. Niepce's trust in Daguerre's tinkering abilities and commercial acumen was to prove well founded. Though the first heliographer died in 1833, before the perfection of his process, his heirs were to profit handsomely from it—though not, to be sure, as much as Daguerre.

Daguerre modestly baptized his improved process the Daguerréotype. With an exposure of four to five minutes, a photographic image could be fixed on a copper plate, which served also to display the rendered, positive image. Thus the Daguerréotype was not itself mechanically reproducible, though it could be traced and then reproduced via lithography, with an inevitable loss of shading and detail. The first Daguerréotype probably dates from 1837. Daguerre and Isidore Niepce, son of the original inventor, attempted to market the process by subscription, but sales were minimal. In a stunning commercial coup, Daguerre managed to sell the process to the French government, as an investment in the public interest. Isidore Niepce received an annuity of 4000 francs per year and Daguerre one of

6000 francs. (Daguerre's extra benefits were for, of all things, disclosure of the "secrets" of the Diorama.) The government made the process public in August 1839, and the Daguerréotype rush was on.

In this story, as elsewhere in the development of cinema, emphasis should be placed on entrepreneurial ability at least as much as on technical acumen. Although Daguerre developed the photographic process which dominated European society for several decades, he was in no way a lonely pioneer. In the late 1830s many other individuals published or exhibited the results of similar photochemical processes. Hippolyte Bayard demonstrated a viable paper-positive process in Paris one full month before the public disclosure of the Daguerre method. Earlier in the same year in England, William Henry Fox Talbot had described his Calotype. Both of these processes, by creating separate positive and negative images, had the enormous technical and commercial advantage of being mechanically reproducible: one negative could be used to produce an almost limitless number of identical positive images. Nonetheless both were swept away, at least for the moment, by the momentum of the Daguerréotype. In the history of technology, being first or being best is not the essential secret for staying in the mainstream of development. What counts is the ability to disseminate a process and make it stick. France is the site of so many important developments in the prehistory of the cinema not (or not solely) because of a national aptitude for technological innovation, but thanks to the remarkable ability of so many of its inventors/entrepreneurs/showmen, such as Daguerre, to get a running start on the competition.

Like photography, the optical synthesis of motion was widely essayed in the 1820s and 1830s. The major stimulus for this was Peter Mark Roget's paper on the effects of stroboscopic viewing on the perception of objects in motion. Many people had observed the illusion of stasis that can occur when a moving wheel is seen, for example, through the openings in a fence, but Roget was the first to explain the phenomenon. His explanation led the Belgian Joseph Plateau to extensive study of the persistence of visual impressions, on which he wrote a doctoral dissertation (in French) for the University of Liège in 1829. Three years later, inspired by a discovery of the English physicist Faraday, Plateau constructed the first apparatus for the synthesis of motion. He called his device, a rotating slotted disc with a series of

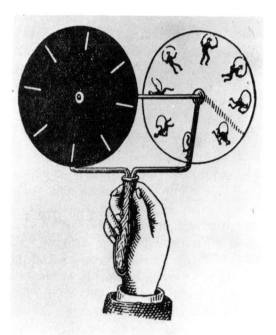

Phénakistiscope de Plateau.

Early moving-image technology was subject to constant *bricolage*, both great and small. In this later version of the Phénakistoscope, a second disk has made the use of a mirror unnecessary.

drawings on its back, the Phénakistoscope. When observed in a mirror, through its own rotating slots, the device intermittently presented successive phases of a simple motion, which was perceived as continuous. At roughly the same time (the winter of 1832–33), the same discovery was made by the Viennese professor of geometry Simon Stampfer.

About a year later, several *bricoleurs* in England and on the Continent developed the mirrorless, cylindrical variant on the device known as the Zoëtrope. If Plateau's device was a true invention, the creation of a new type of productive capability, the more serviceable Zoëtrope was definitely not. It redeployed the elements of the Phénakistoscope to use them to better advantage (elimination of the mirror, suitability to group viewing) and was thus a clear, though minor, example of *bricolage*. Simple as they were, these devices for motion synthesis represented a striking intellectual accomplishment, perhaps best attributed as much to the times as to particular individuals. Mate-

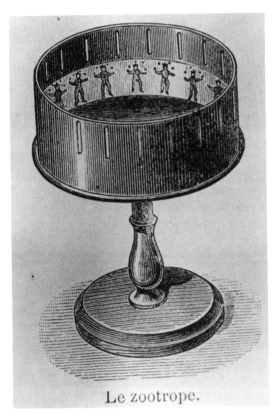

Le zootrope.

The Zoëtrope redeploys the elements of the original Phénakistoscope to eliminate the need for a mirror and to produce a new capability: group viewing.

rially, anyone could have come up with them from the Greeks on, and perhaps even earlier. But apparently they were not *thinkable* until the early nineteenth century. From the 1830s on, Europeans, and particularly the French, were captivated by these simple toys. Twenty years after Plateau's first demonstration of the Phénakistoscope, Charles Baudelaire described it carefully and precisely in his essay "Morale du joujou" ("Morality of the Toy"), in which he called it a "philosophical plaything" *(joujou philosophique)*.

Scientists often make good inventors but bad *bricoleurs*. Once he had given adequate form to his Phénakistoscope to make it demonstrate forcefully the persistence of visual impressions, Plateau seems to have been little troubled by the practical limitations of his philosophical toy. These were twofold: first, only a limited number of drawings would fit on a disc of manageable size, and so only short motions could be synthesized; second, the slits only illuminated the figures for a brief period, and thus the perceived image was dim and not completely stable. When Plateau, Faraday, Stampfer, and their counterparts had moved on to other scientific pastures, these difficulties attracted the attention of Emile Reynaud, "science professor" of the night school of the municipality of Puy-en-Velay, in South Central France.

Reynaud reminds one of Niepce: an autodidact from an obscure provincial town, interested in many fields, a born *bricoleur*. He first improved the luminescence and stability of synthesized motion by combining the mirror essential to the viewing of the Phénakistoscope with the horizontal, cylindrical form of the Zoëtrope. By virtue of small rotating mirrors, one facing each image, Reynaud's Praxinoscope allowed each image to remain before the eye until replaced by the next one. This allowed vastly brighter images; in fact it allowed for them to be projected on a screen. The Praxinoscope was patented in 1877, and the following year Reynaud gave up night school to move to Paris to manufacture and market his device. He won an honorable mention at the exposition of 1878. Articles were written. Orders flowed in.

In his patent application Reynaud had foreseen the possibility of throwing his animated images on a screen, but it was only in 1880 that he created the Projecting Praxinoscope. The problem of the brevity of the image series remained, however. This occupied Reynaud from 1880 on, and in 1888 he demonstrated his Théâtre Optique, or Optical Theatre. This was a sort of Praxinoscope in which the images, instead of being fixed to the inner surface of the apparatus, were assembled in a long strip which wrapped around the rotating drum. There was a feed reel and a takeup reel, and the images were transparent rather than opaque as in the Praxinoscope. Reynaud began work on this machine almost a decade before the general availability of strips of flexible celluloid, which explains why his bands of images had to be assembled by hand and fitted into a large holes on a leather belt. Registration was assured by small holes in the leather, which meshed with protruding teeth on the rotating drum. Georges Sadoul has persuasively argued that the strong analogy this arrangement suggests with the bicycle wheel and chain is far from coincidental.[4] Indeed, the "safety bicycle" was perfected by English inventors and manufacturers in the 1880s and swept the Continent in the very years that Reynaud was perfecting his machine. This was in effect the most concentrated form of *bricolage:* the direct adaptation of a device from one field to solve a technical problem in another.

In 1892 Reynaud was ready for the public, and he signed a contract with the Musée Grévin, the most celebrated wax museum in Paris. Such institutions during the period offered a potpourri of popular visual entertainments: magic shows, pantomimes, marionettes, and—just a few years later—the cinema. For 500 francs per month plus 10 percent of the museum's revenue from its Cabinet Fantastique, Reynaud performed between five and twelve shows per day and agreed not to sell or exhibit his spectacle anywhere else in France. He began with three different "films," *Poor Pierrot, A Good Glass,* and *The Clown and His Dogs.* These were animated pantomimes of six to fifteen minutes in length—which could vary according to the performance. The first two were also fairly elaborate narratives. The complete show lasted roughly thirty minutes and must have attracted good crowds, because the management kept it running almost continuously, despite serious technical problems and Reynaud's chronic lateness in creating new "films." It lasted for eight years, during the last five of which it competed directly with the "real" cinema.

This attraction was quite prominent at the very time of the emergence of the cinema. The Musée Grévin was covered in both the popular press and in trade publications, and the success of the Reynaud presentations cannot have been lost on aspiring entrepreneurs of the spectacle. On a small but significant scale Reynaud established that the Parisian public would pay to see mechanized images of the same sort of show they could see just down the street with live players. He also fixed or anticipated many features of early cinema: the length of the show (roughly 30 minutes), and of its individual units (6 to 15 minutes); the mixture of narrative modes and straight performance; and the addition of music, in the form of an original score by one Gaston Paulin. This last feature gave rise to the world's first proto-cinematic merchandising "tie-in," in the form of sheet music sold in the lobby for the sum of two francs.

Given the way the Théâtre Optique showed the potential and reaped the profits of projected, synthesized movement, and given that animated cartoons are normally thought of as "cinema" in an extended sense, it might be tempting to date the beginning of French film in 1892 with Reynaud, rather than in 1895 as is normally done. But compared with the true cinema, the spectacle at the Musée

Grévin was *incompletely mechanized:* Reynaud gave performances rather than mere projections. He ran his bands at varying speeds, frequently stopping on one image, sometimes reversing and then repeating motions (often for comic effect).[5] This was the great difference between the Théâtre Optique and the cinema that was to follow, not the use of drawings. In fact the spectacle's later bands, such as *William Tell* (1896), were composed of photographs rather than drawings, but they were still intricate, repetitive performances of a relatively small number of images. Reynaud had marked a place for the cinema in the highly competitive business of French popular entertainments, but he did not give birth to the new medium. The continuing line of development lay elsewhere.

▧ If the nineteenth century marked a kind of cultural birth or rebirth of vision, one favorite object of society's collective gaze was the phenomenon of movement. One reason for this, no doubt, was the recent development of the sewing machine, the mechanical loom, and many other devices that could perform simple actions very quickly. The rhythm of life in society had begun inexorably to accelerate. From Plateau through Reynaud, one line of scientific and mechanical research lay in the optical synthesis of motion. But one can only synthesize what has first been analyzed, and men and women of the period were astonished to discover how very little they actually knew about the way things moved. Animal and human motions, in particular, were the subject of lively controversy. For centuries painters, for example, had depicted horses in gallop as having fore and hind limbs fully extended in opposite directions, all off the ground at the same time. So culturally entrenched was this pose that one encounters it to this day in some animated cartoons. But around the middle of the century, astute observers began to question received wisdom on the subject. Probably the first to publish a correct description of equestrian motion was a Lieutenant L. Wachter, of the Seventh Cavalry Regiment of the French army. Using only his eyes, Wachter managed to discern that at no time did the horse in gallop assume the pose depicted in paintings. Wachter published his analysis in 1862 in a book called *Aperçus équestres* ("Equestrian Perceptions"). To prove that his strange looking drawings did indeed accurately represent the horse in motion, he "submitted [them] to the test of the Phénakistoscope," as he stated in the legend of the disk he produced for that apparatus. Fifteen years before the much better known photographs of Eadweard Muybridge, the secret of the horse's movement had been discovered and also represented by the optical synthesis of apparent motion.[6]

A few years after the lieutenant wrote, a much less obscure figure, Etienne-Jules Marey, became interested in the same problem. Marey was born in Beaune, a medium-sized town in Burgundy, but like so many ambitious provincials he was drawn to Paris. He became a doctor and in the 1860s he worked in the capital's municipal hospitals. His specialty was the circulation of the blood, through which he became interested in the graphic recording of motion. Having developed an apparatus for the mechanical recording of the pulse (which was rendered graphically by pen tracings on a moving paper strip), he sought other areas which his machine could be used to investigate. Almost inevitably he was led in 1867 to the problem of the horse in motion, and by 1870 he had established the exact movements of the trot and the gallop. Graphic renderings of his research, which like that of Lieutenant Wachter involved no photography at this point, were published shortly thereafter.

Whether Marey knew Wachter's work or not—and it seems more likely that he did—his own studies represented a scientific if not graphic advance, since his analysis was based on more than mere eyesight. However Marey's work, like Wachter's, resulted in images that seemed bizarre and incorrect to most contemporary eyes. Horse fanciers, of which there were an astonishing number among the very wealthy, took notice but were not necessarily convinced. These were mere drawings, they thought, dependent on the intervention of an artist. It was presumably either Wachter's work or Marey's, or both, that aroused the attention of horse lover and man of leisure Leland Stanford, in the state of California, U.S.A. In his book *La Chronophotographie* (1899) Marey says definitely that Stanford received drawings based on his experiments in the early 1870s, but he does not say how he knows this. (Nor does he mention Lieutenant Wachter. The fight over who "invented cinema" was already on, and Marey was never one given to self-effacement.)

Stanford, who had many contacts in France, chose at this point to become interested in the horse in motion and to engage the services of the noted English photographer Eadweard Muybridge.[7] By 1878 Muybridge had produced several photographic analyses of the horse in motion, and these quickly reached Europe and created a journalistic and intellectual sensation. Muybridge's photographic technique, which confirmed Wachter and Marey's results, convinced the skeptics and aroused great popular interest in motion study. In 1881 the English photographer visited Europe and became the sensation of the season in Parisian artistic and intellectual circles. The enormous success of this visit was far from lost on Marey, who hosted a soirée for Muybridge in his new home in the fashionable Trocadero district. In the carefully orchestrated press coverage of this event, the French scientist tactfully conveyed his opinion that Muybridge had only confirmed Marey's own studies and not established much that was really new.

Nevertheless, after Muybridge left Paris Marey turned with almost indecent haste to the photographic study of motion, abandoning his earlier, mechanical recording techniques. The French scientist was proud and ambitious, and he probably looked with resentment on the meteoric success of an upstart from the Wild West. In 1881 he set out to beat Muybridge at his own game, and in so doing he unwittingly began the chain of developments that would culminate in the Lumière Cinématographe. Marey had pointed out that Muybridge's photos were of little direct use to the study of anatomy and physiology because there was no precise common frame of reference in them. The Englishman's studies were done with a battery of separate cameras activated in quick succession. And so there was no way to measure precisely, say, the exact distance moved by a bird's wing from one image to the next. The only certain remedy for this problem was to record all images through a single, fixed lens. Marey had no need to invent such a technology, however, since he could adapt an existing machine to his needs. The astronomer Pierre-Jules-César Janssen had developed a *fusil photographique,* or "photographic gun," to study eclipses and other celestial phenomena; this was a camera in which the photographic plate was in the form of a revolving disc, which moved between exposures in the same manner as did the chambers of a revolver.

The *fusil photographique* is a lovely example of extended *bricolage.* Janssen had adapted the mechanism of the revolver to the needs of astronomical photography. Marey kept the basic idea and form of the device while adapting it to the additional problem of performing its work very rapidly. He developed a shutter that could provide regularly spaced exposures up to twelve times per second, and an intermittent motion device to turn the sensitized disc in precise synchronization. But the number of photographs he could take was limited

Marey's *fusil photographique* offers a stunningly clear example of *bricolage*—in this case of the photographic camera and a gun with revolving ammunition chamber.

by the size of the photographic plate, which had to be small enough so that its intermittent motion would not cause excessive vibration of the apparatus. In effect, Marey was limited to series of twelve images or so, far too few for most of the motions he wished to study. In 1888 he hit upon what today seems the obvious solution. Instead of arranging his images in a circle on a round plate, he took them sequentially on a flexible, continuous strip of sensitized paper. This idea was also a bit of *bricolage:* in 1885 George Eastman had launched flexible roll film for amateur still photography. Marey combined his photographic gun with George Eastman's Kodak camera, and thus was born the world's first movie camera, the Chronophotographe.

But if Marey had concocted the first camera in the history of cinema, there was one final step he could not or would not take, to assure that his motion studies could be projected on a screen. The problem was that the Chronophotographe had no system for exact registration of images, and so they could not be projected to give the effect of apparent motion because they could not be made to match up precisely on the screen. The irony is that Emile Reynaud had solved this very problem in the same year of 1888 in his Théâtre Optique. Had Reynaud and Marey somehow gotten together, the cinema would not have had to leave France for this crucial stage of its development.

▧ The American Thomas Alva Edison, the only figure in these developments who could give the French pioneers a run for their

money in both tinkering and in self-publicizing, saw a lecture-perfor-
mance by Eadweard Muybridge in the same year of 1888. He was
inspired by the projected animated drawings to conceive a visual
equivalent of his phonograph. Edison was quite literal in this idea,
imagining microscopic images arranged in a spiral on a moving cylinder—the bringing together of the early phonograph with the optical synthesis of motion. Edison often contented himself with having
ideas like this one (one is tempted to call them urges, or impulses) and
assigning the actual work to subordinates, in this case his assistant
W. K. L. Dickson. A year passed with little progress on the project,
and Edison went to Paris to attend the World's Fair. There he met
Marey, who showed him prints from his Chronophotographe. Upon
returning to the United States, Edison immediately filed a "caveat"
with the patent office in which he proposed a new apparatus based
on Marey's technique. Dickson apparently continued to work on the
cylinder idea, however, and it was two years before Marey's device
became the basis for a new American "invention." There is nothing
unfair or particularly unscrupulous in Edison's appropriation of the
French apparatus, particularly since his work entailed several important technical advances. Marey was interested primarily in the analysis
of motion, while Edison was setting out to mass market its reproduction. What one may find a bit distasteful, however, are Edison and
Dickson's sustained later efforts to deny the French scientist's crucial
input in the development of their device.[8]

In 1891 Edison unveiled the Kinetoscope, the first device in which
the optical synthesis of photographically analyzed movement was
accomplished for a sustained period of time. The three technologies
had finally come together. Edison solved Marey's registration problem
by punching holes in his film material, which was no longer paper as
it had been for Marey, but flexible celluloid. His camera was based on
Marey's, but with better registration and smoother intermittent movement of the film strip. The Kinetoscope, Edison's exhibition device,
on the other hand, was a throwback to Plateau's Phénakistoscope: the
images were viewed through a rotating slotted disc. For this reason
they were not very bright and could not be projected. This apparently
did not seem an important limitation to Edison, who made no effort
to correct it until competition from the Lumières and others began to
eat into his profits.

Because of material and organizational difficulties in fabricating the
machines, commercial exploitation of the Kinetoscope did not begin

until April 1894 in New York City, and later that summer in Europe. At this point, cinema history migrated, as it were, back across the Atlantic. Presumably because he was aware of his debt to Marey, who had obtained a patent for his Chronophotographe, Edison did not apply for European patent protection for the Kinetoscope, and so its development and elaboration there were unchecked by the American inventor's notorious techniques of legal and illegal harassment of his competition. From the day the first Kinetoscopes appeared in London, and shortly thereafter in Paris, a race began among entrepreneurs and *bricoleurs* to exploit and develop the new technology. This was all the more tempting a prospect because Edison's agents were selling Kinetoscopes and films for them at astonishingly high prices, given the relative simplicity of the machines and the low cost of the materials for their construction. The first unauthorized Kinetoscopes appeared in England, manufactured by Robert W. Paul. Though his agents strongly urged taking action against this piracy, Edison did nothing, effectively renouncing the European market.

In France the Kinetoscope attracted the attention of Antoine Lumière, who with his two sons operated a flourishing enterprise making photographic plates in the city of Lyon. Antoine Lumière had begun his working life as a sign painter in the Franche Comté, that mountainous part of Eastern Central France where Stendhal set *The Red and the Black*. In his early twenties he taught himself photography and set up business as a "portraitist" in Besançon. The business prospered, probably more because of Lumière's gregariousness than his business sense. In the 1870s he moved to Lyon, then as now France's second important commercial and industrial center after Paris, where he continued portrait work and later set up a factory for the production of the new "dry" photographic plates then coming into widespread use. By all acounts, Antoine Lumière was better at having ideas than at implementing them, and the factory nearly went bankrupt. It was saved by the concerted efforts of his two sons, Louis and Auguste. Their father was discreetly "kicked upstairs" in the business and given little responsibility for its day to day operation.

It was Lumière *père,* however, who had the commercial vision of the family, and he saw great potential in animated photographic images. In 1893, well before the success of the Kinetoscope, he was one of a number of entrepreneurs who considered backing Georges Demenÿ's Phonoscope, a motion synthesis device adapted from Marey's work. As it turned out, it was the future cinema tycoon Léon Gaumont who bought the rights to Demenÿ's device, not Antoine Lumière, probably because of opposition from his sons. Louis and Auguste Lumière may have resisted the charms of the Phonoscope (and rightly so, given the subsequent history of cinema technology), but they did recognize a good business opportunity in moving images when it finally came knocking at their father's door. Eugène Molsson, chief mechanic at the Lyon photographic works, recalled the decisive event: "It was in Summer 1894. Papa Lumière entered my office where I was with Louis and took out of his pocket a bit of a Kinetoscope film that he had gotten from Edison's agents and said to Louis: 'This is what you should make, because Edison sells it at insane prices and his representatives are looking to make them here in France to have a better deal.'"[9] To make films for the Kinetoscope, however, the Lumières needed a camera. It was Auguste who first tried his hand at this task, patterning his work after Marey's (which was all the more familiar since the family was the celebrated scientist's supplier of photographic plates). His efforts led nowhere, and so his brother took on the job.

Louis Lumière was not quite thirty years old when his father put him on the track of cinema. It was he who had developed, as a boy of sixteen, the dry-plate process that made the family fortune. Louis seems somewhat out of place in the confident, self-satisfied world of the nineteenth century bourgeoisie. Psychologically, the figure he most ressembles in this story is Edison's assistant W. K. L. Dickson. Both men were probably what doctors of the day called "neurasthenic." The development of Edison's Kinetoscope was once deferred because of Dickson's "nervous breakdown"; throughout his life Louis Lumière's projects were frequently interrupted by terrible headaches, which had been so severe when he was a teenager that he had to cut short a very promising academic career. Louis was the real technical genius of the Lumière organization, just as Dickson was the linchpin of Edison's Kinetoscope operation. Unlike Dickson, Louis Lumière did eventually get credit in his lifetime for what he did in cinema, though not before having patented everything in both his and his brother's name. The Lumières were a tightly knit group, probably too much so by modern standards. Louis and his brother Auguste not only shared scientific credits but they also married two sisters, the daughters of a close friend of their father. Antoine Lumière built for the two households an enclosed, symmetrical duplex mansion which one might take as a symbol of the family structure, with a broad central staircase from the common rooms below branching in two at upper levels, leading to mirror-image private apartments.[10]

Along with headaches, Louis Lumière suffered from chronic insomnia. As his brother recalled:

> One morning, near the end of 1894, I entered the room of my brother who, a bit sick, had had to stay in bed. He told me that not being able to sleep he had, in the calm of the night, specified the conditions that had to be met to attain our desired goal and had imagined a mechanism capable of satisfying them. It consisted, he explained, of a set of movable claws that was given an intermittent movement by a mechanism analogous to that of the sewing machine. The claws entered, at the top of their trajectory, into perforations at the side of the film, then carried the image along, withdrawing at the bottom of their course, leaving the film immobile during their return in the opposite direction. This was a revelation, and I immediately understood that I had to abandon the vague solution that I had been working on. My brother, in one night, had just invented the Cinématographe.[11]

Louis had realized that his principal difficulty was the intermittent motion required for the film strip. Marey and Demenÿ had already developed one such system (as he must have been aware), and so—though he did not know its mechanism—had W. K. L. Dickson. But intermittent motion was also an essential ingredient of the industrial revolution's flagship industry, textiles and clothing manufacture. Once he had thought of it, all Lumière really had to do was to combine two things: the fits-and-starts motion imparted to fabric in the sewing machine, and the sprocket drive of the Kinetoscope. (Without sprocket holes, precise registration is impossible. This is literally the only significant contribution by Edison/Dickson to the cinema in France, but it was crucial.) The Cinématographe is like a new recipe using known ingredients; it is not to be compared with a newly discovered food source. Though patentable, it was not an invention in any strict sense but one of the nineteenth century's most genial bits of *bricolage*.

Louis Lumière returned to technical and material fundamentals when he devised the Cinématographe. His complete ignorance of Dickson and Edison's camera was, ironically, enormously helpful in the creation of a more useful machine, for the American device was heavy and bulky, like its companion Kinetoscope. Edison and his assistant worked in the context of the former's large, integrated industrial enterprise, which was geared to mass production and sales. Their cinema apparatus was designed along the lines of heavy industrial equipment, for centralized production and exhibition. The smaller French company served a relatively limited clientele of amateur and professional photographers. Louis Lumière designed his device on the model of the portable still cameras which his clients utilized. It was almost a hundred times lighter than the Edison machines, and mechanically simpler. Because of his bias toward simplicity and ease of operation, Lumière took an enormously significant, yet in retrospect obvious, step: he made his machine "reversible," capable not only of taking cinematographic views, but of projecting them as well. (The same machine also served as a contact printer, for making positive prints from the original negatives.) He thus took the final steps for the realization of cinema in the technical sense which the word now has: photographic images on long celluloid strips, in apparent motion, projected upon a screen. His apparatus was also simple and reliable enough to enable his company to be the pioneers of cinema in the *commercial* sense: to project these images before a paying public.

The cinema may have been invented in one night, but that was not the hard thing. In fact, all across the world many others invented it or something very similar at the same time. The trick was to develop the invention so that it was mechanically reliable, and then to publicize and market it. The Lumières were in a privileged position to do both things and quickly, whereas most of their potential competitors were not. Many competing machines by smaller entrepreneurs would be swept away before the triumphant progress of the Cinématographe. Louis immediately gave his design to his head mechanic, Moisson, who built a prototype. While he supervised the elaboration and debugging of this apparatus, Lumière began to concern himself with film stock. He ordered a shipment of celluloid from a New York manufacturer, meanwhile performing tests on his machine using perforated bands of paper. When the celluloid arrived, he had it coated with emulsion in the Lyon factory, but the results were not satisfactory. He asked the Parisian film manufacturer Planchon to study the problem. By late 1895 Planchon had succeeded well enough that he agreed to move his factory to Lyon and to incorporate and expand with capital from the Lumières and their associates (200,000 francs, at a time when a working class household might consider itself lucky to have 1,500 francs a year to live on). At the same time, Louis Lumière and a leading French maker of precision machinery, Jules Carpentier, settled on a reworked version of the apparatus suitable for manufacture. Lumière ordered immediate production of two hundred machines.

Only a large industrial organization could have developed the Ciné- matographe with such rapidity, from summer 1894 (inception of the project) to December 1895 (commercial exploitation). The Lumières had sufficient capital as well as business connections and in-house technical expertise in several interrelated fields. They were well rewarded for their efforts: Louis Lumière later estimated that they made a profit of three million francs on the whole operation. But to succeed, the Cinématographe not only had to come into existence quickly enough to beat the competition, but also to make a strong public impression. And so while technical and logistical problems were being worked out, the apparatus went on the road to be tested and to get some advance publicity. Between its first public demonstration in Paris on March 22, 1895 (at the Society for the Encouragement of National Industry), and the beginning of commercial exploitation on December 28 of that year, the machine went on what could be characterized as the popular science equivalent of today's "talk show" circuit: photographic congresses in Lyon and Brussels, a public demonstration for the magazine *La Revue Générale des Sciences*, conferences of learned societies. The Cinématographe was in this way first publicized and tested not as a simple entertainment but as a "wonder of science," of which there were many in the period. But the machine's scientific status, as several contemporary commentators pointed out, was not at all certain.[12] It was probably for this reason that the Cinématographe made its debut as the second half of a technological double bill, the first part being devoted to Louis Lumière's continuing experiments in color photography.

Lumière's work on color was little advanced in 1895 (he had temporarily abandoned it the year before to follow his father's suggestion about the Kinetoscope films), but the projection of color slides on the same screen as the subsequent moving images gave scientific respectability to the latter while placing it squarely within a larger, implied project of "reproducing reality." Thus the cinema's first target audiences were presumed to be interested in the degree of realism of its images, and not primarily in the images themselves. In choosing to publicize their machine as a wonder of science, the Lumières had little choice but to produce what today we would call documentary films. And so they were, but what was documented was the work of the apparatus itself.

The publicity/try-out campaign was a success, and soon the Cinématographe could stand on its own. A reporter for *Le Moniteur de la Photographie* commented on the June 10 presentation at the Lyon photographic congress: "The prestige of movement triumphs over that of color." At that gathering, the machine scored perhaps its greatest publicity coup. Louis Lumière had filmed congress members disembarking from an excursion boat, and also the celebrated astronomer P.-J.-C. Janssen (the inspirer of Marey's early researches into motion photography) in conversation with a colleague. These two films he projected the next evening, impressing on the delegates the extraordinary capabilities of the apparatus—doubly extraordinary, doubtless, for the implicit flattery of being made subjects of one of its first films. Janssen gave an impressive boost to the Cinématographe's career, in public remarks made after seeing his own image on the screen. He called the Lumière demonstration "the big event of this session"; his words of praise were reprinted in the *Bulletin de la Société Française de Photographie.*[13]

By October of 1895 letters were arriving almost daily in Lyon inquiring about the Cinématographe or asking to purchase one. But by this time the family had come to realize the immense commercial potential, not of films for the Kinetoscope, nor of direct sales of their equipment, but of public exhibition of the Cinématographe as spectacle. They chose to exploit their machine themselves. Only one family member really had the temperament to do this, however, and it was with some misgivings, hints of which appear in their correspondence of the period, that Louis and Auguste let their father organize the machine's commercial debut in Paris. And so neither son was in the capital on December 28, 1895. It was Antoine Lumière who rented the hall, had programs printed, and set the guest list for the inaugural preview that afternoon. Though that show was very well received, Papa Lumière had neglected to arrange any publicity for the general performances that followed, and at the end of the first evening only thirty-three people had paid one franc each to attend the Birth of the Cinema. But more would come, and soon.

❂ 2 ❂

An Industry Begins

Within a few weeks of their début, the Lumière presentations in the "Indian Room" of the Grand Café on the Boulevard des Capucines were playing to large crowds. On some days revenues were 2,500 francs, and policemen were posted to keep order in the lines of waiting customers. Admission was one franc, a relatively high price for thirty minutes' entertainment: fifteen years later, most of the capital's cinemas would charge less than this for the best seats at a much longer show. The first program, much of which had been screened at the earlier previews, was composed of:

> *Sortie d'usine/Workers Leaving the Lumière Factory*[1]
> *Voltige (Horseback Jumping, "French Military View")*
> *Pêche aux poissons rouges (Fishing for Goldfish)*
> *Arrivée des congressistes à Neuville-sur-Saone/Debarcation of Photographic Congress Members at Lyon*
> *Forgerons (The Blacksmiths)*
> *Le Jardinier et le petit espiègle/A Little Trick on the Gardener*[2]
> *Repas de bébé/Feeding the Baby*
> *Saut à la couverture (Blanket Toss, "French Military View")*
> *Place des Cordeliers à Lyon (The Place des Cordeliers at Lyon)*
> *Baignade en mer/The Sea*

There were printed programs for the customers and a piano accompaniment, which helped cover the noise of the apparatus and fill the pauses between films when the operator had to rethread. The programs changed, though not completely, every few weeks. In the course of 1896 other now celebrated early films made their first appearance: *Arrivée d'un train en gare*/*Arrival of a Train at La Ciotat*, *Barque sortant du port* (*Boat Leaving the Port*), *Démolition d'un mur* (*Destruction of a Wall*), *Partie d'écarté*/*Friendly Party in the Garden of Lumière*. All of these first films are by Louis Lumière; during most of 1895 there was only one Cinématographe, and he guarded it jealously. (Brother Auguste got to make only one film, which figures in some compilations and was shown at the Grand Café: *Mauvaises herbes*/*Burning Weeds* [1896].) All told, Louis probably made about sixty films, mostly in 1895. Beginning with the arrival of the two hundred new machines in early 1896, he trained a group of operators who would take over his duties and go literally around the world, giving programs at night and taking new views, as the films were called, during the day. The work of these men was patterned closely on his own. Innovation—except in a few technical areas such as (most strikingly) camera movement—does not seem to have been encouraged.

The most obvious virtue of the Lumière films is their careful composition. Louis Lumière was a devoted amateur photographer and the son of a professional one. The images are balanced, without being mechanically symmetrical. One of his favorite compositional techniques might be called the Lumière diagonal, which as well as a means of structuring an image is a way of suggesting depth. Often the diagonal component will be an axis of motion, as in *Arrivée d'un train*, *Barque sortant du port*, or *Arrivée des congressistes à Neuville-sur-Saone*. Sometimes it is merely a decorative element in an essentially flat composition, as with the villa wall in the background of *Repas de bébé*. Rare are the films, such as *Partie d'écarté*, which are shot head-on, so as to enhance horizontal and vertical elements only. A great deal of care is taken with lighting and exposure values in the films. Louis Lumière and the operators he trained took several versions of each subject, with different exposures and sometimes slight changes in composition. Where there was action, it was repeated without change: these were cinema "takes" in the modern sense. The best shot was selected, and the others discarded. This, and no mysterious sort of genius, explains the consistently high visual quality of the Lumière *oeuvre*.

As well as being composed in space, the Lumière works were often carefully structured in time. As Marshall Deutelbaum has argued, strong "structural patterning" marks many of the films.[3] *Sortie d'usine* begins with the Lumière factory doors opening and ends with their closing, an action which returns the image to precisely its initial configuration. For that matter, there are no stragglers, and the people

The private life of the bourgeoisie as seen by Louis Lumière: *Repas de bébé.*

are very well dressed for turn-of-the-century industrial workers. The film is obviously staged, even rehearsed, and the result is an orderly temporal development. In *Course en sacs* (*Sack Race,* 1896), first one, then immediately afterwards a second group of contestants start the race and exit frame left; the film is over when the last straggler leaves the image. Some of the films have well-structured beginnings but no clear ending, as for example *Repas de bébé.*

The most tightly structured early Lumière film is the short narra-tive, *Le Jardinier et le petit espiègle* (remade as the better known *Arroseur et Arrosé* [*Waterer and Watered,* 1896]). Unlike the many other films which divide into two repetitive sections, in this one the second part, when the gardener punishes the bad boy for his little trick, clearly depends on the events in the first. As Donald Crafton has convinc-ingly demonstrated, this very coherent, influential work did not spring unaided from the head of Louis Lumière, but was inspired by one (or more) contemporary comic strips.[4] (Though the Lumières would sporadically continue to produce short narratives like this one, these never made up a significant portion of their output. The organization remained committed to its basic photographic-documentary model of production.)

One way of summing up the basic formal characteristics of his films would be to say that Louis Lumière was the first great exponent of the strong French tradition of the *integrity of the shot,* which would continue long after he and his operators ceased filming. As Alexandre Astruc once said about F. W. Murnau, though it applies much better to Lumière, Georges Méliès, and to most early French films: "Each image is an unstable equilibrium, better still the destruction of a stable equilibrium brought about by its own élan. So long as this destruction is not accomplished, the image remains on the screen. So long as the movement has not resolved itself no other image can be tolerated."[5] Films by the Lumière operators do not always show Louis's extreme concern for visual and temporal structure, though they occasionally have pleasures all their own. In *Bassin aux Tuileries/Boat-Sailing in the Tuileries* (1896, probably by Auguste Moisson), there is a luminous moment when a young boy unwittingly stands in front of the camera. From frame left, an umbrella or cane enters the image and pushes him out of the way. What is so striking about this event is how rare such intrusions of the aleatory really are in the world according to Louis Lumière.

The formal aspects of Louis Lumière's films mesh well with their major subject matter, the life, times, and attitudes of the turn-of-the-century bourgeoisie. This is almost the last time in French cinema that this social group will be so sympathetically portrayed, although most French filmmakers will continue to come from this social milieu. The recurring players in the domestic scenes are most often family: Auguste Lumière supervises the demolition of a wall; Auguste and his wife feed their baby; Louis's wife awaits the celebrated arriving train; the friendly card party features Antoine Lumière and two of his friends, one of them Louis and Auguste's father-in-law. The only person we never see is Louis Lumière himself, even in films made by others. Perhaps he always had a headache. He was the admiring observer of the confident, unpretentious, provincial bourgeoisie, but it seems that he did not feel himself capable (or, possibly, worthy) of being a part of it.

After 1896 Louis Lumière ceased making films and became a movie producer. His troupe of operators went around the world, giving shows and taking more views in Russia, North Africa, China, Indochina, and elsewhere. Just as the formal parameters of the films changed very little, their content quickly settled into predictable patterns. Though the Lumière family ceased to appear in them, the subsequent films were of a sort that people like them could be expected to like: state ceremonials, military views, carnivals and similar folkloric scenes, panoramas of suitably foreign-looking vistas, and so on. There were no views of the everyday life of poor natives or unfavorable glimpses of police repression. That the Lumière operators made films according to relatively stable formulas (and sometimes literally remade popular successes) marks this as the first, or the second if one counts Edison's early output, of what today we call genre production. It was for a time phenomenally successful. By 1897, however, both the numbers of films produced and the income from them began to fall, and the company issued its first catalog of views for public sale, though production continued sporadically until 1905. A principal reason for the rapid decline in the organization's fortunes was its defeat by the Edison forces in the largest world market, the United States. Though the story is not clear even today, it appears that this involved both economic pressure on exhibitors and threats of physical violence. The Lumière American representative fled the country under an assumed name, in fear for his life (as later American independents would flee to California to evade Edison's "goon squads").

But another reason was probably more important. The Lumières were the first entrepreneurs to reap the inevitable harvest of genre production unrenewed by infusions of new subjects and techniques. Not only did the company rework and remake its own views, but other producers did so as well. Countless views of the sea, untold numbers of babies being fed, of trains arriving, of the military at work or play, paraded across the era's flimsy movie screens. Very soon the one-minute Lumière subject reached commercial saturation in all its markets. This came as no surprise to Louis Lumière. He had told his operators that their jobs would likely last only six months or a year. The family thought it was the cinema itself which, as Papa Lumière put it, had no future. As it turned out, it was only the hugely successful Lumière film operation that began winding down in 1897.

■ If the films, French and otherwise, from before World War I seem alien to us today, it is perhaps because, despite their dates, they are not really from the twentieth century. The nineteenth century had a last, giddy Indian summer that ended abruptly in 1914 and is now called *la belle époque*. The image that remains of it is of a self-confident, expansive sensibility, of which the Lumière family movies give only a small, provincial, and bourgeois sample. After the Lumières' great success, French cinema moved to Paris, where it would mostly remain. And the capital at this time, as Roger Shattuck has forcefully argued, was dominated by a kind of free-floating theatricalization:

> Since Offenbach's era, living had become increasingly a special kind of performance presided over by fashion, innocence, and taste. History provides its own reasons for the gaiety of the era: economic prosperity following rapid recovery from the defeat in 1871, the unexpected stability of this third try at republican government, and innocence of any world conflict of the kind that would put a stop to it all. But such reasons do not explain why almost every book of reminiscences about the period indulges an unashamed nostalgia about a charmed way of life now lost. . . . Paris was a stage where the excitement of performance gave every deed the double significance of private gesture and public action. Doctor and ragpicker alike performed their professional flourishes, and the *crime passionnel* was practiced as a fine art.[6]

What is generally forgotten about *la belle époque* is that it was considerably less *belle* for peasants, factory workers, and servants.[7] Nonetheless Shattuck has ample reason for arguing that both doctor and ragpicker participated in a common sense of social life as public performance. Entertainment had been widely and ever increasingly commercialized since the Revolution. In Paris an entertainment district had consolidated and expanded along the new boulevards, where one found everything from freak shows to wax museums to popular theatrical spectacles like that at the Châtelet. Along these wide thoroughfares, people of all classes strolled to observe each other and to contemplate the various attractions which solicited their patronage. It was there that the Lumière organization first exhibited the Cinématographe, and it was there that Georges Méliès operated a small theatre devoted to conjuring and to fantasy pantomimes.

Méliès did not begin his career in the theatre until the retirement of his father allowed him to do so. Like Louis Lumière, he was the son of a newly well-to-do bourgeois family. Unlike Lumière, he did not contribute to the family fortune, nor did he seem to have much liking for how it was made. Louis Méliès, the *père de famille*, was of petty bourgeois, provincial origins, and he had built up a thriving business in the manufacture of luxury footware, the kind of upscale consumer goods that French entrepreneurs so often excelled in producing. His sons Henri and Gaston were born eight years apart (presumably the result of careful family planning dictated by the family balance sheet) in 1844 and 1852. In 1861, when the family presumably felt it could afford the expense again, Georges was born. He studied at the celebrated Lycée Louis-le-Grand, and though he was already by temperament something of a rebel, he obtained his *baccalauréat*—which would make him the best educated figure in French cinema for some time to come.

Whereas Louis and Auguste Lumière made a place for themselves in their family by becoming the disciplined capitalists that their father could never be, Georges Méliès opted for outright rebellion by aspiring to become an artist. He wanted to study painting at the Ecole des Beaux-Arts; his father wanted him to enter the family business. His father won. Georges was a realist, and he bided his time as machinery supervisor of the boot factory, a position that was to give him valuable mechanical expertise for his later career. He did manage, however, not to marry the third sister of his two older brothers' wives, as the rest of the family wanted (shades of the Lumières). Acting with a characteristic mixture of prudence and audacity, he married the illegitimate daughter of a close friend of his uncle's, thereby securing an ample dowry and a first measure of financial independence. In 1888 his father retired from the business and Georges sold his share in it to his brothers. With this money he bought the Théâtre Robert-Houdin, a small second-floor theatre on the Boulevard des Italiens.

Jean-Eugène Robert-Houdin had been the foremost French magician of the mid-nineteenth century. In 1852 he had designed and equipped the hall of roughly two hundred seats which bore his name. By the time Méliès bought the business, its founder had been dead seventeen years, and the theatre was in genteel decline. From the beginning Méliès planned to revive it not by clever business practices, but by means of his own artistry. One of the hall's performers, a magician named Duperrey, recounted in his diary:

[Today] I went down to the office and brought to M. Méliès's attention the sorry state of business. There were four spectators in the hall at 8:25, sixteen when the curtain went up, forty-eight at the end. I told him that we need to cultivate the newspapers, place advertising, hand out free admissions. He responded that he didn't treat reporters badly. This is false; I know that the opposite is the case.

As for publicity, he told me it is very difficult to lay out copy when one doesn't know what to say. One should imagine an eye-catching gravure, but of what? Only a big gimmick can save the situation; when it exists, great publicity will be arranged.[8]

Méliès's confidence in his gimmicks was based less on their sophistication—he called them his *grosse cavalerie*, meaning that they were not very subtle—than on their rhythm and dramatic development. Old tricks (and a few new ones) could gain in impact by being carefully strung together using bizarre, satirical characters. In his sketch *American Spiritualistic Mediums* (1891), Professor Clodion Barbenfouillis (at times played by Méliès himself) interrupts a magic show and lectures the audience incoherently on occult matters, while the magician and his assistant try to make him stop. The magician, exasperated, pursues the old man with an enormous scimitar, catches him, and cuts his head off (the professor is chased off stage and back on to facilitate the execution of the trick). The head is placed in a bowl, where it continues to talk. The magician shuts it up in a box, but it cries out for air and the doors are opened, whereupon Barbenfouillis recommences his peroration. The doors are closed, but when the magician begins to perform for the audience, the old man's body runs to the box, removes its head, and runs away. Offstage, a skeleton somehow steals Barbenfouillis's head and is pursued back on stage, while the skeleton's skull has latched on to the old man's body. His head, newly detached, is put in another box, the body with skull in a sarcophagus. The magician fires a pistol; presto, the head is back on the body, and the box, opened, is found to be empty. The assistant leads the spiritualist off stage, saying, "This way out, *M'sieu la barbe.*"[9]

This was an enormous change from the elegant, minimal magic pioneered by Robert-Houdin. Méliès got the idea for this kind of show in London, from performances at the Egyptian Hall in Picadilly, but he brought to it his own inventiveness and savage energy, and the public did indeed begin to return to his theatre. Doubtless this could have been accomplished faster if he had followed his employee's advice about better publicity and free tickets, but Méliès balked at working on the purely commercial aspects of his business. The theatre was edging into profitability when, in late December 1895, he was invited to the première of the Cinématographe. He had probably been aware of the apparatus for some time, since Antoine Lumière had briefly rented a work space above the theatre and the machine had had its well-publicized tryouts. After the Grand Café opening,

Méliès is said to have offered to buy a Cinématographe for the astonishing sum of 10,000 francs. The directors of the Folies-Bergère and the Musée Grévin also made offers. The Lumières' refusal led Méliès and others into the search for alternative mechanisms.

How Méliès got his first cinema equipment remains unclear: perhaps from R. W. Paul in England, or from the Isola brothers in Paris, or by his own tinkering. By March 1896 he had a camera, and in April he presented the first film programs in his theatre. Initially he projected Edison Kinetoscope films, but soon he added his own subjects, mostly copied from the Lumières. He had his own arrival of a train, a card game, burning weeds, and so on. He began to experiment with longer forms, beginning with a two-part (two minutes) *Sauvetage en rivière* (*Rescue on the River,* probably May 1896). In his last film of 1896, *Le Manoir du diable/The Haunted Castle,* he spliced together three one-minute film strips to display his very personal narrative imagination in cinema:

> The picture shows a room in a medieval castle; carved stone pillars, low doors and vaulted ceiling. A huge bat flies in and circles around. It is suddenly transformed into Mephistopheles. He walks around, makes a magic pass, and a large cauldron appears and out of it, in a great cloud of smoke, there emerges a beautiful lady. At another magic pass, a little old man comes out of the floor carrying a big book. Then the cauldron disappears. And so it goes on. Cavaliers, ghosts, a skeleton and witches appear and disappear at a sign from the Evil One. Finally one of the cavaliers produces a cross, and Mephistopheles throws up his hands and disappears in a cloud of smoke.[10]

Méliès made four basic types of films: fantastic narratives like *Le Manoir du diable;* straight performance films, with a magician, sketch artist, or dancer playing directly to the camera; Lumière-style views, including a few comic scenes modeled on *Le Jardinier et le petit espiègle;* and phoney newsreels. The latter, of which he was something of a specialist, generally involved no deliberate deception of the audience. It was standard practice in the written press to publish "artist's conceptions" of current events; Méliès only adapted the practice to cinema. He created an *Eruption volcanique à la Martinique/Eruption of Mount Pelée,* 1902) with a paper-maché model mountain and assorted fireworks. His *Le Sacré d'Edouard VII* (*The Coronation of Edward VII,* 1902) was scrupulously recreated (more accurately, pre-created, before the actual ceremony) in his studio with carefully researched décors and costumes, and actors selected to resemble the new English monarch and his court.

Méliès also tried his hand at a few stag films and did some early experiments with filmed advertising. But it is the fantastic narratives that formed the backbone of his production, and into which he poured his abundant imagination. He had already evolved this sort of spectacle in his theatre; he had only to discover the most effective means of transposing it to cinema. He did not first discover his celebrated trick effects and then elaborate a narrative form into which they could fit. He worked in exactly the opposite direction, though in this manner he developed virtually all of the basic optical effects of the cinema: substitution splicing (by which he could simulate sudden appearances, disappearances, and transformations), superimposition through multiple exposures, matting several images together into different parts of a single frame, dissolves, and so on.

The first and, in his own work, the most important effect he mastered in his first year as a filmmaker. This was substitution splicing (sometimes called "stop motion substitution," but which, in fact, involved careful editing).[11] Méliès always claimed that he discovered this accidentally, when he was filming a view of the Place de l'Opéra in Paris. The camera supposedly jammed, and when he managed to continue filming things had changed position, so that a man seemed to change into a woman, a bus into a hearse. Leaving aside the patently Mélièsian flavor of these transformations, one finds no concrete evidence for the story, and much to be said against it. A more likely explanation, advanced by Jacques Deslandes, is that one of the Edison films that Méliès projected in his early screenings was *The Execution of Mary Queen of Scots* (1895), in which a beheading was simulated by stopping the camera and substituting a dummy for the actress at the necessary moment. Méliès would have been all the more interested in this film for its relevance to his stage acts such as the adventures of Professor Barbenfouillis. Close examination of the film strip would have revealed the secret.[12]

At any rate, one of his very early performance films, *Escamotage d'une dame chez Robert-Houdin / The Vanishing Lady* (1896) uses the effect repeatedly and with great proficiency. Its function is to provide an efficient cinematic equivalent of the trap door that was used for this illusion in his theatre. The other optical tricks he exploited were likewise introduced as equivalents of theatrical illusions, though they could later take on a life of their own, producing bizarre effects impossible on the stage. Ghostly figures had been produced in his theatre by means of half-silvered mirrors; in his films they would appear via superimpositions. Decors could "dissolve" on stage by means of double-painted scrims and suitable changes of lighting; in the films, one scene could cinematographically dissolve into another. But the tricks themselves were not the point of his films. As in his stage shows, the illusions were integral parts of a larger narrative whole.

To understand Méliès at all we must remember that, although original, he was not isolated or unique. His stage spectacles had been inspired by acts he saw in England. In Paris itself the *féerie*, or fairy play, had been popular since just after the Revolution. The fairy play was an outgrowth of melodrama, which embellished the genre's extravagant visual effects with sudden transformations, disappearances, instantaneous voyages in time or space, and the like. Severed heads and disembodied bodies were common, as were appearances by the devil himself. Several of Méliès's longer films are particularly close to the *féerie*, such as *Le Royaume des fées* (*In The Kingdom of the Fairies*, 1903).[13] Méliès's real originality has two dimensions. First, in transposing his stage tricks to the screen, he achieved qualitatively more bizarre and unsettling effects. The Robert-Houdin stage could at best produce a ghost or two at a time, or make two disappearances in quick succession. The cinema could multiply these devices, and a controlled, chamber theatre of illusion spawned in film a chaotic nightmare world that anticipated Surrealism and other post-World War I artistic mutations. Méliès was presumably led in this direction by the second, crucial aspect of his originality: the satiric, occasionally brutal tone of most of his work. The *féerie* was, like most early melodrama, a sentimental show in which good triumphed over evil in what turned out to be the best of all possible worlds. In making use of the *féerie* Méliès' recognized that the wicked, disruptive elements were more interesting than the forces of sweetness and light. There is an anarchic, anti-hierarchical side to his personality that often emerges in his films. It is not a coincidence that one of his favorite roles was the devil.

A recurrent pattern in Méliès's works begins with the establishment of an ordered, everyday situation. Fantastic disruption follows. In *Le Revenant/The Ghost and the Candle* (1903, also known as *The Apparition*), a bourgeois traveler tries to read a newspaper by candlelight. At first the candle moves away from him to the other side of the table. When he pulls it back, it retreats again, beginning a series of disruptions that culminates in the candle suddenly becoming six feet tall. This is the revenge of everyday life, the comic problematizing of middle-class comfort. Often the disruption takes the form of a dream, as in the masterful *La Lune à un mètre/The Astronomer's Dream* (1898). Or it can be the devil, or a witch as in *Le Puits fantastique/The Enchanted Well* (1903), in which an old crone curses a farmer's well to undergo incredible transformations, most of them remarkably funny. One suspects that Méliès loves the disorder and finds the victims laughable. Certainly the poor well-owner gets no sympathy, nor does the tormented traveler in search of a night's rest.

The satirical tone of so much of Méliès's work is probably what seems most modern about him. He brought to the cinema the sensibilities of a political cartoonist—which in fact he was, part-time, for much of his life. If irony in film can be simply defined as showing one thing and meaning another, then he was certainly the cinema's first ironist. But we must be wary of making of him an overly modern character. The anti-hierarchical, anarchic side of his work has definite limits. Méliès was, for his day and his class, politically progressive. One of his phoney newsreels was *L'Affaire Dreyfus/Dreyfus Court Martial* (1899), in which his strong Dreyfusard sympathies are clearly in evidence. He often lampooned bourgeois figures, for example the pretentious scientists in *Le Voyage dans la lune* (*A Trip to the Moon*, 1902). But he was by no means a revolutionary. In his everyday life he was distant, even peremptory with his employees, and his liberalism could have its blind sides, as witness the attack on women's suffrage that begins *Le Voyage à travers l'impossible/An Impossible Voyage* (1904).

After his initial efforts, Méliès's work did not significantly change or evolve. Very early on he established his basic tricks and subjects. Particularly in his longer films inspired by the *féerie*, he repeated himself without always making an improvement. Some of the short performance films inspired by his stage magic seem fresher today, particularly *L'Homme à la tête de caoutchouc* (*The Man with the Rubber Head*, 1902) and *Le Mélomane* (*The Melomaniac*, 1903). But these were not *reworkable*, in the sense that the narratives were. In fiction film Méliès established his own variety of genre production. The use of basic stories or configurations whose elements could be varied to produce a new work was the key to the regular renewal of his production. Like the Lumière organization, he could not or would not significantly change his formulas, and so he too eventually fell out of touch with his spectators, whose taste was evolving rapidly.

Méliès's *Le Voyage dans la lune* is not only the first science fiction film; it is also the first *parody* of one. Here, the spacecraft, after being fired from a huge gun, hits a rather unhappy moon.

Méliès contributed mightily to the elaboration of the cinematic institution. In 1897 he constructed the world's first film studio, in the modern sense of the word, modeled on the design of the Robert-Houdin theatre. He pioneered the use of studio-made still photographs for the publicizing and documentation of his work. (Some of the illustrations of Méliès "films" in current use are in fact publicity stills.) And in a real sense he was the first movie star, the main attraction of his most successful works. But he never took the commercial aspect of his work as seriously as he did his "personal compositions," as he liked to call his scenarios and their realization on celluloid. And so his competitors learned from his success and, avoiding his limitations, eventually displaced him.

To whom did Méliès and his competitors sell their films? As an exhibitor, Méliès was, in fact, one of the relatively few entrepreneurs in France to present films as we generally see them today, in permanent halls built for or adapted to that purpose. Most early cinema presentations, however, occurred in contexts which today seem almost as strange as Méliès's oddest works of film fantasy. The medium's first French exhibitors included circus operators, wax museums, "wonders of science" exhibits, operetta theatres, freak shows, and other businesses from among the nation's many small, generally mobile popular spectacles. These operations offered a remarkable variety of entertainments—some respectable (or pretending to be so), some shocking and almost obscene—to the French public. They served a large, though uncentralized, market.

At the turn of the century France was still in many ways a strikingly rural nation. Compared to her neighbors, she had had a very slow population growth; industrially, the nation was well behind Great Britain and Germany. No significant population pressure pushed people out of the rural towns, nor did any great demand for workers (outside of Paris and Lyon) draw them to the larger cities. Most of the population got its entertainment from fairgrounds, either semi-permanent fairs on the outskirts of cities, or traveling troupes making their rural circuits. Some of the larger country fairs could last several months and attract many thousands of customers during their run. When that public was temporarily sated, the fair entrepreneurs would move on to the next location on the circuit. Operators of familiar attractions such as the *métempsychose,* or "transmigration of souls," a magic act based on half-silvered mirrors, could earn a reasonable income. More elaborate and more profitable businesses used a vaudeville-like format of several different attractions. One staple presentation on such programs was the "Loïe Fuller number," in which a young woman dressed in white veils (generally the wife, daughter, or daughter-in-law of the owner) posed while a series of colored images were projected onto her garments. There were also shadow plays, animal acts, and several *aerogynes,* or flying women.

This was a small, relatively closed business community, dominated by a number of prosperous family dynasties. The *raison d'être* of each of these (often sternly patriarchial) families was its commercial enterprise, which could be counted on to provide a comfortable, though not extravagant, standard of living. This was not large-scale capitalism; indeed, in Fernand Braudel's sense of the word, the fairground entrepreneurs were not true capitalists at all, because of the low profit margins in their businesses (a few percent real annual return on capital) and because of their ties to a very specific market.[14] Many of these traveling show people added the cinema to their programs shortly after the equipment became generally available. Some of them eventually developed it into a specialty which dominated their presentations, though it did not generally become their sole attraction.

One reasonably typical example was the business of Nicholas Kobelkoff, the *homme-tronc*, or limbless man. Kobelkoff began his enterprise as a traveling freak show with himself as sole attraction and diversified into cinema in 1905 as a means to support and employ his growing family. Soon the Kobelkoff clan, eight members strong, operated their Giant Cinématographe, a portable theatre complete with organ, "parade" stage, and an auditorium with several hundred seats. The Dulaar family, originally from Belgium, was even more successful, eventually presiding over the Atheneum Theatre, the Théâtre Mondain, and the Excelsior Music Hall (which despite its name showed films, like the others). The average seating capacity of such establishments is said by Georges Sadoul to have been about five hundred, though this figure may be high.[15]

The man who would later preside over the liquidation of Georges Méliès's film business—after he had (or so it seemed) almost single-handedly made a modern industry of the French cinema—had his first business success as one of these (small-time) fairground entrepreneurs. Charles Pathé was that comparative rarity in the France of his day, a man whose major goal in life was to become extremely wealthy. In turn-of-the-century France, at least among the middle and upper classes, the singleminded pursuit of financial gain was often considered suspect, a bit vulgar. One might reasonably strive to become better off than one's parents, of course, but not to seek as much money as possible for its own sake. That was something to be expected of foreigners—or Protestants, or Jews. Sensible people sought a reasonable degree of social and monetary advancement and then settled into an agreeable life of self-cultivation, liberally mixed with eating, drinking, and for the men, the keeping of mistresses. Georges Méliès was a fairly typical example of this world view. But not Charles Pathé.

Pathé's parents came from Alsace, where Charles was born in 1863, and had worked their way up in life to operating a butcher and sausage-making shop in the Paris suburb of Vincennes. The boy went to school there and worked long hours in the business. He recalled that for a long time his only real shoes were his mother's, which he borrowed once a week to go to mass. At the age of fourteen he left school and was an apprentice butcher until his military service. He left the

French army in extremely poor health and with an extraordinary will to advance himself. Throughout his life various physical ailments challenged his strong drive to succeed. Pathé knew how to dream big and to take big chances. He went to South America to make his fortune, only to return hastily in 1891, fleeing an epidemic of yellow fever. In 1894 a friend told him of the Edison Phonograph, then just beginning its commercial career on French fairgrounds. Customers paid a tenth of a franc each to listen to a recording; the machines had 18 or 20 earpieces. Pathé added up the figures: a maximum of two francs every few minutes. In three or four hours, fifty or sixty francs. In his memoirs he recalled being "haunted" by the prospect of buying a machine. His family refused to advance him the money, suggesting instead he go into something more serious—like a butcher shop, for example. But he persisted, and when he managed to buy his phonograph he worked at fairs only briefly before accumulating enough capital to set up a shop selling the machines to small exhibitors.

It goes without saying that Pathé's phonograph business prospered because he worked hard at it. But also, he had found an ideal social niche, selling to people he understood. For despite the odd nature of their business, most of the fairground entrepreneurs were at heart not that different from small-town butchers, and Pathé's success with them was undoubtedly at least partly the result of his similar social origins in the *petite bourgeoisie*, the class of small shopkeepers and low-level functionaries. But his sympathy for his clients had its limits: although he first cultivated the cinema in this archetypal petty bourgeois milieu, he would later pull it up and transplant it elsewhere, as we will see in the next chapter. In early 1895 Pathé began to sell counterfeit Kinetoscopes from England to his clients, and in this manner he came in contact with Henri Joseph Joly. Having come to buy a machine, Joly suggested that because the films were so expensive it would be a simple matter to manufacture and sell them at a good profit. Pathé offered financial backing, and by the fall of 1895 Joly had produced an apparatus and begun to make films. Like the Lumière Cinématographe, his machine could also project its images on a screen.

Depending on whom one believes, Pathé then tricked Joly, or the latter attempted to welch on his agreements with Pathé, or a bit of both. Right or wrong, Pathé confiscated a Joly prototype and set about to manufacture it in small numbers. It did not sell well at first because of technical problems, chiefly poor registration of the images. But

Pathé was not easily discouraged, since his phonographs were selling well and could cover the cinema expenses. By this time he doubtless had a good pair of shoes, but probably not more than one: all extra cash went right back into the business. At the end of 1896 Pathé's mother died, and his three brothers, convinced by now of the serious nature of Charles's business, pooled their inheritance and formed the Société Pathé Frères. Very soon, however, brothers Théophile and Jacques withdrew, fearing ruin in a lawsuit for nondelivery of merchandise.[16]

Charles and his third brother Emile carried on alone, though not for long. It is often said that industrial development in France was retarded because of the extreme difficulty of obtaining capital, particularly from banks. The Pathé brothers' story suggests that the problem was, rather, one of big capital's finding sufficiently ambitious and persistent entrepreneurs, such as Charles and Emile. Just when most bourgeois Frenchmen would have been content to slow their business growth and settle back to a life of big dinners and good cigars, the Pathés were ready to redouble their efforts. They did not have to go looking for financial backing; it came to them, in the person of the industrialist and amateur magician Claude-Agricol-Louis Grivolas. After what seem today to have been shockingly brief negotiations, Grivolas presided over the formation of the Compagnie Générale des Cinématographes, Phonographes, et Pellicules in December 1897. The cinema was barely two years old. It had found, though no one knew it yet except perhaps Charles Pathé, its first Master Capitalist.

To say that Pathé Frères, as the company continued to be called, prospered immediately is to make a monstrous understatement. After the first year of operation, shares that had sold for 100 francs returned a dividend of 17¼ francs. Over the next decade, these payments ranged between 8 percent and 90 percent of the company's book value. There was never a loss. Emile Pathé took care of the enterprise's phonograph operation. Charles began, with his vastly expanded resources, to regularize and expand its cinema business. His first concern was not the production of films, but technical matters such as printing, developing, perforating raw stock, and the development and marketing of cameras and projectors. (The company eventually bought the rights to the Lumière patents and took over, via a stock swap, a leading French manufacturer of precision optical instruments.)

For the first three years of the corporation's life, film production was minimal and haphazard. Charles Pathé had begun, before Grivolas augmented his capital, by duping Edison Kinetoscope films. By 1899 "original" subjects such as an arrival of a train, a children's breakfast, and so on, made their way into the firm's catalogs. But pseudo-Lumière views had basically exhausted their appeal to the public by this time, and the company turned to the production of other sorts of imagery. To this end, Pathé hired Ferdinand Zecca who, beginning in 1900 produced, directed, and acted in thousands of short (five to fifteen minute) works. Pathé apparently took little interest in the films themselves; he preferred to work on technical, logistical, and marketing problems. There was a severely practical reason for this. At the time, the company's film production was a minor adjunct to its vastly more profitable sales of equipment—which were, in turn, dwarfed by the roughly ten times more lucrative phonograph business. Zecca's background made him the urban equivalent of Pathé's first customers. His parents were the *concièrges* (doorkeepers/caretakers) at the Ambigu theatre in Paris: a better combination of popular theatrical milieu and petty bourgeois values can hardly be imagined. Zecca and Pathé seem to have had similar methods and intensity of involvement in their work. Their formula for success was: try everything, then try it all again; stick with what works, but never let a fixed way of doing things get in the way of borrowing from your competition. And so, unlike the Lumière and Méliès operations, Pathé Frères was not doomed by any maladaptive compulsion to repeat film subjects, or other commercial strategies, once their profit potential began to decline.

Zecca proceeded to copy everything in sight. He reworked subjects from Méliès—sometimes closely, sometimes freely—as well as from the innovative English filmmakers R. W. Paul and G. A. Smith. (In turn, others borrowed from the Pathé films, sometimes reappropriating variations on their own earlier material.) Of course, no one who is in a genuine hurry can or wants to copy exactly the work of others. Probably as much by accident as by design, Zecca brought changes and variations to his reworkings, as did those who in turn borrowed from him. The whole process suggests an industrialized, speeded-up parody of the workings of the traditional "oral" cultures. It also makes for great trouble in arriving at critical judgments of works of the period, since assessments of originality so often turn out to be uncertain or beside the point. Yet it is also difficult to evaluate the works as films, since they date from a time when conventions of film making and viewing were not at all consistent and were also quite different from those of today. Whether Zecca and most other early filmmakers should be considered "artists" in the same way that one thinks of Lumière or Méliès will probably always remain an open question.

Artist or not, probably no other person in the history of cinema contributed as much or as fast to its evolution as did Ferdinand Zecca. Apart from his borrowings from other filmmakers, he proceeded systematically to adapt and transform material from other media. He looked almost *everywhere* for material: music hall skits, soft-core postcard pornography, dance, sports, biblical illustration, dirty stories. Many of these areas had been haphazardly explored by others, but it was Zecca who systematically exploited them and allowed them, eventually, to interbreed. For perhaps the most striking characteristic of early cinema production is how utterly distinct the various kinds of films could be. Among the early "series" (as the studios called their film genres), performance styles, decor, camerawork, narrative structure, and so on varied widely, mainly because of their extremely diverse origins. Only slowly would a relatively homogeneous sector that one can call "the cinema" emerge from this heteroclitic mess. Pathé Frères was the caldron in which much of this cooking was done, and Ferdinand Zecca was the hand that stirred the pot.

In 1902 Pathé Frères' advertising enumerated the genres recognized by the studio:

1st Series—Outdoor Views
2nd Series—Comic Scenes
3rd Series—Trick Films [featuring Mélièsian magical effects]
4th Series—Sports and Acrobatics
5th Series—Historical Scenes, Newsreels, and Military Scenes
6th Series—Soft-Core Stag Films ("Scènes grivoises d'un caractère piquant")
7th Series—Dances and Ballets
8th Series—Dramatic and Realist Scenes
9th Series—Fairy Tales and *Féeries*
10th Series—Religious and Biblical Scenes
11th Series—Cinéphonographic Scenes [an early sound process]
12th Series—Miscellaneous Scenes[17]

In terms of later genre history, Zecca's greatest single success at series elaboration was the eighth category: Dramatic and Realist Scenes. These were Zolaesque looks at the lives, loves, and tragic destinies of workers, peasants, and other characters from the lower orders of French society. They are more appropriately called Naturalist rather than realist, if by the latter we mean anything like a documentary impulse. Like the Naturalist journalists and artists of his day, Zecca in this series offered a superficial representation of the mechanics of everyday life in the lower classes, in which explicit political consciousness of class was deemphasized in favor of emotional conflict. How a character felt about being executed, for example, was more important than why this was happening or whether it should happen.

The big early success in this genre was *Histoire d'un crime* (*Story of a Crime*, 1901). The film was 110 meters long, running roughly five to six minutes at early silent speed. It was composed of six scenes, each of which was a single shot:

1. Murder of a Bank Employee
2. Arrest of the Criminal in a Café
3. Confrontation with the Corpse of the Victim at the Morgue
4. In Prison: Dream of the Past
5. Arrival of the Executioner; the Prisoner's Preparations
6. At the Guillotine; the Fall of the Blade.[18]

What is probably most interesting about this film is its source material, a set of tableaux from the Musée Grévin. The waxworks show was itself inspired by yet another medium, as the Museum's catalog made clear: "The Musée Grévin has justly been thought of as a newspaper in wax. In all newspapers, one of the successful elements that is most sought after is the serial novel. The Musée Grévin also has its own such series, more striking, more dramatic in its living reality than any written work. This is *The Story of a Crime*." For the spectacle's third tableau, the catalog gave the following description: "Here is the Morgue, exactly copied with its damp slabs and its sinister collection of bloody rags; the body of the unfortunate bank employee is laid out on the slab. In the presence of the examining magistrate and the judges, the accused is brought forth, shivering and becoming pale in the presence of his victim. Henceforth the proof has been shown, and his attitude before this terrible spectacle reduces to nothing his protestations of innocence."[19] Zecca made few modifications in the Grévin spectacle in adapting it to film. Indeed, few were necessary; the catalog copy itself reads like an early film script.

This was probably the first appearance in French filmmaking of the Naturalist tendency that was to surface periodically in its later history.

But the larger point to be noted here is that the early cinema's creation of genres proceded in a manner reminiscent of the development of its machinery—by various episodes of (here cultural, Lévi-Straussian) *bricolage*. Forms and content areas from other media were systematically borrowed and adapted. Those that proved both marketable and capable of mass production at a predictable rate of expense would survive, if sometimes only briefly. Some would flourish beyond their creators' wildest dreams, and provide the bases for the worldwide industry that was beginning to stir. Later, others would guide it beyond the reach of the French pioneers who assisted at its birth.

⧫ 3 ⧫

Growth and Diversification

Until about 1905 film exhibition in France was typically a mobile show, provided by traveling entertainers equipped with films and projection equipment of diverse origins and varying degrees of mechanical reliability. Even leading manufacturers were often obliged to market their wares in temporary exhibition sites, for the simple reason that there were as yet few fixed sites for cinema exhibition. The Paris World's Fair of 1900, for example, gave the first exhibition of the Lumières' Cinématographe Géant, an apparatus which represented the first major attempt to change the proportions of the film image. This had been set by Edison for his Kinetoscope and would stubbornly resist all such proposed modifications until the 1950s.

The 1900 World's Fair was a privileged moment in the elaboration of the cinematic spectacle, drawing together by virtue of its prestige and its large audiences all manner of entrepreneurs large and small, and a startling number of proposed technological innovations. In addition to the new Lumière apparatus, one could also attend the premières of the Phono-Cinéma-Théâtre, a briefly successful sound film system, as well as the Maréorama, a kind of filmic version of the Diorama devoted to sea voyages, and Raoul Grimoin-Samson's ambitious but doomed Ballon-Cinéorama. The latter apparatus, fitted out with ten seventy-millimeter synchronized projectors (!) throwing images onto a circular screen surrounding the audience, was designed to give simulated hot-air balloon voyages. Unfortunately for Grimoin-Samson and his backers, the projectors generated too much heat, and the attraction was closed as unsafe by the Paris police—who had, as we will see, good reason to worry about such matters. Although all of these experiments in alternative formats and technologies were destined, at least for the moment, to commercial oblivion, they provide clear evidence of the extent to which French cinema at the beginning of the century still remained to be defined, commercially as well as technologically.

The very existence of the industry had depended from its early days on the vigor and acumen of its first exhibitors, who were mostly the same fairground entertainers to whom Charles Pathé had sold his phonographs, and to whom he now also sold projectors and the films produced by Ferdinand Zecca. But it soon became apparent that more intensive, fixed film exhibition in cities and towns could provide an alternative means of selling cinema entertainment to the French public. In 1904, for example, Madame Léon Richebé and her family opened a French precursor of the nickelodeon theatre, the Populaire Cinéma, in the old waterfront district of Marseilles (the setting of Marcel Pagnol's *Marius*). Admission was three sous, the price of a draft beer in a café, and thus well within the reach of a working-class clientele. The business flourished, and in the space of a few years the family opened several other cinemas. Madame Richebé's son Roger, who later became a major film producer, recalled in his memoirs that at about the same time the city's Brasserie de la Bohème transformed its basement into a cinema. Two enormous pillars divided the space in half, with spectators seated on the "good" side of the translucent screen paying a higher admission price.

In all parts of France the rapidity with which fixed exhibition established itself depended on population density. The Richebés and their competitors were typical of entrepreneurs in larger provincial cities. But in Perpignan, a modest provincial capital near the Spanish border, the first permanent cinema did not open until 1911. Before that, the local population could see films only at traveling fairground attractions and at the local vaudeville houses, where visiting operators with their own films and equipment would periodically fill the bill. In Paris, on the other hand, fixed exhibition had become established almost immediately. The Lumières continued their Grand Café operation only until 1900, but in the spring of 1896 they opened three more theatres, one of which (situated in a working class neighborhood near the Porte St. Martin) continued operation through two World Wars under a series of owners.

Rival entertainment concerns frequently chose to join the cinema rather than be beaten by it. On the Boulevard Bonne Nouvelle, the

Most early cinema was exhibited in portable, fairground theatres, either on rural circuits or in quasi-permanent urban locations, as witness the buildings seen here behind the Théâtre Vignard in 1905.

Musée de la Porte St. Denis, an established wax museum also equipped with phonographs, do-it-yourself X-rays, and other amusements, was remodeled and converted into a permanent cinema in 1904. The most spectacular such conversion was the creation in 1907 of a 6,000 seat cinema in the shell of the old Hippodrome arena. Revenues were not as high as anticipated, however, and the site was transformed into a giant indoor skating rink in 1909, only to be bought by the Gaumont company for its flagship cinema, the Gaumont Palace, in 1911. During this period a number of more expensive, luxury cinemas, especially built for the purpose also opened in the capital, though Perpignan and smaller cities and towns like it continued to have no permanent film theatres at all until Paris had over a hundred.

During the century's first decade, then, French film exhibition had a dual nature. The larger cities were served by fixed exhibitors, the towns and rural areas by the traveling entrepreneurs. Though their days were obviously numbered after 1907, the fairground exhibitors continued to be a significant presence in the industry until the years of the Great War. Several factors contributed to their slow decline.

The most important was demographic. With the turn of the century, relatively continuous if irregular economic expansion achieved what the entire nineteenth century had not: it moved most of the population into urban areas. By 1920 the majority of French citizens lived in cities. Even then the fairground cinema might have continued to exist in attenuated form (there were still active fairgrounds on most city outskirts), had it not been for another factor, the fear of fire.

One of the earliest, and certainly the best known of the catastrophic fires in temporary cinemas occurred in the capital at the 1897 Charity Bazaar. This event was an annual fundraiser for good causes organized by the Catholic *haute bourgeoisie* and attended by *le tout Paris*. That year it was held in a narrow vacant lot on the Rue Jean-Goujon. The entire site was covered with a flammable vellum tarp supported by poles of varnished pine. Underneath, a cardboard and papermaché decor represented a market section of prerevolutionary Paris. Ladies and gentlemen of the upper classes amused themselves by playing the parts of small shopkeepers. Most of their costumes, like everything else, were highly flammable. In one corner of this disaster waiting to happen was a small cinema, whose projector used an ether vapor lamp as a light source. After fewer than two hours of operation on the event's first day, this lamp faded and went out. A moment later the operator lit a match in the by then ether-filled projection booth to see what was wrong. Within minutes 140 people were dead, and the site was leveled. There was a special mass for the victims at Notre Dame cathedral.

This was by no means the only catastrophic fire associated with the early cinema, merely the best known because of the social standing of the victims and the massive attendant publicity. Some historians, probably influenced by Charles Pathé's assertions in his memoirs, have contended that this event almost stopped the nascent film industry in its tracks. Yet Pathé's own income figures given in his book show no slackening of cinema activity in 1897 or immediately thereafter.[1] In fact, aside from heated rhetoric on all sides, the Charity Bazaar fire in and of itself had little real impact on the French cinema.[2] Nonetheless, such disasters continued to occur, and eventually local fire ordinances began seriously to trouble the fairground enterprises. However much one may wish to defend them as victims of big government and big capitalism, these operations probably *were* unsafe, though (as in the case of the Charity Bazaar) the major dangers arose not from their cinema equipment, but from flimsy, flammable building materials and a lack of concern for such matters as emergency exits. The traveling showmen tried to organize and fight the growing trend toward regulation of their facilities, but with little success. They were, in any event, already weakened and vulnerable, victims of the country's continuing demographic shift, and also of a campaign against them led by Monsieur Charles Pathé.

Pathé's career as France's leading media industrialist had four phases. First, he worked briefly as a fairground exhibitor (of the phonograph). Subsequently, he abandoned exhibition to sell equipment and entertainment products to others, mostly small entrepreneurs as he had been. In the third phase, which concerns us here, he continued as a producer and manufacturer but also moved back into exhibition. In so doing he waged economic war on the weakest sector of that area of the industry, the fairground cinemas. In the last phase of his career—which, in its entirety, lasted barely over thirty years—Pathé abandoned the production of films and equipment almost completely, concentrating on distribution and exhibition. These two last moves, back into exhibition and then, after World War I, out of production, caused great upheaval and lamentation in the industry. Both also made a great deal of money for Pathé and his beloved investors.

In retrospect, it seems clear that conflict between a true capitalist like Charles Pathé and the traveling cinema operators was inevitable. From Pathé's point of view, the fairground operators were simply not exploiting the medium intensively and efficiently enough. It was rarely their sole attraction: Abraham Dulaar's Athenium Théâtre, for example, also featured an *aerogyne*, or flying woman; his brother Jérome's Théâtre Mondain often employed performers from the *café-concert* circuit. Because they moved about, these exhibitors did not need very many films. They could play a given location to saturation with a single program and then move on. Like everyone else in France, they bought rather than rented their films, which they often colored by hand or otherwise modified to fit their own particular needs. Producers like Pathé and Méliès had no control over the final, projected form of their products. (They also offered their own, mass-produced colored prints, which they would have preferred exhibitors to acquire.) Moreover, the first decade of this century was a period of highly uneven economic development, with two full-scale recessions before the beginning of sustained growth in 1909. The fairground cinemas had a foolproof strategy for hard times: they retrenched, cut back expenses, and bought no new films until prosperity returned. But this way of coping was bad for film producers. First, film production had to be cut back during economic downturns. Second, films were periodically horribly overused, sometimes becoming less photographic images than collections of scratches and splices—a state of affairs which did not make new friends for the medium among disgruntled spectators.

The high watermark of the fairground cinema was probably reached during 1907, a prosperous time sandwiched between two recessions. But in that year came the shot heard round the cinema world: Pathé Frères would entirely cease the sale of its films. Henceforth, the largest film producer in the world would only *rent* films in its home market and, furthermore, only to five franchised companies, each with an assigned geographical territory. In one case, the appropriately named Cinéma-Monopole, this amounted to Pathé only renting to itself. The fairground operators interpreted this move, correctly, as an attempt to drive them out of business. It is perhaps not a coincidence that in the very next year, 1908, the Motion Picture Patents Company established a similar, if more elaborately structured attempt at vertical monopolization in the United States. In fact, one of the participants in the M.P.P.C. was none other than Pathé Frères, whose shining example probably served as a beacon to the American capitalists, and principally to Thomas Alva Edison, in the dark night of the free market economy.

This daring move had two related consequences. The first was to strengthen the position of Pathé Frères in the battle to control and profit from the increasingly lucrative business of film exhibition. This was a field the company had entered well before 1907, though many aspects of these operations are for the moment difficult to specify precisely.[3] Film exhibition was to become so profitable that it ultimately became the major profit center of the organization and was spun off as a separate business entity. But paradoxically, the second consequence of Pathé's bid for monopoly was to encourage the competition. For if the company would no longer sell films to the growing number of French exhibitors, other businesses asked nothing more than to do just that. Charles Pathé had strengthened his company's position in exhibition while weakening it in the area of production, a move which foreshadowed his complete withdrawal, little more than a decade later, from the manufacture of films.

The major beneficiary of this new state of affairs was Pathé's only substantial rival, Léon Gaumont. These two men were in many ways complementary figures. Pathé, a petit bourgeois Alsatian just a year younger than Gaumont, willingly labeled himself a *parvenu*, which might be translated as "self-made upstart." His company, and most of its employees (such as Ferdinand Zecca), had the ethos and methods of its founder's social position. Gaumont, on the other hand, aspired to—though he had not been born into—the classic, Parisian *haute bourgeoisie*. Of even more humble origins than Pathé (his mother was a chambermaid, his father a cab driver), he was obliged to earn his own living at an early age, though a strong interest in science led him to take night courses at various scholarly societies. Through his attendance at one of these, he was recommended as a young man of promise to Jules Carpentier, who would later mass manufacture the Lumières' Cinématographes. Gaumont began work as an office boy at the Carpentier machine works in 1881, beginning a career in French visual media which was to be second in importance only to Charles Pathé's. By 1893, at twenty-nine years of age, he was the managing director of the Comptoir Général de Photographie, a prestigious photographic products supplier with offices just off the Avenue de l'Opéra. Following its owners' loss of a disastrous lawsuit, the establishment was put up for sale. Gaumont borrowed 50,000 francs from family and friends (he had married a woman with a substantial dowry) and found partners among the firm's wealthier customers to put up an additional 150,000 francs. The firm became the Comptoir Général de Photographie Léon Gaumont et Cie. Gaumont embarked on a program of expansion of the business, and well before the first Lumière shows at the Grand Café the company had bought the rights to two proto-cinematic apparatuses based on Marey's work, from that scientist's collaborator Georges Demenÿ.

Like Pathé, Gaumont was more interested in the equipment side of the business than in film production. This latter task he quickly assigned to his own equivalent of Ferdinand Zecca: Alice Guy, known to all as Mademoiselle Alice. Guy had been Gaumont's personal secretary and an extremely competent one, but this alone hardly accounts for his extraordinary decision to assign such an important position to a woman. This was fifty years before women in France had the vote, and Georges Méliès was probably far more representative of attitudes within the nascent film industry when he made his repeated attacks on the contemporary women's movement. But there was a sympathy between Gaumont and Guy, which possibly had its roots in similar self-images and social aspirations. This, combined with the fact that at the time no one dreamed how important film production would become for companies like Gaumont, probably accounts for the remarkable opportunity Monsieur Gaumont gave to Mademoiselle Alice.

Though Alice Guy was born in Paris in 1873, she was raised first in a suburb of Geneva, moved to Valparaiso, Chile, and finally attended a small, ultraconservative convent (where every year Bastille Day was an occasion for deep mourning) near the French border in Switzerland. She lived a life of privilege, if not always of ease, until she was sixteen, when her family's fortunes were suddenly destroyed, and she and her mother had to earn their own living in Paris. She enrolled in lessons in typing and dictation, which she quickly mastered, and obtained the important post of secretary to the directors at the Comptoir Général de Photographie shortly before Léon Gaumont acquired control of the company. Guy's bourgeois background and her many travels must certainly have helped her to fit in with the firm and its generally wealthy, sophisticated clientele. Her ambition to reenter the bourgeoisie from which she had fallen would have endeared her to the enterprise's new owner. She and he both combined the drive and flexibility of the *parvenu* with the cultural and intellectual values of the bourgeoisie. Gaumont would hardly have relished hiring someone like the plain-spoken and exuberant Ferdinand Zecca to make his films. In Miss Alice Guy he found a will of steel and a devotion both to the company and to her own career, the whole overlaid with a convent education and good royalist connections.

Alice Guy is one of the most significant figures in the entire history of French cinema. Despite her great influence, frustratingly little is known about her actual work at Gaumont. She did write a lively autobiography which, like all such works, does not always address the questions that one would like to have answered and suffers from occasional lapses of memory. Until historians carefully examine the extant Gaumont films and written records from 1895 to 1907 (the year she left its Paris operation, though not the company), any account of Guy's work there will be mainly conjectural. Her importance for French cinema, in any event, is not limited to or even necessarily dependent on the quality of her own early films (about which we know very little).[4] She was, like Zecca, not only a director but also one of the earliest French producers. As such she did two supremely important things: she created, over time, the Gaumont "house style," and she developed and trained a team of filmmakers who would be, quite simply, the best in the business, including perhaps most notably her successor as head of production at the company, the great Louis Feuillade. But if Feuillade, and others of the new generation which came to prominence around 1907–08, achieved greatness, it was by standing, as it were, on the shoulders of Alice Guy.

With a little practice, one can generally tell the difference between a Pathé film from the first decade of this century and one from Gaumont of the same period. In a sense, the true film authors at Pathé Frères were the set designers. Following and developing strategies first explored by Méliès, the Pathé filmmakers employed carefully painted *trompe-l'oeil* backgrounds, which often give the impression of being at least as important as the films' stories. The company's 1904 catalog was quite specific on this point: "Set designers, under exclusive contract to us, permit us to vary infinitely the décor of our scenes, and you know that this particularity has its value. Without exception, *each of our scenes has its own special decor.*"[5] The studio's output frequently employed slow lateral panning shots, quite unusual for the period, which seem to have as their principal function to show that the sets do not stop just out of camera range. One notable example occurs in *Au bagne/Scenes of Convict Life* (1905, probably directed by Zecca), a film that in many ways exemplifies the Pathé set design style and its careful attention to perspective and general visual homogeneity.[6]

Early Gaumont films are more likely to use real locations than are the Pathé productions.[7] When they do use painted backdrops, these are typically somewhat crude and schematic when compared with Pathé's precise, detailed designs. The Gaumont works' art direction is less refined, but generally also more flexible and expressive. On occasion noticeable visual conflict arises between the backdrop in one scene and location shooting in another, and sometimes also between one backdrop and the next. It is beyond doubt that these characteristics of the company's visual style were developed by Alice Guy and not by Louis Feuillade. Guy was the first producer/director methodically to scout for locations, and she often made up a film story to fit a visually interesting location or event. In this she began a tradition of photographic verisimilitude in French commercial narrative cinema that would continue down to the days of the New Wave. When she used painted backdrops, she experimented with different visual styles and arrangements of materials. She did not content herself with the elaboration of an established, homogenous style such as characterized the productions of Pathé Frères.

In part, both of these strategies were designed to save money. At least once Guy bought an entire set of used scene backgrounds from a theatre that had no more use for them, and then figured out ways to employ them in her films. She preferred to order her backdrops by the piece from different designers, rather than employ a salaried design department—which probably saved a great deal of money. Location shooting, of course, can also serve as a means of keeping expenses down. Like so many creative people once marked by the experience of (in her case, relative) poverty, Alice Guy never forgot how to economize. But she also obviously liked the *challenge* of cinema, which was even more daunting when it had to be met mainly with found materials. And she liked to be surprised, sometimes pleasantly, sometimes unpleasantly, at what she ended up doing. For Guy, cinema was a process of discovery; for Zecca it was a way to earn a good living while expressing something of his own values and personality. In her memoirs Guy recalls thinking of early cinema as of "a fresh, limpid spring, joyously reflecting the grasses, the cresses, and the willows that bordered it; we had only to wet our lips in it in order to slake our thirst. Its eddies murmured things to us, banal things no doubt, that it urged us to pass on in our turn, a first message to those who could not reach it and refresh themselves."[8]

We will never know for certain, but it was presumably Alice Guy who created and nurtured the mood of excitement and sheer aesthetic pleasure that one senses in so many prewar Gaumont films, including the ones made after her departure from the Paris studio. It is this, finally, which distinguishes the larger and more profitable Pathé film operation from the smaller one founded by Léon Gaumont and shaped by Alice Guy: the people at the latter company took more risks, had more joy in their work. Ideologically, Pathé Frères was far more liberal (Gaumont, Guy, and later Feuillade all had pronounced right-wing leanings); humanly, the Gaumont company was the more liberated, its films ultimately more liberating.

▨ By around 1908 French cinema had stabilized, if not become entirely fixed. Film programs were composed of a number of short works of varying lengths and types. In the nearly established urban cinemas, which were becoming the norm, an average program might run two hours and include travelogues, comedies, fantastic narratives, melodramas, perhaps a newsreel, and sometimes audience sing-alongs and even live performers. There was always musical accompaniment of sorts, and most of the films had some (nonnaturalistic) color, either by means of tints applied to the whole film strip or by hand- or stencil-coloring of objects within the frame. The hodge-podge nature of these programs must be emphasized, as must the utter strangeness, to modern spectators, of most of them. A popular favorite was the scientific cinema, most notably the medical film and the botanical film. The undisputed master in this area, as celebrated in his day as he is forgotten in ours, was Doctor Jean Comandon, who had the distinction of being one of a handful of film producers, aside from Ferdinand Zecca, funded and overseen directly by Charles Pathé. Comandon started with time-lapse cinematography and went on to explore other capabilities of the movie camera. His microcine-matographic views of cholera germs, human sperm, fleas, plant pol-lination, and other subjects became something of a fad in the early teens, to the point that the Gaumont company hired its own compet-ing scientist-filmmaker, one Mademoiselle Chevroton. Ethnographic films were also quite popular. The tremendous range of so-called "primitive" cinema is astonishing.

One type of work dominated, however. This was the comic film, which arguably can be traced back to *Le Jardinier et le petit espiègle*, though neither its director Louis Lumière nor his collaborators did much to develop the genre. Georges Méliès's work had always been humorous, of course, and his films undoubtedly had some influence on the French comic school, but a great deal of the impetus to its development seems to have come from England, where the cinema had a brief but internationally influential burst of development in the decade between 1897 and 1907. By 1905 English directors (such as George Albert Smith and James Williamson) were arguably the lead-ing comic filmmakers in the world.[9] Their works were quickly adapted and elaborated upon by the major French producers. Pathé Frères even saw fit to abandon its famous studios and set designers to imitate the English films' frequent location shooting—as in, for exam-ple, the extremely successful *Dix Femmes pour un mari* (*Ten Women for One Husband*, 1905), a blatant knock-off of Alf Collins's *Personal* (1904). The Gaumont company, which distributed *Personal* in France, also exploited the English mode of comic actions in real locations, perhaps more innovatively than did Pathé. Works such as Feuillade's *Une Dame vraiment bien* (*A Really Swell Lady*, 1908) and *L'Homme aimanté* (*The Magnetized Man*, 1907) are, structurally, comic chases in the English manner: a catastrophic situation moves, inexorably, from place to (real) place, wreaking havoc as it proceeds. Pathé Frères, for its part, was quicker to exploit a more profitable and easily standardized form of comedy, one based on the growing importance of the movie star.

Early French comic stars were inseparable from the fixed, stereotyped roles that they played. André Deed, whose real name was André de Chapais, was a singer and acrobat before he appeared in a number of Pathé chase comedies. Beginning in 1906, he became the studio's first identified running comic character, "Boireau," a very broadly drawn figure with unsubtle and hypertheatrical makeup who typically blundered into things and provoked laughs by absurdly clutzy behavior. Most of Deed's, as well as similar films with other actors from Pathé and competing studios, are close to unwatchable today, though they were wildly popular in their time. The first of these series stars to bring some subtlety and genuine inventiveness to the comic character film was Max Linder, Pathé's—indeed the entire French cinema's—greatest star of the prewar period.

Linder's real name was Gabriel-Maximilien Leuvielle. He was born in a village in the Gironde, in the heart of Bordeaux, where his parents raised grapes for wine making. Against the wishes of his family (to have him grow or deal in grapes, like any sane human being), he enrolled in drama courses at the Bordeaux Conservatory and later played small stage roles in that city. In 1904 he went to Paris, where three times he took the yearly entrance exam for the Conservatory, and three times he failed. By this time Gabriel Leuvielle had definitively adopted the stage name of Max Linder, and under that name he was engaged at the Ambigu theatre—a recruiting ground for Pathé Frères because of Zecca's family connection with the establishment—and played various walk-on and secondary roles in melodrama. The Ambigu's extras coordinator, Louis Gasnier, who directed for Pathé in his spare time, engaged the young man for a number of films beginning in 1905 with *La Première Sortie d'un collégien* (*The School Boy's First Outing*).

Like Charles Chaplin after him (on whom the French comic had an enormous influence), Linder did not begin in cinema with his trademark character. He played various roles, but never that of the blasé young dandy. That character was the exclusive property of the actor Gréhan, who was, with André Deed, one of the studio's most successful series comics. In 1907 Gréhan got a better offer at a new competing studio, and his departure left a big gap in the company's production schedule. Linder was chosen to fill Gréhan's shoes, as well as his evening coat, dress shirt, and tie. Assuming the costume and much of the manner of Gréhan's character "Gontran," Linder made, under Gasnier's direction, *Les Débuts d'un patineur/Max Learns to Skate* (1907), the first work in which he becomes, recognizably, "Max." The film was not a hit either with audiences or with Pathé executives, however. For two years it remained without a sequel, while Linder continued to perform as a lead or secondary character in various other projects for the studio.

Linder finally got another chance at comic stardom in 1909, again with a variant on Gréhan's dandy. (Gréhan, who had brought the character with him to Pathé from the theatre, had meanwhile taken it along with him to the Eclair studios.) The new Max films were enormously successful, and he continued making works in the series, generally one every two weeks, until war broke out in 1914. This rate of production was one-half that of most other notable series comics; Prince (Pathé's "Rigadin" after 1910), for example, later claimed to have starred in the greatest number of comic films of any artist of the period, the eye-opening but not impossible figure of 582.[10] Despite Linder's less frequent screen appearances, few stars were as loved as he, and few were paid so well. He made tours of Spain, Russia, Germany, Eastern Europe. Everywhere he was mobbed. Women were said to contemplate suicide at the thought of his inaccessibility. Much later, in 1925, he and his young wife would themselves commit a spectacular double suicide, apparently provoked in part by the sudden loss of the public's love Max had once enjoyed.

One secret of Linder's success was that he put twice as much time, effort, and thought into each film as did his competitors.[11] Another equally important attraction was that his gestures were smaller, his pace much less frenetic compared to the other comic stars of his day. His great appeal to audiences can be seen as one of several key signs of the reentry of middle-class values into the cinema—moderation in all things, including comedy—in the years between 1907 and 1910. (Aside from Linder, such phenomena included, most prominently, the *film d'art* and the rise to prominence of the American director D. W. Griffith.) Broad slapstick would in any event have been out of place with the Max character, a distracted bourgeois dandy played with a real sense of what it meant to belong to the bourgeoisie.

It has been said that in Linder's films there is no necessary connection between character and comic effects, and yet this is clearly not entirely the case. Much of the films' humor springs from the conflict between Max's extreme self-confidence, an aspect of his social position, and his incompetence at even the simplest tasks. For the viewer familiar with the character, the films' titles announce this contradiction: *Max joue le drame* (*Max Plays at Drama,* 1910) and *Max jongleur par amour/A Tantalizing Young Lady* (1909), for example, demonstrate that Max can neither play drama (his wig falls off) nor juggle (he hires a professional to be his "hands," a trick that is quickly unmasked). Not only could the bourgeoisie itself be amused by the antics of this idiot son—he shouldn't try all these silly things anyway: where's *Max Joins the Family Business* or *Max Marries Well?*—but viewers from other classes could laugh at him insofar as he symbolized (and ridiculed) the whole bourgeoisie. Linder was appealing, a true star, in part because he could seem funny to different people in different ways. However, beyond his class status, it is true that Max has no individuating characteristics, except for generic comic tendencies to get drunk and fall madly in love. It would be for Chaplin to add this final development to the Linder persona, as Linder himself had modified Gréhan's. Chaplin's Tramp is a down-and-out figure who would desperately like to be a Max-like bourgeois dandy. Thus many of his difficulties have an interior, properly psychological dimension. The character is, to borrow E. M. Forster's distinction, more "round" than the essentially "flat" Max. At the same time, Chaplin—at least in his later films—can also be seen as excising most of the class content from Linder's characterization and replacing it with individualistic sentimentality.[12]

Although he expanded and developed Max's comic persona, Chaplin would borrow virtually intact Linder's restrained, minimal methods in using the film medium. Linder and the Pathé technicians who worked for him knew very well how to use match-on-action cutting (*Max victime du quinquina/Max and the Quinquina,* 1912), split-screen effects (*Max et son chien* [*Max and his Dog*], 1912), glance/object editing (*Max joue le drame*), and other elements of the so-called "language of cinema." But these devices they employed sparingly, and only when appropriate to a particular comic point. The normal Linder scene is played in full shot, straight at the camera in the manner of Georges Méliès's orchestra seat view, with no unnecessary cutting. At the same time that D. W. Griffith was flamboyantly exploring the medium's many resources in the United States, Linder was continuing the traditional French concern for the integrity of the shot. Griffith's extensive editing and other cinematic manipulations often had the effect of breaking down real, physical space into an abstract, mentalist geog-

MAX WANTS A DIVORCE.

During part of World War I Max Linder worked in the United States, his screen persona and filmmaking methods essentially unchanged. Unfortunately, American-made films like *Max Wants a Divorce* (Essenay, 1917) did little for his by then fading stardom.

raphy. Linder, conversely, was always scrupulously clear and literal in his use of space: if he edited two shots together, their relationship was always immediately comprehensible. In terms of the classical scene construction that would later dominate world cinema, it was not the celebrated American director's work, but the Linder films and others like them, with their invisible, always dramatically motivated and spatially logical joining of shots, which contributed the most to the evolving conventions of commercial narrative film. Histories of cinema too often focus on Griffith's extensive and extravagant use of the "language of cinema" at the expense of figures like Linder (or the makers of the *film d'art*, which we will examine next), who used the medium's resources less, but no less well, and above all, differently.

By its sheer volume and extraordinary box office returns, film comedy dominated French cinema until 1914. We must keep this fact in mind when considering three other important currents of the period: the *film d'art*, the serial, and pictorialist melodrama. The *film d'art* was significant, from its very conception, by being aimed at a different, socially more elevated audience than was the comic school. This was certainly not the first time that the cinema attempted specifically to interest the upper middle class: that distinction rests with Louis Lumière's works. But it marked the first time that the medium presumed to interest elite audiences not in itself as novelty but in the stories it could tell.

The words *film d'art* refer both to a type of filmmaking and to a specific production company. The company was founded in 1907, the marriage of the entrepreneurial acumen of Paul Lafitte (managing director) and the aesthetic vision and theatrical connections of Charles Le Bargy, a well-known Parisian actor (artistic director). The idea to film famous players from the Comédie Française and from the boulevard stage in recognizably highbrow (though not avant-garde) subjects was not the exclusive creation of Messieurs Lafitte and Le Bargy. But they were unique in founding a production company solely for this purpose, and in being past masters of the genteel art of gaining media attention:

> Monsieur Alfred Capus is in his home, practically speechless [wrote Covielle, in *Le Matin*]. I run to seize him by the neck, offering him some throat lozenges. I ask:
> "So you are working for that great cinema, the third and very soon the only French theatre?"
> "Make your jokes," replies the author of *Two Men*. "Make jokes about the cinématographe, but there's always something left standing . . . I have already begun a play for De Féraudy and Lavallière. It's a series of very short tableaux of the different sorts of Parisian life. Of course, I don't write all the characters' dialogue, since it's a pantomime. The actors will nonetheless be obliged to learn their parts and to rehearse. This will require two or three sessions, in any event, made agreeable perhaps by the roles, and certainly by the fee paid for each rehearsal."
> The beautiful poster, on which the names of Sarah [Bernhardt], Réjane, Granier, Mounet-Sully, Guitry, would be side by side, was to appear that night. The duel between the cinema and the theatre has begun. Provided that the one does not kill the other![13]

One fascinating aspect of the extensive newspaper coverage of the *film d'art* (sometimes genuine reporting, sometimes fantasy, very often obviously rehashed publicity texts) is how it seems to rehearse in miniature the debate over film and theatre that was to rage in the early

1930s on the occasion of the coming of synchronized sound to cinema. The Guitry of Covielle's (probably imaginary) poster was Lucien Guitry, a European stage idol; a generation later his son Sacha would also argue, with much coverage in the French press, that a struggle between cinema and stage had begun, and that film would be the theatre of the future. More immediately significant than this foreshadowing of later debates was the company's careful exploitation of the publicity channels of bourgeois theatre. The studio got its films reviewed, their preparation and rehearsals covered, as if they were boulevard plays. Today, with the massive publicity apparatus of cinema in place, this seems unsurprising. But before the *film d'art*, cinema simply did not get this sort (or this quantity) of press coverage. At this point all channels of theatre publicizing were brought into play: reports on business aspects of the productions, reviews of the works, bits of gossip about their actors and writers. In this sense, modern cinema publicity methods were born with the *film d'art*.

Although many histories of cinema reject the Film d'Art company's productions as crude, uncinematic, and an artistic dead end, such evaluations seem mainly based on secondary sources that repeat judgments from other secondary sources, or on hasty viewings of corrupt prints. Although it quickly encountered unsurmountable financial difficulties, the enterprise in its first years produced significant works that had a lasting influence on French, and world, cinema. Its first public program was presented to a select invited audience on November 17, 1908. The featured work was *La Mort du duc de Guise/The Assasination of the Duc de Guise*, directed by Le Bargy and André Calmettes, with a scenario by Henri Lavedan and with a music score for the live orchestra by Camille Saint-Saëns. Lavedan, a member of the Académie Française, was at the time one of the country's most celebrated writers, though today he is virtually forgotten. His participation helped distinguish the work from previous filmings of the same story, for the Lumières and Pathé Frères had already produced their own versions of the Duke's death. The new work was well received by the critics, as were most of the other films which followed.

After the first public program, Charles Pathé is said to have complimented Lafitte and Le Bargy, "Ah, gentlemen, you have gone well beyond the rest of us!" Pathé could well afford to be generous because he stood to profit from the films' success (he had acquired, on very good terms, exclusive distribution rights) and because he was already working to assure the company's downfall, having set up a similar, competing business, the Société Cinématographique des Auteurs et Gens de Lettres, whose films he would also distribute. But with or without Pathé's kind ministrations, the enterprise in its original form was probably doomed. Enormous sums had been invested in a new studio in the Paris suburb of Neuilly and in large payments (though not as large as reported in the press) to authors and actors. The films cost too much money; the public they aimed to reach did not yet go to the movies in large numbers; production was far too artisanal for the company to have a regular, predictable flow of product. In June of 1909 business was so bad that Lafitte and Le Bargy were fired by the company they had created, and a new director was hired to try to revive it. The distribution contract with Pathé was abrogated (and a lawsuit instituted against him). Film budgets were slashed. But the effort was unsuccessful, and in 1911 the bankrupt organization was taken over by its distributor, Charles Delac. Although Delac was to go on to be an important independent film producer in the postwar period, the name Film d'Art soon ceased to be anything more than a trademark for his varied productions.

The most striking characteristic of all the company's "art" films is their restrained, efficient, and expressive acting. Gestures are economical—certainly more restrained than they would have been on stage—and they have been carefully planned for the camera. When an important action occurs, it is the only motion within the frame; when another character reacts, the first becomes immobile, more so than would be necessary on the stage. In Henri Pouctal's *La Dame aux camélias/Camille* (1911, after Alexandre Dumas *fils*), when the doomed courtesan, played by an aging Sarah Bernhardt, dies in the arms of her former lover, the viewer's attention is directed to one strategically placed hand; the rest of her figure is immobile, and partially obscured by the other actor. The hand clenches, then falls. Stunned, the lover suddenly pivots to give the camera a good view of her dead body. The effect is impressive, but it is as much a directorial triumph as the result of good acting.[14] (It is absolutely essential in judging such effects to view the films at sixteen or eighteen frames per second; at modern "sound speed" the players' movements become jittery and hysterical.) That such effects are achievable in narrative cinema may seem obvious today, but it was not so evident in the context of *belle époque* cinema.

Another remarkable aspect of the films is their use of depth. Although the sets are obviously theatrical-style "flats," they are arranged in three dimensions and have been built to allow entrances and exits from the back as well as from the sides, and to facilitate the use of multiple planes of action. *La Mort du duc de Guise* displays a remarkable cinematic progress through several sets via movement in depth: characters exit at the rear of one set, are seen entering through what appears to be the same door at the back of another, and so on. The narrative carefully and methodically progresses through the royal palace, a fictional space that always extends beyond the screen, and in depth relative to it. Directional matches are always correct, even by today's standards—which cannot always be said of other works of the period, for example Griffith's. What the films lack, generally, is editing within scenes and any real variety of shot scale (except for occasional close-up insert shots). *La Mort du duc de Guise* handles these limitations by keeping its scenes (that is, shots) relatively brief, and by the momentum generated by its action-matched passages from one set to the next. The company's later works, by contrast, become more and more obviously stagebound, at just the point in film history when the American cinema was discovering the psychological power resulting from motion.

But even as the Film d'Art company began its commercial and artistic decline, French cinema still dominated the world film market. Many of the other studios' "art series" (*séries d'art*) were quite successful, in France and elsewhere, although—perhaps because—they were less innovative. The nation excelled in the area of film comedy, with Max Linder the world's leading comic star. And a new French film genre was remarkably successful: the serial melodrama. All of Europe had been in the grip of American or American-style "novels" that were published in weekly installments, lavishly and sometimes grotesquely illustrated. (This is a phenomenon later lovingly recalled in Renoir and Prévert's *Le Crime de Monsieur Lange*.) The idea of transferring these stories to the cinema screen must have seemed obvious to many observers, but not, at first, to the massive, highly bureaucratized Pathé company, nor to its chief rival, Gaumont.

Former Gaumont director Victorin Jasset directed the first important French serial, *Nick Carter* (six episodes, 1908), for the Eclair company, one of the many new enterprises founded in the wake of Pathé's restructuring as a vertical monopoly. Eclair made a specialty of crime subjects and courted a distinctly lower-class audience. For a time its serials had great success and then, for several years, the genre faded away almost to nothing, before returning to prominence in 1911.

Among the larger-than-life figures in this second wave of serial mania were a resourceful detective named Nat Pinkerton (at Eclipse, another small company) and a master criminal called Zigomar who committed his crimes for Eclair. This time around, Pathé Frères partipated with a serial hero named Nick Winter. But the genre's biggest success, financially and artistically, was Gaumont's *Fantômas* (five episodes, 1913–14), directed by the company's head of production, Louis Feuillade.

Feuillade was born in 1873 in Lunel, a village in the Midi, the sun-baked South of France. His parents and relatives were all wine brokers, big people in a small world. The family was devoutly Catholic and fiercely anti-republican, attitudes the director was to keep all his life. After his military service, he married the daughter of a local fruit merchant and set himself up as a wine broker, passing much of his time writing poems and reciting them at banquets and in the village café. His destiny changed with the deaths of his father in 1896 and his mother in 1898. At the age of twenty-five Feuillade no longer felt bound to his native region and left for Paris with his wife. As before, he seems to have put more energy into his intellectual and social life than into his career, which for several years was little more than a series of dead-end jobs. Unlike the energetic young Balzacian provincial who moves to the capital to win fame and fortune, Feuillade seems to have gone there mainly to get away from home and to have more people of like mind to associate with—monarchist, anti-democratic attitudes being relatively unusual in the Midi.

It was by accident and not design that he finally did win fame and fortune in the cinema. While working as an assistant editor on the right-wing *Revue Mondiale,* he was struck by the sudden prosperity of an old friend who had begun work as a scenario writer for Pathé Frères. His friend got him an interview with Ferdinand Zecca, but nothing came of it: it is hard to imagine the arch-royalist Feuillade getting along with the populist Dreyfusard Zecca. He then approached the next most prosperous French studio, and in December 1905 he was engaged at Gaumont as a scenario writer and first assistant (the second assistant was Victorin Jasset) to Alice Guy. Feuillade, up to this point showing little interest in hard work of any sort, quickly became an assiduous and energetic writer, director, and later head of production for the firm when Guy left Paris with her new husband in 1907. This transformation seems more due to the particularly good meshing of three strong personalities—Guy, Léon Gaumont, and

Feuillade—than to any immediate predilection of the latter for the moving image. Also, the Gaumont company valued hard work and compensated it well. The young assistant worked for the substantial salary of one hundred francs a week, and he believed that in return he should give good value. Feuillade, in short, was no social rebel. But his imagination was to prove as exuberant, in its own way, as that of Georges Méliès, and his films were eventually prized by viewers (such as the Surrealists) whom he never would have dreamed of addressing socially or artistically.

Before becoming a specialist in the crime serial, Feuillade worked in most of the genres produced by Gaumont: the comic chase, the historical film, domestic drama (sometimes also called "family melo-drama," though it has little to do with pure young maidens tied to railroad tracks), jungle pictures, religious scenes, and comic character series. He wrote all of the films (and directed many of them) in the series *La Vie telle qu'elle est* ("Life as It Really Is"), which studio publicity promoted as a significant advance in cinema subject matter: "These scenes are intended to be *slices of life* . . . They shun all fantasy, and represent people and things as they are and not as they should be."[15] A recurrent theme in these domestic dramas, at least in the surviving examples analyzed and described by Richard Abel, is that social and sexual stereotypes are often misleading, tragically masking the true character of innocent individuals caught in a society too quick to cate-gorize and to condemn.[16] If one takes the publicity texts seriously, Feuillade intended these films as a reaction against the (socially deter-minist) neo-Naturalist works that had long been a staple of the Pathé output. The *Fantômas* serial was his next major project after *La Vie telle qu'elle est*, and in a sense it was the better response—a naturalis-tically presented fictional world in which fantastic, spiritually charged events occur, and where God and the devil fight a duel to the death on a quiet city street.

The enormous success of *Fantômas* and other serials may on one level be interpreted as a reaction against the scientific, rationalist, progressivist thought which dominated the late nineteenth century and *la belle époque* and formed the ideological backbone of literary Naturalism.[17] Master criminals and master detectives could not be explained by formulas such as Taine's *la race, le milieu, et le moment*, nor by Berthelot's "scientific" basis of morality. This was probably the basis of their appeal to the radical fringes of the intelligentsia, such as the circle surrounding the poet Guillaume Apollinaire, who created a "Society of the Friends of Fantômas." But the films were also eminently traditional as popular entertainments, continuing and transforming the traditions of the popular French stage. Traditional melodrama was typified by extreme polarization of characters, with absolute distinctions between Good and Evil; by episodic, improbable plots involving bizarre coincidences and sudden discoveries (of a character's unknown aristocratic ancestry, for example, via a locket or similar artifact); by a strong emphasis on sensory elements (music, other sounds, scenic effects) at the expense of dialogue; and by dramatic climaxes confronting Good and Evil against a spectacular background (an earthquake, a flaming dungeon, a runaway train about to massacre countless innocents).

What is unusual in Feuillade's work in the genre is its visual matter-of-factness; one would be tempted to say "realism" if it were not for the impossible characters and events. Location shooting is frequent, not only in *Fantômas* but in his masterpiece *Les Vampires* (1915–16) and in later works. Where used, sets are functional and only minimally expressive. Acting is sober and restrained, its rhythms slow and precise (Feuillade had learned the lessons of the *film d'art*). Editing and the elaboration of cinematic space are accurate and logical. In the midst of this carefully constructed, plausible world, strange things happen. Investigative reporter Philippe Guérande, on the track of the criminal band "The Vampires," leans out of the second story window of his room in a (very real location shot) villa in the Midi. Suddenly a noose is placed around his neck by a mechanism operated from the ground via a long pole, and he is dragged out of the window and falls, literally, into the hands of his enemies. In *Fantômas*, Inspector Juve awaits an unknown assassin in his bedroom, a studio set in this instance, but no more or less attractive or sinister than a real contemporary bedroom. A dark car stops in the (real) street below, and the killer emerges: a huge python.

In his crime serials Feuillade elaborated an aesthetics of cinematic paranoia. As in traditional stage melodrama, there is Good versus Evil. One is more powerful than the other, though generally (most clearly in *Judex* [1917]) the balance of power shifts back and forth. The director typically tells his story from the restricted point of view of the less powerful side: at any given moment the character whose actions lead us through the narrative will be, as it were, swimming against a strong current. When Juve, who has served as the narrative center of most of the second episode of *Fantômas*, has at last trapped

In Feuillade's work danger often strikes in the midst of reassuring, ordinary surroundings, as here, with the hero sitting unawares in an automobile on a sunny day in *La Nouvelle Mission de Judex* (*Judex's New Mission*, 1917).

the master criminal in Lady Beltham's villa, we switch to the villain's point of view until he escapes and regains the upper hand (and the episode ends). Visually, the films reinforce their paranoid structure with an unstable dialectic of the subjective and the objective. As with so many prewar French films, the Feuillade serials generally avoid editing except for changes of scene, with one huge exception. There are frequent insert shots, point-of-view close-ups of letters, significant objects, *clues* to the activity of the other side. Typically, the meaning of these artifacts is either unknown or misleading. There are no mediating, semi-subjective medium shots like the ones the classic Hollywood cinema would later employ to blunt this opposition. But the "objective" shots can sometimes prove as limited and potentially deceptive as the "subjective" ones, as when the noose contraption suddenly snares Philippe Guérande, coming from outside not only his point of view, but ours as well.

Feuillade went on making serial melodramas until his death in 1925, though his period of greatest creativity in the genre coincided almost exactly with the years of the Great War, which also saw the peak of public interest in the genre. After the war serials continued to be produced, but their heyday had clearly passed. However, a related type of filmmaking, brought to first perfection by a contemporary and coworker of Feuillade's, pointed the way to significant later developments in the very different postwar environment. This was a type of filmmaking which here will be labeled "pictorialist melodrama"; before the Great War its master was Léonce Perret.[18] Perret, who was seven years younger than Feuillade and would continue making films into the early sound period, had come to the Gaumont studio in Feuillade's first year as artistic director, working first as an actor and then also as a director. He was best known to the early cinema public as "Léonce" of the innovative comic series of the same name. Henri Fescourt, who was there at the time, reports that Perret's standing at the studio sometimes threatened to eclipse even Feuillade's.

It has been estimated that between 70 and 90 percent of prewar French films have been irretrievably lost. Thus any judgment of Perret's originality or relative value as an early feature film director must be severely qualified. But there are few known works of prewar world cinema which are the equals—technically, aesthetically, and in the degree to which they anticipate the best of later commercial narrative cinema—of his *L'Enfant de Paris* (*Child of Paris*, 1913) and *Le Roman d'un mousse* (*Story of a Cabin Boy*, 1914). Both of these works are traditional melodramas of feature film length, belonging to the quite popular subgenre in which the protagonist is a child or adolescent. The "child of Paris" is the kidnapped young daughter of an aristocratic military officer. In the course of an approximately ninety-minute film, she is hidden in a large wicker basket, locked in various rooms, spirited away from the police who are looking for her, and taken on a cinematic tour of the Midi before being rescued by a plucky orphan boy. In *Le Roman d'un mousse*, Perret's cabin boy is taken on a comparable odyssey in a little over two hours of screen time. The son by a first marriage of a wealthy countess, he is abducted by the moneylender to his mother's debt-ridden second husband and delivered to the unscrupulous captain of a ship sailing for Iceland. The captain is to dispose of the boy during the voyage, but he escapes with the help of a sympathetic old sailor and eventually turns up at his mother's trial for murder in Paris. He clears her of the crime, the moneylender is arrested, and a symbolic new family is forged of mother, child, and old sailor.

Not surprisingly, Perret's work resembles Feuillade's in many ways, most notably in its extensive use of location shooting and naturalistic set design. But unlike Feuillade (at least the Feuillade of the great serial melodramas), Perret created a cinematic world based on homogeneity and continuity rather than on contradiction and rupture.[19] A striking characteristic of both *L'Enfant de Paris* and *Le Roman d'un mousse* is their effective use of light. Perret could make people and things *shimmer* in his images, seem to float on the very light by which one sees them. There is an airy, pleasing quality, an expressivity even in scenes of great tension, much of it produced by extensive use of backlighting (which creates a halo effect around characters). He frequently employed water or leaves in motion as a background in his shots, which gave them an attractive, textured look. His visual compositions were carefully constructed to be pleasing in and of themselves (whereas Feuillade's tended to be more strictly functional). The director's emphasis on the beauty of the image for its own sake and also as a means of romanticizing its contents arguably makes him one of the first masters of French cinematic pictorialism, a tendency that recurs periodically in different guises in the history of the medium.

Perret's films systematically deploy their dramatic situations in depth, continuing in the tradition of the Film d'Art. His films were probably among the first in France consistently to employ the so-called American shot, thus named by the French because they first saw it in films from the Vitagraph studio. (This shot cuts characters off somewhere between the ankles and the chest; contemporary French observers had commented on American film characters "with no feet.") He employed a remarkably large range (vastly larger than Feuillade, who clearly was not interested in this sort of thing) of different types of edits, variations in shooting distance, high angle versus low angle shooting, and other stylistic effects. His work flawlessly combines such sophisticated cinematic means with the basic respect for the integrity of the shot so characteristic of early French cinema.

To argue for Perret and against the often technically less sophisticated but (probably unconsciously) proto-modernist Feuillade, or vice versa, is of course possible, but finally unhelpful. Despite superficial similarities, the two filmmakers had wholly different goals and visions. Their works suggest two neighboring summits in the high mountain range of French cinema in its influential two decades of world hegemony.[20] But this metaphor is misleading, for mountain ranges are not knocked down almost to level ground in the course of a few years. And this was to be the fate of the once mighty French film industry. The first modern audio-visual mass media empire, it was to be one of the many casualties of Europe's first terrifyingly modern war.

II

The Golden Age of the Silent Film

4

Decline and Mutation

The disaster which struck the French cinema in the early years of World War I was not a unique, isolated event. Automobile and airplane manufacturing suffered similarly catastrophic declines in their share of the world market, as did many other sectors of the nation's industrial economy. The crisis began with the total mobilization of ablebodied Frenchmen to fight what was initially envisioned as a brief conflict. Virtually all industries unrelated to the war were shut down until further notice. But the conflict dragged on, with little progress except in the numbers of the dead. Meanwhile, demand for films continued unabated in the world market (as for automobiles, airplanes, and other products), and enterprises from other countries, many of them newly created or expanded to take advantage of the situation, stepped in to fill the void. By the time the French government realized that the war would not be quickly won and allowed some industrial activity to start up again, severe damage had been done.

But the French cinema's decline would not have been so precipitous had the industry not already been in an inherently unstable position. France was a small country, effectively even smaller because it was still remarkably rural compared to other Western nations. The film industry depended heavily on exports, and by far its most significant foreign market was the United States. French companies had important American subsidiaries or branch offices; industrialists such as Charles Pathé and Léon Gaumont regularly made the long sea voyage to this distant and strange land. From New York in 1908, Gaumont wrote to his new production head Louis Feuillade about what to do and not to do to maintain the company's position: "*The Iron Worker's Daughter* and

The Piano Mistress are marvelous in their action, their photography, but unshowable in the American market. The subject offends public morality here. It's a great pity, it's frightening, but that's the way things are. You see, my dear Feuillade, that your job is far from simple."[1] It was essential to produce films which could be successfully marketed at home and abroad. Comedies and Méliès-style trick films played well on both sides of the Atlantic, as did travelogues and most other nonfiction subjects. Although today it seems bizarre, French producers pioneered the Western film with the help of France's own Joe Hammon, who, along with "Bronco Billy" Anderson, was one of the screen's original cowboy stars. (Both men began making Westerns in 1907.) Hammon had lived in Montana and South Dakota as a teenager, and there had learned to ride, rope cattle, and look and act the part of the cowboy. By the early teens he was one of the French cinema's most popular stars in its home market—in retrospect an ominous portent of the nation's later infatuation with American mass culture.

Producing films in the United States through a French-financed and managed subsidiary was an alternate strategy. Even Georges Méliès, in his last years in the industry, had an American affiliate headed by his brother Gaston, the Méliès Manufacturing Company, located first in Fort Lee, New Jersey, and subsequently on a ranch in San Antonio, Texas (the company made mostly Westerns). Pathé Frères inagurated their American production in 1910 with *The Girl from Arizona,* filmed in the wilds of deepest New Jersey. (It was in the interest of greater visual authenticity that the Méliès operation had moved to Texas.) Gaumont and Eclair, among others, also had American studios. But as the French companies developed their various overseas operations, already their share of the American market was beginning to decline.

The nickelodeon boom that had begun in 1907 vastly increased the extent both of American film exhibition and of direct, often cutthroat competition within it. For several years French producers held on to a large share of this booming market. However, new American production companies were formed and smaller ones expanded to respond to the ever growing, but also increasingly selective, demand for product. Foreign producers quickly became the targets of cultural and economic nationalism. American social reformers denounced European films as immoral. Several independent domestic producers launched a "buy American" campaign in the industry press. The

French grip on the American market began to loosen. Eclair American merged with a larger U.S. studio in 1912, and in 1914 what remained of the company ceased operations entirely after a disastrous fire. The Pathé subsidiary sold off its real estate and equipment in 1914, regressing in effect from full-fledged studio to independent production company. The American film industry was poised to move West (some of it already had); most of the remaining French affiliates stayed on in New York and New Jersey and faded slowly from the scene.

The French companies' final years of significant American activity were greatly complicated by the assiduous efforts of Thomas Alva Edison to dominate the U.S. film industry. In 1908 Edison masterminded the formation of the Motion Picture Patents Company. The M.P.P.C. included seven major American producers, plus Pathé Frères, Méliès's American subsidiary, and George Kleine, an importer of European films. The organization's aim was nothing short of a complete monopoly of all motion picture production and distribution in the United States, with a large share of the proceeds going to Edison (for his supposedly unassailable patents). But in 1912 the U.S. Justice Department filed an anti-trust suit against the M.P.P.C. In 1913 the case went to trial, and in 1915 a federal district court ruled the Edison trust illegal. Although the M.P.P.C. had not achieved its lofty goal of industrial hegemony, it had for four years succeeded in slowing the rise of the new independent producers who were to become the major powers of the American industry. Without the trust, which included one major and one minor French producer directly and the agent—Kleine—of several others, France's fall to a poor second place in the world cinema industry might well have occurred earlier than it did. However, to make this argument is to speak, somewhat misleadingly, of the French industry as a whole: the Edison trust benefited some producers—above all, Pathé—at the expense of others, many of which joined in the growing rebellion against it. As it happened, the interruption of film production in France and the final unfettering of the American independents occurred almost simultaneously, an unhappy coincidence which made the French producers' difficulties all the more spectacular and sudden.

In the years just before the French producers' fall from industrial grace, a new factor raised the stakes in the international struggle over the world film market: feature film production. Films of more (eventually much more) than twenty minutes in length achieved broad audience acceptance in Europe before they reached American audiences in large numbers. Their box-office revenues could be very substantial, a compellingly attractive feature to vertically integrated companies like Pathé Frères, which were heavily involved in exhibition. The larger studios poured increasing sums of money into their feature productions, and found that revenues grew even more than the film budgets. In contemporary terms, features became the A pictures of the day, with the shorter works mostly relegated to B status. But European producers, with their small home markets, needed to sell such big budget productions in the American market if they were to realize profits on them. French firms in particular aggressively marketed their features in the United States. Pathé, which was increasingly involved in feature production, operated within the conservative, generally anti-feature Edison trust, while most other firms worked outside of it, through independent American distributors and exhibitors.[2]

American exhibitors and most of the country's producers did not want the feature film to become the industry standard. The numerous small nickelodeon theatres were geared to brief programs of many short films; their working-class audiences did not have the time to attend longer presentations—or so it was thought. Many features were screened outside the nickelodeon circuit, as "road shows" in theatres that normally presented plays. In the early teens, the success of several of these efforts began to change minds within the industry. The future movie mogul Adolph Zukor paid what many Americans found the astonishing sum of $35,000 for the rights to an obscure, independently produced four-reel picture, *La Reine Elizabeth* (*Queen Elizabeth*, 1912). This was one of the last French *film d'art* spinoffs, starring Sarah Bernhardt. It had not had significant impact in the European market, where it appeared clumsy and antiquated by comparison with the newer, better features. But in the American market it was an enormous hit, providing the seed capital for what would later become Paramount Pictures, and changing many minds about the shape of the emerging American film industry.

La Reine Elizabeth was the best known, though by no means the only example of a French feature work which helped to stimulate American companies' interest in the production of longer films. However, U.S. companies which began to produce features found themselves, in their turn, in need of increased revenues to amortize these more expensive products. They sought to expand their own market share, sending their films across the Atlantic in search of their own foreign revenues. The economic chaos of the early years of World War I gave them their golden opportunity to make the French market a colony of the American industry as the United States had once been for France. From figures provided by Pierre Bachlin, one can calculate that French national film production, by meters of film per week, accounted for 38 percent of the country's total supply of films in 1914. In 1916, only halfway through the war, the figure had fallen to 18 percent.[3] These numbers are very tricky, for they measure quantities of film, not showings on movie screens or box office returns. But comparatively, they give a clear picture of the industry's decline, which was very grave indeed. In two years its share of its home market was probably cut in half.

If French producers had lost their former position in their home market, this was not merely because the industry had shut down for several months before resuming with reduced manpower. French cinema also confronted a sudden shift in allegiance by the nation's film-going public, which found in the American works a respite from the long, bloody war. Sharing this new taste were the country's artists and intellectuals, for whom the sensation of the Paris screen in 1916 was an American import, Cecil B. De Mille's *The Cheat* (1915), known in France as *Forfaiture*. Colette, one of many distinguished writers to comment on the film, reviewed it explicitly in terms of what she saw as the contemporary French cinema's failings:

> To the genius of an oriental actor, Sessue Hayakawa, is added that of a director probably without equal. The heroine of the piece—vital, luminous, intelligent—almost completely escapes any sins of theatrical brusqueness or excess. There is a beautiful luxuriating in lace, silk, furs—not to mention the expanses of skin and the tangle of limbs in the final melee, in which the principals hurl themselves unrestrainedly against each other. We cry, "Miracle!" Not only do we have millionaires who don't look as if they've rented their tuxedos by the week [as in French films], but we also have characters on screen who are followed by their own shadows, their actual shadows, tragic or grotesque, of which until now the useless multiplicity of arc lamps has robbed us.[4]

De Mille's film looked *new*. It had an unusual, highly visible cinematographic style. And it had what Colette, in an essay on French cinema published two years after its release, called *du lusque*, which has been aptly translated as "luggsury":

> The longer the war lasts, the more we lack sugar and bread and gasoline, the more [the cinema manager] will ask, on behalf of his audience in

worn-out jackets and spongy, broken-down shoes, for *luggsury* and still more *luggsury*. I won't try to explain this need simply by the thirst for superfluity that torments human beings deprived of necessities. The source of it must be found in the progressive impoverishment of the theaters and the music halls. For three years we have lived in an increasing shadow. Artificial light, dimmer every day, no longer inundates the stages or our private homes . . . What is left for the public? Where can it bathe itself in decorative illusion, adventure and romance, high life, society, inexhaustible splendor? At the cinema. Only the cinema spends, wastes, destroys or miraculously builds, mobilizes hordes of extras, rips embroidered cloth, spatters with blood or ink thousand-franc dresses; only there will you see a gentleman in a white tie not giving an instant's thought to his three-hundred-franc evening clothes when he grapples with a bandit—and triumphs, in rags.[5]

American films had two enormous advantages over domestic productions: their "luggsury" was all the more striking for being unfamiliar, and it could be more extravagant thanks to the larger budgets in which the American companies could now indulge. The two major powers of the French cinema, Pathé and Gaumont, were vertically integrated, combining production, distribution, and exhibition. The huge success of the imports presented them with a conflict of interest, which they rapidly resolved at the expense of their own production operations. First, they distributed and exhibited more and more American works, and then they cut back on the number and scale of films they themselves produced because these were less and less profitable. In 1918 Pathé Frères announced it was giving up all production activity, though it took until 1920 for the corporation to make its last films. The company retained, in reorganized form, its profitable phonograph and cinema exhibition operations. The by now only marginally profitable production operation was spun off as a much smaller company, Pathé-Consortium, which continued to make films during the rest of the silent period (after 1925 through its Cinéromans affiliate), but without the benefit of the older conglomerate's enormous cash flow and political clout. The Gaumont company remained intact but drastically scaled back its production schedule. Its studio in Nice, constructed just before the outbreak of hostilities, remained in limited operation, and it was there that Louis Feuillade continued to make films until his death in 1925. The smaller companies, many of which did not have profitable theatre chains to fall back on, also retreated from production, though not as rapidly as the two majors.

It is easy enough to denounce the big powers of prewar French cinema for acting as they did. Yet they only operated as true capitalists always do when confronted with a sudden change of circumstances: big capital shifts to areas of greatest return. To the extent that it does not do this, it cannot remain big capital. The vertical integration of the film business, with its implicit protection of production, did not die, however: it had migrated to the United States, where it would remain in place until ruled in violation of anti-trust laws several decades later. At the end of World War I the French film industry resembled, ironically, the American industry of today. (The big difference—and it has enormous consequences—is that modern film production is much more capital intensive.) Production was fragmented, its return on capital uncertain. Distribution and exhibition were enormously, and reliably, profitable. Relations between film production and the rest of the industry were, in a word, adversarial.

But as Fernand Braudel has persuasively argued, capitalism is rarely "on home ground" in the sphere of production. The highest returns on investment are most often in distribution and sales.[6] From this perspective, the French film industry's financial and organizational debacle in the war years made it (ironically) more "modern," more mature than the newly consolidating American industry—which would remain anachronistically tied to production for many years, until the U.S. Justice Department forced it to deregulate itself. And the upheaval did not cause the complete end of production activity, nor any sudden loss of aesthetic merit in the films that managed to be produced. On the contrary, this was to be remembered as *l'age d'or du cinéma muet*—the golden age of the silent film.

▓ The war drove the French cinema into the first of the major crises in its long and varied history. The pattern of that history, from that point on, was an alternation of periods of slow evolution—for example, from the end of World War I to 1929—with short bursts of cataclysmic change. Until the coming of the sound film threw everything into question again, French film production changed comparatively little during this golden age. One recurrent aspect of these periodic upheavals is a significant, though by no means total, change of industry personnel. Many of the most important figures of prewar French cinema remained active in the postwar period—including Louis Feuillade, Henri Fescourt, and Henri Pouctal, to mention only directors. But others left, often for the newly dominant American industry (Max Linder, Léonce Perret). Still others retired, or worked less often. Their places were quickly filled. It is convenient, if not strictly accurate, to speak of "new generations" of stars, directors, writers, and other creative individuals who enter the industry at times of sudden change, drawn to it precisely by the chaos that creates opportunity, or recruited as "new blood" to meet new challenges. Among the most visible, if not always the most successful, of these newcomers in the postwar period were the so-called "impressionist" filmmakers. And of these, possibly the most ambitious and successful, and certainly the most charismatic, was the young Abel Gance.

Gance had begun his cinema career just before the war, though in a desultory manner. He was ready and in place, the earliest of his generation, for the opportunities and challenges of the industry's new circumstances. His career before becoming a filmmaker was aleatory, like Louis Feuillade's. But he suffered from a burden that Feuillade could only imagine, though it was the stuff of one of Gaumont's "Life as It Really Is" films. Gance was the illegitimate son of a well-to-do Parisian doctor. At the time of his birth his mother, Françoise Perthon, was living with a chauffeur and automobile mechanic named Adolphe Gance. Three years later the couple married, and his mother's husband adopted young Abel Perthon, who became Abel Gance. The child was aware of his parentage, and throughout his early life he received financial support and personal encouragement from his biological father. How he felt about the matter is suggested by the fact that until his death he steadfastly maintained that he was the son of a Doctor Gance, and that he had had a normal, unproblematic, bourgeois childhood. Some of the director's intimates knew the truth but carefully helped sustain the deception.[7]

The two poles of Gance's childhood were his biological father's home in the center of Paris (the first *arrondissement*) and his mother and adoptive father's various homes in poorer, more geographically and socially marginal neighborhoods of the capital. One feels this division and its effects in much of his work. In his interest in and sympathy for both the upper and lower classes of French society, Gance resembles a later member of his cinematic cohort, Jean Renoir. Unlike Renoir, however, Gance only *imagined* a happy, unified family of origin. Gance's fantasies of social and familial unification, as well as his nightmares of tragic separation and class division, probably find their origins in a childhood wish to piece together his own fragmented, socially split family. A recurrent motif in his films is the unification of a divided group, country, or world by a charismatic artist-leader. Gance has often been accused of being a crypto-fascist for this reason, but the origin of his powerful leader figures probably lies in the stunned incomprehension of a child helplessly wishing to live with both mother and father in a single home. It comes as no surprise that, almost alone among his generation, Gance really *believed* in the extravagant narratives of most of his pictures. While most of his critics and industry peers saw popular domestic drama plots—with their illegitimate children, tormented and possibly unfaithful husbands and wives, and their characters' morbid fear of scandal—merely as a means of reaching a wide public, as conventional structures on which to hang cinematographic experiments and bravura acting, Gance clearly took these stories seriously and thought they could tell great truths. This is probably what makes him both such a great filmmaker and so hard for us to understand today.

Gance's childhood was nomadic and unsettled. He studied at good schools, paid for by his biological father, but he had little aptitude for formal education. In 1904, just before his fifteenth birthday, he entered a Paris law firm as an apprentice clerk. For the rest of his life he would be a passionate autodidact, a stance which perfectly expressed his love of learning and his unease with any form of established authority. He became particularly well read in philosophy and religion. His two years as a law clerk are a testimony both to his perseverance and to the pressures he must have felt to obtain a respectable position in society. One marvels that he held the job that long, for his opinions about the need for radical social and moral change were close to fully formed. The law could only have represented the great Impediment to everything he desired. In 1906, not yet seventeen, Gance renounced the law and decided to become a man of the theatre. His first years as an actor and aspiring playwright brought him neither fame nor fortune, and in 1910 he began to write scenarios and sell them to various film studios. Although these stories were doubtless fairly unsubtle, as was much of the cinema of the day, the young man quickly came to believe that the new medium could become a full fledged art on its own merits. He formed his own independent production company, for which he wrote and directed four short films. The venture ended up in bankruptcy court, as would other Gance endeavors, and he returned to the stage, again with no notable success. It was the shortage of film personnel in 1915 which brought him back to the cinema.

Gance's health was always very delicate, and he was exempted from military service. This was indeed fortunate, for he had already concluded that war was madness itself, though this opinion did not prevent him from being a kind of pacifist nationalist. He wrote a war film scenario and sold it to Film d'Art. The company engaged him to make his next film himself, and the result was *Un Drame au château d'Acre* (*Drama at the Acre Chateau*, 1915), which told a story of jealousy, hypnotism, a major earthquake, an apparent return from the dead, and an ensuing case of total madness. His next film, *La Folie du docteur Tube* (*The Insanity of Doctor Tube*, 1915), is well known today for its anamorphically distorted images, a cinematographic rendering of the madness which always fascinated him, but it was never seen by the public of its day because the artistic director of Film d'Art, Louis Nalpas, was horrified by its confusing imagery. It is a measure of the industry's shortage of personnel, and of Nalpas's faith in Gance, that the young director nonetheless stayed on at the studio and, after directing another, more conventional film to show he could behave himself, got a contract "for the duration of the war."

Gance already felt that the French cinema needed revitalization, and that he was the man for the job. After making ten films for Film d'Art, he journeyed to London to see the latest American productions. Thus he happened to be one of the very few Frenchmen to see D. W. Griffith's *The Birth of a Nation* (1915) before its Paris release (long delayed by government censors) in the early 1920s. Either in London or on his return to Paris, he probably saw *The Cheat*, as well as the other major American films of the season. It would be inaccurate to say that Gance carefully imitated these works, but he unquestionably found much inspiration in them. From Griffith he came to understand that editing could do more than seamlessly join together neighboring spaces or actions. From De Mille and other directors he learned that the delicately lit, pictorial-realist French tradition of cinematography was not the only possible use of camera and light. As we have seen, Colette had praised *The Cheat* for its expressive use of shadows. Many French critics and filmmakers had been quite impressed by De Mille's "Rembrandt lighting"; Gance and many of his peers would follow in this path.

Gance blended these American influences with his own extravagant narrative imagination in a series of highly successful films, including *Mater Dolorosa/The Torture of Silence* (1917) and *La Dixième Symphonie* (*The Tenth Symphony*, 1918). But his reputation as the great filmmaker of the period rests on his last three silent features: *J'Accuse* (*I Accuse*,

1919), *La Roue* (*The Wheel*, 1922), and *Napoléon vu par Abel Gance* (*Napoleon, as seen by Abel Gance*, 1927). These films all pose the same fundamental problem to historians: we can never see them in versions which even approach their original form and scope. Gance himself was largely to blame for this state of affairs. In his films as in his life, the director placed great emphasis on the artistic value of suffering, already a major theme of *La Dixième Symphonie*. He both dreaded and expected the incomprehension of his producers and his public. His own suffering body was to be the site of the resolution of all social and moral contradictions, at the cost of his health and perhaps of his life. In fact though not in fantasy, Gance lived to a ripe old age, and his major films seem to have played the role of his surrogates in this life project. They would tower over the world, bind together the wounds of humanity, and then, like many gods in the religions he studied, be torn apart. In a fit of rage, Gance once threw into the fire several sequences of the famous triptychs from *Napoléon*. This is a horrifying but entirely symptomatic gesture. In other, more prosaic ways as well he mutilated his own best films, in successive releases which reduced them, progressively, to shadows of their former greatness.

J'Accuse tells the story of Jean Diaz, a "poet of fragile health" (like Gance) who loves Edith, a "delicate and bruised spirit" married to the brutal peasant François. Both men go off to fight in the Great War and the jealous husband sends his wife to live with his father, from whose house she is abducted by the Germans. After three years of service, Jean is discharged for poor health and returns home in time to witness his mother's death. He cries, "I accuse! War kills mothers as well as sons!" Edith returns home the same night with an infant, the result of a brutal rape by an enemy officer. "I accuse!" cries the poet again, and he reenlists and returns to the front. In the course of a terrible battle, François is killed and Jean loses what is left of his sanity. He escapes from a hospital and gathers the mothers and widows of his village in Edith's house. He speaks to them of the dead soldiers, and how in a field he heard one of them cry, "My friends, let us go home to see if the living are worthy of us, if our deaths have served some purpose." The poet opens the door to the house and his audience sees a multitude of fallen soldiers returning from the grave. Some onlookers try to flee; all are terribly moved. But this vision has cost the poet too dearly, and he dies.[8]

The first release version of *J'Accuse* was in three feature-length *époques,* or chapters. This format made exhibition in a single showing impractical, and doubtless reduced the film's excellent revenues somewhat, but no producer took the work away from its creator and had it truncated the way Irving Thalberg did, for example, with Erich von Stroheim's *Greed* (1923). Three years after the film's Paris debut, long after the matter would have been of any real concern to a major producer or distributor, Gance himself shortened *J'Accuse* to roughly three hours in length, radically recutting it, rewriting the titles, and altering the nature of its commentary on the Great War. Characteristically, he seems to have excised many of the work's celebrated battle scenes but kept the love triangle basically intact. He did not bother to preserve any copies of the earlier versions of his film, which have apparently been lost forever.

Gance recut *J'Accuse* as a warmup for the editing of *La Roue,* which is probably his masterpiece. But again, once he had completed his new work he continued to reduce and alter it—this time in response to criticism of its length from critics and exhibitors. Until recently, the film only existed in widely divergent, partial prints, but now there is some reason to hope that a satisfactory reconstruction will eventually become generally available.[9] *La Roue*'s extravagant plot revolves around Norma, the "rose of the railroad tracks," who is loved both by her adoptive father Sisif, a train engineer, and his son Elie, a violin maker. (Elie makes his instruments in the family home, which is surrounded on all sides by railroad tracks. Many shots strikingly contrast his activity with the roaring trains seen in the background, an example of the director's extravagant, "unrealistic" image making which many critics found intolerable.) To resist his quasi-incestuous desires, Sisif marries Norma off to a corrupt railroad bureaucrat, who later has a lonely, mountaintop fight with Elie, in which both men are killed. Sisif eventually goes blind and dies, cared for by his melancholy daughter.

Few films in cinema history have triggered such an outpouring of debate as did *La Roue.* As time has passed, however, the people who violently criticized the film have been largely forgotten. Its many supporters, including Fernand Léger, Jean Cocteau, Louis Delluc, and René Clair, have grown in stature to the point that they seem, to many historians, more important than the film they so fervently endorsed. But their advocacy, generally, was not so much for the film as a whole as for certain aspects of it. René Clair wrote in 1923:

> As I see it, the real subject of the film is not its odd plot, but a train, tracks, signals, puffs of steam, a mountain, snow, clouds. From these

great visual themes that dominate his film Mr. Gance has drawn splendid developments. We had already seen trains moving along tracks at a velocity heightened by the obliging movie camera, but we had not yet felt ourselves absorbed—orchestra, seats, auditorium and everything around us—by the screen as by a whirlpool. "That is only a feeling," you will tell me. Maybe. But we had not come there to think. To see and feel is enough for us. Fifty years from now you can talk to me again about the cinema of ideas. This unforgettable passage is not the only one that testifies to Mr. Gance's talents. The catastrophe at the beginning of the film, the first accident Sisif tries to cause, the ascent of the cable car into the mountains, the death of Elie, the bringing down of his body, the round dance of the mountaineers, and that grandiose ending amidst veils of cloud: these are sublime lyrical compositions that owe nothing to the other arts. Seeing them, we forget the quotations from Kipling, Aeschylus and Abel Gance throughout the film, which tend to discourage us. And we start to hope.

Oh, if Mr. Abel Gance would only give up making locomotives say yes and no, lending a railroad engineer the thoughts of a hero of antiquity, and quoting his favorite authors! . . . Oh, if he were willing to give up literature and place his trust in the cinema![10]

The central opposition of Clair's analysis, between "thinking" (literature) and "feeling" (cinema), reveals a profound misunderstanding of—or hostility to—Gance's project. To try to separate out the purely cinematic virtues of *La Roue* from the director's moral messages is, finally, to misread him and make his work radically less interesting and compelling than it can be when read more sympathetically. At his best, Gance was a visionary filmmaker who made no distinction between ideas and feelings. The cinematographic experiments in his works can only fully be understood as expressions, and affective explications, of his philosophical positions. The wheel of the title (explicitly identified in the film's beginning as an instrument of torture, and implicitly identified with locomotives) represents human existence. It is the embodiment of the first truth of Buddhism that all life is suffering, and of the Buddhist and Hindu view that existence is nothing more than the repetitive appearance and decay of illusory phenomena. Gance often situates his hero in relation to Greek mythology. Like his namesake, Sisif (Sisyphus) is doomed to cycles of repetitive behavior until, like Oedipus, he is purified by a suffering ultimately symbolized by blindness. His slow, painful liberation from the torture-wheel of life is figured by the succession of his trains: first a large, powerful one, then a small funicular, and finally a model which he clutches and lets drop to the floor when he dies. This oddly happy death serves as prelude to what is in many ways the most impressive

In *La Roue* the elderly Sisif drives a funicular car up and down a mountain, laboring as did his mythical namesake. When he goes blind, Oedipus-like, he lives out his days playing with a model of the larger train he drove as a young man.

sequence in the film, a perfectly achieved *slow* montage depicting a ritual celebration of the cycles of Nature. As a yearly round dance ascends a mountain peak, going higher than "ever in the memory of the guide" it has gone before, the only circle (wheel) left is that formed by the clouds in the sky around the high summit.

Commentators such as René Clair (and, more recently, Richard Abel) who reject Gance's visionary, philosophical project must inevitably view *La Roue* as a mass of contradictions, a work which combines the supposedly antithetical elements of "pure cinema," literary and philosophical quotations, melodrama, a certain social realism, and so on.[11] But it was the very heart of Gance's life project to overcome contradictions. A huge number of disparate elements are to be found in his films because he put them there deliberately, so that his work could become the site of their reconciliation. Perhaps he did not always succeed, indeed perhaps he never did, but there is no doubt that his was a conscious and in its own way sophisticated endeavor, and not the naive, almost embarrassing primitivism it is sometimes made out to be. Currently available versions of *La Roue* probably seem clumsy and contradictory because too much has been cut from them. Gance structured his film as a poetic visual text, based on extensive formal repetition which figures his characters' plight. The wheel, its complementary motif the cross, blackness, whiteness, hands, impressions of speed or slowness, and many other elements are repeated, varied, and combined in different ways. To understand the film, to allow the necessary, and for many viewers difficult, suspension of (philosophical) disbelief, we will have to see it in a version as close as possible to its original proportions.

The situation is very different with *Napoléon*, thanks to Kevin Brownlow's careful reconstruction, the most complete version of which (for the Cinémathèque Française) now includes virtually all extant footage of the work, though it still falls short of the original in many ways.[12] If most modern viewers know Gance at all, it is thanks to this film, his biggest but in some ways least characteristic project of the silent era. The director's works had been getting longer and longer. *Mater Dolorosa* and *La Dixième Symphonie* were of ordinary feature length. *J'Accuse*, initially, was three times as long as they, and the first release version of *La Roue* (in four *époques*) was twice as long as *that*. From its inception, Gance's Napoleon saga was to unfold in six films, each of which would be longer than *La Roue*. But because Gance only got to make the first installment of his epic, it remains, compared to the rest of his work, emotionally incomplete. Its triumphal tone was to give way to paranoia, depression, and defeat in later chapters. Throughout the 1927 work, Gance carefully laid the ground for these later, somber developments, most obviously in his depiction of the relations between Napoleon and Josephine.

But as it stands, the film ends happily, with little hint of the intense suffering and madness which the director considered to be the necessary consequence of the artist-hero's vision. Contemporary observers who didn't like the film (and there were many) often worried about what they saw as its demagogic glorification of the strong leader. Those on the extreme Left were generally the most troubled, as for example Léon Moussinac, writing in *L'Humanité:*

> *Napoléon* is addressed to the masses. The masses will rush to see it because of the title, because of Abel Gance, because of the advertising.

Well I challenge these masses not to be convinced by this film that the French Revolution . . . only destroyed whatever "good" had been done under the *ancien régime*, that all it did was to kill off poets [André Chénier, sent to his death when Josephine does not have to go to hers], scientists, and good-hearted innocents, that it was led by lunatics, maniacs and crazies, and that Napoleon Bonaparte happened on the scene at the right moment to re-establish order in the good name of discipline, authority, and country: in a word, military dictatorship.[13]

Perhaps Moussinac and others would have felt obliged, at least in part, to rethink their reactions to the first film had Gance been able to continue. There is no doubt that his later Napoleon would have been a spiritual cousin of *J'Accuse*'s Jean Diaz. For Gance viewed his character as an *artist* (also, in one scene, a mathematician—a connection the director would make in other films): a military artist to be sure, but an artist nonetheless, a visionary. The point was not just that ordinary men and women could be galvanized by a strong leader, able to immobilize a hostile crowd with a single, steely glance. For until all humanity came to see the world in a new way, such exceptional men's insights would ultimately bring to them only madness and death, and to society at large painfully little lasting change.

In terms of film genre, *Napoléon* was one of Gance's most conventional and "safe" silent works. Gance's backers, who put enormous sums of money into the production, knew that well-made historical epics had excellent box office prospects both in the French market and aboad. In his earlier work the director had excelled at depicting hyperemotional situations involving a small number of intimately related people: the husband, the wife, and the blackmailer; or the working-class father, his son and adopted daughter, and the corrupt bourgeois bureaucrat. These films were psychological dramas, not subject to the constraints of historical verisimilitude. Because of the film genre within which he worked, Gance's narrative imagination was much more restrained in *Napoléon* than in his earlier work—though many viewers may find this limitation beneficial. As René Clair had requested, Gance gave up locomotives that talked and reduced his dependence on quotations. There was only one continuing, really intrusive bit of symbol-making in the film: the eagle, sometimes seen accompanying the hero, sometimes intercut with him. The director chose to opt for more "whirlpool"-like passages of pure feeling, and to restrain his interest in a cinema of ideas. He devised, for example, a kinetic chase on horseback (Napoleon's departure from Corsica) that might have come straight out of an American Western, complete with the hero jumping into his saddle from a second story balcony and riding furiously off with other horsemen in hot pursuit.

Many of the moments of "pure cinema" in *Napoléon* are stunning and fully achieved. In at least one case, Gance inspired a notable example of filmic rewriting and imitation. His pillow fight sequence (Napoleon's youth at Brienne) obviously impressed the young Jean Vigo, who partly recreated it in his *Zéro de conduite* six years later. And Jean Cocteau was possibly inspired by the work's celebrated snowball fight scene when he filmed a similar situation in *Le Sang d'un poète* (1930). But such *hommages* in subject matter are exceptional; most film artists preferred to emulate Gance in the area of technique. His greatest contribution to the French silent cinema's golden age was the subjective or quasi-subjective rapid editing sequence. After his extraordinarily effective experiments in *La Roue,* the filming of sustained bursts of brief, disparate images became a sort of litmus test for membership in the "impressionist" school of French cinema, and a mark of artistic commitment to the progress of the medium.[14]

Gance was extremely aware, and proud, of his impact on the French cinematic impressionists, whose work we will consider in the next chapter. Beyond the area of cinematographic technique, he also hoped to influence the development of film technology. Already in 1913 he had tried to interest Pathé Frères in a chromatic "alphabet" of his devising which would enable filmmakers to "write in colors." Other ways of expanding the cinema's technological base continued to interest him throughout his career. In the silent period, his most notable research was in triple-screen images for *Napoléon.* Only the last such sequence of the film survives, but it gives us a good idea of what he could do with the process. Its formal possibilities are explored with remarkable thoroughness, given the sequence's brevity. Sometimes a single panoramic scene appears, photographed with three synchronized cameras in an array built to Gance's specifications. More often, presumably because he had the idea of the triple screen late in the production and little panoramic footage was shot, all three images are different, or a central image is flanked by a second one and its reversal, or by two dark screens. Titles sometimes appear only on the central screen, and sometimes they spread out on all three. At the film's end, the outer images are tinted red and blue, forming a filmic equivalent of the French flag.

Gance had great hopes for his Polyvision system, but it was not until the 1950s that it was briefly imitated, in the American process called Cinerama—which later ceased to be a three-image process, perhaps because of the stylistic timidity with which it was used. His experiments with different images on the three visual systems, perhaps the most remarkable possibility of the apparatus, were not emulated. In technology as (within a few years) in cinematographic technique, Gance filled the role of one of his own heroes. He could mesmerize, he could agitate and temporarily control his viewers, but he could not effect lasting change, because audiences and other film artists did not long for transformation as deeply as he did.

Abel Gance was among the best known of the postwar film artists, despite the comparatively small number of works he made. The lavish attention he received did not come simply out of respect for his films, or for their generally good box office revenues. He became one of the French silent cinema's few authentic culture heroes, interesting—or dangerous—for his character, his dreams, and for the wider symbolism that was perceived in them. Other members of the French film community (such as Marcel L'Herbier) aspired to this status, but few achieved it. One of those who did, though most fully only after his early death, was Louis Delluc, then as now better known as a critic than as a filmmaker. Both men are often classified as cinematic impressionists, though they were not so much members of this school as two important points around which it crystallized. Delluc is often said to have "invented film criticism," though this claim tells more about his status as a cinema culture hero than about actual historical priority.[15] Even before his death, Delluc became something of a symbol of the French film industry's efforts to find its way in the confusing postwar environment.

Delluc was born in 1890, five years before the official birth of cinema, in a small town in the Dordogne, a primarily agricultural region of Southwest France. His father was the town pharmacist and assistant mayor. Louis seems to have been the center of his parents' life, and he followed the classic trajectory of upwardly mobile provincial French citizens—from small town to provincial capital and finally to Paris—not because of his own ambition but because of theirs for him. When he was eight the family moved to Bordeaux where, after a year of preparatory studies, the boy was admitted to the Lycée de Bordeaux. After four years of excellent studies there, in 1903 he entered the Lycée Charlemagne in Paris, where the family had moved to further his academic career. Five years later he obtained his *baccalauréat* and began preparatory studies at the Lycée Henri IV for the entrance exam to the Paris Ecole Normale Supérieure. But the following year he suddenly abandoned his studies and decided to become a journalist. This is a rather surprising end to that story: Delluc had been, quite simply, on the track that leads to entrance into France's ruling class. In theory, the capital's Ecole Normale trains teachers. In practice, it trains the country's intellectual and political elite. To abandon a chance at entering the school, after the years of hard work necessary to get as close as Delluc got to it, and for journalism, of all professions, has the ring of a declaration of moral independence, though doubtless not a wholly conscious one. Probably a combination of ill health, a repressed sense of inadequacy, and a dislike of being the vehicle of his parents' social climbing all contributed to this result.

One theme which runs through the lives of many of this period's new filmmakers is poor health. The reasons for this are simple enough. One group of young Frenchmen, including Gance and Delluc, found their careers facilitated in the years of the Great War when they, unlike most of their contemporaries, were exempted or discharged from military service because of physical disabilities. Delluc had a bad heart, as well as other health problems that would plague him until his untimely death of consumption in 1924, when he was not yet thirty-four. He served his country only briefly, in an army hospital near the end of the war. Other young men fought in the world's first truly mechanized conflict, without benefit of antibiotics, with frequent attacks of poison gas, and were discharged with health problems of varying degrees of severity, often with shattered nerves: René Clair is but one of many examples. Rare, in the upper echelons of the French cinema at least, were veterans who got home with minimal physical damage and in possession of their health and mental equilibrium.

In spite of his physical condition, or perhaps because of it, Delluc worked compulsively at whatever he did. He wrote for and eventually became managing editor of *Comoedia Illustré*, a glossy weekly magazine covering the arts and life in Paris, but until 1916 he took no great interest in the cinema. On the insistence of his friend and companion (later wife), the actress Eve Francis, he went to films occasionally, but it was not until he saw *The Cheat* and the first Chaplin films released in France that he took the medium seriously. When *Comoedia* was forced to cease publication because of the war, Delluc plunged into his new interest. In 1917 he became editor in chief of *Le Film*, a weekly cinema magazine, and until the end of his short life he devoted himself almost exclusively to his enthusiasm for the moving image. He wrote a film scenario that year and sold it to Louis Nalpas, former head of the Film d'Art and now one of the period's many independent producers. Nalpas hired one of the war years' many newcomers to the industry to direct *La Fête espagnole* (*Spanish Festival*, 1919): Delluc's contemporary and later rival, Germaine Dulac.

In 1918 a change of management at *Le Film* forced Delluc to give up his editorship of the magazine, but he had no trouble finding other work. In 1919 he published a war novel based on his brief military experiences as well as his first book on film, *Cinéma et Cie.* ("Cinema and Company"). This was a collection of the columns he had written for *Le Film* during 1917. Although today collections like these are anything but rare, Delluc's book was the first example of such recycling by a French film critic; it was successful enough to be followed by other, similar efforts. If he did not actually invent film criticism, he was the first to exploit it in this particular, commercially significant manner. All five of his film books, with the only partial exception of his second, *Photogénie* (1920), were pieced together from preexisting material. The last, *Drames du cinéma* (1923), was a collection of his film scripts. For in the same brief period before his death when he became, for many cinema enthusiasts, France's leading film critic, he also wrote and directed six films, among them *Fièvre* (*Fever*, 1921), *La Femme de nulle part* (*The Woman from Nowhere*, 1922), and *L'Inondation* (*The Flood*, 1924).

Delluc's central position in the French silent cinema's golden age was assured by his three coordinated and complementary roles: he worked simultaneously as a filmmaker, as a critic, and—crucially—as an organizer. In large measure because of the decline in importance of the major film studios, the French film community after the Great War was less coherent and more contentious than it had been before. Activists like Delluc tried to influence the evolution of French cinema to ensure the success of artists and films they respected, as well as to consolidate their own standing in the industry. In maneuvering for power and position within the film community, Delluc's greatest weapon was his criticism. But he and his allies also worked to expand the boundaries of the film community, to extend it beyond the small circle of people who worked in the industry. Delluc was one of the most influential and tireless founders of the *ciné-club* movement in France, which was at the heart of what became an organized, alternative film culture that attempted to influence the nation's filmmaking by bringing into the dialogue on its evolution not only artists and businessmen, but enlightened consumers as well. *Ciné-club* is sometimes translated as "film society," but that term has rather passive, defensive connotations which ill suit the activist, cinema consumers'-rights orientation of the French organizations. The clubs defended (in discussions, but also in their many publications) and illustrated (by screenings, often of works that could not be seen otherwise) the kind of cinema their members thought should be made.[16]

The alternative film culture of the 1920s would presumably have existed without Louis Delluc, but he was at its very center, and he helped to define its goals and its tastes. He is most often invoked today as a critic, ocasionally by writers who do not seem to have read his criticism. For example, he is sometimes said to have invented the word *photogénie* to describe a certain ineffable quality of the photographic or cinematographic image. While it is true that he did not shrink from coining words—*cinéaste* is his, meaning anyone involved with the creative process of filmmaking—he claimed no credit for *photogénie*, which is found in many late nineteenth century dictionaries. But Delluc did choose it as the title of his only quasi-theoretical work on cinema, and his use of the word shows something of what he was about: "In the dubious jargon of the cinematizers, *photogénie* means mediocrity, or rather—excuse me—the *juste milieu*. Mademoiselle Huguette Duflos is called photogenic, who is [only] pretty; Monsieur Mathot is called photogenic, who is, in sum, a nice looking boy. You see, they are always photogenic, and one may confidently employ them in any film, even if the light is bad, the cameraman an hysteric . . . all is saved if the actors are photogenic. This concept of *photogénie* is not without problems. It threatens us with a profound monotony."[17] To this received, corrupt notion of *photogénie*, Delluc opposes an authentic sense of the word which, unfortunately, he never defines in any precise way. Authentically photogenic actors have "character." Most well-known French screen stars don't have it, but Sessue Hayakawa, star of *The Cheat*, does, as do most American actors Delluc speaks of. The Midi, favorite region for French location shooting, is not photogenic, but the Basque country is: "It doesn't pose." It is the only region of France almost as photogenic as California. And French telephones? "France is without doubt the one country where almost everyone is agreed that a telephone receiver should be an ugly thing."[18]

These summary judgments are delivered in a detached, untranslatably witty language. One reason people liked to read Delluc was that he was never dull. He did not hesitate to mount a frontal attack on a notable figure, generally from the French filmmaking establishment, and compare him or her unfavorably with someone else, either an American (De Mille, Thomas Ince, Chaplin) or one of his young French friends or associates. He was an *enfant terrible*, and in many ways he reminds one of the young François Truffaut. If there had been a Cannes film festival in his day, Delluc might possibly have got himself barred from it as would Truffaut over thirty years later, and for the same reason: saying bad things about his elders and betters, and saying them intemperately but very well. Delluc's situation differed profoundly from Truffaut's, however, in that what he was saying accorded so precisely with the sentiments of the big powers in the industry, the distributors and exhibitors. Criticizing the French cinema and praising American films was at this time a bit like kicking a blind man who is on the ground in an epileptic fit. But Delluc was not merely being sadistic or casually destructive. He was trying to legitimate the works of his favorite, mostly young filmmakers (and his own as well) by positing them as the real successors to the American achievements.

As a filmmaker Delluc is hard to evaluate because he made so few films, and because they show no consistent orientation. Certainly his work was widely commented upon, and held to be very influential, by young French filmmakers, but one may suspect that at least some of this praise had to do with not wanting to be on Delluc's bad side—a very bad place to be. *Fièvre* is currently available to most viewers only through copies of the titleless print from the Cinémathèque Française. This version of the film provides ample evidence for the proposition that titles were an essential aesthetic component of most silent films, even highly visual ones. One follows the film's story only with great difficulty; furthermore, its rhythm has been completely destroyed (and cinematic rhythm was one of Delluc's major concerns, to judge by his criticism). What one can still see of *Fièvre* suggests that its creator was still feeling his way. Much of the film looks derivative of the American directors Delluc so admired, in particular D. W. Griffith. Its climax involves some Abel Gance-like symbol making. An Asian woman, wife of a sailor now back home in Marseilles and confronting his old girlfriend, concentrates visually and emotionally on a flower in a vase in the waterfront bar where this confrontation takes place. Around her a brawl rages. She draws closer and closer to the flower, while the fighting escalates (as does the rhythm of its depiction). She finally realizes that it is artificial, a symbol perhaps of her

Eve Francis, as Louis Delluc's *La Femme de nulle part,* wanders through one of the many picturesque landscapes from the golden age of French silent cinema.

dashed hopes for a new life. (Audiences seeing the titleless print don't learn that the flower is a fake.)

Fièvre, his third film and second as solo director, was a kind of exercise in style for Delluc, an extended (forty-five minutes, with titles) cinematic experiment. *La Femme de nulle part* and *L'Inondation,* both feature length, are very different films. It is unfortunate that they are not widely viewable, outside of archive showings. Delluc was still experimenting there, with uneven results, but beginning to find his way to a new, perhaps more personal style. To some extent he turned his back on his American masters and on Gance and began to work with the simple, evocative landscapes of the French pictorialist tradition. Stylistically, he seems to have been on the verge of changing sides in the period's undeclared war of filmmaking generations, from the camp of Gance, Dulac, and the other cinematic impressionists to the side of the earlier, but still vital pictorialist and naturalist tendencies of French cinema, as united and developed in the highly influential work of André Antoine and his followers.

We will never know whether Delluc would have shifted his film-making practices completely, following Antoine's example and rejecting Gance. Given his independent nature, it is perhaps unlikely, for he preferred the role of leader to that of follower. The stylistic uncertainty of his last films serves as one condensed example of the distinction which existed in the French silent film's golden age between cinematic impressionism and what in this book will be called pictorialist naturalism. This was both a conflict of generations and a conflict of world views, and it will be the subject of the next chapter. It was not of vital interest to all *cinéastes* of the time, however. The modernist independents, such as Luis Buñuel, had little interest in either position. And other, more pragmatic and eclectic young filmmakers, including such soon to be important figures such as René Clair and Jean Renoir, were slowly gaining experience that would prepare them for a vanguard position in the French cinema after its next great crisis.

5

The Mental and the Physical

The label "impressionist" to designate the work of the young film-makers promoted by Louis Delluc (including Abel Gance, who was not so much member as model for the group) was probably first employed in print by Germaine Dulac in 1926. Dulac argued that until the 1920s French cinema had been dominated by "realist" works, of which (curiously) she considered *Fièvre* the culmination. After that:

> Another era arrived, that of the psychological and impressionist film. It seemed childish to place a character in a given situation without penetrating the secret domain of his inner life, and the actor's performance was annotated with the play of his thoughts and his visualized feelings. When one added to the unambiguous facts of the drama the description of multiple and contradictory impressions—actions being only the consequence of a mental condition, or vice versa—imperceptibly a dual development ensued which, to remain harmonious, had to follow a clearly established rhythm.
>
> I remember that in 1920, in *La Mort du soleil* [*Death of the Sun*], having to depict the despair of a scientist who regains consciousness after having been felled by a stroke, I used, in addition to facial expressions, his paralyzed arm, and the objects, lights, and shadows surrounding him, and I gave these elements a visual value equivalent in intensity and cadence to the physical and mental condition of the character.
>
> Of course, this passage was cut; spectators were not willing to endure an action slowed down by a sensorial commentary. Nonetheless, the era of impressionism had begun. Suggestions began to prolong the action, thereby creating a domain of emotion more vast because it was no longer confined within the limits of unambiguous facts.[1]

This remarkable text contains many necessary elements not only for a description of impressionist practices, but also for their critique.

Dulac was one of the movement's most articulate members, but she was also one of the first to abandon it. By the time she wrote this, she considered herself in the forefront of the cinema's next great movement, the "abstract" or "pure" (nonnarrative) film. And so it is an ex-practitioner that she points out the fundamental aesthetic problem of so much impressionist cinema: its dualism. The solution she envisions to the dichotomy of reality and impressions is a purely formal one: cinematic rhythm. But rhythm alone cannot integrate an entire narrative film. And so many (though not all) works produced by the movement alternate almost mechanically between storytelling, factual sequences and psychological, imagistic ones.

One obvious exception to this criticism is Gance. Everything in one of his major works is to be taken as the emanation, or series of impressions, of an (offscreen) character: the director himself. Monstrous egotism does apparently have its compensations. In his useful monograph on the cinematic impressionists, David Bordwell goes a step beyond Dulac and argues that their style "renders the film-maker's, or a character's impressions of a situation." Bordwell has constructed a model or paradigm of the stylistic means typically employed in cinematic impressionism. These include (1) close-ups, either as narrational figures (synecdoches and symbols) or as overtly subjective images; (2) camera movement, either as a purely graphic, narrational effect or as the physical point of view of a character in motion; (3) optical devices (masks, superimpositions, and so on), as decoration, or to convey abstract meanings or indicate a character's mental imagery; (4) marked displacement within the visual field, as when shadows indicate off-screen presences, or within the progress of the story (flashbacks or fantasy); (5) nonlinear editing patterns, either making a point about the story or indicating a character's psychological state within it.[2]

Bordwell's distinction between the (implicit) filmmaker's impressions as conveyed in a film, and those of its fictional characters, is useful because it points up some of the many variations that can be observed within cinematic impressionism. For these are two rather different sorts of impressions. A basic division that results from the difference is between films—like Gance's—with a strong sense of narrational presence (the filmmaker's impressions), with or without irruptions of subjectivity from within the narrative, and films in which a self-effacing narrator is periodically displaced by strong impressions from a fictional character. By making this distinction we can pose the historical question: which kind of filmic subjectivity came first? It seems clear that, in general, it was the implicit filmic narrator who first offered psychological and moral impressions in French film. In this area the cinematic impressionists seem to have been greatly inspired by D. W. Griffith, and the movement can be thought of as the development and extension of the American director's work just at the moment, ironically, when his influence was definitely on the wane in the United States.

Character subjectivity came later. For example, the rapid, rhythmic editing conventionally employed to convey drunkenness, illness, fits of insanity, and so on, was not done until 1922 with Gance's *La Roue*, though Dulac's claim to have had the idea two years before is not to be discarded out of hand. Such sequences would become common (in fact, they became something of a cliché) a few years later. Stylistically, cinematic impressionism was anything but stable—a fact which Bordwell's otherwise useful analysis tends to obscure. We can get some sense of the movement's variations and evolution by following the progress of perhaps the most consistently impressionist director, one of Louis Delluc's principal examples of a French filmmaker worthy of the Americans' artistic mantle: Marcel L'Herbier.

L'Herbier was born in 1888, two years before Delluc and one year before Gance.[3] His father was a high-ranking diplomat, his family part of the Parisian *haute bourgeoisie*—that sector of French society that Delluc's projected studies at the Ecole Normale Supérieure might have permitted him to join. One might suppose that such a privileged background would result in a high degree of satisfaction with one's lot in life, but in L'Herbier's case (and he is not wholly atypical) it did not. The *belle époque* was witness to the final flowering of the French aristocracy, of which we have one important record in Marcel Proust's *A la recherche du temps perdu*. In fact, L'Herbier and Proust had a number of traits in common, most notably a profound ambivalence about their own social class and the one above it. The director's memoirs contain some veiled but nasty comments about his aristocratic friends, and it is clear that he could find them bright and clever or else unworthy of their status, but he could never forget their position in society, and his own.

L'Herbier's father wanted him to become a lawyer or a diplomat, and at the age of twenty Marcel finished his *maîtrise* in law. But once he obtained this bourgeois credential, the young man went on to graduate study of literature and music. He began to publish essays on various arts. He lived in an extravagantly decorated apartment with colored lights, enormous brightly colored sofas, a glass spider hanging from the ceiling. This sort of life, reminiscent of that described in Huysmans's novel *A Rebours*, was probably his means of asserting a social position above that to which he had been born. It was certainly a rejection of the classic values of the bourgeoisie: comfort, tradition, the *juste milieu.*

L'Herbier had done his obligatory military service well before World War I and been discharged for injuries sustained in a battle exercise. He thus spent the first year and a half of the conflict out of uniform. Like other Parisians of the time, he went to the movies—there was little other entertainment—and discovered the American cinema. Previously he had despised the new medium; now he became an enthusiast. But the supply of ablebodied young men soon dwindled, and cases such as his were reevaluated. He was called up and eventually assigned to the French army's Cinema Service, in which he served for the rest of the war without having to leave Paris. Family connections were probably involved; L'Herbier *père* would have had little trouble arranging this calm, out-of-the-way assignment for his son. L'Herbier ultimately made a film for the army, with the assistance of Léon Gaumont. *Rose-France* (1919) was a mixture of *fin-de-siècle* symbolism and nationalist propaganda. By the time it was released the Great War was over; the work nevertheless received praise from many critics, including Louis Delluc.

Gaumont was still an active producer, and he offered L'Herbier a two film contract provided that budgets be kept very low. The two-films eventually became six, of which *L'Homme du large* (*Man of the Sea*, 1920) and *El Dorado* (1921) are probably the most important. *L'Homme du large* shows that, unlike Delluc, L'Herbier found his chosen path almost immediately. It tells the simple story of a virtuous old sailor for whom the ocean represents an ideal of absolute purity. He condemns his only son for a horrible crime against the family, ties him to the bottom of a small boat, and lets it drift out to sea. The son eventually returns, purified by his voyage and by a near-miraculous rescue, and the family is reconstituted. This story is narrated with an incredible array of titles (some separate from images of the fiction, many integrated with them in various ways) and optical effects, and some impressive location shooting. The film is very self-consciously aestheticized, but it is also movingly beautiful in much the same way that the best of Griffith's work can be. Despite his "decadent" inclinations, L'Herbier could be very effective with this sort of simple moral fable.

In *El Dorado* L'Herbier experimented with what David Bordwell calls semi-subjective images. The most celebrated of these is set in a cabaret where a dancer, played by Louis Delluc's wife Eve Francis, distractedly sits with other women, thinking about her sick young son. She is out of focus, the other characters perfectly in focus. Various other subjective and semi-subjective optical distortions occur in the film, as do many overt markers of a narrator's presence. In fact, in terms of Bordwell's model, *El Dorado* is one of the most impressionist films ever made. (Producer Léon Gaumont, when he first saw it, was disturbed by what he thought were "poor quality" images.) However, it was not a case of the films' being made to fit the director's style. He seems, rather, to have suited his use of the cinema's resources to the varying demands of his subject matter. Often, the result seems to typify cinematic impressionism; sometimes it does not.

L'Inhumaine/The New Enchantment (1924), made by L'Herbier's own production company, abandoned *El Dorado*'s concern with subjectivity to experiment extensively with filmic narration. The director deliberately chose an awkward science fiction plot in which a brilliant young scientist literally brings back from the dead the woman he loves, who has been murdered by an evil maharajah. This story serves as the pretext for some virtuoso displays of cinematographic virtuosity, and as the narrative justification for some some remarkable décors designed by the painter Fernand Léger, the architect Robert Mallet-Stevens, and future film directors Alberto Cavalcanti and Claude Autant-Lara. The sets are a microcosm of the whole film: they are in very different styles, and going from one to the next produces an almost physical shock. The film was very poorly received, both by critics and by the public, and one can see why. It is arguably the first great example in the narrative cinema of the so-called post-modernist aesthetic. For the coherence of a stable fictional world with suitably "round" characters who undergo various experiences, *L'Inhumaine* substitutes a fundamentally incoherent world of pastiche, parody, and quotation. Its flat characters provide no stability; they are but puppets in the hands of an unpredictable, perhaps even mad storyteller. The film uses many devices from the stylistic repertoire of cinematic impressionism, but rather than amplifying and explicating the narrative, they serve instead to call it into question.

The film by L'Herbier best known to most modern viewers is one

Fernand Léger's laboratory set of L'Herbier's *L'Inhumaine* is one of several distinct and striking visual environments in the film. The work later inspired the painter to create his celebrated essay in cinematic modernism, *Ballet mécanique.*

of his least impressionist: *Feu Mathias Pascal* (*The Late Mathias Pascal,* 1925). L'Herbier had seen a production of Luigi Pirandello's *Six Characters in Search of an Author* in 1923 and was sufficiently impressed to search among its author's works for something more accessible to average filmgoers. An associate recommended *Mathias Pascal,* which the director described as "the story of a man who starts by fleeing himself and in the end finds himself through his double."[4] Unfortunately for L'Herbier and the financial health of Cinégraphic, his production company, the film did very poorly at the box office, despite the presence of the popular Russian actor Ivan Mosjoukine in the title role. *Feu Mathias Pascal* is one of L'Herbier's most visually restrained films of the silent period. He understood that its uncanny world—in which a man who fakes suicide finds it more difficult than he had imagined to live with no official identity—would be best served by a relatively self-effacing, though by no means invisible, filmic narrator. As a result, viewers who know the director's work only through this film inevitably have a somewhat misleading idea of his typical interests and tactics.

L'Herbier's final film of the period was a superproduction, *L'Argent* (*Money,* 1929, after Emile Zola). Undoubtedly influenced by Abel Gance's experiments with camera mobility in *Napoléon,* L'Herbier turned this very free, modern-day version of Zola's celebrated novel into a series of pretexts for outbursts of striking cinematic excess. The result is a film resolutely split between narrative and spectacle, between straightforward storytelling scenes typically dominated by shot-reverse shot cutting and chaotic, exciting impressionist sequences, as when, at the Paris stock market (shot on location) a camera hanging from a pulley apparatus high above the trading floor sweeps down on the traders. (The effect, presumably, means to evoke the irrational frenzy of capitalist speculation. But L'Herbier's *L'Argent,* unlike Zola's, criticizes capitalism from a decidedly right-wing perspective.) The undisguised discontinuity in *L'Argent* between narrative sections and passages of cinematic excess may be viewed either as a fatal flaw of cinematographic form, or (for example, by Noël Burch) as a radical critique and exploration of film narrative.[5] In either case the film demonstrates that cinematic impressionism within the commercial narrative cinema of the late 1920s had become problematic, potentially unstable. Perhaps this was one of the reasons for the movement to all but vanish with the coming to cinema of recorded sound.

L'Herbier, Gance, and Delluc were by no means the only major cinematic impressionists. Jean Epstein and Germaine Dulac also made important contributions to the movement, though as we will see their careers ultimately turned in other directions. In any case, cinematic impressionism was not a kind of club to which one either did or did not belong. Its boundaries were fluid: directors as different as Jean Renoir and Jacques Feyder could draw on its resources and effects. In addition to Gance, Delluc, L'Herbier, Dulac, and Epstein, however, the most sustained exploration of the movement's possibilities came from a tightly knit community of Russian expatriate filmmakers.

It is too often forgotten that Russia had a healthy, if relatively small film industry before the establishment of the Soviet state. This industry had come into existence through the activities of French film companies and their representatives, beginning with the Lumières, but it did not really flourish until World War I. As fewer foreign films became available because of the conflict, domestic demand grew. The resulting financial hothouse atmosphere led to the founding of new firms and the expansion of older ones. By 1916 there were 164 domestic production and distribution companies. The Revolution of February 1917 was greeted with enthusiasm by most of the film industry, which solidly threw its weight behind the provisional government. The *coup d'état* by the Bolsheviks in October of the same year was another matter, however.

One of the first actions of the new government was to abolish most forms of private property. As a result, anything transportable and of any value immediately was spirited to areas of the country not controlled by the Bolsheviks. Cinema equipment, film stock, and negative and positive prints of films were all removed from Moscow. Most cinema personnel felt they had no choice but to follow, and the Russian film industry relocated in the South, mainly in Odessa and Yalta. Civil war between the Bolsheviks, or Reds, and anti-Bolsheviks, the Whites, raged while film production fitfully continued. The industry, of course, was solidly White. Eugène Lourié, who would later become an important set designer in the French industry, remembered a brief stint in Yalta as an extra in an anti-Bolshevik film called *Black Crows*. The director, Alexander Volkov, who was also to have an important French career, instructed the extras playing vicious Reds invading the property of a country landlord: "Be savage. Be beastly. Be realistic."[6] By the time the Bolsheviks had won the civil war in 1920, most members of the old Russian film community had fled the country along with the other Whites. According to Jay Leyda, one British ship carrying refugees to the relative security of Constantinople included among its passengers the producer Yermoliev (who would spell his name Ermoliev in France), the directors Volkov and Protozanov, and film stars Ivan Mozhukhin (later Mosjoukine) and Nathalie Lissenko.[7]

Constantinople was but a way station, however. Some of the Russians went directly to Paris, while others went there after some time in Berlin. (Still others stayed in Berlin, but were generally less successful than the French contingent.) Thus it happened that the potential personnel for several independent production companies, including camera operators, actors, writers, directors, and set designers, arrived *en masse* in the French capital. It was easy enough to recruit more Russians as needed, for there were many other White refugees already in Paris—such as Lourié, who got his start in the French industry painting sets for a Mosjoukine film. The producer Joseph Ermoliev rented the former Pathé Frères studio in the suburb of Montreuil and set to work preparing French release versions of his Russian successes and completing unfinished projects. (Some of these had begun in Yalta, continued in Constantinople, and were finally finished in Montreuil.) Ermoliev's biggest asset was Mosjoukine, who quickly became one of the biggest French cinema stars of the 1920s.

From the very beginning, the Russians filmmakers had many enthusiastic French supporters, including perhaps most notably Louis Delluc. Many of the immigrants, such as Mosjoukine and Lissenko, were the same age as Delluc and his associates. Both groups were industry outsiders hoping to become insiders. Thanks to the preference for French language and culture among prerevolutionary Russia's middle and upper classes, they had also read and admired many of the same books. An alliance and partial fusing of the two groups was almost inevitable. The exact role of the Russians in the development of cinematic impressionism is for the moment hard to establish. Jay Leyda argues that L'Herbier in particular was influenced by their work, and that Delluc modeled his direction of Eve Francis on Protozanov's work with Lissenko. Most French authors, on the other hand, assume that the Russians came to France and adopted cinematic impressionism as the style they found closest to their own, though modified to their own ends and in a more commercial vein. Probably the influences operated in both directions, the French following the Russians' lead in acting and use of decor, the Russians emulating the French in editing, optical tricks, and possibly narrative structure. There was, in any case, considerable professional and social interaction. Both Marcel L'Herbier and Jean Epstein directed films starring Mosjoukine and produced by the reorganized Ermoliev company, renamed Films Albatros and headed by another refugee White, Alexandre Kamenka. Film historian Jean Mitry, a friend of Delluc and his circle, recalls drinking sprees in the Russian night clubs of Montparnasse in the company of Epstein, Mosjoukine, Lissenko, and others.

The high watermark of the Russian efforts in France probably came in 1923 and 1924, which may also be considered the peak years of cinematic impressionism as a movement. Mosjoukine wrote, starred in, and codirected with Alexander Volkov *Le Brasier ardent* (*The Fiery Furnace,* 1923). The next year he starred in Volkov's *Kean* (1924, after Alexandre Dumas *fils*). Both films costarred Nathalie Lissenko; she and Mosjoukine formed a kind of ideal exotic couple for the period. *Le Brasier ardent* begins exceptionally well, but soon becomes a relatively conventional light romantic comedy enlivened by more than a few bizarre touches.[8] Its long opening sequence depicts a nightmare of the Lissenko character in which she is pursued by a man (Mosjoukine) who appears in various roles and costumes. Cinematic space expands, contracts, changes suddenly without warning. The film's sets—a deserted street at night, an opium den, a cathedral—are clearly influenced by German cinematic expressionism. The dream's subject matter is conventionally but effectively out of the ordinary: fire, murder, theft, prostitution—in sum, transgression. This part of the film, impossible to describe in a few words, has a stark surreal quality that the remainder rarely lives up to, though periodically it tries. (If only the characters had gone back to sleep!)

Kean is a more serious and consistent work, though its Dumas plot suffers from near-terminal romanticism. The actor Edmund Kean, idol of the London stage and friend of the Prince of Wales, falls in love with the exotic Countess of Koefeld. The actor is driven to a jealous rage and interrupts a Shakespeare performance when he realizes that the lady is his friend's lover, and that the prince will not give up his *droit de seigneur.* Kean dies of madness and frustrated love in a hovel outside of London, visited in his last moments by his beloved. The three kinds of sequences in the film are straight narrative scenes, theatrical performances, and bravura sequences of "impressionist" fireworks. The most celebrated of the latter is Kean's drunken frenzy in the Coaly Hole tavern, subjectively rendered by superimpositions and rapid, rhythmic editing. Germaine Dulac so admired this sequence that she showed it, minus the rest of the film, to illustrate several lectures on cinema art that she gave during the 1920s. This is perhaps one sign of weakness: the film is excerptable. But the work's major impressionist sequences, including the widely admired scene of the hero's death in the midst of an appropriately Shakespearean storm, are carefully prepared, the logical culminations of the drama that has preceded them. For this reason, the film does not seem arbitrary in its exploration of cinematic possibilities, in the way L'Herbier's *L'Argent* does. Of course, this also marks *Kean* as a more safely commercial film than *L'Argent*.

But few, if any, of the cinematic impressionists thought that commercial success was incompatible with artistic merit. Sometimes the filmmakers miscalculated public taste—as with *Le Brasier ardent* and *L'Inhumaine*, both financial disasters—but often they produced genuine hits (*J'Accuse, L'Homme du large*), and solid successes such as *Kean* and *Napoléon*. The Mosjoukine films were arguably the most obviously commercial of such films in intent, but not always in final result. In their use of the film medium's resources, the Russian efforts seem to take cinematic impressionism to one kind of logical, if mass-audience oriented, conclusion. By David Bordwell's criteria, they are among the most impressionist films made during the period. Mosjoukine himself became a kind of exemplary figure for the movement. His face had the mask-like quality that Delluc and others admired so much in performers like Sessue Hayakawa and William S. Hart. The actor's gestures had the economical, Kabuki-like quality associated with prewar Russian experimental theatre, and which young French players of the 1920s, such as Jacque Catelan, would emulate.

Mosjoukine also exemplified the movement in another way. His typical roles often involved the splitting of the self or its response to the threat of dissolution. Frequently his characters played many parts (*Kean, Le Brasier ardent*), or looked for parts to play (*Feu Mathias Pascal*), or hid their identity from a hostile force (Jean Epstein's *Le Lion des Mogols* [*Lion of the Mogols*, 1924]). Mosjoukine's star image demonstrates that although cinematic impressionism was committed to rendering the impressions and sentiments of fictional characters and/ or of filmic narrators, its practitioners did not think that the selves from which these feeling states emanated were stable, easily definable entities. To the contrary: the impressionist filmmakers were interested in feeling states precisely because they thought that selves were shifting, contradictory phenomena.

Commenting on the original Impressionist painters, Théophile

Gautier wondered, ironically, "whether it is in fact possible to understand any art other than that with which one is contemporary, that is to say the art with which one shared one's twentieth birthday."[9] In this perspective, the cinematic impressionists were indeed making contemporary art, the art with which *they* had shared their twentieth birthdays—which clustered around the year 1910. The major influences on their intellectual, artistic, and moral development were the Symbolist and decadent movements in literature, their great heroes Oscar Wilde and Maurice Barrès. Barrès, in particular, had written of the *culte du moi*, the cult of the self, but he did not mean "self" as a single, unified field of consciousness, but a multiple, shifting, finally *theatrical* construct. Only this sort of *moi* could successfully navigate through the treacherous yet seductive new freedom of a world where social barriers, once the guarantors of unified personalities, had fallen.[10]

Their interest in the various possibilities and positions of the self led the cinematic impressionists to an interest in fictional characters from all social classes, often from the lower reaches of society. This is one important way in which their work differs markedly from the mainstream commercial cinema of their day. Yet they were not, in general, sympathetic to the political Left. (Major exceptions were Delluc and Dulac.) The radically conservative politics of prewar thinkers like Barrès were much more to their liking. Their interest in the vicissitudes of the self in a world without clear boundaries led them to place their characters in stories involving extreme mental states such as insanity, uncontrollable rage or jealousy, dreaming, drunkenness, and the passage from life to death. Their cinema was at once self-therapy and wish fulfillment, a decadent prefiguring of Borges's "Lottery in Babylon."[11] Theirs was a powerful vision, but it was in many ways already an anachronism, and its days were numbered. Even without the coming of sound, cinematic impressionism would probably have faded from the French scene in the early 1930s, as more and more audience members' idea of "contemporary" culture, that with which they had shared their own twentieth birthdays, moved inexorably from *la belle époque* to the very different postwar sense of the world and its problems.

▨ Cinematic impressionism is arguably the most significant artistic trend in 1920s French film. It alone had the coherence, both in terms of its participants' goals and methods and of their backgrounds and relations, that made it comparable to German cinematic expressionism, or to the Soviet montage school of roughly the same period. However, as with these other, more celebrated cinema art movements, the actual number of impressionist films is comparatively small. David Bordwell, for example, arrives at a list of thirty-five films that may be clearly ascribed to the movement. By comparison, Raymond Chirat and Roger Icart's catalog of French fiction feature films from 1919 to 1929 lists some 1,055 titles.[12] Little is known about many of these films, for some of which Chirat and Icart are unable even to provide plot summaries. Cinematic impressionism as a cultural phenomenon, in contrast, had what symbolic interactionist theorists call "social reality" that was far out of proportion to its physical reality. The coherence of this small group of filmmakers, their access to the media, their showcasing of a common group of favorite actors and actresses, their discussions of and *hommages* to each other's works, all gave them a weight, a critical mass (at least in terms of the later writing of film history) that they could never have had as isolated individuals.

Between cinematic impressionism and the most undistinguished commercial productions of the postwar silent era lies a middle ground, a territory where trends may be distinguished, notable film artists identified, but in which one cannot easily speak of movements or schools, only of recurring tendencies, interests, and strategies. What will here be called pictorialist naturalism is arguably the period's most important such secondary trend or artistic focus, though until recently it has rarely been the object of close historical examination.[13] A major reason for this neglect lies in the evolution of the writing of French film history. Most of the country's first serious film critics and historians were either of the same age as Louis Delluc and his allies or a few years younger. Pictorialist naturalism, on the other hand, was largely the domain of an earlier generation, the working out of an earlier aesthetic for which these young writers had, in general, relatively little interest or sympathy. Because so many film historians work by recasting and reevaluating selected, supposedly authoritative written texts from the periods which they study, the original, generationally caused neglect of pictorialist naturalism has been widely perpetuated in accounts of the evolution of French filmmaking.[14]

The man most directly responsible for the pictorialist naturalist trend was André Antoine. Antoine was a famous (in many quarters, infamous) theatre director before he became, briefly, a highly influential and respected film artist. His theatrical practices, however, had already had a major impact on French cinema before he began making films during the war years. When the Gaumont company used the words "slices of life" to publicize Feuillade's "Life as It Really Is" series, the phrase was already well known as a slogan describing Antoine's Naturalist theatre productions. More significantly, the director's protégés were influential in the Film d'Art and its many imitators. Henri Pouctal and several other actors and directors hired by Lafitte and Le Bargy had worked under Antoine at his Théâtre-Libre. The Pathé company's Société Cinématographique des Auteurs et Gens de Lettres had as its artistic director and principal filmmaker Albert Capellani, who had learned his craft with Antoine. Although the founder of Naturalist theatre cannot be held responsible for the work of his former associates, many of whom in various ways departed from his example, much of their interest in painterly cinematic compositions and in the use of simple, direct gestures in acting is clearly a sign of his influence.

Antoine was born in 1858 in Limoges, an industrial city (shoes and fine porcelain) in West Central France. He was several years older than Lumière and Méliès, and he is in some ways the most thoroughly nineteenth century figure in the history of French cinema. By the time of his birth his family had, over several generations, worked its way up from peasant origins to the lower fringes of the petty bourgeoisie. His father was a clerk in one of the country's new railroad companies. When he was eight years old the family moved to the capital, where his father took a job with the municipal gas company. In this period the petty bourgeoisie could be extremely poor, poorer in fact than the upper reaches of the working class. Such was the case with the Antoines. When André was thirteen, his brilliant academic performance won him a scholarship to the Lycée Charlemagne, and he would have been one of the era's rare underprivileged youths to rise socially through the French education system had it not been for his father. Even with the scholarship, André's education would have strained the family finances, and Antoine *père* insisted that his son renounce the dream of a *baccalauréat* and go to work—as a petty bureaucrat of some sort, of course. This edict must have seemed spectacularly unfair to a boy who loved learning and already hated the grinding routine which his father insisted he embrace. The older man probably feared that André's education would not only entail ruinous sacrifice for the family, but also would produce an offspring with almost nothing in common with the rest of them. Ironically, this is what happened anyway.

His biographer Mateï Roussou compares Antoine's early life to something straight out of the work of Maxim Gorky. Certainly, if anyone's life demonstrated the pitfalls and dead ends that late nineteenth century industrial society could have in store for the lower orders, it was André Antoine's. He served five horrible years in the military. At age twenty-five, his health broken, he left military service to work at the gas company. He worked twelve-to fourteen-hour days and earned less than a skilled worker would in his home town. He married a milliner for whom he had no real love, and whose health was even worse than his own. But fortunately, his life did not remain the raw material for a Gorky play. When he was twenty-seven, his love of the theatre (which had fascinated him since childhood) led him to join the Cercle Gaulois, an amateur theatrical club in Montmartre. He quickly became the club's dominant personality, for Antoine was one of those rare individuals whom one may call, without any exaggeration, charismatic. He was soon operating his own, subscription-only theatre season which he called the Théâtre-Libre, since the subscription format made it free of interference from government censorship. He was able to quit the hated gas company.

Antoine quite simply revolutionized theatrical practice. From his very first "free theatre" program in 1887, he rejected the traditional artifice of the French stage. His actors spoke and moved as naturally as possible. They did not play to the audience: the director maintained that the proscenium should be treated as if it were a "fourth wall" through which spectators could somehow see. When Antoine himself actually *turned his back* on the audience in an early performance, this simple act was both a revelation and the beginning of an aesthetic revolution. He also believed in making sets as true to life as possible. Previously, parts of a set not used by actors, such as books in a bookcase, were only painted on flat backdrops. Antoine insisted on the physical reality and authenticity of scenic objects. His use of actual sides of beef for the set of a play called *The Butchers* scandalized the theatrical world.

Antoine would have had some difficulty applying his methods to "well-made plays" by writers like Eugène Scribe. He had to develop a new dramatic literature to fit his new orientation. At his first evening of free theatre, the big success was an adaptation of a short story by Emile Zola. Although not all of his repertoire was as clearly allied with the Naturalist movement, Antoine's debts to Zola and his disciples were historically perhaps the most significant. Naturalism stressed the ways in which human beings are shaped by their social and physical environments. Antoine's Naturalist theatre would pay close attention to these relationships. Hence the real sides of beef, the authentic cadences of spoken French as heard in various regions and social classes, and the closely observed gestures. As well as adapting Naturalist fiction to the stage, Antoine also encouraged new, not always strictly Naturalist playwrights, among them Henri Lavedan, author of Film d'Art's *La Mort du duc de Guise*. The work of many of these authors later found its way to the cinema. In 1892, for example, Antoine produced and directed *Blanchette*, a study of love and social class in a small French village. The play, written by Eugène Brieux, son of a cabinet maker and later a member of the Académie Française, was filmed by Antoine's protégé René Hervil in 1921. This was only one of many cinema works of the period adapted from plays originally staged by Antoine, or written by authors with whom he was associated.

Antoine would not have come to cinema at all had it not been for his imprudent financial practices. In 1914 money problems forced him to leave the Odéon theatre, which he had directed since 1906. He was famous, respected, and hopelessly in debt. Pathé's Société Cinématographique des Auteurs et Gens de Lettres, where many of his former actors and assistants were working, offered him a multi-year contract at a high salary, though the outbreak of war delayed his first solo work for the studio by almost a year. In 1915 he completed *Les Frères corses* (*The Corsican Brothers*, after Alexandre Dumas *père*, released in 1917). The film was well received by the critics and the French public. Louis Delluc would often refer to it as an uncharacteristically worthy French production, praising its visual qualities even as he denounced its scenario and its style of acting.

Delluc's approval of Antoine was only provisional, however. Soon the two men were quarreling openly in the French press. Antoine became the advocate of one sort of film, Delluc of another. The older man argued that the cinema should find its subjects in significant works of drama and fiction. While Delluc argued for original scenarios, Antoine's films adapted works by Victor Hugo, Alphonse Daudet, Zola, and (somewhat surprisingly) even the boulevard dramatist Henry Bernstein. But Antoine thought that these works, once chosen, should be treated in ways quite specific to cinema, though by this he did not mean the cinematic impressionists' favored ways of playing with film images. Above all, he insisted on visual authenticity, best obtained by location shooting. He envisioned a new era, "in which the studio will be no more than what it should be—a simple workroom useful for certain kinds of detailed work, trick shots, or for special effects which require stationary equipment."[15] (For the cinematic impressionists, such tricks were almost the very essence of cinema.) Although financial constraints did not always permit him to shoot exactly where he wished, Antoine did follow his own recommendations in most of his films. But his preference for location shooting does not make him a direct precursor of Neorealism and related movements in cinema, because of the tension in his work between physical reality and dramatic artifice, and because of the extreme, painterly care with which he composed his images. In his concern for well-crafted shots that had an aesthetic self-sufficiency (and pointedly did not serve to relay some larger impression of a presence outside of or within them), Antoine joined with and renewed the pictorialist tradition that may be traced back to Léonce Perret and some of his contemporaries, and arguably all the way back to Louis Lumière.

Antoine was far from the only cinema artist of the period to explore this type of filmmaking. He had many admirers within the industry; many of them quickly followed his lead and continued to do so after he made his last film in 1922. The important financial success of his *Les Travailleurs de la mer* (*Those Who Work at Sea*, 1918, after Victor Hugo) was undoubtedly also a factor in this trend. But aside from Antoine, no director specialized exclusively in the pictorialist naturalist film. Louis Mercanton, for example, made both strictly commercial, sentimental fare as well as pictorialist naturalist films. One, set in Spain (*Aux jardins de Murcie* [*In the Gardens of Murcia*, 1923]), was about a peasant feud over water rights); another was about gypsies (*Miarka*, 1920, starring Réjane and shot on location in the Camargue region). Léon Poirier, one of the most versatile and interesting directors of the period, and one of the most neglected today, made *Le Penseur* (*The Thinker*, 1920, inspired by the famous Rodin statue), a film with many impressionist touches, as well as standard studio features about vulnerable rich women married to men who don't understand them, and the like. But he also created one of the most beautiful of all pictorialist naturalist films, *La Brière* (1924), based on a prize-winning contemporary novel and named after its setting, a salt marsh in lower Brittany. Although this film has a clear narrative, it is as much a visual

His producer balked at the extreme visual naturalism and dramatic under-statement of Antoine's *L'Hirondelle et la Mésange* (1920/83, named for the story's two barges). It was never screened publicly until its recent restoration by the Cinémathèque Française.

essay on water, light, fog, and isolation as it is the story of a peasant family dominated by a brutal, embittered patriarch. Poirier also brought the methods and ethos of pictorialist naturalism into the genre of the historical drama in *Jocelyn* (1922, after Lamartine), and later mixed pictorialist techniques with the documentary in *Verdun, visions d'histoire* (*Verdun, Visions of History*, 1928).

Other important pictorialist naturalist works were made by Henri Pouctal and Jacques de Baroncelli. Along with Poirier and Mercanton, they were members of the French cinema's prewar generation. But the appeal of pictorialist naturalism was not limited to people over the age of forty. Because of the structure of the industry, most films were produced by companies which did not own (and hence, did not have to use) studio facilities. That is why many young directors working on limited budgets, such as Jacques Feyder, made occasional contributions to the genre. And there was a clear affinity between pictorialist naturalism and the documentary film, as Poirier's

Verdun attests. In the silent era, as today, documentary was an area in which younger people unable to move directly into fiction film production were able to find work. It was by this route that the last of the great early cinema pictorialists, Jean Grémillon, entered the French film industry.

Grémillon was born in 1901 in Bayeux, a farming community in Brittany, to a good bourgeois family. His father was an industrial engineer for a railway company, and the family expected Jean to follow this profession, or to become a doctor, or to find some other suitably respectable career. But the boy had a passion for music, which he studied with great application, though at first in secret. After his *baccalauréat* and (peacetime) military service—he is the first filmmaker in our story too young to have fought in the Great War—he moved to Paris and studied composition with Vincent D'Indy. To earn his living he played the violin in a cinema orchestra, where he met a fellow musician whose husband, Georges Périnal, was a projectionist and part-time cinematographer. The two men became friends, and in 1923 they collaborated on a short documentary, *Chartres*. Until 1927 they continued to make industrial and travel films about subjects such as the fabrication of synthetic glue, the Auvergne region, and the *Life of Italian Workers in France* (1926, feature length). In late 1924, Grémillon assembled some striking shots from a number of their films into a work he called *Photogénie mécanique* (*Mechanical "Photogenia"*) which was shown at the Vieux-Colombier, an art cinema which was probably the period's most important meeting ground for avant-garde film artists. In 1926 the same theatre presented the first run of his *Un Tour au large* (*A Sea Journey*), a poetic documentary about the voyage of a tuna fishing boat. At the Vieux-Colombier he met the actor Charles Dullin, an important figure in French avant-garde theatre, who was forming his own independent film production company. Dullin asked Grémillon to direct its first feature film, *Maldone* (1928).

Maldone has a rather creaky plot about a canal mule driver, in reality the heir to a large estate, who falls in love with a gypsy girl. The death of his brother forces him to return home to manage the family *domaine*, but he misses his former life and goes a little mad. At the end of the film he abandons riches and security to seek the simpler life he once knew. Like most pictorialist naturalist films, *Maldone* is partly about social class. Its hero can only feel comfortable with gypsies or other social outcasts; for reasons that are never made clear, he cannot accept the limitations of a comfortable, middle class existence.

This simpleminded social analysis, however, is not what makes the film interesting, nor is it Dullin's performance, which seems oddly stylized in the context of the work's stunning canal and mountain compositions. (Unproductive tension between conventional stage acting and very real decor is the major weakness of many pictorialist naturalist films.) But with a simple shift of attention, *Maldone* can be experienced as a film of beautiful landscapes. Its rhythms are slow, its compositions balanced and pleasing. So self-sufficient are many of its shots that they begin and end with fades to and from black. The 1929 *Gardiens de phare* (*The Lighthouse Keepers*), set on an isolated island off the coast of Brittany, confirmed the stunning lyrical gift that Grémillon brought to cinema. Like *Maldone*, it had an implausible, melodramatic plot and used obviously professional actors in equally obviously authentic surroundings. But it also had a masterful, painterly and abstract approach to image making, and an impressive sureness of rhythm. The two films are probably the culmination of the pictorialist naturalist tradition—though its naturalism had by this time become perceptibly diluted with conventional cinema melodrama.

▨ Cinematic impressionism and pictorialist naturalism embody the temptations of idealism and of simple materialism, respectively. As a general rule, the former tended to the political Right, the latter to the Left. It is therefore not surprising that filmmakers strongly associated with one position rarely showed much interest in the other. Such was not the case, however, with one of the period's most fascinating film artists, Jean Epstein, whose career clearly expresses this central tension. Epstein was born in 1897 in Warsaw, the son of a French father and a Polish mother. His father, a mining engineer, died when Jean was not yet ten years old, and after his death the family moved to Switzerland, where Jean received his *baccalauréat*. His father's wish had been for the boy to become an engineer, but when Jean went to the University of Lyon, just at the beginning of the First World War, it was to enter the study of medicine. As a foreign national, Epstein was not obligated to serve in the military, but there is little doubt that the peculiar atmosphere of the war years contributed greatly to his personal and professional evolution: why learn to heal bodies when science itself was finding ever more horrible ways to mutilate them? After a few years of study, he dropped out of medical school.

Unlike L'Herbier, Gance, and other men of their age, the considerably younger Epstein did not first develop a set of interests and then conclude that the cinema could serve as their vehicle. He had long loved the cinema spectacle itself and sought to explore all its possibilities. His was the first generation for which filmgoing was, simply, a fact of life. In his early adolescence he had been fascinated by French comics such as Prince and Max Linder. By the time he got to Lyon, he was going regularly to the movies with his sister Marie and with other students, whether the films were good or bad. Mostly, he thought they were bad, with the notable exception of Chaplin's. He recalled the pleasures of hooting at the leading French stars, and felt that most of the country's films were little more than "albums of poses and catalogues of décors." Then, one evening, "there came a film of William [S.] Hart, a view suddenly given of another world, more lively and more nourishing than the real world, than the world read or heard about."[16] Epstein's experience of the first notable American feature films distributed in France convinced him that the cinema was an essential expression of contemporary culture. By the end of the war his interest in contemporary intellectual life had won out completely over the parental mandate to become a respectable technocrat, and he began to contemplate writing a graduate thesis in modern literature. He had concluded that contemporary culture had suddenly mutated, its evolution accelerated. Poets, the best representatives of new trends, no longer elaborated arguments and planned structures, but presented successions of striking details. Art was no longer distant from its perceivers, but frighteningly close. The old aesthetic goal of perceiving organized wholes had been replaced by a new ideal: perceiving *rapidly*.

Epstein wrote an outline of his ideas and sent it to the poet Blaise Cendrars, whose work he thought particularly representative of this "new state of intelligence." Cendrars responded warmly, and the two men began an extensive correspondence. In 1920 Jean and Marie Epstein spent most of their meager savings on a trip from Lyon to Nice, where Jean delivered his completed manuscript to Cendrars and, thanks to the poet's introduction, brother and sister were able to observe Germaine Dulac directing one of her films. Cendrars also arranged for Epstein to observe second-unit shooting on Abel Gance's *La Roue* and recommended his manuscript to Paul Lafitte. Lafitte, onetime cofounder of the Film d'Art and now proprietor of Les Editions de la Sirène, a short-lived but influential avant-garde publishing house, accepted not only the book on modern poetry but also Epstein's *Bonjour Cinéma* (a collage of essays, poems, and drawings), both of which were published in 1921. Thanks to Lafitte, Epstein was hired by Louis Delluc as assistant director on *Le Tonnerre* (*Thunder*, 1921—one of Delluc's less successful films). Epstein's progress illustrates just how small a world this section of the Parisian intelligentsia really was. Lafitte's recommendation probably carried weight with Delluc because La Sirène had just published his collection of semifictional sketches, *The Cinema Jungle*. Delluc introduced Epstein to Marcel L'Herbier, who tried to find him a job on his next film but could not, supposedly because of opposition from his producer. But this was a rare setback in the young man's career. When he could not find a job and was forced to contemplate leaving Paris, Lafitte hired him as his personal secretary at the publishing house.

Epstein shared an office with Léon Moussinac, also a friend of Delluc's, who was soon to become the French cinema's first major Marxist critic and historian. In an office down the hall, Jean Benoît-Lévy's small production company was preparing a film on the life of Louis Pasteur to commemorate the centenary of the scientist's birth. Lafitte convinced Benoît-Lévy to hire Epstein as the film's director, and *Pasteur* (1922), which today we would call a docudrama, launched his cinema career. After another nonfiction work for Benoît-Lévy, Epstein was hired by Pathé-Consortium to direct four very different projects, most notably a script of his own about an orphan girl in Marseilles who loves an honest dockworker but is forced to live with a brutal thug while her true lover is in prison. This scenario had won two hundred francs in a competition run by Delluc's magazine *Cinéa*, and—calculatedly or not—it contained many elements that Delluc and his allies could admire. In the completed film, *Coeur fidèle* (*Faithful Heart*, 1923), many viewers were greatly impressed by a striking sequence set on a merry-go-round, on which the heroine rides while in a state of extreme mental agitation. Epstein, inspired by Gance's *La Roue*, experimented in this scene with the editing of very short bits of film in regular, rhythmic patterns.

The merry-go-round sequence in *Coeur fidèle* quickly became an accepted "classic" of cinematic impressionism, but the two films Epstein made immediately afterwards were of a very different sort. These were a short documentary on the eruption of Mount Etna, and *La Belle Nivernaise* (1924), whose title is also the name of the river barge on which most of its action takes place. If *Coeur fidèle* was guaranteed to warm the hearts of the cinematic impressionists, *La Belle Nivernaise* had virtually everything necessary to please the followers of André Antoine. The film was based on a novel by Alphonse Daudet, was shot on location on the river Seine, and had spectacularly beautiful landscapes against which the often brutal behavior of its characters emerged with particular clarity. There was only one brief bit of (nonsubjective) rapid editing. Critics who had admired *Coeur fidèle* were disappointed by the lyrical, pictorialist *Belle Nivernaise*.

This reaction is perhaps the main reason that, until the end of the decade, Epstein limited his pictorialist impulses to his documentaries, which he continued to make, and to the striking exteriors in his historical dramas. But he was clearly not interested in following up *Coeur fidèle* with other, calculatedly similar impressionist films. In a 1924 lecture he went so far as to denounce the new sacred cow of cinematic impressionism, rapid rhythmic editing: "The abusive use of rapid editing has now spread even to documentary. Every drama has its scene made out of little pieces, when it's not two or three such scenes. I predict that 1925 will inundate us with films that correspond exactly to the most superficial aspects of our cinematographic ideal of 1923. 1924 is already upon us and in one month we have been presented four films using rapid editing. It's too late. This is no longer interesting, it's a bit ridiculous."[17]

Epstein's efforts to contribute meaningfully to the development of the film medium were often constrained by his producers' notions of what would sell. In 1924 he left Pathé-Consortium for the Albatros company, where he directed Mosjoukine and Lissenko in *Le Lion des Mogols* and Lissenko in *L'Affiche* (*The Poster*, 1924). The latter film, one of his best meldings of cinematic experiment and popular subject matter, was based on a script by his sister Marie. Though the film has several striking instances of subjective cinematic effects, most of the narrative which motivates these sequences is conveyed in smooth, Hollywood-style invisible editing. The film tells the story of an unwed mother who sells the picture of her baby to a soap company. (The idea for the story came from a highly visible, contemporary publicity campaign centered on a baby's picture.) The baby dies, the grieving woman wanders through a Paris filled with images of what she has lost. The obligatory happy ending, in which she is reunited with the baby's father, does not efface the powerful central dilemma: how to live in a world where others may try to impose unwanted meanings on one's own images.

In 1926 Epstein achieved artistic independence with the formation of his own production company. His first project for it, however, was not an occasion for striking cinematic experiments, but a pictorialist variant on the historical drama, a genre he had explored for Pathé-Consortium (the striking, innovative *L'Auberge rouge* [*The Red Inn*, 1923, after Balzac]) and for Albatros (*Les Aventures de Robert Macaire* [*The Adventures of Robert Macaire*], 1925). *Mauprat* (1926, after George Sand) even had a companion documentary short, *Au pays de George Sand* (*In the Country of George Sand*, also 1926). After these lyrical, pictorialist explorations of the Romantic imagination, Epstein again turned to impressionist themes and formal exploration in the feature film *6½ × 11* (1927, scenario by Marie Epstein) and two shorter works, *La Glace à trois faces* (*The Three-Paneled Mirror*, 1927, after Paul Morand) and *La Chute de la maison Usher* (*The Fall of the House of Usher*, 1928, after Edgar Allan Poe). The last two films represent a significant departure from his previous work. In these short works, cinematic and narrative experiments achieve a remarkable density and complexity. Clearly they do not address the general cinema audience, but court the sophisticated viewers of the *ciné-clubs* and specialized art cinemas. They are Epstein's own, very personal summation of the cinematic impressionist movement.

Both films concern the role of human desire in the elaboration of images—an artist's portrait of his wife in *La Chute de la maison Usher*, three women's memories of one man in *La Glace à trois faces*. Richard Abel argues that Epstein reached an aesthetic and philosophical impasse in *La Chute de la maison Usher*, where Nature itself rebels against the artist's need to impose his own vision on his wife's tortured body. Following Poe's "The Oval Portrait," Epstein has the painter's efforts result in his model's death. Later she returns from the grave to lead him out of the family house just before it is destroyed in a terrible storm. This narrative can be read as Epstein's own, perhaps unconscious rejection of "art for art's sake."[18] Conversely, it is sometimes argued that the principal defect of Epstein's work is its reliance on artistic intelligence at the expense of any real emotion.[19] The protagonist of *La Chute de la maison Usher* might then represent something the director never had, or thought he could not have. Perhaps he abandoned cinematic impressionism because he finally realized that his own emotions were not moved by such works, but responded more to the simple, direct portrayal of ordinary people seen against natural landscapes.

In *La Chute de la maison Usher* and *La Glace à trois faces*, Epstein had taken the impressionist film toward its ultimate limits of intelligibility and aesthetic coherence. When he again shifted his artistic course, it was toward the pictorialist tendency that had always been present in his work. This too he took much further than he had done before. *Finis terrae* (*Land's End*, 1929) takes place on a small island off Brittany, inhabited only by a few kelp gatherers. It is about a fight between two men resulting in injury and an infection that threatens the life of one of them. Although this plot is very similar to that of Grémillon's *Gardiens de phare* (in which a lighthouse keeper on a very similar island is stricken with rabies), the two films are very different. Epstein developed his story in cooperation with the islanders themselves and featured them as his players, using no professional actors. While Grémillon's work recalls André Antoine, Epstein's suggests a French pictorialist version of Robert Flaherty.[20] Though his career later faltered, Epstein made three more such films, two short narratives and one feature, during the French cinema's conversion to synchronous sound production. There is a quality of feeling in these works that the director never achieved, or only rarely, in his more aesthetically "advanced" films. Possibly he alone, of all those associated with cinematic impressionism, experienced the end of the silent era and the transition to sound as a period of personal and artistic fulfillment.

🔲 6 🔲

The Commercial and the Esoteric

During the 1920s there were, broadly speaking, three relatively distinct options in the shooting and editing of silent cinema. The oldest of these goes all the way back to Louis Lumière: a shot, and thus the action or situation it depicts, may be allowed to continue until it attains some kind of formal or narrative closure. Taken to the extreme, this respect for the integrity of the shot results in the celebrated long takes of the early films of Orson Welles. But such a shot need not be of long duration if its possibilities are quickly exhausted, as typically happens in the prewar features of Léonce Perret. In postwar French cinema this respect for the integrity of the shot generally characterized the works of the pictorialist naturalist tendency. Another choice was to interrupt an action or situation with action from another space, or with a markedly different view of the same action; in this case the film spectator is obliged to bring unity to the diverse, often conflicting elements of the sequence—to construct it mentally. This option is frequently called *montage*, with the Lumière tradition labeled, by opposition, *mise-en-scène*. It should be remembered, however, that almost all films use montage (editing), and that all depend on some sort of *mise-en-scène* (arrangement of elements within the image). The montage tradition had been extensively explored by the American director D. W. Griffith and, following his example, by the French impressionist filmmakers.

But there was also a third possibility, which had slowly begun to develop even before the war and would soon attain the status of a (worldwide) norm with the transition to sound cinema. That was to use editing in a self-effacing manner, to shift the visual emphasis within a scene, or to give the impression of effortlessly following the progress of a film's story as it evolves in space and time. Although unnoticed by most spectators, this kind of filmmaking requires quite careful planning of fictional geography and temporality, and of the formal characteristics of the image (shot scale, camera direction, and so on).[1] For example, two characters in conversation may be seen from alternating, complementary angles, in the formation known as shot-reverse shot. Or, in a match cut on action, the visual field may shift effortlessly (or so it seems) in relation to the story, allowing us to follow a character through a door, or to get closer to an important bit of business—the change of image appearing as a kind of natural response to the fiction. André Bazin called this orientation *découpage classique,* which might best be translated as "classical scene construction" (but which his American translator renders as "classical editing").[2] Since the early days of the sound film, Bazin argued, this set of practices has served as the stylistic foundation of mainstream commercial cinema, but in the silent era it was still, as it were, under construction. The French director most adept at its use in the 1920s was probably Henri Fescourt. In his style of cutting, shot selection, and no-nonsense approach to storytelling, he often seems a kind of continental version of the American master of action films, Howard Hawks.

If classical scene construction was still, in the French cinema of the 1920s, only one option in a wider repertoire of filmmaking practices, its underlying rationale was already quite clear: what the camera shows the film spectator, where it is, how long shots last on the screen, and so on, is determined not by independent aesthetic criteria but by the varying demands of the fiction. A film's subject matter dictates its cinematographic style, aided by Ockham's razor: one must use only those stylistic devices necessary to a particular narrative effect and no more. Filmmakers such as the cinematic impressionists, who cared more for what they considered the "art of the film" than for the stories they told, presumably found this orientation rather unappealing. Their reluctance to accept the limitations it imposed on them almost certainly accounts in large measure for the difficulties they encountered during the transition to synchronous sound filmmaking, which (as we will see in the next chapter) finally elevated *découpage classique* to the status of a norm.

But in subordinating the formal dimensions of the cinema to the demands of narrative intelligibility, classical scene construction placed a heavy burden on subject matter in a medium that has always had a terrible compulsion to repeat and thus to deplete the impact of its fictions. Because of its industrial organization and its dependence on a mass market, mainstream cinema throughout its history has periodically produced works of a certain originality (and often artistic interest), which are then followed by successive imitations and variations of the successful prototype(s). We call these cycles of repetition and variation film genres.³ With the growing importance of classical scene construction came the crucial, continuing problem of mature commercial cinema: the successful exploitation and periodic renewal of these basic formulas in a medium which increasingly depended for its impact on narrative rather than on spectacle, on characters and their situations rather than on the filmmaker's presentation of them.

In postwar French silent cinema a number of such cycles may be identified, but it should be kept in mind that cross-fertilization and generic parody are always the rule, not the exception.⁴ The serial melodrama, so strikingly elaborated by Feuillade, continued to appeal to audiences until the mid 1920s, though its success was clearly on the wane. The new genres emerged in feature film production, though typically they continued trends from the prewar cinema. In purely financial terms, the most significant trend was inspired by the often hyperemotional family dramas of popular boulevard playwrights. Today it is conventional to call films of this sort domestic melodramas, though in fact they owe little to the stage melodrama and much to the older French tradition of the *drame bourgeois*. Gance's *Mater Dolorosa* is an early example. By the end of the 1920s the French cinema was awash with stories of virtuous wives, domineering husbands, unscrupulous blackmailers, children falsely accused of heinous crimes, and so on. Gance had long since abandoned this type of story by the time it sank, inevitably, into unredeemed kitsch.

Another important, if rather peculiar, category of 1920s commercial cinema was the exotic costume drama. These works told stories of fierce passion and deadly intrigue, generally involving affairs of state and set either in mythical foreign lands or in real places treated as if they were mythic; they generally favored North Africa and the Orient as the settings of their fevered narratives. Jacques Feyder, who would become one of the leading French filmmakers of the early sound era, directed the monster hit of this genre, *L'Atlantide* (1921), which tells the story of the fatally attractive queen of a remote, very decorative civilization in the Sahara, and of the two Frenchmen who fall desperately in love with her. Clearly the success of this and other similar works had something to do with French colonial aspirations and the wish to idealize the empire. At the same time, ambivalence about foreignness also comes through: one of the men in Feyder's film goes mad with desire and kills the other. If only they had stayed home perhaps none of this would have happened—though their wives might have been blackmailed, or their children framed for murder.

During the silent film's golden age, most mainstream French productions paid as little attention to social reality as did exotic costume dramas such as *L'Atlantide.* Then as now commercial cinema generally functioned as an escape from rather than as a mirror of contemporary life. Feuillade's slogan of "la vie telle qu'elle est," life as it is really lived, was a commercially viable ideal only for the pictorialist naturalist films that depicted sectors of French society of which most spectators had little direct knowlege. Pictorialist naturalism existed as a genre as well as an aesthetic orientation—a minor genre, commercially, but virtually the only one in which problems of everyday life could be routinely examined. The rest of commercial cinema dealt with the day-to-day existence of ordinary French men and women indirectly, if at all. Most films were set in a kind of vague present day from which political and social issues were banished; their characters derived largely from theatrical stereotypes: blasé aristocrats, bourgeois *pères de famille,* virtuous wives, meddling mistresses, and innocent children (often poor orphans) at the mercy of an often cruel fate. Working class characters, such as the ones in Epstein's *Coeur fidèle,* were remarkably rare, their problems and social context only somewhat less stereotyped and vague.

The most commercially significant genre with some sense of connection between the characters and the larger world in which they lived was the historical drama, which by definition could comment on contemporary life only through indirection and allegory. Seen today, many of these films hold up surprisingly well. One reason for this is probably the inherent constraint which the genre exerted on the industry's tendency to repeat itself: in treating widely known, quite specific historical events, filmmakers could not with any honesty imitate each other too much, unless they made films about the same subject. These works were big in resources employed and in running time on the screen. France was the favored setting for much of the genre, but interest also extended to northern locales (Flanders, Germany) and to the east (Poland, Russia). Tales set in foreign lands often evoked deliberate parallels with French history. The popularity of the genre probably reflected a continuing need to assert the viability of the nation and the individual in the face of tumultuous change. To judge by its productions, most of the film industry accepted the national consensus: the recent victory over Germany had shown that progress was on the side of France, even if the human cost of its triumph had been high. Most creators and sympathetic observers of mainstream cinema thus took a positive, progressive view of history and considered it worthy subject matter for the medium—in fact, the very height of what enlightened commercial cinema could do.

With clever marketing, the right historical subject could turn an ordinary feature film into a National Event. Raymond Bernard's *Le Miracle des loups* (*Miracle of the Wolves,* 1924), a Joan of Arc-like story of a young woman who saves French national unity and the monarchy as well, had its premiere at the Paris Opera, attended by the President of the Republic—not coincidentally a political moderate trying desperately to assert control over a deeply divided government. At the end of the decade, two very different films on the same subject showed the genre at its two extremes: at its best, and, if not at its worst, at least at its most uninspired. Carl Dreyer's *La Passion de Jeanne d'Arc* (*The Passion of Joan of Arc,* 1928) and Marco de Gastyne's *La Merveilleuse Vie de Jeanne d'Arc* (*The Wondrous Life of Joan of Arc,* 1929) both aimed to exploit the five-hundredth anniversary celebrations of Joan's great series of victories of 1429, but there the resemblance ends. *La Merveilleuse Vie* is lumpy and uneven, close to unwatchable today, whereas *La Passion* is universally considered one of the great achievements of world silent cinema. A more worthy artistic and ethical counterpoint to Dreyer's masterpiece was the widely admired historical film of the decade's end, Gance's *Napoléon.*

Both directors were, broadly speaking, mystical or spiritual filmmakers whose interests probably grew out of oddly similar life histories, though few filmmakers are ultimately more different.[5] Although *La Passion de Jeanne d'Arc* is often considered—like *Napoléon*—an experimental film, its cinematic innovations (high and low angle shots, camera movements, some quite noticeable disruptions of filmic space) are never in the service of flights of lyricism or eruptions of character subjectivity. Rather, they help to direct the viewer's attention to brute, physical facts of the historical reconstruction: faces, costumes, a remarkably ascetic decor, and above all the text, taken from the actual records of Joan's interrogations. Dreyer's film examines the spiritual meanings of its story, but without any easy, comforting recourse to simple idealism or dimestore metaphysics. It is not concerned with the Nation, nor with Great Individuals or the Forces of History, whereas *Napoléon* and more routine works such as Gastyne's *La Merveilleuse Vie de Jeanne d'Arc* are, in large measure, precisely about these things. (Not by chance, Gance and Gastyne's films had greater commercial success than did Dreyer's masterpiece.)[6] This difference is probably the major reason that the Danish director's only French work seems, from today's vantage point, so much more modern than the nation's typical historical epics of the 1920s. The film demonstrates, by its striking, isolated example, the philosophical and aesthetic limitations of its genre during the last glory days of silent cinema.

By the mid-1920s French cinema had recovered, to the extent that it could, from its recent, radical loss of world market position. Although the nation no longer had a powerful, vertically integrated film industry, the fragmented, inchoate nature of its production activities brought with it certain nonmonetary advantages. French filmmaking could sustain efforts to build an art cinema (impressionism, pictorialist naturalism), in a way that the more ordered, rationalized American system could not. Producers were encouraged to court artistic distinction—or cater to specifically French or European tastes—precisely because they had so little hope of success in appealing to the lowest common denominator of world film audiences. To compete directly with the American firms' areas of greatest strength was sheer madness. Largely for this reason, one important film genre remained notably underdeveloped by French producers for most of the decade. Film comedy depended to a remarkable extent on the exploitation of established stars, but in the face of competition from the works of Chaplin, Keaton, Lloyd, Langdon, and others, French cinema had not developed a major comic player since Max Linder. Linder appeared in the very successful *Le Petit Café* (*The Little Cafe*, 1919), a sentimental comedy directed by Raymond Bernard after his father Tristan's play, but this was the country's last major comic film for more than half a decade. French film comedy was finally (though in commercial terms only partially) revived not by a notable performer, but by a young director. When René Clair began making comic films, he had the field almost to himself. Largely free of the precedents and attendant commercial pressures of genre production, he was able to evolve a very personal yet commercially viable approach to the medium which would soon make him one of the leaders of early French sound cinema.

Clair was born René Chomette in Paris in 1898 in the central market district of Les Halles, where his family lived in an apartment above their wholesale soap and hotel supplies business. (His depictions of urban life in films like *Sous les toits de Paris* [1930] would owe much to his childhood experiences in this neighborhood.) Young René attended school first at the Lycée Montaigne and then at Louis-le-Grand. He was an uneven student, but he excelled in French composition and wanted to be a poet. His parents did not discourage this ambition: though they were hard working, successful entrepreneurs, they were neither snobs nor philistines. Thus Clair's involvement with the fine arts, almost uniquely among the film world's bourgeoisie, was not tinged with rebellion against a constricting set of family expectations. War broke out when he was sixteen, forever changing his artistic and intellectual orientation, as it did for most of his generation. His father and his older brother Henri (who would also become a film director) both enlisted in the military; René was left at home, attending school and helping to run the family business. Boys of his age found themselves in a strange situation: they saw the date of their own military service approach, and they heard stories of friends' fathers or older brothers killed or maimed. It was probably at this time that Clair's lifelong anarchist sympathies first began to develop.

René Chomette was declared fit for military service in 1916 and asked to be assigned to an ambulance company. This was neither easy nor safe, for the battleground was a hellish place where medical personnel were not exempt from the terrible dangers of machine gun fire and poison gas. He was soon wounded, given six months to recuperate, and then sent back to the front. In the summer of 1918 he received a new shock: his closest boyhood friend had died in battle. When the Armistice was signed in November, he was just twenty years old—bright, bitter, confused, and probably a bit phobic from his war experiences. He took a job with *L'Intransigent,* an irreverent daily newspaper, beginning as a jack-of-all-trades reporter and eventually moving up to literary subjects. The work seems not to have had much hold on him, to judge by how readily he left it. He acted in a Loïe Fuller film because he was recommended for the role by a friend, and because it paid well. His frail, nervous good looks, reminiscent of Mosjoukine or Jacque Catelan, made him a striking screen presence, even if his technique apparently left something to be desired. He performed in another film, under the direction of the Russian émigré Protozanov, and then went to Nice to be the romantic male lead in two of the last of Louis Feuillade's serials. This experience finally interested him in the cinema as something more than a source of income, though he aspired to be a director or screenwriter, not an actor. For his film career he took the pseudonym of Clair, reserving his family name for the serious literary works that he still saw as his ultimate goal.

In the years following the Great War, opium smoking had a certain vogue among young, often slightly shellshocked intellectuals. Late one night, after having consumed a quantity of the drug, René Clair got the idea for his first film as a director-writer, *Paris qui dort/The Crazy Ray* (short subject, 1924). The story, which supposedly came to him as he looked out over a deserted, motionless city, involves a mad scientist with a device capable of immobilizing all life. Six people accidentally free of the machine's effects track the man down and force him to restart the world, though not before they experience the joys and sorrows of their complete mastery of the immobilized city. The film, which is recognizably about reactions to trauma and ennui (the war still loomed large in Clair's early work), was made with very little money. Clair still earned his living mainly from journalism, and it was as a writer for a magazine cinema supplement and not as a successful filmmaker that he met Francis Picabia and was asked to direct the Dadaist short subject *Entr'acte* (*Intermission*, 1924). That aggressive, deliberately scandalous work was seen by the public six months before *Paris qui dort,* and helped draw attention to his more modest tale of "sleeping Paris."

Both works enjoyed great critical if not commercial success, which helped their director obtain a contract with a small production company for his first feature-length work. *Le Fantôme du Moulin-Rouge* (*The Ghost of the Moulin-Rouge,* 1925) also explored a comic, if at times nightmarish, fantasy. In the film a dissolute young man is persuaded by a mad doctor to submit to an experiment in which his soul is disassociated from his body. The soul escapes, wanders through the capital, and eventually falls in love and wants to return to its body, managing finally to do so just before an autopsy is performed to determine cause of "death." The film was a critical and popular success and even did some business in foreign markets. Encouraged to pursue the same themes, Clair went on to film *Le Voyage imaginaire* (*The Imaginary Voyage*, 1925), most of which was devoted to a complicated dream of its main character, a timid bank employee. Stylistically and emotionally Clair's most complex film to that point, it was a terrible failure both with critics and the public. It marked the end, for the silent period, of his flirtation with the fantastic.

Clair liked small, personal subjects. His early fantasy-comedies probably served as ways of asserting control over a world whose recent history he regarded as shocking and threatening. Most members of his generation who shared this attitude had little direct contact with commercial cinema; their occasional contributions to French filmmaking would be largely limited to the artistic and moral protest of the modernist avant-garde. But unlike more radical filmmakers such as Luis Buñuel or Man Ray, Clair never rejected mainstream filmmaking; rather, he sought workable compromises with its demands. His last three, considerably more conventional, silent films were produced by Kamenka's Films Albatros. One of them, the very popular *Un Chapeau de paille d'Italie* (*An Italian Straw Hat*, 1927), is widely considered one of the best film comedies of the era.

In his adaptation of Feydeau's famous stage farce, Clair kept the first and last acts more or less intact and substituted sight gags and slapstick chase comedy for the playwright's verbal humor in the rest of the play. In terms of cinematic style, this is Clair's most self-effacing, classically constructed film of the silent era. Because Feydeau's narrative could rarely accommodate cinematic tricks such as the superimpositions in *Le Fantôme du Moulin-Rouge* or the play with motion in *Paris qui dort*, Clair used such devices sparingly. Already in 1924 he had criticized Epstein's *Coeur fidèle* for going "astray into technical experiments which the action does not demand. That is the difference between the advanced technique of our school and American film technique, which is completely at the service of the progress of the story."[7] In positing this opposition, Clair clearly had more sympathy with the American position, though he did not identify himself with it completely. This orientation, and not any specific techniques (such as superimpositions or slow motion cinematography—both of which he employed), makes his films quite distinct from those of the cinematic impressionists and more aligned with the commercial mainstream. As befitted his earlier ambitions, Clair developed a *writerly* approach to the film medium, first imagining his tales and then conceiving the means to tell them. This flexibility, and his commitment to narrative as a first principle, would be major advantages when he later faced the challenges of the sound film.

Clair's work demonstrates there was no hard and fast line of demarcation between mainstream commercial cinema and self-consciously artistic filmmaking during the silent film's last decade. French cinema of the 1920s was remarkably diverse, offering a wide range of subject matter and stylistic orientations. Some filmmakers, such as Abel Gance or André Antoine and his disciples, approached their craft with definite, relatively inflexible ideas about what the medium could do. Others, like Clair, were more willing to compromise, exploring different styles and subjects in each new film. Jacques Feyder and Julien Duvivier, for example, produced works of great diversity during the late silent period, as we will see in the next chapter. Their pragmatism and flexibility helped them emerge from relative obscurity to become leading figures of 1930s French cinema. That troubled period's most important film artist was also learning his craft in the late silent era, exploring most of its diverse possibilities. Jean Renoir made comedies and historical dramas, as well as films which defied generic classification. He flirted with both impressionist and pictorialist styles, but was also adept in the self-effacing technique of *découpage classique*. He made works directed to the large audiences of commercial cinemas and to the less numerous, but dedicated spectators of ciné-clubs and small art cinemas. From his own unique vantage point he was, in a sense, the period in microcosm.

Renoir was the second son of Pierre-Auguste Renoir, born in the Montmartre district of Paris in 1894. After years of poverty, the great painter had by the time of Jean's birth achieved both social and artistic recognition and financial security. The family lived alternately in Paris and in a house in Burgundy. Although he was very close to his immediate family, the boy was mostly brought up by his young cousin Gabrielle Renard, a familial *au pair* whose duties were divided between Jean, who received most of her attention, and his father, for whom she posed for many celebrated paintings. With Gabrielle, Jean attended the popular Parisian entertainments of *la belle époque*—puppet shows, pantomime, and of course the cinema. His father tried to encourage him to take his schooling as seriously as these distractions, but Jean was a mediocre student: real life was elsewhere. Although the family officially regretted his attitude, no one wept bitter tears over it. Renoir did pass his *baccalauréat* exams and then, in a fit of patriotism, enlisted in the cavalry just before the Great War. He had the ironically good fortune to suffer a serious leg wound early in the conflict and to spend most of the war years recovering from it.[8] Like everyone else not at the front, he went to the movies. He liked the American cinema, revered Chaplin, and found most French films of little interest. At the end of the war he spent a brief period doing aerial reconnaissance, an experience which would be one source of his *La Grande Illusion* (1937).

At the war's end Renoir did not immediately rush into filmmaking. His career plans were undecided, and at his father's suggestion he tried his hand at ceramics. (Thanks to his great success, the painter's children would all be reasonably well-to-do, and so money was not a major concern.) Renoir *père* was in increasingly poor health, but his last years were brightened by a new young model, Andrée Heuschling. Shortly after his father's death in 1919, Jean Renoir married Heuschling. The quasi-incestuous resonances of this action, and the likelihood that Heuschling also symbolically incarnated the mother/sister figure Gabrielle, hint at the extreme importance that women, all sorts of women, would have in the director's future film work. His very choice of a cinema career, in fact, seems to have been largely determined by his Oedipal "family romance." For Renoir first became a director to make his wife a movie star—hence the equivalent for him of what she had been for his father.

Later Renoir recalled it was *Le Brasier ardent* that convinced him that good films could be made in France, and that he could possibly make some of them. His considerable inheritance, much of it in the form of paintings, assured that he need not worry about financial backing, which he provided himself for his first work. Codirected by Renoir and the actor Albert Dieudonné (Gance's Napoléon), *Catherine*, also known as *Une Vie sans joie* (*A Life Without Joy*, 1924/27) was not a very promising debut either for Renoir or for his wife, who was now known as Catherine Hessling. *La Fille de l'eau/Whirlpool of Fate* (1924), also starring Hessling but with Renoir alone as director, was set on a barge and had both striking pictorialist tableaux and impressionist spurts of rapid montage and subjective optical effects. This second film (the first to be released) had a modest critical and financial success, and it gave Renoir the confidence to stray from French cinematic models he had followed to that point. His third film, *Nana* (1926, after Emile Zola), was initially inspired by Eric von Stroheim's *Foolish Wives*.

Nana is probably the most interesting, noble failure of all French films of the 1920s. Cinematographically, the film follows American rather than continental models: its standard camera setup is the so-called American shot (actors cut off at or near the waist), and there is a great deal of shot-reverse shot cutting and match cuts on action. The acting, however, is another matter entirely. Hessling, in the title role, is a puppet, her gestures abrupt and Kabuki-like. Other characters (for example, Bordenave) are broadly drawn caricatures inspired by the French stage, while still others (Muffat and Vandeuvres) use the minimal, naturalistic playing style of the best American screen actors of the day. Throughout his career Renoir would juxtapose quite different acting styles in a single film, but in *Nana* (in the view of most commentators) the tactic fails utterly. The problem is that the analytic, American-style shooting and editing cuts up the components of the fictional world, so that Nana and the other characters seem to exist in separate spaces with minimal contact. Renoir would make this kind of mixed economy of acting styles work in his later films precisely when he strayed from *découpage classique*. Put the various players in *Nana* in the depth-composed shots of his films of the late 1930s, and you would have another film entirely. Even so, this failed, ambitious work has a fascination that more modest films of the period cannot match.

Nana was a commercial and critical disaster. Renoir lost a great deal of his own money, and he could no longer afford the luxury of financial (hence artistic) independence in making feature films. Inevitably, the result was that he was pushed toward mainstream commercial film on the one hand (where others would bankroll the right projects) and toward the ciné-club and art house circuit on the other (showing generally short and cheaply made films). *Charleston* (1927) was a brief exercise in social satire made with leftover film stock from *Nana* and probably only shown a few times at the Vieux-Colombier cinema. In 1928 Renoir and Jean Tedesco arranged a primitive studio in the attic of the small cinema. There Renoir shot *La Petite Marchande d'allumettes / The Little Match Girl* (1928/30), a work which is either a grimly comic impressionist film, or a parody of one, or both. Little in it prefigures Renoir's later work in the way that *Nana* often does, though as Alexander Sesonske argues, the film "represents the first full flowering of . . . Renoir's tendency to create an atmosphere of strangeness an unreality, to evoke the quality the French call *féerique*."[9]

Renoir did the rest of his work in the silent era for mainstream commercial producers, and in truth the films would be of little interest today if he had not made them. The best is probably *Tire au flanc* (1928), a military comedy based on a long-running Boulevard play and featuring the young Michel Simon. It has the improvised (yet deft) feel of his best work of the 1930s, and in retrospect one can see that here was a director who would do well in the very different aesthetic world of the sound cinema. Renoir continued to use the basic figures of invisible editing, but already he was trying to expand the expressive possibilities of the style, with experiments in panning, novel uses of offscreen space, and some scenes with careful composition in depth (marred, in the absence of fast enough film stock, by clumsy refocusing within shots). Ironically, it was in such purely commercial efforts that he began slowly to find the style and even the subject matter of his great sound features. By the time of *Tire au flanc*, Renoir had already begun to explore the visual style he would elaborate throughout the first decade of the sound cinema.

One must be wary of ascribing too much explanatory power to labels such as impressionism and pictorialist naturalism: they are typically of little help in the interpretation or analysis of particular films.[10] But the terms are useful in sorting out the era's conflicting visions of what the film medium was and how it ought to evolve. The political metaphor implied in this book's title is meant, in this case, to be taken almost literally. One may think of impressionism and pictorialist naturalism as being the aesthetic equivalent of political parties, or perhaps pressure groups, within the film community. They represent an important form of collective action by particular, relatively coherent networks of individuals. The metaphor may be taken a step farther if one internationalizes it. For if the French cinema was at this time a kind of imperfect republic (though we should keep in mind that not all groups get represented in republics, only those that can establish a sufficient power base and organize it effectively), the American cinema of the same period was more like a one-party state, its rulers being the apparatchiks of the large studios. It was easier to innovate and to have one's innovations matter in France, where power was more evenly and more fluidly distributed.

For this reason, and because Paris was already the center of a large and active community of avant-garde artists in other media, French cinema of the 1920s was the site of many attempts either to extend the artistic limits of commercial narrative filmmaking (cinematic impressionism) or to ignore them entirely in an attempt to develop a new kind of cinema art (what today we would call experimental cinema). Because of their disdain for the industry establishment, and

Nana (Catherine Hessling) and Vendeuvres (Jean Angelo) have an important day at the races in Renoir's stylized adaptation of Emile Zola's *Nana*.

because they were allied with self-consciously modern artists in other media, artists of the latter orientation may be called modernist independents. This group included diverse, idosyncratic figures such as Luis Buñuel, Man Ray, and Fernand Léger. Defining their filmmaking practices in any general way is problematic. Even the use of the word "modernist" to define them is, strictly speaking, inadequate. The modernist impulse developed in a series of distinct phases, with one crucial dividing point being the Great War. Cinematic impressionists such as Gance or L'Herbier were heavily influenced by the early manifestations of literary modernism; in the mid-1920s, however, their claims to an aesthetic vanguard position in French filmmaking were challenged by a new group of artists inspired by more recent trends in the visual and performance arts. Here, as elsewhere, the distinction was one of cultural, though not always literal, generations. Age was not as important as artistic self-definition, the choice of one's friends and enemies. Thus Jean Epstein broke off relations with Luis Buñuel, his assistant director on *La Chute de la maison Usher* and less than three years his junior, when the latter called the impressionists' hero Abel Gance a *vieux con* (roughly: "old shithead").

As this incident suggests, relations between the cinematic impressionists and the modernist independents were often strained. The latter group generally admired the prewar films that the former had found so uninspired. Jacques Brunius, one of the younger artists' first historians, characterized early cinema as a "poetic pastime, the magical manner of *wasting one's time.*"[11] Brunius and his associates also agreed that the serious commercial cinema of the 1920s was offensively pretentious. Robert Desnos said that the mere photographic image of Jacques Catelain, leading man of many L'Herbier films, was convincing proof of the performer's "grotesqueness and vanity, which make him the prototype of the 'advanced' actor, as Monsieur Marcel L'Herbier is among directors."[12] L'Herbier and Catelain, perhaps in return for such courtesies, sometimes went to screenings or performances of their opposition and created disturbances, yelling insults or walking out in disgust at appropriate moments.

In both production circumstances and exhibition, the modernist independents' works departed from normal industry practices. Their films were brief, produced cheaply and by few hands. There was little of the careful division of labor that characterized feature film making. Once made, the films were exhibited as art works in galleries or private shows, shown as part of multi-media spectacles, or screened in specialized art cinemas or ciné-clubs. Making money was not a major goal for most of the independents, beyond the simple wish to continue to live and make art. The commercial cinema represented the hated society that had so blithely sent them and their fallen friends off to the recent slaughter. The most radical of the independents saw art as a way of changing the world. For the less radical, or perhaps the less hopeful, it probably represented retreat to a world unsullied by violence and greed. Such an impulse did not, probably could not originate or sustain itself within the cinema community alone. Cinematic modernism may perhaps best be thought of as the meeting points between the most radical elements of the French film community and the modernist avant-garde of the other arts.

The history of this sector of French cinema is thus by definition fragmented, plural. It can be conceived in various ways: from the side of the film community, from the perspectives of the various artists and art movements which made contact with the cinema, or in terms of its posterity. The last point of view probably accounts for the curious fact that the modernist independent works loom very large in English language histories of film, but get comparatively little attention from French scholars. For the films' most lasting impact was to be felt in the United States where, over a decade after their heyday (when they had been all but forgotten by European *cinéastes*), their revival and study played a major role in the first flowering of American experimental filmmaking.[13] In the United States this kind of cinema became by the 1950s what it had never managed to be in France: the work of a community of film artists whose coherence—which often found expression in aesthetic tensions and personal antagonisms—did not depend on issues, personnel, and sheer momentum from other media. In retrospect, this outcome is anything but surprising: many of the most notable French modernist independent works were made by foreigners.

The cinema was one of the last of the arts to be touched by postwar modernism. It was probably in 1920 that Marcel Duchamp, assisted by the American artist Man Ray, attempted a stereoscopic film. Unfortunately, only a few frames of that work survived a primitive, homemade developing process. In 1923, when one can begin to speak of a movement rather than of isolated endeavors, Man Ray made (or perhaps more accurately, assembled) *Le Retour à la raison* (*The Return to Reason*), a five-minute mixture of live action footage and "rayographs," or images made by laying objects such as thumbtacks or grains of salt directly on unprocessed film and exposing it to light. The film was conceived for a Dada evening called "The Bearded Heart," organized by Tristan Tzara. When two of Ray's homemade splices gave way and interrupted the projection, the ensuing melée caused the police to intervene and stop the spectacle, a most satisfactory Dada end to the proceedings. The year 1923 marked another important beginning, with a number of highly visible programs of short artistic films, mainly excerpts from commercial features. These were shown and discussed, sometimes in the context of lectures, at ciné-club meetings and other public forums. By 1924 an unofficial canon of such works included the opening train crash from *La Roue*, the tavern dance from *Kean*, and the merry-go-round scene from *Coeur fidèle*. In the same year, Jean Epstein's *Photogénie* and Jean Grémillon's *Photogénie mécanique* were among the first works made specifically for this new audience and exhibition format. At the end of the year, Jean Tedesco opened the Vieux-Colombier, the first of the Parisian art houses.

The two most important modernist works of 1924, however, initially had little contact with the film community's celebrations of cinema art. Inspired by the rapid, rhythmic train sequences of *La Roue* and *L'Inhumaine* (for which he had designed the set for the climactic laboratory scene) the painter Fernand Léger made his only film, *Ballet mécanique*, in collaboration with the American filmmaker Dudley Murphy. Léger submitted the work to Jean Tedesco for the Vieux-Colombier's first season, but Tedesco refused it outright, preferring established figures such as Gance and Epstein for his programming. One imagines him saying to himself: Léger can paint, but he knows nothing of cinema! Nonetheless, by the end of the decade *Ballet mécanique* had become a classic of the art house and ciné-club circuit, though by then audiences had had to get used to much stronger stuff. Léger's film is sometimes called a Cubist work. While this is a useful formulation, it is more accurate to say that it exploits many of the painter's typical subjects and formal strategies, and that these often suggest his own version of analytic Cubism.

Like so many modern artists, Léger was profoundly affected by the Great War. Before the conflict, his subjects, like those of Picasso and the other Cubists, were traditional French painterly ones: landscapes, nudes, and so on. After the war, though he continued to paint nudes and landscapes, he also became obsessed with mechanization; much of the reflective tranquillity of the *belle époque* had been forever shattered by tanks, planes, and heavy artillery. *Ballet mécanique* is a film about machinery: how it looks and what its rhythms are like, how people can be seen as mechanisms, and how the cinema experience itself is machine-like. At one point in the film, a washerwoman with a laundry bag over one shoulder is seen, from above, climbing a stone staircase toward the camera. Near the top, she begins to gesture, as if to say, "Well?"—and suddenly she is at the bottom again, climbing the same stairs as the footage is repeated again and again (a total of seven times), before we see a different, close-up shot of a mouth that suddenly, *mechanically* smiles. Then back to the washerwoman several times more, then a close-up of a machine part in motion (that is, the mouth, formally), then a final burst of the washerwoman's Sisyphus-like progress, followed finally by a dark screen. The sequence is funny and moving at the same time: the woman, trapped by the film and probably by life itself, still half-smiles and gestures: "Well? So what?"

Although *Ballet mécanique* is constructed from quite diverse visual materials (as in the sequence just described), Léger imposes on them his unifying vision of a world built from a limited repertoire of forms and movements. In this way the film manages to recapture the detachment and (kinetic) balance of prewar Cubism in the service of new, potentially disturbing subject matter. *Entr'acte*, the other landmark modernist film of 1924, is anything but balanced and detached. Both films depend heavily on graphic editing, the setting into play of geometric relations between adjacent images. *Ballet mécanique* makes this strategy explicit in a set of alternations between a circle form and a triangle. Léger presumably meant to suggest that the material world, however complex it may seem, has an underlying, geometric logic, laid bare in the workings of the machine. In *Entr'acte* this logic is exposed as arbitrary, as a *trap*. In the world of Dada, the world of nonsense masquerading as reason, we are all victims of the demented pseudo-rationality of the World Machine.

Entr'acte was directed by René Clair, as part of *Relâche* ("No Performance"), a Dada spectacle performed by the Ballets Suédois with music by Eric Satie, choreography by Jean Borlin, and sets and film scenario by the Spaniard Francis Picabia. The show opened with a brief film prologue, in which Satie and Picabia were seen cavorting on a rooftop and eventually firing a World War I vintage cannon directly at the audience. Then came the first part of the stage presentation. The bulk of today's *Entr'acte*, which means "intermission," was projected during the interval between the live spectacle's two acts. The intermission film itself (the second, longer section of modern prints) falls into two parts, the first assembling a number of disconnected, graphically contrasting views of Paris, a subway car seen in Méliès-style miniature, and a rooftop scene in which Marcel Duchamp and Man Ray are seen playing chess. Out of this deliberately incoherent mass of images, the second half of the *entr'acte* suddenly emerges. A young man aims a rifle at an egg balanced on a plume of water. Another man shoots him and he falls from a rooftop into his own funeral procession, the hearse drawn by a camel. From this point on, the film becomes the Dada rewriting of a prewar chase comedy, as the hearse, suddenly without the camel or any other means of locomotion, careens through the streets of Paris, followed by a crowd of bourgeois mourners in hot pursuit.

Ballet mécanique and *Entr'acte* neatly summarize the two directions that the modernist independent cinema was to take during the remainder of the 1920s. One direction, typically more attractive to those with experience in commercial filmmaking, was called pure or abstract cinema. Films of this sort tended to echo Léger's almost meditative stance, striving for a unity of mood, theme, or cinematic strategy—even when the results sometimes confused the unprepared spectator. The other direction led to confrontation, to deliberate disunification. The result was films which thumbed their noses at the spectator, careening wildly from one thing to the next, like *Entr'acte*'s miraculously mobile coffin, which opens at that film's end to reveal the young hero, now very much alive and wielding a magic wand. One by one, he makes the stunned remaining mourners disappear, and then himself. Picabia's 1924 scenario has the feeling of a dream logic, as if the shift from Dada to Surrealism were already inscribed in this last, strange narrative turn.

■ Modernist independent film was a splinter movement within a chaotic and often divided film community. Few figures could be or even wished to be known primarily for their work in such a limited domain. Thus the most notable public advocate of the trend was also one of the period's most successful commercial filmmakers: Germaine Dulac. Dulac was born Charlotte-Elisabeth-Germaine Saisset-Schneider in 1882 in Amiens, an important industrial and commercial city in Northern France. She came from a family which, like L'Herbier's, belonged to the upper strata of the *grande bourgeoisie;* her father was a career military officer, as were most of the men in the family who were not industrialists. His career necessitated living in small garrison towns not always suitable to a young girl of good family, and Germaine was eventually sent to live with her grandmother in Paris. She studied theatre, art, and music; for much of her adolescence she took an impassioned interest in the operas of Richard Wagner.

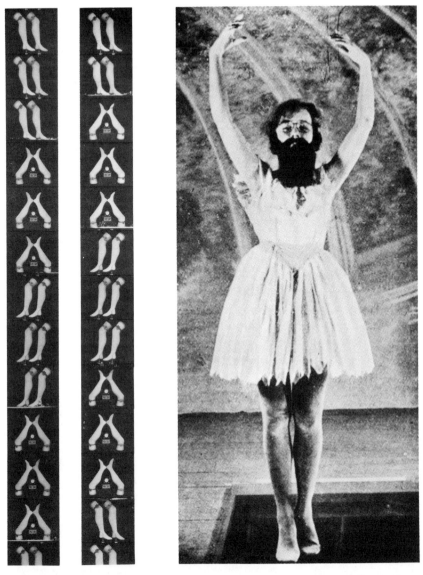

Left: detached mannequin's legs do a manic montage dance in Léger's *Ballet mécanique*. (These frames compose about 1½ seconds of the film.)
Right: a very different dance scene occurs in Clair and Picabia's *Entr'acte*, where clever editing smoothly substitutes a bearded man for a ballerina.

In 1905 Germaine Saisset-Schneider married Louis Albert-Dulac, an agricultural engineer with a similar class background. The couple's privileged financial and cultural position presumably played some part in Germaine Dulac's great independence and commitment to causes that she believed in, notably feminism and radical social theory. In 1909 she began to work with and write regularly for *La Française*, a feminist magazine for which she eventually became the drama critic. Through this position she first made serious contact with the cinema. In 1914, just before the war, she accompanied a friend, the actress Stacia de Napierkowska, on a voyage to Italy where Napierkowska was to act in a Film d'Art production. When Dulac returned to France, she had acquired not only a basic knowledge of the new medium, but also the strong desire to involve herself in its future. The war gave her the opportunity to do so. With her husband's financial and administrative participation, she and the writer Irene Hillel-Erlanger founded D. H. Films. The company produced three films in 1915 and 1916, all directed by Dulac with scenarios by Hillel-Erlanger.

In 1918, with *Ames de fous* (*Madmen's Souls*), Dulac became a noteworthy presence in the industry. That film, a serial melodrama with a scenario of Dulac's own devising, gave the director her first sustained opportunity to experiment with the cinema's expressive possibilities. She was even mildly criticized by one reviewer for her "overuse of back lighting, which plunges the artists into a regrettable darkness; we no longer see their faces, and it is silhouettes that do the acting."[14] Dulac, however, remembered the work as her first lesson that "the value of the film resides less in the action than in the subleties which emerge from it . . . Lighting, camera position, and editing seemed to me elements more important than the simple workings of a scene played in accordance with the laws of the stage."[15]

Ames de fous is probably most noteworthy for film history as the first screen appearance of the noted stage actress Eve Francis. Through Francis, who was to become one of the most important players in the impressionist cinema, Dulac met Louis Delluc, who had just written *La Fête espagnole*. Dulac was hired to direct the script, and the film was released in 1920. It is sometimes cited as one of the decade's most influential works, but unfortunately only about ten minutes of excerpts have survived, and so its actual role in the evolution of French film form and style must remain something of a mystery. During the next three years Dulac made a series of commercial feature films for her own company and for other organizations, most with conventional love triangle plots set among the higher social orders. Dulac, like many of her peers, thought that her films' subject matter was less important than the stylistic effects she explored, and that it was important to "keep one's hand in" the profession, rather than to wait for an ideal project.

Dulac is best known today for her short impressionist narrative, *La Souriante Madame Beudet* (*The Smiling Madame Beudet*, 1923). The film tells the story of a bored, petty bourgeois housewife in a provincial town. She never really smiles at all: the title is thus a notable example of the film's many ironies. Mme. Beudet's coarse, remarkably insensitive husband has the lamentable habit of putting an unloaded handgun to his head and feigning suicide. One night, pushed to the limit by his boorish behavior, she loads the gun. The next day, she narrowly escapes becoming the victim of her murderous project, but the husband, incapable of conceiving that his wife could wish to kill *him*, concludes that she has tried to arrange for him to kill her. He clumsily tries to comfort her, and the film ends as it began, with shots of the small provincial town where the couple will remain, "united for all time."

Dulac adapted *Madame Beudet* from a contemporary avant-garde play, but its most striking resonances are traditional and literary. Madame Beudet is clearly a comic (perhaps one should say, less grimly comic) Madame Bovary. The film's characters and provincial setting are remarkably Flaubertian, but even more so is Dulac's relentless irony. Although the film does not contradict Madame Beudet's view of her spouse as a lamentable buffoon, her reactions to him are shown to be neurotic and pathetically inadequate. An unspoken disagreement over where a vase should rest on a table becomes a continuing war of nerves. Much of the film's irony stems from the disparity between trivial provocations and heavy, doom laden responses by the heroine. Dulac's protagonist, like Flaubert's, experiences her life through an overdeveloped but undernourished Romantic sensibility. Even her fantasy life suffers from cultural anemia, as when she dreams (via numerous optical effects) of a tennis player she has seen in a magazine illustration. Despite its implicit critique of its central character, however, *Madame Beudet* remains true to its director's radical feminism. For the ultimate tragedy lurking beneath the surface of this subtly comic film is that the heroine has internalized her oppressive situation so completely that the ways in which she can rebel against it (moving the vase, indulging in mass-marketed reverie) only serve as humorous illustrations of her terrible psychic imprisonment. Although *La Souriante Madame Beudet* is widely accepted as one of the landmark works of the period, Dulac never again made a film very much like it. Perhaps she had already decided that the era of the impressionist film was over, a change of orientation probably helped along by her quarrel with Louis Delluc over an unproduced screen-play. Rejecting the kind of cinema he promoted would have been one way for Dulac to distinguish herself from her younger but better known colleague and rival. For Delluc and Dulac were in many ways quite alike. She, like he, was at least as important an organizer and proselytizer as a director. Both were, unlike Gance, L'Herbier, and most of the Russians, drawn to the political Left. Both refused to set-tle down to explore a single, personal style in their filmmaking. After Delluc's death, Dulac took over his role as self-appointed lobbyist for the art of the film. She wrote articles, lectured, was active in the ciné-club movement. She continued to make commercial features. One of these, *Le Diable dans la ville* (*Devil in the City*, 1924), shows up on some lists of important impressionist works, but it seems at least equally influenced by German cinematic expressionism (particularly by Paul Wegener's 1920 version of *The Golem*) and completely lacks the deli-cate ironies of *Madame Beudet*.

In 1927 Dulac directed *La Coquille et le Clergyman* (*The Seashell and the Clergyman*) after a scenario by Antonin Artaud. If Dulac is famous for *Madame Beudet*, she is in many quarters still infamous for *La Coquille et le Clergyman*. Some commentators assert that Artaud him-self complained about Dulac's having "feminized" his scenario, but nothing in the historical record substantiates this charge. Ironically, although by then Artaud had been all but expelled from their move-ment, it was mainly the Surrealists who denounced Dulac for betray-ing the true spirit of their movement as supposedly embodied in his original script. Their reactions clearly arose mainly from sheer hostil-ity to Dulac, for even a cursory comparison of scenario and finished film demonstrates that she was faithful, often slavishly so, to the author's stated intent.[16]

La Coquille et le Clergyman is loaded to the gills with optical effects, bravura editing, and other markers of authorial interpretation. But this is, arguably, what is wrong with it as a Surrealist work. Here the reality in front of the camera, the material world of the fiction is never allowed to seem strange in and of itself: a sense of the surreal is imposed, not found. Truly great examples of Surrealist filmmaking (such as Buñuel's works) generally eschew optical effects and complex editing for this very reason. Such techniques do not *create* the shock of the uncanny; rather, they *suggest* the uncanny or construct its equivalent. Dulac never made another film remotely like *La Coquille et le Clergyman*, and given the fierce hostility it provoked she presumably never wanted to. During the rest of the decade, in addition to projects made strictly to earn money, she produced and directed a series of short essays in what she and others called pure or abstract cinema, including *L'Invitation au voyage* (1927, inspired by Baudelaire's famous poem) as well as *Disque 927* and *Thèmes et variations* (both 1928). Although these works found much more favorable public and critical response than had *La Coquille et le clergyman*, some recent historians have found them rather mechanical and uninspired. Dulac may have been too much of a Cartesian rationalist for such meditative, poetic works. With the benefit of hindsight, one may wonder to what degree she herself was committed to them. When, at the end of the decade, the coming of synchronized recorded sound shocked and bewildered most of the French film community, she took part in the debates about the future of the medium but did not try to continue her explorations of pure cinema using the new technology. Beset by ill health and probably discouraged by the rapid decline of experimental filmmaking, she accepted an administrative position with the Gaumont company, for which she created and supervised the influential sound newsreel, *France-Actualités-Gaumont*.

Possibly Dulac's very success in the industry made it difficult for her to create viable works outside the mainstream. This, in any case, is the argument made by many of today's avant-garde filmmakers: one must choose between entering the system to make money, and staying away to make art. Dimitri Kirsanov, of all the figures studied here most resembling early American experimentalists such as Maya Deren or Kenneth Anger, provides an example of an independent film artist who had little contact with the industry mainstream during the silent era and made a few great works, in splendid isolation and self-absorption. Kirsanov was a young White Russian, but he claimed never even to have met the large community of his compatriots who made commercial films. He came to France in 1919, at the age of twenty, to study the 'cello at the Paris Conservatory. Like Jean Grémillon, he played in cinema orchestras to earn a living. The films he saw convinced him that the medium had great, untapped artistic potential, but he did not make the rounds of the Paris studios looking for a job. Instead, he produced, wrote, and directed *L'Ironie du destin* (*The Irony of Fate*, 1924). That film, now lost, told the story of an old man and an old woman (played by Kirsanov and his wife, Nadia Sibirskaia) who knew and secretly loved each other in their youth, meet by accident on a park bench, and tell each other the sad stories of their lives. The film was a commercial failure but it caught the eye of Jean Tedesco. When Kirsanov's next film had trouble getting distribution, Tedesco booked it as the opening work for the Vieux-Colombier cinema's second season. *Ménilmontant* (1926) was, in the modest context of the alternative cinema circuit, a smash hit. Its great success allowed Kirsanov to go on making films, and also helped Tedesco to stay in business as an exhibitor.

Like Kirsanov's first film, *Ménilmontant* tells a story without the use of inter-titles. It is often said that the director's cinema is poetic, but one must add that in his second film he explored the poetics of violence and degradation. The story begins and ends with two unrelated, but similarly filmed and edited murders. In each case, the grisly event does not grow organically out of the plot, but seems to surge out of a world welling with violent impulses. *Ménilmontant* uses practically all of the typical stylistic devices of cinematic impressionism, but it is hard to consider it as in any way representative of the movement. Its overwhelming, virtually unrelieved violence and despair seem to infect its own storytelling agency, upsetting what in other directors' works would be clearly delineated relations of parts to the whole. The film contains several bursts of rapid editing, for example, but they are not rhythmic in any simple, narratively justified way (in the manner of Abel Gance, for example); their meter is complicated and unsettling, worthy of an Igor Stravinsky. The film offers several notable examples of subjective camera work, but typically these become slightly unhinged, with no absolute certainty as to which character's experience is being rendered. *Ménilmontant* is, quite deliberately, a film in which the formal center cannot hold, because it is about a world in which this is also true. Although certainly not a Surrealist work, it shares with Surrealism not only a fascination with violence and sexuality, but also a display of forces that transcend, and question the boundaries of, individual human consciousness.

After the great success of *Ménilmontant*, Kirsanov directed two more straightforward, narrative features for independent production companies. In 1929 he made a short lyrical work generally considered his second masterpiece of the silent era, *Brumes d'automne* (*Autumn Mists*), again starring Sibirskaia as the one human figure in a melancholy setting of water, fog, and deserted walkways. It is a mood piece that implies, but does not impose or explain, a narrative context. We might usefully compare it to the haiku, which Roland Barthes argues (and he might as well be speaking of Kirsanov's film) is "undevelopable: everything is given, without provoking the desire for or even the possibility of a rhetorical expansion . . . we may (we must) speak of an *intense immobility*."[17] The film has a formal perfection rarely found in the cinema, a balance and consistency of mood and means as far removed from the Surrealist impulse as *Ménilmontant* is, in many ways, close to it.

In the same year that Kirsanov made his first film, André Breton published his first *Surrealist Manifesto* (1924), and by the time of *Brumes d'automne* the movement had become the most visible and contentious point of contact between French cinema and the modernist avant-garde of other media. Although the Surrealists took a great interest in the cinema as spectators and occasionally as critics (for example, Philippe Soupault), most of them were not tempted much by filmmaking itself. The major exceptions were two expatriates, the American Man Ray and the Spaniard Luis Buñuel. Man Ray was born in Philadelphia in 1890; he had been active in the Dada movement in New York before arriving in Paris at the beginning of the 1920s. To earn money, he worked as a commercial photographer, and it was by accident that one day he discovered the principle of the "rayograph," which he later used in *Le Retour à la raison*. Along with the young Marc Allégret, Ray assisted Marcel Duchamp in the making of *Anemic Cinema* (1926), a sort of minimalist Dada work in which shots of nine revolving discs with spiraling puns and nonsense rhymes (*bains de gros thé pour grains de beauté sans trop de bengué*) alternate with images of ten revolving discs of optical patterns. (Duchamp professed not to be interested in the cinema as such, but found it the best form of presentation of the particular effects he wished to obtain in this work. *Anemic Cinema* was his only completed film.)

By 1926 Ray's own work had turned, along with that of most of his friends and associates, from Dada to Surrealism. His *Emak Bakia* (1926—the title means "leave me alone" in Basque) is still marked, however, by the spirit of Dadaist anarchy. It assembles a wide range of disparate elements: rayographs, shots that recycle themes and techniques from Ray's photographs, and some striking allusions to (or parodies of) *Ballet mécanique* and *Entr'acte*. Perhaps because of the film's uninhibitedly omnivorous spirit, the other Surrealists did not admire *Emak Bakia*. Ray's next film, *L'Etoile de mer* (*The Starfish*, 1928, after an unpublished poem by Robert Desnos), was more disciplined, taking its lead from the Desnos text, "as seen by Man Ray." The film's many soft-focus shots, however, give it an ethereal feeling curiously reminiscent of *La Coquille et le Clergyman*. Like Dulac and Artaud's work, *L'Etoile de mer* posits, rather than creates, a sense of the surreal. Ray's last film, *Le Mystère du chateau de dés* (*Mystery of the Chateau of Dice*, 1929), a mélange of parodic narrative and themes from Mallarmé's poem "Un Coup de dés n'abolira jamais le hasard," was the first of three important modernist films to be financed by one of France's most famous patrons of the arts, the Vicomte de Noailles. The vicomte was so pleased with the finished work that he offered to commission a feature-length film, but Ray refused. As if anticipating the coming disolution of the modernist independent cinema, he returned full-time to his work in other media.

For Luis Buñuel, in contrast, the meeting of Surrealism and the cinema was to spark a life's involvement with the medium. Buñuel was born in 1900 in Calanda, a village in Northern Spain, the first son of a good provincial bourgeois family. During his childhood and adolescence he developed a love of animals and insects, and of sado-masochistic play. He studied for his secondary diploma at a Jesuit school—an experience which, to say the least, he did not enjoy. One must remember that for a Spaniard of this period religion was a very serious matter. The easy anti-clericalism of the French bourgeoisie was impossible for someone like Buñuel, and the angry denunciations of Catholicism in his films have the ring of deeply personal statements. At the age of seventeen he went to Madrid and, at his father's insistence, studied agricultural engineering, though he had wanted to pursue music. Engineering held little charm for him, and he drifted from it to the study of entomology and then to philosophy, in which he finally obtained a graduate degree in 1924. His father had died the year before, and Buñuel was adrift, personally and intellectually. In 1925 he decided to move to Paris, though with no clear idea of what he would do there. He had always gone to the movies, but now he went as often as three times a day. He decided to try to enter the industry and enrolled in a private film school run by Jean Epstein and several associates. Buñuel worked briefly as an extra on Epstein's *Mauprat*, then as assistant director on *La Chute de la maison Usher*.

When Epstein wanted to recommend him for similar work on Gance's *Napoléon*, Buñuel refused to consider working on the project and decided to make his own film.

Buñuel wrote the scenario of *Un Chien andalou* (*An Andalusian Dog*, 1929) with his friend Salvador Dali, during one of Buñuel's trips back to Spain. He produced and directed the film in Paris, with money provided by his mother. Dali had by that time also moved to the French capital, but he participated very little in the shooting and not at all in the editing. Although the film must be considered a truly collaborative work given the crucial importance of its bizarre scenario, Buñuel's precise, technically proficient direction was almost certainly the decisive factor in the successful creation of a Surreal fictional world. Unlike *La Coquille et le Clergyman* and *L'Etoile de mer* (many of whose shots were deliberately blurred by a homemade gelatine filter), *Un Chien andalou* is a hard-edged film, both in its cinematography and in the precise way it moves from one shot to the next. Buñuel's film school studies, or perhaps his extensive moviegoing, had taught him methods of editing at that time little exploited in France, though common in the American cinema. The film is filled with perfect match cuts on action, frequent glance/object edits, and effortless changes of shot scale and angle which never violate established filmic geography. These devices of Hollywood editing are used in the service of the scenario's remarkable transformations, in which, for example, a small room suddenly becomes large enough to accommodate two grand pianos with dead donkeys sprawled upon them and priests hanging from the ropes that pull them. Spaces also change in relation to other spaces: the door to an upper-story flat suddenly opens onto a beach.

Though the film has the hard-edged feel of unadorned reportage, with few of the stylistic flourishes of "artistic" works of the period, its content is compellingly dream-like. Its sense of the Surreal seems to arise from the fictional world itself, and not from anyone's impression of it. In this way *Un Chien andalou* announces the death of 1920s art cinema. Or rather, it tries to do so. Buñuel was distressed when the film quickly became a smash hit on the ciné-club and art cinema circuit. He protested, to no avail, that his work was meant not as art but as a call for revolutionary violence. To set the record straight, he accepted the Vicomte de Noailles's offer, which Man Ray had refused, to finance a Surrealist feature film. *L'Age d'or* (*The Age of Gold*, 1930) was one of the earliest, and certainly one of the strangest, French sound films. It was also to be one of the last works of modernist independent filmmaking, though not, as Buñuel intended, because it succeeded in galvanizing its spectators to transform their society (making conventional art unnecessary). The modernist impulse in French cinema would quickly wither away, the victim of new social circumstances and of the vastly more expensive technology of the sound film. The modernist independents thought of themselves as heralding the future not only of cinema, but of society. But their day had all but passed by decade's end, as had that of the cinematic impressionists and the pictorialist naturalists. With few exceptions, the future of French cinema would belong to less celebrated, commercial artisans of the mainstream filmmaking, and to narrative-oriented, independent pragmatists such as René Clair and Jean Renoir.

III

The Golden Age of
the Sound Cinema

❖ 7 ❖

An Unexpected Upheaval

Perhaps the most surprising aspect of the coming of synchronized recorded sound to the cinema worldwide is how profound and swift was the resultant transformation of the industry and of its product. One factor which greatly intensified the sudden, massive change came from outside the film industry, in one of the frequent historical synchronicities which often characterize the development of modern mass media.[1] The changeover to the "talkies" from so-called "silent" film (the French label, *cinéma muet* or "voiceless cinema," is more accurate) coincided almost exactly with a worldwide socioeconomic transformation, from the heady prosperity and expansion of the 1920s to the retrenchment and social polarization of the 1930s.

But the upheaval in film production was more directly the result of the inertia which has always characterized mature industrial capitalism. Large bureaucratized organizations have little incentive to innovate as long as they may make profits using existing resources and established production and marketing practices. They have, in essence, a vested interest in ignoring for as long as possible the necessity, and even the possible long-term benefits, of almost any sort of change. To judge by the events of the late 1920s, many filmgoers must have been growing restive, ready for something new, though the overwhelming majority of industry insiders could not conceive of such a possibility.[2] And so it came as a terribly unwelcome surprise that audiences throughout the world fervently embraced a variety of cinematic spectacle which they had previously, and repeatedly, rejected.

The Paris World's Fair of 1900 was the first site of what would be a long series of attempts to market synchronized sound films. But the

Phonorama, also known as the Phono-Cinéma-Théâtre, had only a brief commercial success, although its mechanical synchronization system seems to have functioned well enough. Later in the decade, both Pathé Frères and the Gaumont company tried to market their own sound film processes, again with no lasting success. There was as yet no electrical amplification of recorded sound, but systems based on compressed air, amplifying sound signals in a manner analogous to the way power steering reinforces the motions of an automobile's steering wheel, were completely practical. Many of Gaumont's sound films were screened in Paris at the Gaumont Palace, before audiences of up to 5,000 people. The problem, film producers agreed, was that the public simply was not interested, beyond a brief flurry of box office activity provoked by each new system. After these early commercial failures French companies abandoned the sound cinema entirely, only to discover to their horror, two decades later, that it was to be imposed upon them from abroad.

In the United States before World War I, few organizations had the capital and the sheer ambition to attempt to exploit this apparently unpromising area. The exception was Thomas Alva Edison. Beginning in 1911 and using a technology that was initially quite primitive compared to the French efforts, Edison launched, with lavish publicity, a series of short sound films. Again public response was cold, in this case in part because synchronization between sound and image was imperfect, regulated manually by the projectionist during each screening and subject to frequent breakdowns. Edison abandoned the enterprise, declaring that the sound film was unworthy of further development. By the time modern, electrically synchronized and amplified sound cinema was possible, industry opinion on both sides of the Atlantic was that the new medium had already been tried, and found wanting.

When the American inventor Lee De Forest developed a viable, electrically recorded and reproduced sound-on-film process in the early 1920s, no one was interested. De Forest financed and produced a number of short films with his process, but with insufficient capital for such a project, and no experience in marketing, all he ultimately accomplished was his own financial ruin. The Western Electric company, which had greater resources than De Forest and, like he, had the optimism that could only spring from a position outside the film industry, perfected its own cinema sound process in 1924, based on the electro-mechanical synchronization of images on film with sound on discs. The firm did not propose to make any films itself, however, but to find a company that would do so under license to its patents.

The major American studios remained convinced that sound films were "box-office poison" and dismissed the Western Electric proposals. Only Warner Brothers, a small concern with great ambitions and little to lose, decided to take what by now appeared almost a hopeless gamble. But the Warners did not set out to revolutionize the cinema, for all their entrepreneurial drive. For them, sound technology was appealing solely as a cost cutting technique. Most major cinemas in the United States employed vaudeville acts as part of their programs, and the Warners reasoned that short sound films could cheaply and profitably replace live singers, dancers, and instrumentalists. In addition, the musical accompaniments to silent features were expensive, and similarly open to replacement by a cheaper, prerecorded orchestral score. And so the studio concentrated its efforts in the two areas of filmed vaudeville short subjects and conventional "silent" features with recorded musical accompaniments plus sound effects such as clashing swords, crowd noises, and so on.

A logical extension of Warner Brothers' strategy was to produce a work combining these two uses of synchronized sound. Following up on the good reviews and favorable audience reactions to its early efforts, the studio thus made the film which finally, and irretrievably, altered the course of cinema history. The enormous success of *The Jazz Singer* (1927) came as a surprise to almost everyone, except perhaps to its uninhibited star. Al Jolson was an irrepressible ad libber, and he interpolated a few lines of spoken dialogue, supposedly in defiance of the express prohibition of his director, into two of his sync sound musical numbers. (The rest of the film was a conventional silent feature, with written titles and recorded musical score.) Public reaction to the brief bits of recorded talk was swift and startling. For reasons that are still difficult to understand over six decades later, audiences finally clamored for what they had previously rejected: fictional characters who spoke, sounds that emanated from the narrative world. The formerly mute cinema had finally found its voice, and it said, prophetically, "You ain't heard nothin' yet."

For a time, European production of silent films continued unabated, despite the mad rush to convert to sound that gripped the United States in the wake of *The Jazz Singer.* French producers and exhibitors were as unenthusiastic about sound cinema as the large American studios had been just a few years before. But the storm was approaching. Because of its weak domestic film industry and lack of any serious language barrier, England served as the soft, vulnerable underbelly of the European market for the American companies' marketing efforts. By late 1928 *The Jazz Singer* and a number of other "talking pictures" (many of them still only partly filmed in synchronous sound) were playing there to packed houses in the growing number of cinemas newly converted to exhibit them, and the first English film studios had been equipped for sound recording. French producers, exhibitors, directors, and critics took the boat train to London to evaluate the new phenomenon. Their initial reports were uniformly gloomy. The critic Alexandre Arnoux wrote of his first impressions:

> Right at the start the general effect is rather disconcerting. Since the loudspeaker installed behind the screen never changes its locus of sound propagation, the voice always comes from the same spot no matter which character is speaking . . . We are faced with a strange comedy, in which the actors are closely miming the lines with their mouths, while a mysterious ventriloquistic chorus leader, rigid and motionless in the center of the screen, at a certain depth, takes charge of the audible part of their silent speeches.
>
> To palliate this shortcoming, no doubt, and perhaps also because of technical difficulties, the director has avoided, as much as possible, changing shots and looking for varied camera angles, at least during conversations . . . I am making an effort to be impartial. Perhaps I am not succeeding very well. How can a man travel and see things without bringing along himself and his prejudices? I love the cinema deeply. Its interplay of black and white, its silence, its linked rhythms of images, its relegation of speech, that old human bondage, to the background, seem to me the promises of a wonderful art. And now a savage invention has come along to destroy everything. I may be pardoned some bitterness and unfairness.[3]

In January of 1929 *The Jazz Singer* opened in France. There were only two cinemas in the entire country equipped to show it, and no studios at all for the production of sound films. The French public embraced Jolson and *The Jazz Singer* as fervently as had the Americans and the English, all but annihilating the last vain hopes that the new "savage" technology would not take hold in France. But very soon there came a film that gave many critical observers some cause for optimism—not that the silent cinema could be revived, but that the sound film could do interesting things after all. Metro-Goldwyn-Mayer's *Broadway Melody of 1929* was to the talkies in France what *The*

Cheat had been to the early silent feature film. René Clair returned from London with one of the first reviews:

> With *The Broadway Melody* the talking picture has found its form for the first time: neither cinema nor theater, but a new genre. The immobility of the shots—that flaw of the talking picture—has disappeared. The camera is as mobile, the shots as varied, as in a good silent film . . . The sound effects are used with intelligence, and if some of them still seem superfluous, others can be held up as models . . .
>
> [In one scene] Bessie Love is in bed, sad and pensive; you feel she is about to cry: she puckers up her face, but it disappears into the shadow of a fadeout, and from the screen, which has turned black, issues the sound of a single sob. [In this example] it will be noted that at the right moment sound has replaced the image. It seems that it is in this economy of its means of expression that the sound cinema has a chance to find original effects.[4]

But the new possibilities that Clair and others, such as Jean Renoir, saw displayed in *Broadway Melody of 1929* were to remain, for the moment, entirely theoretical for most French film artists. Since the country had no studios equipped for sound film production, rapid progress in this area could hardly be expected. Western Electric and other American companies controlled one crucial set of patents; the German company Tobis Klangfilm had its own sound system, also with ample patent protection. The only French system, the Gaumont-Peterson-Poulsen process, had markedly inferior sound quality, and its patents were quickly (and profitably, for Gaumont) merged with the Tobis ones. The licensing fees for any sort of sound were high, as was the cost of equipping a studio. Capital reserves of the French producers were low. The first French "sound picture," *Le Collier de la reine* (*The Queen's Necklace*, 1929, after Alexandre Dumas *père*) was in reality a silent film with a recorded music score, some sound effects, and a small number of interpolated, synchronous sound close-ups which replaced some of the title cards in the alternate, silent version. The film's music and effects track and its minimal sound shooting were done in the Tobis company's newly equipped studio in the Paris suburb of Epinay, where one year later René Clair would shoot his first sound film. Despite the dubiousness of its classification as a *film sonore et parlant*, *Le Collier de la reine* got a great deal of attention in the French press, and audiences flocked to see it.

The first real French talkie, *Les Trois Masques* (*The Three Masks*, 1929, directed by André Hugon after a play by Charles Méré) was shot in a rented studio in England. Its great box office success, coming just after the release of *Le Collier de la reine*, confirmed that the sound film was in no danger of an early death, as some in France still hoped. By comparison with the American talkies of the same year *Les Trois Masques* seems rather stagebound, and it is generally treated harshly by film historians. Still, it shows surprisingly good technical mastery of the new medium. The early talkies' inevitable array of several synchronized cameras (which often produced a television-like look) are used effectively, and sometimes even imaginatively. Different takes are edited together smoothly, aside from some noticeable clicks and pops, and changes of sound level. Unfortunately, technique alone cannot hide vapid content. The biggest problem with the film is its kitschy theatricality. To ears accustomed, for example, to Marcel Pagnol's loving attention to regional speech, it is shocking indeed to hear a Corsican peasant say, in a perfect Parisian accent, "*J'avais peur que tu ne puisses pas venir.*"[5]

Most of the other early French talkies were also produced abroad, either in England (*La Route est belle* [*The Road Is Beautiful*, 1929], directed by Robert Florey and produced by Pierre Braunberger) or in Germany (*La Nuit est à nous* [*The Night Is Ours*, 1929], an early multi-language production with a German version of the same script directed by Carl Froelich). Henri Chomette, brother of René Clair, directed *Le Requin* (*The Swindler*, 1929) in the Tobis company's Epinay studios, but that film was only a part-talkie with a few musical numbers and one synchronously recorded dialogue sequence at the end. Few of these early French efforts gladdened the hearts of those who had glimpsed the new possibilities of *Broadway Melody of 1929*. Most of the industry remained glumly inactive during 1929, when, counting *Le Collier de la reine*, a grand total of eight sound pictures were made for the French market. Much more activity took place in 1930: 98 feature films with some sort of recorded sound (by Raymond Chirat's tabulation)—not bad compared to the level of activity of the 1920s but still well below the rest of the decade's average of roughly 150 feature films per year.[6] Many of the works of 1930 were, inevitably, unimaginative cinematic records of mediocre stage plays. But there were also several notable attempts to go beyond the simple, theatrical textures of *Les Trois Masques* and its stagebound successors. The sound film, in the view of the more adventurous members of the film community, had yet to be defined. The various fates of those who tried to do this served as moral and practical lessons to those who would follow.

The most spectacular of these all too public dramas was probably the case of Abel Gance. Gance had meditated on the basic idea of his *La Fin du monde* (*The End of the World*, 1931) since 1913. The financial success of *Napoléon* gave him the courage, and his backers the confidence, to envision a much more personal, evangelical and mystical work. His story would show how humanity could one day escape the repetitive cycles of suffering and obsession that he had studied in *La Roue*. *La Fin du monde*'s protagonist, a charismatic mystic played by Gance himself, goes mad and disappears after producing a body of texts that become the basis of mankind's spiritual salvation when the earth is menaced by destruction by a huge comet. When this danger miraculously passes, and the prophet's book has become the Bible of a new society, he reappears, sane again, only to vanish into the crowd so as not to trouble the new, wondrous order. The film also includes a subplot about two evil financiers and a visionary scientist (the mystic's brother).

This was vintage Gance, but no one involved in the project seems to have worried about how this peculiar vision would translate into the new medium of the talking picture. For although Gance later claimed, self-servingly, that he planned and shot most of *La Fin du monde* as a silent film, the truth is that well before production began he had rewritten and reconceived it as a sound picture.[7] The director obviously wanted to demonstrate that, *Napoléon* and *La Roue* to the contrary, he could work quickly and efficiently in the high-cost, high-risk environment of the sound cinema. Shooting began in mid-1929 and was completed roughly a year later. In late 1930 (again, Gance made unprecedented efforts to stay on schedule), the film had been edited to a running time of just over three hours. But meanwhile the rights had been sold to an unsympathetic distributor who cut the work, without Gance's participation, to 100 minutes. This truncated version premiered in January 1931, to a disastrous reception by critics and the public alike.

No doubt many of the problems of *La Fin du monde* stem from its brutal abridgement. But the film had other troubles as well. Its dialogue, recorded with the Gaumont-Peterson-Poulsen process, was frequently unintelligible. When the actors could be understood, their apocalyptic pronouncements provoked jeers from audiences rather than awed understanding. Gance had approached film sound as another layer of formal possibilities that could be *added* to his cinematic visions, rather than as requiring their recasting in new forms. He also failed to understand that audience preferences had shifted dramatically in a very short time to intimate, personal dramas set in more plausible fictional worlds. The mistake was, in retrospect, predictable. Gance's main handicap was his own great stature at the end of the silent era, which allowed him to speed ahead into unknown territory, like one of *La Roue*'s runaway locomotives, without worrying about the warning signals *(The Jazz Singer, Les Trois Masques)* that dictated caution, or a full stop until the dangers were acknowledged and the track was clear.

Jean Grémillon, in contrast, saw clearly that the new medium required a complete rethinking of aesthetic means and priorities. "The talking film poses anew the question of the construction of the drama, and its means of expression," he wrote in 1931. "Almost none of the traditional methods of the silent film can survive, beginning with scene construction [*découpage*] and editing."[8] This insight, however, did not save Grémillon from his own, very different early talkie disaster. If Gance was aesthetically caught in the cinema's past, Grémillon was, perhaps tragically, ahead of his time. *La Petite Lise (Little Lisa,* 1930) uncannily anticipated the subject matter and mood of what would later be aclaimed as "poetic realism." Charles Spaak's scenario features a doomed working-class hero, a world of petty criminals and sleazy night clubs, and scenes that take place at night or in claustrophobic, darkened rooms. The visual texture of the film completely abandons the pictorialist landscapes of Grémillon's silent feature films in favor of constrained, gloomy, urban spaces in which its characters are trapped. Sound, rather than opening up their world, points out the horrifying dimensions of their confinement. Train sounds are heard contrapuntally over images of the hero's room in the Hôtel du Nord (that name was the title of one of the best-known later poetic realist films), and piercing lathe noises issue from his workshop (foreshadowing Jean Gabin's sandblasting job in Carné and Prévert's *Le Jour se lève*).

Even today, Grémillon's cinematographic style seems strikingly modern in its stark contrasts between images and sounds, and in the way the soundtrack is composed of large, disparate blocks of aural materials. A native song, heard at the film's beginning over shots of a prison in Cayenne, recurs on the soundtrack over urban images of the prisoner-hero's daughter, a Paris prostitute. The song returns when the protagonist learns that his daughter has murdered a pawnbroker; this time it is heard over the first shots of a nightclub where black musicians are playing. Their music replaces it on the soundtrack as the hero has a vision of his return to prison (he decides to confess to his daughter's crime, realizing that his own murder of her mother has driven her to her sorry state). The sequence thus has an elegant, quasi-poetic structure: prison (music)/Paris (images), followed by Paris (music)/prison (image).

Unfortunately, Grémillon made this complex, daring work for the recently reorganized Pathé-Natan company. After seeing the final cut, studio head Bernard Natan (universally regarded as one of the few true philistines among French producers) reportedly said to the director: "Monsieur, you will never work for me again," in such a violent manner that Grémillon went out into the street and vomited. Had Natan not so thoroughly disliked the film, it probably would have reached more spectators and impressed them more favorably. After all, its subject matter and much of its visual style would become virtually mainstream commercial fare at the end of the decade. But released with little fanfare, and quickly withdrawn when its reception seemed to confirm the studio head's opinion, *La Petite Lise* quickly faded into an obscurity from which it has never completely emerged.

Both Grémillon and Gance had great difficulty recovering from these early setbacks in sound cinema, though recover they eventually did, in different ways. Grémillon would become a leading filmmaker of the late 1930s and the Occupation years. Gance, though he continued making films, was forced (with only one major exception) to limit his pursuit of aesthetic experiment and cinematic self-expression. The older man's fate was typical of what befell the leading filmmakers of his generation, many of whom retreated into partial or complete inactivity with the coming of the talkies. The new era brought prominence and artistic leadership to a group of younger, formerly less celebrated directors who had begun work in the industry during the late silent period. Jean Renoir and René Clair, for example, already had demonstrated the artistic pragmatism and the interest in storytelling which would be crucial assets during the transition to sound. But they also had, by temperament and by their associations with avant-garde filmmaking in the 1920s, a strong desire to test the limits of the new medium. Their early sound features gave notable proof that commercial success and artistic innovation need not be incompatible in the talkies.

Renoir shot his first sound film in 1931. He probably would have had to wait even longer than that had he not been a friend of Pierre Braunberger, producer of the immensely profitable *La Route est belle*. Braunberger had cofounded a vertically integrated film company combining production, distribution, and exhibition with Roger Richebé, whose family owned an important circuit of theatres in the South. (Richebé's Capitole in Marseille had been one of the two French cinemas to play *The Jazz Singer* on its initial run. Profits were enormous.) Renoir wanted to make a film of Georges de la Fouchardière's bestselling novel *La Chienne*, published in 1930. This would be a complicated, costly project, and Braunberger and Richebé demanded that the director first prove himself by filming a Feydeau farce for which it already owned the rights. Renoir agreed, and he shot *On purge bébé* (*Baby Gets a Laxative*, 1931) in a few days. The work has an important place in film history not for what it is—a fairly straightforward piece of "canned theatre"—but for what it taught Jean Renoir: "At first I was interested mainly in working out the story. Then I became fascinated with techniques and dreamed of making pictures filled with nothing but tricks. Only when the actors began to talk did I gradually realize the possibility of getting to the truth of character. It was when I began to make talking pictures that I had the revelation that what I was most deeply concerned about was character."[9] Renoir discovered the crucial role *speech* could play in his cinema—not so much the words themselves, but how the characters used them: tone of voice, rhythm, emotional undertones.

Having shown he could make a commercially acceptable talkie, Renoir went on to film *La Chienne* (*The Bitch*, 1931) with almost complete freedom. (His producers did require that he cast Janie Marèze, not Catherine Hessling, in the film's title role. Renoir later cited his acquiescence in this as the beginning of the end of their marriage.) By this time Roger Richebé was in complete control of Braunberger-Richebé, and his reaction to the finished film was similar to Bernard Natan's feelings about *La Petite Lise*. Fortunately for Renoir, Braunberger-Richebé did not botch the promotion and distribution of his film as badly, or as deliberately, as Pathé-Natan did with *La Petite Lise* (which probably accounts for much of the disparity between the two works' commercial careers). After a poor initial reception, the work

Janie Marèze and Michel Simon in *La Chienne*. The difference between this couple and the one of *Nana* hint at the transformation of Jean Renoir's work, and of French cinema in general, in the wake of the talkies.

became a hit thanks to a new publicity campaign devised by a sympathetic cinema owner. The differences between Renoir's film and Grémillon's are instructive: *La Chienne*, though set in much the same milieu as *La Petite Lise*, has a lighter, more detached and ironic tone, and its frequent uses of sound as commentary on its story always come from within the narrative world, rather than being imposed by an implicit narrator. Visually, Renoir's film has the stunning simplicity and elegance of his later work. Several scenes are done entirely in one shot, and editing is used mainly when it is the simplest way to obtain a particular effect or shift of emphasis.

In making his sound cinema center on the study of character, Renoir began his lifelong love affair with actors. But he did not make a fetish of his players, immobilizing them with a controlling gaze in the manner of a von Sternberg. He strove, instead, to create an optimum, focused field in which their behaviors could resound and take on multiple meanings. In the curious Punch and Judy prologue to *La Chienne*, a puppet announces to the film audience: "The work we present to you has no moral intentions, and it will prove nothing at all. The characters are neither heroes nor villains. They are just poor human beings like you and me." This is a bit of an exaggeration, for *La Chienne* will have a hero—a petit-bourgeois patsy played by Michel Simon—and a number of crass, vicious characters. But even the most unsympathetic of these are treated with an almost palpable directorial *politesse*. Such politeness, however, is a way of showing respect for human beings while at the same time asserting distance from them, a distance which frequently can suggest authorial irony. In this way, Renoir's filmmaking after 1931 is the very antithesis of cinematic impressionism, which was completely caught up with the project of merging filmic narration with fictional characters' points of view. When his characters began to speak, Renoir became interested not in how people view the world, but in what goes on *between* people. That, he seems to suggest, is what reveals the most about them—more than they themselves can ever know.

Jean Renoir's early work with the new medium is more significant as the point of departure for his brilliant career in the French sound film's golden age than as an important example to his contemporaries of how to succeed in the talkies. His greatest critical and commercial triumphs would come later in the decade. René Clair, on the other hand, became quickly (though briefly) a highly visible master of the new medium, though his first contact with the talkies was far from promising. After signing a contract with Sofar, a small German firm, Clair developed a story idea of G. W. Pabst's about a young working-class woman who wins a beauty contest and becomes a film star. The film was to feature the American actress Louise Brooks, who had appeared in two of Pabst's most striking silent films. Before production began, however, a dispute with the producer over his treatment led Clair to resign from the project, which was completed by the Italian director Augusto Genina. Genina retained some elements of Clair's scenario, most notably the film's final sequence in which the Brooks character is shot by her former lover during the projection of her first film. As the film-within-the-film character continues to sing, the dead actress is seen in the foreground, slumped in a screening room seat. *Prix de beauté/Miss Europe* (1930) was released in France with the credit, "after an idea by René Clair," perhaps in recognition of this important contribution. The rest of the film, however, was a badly postsynchronized, occasionally awkward part-talkie.

After this false start, Clair was hired by the French branch of the Tobis Klangfilm company to direct their next sound feature after his brother's *Le Requin*. In Tobis Clair found a producer more to his liking. The company was at least as interested in demonstrating its sound system as in making money at the box office, and Clair was able to write and direct a project that other companies might have judged too risky. He conceived a story set in a (studio built) working-class Parisian neighborhood much like the one in which he had grown up, though he may also have taken some inspiration from the urban imagery—and use of music—in *The Jazz Singer* and *Broadway Melody of 1929*. *Sous les toits de Paris* (*Under the Roofs of Paris*, 1930) tells of the lives and loves of a poor street singer and his friends, all of whom live on the higher, and therefore cheaper, floors of the neighborhood's apartment houses. Shots of rooftops and the cramped rooms beneath them punctuate the film's narrative. Music, which almost completely dominates the soundtrack, often masks dialogue.

Sometimes this aural intrusion is justified physically, as when characters are seen talking and gesturing through cafe windows. On other occasions there is no such sonic alibi, as when a gangster punches one of his henchmen and we hear a dissonant piano chord on the soundtrack.[10] The film's acoustic universe is poetic rather than realist—almost as much so as in Grémillon's *La Petite Lise*, though in a comic rather than melodramatic emotional register. Perhaps because of its departures from aural plausibility or its setting in the lower social order (characteristics it shared with Grémillon's doomed work), Clair's film had a notably poor reception on its initial Paris presentation. Nonetheless, Tobis arranged a gala presentation of the work in Berlin, probably more as a demonstration of its technical accomplishments—most notably, some remarkable movements of camera and microphones—than in the hope of a better response to the film itself. Berlin's moviegoers and critics were wildly enthusiastic, and on the strength of this success the work reopened in a major Paris cinema and had a profitable run.

Probably the greater initial German sympathy for his first sound film led Clair to develop his next film in the way that he did. The plot of *Le Million* (*The Million* [*Francs*], 1931) comes straight out of the great tradition of silent film comedy: a winning lottery ticket left in a tattered coat gives rise to a series of cinematic chases and comic misunderstandings. The story, adapted from a stage farce, is told in operetta form, but with a very modern Brechtian twist. This aspect of the film probably grew out of the director's German contacts. The German branch of Tobis Klangfilm had produced Pabst's rather free version of Brecht and Weill's *Threepenny Opera*, with a parallel French version starring the music hall singer Florelle, in 1930. Clair had traveled to Germany several times and almost certainly saw the stage version of the celebrated musical play. In *Le Million*, a clearly Brechtian master criminal named Père La Tulipe (Father Tulip) has a band of henchmen who sing about the joys of living outside the law. A basic premise of the plot, that a good friend will sell out his comrade for enough money, also has Brechtian resonances. The film's detached, boisterously satiric tone, much of which shows a decidedly leftist bent in its use of class stereotypes, is quite unlike the straightforward populist sentimentality of *Sous les toits de Paris*.

The ironic, distanced narration of *Le Million* allowed Clair's continuing experiments with sound to seem less disturbingly arbitrary than those of *Sous les toits*. When assorted characters vie for the valuable coat, tossing it back and forth and running with it, we hear crowd reactions worthy of a rugby match. Here the obvious presence of an arbitrary narrator, who provides sounds only accessible to the film spectator, clarifies and strengthens the joke. When the hapless lottery winner and his momentarily estranged girlfriend are trapped behind scenery at an opera performance, the onstage performers, grotesque pseudo-Wagnerian figures who hate each other, sing of undying love. The words, so inappropriate to the singers, seem to come as a narrator-sent message to the lovers, and by the song's end they are in each other's arms. Visually, Clair juxtaposes costumes and behaviors grounded in social reality (or at least in commonly accepted class stereotypes) with sets that are remarkably nonnaturalistic. A hilarious "wanted" poster of a notorious criminal's handprint in the police station is only one of the film's many reminders that its own construction of social relations must be taken as arbitrary, a game.

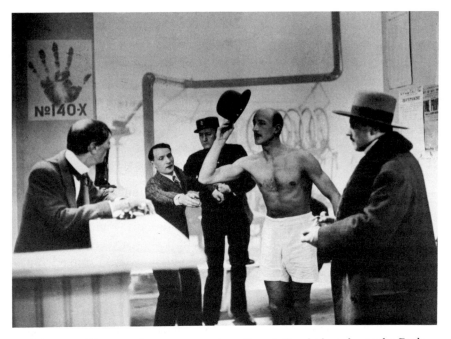

Clair's *Le Million* pays homage not only to Bertolt Brecht but also to the Dada movement; witness the "wanted" poster in this strange police station, and the man wearing only underwear and a bowler.

Clair's second film for Tobis was also a popular and critical success, this time without the initial skepticism that had greeted *Sous les toits de Paris*. He immediately began work on a third sound film, with most of the technical and artistic team that had worked with him on the first two. *A Nous la liberté* (*Give Us Liberty,* 1931) sprang, as did many of the director's original scenarios, from an image seen in life and expanded into a story. The Tobis studio was near a suburban industrial region of dark factory chimneys in the midst of fields full of weeds and wildflowers. The contrast between nature and industry, organic growth and mechanical regimentation—the latter quite possibly reinforcing memories of the mechanized warfare of little more than a decade before—led Clair to imagine a fictional world split between these two poles. In the finished film factories are equated with prisons, most obviously in terms of set design and scene construction; nature is identified with freedom-loving tramps and (less consistently) with the working class. *A Nous la liberté* has often been criticized for its simpleminded social analysis, but its admitted ideological weaknesses probably result from its being one of Clair's most directly personal works. In one of the film's most striking uses of non-naturalistic sound, a flower sings a lullabye to a sleepy tramp, only to have its offer of protection brutally mocked by the appearance of two factory security guards who arrest the wanderer for vagrancy. The purpose of this scene is less to convince us of the rightness of Clair's social vision than to express in narrative terms the emotional meaning of his image of the polluting factory surrounded by uncultivated Nature.

A Nous la liberté contains some of Clair's most daring experiments in the sound film. When the guards confront Emile, the tramp, they exclaim, "You're not working? Don't you know that . . ." Cut to a shot of a public school teacher dictating to his students, "One must work, because work is freedom." This shock cut, fully ten years before *Citizen Kane's* "Merry Christmas (cut to half a lifetime later), and a happy new year," has the same exhilarating effect and subversive irony as Welles and Mankiewicz's more celebrated leap in time and space. As in *Citizen Kane*, another deeply personal film often criticized for political naiveté, such intrusions by an implicit narrator produced a feeling of almost reckless mastery of a dangerous world.

Danger in *A Nous la liberté* often comes in the form of prophetic images of militaristic domination: the factory guards wear proto-fascist armbands and uniforms. The film equates authoritarianism with capitalist exploitation of the working class. Emile's onetime fellow prisoner, Louis, becomes a wealthy industrialist and builds a factory modeled on the prison from which he once escaped. But Emile is the Dada remedy to Louis's capitalist order. Everywhere he goes, straight lines collapse in confusion, mass production comes to a standstill. The spirit of Dadaist revolt against sterile order also surfaces in other ways. The film's penultimate sequence becomes the politicized rewriting of the end of Clair and Picabia's *Entr'acte:* an orderly assembly of bourgeois gentlemen in dress coats and top hats suddenly and frantically begins to chase after bank notes scattered by the wind, while a senile politician vainly tries to read a speech commemorating Louis's last bourgeois achievement, a completely mechanized factory.

A Nous la liberté opened to favorable reviews—with some of the highest praise coming, curiously, from the extreme right-wing paper *Action Française*—but mediocre box office returns. Its commercial career was further damaged by its suppression, as politically dangerous, in Hungary, Portugal, Italy, and the Soviet Union.[11] Clair had no wish to be a controversial political pundit, much less one who made unprofitable films. And so for his next project he returned to the nostalgic, less tendentious world of *Sous les toits de Paris*. *Quatorze Juillet* (*Bastille Day*, 1932) tells the simple story of a taxi driver, a flower seller, and the people they encounter in a few days' time in a working-class neighborhood: young toughs; a luckless, comic bourgeois family; a rich eccentric; and, of course, the Other Woman. But plot is rarely what counts in the film, serving mainly to set up sight gags and sentimental vignettes. Overt experiments with sound, and expressive contrasts of style within the image are rare; the film's narrative and cinematic rhythm often seem halting and unsure. Some critics and industry insiders praised the film publicly while privately fretting that Clair had ceased to grow artistically. Perhaps in reaction to such worries, the director chose to return in his next film, for the second and last time, to overtly political subject matter, and also to the greater flights of fantasy that had characterized *Le Million* and *A Nous la liberté*.

Le Dernier Milliardaire (*The Last Billionaire*, 1934), tells the story of a small, mythical European country suddenly subjected to the whims of a mad dictator. Tobis Klangfilm refused to bankroll the project on political grounds, worried that it could be considered a commentary on Hitler's recent seizure of power in Germany. (Clair's script also contained some fairly overt parodic references to Mussolini.) And so the (by now financially ailing) Pathé-Natan company had the bad fortune to produce what most observers consider the one complete failure among all of Clair's works, a film scorned by audiences and critics alike as unfunny, tasteless, and cinematographically inept. Unnerved by this commercial and critical disaster, Clair left France for an artistic exile in England and, during the war years, the United States.[12] It would be thirteen eventful years before his return to the French cinema, as an old master in the postwar Tradition of Quality. But in the sound cinema's difficult early days he had shown, four times over in quite different ways, that simple filmed theatre was not the only, nor the best, recipe for success in the new world of the talkies.

▧ If he were to forget recent European history, the *cinéaste* of the early 1930s could find much to applaud in the German presence in French film, and much to fear from the Americans. Like the much smaller Tobis Klangfilm, the German giant UFA (Universum Film

Aktien Gesellschaft) took its French-language productions very seriously. They were made in Berlin, using (until 1936) the same sets and basic scenarios of the studio's German-language productions. That UFA could profitably continue multi-language shooting, long after other companies abandoned the technique as unprofitable, tells a great deal about the quality of the company's French films. Casting, in particular, was done with great care and financial largesse. The studio's head of French-language production, Raoul Ploquin, had a notable gift for choosing—and making—film stars, and the list of players for the UFA productions reads like a Who's Who of French cinema: Jules Berry, Gaston Modot, Anabella, Marie Bell, Albert Préjean, Danielle Darrieux, Pierre Brasseur, Edwige Feuillère, and many more. Among the directors and scriptwriters hired by the company for its francophone production, two young filmmakers who learned their craft with the studio would later have important French careers: the unjustly neglected Serge de Poligny and the most notorious filmmaker of the Occupation years, Henri-Georges Clouzot.

The German studios obviously realized that the sound film required great attention to the cultural specificity of foreign markets, even if in UFA's case this problem was mainly addressed (until late in the decade) in terms of actors and actresses. By recognizing this simple truth, as well as maintaining a fiscal policy that did not attempt to buy success too cheaply, Tobis and UFA were able to remain major presences in the French market through most of the 1930s. The American studios, on the other hand, were far less sensitive to the cultural dimensions of the sound film and often too eager to cut costs. The first French films produced by American companies were made by Europeans in Hollywood. In 1930 Jacques Feyder quickly remade two Metro-Goldwyn-Mayer talkies directed by Lionel Barrymore in 1929: *His Glorious Night* became *Si l'empereur savait ça,* and *The Unholy Night* was reborn as *Le Spectre vert.* In the same year Yvan Noé codirected MGM's *Le Chanteur de Seville,* MGM's French edition of *Call of the Flesh.* (Both films starred Ramon Novarro, who also directed and acted in a Spanish version of the same work. Novarro's career quickly faded, in all three languages.) In 1931 Claude Autant-Lara codirected the French version of *Parlor, Bedroom, and Bath,* with Buster Keaton. As these very diverse examples indicate, MGM adopted a "try everything, see what works" policy for its initially abundant French production schedule. Unfortunately, almost nothing really worked. Other, similar Hollywood forays into francophone production were made by Warner Brothers, Fox, and even by United Artists, also with little success.

By far the most substantial American attempt to enter the European sound film market was made by Paramount (which had a history of sporadic production activity in France dating back to the early 1920s). In April 1930 the company took possession of the old Aubert studios in the Paris suburb of Joinville, quickly reequipped two shooting stages for sync sound recording, and began making films. A few months later the studio had built six additional soundstages on the site and begun hiring teams of actors and directors fluent in, all told, fourteen European languages. Mass production began. Paramount at Joinville, which the screenwriter Henri Jeanson dubbed "Babel by the Seine," turned out quickie talkies in enormous quantity.[13] The films were on the whole technically adept, but they had a kind of cultural facelessness that stemmed from the need to translate each script into up to thirteen different languages and cultural contexts. Because they were so quickly made and generally employed second-rate actors (with a few notable exceptions), the works did not even have the UFA films' major saving grace of interesting performances.

French Paramount and its chief, the American Robert T. Kane, obviously believed that massive publicity could sell almost any product. As a side benefit of its lavish paid advertisements in publications such as *Cinémagazine, Ciné-Journal,* and the corporate *Cinématographie Française,* the studio's publicity department concocted long press releases that appeared—sometimes, it seems, with little or no modification—as articles in the same magazines. If one only read the corporate press in 1930 through 1932, one would think that Paramount could do no wrong, commercially or artistically. But audiences, as Mr. Kane and his team of flacks soon learned, were not so easily led. From the beginning, most of the Paramount quickies fared badly at the box office. A brief look at how the films were made goes a long way toward explaining why. Scripts, generally from successful American films, were translated into various European languages. Sets were built and contract players chosen. Then the directors were shown the original release and told to duplicate it as closely as possible. There was very little rehearsal.

Toute Sa Vie (All Her Life, 1930), for example, was one of six parallel remakes of *Sarah and Son* (1930), an American Paramount film directed by Dorothy Arzner and starring Ruth Chatterton and Frederic March. In addition to the French version, the script was also produced in Spanish, Italian, Portuguese, Swedish, and Polish. The story concerns a desperately poor singer living in Brooklyn (!) with her unloved and unlovable husband and her darling son. One day the husband abducts the child, whom he leaves with a rich English couple before going off to fight in World War I. The heroine meets him by chance when he is on his death bed and learns the name of her son's new parents. With the help of their sympathetic young lawyer, she eventually manages to establish that the child is indeed hers, and everything ends well. Now a rich and celebrated performer, she will marry the nice young man who has helped her, and who is already good friends with her son.

This plot, the stuff of countless silent era domestic dramas, was the kind of material into which Dorothy Arzner could breathe a kind of life, though *Sarah and Son* is not generally considered one of her best films. One is surprised to find it, in the French and also in the Portuguese versions, in the hands of director Alberto Cavalcanti. Cavalcanti, born in Brazil and educated in Switzerland, began his cinema career in France as a set designer for Louis Delluc and Marcel L'Herbier. He had directed the modernist "city symphony" *Rien que les heures* (*Only the Hours*, 1927), as well as several silent fiction films, some of them starring his friends Catherine Hessling and Jean Renoir. Obviously he hoped to make his Paramount quickies serve the same function that *On purge bébé* would perform for Renoir: a demonstration that he could be trusted with more adventurous projects. But Cavalcanti was not so lucky as Renoir, and after his Paramount contract he found that he could only get work doing more of the same. In 1934 he accepted an offer from John Grierson to come to England as a member of the G.P.O. filmmaking unit, and became one of the most influential and innovative members of the British documentary school.

Toute sa vie is reasonably representative of French Paramount's first productions. But even in its early days there were scattered exceptions to the studio's policy of remaking American originals. *Un trou dans le mur* (*A Hole in the Wall*, 1931), for example, was adapted from a boulevard comedy by the popular playwright Yves Mirande. One curious detail reveals the extent of the studio's lack of concern for artistic integrity: into this film, and into the parallel Swedish and Spanish versions, were incorporated bits of several production numbers from American Paramount's *The Cocoanuts*, a 1929 Marx Brothers feature. *Un trou dans le mur* had been a notable exception to the studio's initial production policy. But when the multi-language remakes of American films proved capable of producing only mediocre box office returns, in France and throughout Europe, Paramount shifted policy. French boulevard theatre quickly became its dominant source of subject matter, and the company began steadily to reduce the number of parallel versions in other languages. Original scenarios and adaptations from other media (most with a decidedly boulevard tone) quickly followed, many written by established dramatists such as Mirande and Marcel Achard. Paramount had belatedly discovered that to sell films to a given market one had to be culturally, even geographically, in touch with it. In 1932 only two of the studio's two dozen French language films were also made in another language. The days of Babel by the Seine were over.

French Paramount was now in the industry mainstream, producing one lighthearted comedy after another, generally about love and bizarre misunderstandings among the upper classes. The studio's films were probably earning respectable grosses, but the operation had not become the source of windfall profits that the company had hoped for, since the multi-language productions' great economies of scale had been entirely lost. In early 1933 the disappointing return on its large investment, plus retrenchment and depression-strained resources at home, led Paramount to close most of the Joinville studios, except for a few stages used to postsynchronize American films for the European market. But if the modest profits from works such as *Rien que des mensonges* (*Nothing but Lies*, 1932: two husbands pretend to be freemasons to explain nighttime visits to their mistresses) and *Le Fils improvisé* (*The Improvised Son*, 1932: the "son" is really a woman's secret lover) did not tempt the American studio, they were more than sufficient to interest many smaller domestic producers. The Joinville operation's brief life had given tremendous impetus, both as financial example and in the domain of public relations, to the industry's reliance on boulevard-style comedies. Such works would continue to be a massive presence in French cinema of the 1930s until their partial eclipse during the time of the Popular Front and the growing menace of another World War.

■ One immediate effect of the coming of synchronized sound to the French cinema was the rupture and virtual death of the medium's tenuous alliance with the modernist avant-garde. The great expense of sound film production, and its dependence on specialized technicians and equipment, meant that artists working in relative isolation could no longer make a film as they had been able to do in the silent era. Moreover, the political climate of the new decade had its effects on the art world. Struggles within the political Left bitterly divided the Surrealists, and the movement's influence began to wane by 1931. Artists of any orientation who chose to associate with Communists were exposed to the doctrine of Soviet socialist realism, with its hostility to formal experiment. As a result, much new art of the period turned its back on the modernist impulse and looked to older traditions for its inspiration. Modernism did not die, certainly, but its place in French cultural life became noticeably less prominent. But before vanishing almost without a trace, modernist independent cinema gave the film community two striking essays on the sound film and its possibilities: Luis Buñuel's *L'Age d'or* (*The Golden Age*, 1930) and Jean Cocteau's *Le Sang d'un poète* (*Blood of a Poet*, 1930). Both works were among the very first French sound films, and both were financed by that great patron of the arts, the Vicomte de Noailles.

L'Age d'or extends and clarifies Buñuel and Dali's first, revolutionary Surrealist vision. Dali collaborated briefly on the film's scenario, but unlike *Un Chien andalou, L'Age d'or* is essentially Buñuel's film. Its central narrative concerns an exemplary Surrealist couple, whose desires are periodically thwarted but not extinguished by bourgeois civilization. Sigmund Freud, whose *Civilization and Its Discontents* was published in the same year that Buñuel made his film, is an obvious and pervasive point of reference. Buñuel clearly agreed with Freud that civilization imposes a terrible price for its repression of basic psychic drives (sex and aggression), but the Spaniard didn't like this bargain and wanted out. His liberated protagonist, played by Gaston Modot (who later became something of an icon for left-wing films), growls at dogs, kicks a blind man in the street, and assaults a nice old lady at a very proper cocktail party. *L'Age d'or* is a modernist part-talkie, mixing silent sequences accompanied by music (some complete with title cards) with a few scenes involving synchronized dialogue. The limited use of the new technology hardly matters for this particular film: speech, that ultimate example of civilized behavior, has little place in a work that denounces civilization. Although there are a few remarkable sound effects, most notoriously a flushing toilet heard at a moment of high passion, in general the film's audio track is as straightforward and uncomplicated as its image construction.

Cocteau's *Le Sang d'un poète,* conversely, was just the kind of "artistic" work that Buñuel and his friends could love to hate. The film is very elaborate in form and cinematic style, and includes a poetic voice-over narration, written titles and handwritten graphics, abundant special effects, and bits and pieces of art from many diverse media. But its great formal diversity is at the service of the most limited and self-reflexive of subjects: the struggle between the artist and his artwork. The film defines artistic creation as the product of real or metaphorical *wounds* in the body of the artist. Once given independent existence, the wound/artwork becomes a rebellious, hostile part of the creator's self, attempting to dictate his conduct, fighting back when mistreated. Many modern viewers find the film's general air of narcissism repellent, but *Le Sang d'un poète* was a revelation to young, aspiring independent filmmakers throughout the world in the late 1930s and early 1940s, and its influence on the American avant-garde film community continues to this day. *L'Age d'or,* in many ways the more radical of the two films, had a very different posterity. Its first showings aroused the ire of the extreme Right and provoked hostile responses by several of the recently organized fascist leagues. The film was banned by government censors after a few days of sporadic violence at the cinema where it was screened, and aside from rare archive presentations it was not widely seen again until the late 1970s.

The virtual demise of modernist cinema is but a small, though highly symptomatic aspect of the great transformation in French filmmaking from 1929 to roughly 1932 produced by the conversion to sound and the change of sociopolitical climate. The most significant effects of recorded sound on the film industry as a whole, both positive and negative, were at first mainly economic. The high cost of refitting studios and cinemas for the new technology, which amounted to a substantial export of capital to the United States and to Germany, was obviously quite disruptive. Confusion within the industry over what type of product would sell, and who was best suited to make it, also resulted in some notable financial setbacks. At the same time the sound film strengthened the position of French producers, because foreign companies suddenly faced a language barrier which postsynchronization and multi-language production could only partially overcome. Even more significant in the short run, though ironically damaging in the long term, was that income from film exhibition rose dramatically. New audiences, largely though not exclusively from the middle classes, began to attend, or attend more regularly, the new talking pictures, and the industry went on a veritable binge of cinema construction to meet this new demand. Smaller cities, which had been served by traveling exhibitors showing films one or two nights a week in a local cafe, now got their own cinemas. Large cities got more and bigger movie theatres.

Economic history and capitalism's celebrated tendency to alternate boom and bust combined, however, to write a sorry end to this story of entrepreneurial zeal. Too many cinemas were built, and at precisely the wrong time. For the great Depression, though it was not to devastate France as badly as it did the United States, began seriously to contract disposable incomes at a time the new film theatres most desperately needed patrons. The result was frenzied competition and price cutting. As the decade wore on, ticket prices did not keep pace with inflation. Single feature (plus short subjects) programming gave way to the double feature. Live performers, once banished by canned vaudeville shorts, reappeared in many markets. In some suburban areas, patrons could see a film for one franc—roughly the top price of a program before the Great War, at a time when the currency was worth roughly one-tenth as much. Profit margins were cut to the bone. Some exhibitors had to declare bankruptcy, and others just got by.

This crisis in exhibition, which began to be felt in 1932 and steadily worsened through the rest of the decade, had a profound impact on film production. Integrated companies that owned cinema chains, such as Pathé-Natan and the recently reorganized Gaumont-Franco Film-Aubert, found that what had once been a source of (production subsidizing) cash suddenly became a terrible drain on capital. Smaller production companies which owned no film theatres also suffered, when low ticket prices and double feature-induced splitting of the take reduced their profit (which was calculated on a percentage of box-office returns). In this way, the conversion to sound weakened the entire film industry at the worst possible time, the beginning of the prolonged economic crisis of the 1930s. Still, sound technology had mainly accentuated weaknesses that were already present: the French market was too small, the industry too fragmented.

The impact of synchronized sound on the aesthetics of the fiction film (for documentaries, which continued to be shot as if silent films, were little changed) seems both more radical and more immediate. Although, as partisans of the older "art of silence" never tired of pointing out, nothing purely technological prevented sound from becoming simply one more resource at the filmmaker's disposal, in actual practice the addition of sound reduced the flexibility and complexity of the image track. Some of the cinematic impressionists' favorite devices, such as rapid editing, subjective images, and optical effects such as superimpositions and out-of-focus shots were immediate casualties. The reasons for this striking retreat from overt visual complexity are not completely clear, though the greater expense of talkie production and the overwhelming use of theatrical material obviously played a part.

There is also, however, a qualitative difference between images of a set of events (accompanied by music and other sounds during projection) and simultaneous image and sound presentation of the same events. Synchronized sound and image give greater weight and presence to represented objects and actions. For this and other reasons, some theorists speak of the sound film's great realism. Aesthetically adventurous silent films typically played on the very flatness of the cinema image: one could see it either as two-or three-dimensional. Decor, blocking, and composition were often conceived mainly in pictorial (as opposed to dramatic) terms. The addition of recorded sound seems to have upset this delicate balance, making the image harder to see *as image,* as something with its own (two-dimensional) pictorial integrity. Now all aspects of cinematic style had to refer in the first instance to the logic of the fiction, rather than to the style of its presentation, and the visual experiments so characteristic of silent filmmaking were more likely to be experienced as unwelcome intrusions.

Aside from this general reduction of the complexity of the image track, the most striking aesthetic change associated with the sound film was in the area of editing. Analytic, or classical editing *(découpage classique)* now became the dominant, indeed virtually the only acceptable means of linking shots within a scene. Here, too, the increased psychological presence of the fictional world was probably of crucial importance. Analytic editing seems to follow the logic of narrative events rather than the dictates of a narrator. It scrupulously respects (indeed, it depends upon) the logic of spatial relations within the fictional world. Sound fiction filmmaking did retain rapid montage editing as a stylistic option (to represent earthquakes, for example, or other unusual events), though only in isolated, measured doses. The silent era's tradition of respect for the integrity of the shot likewise became a possible variant on classical sound film construction, notably so by decade's end. Jean Renoir and Pierre Chenal, among others, would experiment with composition in depth and elaborate camera movements as ways of minimizing shot changes, but when they did edit it was in accordance with the rules of *découpage classique*. Their styles were not so much challenges to the dominant model as subtle variations on it.

At a more general level, this triumph of classical editing was but one aspect of the most pervasive change brought about by the conversion to synchronized sound: increased standardization. The silent film spectacle had been a notoriously variable phenomenon. Films could be projected at different speeds, with operators sometimes varying the rhythm of projection within a given film. A single work could exist in different versions: black and white, or colored; long and short and medium-length. Music and other sound could also vary, from full orchestra accompaniment with elaborate sound effects in first-run cinemas to a single drunken piano player in cheaper houses. From one fiction film to another great variations could be seen, most notably in running time. Dulac's *La Souriante Madame Beudet* was one-twentieth as long as some versions of Gance's *Napoléon*. Acting styles, set design, and other elements of film style also varied widely.

The transition to sound reduced most of this remarkable complexity to a tidy set of fairly limited options. Projection speed was fixed at twenty-four frames per second. Although some medium-length films *(moyens métrages)* continued to be made, the overwhelming majority of French productions fell into the categories of "short subjects" and "feature films." The feature was, with a very few notable exceptions, standardized at seventy-five minutes to two hours in length. Music and sound effects were fixed once and for all by the original production. Color tinting and toning of the image were largely abandoned. Because editing was more difficult and costly, films almost always appeared only in one version. There was less variation in cinematic style from one feature film to another. Thus the cinema finally became a fully rationalized, mass-produced spectacle. Every proper showing of a given film was like every other showing. Each film was also more like the next than had been the case in the silent era—in length, style, presentation, even (perhaps) subject matter. In many ways, this sea change is precisely what disillusioned film artists such as Marcel L'Herbier argued—a tragic loss of the twentieth century's most peculiar and endearingly mixed art form. But it was the silent cinema's impure, incompletely rationalized nature that allowed it to be (at its best) what it was. The miracle is that it survived as long as it did, in the era of mass production and mechanical reproduction.

But with the coming of sound, the art of the film did not die, as many predicted it would. Within the aesthetically narrower confines of the sound cinema, much could be done, but to very different ends, and by different people. The second great crisis of French cinema, like the first, brought with it a new generation of film artists.[14] Some of them came to cinema for the first time after 1930. Others had already begun their careers as relatively unsung artisans of the silent era. Their challenge was to discover what could be done with the new, and surprisingly different medium, and to conceive their work in terms of a very different social climate. Their responses would be more directly influenced by politics and less immediately by purely aesthetic questions. For troubled times lay ahead, and the cinema would have to respond to them.

8

Art and Entertainment
in the Sound Film

The transition to recorded sound caused an upheaval in the film industry even greater than the crisis that had occurred during the first years of the Great War. As before, one of the most visible aspects of the transformation was in the area of personnel, where the most public dramas concerned actors and actresses. Some careers went into eclipse, others suddenly blossomed. Ivan Mosjoukine, not surprisingly, had a strong Russian accent which hindered the intelligibility of his dialogue. His career quickly faded, as did those of most of his compatriots. Even native speakers with trained voices could find themselves in trouble. Charles Dullin (Jean Grémillon's *Maldone*), a leading stage actor and onetime film star, got only bit film parts—often, none at all—in the next decade, as did Jacques Catelan, Gina Manès (star of Epstein's *Coeur fidèle*) and many others. At the same time the careers of relatively minor players, most of them also a few years younger than these former stars, were quickly taking off: Michel Simon, Charles Vanel, Albert Préjean, and Florelle are just a few examples. In general, the survivors had more restrained acting styles and had been associated with less extravagant or emotive roles. Players who specialized in comedy or light drama fared uniformly better than those associated with heavy melodrama. Public taste, as well as technology, had changed.

After the dust had settled, a kind of cinema repertory company emerged, composed of perhaps a hundred notable members who could be seen in film after film, often in bit parts but always with a line or two and a bit of business to characterize them. The newcomers among them came mainly from the boulevard stage and from the music hall and café-concert circuit. An underlying class consciousness helped shape the new actors' roles and images: those who had appeared in bourgeois theatre generally played upper- and middle-class parts (Louis Jouvet, for example), whereas ex-vaudevillians (Julien Carette, Jean Gabin, and many others) mostly played workers and members of the underclass. The French cinema of the 1930s is often called actors' cinema because of the noteworthy contribution made by its players, but it is important to point out the heterogeneous nature of their efforts. A stylized, hypertheatrical actor like Jouvet could easily appear in the same film universe with ex-song and dance man (and archetypal proletarian hero) Gabin, and one could savor the equally odd juxtaposition of former stage actress Françoise Rosay with the music hall star Arletty. It was the cultural and stylistic diversity of the actors, as well as their talent, which made their presence so notable.

The period's notable use of players reflects the first requirement of a successful talkie director: competence in the direction of actors. Experience in the theatre was helpful, if not absolutely essential. (A notable exception was Jean Renoir, who became an "actors' director" *par excellence* despite his lack of stage experience). A second, at least equally important qualification was a director's orientation toward narrative as the dominant, structuring principle of a film. The directors who adapted most easily to the sound film were those whose primary interest was in telling a story clearly and efficiently. Seemingly restrictive, this commitment to narrative could, as in the case of René Clair, entail ample use of the cinema's formal resources.

Many filmmakers who already met these requirements survived the transition from the silent film to the sound era with their standing in the industry virtually unchanged, often continuing to make the same kinds of films as they had before. Henri Fescourt—whose career and work made him a kind of European version of Howard Hawks or perhaps Michael Curtiz—continued to make his energetic, carefully crafted (and American-looking) films throughout the 1930s, though today he is better known for his invaluable memoir of the French film community.[1] Raymond Bernard, who had enjoyed a somewhat higher standing in the industry and with the critics than did Fescourt, continued to enjoy the same reputation, winning particular praise for his big-budget historical films. Bernard's greatest work of the decade is probably his three-part adaptation of Hugo's *Les Misérables* (1933), starring Harry Baur as Jean Valjean. Though known today largely in one- or two-part versions that eliminate substantial amounts of the five-and-a-half hour original, Bernard's *Les Misérables* arguably remains one of the few truly great adaptations of a nineteenth century novel to the cinema screen.

But if Bernard, Fescourt, and others went on making the same sorts of films and getting much the same reception as before the transition to sound, such was not the case with the four new leading directors who had begun work in the silent era: René Clair, Jean Renoir, Julien Duvivier, and Jacques Feyder. Sound film changed these men's work, bringing to it consistency, force, and new means of storytelling that audiences and critics alike found compelling and satisfying. Though they have much in common in their career trajectories, the development of their personal issues and cinematic styles led them in different directions. Renoir and Clair had formal and ideological interests that showed up in various ways in their films, whereas Feyder and Duvivier were mainly concerned to be good storytellers. All four made highly personal films, but Feyder and Duvivier's works were often less obviously so.

Jacques Feyder was forty-four years old in 1929, thirteen years older than René Clair, nine years older than Jean Renoir, and far more successful in his chosen profession than either of them. He had directed one of the silent era's great popular hits, *L'Atlantide* (1921), and had made seven more silent films in France, carefully conceived projects which did not always succeed with the public or the critics, but were invariably recognized as serious works of cinema. Feyder had not adopted a single, recognizable style in the 1920s. His films were eclectic, exploring subjective distortions of time and space in *Crainquebille/Old Bill of Paris* (1925, after Anatole France), employing American-style scene construction in *Gribiche* (1925), and making a not wholly successful attempt at a filmic naturalism *à la* Prosper Mer-imée in *Carmen* (1926). Most contemporary critics considered his best silent work to be his brooding, German-produced *Thérèse Raquin* (1928, after Zola), all copies of which appear to have been lost. Throughout the silent era Feyder's work was characterized by careful craftsmanship and intelligent visual experiment, but also by a certain distance, a reluctance to make a commitment, whether to a style or to a set of issues. Then, with the coming of the talkies, Feyder began to make films which were not only more stylistically consistent, but which also shared a common atmosphere and world view. In his mid-forties he finally joined the ranks of *les grands*, the great masters of the French cinema.

Jacques Feyder was born Jacques Frederix in 1885 in Ixelles, an industrial suburb of Brussels. His family was typical, almost a parody, of the Belgian Protestant bourgeoisie of the day.[2] It had a strong tradition of military service dating back four generations, and an equally important tradition of accumulating capital and making it grow—though not to the exclusion of other interests. Jacques's father easily combined a strong involvement with the arts with his job as director of the Brussels branch of the Société des Wagons-lits, and his son was the perhaps inevitable rebellious offspring who arrives to trouble such a carefully contrived equilibrium. The boy received a traditional bourgeois education and at the age of twenty was sent to the Military Academy at Nivelles to continue the family obsession with *grandeur militaire*. But young Jacques had no military music in his soul, and he soon left the school with a reputation as an insubordinate prankster. His family then sent him to work for the Liège canon foundry once administered by his great-grandfather. This part of his heritage also had little appeal for him, except for the job of showing visiting clients the city's night life. At this point in his life Feyder's mother died, and the young man went to his father to announce his intention of becoming an actor. The elder Frederix reacted violently to the idea, forbidding his son to use the family name in such a scandalous profession. Jacques Frederix obediently altered his last name and went to Paris to pursue his new ambition.[3]

In the French capital Feyder managed to get a few acting jobs, but only in small roles. He was tall, graceful, and handsome, but he was never entirely at ease before live audiences. And so, in the early teens, he began to act in films, under the direction of Victorin Jasset and Louis Feuillade, among others. During a theatrical engagement, he met his future wife, Françoise Bandy de Nalèche, who would much later achieve cinema stardom under the name of Françoise Rosay. The young Belgian became a film director, like so many others, thanks to the Great War, and also because of his foreign nationality. Gaston Ravel, a protégé of Feuillade's and a Gaumont contract director, was called up to fight in the conflict. He suggested Feyder to replace him, in an unusual arrangement where Ravel effectively got a percentage of the younger man's earnings. And earn he did: in the next year and a half, before his own reserve unit of the Belgian army was mobilized, Feyder directed fourteen films for Gaumont, one of them a four-part serial. Just before he left for the front, Feyder married Françoise Bandy de Nalèche, and in good bourgeois fashion she abandoned a promising stage career to devote herself to her husband and family.

When Feyder returned from the war, his second film, released through Gaumont but financed by a Belgian bank administered by two of his cousins, was *L'Atlantide*. That film had much more success with the public than with the critics, who admired its stunning (and real) desert landscapes but severely criticized its leading lady's acting and its unsubtle scenario. But despite its enormous box-office earnings, *L'Atlantide* gave Feyder a troublesome reputation as a big spender: his cousins' bank had had to triple its original investment before the film was finally released. As a result the director did not find hordes of producers knocking at his door. Most of his remaining silent films were made for small, typically foreign companies. By the end of the decade he was growing discouraged. His last French silent film, *Les Nouveaux Messieurs* (*The New Gentlemen*, 1929) even ran into trouble with the normally lethargic French censors, and had to have several sequences removed because they were held to show members of the government in a bad light. Even before this final setback, however, the director had signed a contract with Metro-Goldwyn-Mayer, and while the film's producer negotiated for its release the Feyders were on a ship bound for the United States. By the time of his arrival in Southern California, the director had been a naturalized French citizen for a little over a year.

Hollywood, as it turned out, was not the answer to Feyder's problems. After directing Greta Garbo in *The Kiss,* (1929), one of MGM's last silent films, he directed French, German, and Swedish versions of several of the studio's early talkies, and then made two works in English as part of MGM's last vain efforts to salvage the career of Ramon Novarro. Feyder was accustomed to writing (or rewriting) his own screenplays, choosing his cast, and carefully controlling the visual style of each of his films. The highly developed division of labor of the American studio system, in which the director often had little if any choice in these matters, was not to his liking. In despair, he returned to France and eventually bought out the remainder of his MGM contract rather than make even one more film under such conditions.

The France to which the Feyders returned was much changed in the three years they had been away. In 1932 the first effects of the Depression could be felt, and the film industry was beginning its long, slow economic decline that would mark the rest of the decade. Like most of his contemporaries, Feyder found that dealing with producers could be even more difficult than it had been during the 1920s, and he was unable to complete several projects, most notably a political satire called *1940* (set in a hypothetical France in which—shockingly—women could vote) and an adaptation of *Madame Bovary* (eventually directed, with a different script, by Jean Renoir). Finally he turned to an idea that had fascinated him for some time: to use the new medium to portray two characters, played by the same actress but with two different voices, in a Pirandellian play of questions of identity. He wrote the basic treatment quickly, and then elaborated the scenario for *Le Grand Jeu* (*The Great Game*, 1934) with his friend and fellow ex-Belgian bourgeois, Charles Spaak.

Feyder's first French sound film—more accurately, the first one he made in France—tells the story of Pierre (Pierre Richard-Willm), who loves and bankrupts himself for the beautiful courtesan Florence (Marie Bell, as a blonde and with her own voice). Forced by his family to leave both his love and his country, Pierre enlists in the Foreign Legion and ends up in a small garrison town where he meets Irma (Marie Bell, brunette this time and dubbed with another, quite different voice), a cabaret singer with no memory of her past. The two women are so alike, yet so different. Is Irma really Florence, transformed by some horrible trauma? If not—or if so—can Pierre still love her? The plot of *Le Grand Jeu* is complicated, well narrated, and ultimately less important than the film's almost palpably uncanny atmosphere. Feyder and Spaak's North Africa is a kind of dream zone in which characters find themselves acting out an unknown script, not sure of their own or others' real natures. This strange atmosphere is created with quite simple cinematic and narrative means: the dubbing of Bell's voice, some discreetly expressionistic lighting, and the uncannily accurate yet deceptive fortunes told by a jaded boarding-house proprietor (Françoise Rosay).

Le Grand Jeu was an immediate hit with critics and the public, and for the rest of the decade Feyder's problems with producers were over. The French branch of Tobis Klangfilm produced his next two films, *Pension Mimosas* (*Hotel Mimosa*, 1935) and *La Kermesse héroique/*

Carnival in Flanders (also 1935, with a parallel German version, Die
klugen Frauen), each with an original screenplay by Feyder and Spaak.
Pension Mimosas tells the story of a petty bourgeois wife and hotel proprietor (Françoise Rosay) who loves, with a growing passion, the weak,
manipulative small-time criminal who was once her foster son. She
tries to save him from his dangerous associates, mainly from a woman
of doubtful virtue (Arletty), but she ends up indirectly causing his
death. As in Le Grand Jeu, the plot, though well elaborated, is less
important than atmosphere. The Hotel Mimosa serves as a refuge for
compulsive gamblers who play at the nearby casino, and the Rosay
character's husband works there as a croupier. Pension Mimosas is
largely about the contamination and breakdown of the opposition
between the bourgeois home and the world of gamblers and criminals. At the end, Rosay gives a bravura portrayal of a woman whose
very moral core has been irretrievably shattered, in one of Feyder's
most effective and bleakest scenes. As the distraught woman sobs over
the dead body of her too well-loved "son," banknotes that she has won
at the casino (after preaching against gambling throughout the film)
swirl about the room, lifted by the winds of a violent, quasi-Shake-
spearean storm. Feyder's tragic characters—this frustrated wife or
Pierre in Le Grand Jeu—exist in a kind of moral vacuum they are
finally forced to confront. Even love will not fill the void.

Possibly because the original idea came from Spaak and not Feyder,
La Kermesse héroique has a lighter tone, even if its ultimate view of life
is not a great deal more optimistic. Feyder had tried to interest producers in the Spaak story ten years earlier, but to no avail. Now, with
two hits to his credit, he had no trouble getting Tobis's approval. La
Kermesse héroique is probably the best known of the director's works,
but, as so often happens, it is not particularly representative of them.
Feyder himself saw it as a kind of divertissement after the hard subjects
he had just filmed. The story likewise concerns bourgeois values (here
found in seventeenth-century Flanders) at the limit of their viability—
in this case, threatened by the one-day sojourn of a Spanish army unit
in a peaceful small town. The men of Boom (!) collapse and dither
when the occupiers arrive, and the women, led by the mayor's wife,
must save the day. They succeed, not only in preventing rape and
pillage, but also in gaining Boom a one-year tax exemption and in
marrying off the film's young lovers (one of them a struggling artist
named Breugel), whose union had been opposed by the cowardly,
pompous mayor. La Kermesse héroique indulges in some fairly typical

1930s bourgeoisie-bashing, but it is all done with a deft touch and in a visual style which invokes classical Flemish painting without becoming ponderously academic. The film is a splendid collection of actors' *tours de force*, most notably by Louis Jouvet as a sinister Spanish priest, André Alerme as the mayor, and Françoise Rosay as his wife. The cast members' playing styles are quite uniform, unusually so for the period, and mesh together almost too well. In its seamless look and feel, *La Kermesse héroique* anticipates the later "tradition of quality," which is to say that its sleek consistency looks a bit out of place in the generally more informal, variegated French cinema in the 1930s.

In his first three French sound films, Feyder arguably reached the peak of his achievement as a director. It is probably not a coincidence that when he continued working without the collaboration of Charles Spaak—with whom he quarrelled just before production of *La Kermesse héroique*—his films, though still of great interest, lost some of their consistency and subtlety. (Feyder and Spaak were the first of the notable director-writer teams that would make their mark in the industry; later examples would include Feyder protégé Marcel Carné's celebrated partnership with the poet Jacques Prévert, and Claude Autant-Lara's collaboration with the writing team of Jean Aurenche and Pierre Bost.) Feyder's last film released before World War II was *Les Gens du voyage* (*People of the Road*, 1938, with a parallel German version, *Fahrendes Volk*), again produced by Tobis. That work is in many ways resembles *Pension Mimosas*, with a traveling circus in lieu of the gambling casino, and Françoise Rosay's character disturbed by a criminal lover instead of a foster son.

It is noteworthy that the moral centers of most of Feyder's great films are women, children, and very young adults. The mature men in his works tend to be stick figures, comic or dangerous but not complex or ambivalent. Perhaps he was too much a classic *père de famille* to be interested in other *pères de famille*. But his consistent focus on the weaker members of bourgeois families does not necessarily make him a rebel against middle-class life. His interest in women and young people is like that of a kindly, though troubled, father. Feyder saw his characters as isolated though not always completely stable entities. If he is one of the directors of the 1930s most consistently interested in family relations, he remains, in the last analysis, an unrepentant bourgeois individualist.

Julien Duvivier, whose career in many ways resembles Feyder's, shared his interest in the often tragic plights of isolated individuals, while generally placing these concerns in more directly social contexts. Duvivier was also a successful though not renowned director in the silent era. It was with the coming of recorded sound that he too became one of the film community's "greats," though he has not fared nearly as well as Feyder with critics and historians of today. Duvivier was born in 1896 in Lille, the commercial, industrial, and political capital of the French North. His education began at the Jesuit *collège* there (which probably accounts for his periodic interest in religious subjects) and continued in Paris. Amid the political and moral confusion of the First World War, he met a former classmate, at that time an actor at the Odéon theatre, who suggested that he try his hand at acting. By 1916 Duvivier too was working at the Odéon, his career aided by the wartime shortage of young men. Success in acting came easily to him, but it was not a profession that he particularly liked. The French cinema was in desperate need of personnel, and the young actor had no trouble making the shift to assistant film director, in which capacity he worked for the great Louis Feuillade, among others.

In 1919 Duvivier wrote and directed an independently produced feature film (starring Séverin-Mars) with financing provided by a Bordeaux mustard manufacturer, one of many similar efforts at the time to fill the void left by the major studios' retreat from production. The enterprise failed, however, when the negative of his second film was destroyed in a fire, and Duvivier resumed work as a director's assistant. In 1922 he was able to return to directing, first for a series of small, unstable companies and then, beginning in 1925, for the Film d'Art. Duvivier's silent work is more abundant than Feyder's (21 films, including the one destroyed by fire) and even more varied—though one must judge mainly by descriptions of films that have been lost. He filmed a (presumably) naturalistic peasant drama (*Coeurs farouches,* 1924); a tale of confused identities with many impressionist touches (*Le Reflet de Claude Mercour,* 1923); a moralizing story of religious fervor conquering vile materialism (*Credo, ou la tragédie de Lourdes,* 1923), as well as other more straightforward commercial projects. He directed a harrowing, psychologically and cinematically violent *Poil de Carotte* (*Carrot Head,* 1925) from Jacques Feyder's adaptation of Jules Renard's works, after the film's producer removed Feyder from the project. (When he remade the film in 1932 as a talkie, Duvivier wrote his own more restrained, tactful adaptation of the Renard stories.)

Few observers would have predicted on the basis of his silent work that Duvivier would become one of the best known directors of the

1930s. As it turned out, however, the new demands of the sound cinema suited him extremely well. Commercially successful talkies placed heavy emphasis on narrative clarity and dramatic construction, often at the expense of stylistic effect and formal experiment. Duvivier managed to excel at the former without neglecting the latter. *David Golder* (1931), his tale of an unhappy Jewish patriarch (from a novel by Irène Nimirowsky), employed a wide variety of expressive techniques, including Soviet-style montage, expressionist lighting and camera movement, American-style dialogue editing, and some remarkable landscapes. It was an impressive new beginning for a career that would not falter or vary a great deal in its level of achievement until the Occupation, when the director left France rather than live and work under the Germans.

Duvivier is often accused of being an eclectic, if highly competent craftsman who brought little personal commitment to his work. He typically found his subject matter in popular fiction, and his cinematic style could vary enormously, depending on his material. *Maria Chapdelaine* (1934), for example, was adapted from a best-selling novel about French Canadians struggling against the rigors of life in the wilderness. The film is relatively unusual for the 1930s in drawing on cinematic impressionist techniques more typical of the 1920s, particularly a long hallucination sequence in which a character played by Jean Gabin dies in a blizzard while thinking desperately of his one true love. More characteristic of its period, *Pépé le Moko* (1937, from a popular crime novel) is generally categorized as a poetic realist work, because of its claustrophobic, threatening cityscapes and its doomed hero (Jean Gabin, in a very different role) lit by focused spotlights in the midst of expressionistic pools of darkness. *La Fin du jour* (*Day's End*, 1939, based—atypically—on an original story by Duvivier), on the other hand, is visually self-effacing, all the better to highlight a remarkable set of performances (Louis Jouvet, Michel Simon, and others as former actors in an old age home) in what may be the director's best and most unjustly neglected film of the decade.

The versatile Duvivier was by no means unconcerned with film form and subject matter. The very aesthetic diversity of his work, in fact, demonstrates how seriously he took questions of film style. And Pierre Leprohon has forcefully argued that the director's favorite subject is the failure of an embattled individual trying to break out of some sort of trap.[4] Although Duvivier had an obvious penchant for this kind of story—hence his association with the poetic realist tendency we will consider in the next chapter—it does not suffice for a general account of his work. But virtually all of his French sound films, even those that end happily, are bathed in a pervasive, ultimately nihilistic pessimism—which may explain why so many liberal, humanistic critics take such pleasure in denouncing him as little more than a talented hack. The retired actors in *La Fin du jour* have material comfort (unlike most older French citizens of the day), but they finish their lives in rivalry and petty bickering. In *Un Carnet de bal* (*A Dance Program*, 1937, the director's other original story idea of the decade), a young widow decides to visit the men who danced with her at her first ball. One has become an abortionist, another a disbarred lawyer, and so on.

Un Carnet de bal was enormously popular, and it was named best foreign film at the Venice film festival. This work's great success suggests that Duvivier's generally bleak view of life had much to do with his films' wide appeal for audiences and critics of the 1930s. Like Feyder, he told grim, fatalistic stories during a particularly grim decade. Neither man's work suggested that much could be done to change things, for their characters' problems arose from the human condition itself, not from a particular set of sociopolitical conditions one might perhaps try to alter. Duvivier probably took a certain cynical pleasure in the way his own situation at the end of the decade placed him in his own personal trap. Like Feyder, he had had his own flirtation with Hollywood, making *The Great Waltz* (1938, based on the life of Johann Strauss, Jr.) for MGM and returning home with much the same opinion as Feyder of the terrible constraints on directors in the United States. In an ironic twist of fate that could have come out of one of his own films, because of his unwillingness to work under the German Occupation Duvivier found himself again working in the American studio system only three years after he had rejected everything it stood for.

◼ Unlike pragmatic, eclectic figures such as Duvivier and Feyder, the film artists who approached the sound film with strong aesthetic orientations formed during the silent era did not usually fare well with the new medium. This does not mean, however, that they could not work at all. Abel Gance, for example, made twelve films between *La Fin du monde* and the beginning of the Second World War, including new versions of *Mater Dolorosa* (1932, shot in only 18 days) and *J'accuse* (1937, its story much changed from the original), as well as a "sonorisation," with some new footage, of his silent *Napoléon* (1935), for which he devised a proto-stereophonic sound system two decades ahead of its time. The one Gance work of the decade which approached the level of his great silent films was *Un Grand Amour de Beethoven*/*Beethoven* (1935), starring Harry Baur as the composer. Most of Gance's favorite themes are to be found in the film: the importance of suffering to the artist; his ability to galvanize audiences, giving them a new vision of life; his ultimate solitude redeemed by his work. There are some remarkable sequences of audio-visual montage, particularly when Gance gives a subjective rendering of the composer's deafness. But for most spectators the film remained an artistic anachronism, and it did not serve to reestablish its director as a cinema artist of the first order.

Marcel L'Herbier fared somewhat better than Gance: he had more work during the decade, and many of his films were notable successes with critics and the filmgoing public. Beginning with a quickly made piece of canned theatre, *L'Enfant de l'amour* (*Child of Love*, 1930, with parallel versions in English and German), he made nineteen feature films and two short subjects before World War II. Of these, only *Le Bonheur* (*Happiness*, 1934), *Nuits de feu*/*The Living Corpse* (1937, after Tolstoy), and perhaps one or two others are today generally considered worthy of revival.[5] Both L'Herbier and Gance worked more often and received greater recognition than did Jean Epstein. After *L'Or des mers* (*Gold of the Seas*, 1932), a semi-fictional film acted in real locations by Breton fishermen, Epstein's work oscillated between nondescript fiction features and educational short subjects, most of the latter made for his first producer, Jean Benoît-Lévy.

But there were important exceptions to the generally lackluster work of the aesthetically committed generation of the 1920s. One such is Léon Poirier, whose work in the 1930s is currently almost as little known as his films of the 1920s. This situation may have as much to do with politics as with aesthetics (to the extent that the two may be separated): Poirier's work gravitated, as did Gance's, to the political Right as the decade progressed, whereas much contemporary film history is written by scholars with left-wing sympathies. If late twentieth century film historical trends have not worked to Poirier's advantage, they have on the other hand helped to revive interest in the team of Jean Benoît-Lévy and Marie Epstein. Their collaboration began after Epstein's brother Jean left Benoît-Lévy's production company to work for Pathé-Consortium. Marie Epstein later recalled that the producer was "a bit aggravated that my brother was leaving him, and my brother told him: 'Well, I'll leave you my sister in my place.' That's how it happened, as simple as that."[6]

Whether this story is entirely true or not, it points to a problem in evaluating Marie Epstein's work: she herself and most subsequent commentators tended to see her work as a slightly inferior, more pliable version of her brother's. The fact is that by the time of the team's first film, *Ames d'enfants* (*Children's Souls*, 1927), she was remarkably well qualified in her own right, particularly in the area of scenario writing. Sandy Flitterman-Lewis has persuasively argued that although Benoît-Lévy is often considered the real director of their works, with Epstein as his assistant, in fact their collaboration proceeded on a "perfectly egalitarian basis (perhaps a little too perfect, in terms of a blend that has historically molded them into one '*auteur*' with the name of Jean Benoît-Lévy)."[7] Epstein and Benoît-Lévy made three silent films together and then survived the transition to sound with little trouble or apparent aesthetic indecision.

One likely reason that they fared so much better than Marie's brother at this point was their penchant for making films with important ideological agendas. *Ames d'enfants*, for example, contrasts the children of two poor families; the film sets out to demonstrate the importance of proper parenting by a starkly drawn contrast between neglected children and well-supervised ones. Although not all of Epstein and Benoît-Lévy's work is so obviously propagandistic, it always pays careful attention to the moral choices required by particular social conditions. But they were concerned with aesthetic as well as social issues. Their best-known film, *La Maternelle* (*Nursery School*, 1933), infuses a relatively unpromising, domestic drama plot with an important social dimension and an exciting sense of formal experiment. In its stylized insistence on physical environment and its naturalistic observation of the behavior and appearance of its (entirely authentic) slum children, *La Maternelle* anticipates both French poetic realism and Italian Neorealism. But if the film looks ahead in this way, it also looks back, to the tradition of cinematic impressionism. Several extended examples of subjective editing give striking cinematic rendering to traumatic events in the life of a neglected slum child. Near the end of the film, Epstein and Benoît-Lévy render her attempted suicide in a rapid sequence of disparate images that could have been shown and appreciated in the ciné-clubs during the previous decade. But *La Maternelle* does not give most viewers the impression of being

The idealistic heroine of *La Maternelle* (Madeleine Renaud) brings a rabbit for her young charges to observe. The gentle, timid animal—which is destined to be eaten later—functions subtly as a symbol of the children.

an aesthetic anachronism, for all its debts to earlier practices. Its strong commitment to social issues and its effective mixture of non-professional and professional players make it very much a film of, and even ahead of, its time.

The threads of continuity running through all of Epstein and Benoît-Lévy's films lie more in subject matter—childhood, taking responsibility for one's acts, the social dimensions of moral choices and vice versa—than in the domain of film aesthetics. Their other films could and often did look and feel quite different from *La Maternelle*. This versatility and willingness to put form and style in the service of content and ideological project go a long way toward explaining their success in the sound film's first decade. They did not have to relearn their craft, reassess their aesthetic orientation, or wait for industry conditions and public taste to evolve. In this they were typical of the most successful members of their professional generation.

One striking exception to the general pattern of transition is Jean Grémillon. A virtual pariah in the early 1930s after his promising début in the late silent era, he became one of France's most respected and influential filmmakers by the decade's end. As we have seen, Grémillon began his work in the talkies with an unmitigated commercial disaster, *La Petite Lise*. As a result, he had few choices and little creative control over subsequent projects. After his first sound film, he directed two cliché-ridden, purely commercial features, the second of which was cut and reedited so extensively by its producer that he refused to allow his name to appear on the credits. He was reduced to making fiction short subjects of little merit before he left France in disgust—not for Hollywood but for Spain, where he worked in obscurity for over two years. His rehabilitation in the French film community began in Berlin, with what amounted to a directorial apprenticeship under the supervision of Raoul Ploquin, UFA's head of French-language productions.

Encouraged by the results, Ploquin did what probably no domestic French producer of the time would or could do: he assigned to Grémillon an important, if still relatively conventional project. *Gueule d'amour* (*Love Face*, 1937, filmed in Berlin in French, with no parallel German version) cannily exploited the great success of Duvivier's *Pépé le Moko;* it featured *Pépé's* two stars, Jean Gabin and Mireille Balin, and a plot and atmosphere which strongly recalled the earlier work. Unlike most such efforts, Grémillon's film managed to transcend and in some ways improve upon its model. While *Pépé le Moko* is, like all of Duvivier's work, crafted with great care and infused with a kind of latent nervous energy, Grémillon's film is more meditative and stylistically subtle. Charles Spaak's scenario serves as the basis for a cinematic essay on the Jean Gabin persona, paying careful attention to the character's disturbing anger and violence.

After the success of *Gueule d'amour*, Grémillon finally got to make the kind of complex, stylistically polyphonic work that he had attempted at the decade's beginning. Although it does not resemble *La Petite Lise* in any obvious way, *L'Etrange Monsieur Victor* (*The Strange Monsieur Victor*, 1938, again filmed in French in Berlin) shares the earlier work's quasi-musical structure. One can look at the film many times, to watch the camera movement, composition, blocking of the actors; to note speech rhythms, patterns of dominance and submission in relations between the characters; or to observe the way one sequence calls forth the next. Raimu, one of the French cinema's greatest box office draws of the time and one of its best actors when he got the right sort of role, gives a stunning performance as the title character, a receiver of stolen goods who pretends to be a respectable bourgeois. Grémillon was able to return to France at the top of his profession. He was at work on a new film with Gabin in 1939 when the "phony war" halted all production. He would remain one of his country's leading filmmakers during the troubled times of the German Occupation.

New people, of course, also came upon the scene. As normally happens at such transition points in cinema history, the newcomers were less numerous than the veterans who had practiced their craft during the silent era, but highly visible. Many aspiring directors, writers, and producers had been on the fringes of the industry, or in menial positions, and found that with the arrival of the talkies they could finally work as they wished. André Gide's nephew Marc Allégret had made a documentary based on his uncle's trip to Africa (*Voyage au Congo,* 1927) and had worked briefly as an assistant director and set designer on several early sound films before getting to direct *Mam'zelle Nitouche* (1931), an operetta adaptation coproduced in French and German versions by two small companies, one from each country. He quickly acquired a reputation as a reliable craftsman and canny discoverer/developer of cinema stars. Today he is probably best known for *Lac aux dames* (*Lake of Ladies,* 1934, adapted from a popular novel, with dialogue by Colette). This sentimental comedy-drama posed the burning question: will a handsome but poor young engineer be allowed to marry a millionaire's daughter? Sociopolitical analysis was not Allégret's forte, but glamour photography, abetted by liberal doses of cheesecake and beefcake, clearly was. As a director, he was typically only as good, or as bad, as the scripts he directed (and he did get some much better ones—most notably *Gribouille* [1937], written by Marcel Achard).

Many other aspiring filmmakers also profited from the coming of the talkies. Most of them ended up working on program-fillers for the *cinéma de sam'di soir*—films to pass a Saturday night and little remembered on Sunday morning, much less today. An exception to this general mediocrity was Claude Autant-Lara, who would have much more impact on the French cinema than Marc Allégret. His career took off when Allégret's began to fade, during the Occupation and the Tradition of Quality. As a subject for further research, we should also cite the case of Edmond T. Gréville, bilingual son of an English father and a French mother, who had been a ciné-club activist and made a number of short avant-garde and advertising films in the late silent era. Gréville is perhaps the ultimate *cinéaste maudit*, a jinxed film artist whose difficulties make Jean Grémillon's career look easy by comparison. He had an almost fatal attraction for subject matter most audiences found bizarre or distasteful, and as a result he often worked on what today we call exploitation films.[8]

The most widely noticed newcomers to the sound cinema scene were the playwrights. Their presence was important mainly as a symbol of the cinema's new subjugation to the spoken word. Not only did these new arrivals profit handsomely from the silent film's untimely demise; some dramatists also had the effrontery to *lecture* established filmmakers on what they were doing wrong. Marcel Pagnol, for example, published a tendentious series of articles arguing the heretical proposition that "the talking picture is the art of recording, preserving, and diffusing the theatre."[9] René Clair, one of the most vocal opponents of this position, responded: "The most striking thing in the writings of Marcel Pagnol and most of his colleagues who have joined this debate is their cockiness and their astonishing ignorance of the cinema."[10] The debate continued, as French intellectual disputes can, generating more heat than light throughout the first half of the decade.

Given this context, it is not surprising that the most visible playwright-filmmakers did not integrate easily into the larger film community. Pagnol and Sacha Guitry, in particular, developed their own actors and technical teams, and for many years their works were widely thought to constitute a separate, less interesting domain than the "real" cinema of Clair and his colleagues. Aside from their beliefs about cinema and theatre, another reason for Pagnol and Guitry's isolation within the film community was their relatively odd social background and attitudes, at a time when the dominant personalities of French cinema came almost exclusively from the middle and upper bourgeoisie. Marcel Pagnol was not only not a true bourgeois, but he was also something of a cultural separatist. A son of the Midi proud of his roots—he spoke fluent Provençal—he was not at all eager (unlike the stereotypical upwardly mobile provincial) to jettison his heritage in order to integrate into polite Parisian society.

Pagnol was born in 1895 in Aubagne, a semi-industrial town near the great port city of Marseilles. In family background the only figure in these pages he resembles is André Antoine. Pagnol's father, like Antoine's, had by dint of great effort managed to rise from humble origins to the lower reaches of the petty bourgeoisie via the classic route of becoming an elementary schoolteacher. Unlike Antoine, however, Pagnol dearly loved and emulated his father, and for a long time he faithfully followed in the older man's footsteps—though rising higher, of course. At the age of nineteen, he took the first of a series of teaching jobs that culminated in a move to Paris and employment as a professor of English at a *lycée*. But Pagnol's real ambition was to become a writer; in the same year he moved to the capital he joined the staff of *Comoedia Illustré*. He continued teaching, however, until 1927, the year after his first big success as a playwright. As a kind of lighthearted poison-pen letter to the profession he could finally abandon, he wrote *Topaze* (play, 1928), a satiric comedy about a naive and exploited schoolteacher who sees the light and learns how to succeed in the real world of corrupt business and politics. The work was an enormous hit on the Parisian stage, as was *Marius* (play, 1929), his bittersweet drama about a young *marseillais* torn between his love for a woman and his wish to go to sea.

Marius had an exceptionally long and profitable Parisian run; few spectacles in the capital could compete with it financially, or as a subject of polite conversation. One strong competitor, however, was Warner Brothers' *The Jazz Singer*, and Pagnol quickly became passionately interested in the talkies. He began writing his controversial assessments of the new medium; in the course of his informal research he met Robert T. Kane, the head of the Paramount company's new French studios. Pagnol became one of the few Frenchmen Kane really could get to know, because he spoke fluent English and the American executive spoke virtually no French. Thanks to Kane, Pagnol was allowed to observe all aspects of filmmaking at Paramount. Many years afterward, when he wrote a blistering (and probably accurate) description of the company's inefficient, rigidly hierarchical structure, he reported that "If I was later able to direct films, while at the same time administering a laboratory, studio facilities, and distribution agencies, I owe it to the friendship of Robert T. Kane."[11]

At Kane's request, Pagnol helped choose and organize Paramount's

Literary Committee, a group of celebrated authors theoretically constituted to advise the studio but in reality only a clever public relations ploy. Paramount's only real interest in authors was in getting them to sell their most popular works for film adaptation. Pagnol eventually sold the studio the rights to *Marius* and *Topaze*, which were filmed in quite different ways. For *Marius* (film, 1931) Pagnol insisted upon a measure of creative control, and succeeded in getting it with the backing of the director Alexander Korda. *Topaze* (first film version, 1932), however, was made with little or no consultation with its author, who was so dissatisfied with the result that he made two subsequent film versions of his own (1936 and 1951).

Paramount's *Topaze* attempts to conceal its theatrical origins. The play has been "opened out," with scenes originally played in one set moving frenetically from one location to another. Dialogue is treated American-style, with extensive, generally unnecessary cutting from one character to another, in an obvious attempt to infuse a sense of movement into basically static situations. *Marius*, on the contrary— partly because it was made a year earlier but mainly because Pagnol and Korda wanted it that way—does not attempt, with rare but effective exceptions, to "make cinema." The film is a reasonably faithful reproduction of the play, complete with its original stage stars: Raimu, Orane Demazis, and the young Pierre Fresnay. Although *Topaze* has undeniable charms, chiefly the performances of Louis Jouvet and Edwige Feuillère and some eye-opening art deco sets, it is finally a less compelling film. Pagnol and Korda recognized instinctively the point André Bazin would carefully argue more than two decades later: if one attempts to render a theatrical work "cinematic," one almost inevitably ends up with neither good theatre nor good cinema.[12]

Although *Marius* was intended to be a complete work, its open-ended conclusion allowed Pagnol to write two sequels, *Fanny* (play, 1931; film, 1932, directed by Marc Allégret) and *César* (film only, 1936, directed by Pagnol). Although the "trilogy" became increasingly sophisticated cinematically, it is the stage-bound *Marius* which has the most power and artistic originality—though public response to the later works was overwhelmingly positive. In association with Braunberger-Richebé, Pagnol for the first time became a film producer with *Fanny*. In 1933, he took the next logical step and formed his own independent production company, Les Auteurs Associés, soon renamed La Société des Films Marcel Pagnol. At this point his career abruptly took a new direction. Judging by his previous work and his articles, one might have expected Pagnol to continue filming plays in the manner of *Marius* and *Fanny*. Instead he began to write directly for the cinema, at first adapting novels and short stories. He shot these scripts in a manner that strikingly anticipated the Neorealist movement in cinema that would flourish after the Second World War.

In retrospect, it is likely that Pagnol did not specialize in conventional filmed theatre because success on the Parisian stage, and everything it entailed, was not his final goal. It was certainly a more pleasant way of earning money than teaching English, but like that profession it was mainly a means to an end. Pagnol ultimately wanted to be an artist who spoke for his native Provence. Boulevard theatre, as the cinema which exploited it, was basically a Parisian phenomenon, even when it played in the hinterland. It was a manifestation of the cultural centralism that self-consciously regional artists rejected. To be the national stage's token Southerner, writing conventional plays and films about the Midi, even having them performed (like *Marius* and *Fanny*) mainly by natives of the region, did not satisfy Pagnol.

And so he left Paris and established himself as an independent producer-director in Marseilles, becoming a lonely, proud exception to the French sound cinema's basically Parisian nature. But perhaps because he lacked complete confidence in his own literary Southernness, and certainly because he felt that his new enterprise needed the imprimatur of an older, more firmly established reputation, Pagnol sought and obtained a contract with Jean Giono. The celebrated novelist was to receive a percentage of the earnings of films adapted from his works and would collaborate on their screenplays. Pagnol produced, scripted, and directed four films based on Giono's novels and short narratives, but the author did not, for reasons which are still unclear, work on the scripts. As a result, Pagnol did not pay him as specified in the contract, and their collaboration ended unhappily with a lawsuit brought by Giono in 1941.[13]

Pagnol made other films during the 1930s and afterwards, but his Giono adaptations are generally held to be his best works. *Jofroi* (medium length, 1933) and *Regain/Harvest* (1937) are close in story and spirit to their sources; *Angèle* (1934) and *La Femme du boulanger* (*The Baker's Wife*, 1938) stray more from the originals and have a more obviously Pagnolian feel to them. All four works, and the rest of Pagnol's films except for a few play adaptations, employ extensive exterior scenes shot on location, actors mostly from the Midi (including some nonprofessionals), and sober, unflamboyant shooting and editing styles which place emphasis on image-content rather than on the film as storytelling agency. His soundtracks feature direct, synchronous recording of dialogue (even in windy locations) and place great emphasis on the rhythmic musicality of his characters' speech. The director was said often to choose the "take" of a sequence by listening first to the soundtrack. A proponent of "visual" cinema such as René Clair might consider this as heresy, but in Pagnol's speech-oriented fictional universe it is perfectly logical.

Pagnol liked simple stories in which there was time for narrative digression and observation of social rituals. His cinema is based on a set of recurring character positions and types. One typically finds proud, repressed fathers and loving but often rebellious children; unfaithful wives and kindly but cuckolded husbands; illegitimate children and the fallen women who bear them; people who take pleasure in working hard, and others who find pleasure in doing nothing at all; people who talk for the love of talking, or lie for the love of lying, or both. In Pagnol's more Gionoesque works, a major theme is the Land and its relation to Woman: both can be barren or fertile, unforgiving or kind, depending on circumstance and how one treats them. (Even forgiving feminists will find *Regain*, in particular, extremely disturbing.) The earth's fertility is often symbolized by spring water and traditionally baked bread; their absence indicates a world out of joint. Pagnol liked to celebrate the testing and renewal of human bonds; along with Jacques Feyder but in an entirely different, affirmative register, he is one of the French cinema's great observers of the family.

Pagnol clearly wanted to give his stories of provincial life as great a sense of authenticity as he could, most obviously by his use of players with convincing regional accents and behavior and his avoidance of studio-fabricated exteriors. He arguably could not have made the films he did without the earlier example of André Antoine and the other pictorialist naturalist filmmakers of the silent era. Antoine's manifestos of almost two decades before, not Pagnol's own polemical articles of the early 1930s, are the true theoretical preludes to *Regain* or *La Femme du boulanger*. Beyond the two men's insistence on visual authenticity, their films share a pleasing, productive tension between naturalistic observation and theatrical artifice. Antoine's influence on Pagnol was probably direct and personal. In the late 1920s Pagnol was a member of an informal club called Les Moins de Trente Ans ("The Under Thirties") which held monthly banquets where young, mostly little-known playwrights discussed and criticized each other's work.

The protagonist of *Regain* (Gabriel Gabrio) has brought an abandoned village back to life. One symbol of fertility and harmony is the fresh bread he carries across a sunny, location-shot field in the Midi.

The great Naturalist director, by then in his seventies, was an important patron of the group; Pagnol dedicated the published text of his first stage hit, *Topaze*, to him.

The Moins de Trente Ans group is fascinating in the context of cinema history in another way, for, with the prominent exception of Sacha Guitry, most of the notable playwright-filmmakers of the 1930s participated. Few of them became as intensely committed to cinema as did Pagnol, but their collective contribution to the medium was enormous. They included: André Antoine's son André-Paul Antoine, who wrote the original stage play and the dialogue for Max Ophuls's *La Tendre Ennemie* and the dialogue for the same director's *Sans lendemain;* Stève Passeur, author of many adapted plays, original scenarios, and the dialogue for four Abel Gance films, including *Beethoven;* Jacques Natanson, who became an active producer, director, and scriptwriter; and Jacques Deval, who briefly became a writer-producer-director of international repute. In addition to Pagnol, the writers whose reputations have held up the best in the cruel light of history are probably Marcel Achard, who wrote the screenplays for Pierre Chenal's *L'Alibi* and Marc Allégret's *Gribouille,* and Henri Jeanson, whose best-known screenplay of the 1930s was *Pépé le Moko.*

Pagnol's fellow playwrights of the Moins de Trente Ans generally adapted themselves to the French film industry as they found it and did not try, as he did, to make of it something different and more personally fulfilling. The other major playwright-filmmaker of the period who shared Pagnol's obstinate quest for a cinema cut to his own, though very different measure, was one of the theatre's great *monstres sacrés:* Sacha Guitry. Guitry did not attend the meetings of the Moins de Trente Ans, mainly because he didn't need to break into a theatrical community in which he was, almost by birthright, firmly placed. He also was too much of an ardent individualist—some would say a self-contented narcissist—to have listened to the opinions of his peers. The only voices of approval or disapproval that mattered to him, and they mattered enormously, were those of his spectators. Toward the opening of a 1932 lecture entitled, significantly, "For the Theatre and against the Cinema," he felt compelled to report: "On one side, there is you, the Public; on the other side, I . . . I can assert without lying that I have spent the greatest part of my life thinking only of you, concerning myself only with you—which gives me, perhaps, the right to speak directly to you and to make a declaration, a true declaration. This declaration—specific, brutal—is this: I LOVE YOU!"[14]

Sacha Guitry was born in 1885 in Saint Petersburg, Russia, where his father Lucien Guitry, whom many considered the finest actor of his generation, was making a winter tour of the country's Imperial Theatres. (The child's exotic sounding first name was apparently suggested by his Russian nursemaid.) When the boy was four years old, his·father's many infidelities led to a bitter divorce, and Sacha went to live with his mother. The next year, Lucien Guitry kidnapped his (willing) son and took him on his last theatrical tour of Russia. Given this turbulent background, it is hardly surprising that after his mother reclaimed him young Sacha was anything but a model student at the series of boarding schools which he attended while she pursued her own stage career—schools from which, sooner or later and generally sooner, he was expelled for bad conduct. At the age of seventeen, his studies so inadequate that he faced at least six more years of school before he could take his *baccalauréat* exams, he abandoned his education to devote himself to his two great loves: the theatre and women.

By the time *The Jazz Singer* opened in Paris, Guitry was forty-four years old and the rage of the capital, acting in and directing a brilliant series of his own light comedies, typically with three main roles: the husband, the wife, and the lover. Unlike Marcel Pagnol, Guitry was at first highly critical of the new medium, as one can see from the title of the lecture cited above. Nonetheless, he finally overcame his dislike of the talkies and, with characteristic energy, directed and starred in two of them in the same year: *Pasteur* (1935, after his historical drama of the same name) and *Bonne Chance* (*Good Luck,* 1935, an original scenario). "From the instant I came to the cinema, from the instant I made myself up for it," he soon reported, "I loved it and I only thought of doing my best at it, because I can't conceive that one can do something in any way other than passionately."[15] Guitry loved the cinema, but he still also loved the theatre, and so he did not move definitively into filmmaking as Pagnol did, though he produced more films than new plays in the remaining twenty-two years of his life. More than half of his cinema work consists of adaptations of his stage plays (including some written long before the coming of the talkies). In these films he shrewdly refused, like Pagnol and Korda in *Marius,* to "make cinema," at least in conventional ways. He chose instead to use the medium to insist and, implicitly, to comment upon the works' very theatricality. Even in these adaptations he loved to indulge in breathtaking, unconventional eruptions of cinematic play, most prominently in the elaborate credit sequences of which he was particularly fond, and in some remarkable experiments with camera movement.

In his original screenplays, particularly the early ones, Guitry pushed his formal investigations much further. In *Le Roman d'un tricheur*/*The Story of a Cheat* (1936, after his novel) the title character—

played, it goes without saying, by Guitry himself—tells the story of his lamentable life, narrating a series of flashbacks in voice-over. The characters in the flashbacks are never heard; the narrator speaks for them, assuming a variety of attitudes and relations to them. The work of the film is perpetually on display; even the passages in "the present" seem strange in such a context. In *Les Perles de la couronne* (*The Pearls of the Crown*, 1937), Guitry experimented with a form which other filmmakers had briefly explored in the early 1930s, the polyglot film. An international cast, speaking French, English, and Italian, plays the successive owners and admirers of three black pearls. Guitry wrote the screenplay so that the film would be comprehensible to spectators in all three countries without the necessity of dubbing or subtitles. In this form, the film works best for francophone audiences, and modern English prints are subtitled. Although this procedure subverts the director's formal play with language, the film has other strange joys, in particular some extremely eccentric casting (for example, Arletty as an African queen speaking a gibberish created by running her vocal track backwards). Guitry not only plays the (briefly visible) narrator, but three other roles within the story, and the effect of his presence in these two distinct levels, is, to say the least, disorienting.

Guitry's film work has been criticized as all form and no substance, and it is true that the stories he chose to tell typically were, like *Les Perles de la couronne*, pretexts for his seemingly self-indulgent formal play. Such criticism generally comes from the very vocal minority of viewers who take an instant, almost visceral dislike to the director's personality. For his films are finally not about pearls, nor romantic triangles, nor French history (which became one of his favorite cinema subjects). They are about Guitry himself, as an actor and storyteller who can continually surprise and please his public. In a sense he always remained a little child seeking the love of his parents—now the audience—by being clever. This is perhaps a bit sad, and not a good moral example for us all (Guitry loved setting bad examples), but the fact remains that he was truly, extravagantly clever, to the point where his cleverness became a kind of brittle art. And his cinematic posterity argues persuasively for him. When the young aspiring directors of the New Wave looked beyond what they saw as the tradition-bound *cinéma de papa* (freely: "the old men's cinema"), they looked on Guitry (and Pagnol, and other outsiders) as potential models. Alain Resnais, one of the most formally innovative directors of post-World War II French cinema, cited *Le Roman d'un tricheur* as a seminal work in his understanding of what the film medium could really do.

▨ France has always taken pride in being a safe haven for exiles of all sorts. In the silent era, the Russian emigré filmmakers were an important presence in the film community. In the 1930s they were succeeded by a rather different group of expatriates: refugees fleeing fascism, mainly from Germany and Austria. Major filmmakers such as Billy Wilder, Robert Siodmak, Fritz Lang, G. W. Pabst, Anatole Litvak, and many others joined the French film community during the decade, though not all of its members welcomed their arrival or wished them well. For most of these men France became a way station on an unpredictable, often difficult journey to Hollywood, but during their brief residence the new emigrés expanded the range of expressive possibilities open to the French sound film, and a few made their mark in lasting ways.

There is little doubt, in retrospect, about naming the single expatriate who adapted the best and contributed the most to the French cinema. Although he too eventually left for Hollywood, Max Ophuls did not do so willingly, and, unique among the anti-Nazi refugees, he returned after the war to become one of the leading exponents of the Tradition of Quality. Ophuls was born Maximilian Oppenheimer in 1902 in the industrial German city of Saarbrücken, just a few miles from the French border. By its proximity to the province of Lorraine, and its brief occupation by the French in the early nineteenth century, the Saar region had significant cultural and commercial ties with its neighbor, though most of its inhabitants, like the Oppenheimers, spoke German. In the aftermath of World War I, the area was again occupied by the French; when he traveled, Ophuls used a League of Nations passport and was, until 1935, literally a man without a country. The Oppenheimers were prominent members of the region's Jewish bourgeoisie, and their son was expected, after suitably brilliant studies, to join the family textile business.

But the young man's education revealed to him a world vastly more interesting than manufacturing and sales, and this, along with his growing interest in the opposite sex, made him yearn for a different, less constricted and ordered life. The confusion of the First World War doubtless also contributed to his rejection of bourgeois values, and beginning in 1919 he became first a drama critic, then an actor, and finally, in 1923, a theatre director. To avoid embarrassing his family by his unacceptable profession, he took the pseudonym Ophüls (which would become Ophuls in France and Opuls in the United States). Although he recalled in his memoirs that he began to direct at the insistence of an outraged theatre manager who had little regard for his acting, Ophuls was immediately and extraordinarily successful in his new work. He moved from city to city, directing plays by Shakespeare, Molière, and Kleist, but also modern fare by authors as diverse as Arthur Schnitzler, Marcel Pagnol, Edna Ferber, and even Jacques Natanson and André-Paul Antoine, future collaborators on his French film work.

Aesthetically and politically, Ophuls was a radical (though not quite a revolutionary). In the heady theatrical world of the Weimar Republic he was one of many *enfants terribles* who sought not only to find new solutions to old problems, but also to find new problems and to make his public confront them. The center of progressive German theatre culture was Berlin, where he arrived in 1930 at the age of twenty-eight to direct a play on the invitation of an avant-garde troupe. In the German capital Ophuls, like many of his peers, became interested in the talkies. His first cinema job was as assistant director at UFA for Anatole Litvak, a Russian Jew of the same age, and with a similar background in (Soviet) avant-garde theatre. Such was the demand for competent personnel that the giant studio almost immediately offered Ophuls a comedy short subject to direct. After this brief apprenticeship, in the two remaining years before the abrupt end of his German film career Ophuls directed four features, in two of which—*Die verkaufte Braut* (*The Bartered Bride*, 1932) and *Liebelei* (*Flirtation*, 1933, after Arthur Schnitzler)—he explored virtually all the themes and stylistic interests of his celebrated later cinema work.

Like the Russian emigrés before them, most of the new refugees came to France in a sudden wave, following the 1933 Reichstag fire and the new Nazi government's swift consolidation of absolute power. Communists, Jews, and other "undesirables" suddenly found themselves in danger of losing not only their jobs, but in many cases their lives. Ophuls, a Jew with well-known leftist associations, did not wait long before leaving Germany with his family, abandoning, as did so many others, most of his possessions. He had the great fortune, however, to arrive in France just before the Paris opening of *Liebelei*. The film became one of the 1933–34 season's biggest box office successes, first in its original form and then in a hastily made, partly dubbed French version that Ophuls directed and reassembled with the participation of most of the original cast, now refugees like himself. Many of his compatriots were not so lucky. Billy Wilder, for example, had to borrow money from friends and work surreptitiously because he could not get a labor permit. Wilder finally directed *Mauvaise Graine* (*Bad Seed*, 1934) just before leaving for Hollywood with the help of his friend and compatriot, the producer Joe May—who also had made only one French film before crossing the Atlantic to begin his American career.

Even after the success of *Liebelei*, Max Ophuls did not find it easy to get work in France. However, another emigré, the former UFA executive Erich Pommer (the producer of many francophone films made in Germany before 1933), had contracted with 20th Century Fox to make films for the French market. Pommer's first two projects were Ophuls's *On a volé un homme* (*A Man Has Been Stolen*, 1934) and Fritz Lang's *Liliom* (1934, after Ferenc Molnàr). Unfortunately, both films did badly at the box office, and both Pommer and Lang moved on to Hollywood. Ophuls and his friend and *Liebelei* coscriptwriter Curt Alexander traveled to Italy to make *La Signora di tutti* (*Everybody's Lady*, 1934), widely regarded as his best film of the decade. After this project (except for work on an odd, underrated comedy made in Holland in 1936), he remained in France, making six features and two musical short subjects for domestic producers before fleeing the Nazis a second time in 1940.

Most of Ophuls's 1930s French films are rarely seen today (and *On a volé un homme* has apparently been lost forever, probably a victim of its "undesirable" origins during the German Occupation). Audiences and reviewers of the period considered the director's two best French films to be *La Tendre Ennemie* (*The Sweet Enemy*, 1936, after André-Paul Antoine) and *Sans lendemain* (*No Tomorrow*, 1939). Less successful at the box office but admired in some quarters were *Divine* (1935, after Colette) and *Werther* (1938, freely adapted from Goethe). *Yoshiwara* (1937) and *De Mayerling à Sarajevo* (*From Mayerling to Sarajevo*, 1940) were generally considered failures—particularly the former, a tale of doomed interracial love set in the geisha district of nineteenth century Tokyo. In retrospect, *La Tendre Ennemie* and *Sans lendemain* are arguably his most conventional, unadventurous works of the decade, though they do prominently feature the breathtaking mobile camerawork that was already an Ophuls trademark. The two supposed disasters, on the other hand, if not completely successful films, are much more complex in tone and form and anticipate more forcefully his great postwar work.

Ophuls integrated quite well into the French film community, better than the other anti-Fascist refugees. Only G. W. Pabst and Robert Siodmak worked in France as long as he did, and they were forced to deal with much more marginal projects. Only Anatole Litvak briefly matched Ophuls's critical and box office success, with *Mayerling* (1936, to which *De Mayerling à Sarajevo* is a sequel of sorts). Ophuls spoke fluent, if noticeably accented French, and his sympathy with and understanding of actors—and particularly actresses—was legendary. In 1935, when the majority of the residents of the Saar region voted for union with Germany, he accepted the French government's offer of citizenship for those who disagreed. He remained loyal to old friends and associates who were less fortunate than he: in addition to Curt Alexander, he also worked when he could with the great cinematographers Eugen Schufftan and Franz (later Frank) Planer. These associations, and his Jewishness, and his notorious propensity to become romantically involved with (Gentile) actresses, earned him some quite nasty comments in the increasingly anti-Semitic right-wing French press of the late 1930s.

But despite these diatribes Ophuls had little immediate cause for fear, and he had experienced more virulent anti-Semitism before, in Austria and Germany. His new citizenship protected him from the threat of expulsion, widely discussed in France as proper treatment of undesirables, and he continued to work on personally meaningful projects. His fellow refugees had more cause for alarm. By the last years of the decade, Jewish or even simply German sounding names were routinely altered to seem more French in film credits. Few among the flood of emigrés remained in the country, except for those who could not get money or papers to leave, and fewer still could find steady work. The small number still in the country in mid-1940 had to go into hiding, but such was the solidarity of the film community that most of them survived, physically if not always psychologically, until the Liberation. The major exception was Curt Alexander, who was arrested and sent to a concentration camp late in the Occupation, never to return.

☙ 9 ❧

Politics, Poetics, and the Cinema

The swift transition to synchronized recorded sound, and the slower, but no less dramatic shift in social circumstances that took place at roughly the same time profoundly altered French filmmaking in the early 1930s. Although most industry insiders probably took little notice of it, one important symptom of the change was the virtual disappearance of modernist avant-garde cinema as the source of an alternative vision of the medium. But its eclipse did not mean that all film artists and viewers now agreed that mainstream commercial cinema was the best of all possible mechanically reproduced worlds. Rather than disappearing, the opposition shifted ground. As most modernist artists lost interest in the medium, new energies flowed into the ongoing debate about its future. The ciné-club movement became less significant, both in the size of its public and in the notice taken of it by the press and the film industry. Meanwhile, new, explicitly political directions in all the arts, quite prominently including the cinema, were encouraged and exploited by a wide range of organizations which had their own public forums and media outlets. The Communist party soon emerged as a dominant force in what one might call the aesthetics of social opposition.

In retrospect, political filmmaking in the 1930s seems almost exclusively a creation of the Left, and since Communists, Socialists, and assorted *gauchistes* will dominate the pages which follow, it is worth posing the question: what of the Right? Royalist, hypernationalist, and proto-fascist organizations existed in their own subcultures, held meetings, and issued specialized publications to promote their own favored approaches to the film medium. They had their own sympathizers in the industry (and we will see how important this was for Communists and other leftists). Why then did they not attempt to exploit the cinema? It is sometimes argued that an overt effort to do so was not necessary because mainstream commercial cinema, since it must posit reasonably stable characters and social configurations to tell its stories, is by definition a tool of bourgeois ideology and hence a creature of the Right, regardless of how superficially varied its politics may seem. Whatever the merits of this argument in general, it is of relatively little use in examining the political culture of the 1930s, when the extreme Right was uniformly more hostile to bourgeois individualism and to the dominant cinema which perpetuated it than was most of the Left.

In one of the very few studies of the extreme Right and the cinema, Alice Yeager Kaplan has argued that Maurice Bardèche and Robert Brasillach's *Histoire du cinéma*—a work of almost impeccable fascist credentials, given that Brasillach was executed after the Liberation for his ardent collaboration with the Nazis—demonstrates an insistent hostility to mainstream, theatrically inspired sound cinema, which its authors viewed as completely out of touch with the medium's real mission: "The worst kind of film [for Bardèche and Brasillach] is one that uses stage technique and stage actors: plays are for and about individuals, movies for and about groups, and the attempt to film theatre is a gross misunderstanding of the form. Crowds watching films [should] learn from the screen to know themselves as a crowd: moviegoing becomes a group rite, or a place where strangers gather to dream together. The crowd comes to know itself as film."[1] Kaplan's penetrating analysis of the theoretical underpinnings of fascist film aesthetics is more compact and coherent than that of Bardèche and Brasillach. The two young historians were much better at saying what they liked and didn't like. And with few exceptions, they didn't like commercial sound films; the only areas of 1930s filmmaking that consistently pleased them were those that had stayed closest to the historians' beloved silent cinema: documentary and newsreels.

After 1937, most French fascists and fascist sympathizers had no problem naming their favorite sound film: Leni Riefenstahl's *Triumph des Willens* (*Triumph of the Will*, 1935), which had been shown to an often tumultuous reception at the German Pavilion of the 1937 Paris World's Fair. But why, even then, did none of them think to attempt their own such work? One reason, almost certainly, was that there was no French equivalent of Adolph Hitler, around whom Riefenstahl's work is carefully built, though there were by that time enough aspiring candidates. The fascist hero, the Leader who belongs totally to the Nation, and by this belonging causes the collectivity to speak with one voice (his own), casting out impurities from its sacred body—this was too serious a matter to be presented as anything but a *fait accompli*. And so the most visible points of contact between the French extreme Right and the cinema were the abundant and virulent denunciations of supposedly Left- and Jewish-influenced filmmaking by writers such as Louis Ferdinand Céline and radio commentators like Lucien Rebatet, and the mini-demonstrations sometimes provoked by newsreels.[2] Jean Renoir felt compelled to ask, in a 1937 newspaper column, why the recently active French censor did not pay more attention to curbing the excesses of "heroic young people, always the same ones, [who] make manifest a disorderly enthusiasm at the appearance on the screen of Mussolini, Hitler, or Franco's army."[3]

▨ Probably the most important reason that the Right had so little direct contact with French filmmaking was its fragmentation, as compared to the Left. Fascists and monarchists did not willingly form alliances; right-wing anarchists found little sympathy from either group. On the Left, however, Communists, Socialists, anarchists, and assorted syndicalists were more willing to establish contacts, make compromises, and build coalitions—at least in the arts and letters if not, until roughly mid-decade, at the higher levels of political leadership. In the cinema and other media, the Left's Popular Front against fascism had been taking shape well before its consolidation as a political strategy. Left-wing artists and organizers who could not forge a program of common actions could agree, implicitly, to support each other and new figures who opposed the status quo in the area of artistic expression. Young Jean Vigo, for example, received crucial aid from established and aspiring members of the film community who had quite diverse relations to Left politics. Without this support, he probably could not have made his most important films before his death at the age of twenty-nine. Much later, after World War II, his status as an icon of the broad Left would play a major role in the revival, restoration, and critical praise of his works. Only then did they finally find the wider audiences he had sought during his brief life.

Jean Vigo was the son of the notorious left-wing anarchist Eugène

Bonaventure de Vigo, who was better known under the pseudonym of Almereyda, an anagram for "[il] y a [de] la merde," or "there is shit." Almereyda's only son was born in 1905, out of wedlock it goes almost without saying, in a crowded attic room that was usually full of cats and kittens and the sound of laughter and feverish talk of revolution. Almereyda had pursued an exemplary career as a political agitator, being arrested once (before Jean's birth) for constructing crude bombs, and again (when the boy was three) for purveying revolutionary propaganda. Though he eventually joined the Socialist party and became an influential Left establishment journalist and publisher, he did not entirely shed his earlier reputation as a political extremist. The family had become remarkably prosperous—probably thanks to covert contributions from illegal, perhaps even treasonable sources (the country was at war)—when Almereyda was again arrested in August 1917. Less than a week later he was found dead in his prison cell, possibly murdered (or so his supporters thought) to prevent him from compromising members of the government, which was said to have been secretly involved in his activities. After Almereyda's death, custody of his child was awarded to the boy's paternal grandmother and step-grandfather. Such was his father's reputation—he had been accused of being a German agent—that Jean could not live untroubled with his grandparents. He was sent away, under an assumed name, to a village boarding school, an unhappy place which would later be the model for the school in his *Zéro de conduite*.

Jean Vigo had a scholarly inclination but (already always the rebel) he did not complete the last part of his *baccalauréat* exam. Continuing his education on his own terms, he audited courses at the Sorbonne until he fell ill with tuberculosis, at the age of twenty-one. In a sanatorium in the Pyrenees he met a fellow patient, Elisabeth ("Lydou") Lozinska, the beautiful, fragile, and nervous daughter of a bourgeois Polish Jewish family from the city of Lodz. The couple lived together and traveled briefly before marrying and settling in Nice, which had the climate their health required and was also the only viable non-Parisian outpost of the French film industry. This advantage was necessary because Vigo had decided just before his illness to become a filmmaker. Through an old friend of his father's he met the future director Claude Autant-Lara, a young man of left-wing anarchist sympathies who was a bit further along in the difficult project of entering the industry. Autant-Lara got Vigo a low-paying job as assistant cameraman on a Franco-Film production, but after that, despite support from Germaine Dulac, also a friend of a (Left pacifist) friend, he was unable to find more film work.

The Vigos were in financial difficulty when Lydou's father gave them a delayed wedding present of 100,000 francs—an important sum for the period, enough for some working-class families to live on for a decade. Jean bought a camera and began working on *A Propos de Nice* (*On the Subject of Nice*, 1930), first alone and then with the collaboration of the Russian emigré cinematographer Boris Kaufman. After a few false starts, Vigo's *point de vue documenté* ("documented point of view") on Nice emerged as a Soviet-style parodic montage commentary on the city and the bourgeois tourists it pampers, only to devour. Unfortunately, only about two-thirds of the original survives in existing prints, and the film as one can see it today requires P. E. Sallès-Gomes's careful commentary on its origins and original form to make much sense.[4]

Vigo went to Paris to promote his work, which had the great disadvantage of being a silent film in the first full year of French sound cinema. At first his only results were two noncommercial screenings and some favorable reviews, mainly in the Left press and most notably by Léon Moussinac in the Communist daily *L'Humanité*. But Moussinac was also a friend of a friend, and Vigo began to despair of achieving any general, more disinterested recognition of his talents. Finally the film was accepted for a run at a small art cinema. It was not this limited success that got its maker his first commercial filmmaking contract, however, but rather the intervention of Autant-Lara, Dulac, and Moussinac. With their support he was hired to make a short sports film about a swimming champion. *Taris* (1931) was well enough received that Vigo was engaged to make a second, similar work. Unfortunately, that project failed to materialize, and by mid-1932 he was again unemployed, except for running a ciné-club he had organized in Nice, and the couple was living on another generous gift from Lydou's father.

One of the admirers of *A Propos de Nice* had been the left-wing actor René Lefèvre, future star of Renoir's *Le Crime de Monsieur Lange* and a major figure in the Resistance during the German Occupation. Lefèvre recommended Vigo as a director to a left-connected businessman who wanted to produce medium-length films (*moyens métrages*, of roughly forty-five minutes to an hour in length) to accompany feature film presentations. Vigo proposed, among other projects, an autobiographical scenario which became *Zéro de conduite* (*Zero for Conduct*, 1933). In this film Vigo tapped his childhood memories of the small town boarding school he had attended and the rage he had felt against the adults who, in his view, had murdered and defamed his father. Partly because of his small budget, but also because he wanted to avoid theatrical artifice, he chose mainly non-professional actors for his film. Most of the children were found in poorer Paris neighborhoods, and they speak and act accordingly, which adds an implicit layer of class conflict to the work's main opposition between grotesque adulthood (the school principal is a bearded dwarf dressed in formal bourgeois garb) and the magical world of childhood.

Zéro de conduite is widely accepted as one of the genuine masterpieces of world cinema, and like most masterpieces it is difficult to classify or explain meaningfully in terms of its period. It can arguably be called a Left anarchist film, and one can also point out its many debts to Surrealism; these labels might be of some use if one were interested in how contemporary audiences reacted to it. But very few people in France ever saw it during the 1930s, because it was almost immediately banned by the government, for reasons that will probably never be fully understood. Certainly the censors were more attuned to the work's political overtones (the children's revolt against their school as metaphor for revolution) than are most contemporary spectators. Today we see *Zéro de conduite* as a strikingly original, personal work, which it certainly is, but in 1933 it was also an early, deliberate salvo in the rapidly escalating war against polite society and the rule of (bourgeois) law.

Vigo's first fiction film would certainly never have been made if its producer, J.-L. Nounez, had been an industry insider. Few films have been more obvious candidates for commercial oblivion in both subject and technique (the work has some terrible problems with continuity and very poor sound recording). After its suppression Nounez, quite foolishly in the view of most of his associates, insisted on employing Vigo to direct a new, feature-length film that would, he hoped, recoup the investment lost on *Zéro de conduite*. But this time the young director would not be allowed to devise his own scenario, and he would have to employ professional actors, at least in the leading roles. Michel Simon, on the verge of becoming one of the industry's most popular stars, accepted a supporting role in *L'Atalante* (1934), apparently because he liked the idea of working for the director of a banned, reputedly subversive film. For this project Vigo had a budget five

In *Zéro de conduite*, a provincial school becomes a metaphor for society at large. Anarchy must not be tolerated; the authorities intervene in a chaotic classroom and hierarchy is restored, if only for a time.

times the one for *Zéro de conduite*. He could rehearse adequately and shoot enough film (with a better sound system) to avoid the technical problems that had plagued him the year before.

Vigo clearly made a real effort to follow his producer's guidelines, but he also subtly transformed the original project. He added to the original script's quite conventional story of love, separation, and reconciliation a magical, surreal quality, and at the same time he included several glimpses of contemporary social conditions (for example, unemployed workers in search of work outside a factory). After one corporate screening to a mixed but not disastrous reception, the film's distributor insisted on massive changes to make it more commercial. Nounez eventually capitulated, and the film was drastically cut and reedited, with a vapid popular song replacing most of Maurice Jaubert's original score (today considered a landmark work of French film music). The result was the same as for other, similarly misguided rescue efforts (such as the reworkings of Ophuls' *Lola Montès* or Renoir's

La Règle du jeu): a film that was neither commercially nor artistically viable.

Like *Zéro de conduite*, *L'Atalante* was seen by very few French viewers during the 1930s, though it too would be considered a masterpiece on its rerelease after the war, serving as a model for personal film-making for the future directors of the New Wave. Even in its restored original version, Vigo's second and last fiction film is much closer to the successful commercial cinema of its day than was *Zéro de conduite*, which is hardly surprising or a matter for lamentation. Had it been released in 1934 as Vigo completed it, he might, paradoxically, have been a less potent figure in cinema history, a director who followed up a banned, radical film with a safer, more conventional one. But the mutilated film's swift failure at the box office, and its director's death a few weeks later from blood poisoning, wrote for many observers the final chapters in the ultimate cinema version of the myth of the Romantic artist, the heroic loner doomed to death and despair by an unfeeling, uncomprehending society. Yet the real significance of Vigo's story is probably that he got to make his films at all, thanks to the support of people who admired his artistic integrity and the social and moral values he (and his father) stood for.

Jean Vigo was not a unique, isolated figure in the French film community of the early 1930s. René Clair and Jean Renoir, sensitive to the changing tenor of the times, quickly began to explore social themes in their early sound films, more tentatively to be sure, and with diametrically opposed outcomes: Clair retreated into purely commercial projects by mid-decade, at the same time that Renoir deepened his commitment. Renoir's growing involvement with polit-ically progressive films reflected more than merely the continuing evolution of his own attitudes. His work also expressed, and in part served to consolidate, the growing influence of an increasingly coher-ent political subculture of the Left within the film community. The most important elements of this subculture could not have evolved as early or as effectively as they did without careful nurturing, which was principally provided by the Parti Communiste Français, or P.C.F. To understand how this took place, one must bear in mind a curious contradiction between the Party's cultural policies and its strictly polit-ical orientation.

The P.C.F. had formed as an independent entity only in 1920, and in its first years it slowly consolidated, under close direction from Moscow, as a small, tightly organized and centrally directed unit. Members unwilling to submit to strict Party discipline were gradually eliminated, even at the highest levels. A deliberate policy evolved of promoting men and women of proletarian origins, while deemphasizing the role of (even quite committed) members from the bourgeoisie. During this period, which ended in 1934, the P.C.F. avoided compromises or meaningful alliances with other Left parties. As a political force in the early 1930s, the Party lived up to most of the stereotypes of Stalinism. Most of the non-Communist French Left generally regarded it as hypocritical and untrustworthy. Yet the Party engaged in a cultural politics of alliances and pluralism, ironically at the same time that artistic and intellectual life in the U.S.S.R. was undergoing a process of radical reversal of pluralization, and celebrated figures of the 1920s such as Sergei Eisenstein came under withering attack. In its cultural activities the P.C.F. encouraged the participation of people who would have been excluded from its political meetings—and who, in the Soviet Union, would probably have simply disappeared to the gulag or to unmarked graves. Curiously, the Party at first placed little emphasis on cinema, emphasizing instead literature and theatre as ideological vehicles. Though Communists and fellow travelers could and did applaud Jean Vigo's work, for example, their first direct contact with filmmaking came about indirectly, through the Party's extensive efforts to establish an alternative theatrical culture.

The P.C.F. probably emphasized theatre for two reasons: it was a way of seeking working-class recruits, drawn by the lure of the stage, and it involved collective effort and group discipline, both strong Party ideals. To avoid the taint of bourgeois individualism, most performances emphasized choral pieces, in which young proletarians declaimed or sang edifying, generally political texts in unison. One theatre group, named Prémices, harbored a number of dissatisfied members: "We didn't want to make theatre," one recalled, "but to make the Revolution."[5] This dissident faction either left or was expelled in 1932, and they sought a patron to help them organize their own group. They were referred to the film critic Léon Moussinac, who in turn suggested they enlist the help of the anarchist poet and former Surrealist (and non-Communist) Jacques Prévert. Prévert and his friend Jean-Paul Dreyfus—in 1936 he adopted the less controversial pseudonym Le Chanois for his film work—quickly elaborated a satirical sketch about the bourgeois press. During rehearsals of the piece the group established a lasting feeling of solidarity and named itself the Groupe Octobre (October Group) to indicate its dedication to the Revolution and to the Soviet example.

There is little doubt that from his first contact with the group Prévert became its dominant personality. He wrote or collaborated on most of its scripts and brought in many of his friends, transforming a largely proletarian entity into a conglomerate of people from different classes and left-wing political points of view. But there were no secessions or expulsions from the group, because Prévert was no autocrat. On the contrary, he was fascinated by group process and by the artistic possibilities to be found in continuous close contact with political and social reality. He did not direct or manipulate the group but sought to focus its energies, while never suppressing his own. During one performance of *La Bataille de Fontenoy*, a nervous young actor playing a policeman was supposed to exclaim, "Méfiez-vous! Les oreilles ennemies vous écoutent!" ("Be careful! The enemy's ears are listening!"), but instead he announced: "Les oreilles ennemies vous contemplent!" ("The enemy's ears are watching!"). The poet, enchanted, kept the new (and very Prévertian) line in his sketch at all subsequent performances.[6]

Today Prévert is best known for his less political poems and the later poetic realist screenplays. His most directly ideological work is often neglected, possibly because the poet as political activist fits badly with modern notions of both poetry and political struggle. In common with Jean Renoir, he had both a strong sympathy for the Left and a great openness and sensitivity to the people around him. In the company of optimistic, joyful revolutionaries of all persuasions (there were Stalinists, Trotskyites, anarchists, and other *gauchistes* in the group) he wrote agit-prop vaudeville texts, with a lingering hint of Surrealism. With little of the uncompromising singlemindedness of a Vigo or a Luis Buñuel, his writing could change in register and purpose in new contexts, such as the commercial cinema.

All but the last of the October Group's various adventures in filmmaking came about as a result of Jacques's and his brother Pierre's fascination with the medium and their friendships with similarly inclined leftist artists. The Préverts had already attempted to interest film producers in at least two scenarios, and the poet had been at work on a script with his friend Pierre Batcheff (best known for his role in

Buñuel's *Un Chien andalou*) when the actor suddenly committed suicide. Shortly after the October Group's formation, the brothers
arranged with a friend who worked for Pathé-Nathan to make a
medium-length film for the studio using sets already constructed for
another project. The result was *L'Affaire est dans le sac* (*The Deal is in
the Bag*, 1932), written by Jacques Prévert, directed by his brother, and
starring group members. Unfortunately Pathé-Nathan did not appreciate the finished product, a hectic farce about mad love, kidnapping,
and hats, and all copies were ordered destroyed. Happily, the film has
survived and pleases audiences to this day, though it gives only a limited notion of what the group was up to. The Préverts honestly tried
to make a commercially viable film; the work's only reference to politics is the periodic appearance of an angry petit bourgeois type,
played by Jacques Brunius, who always asks to buy a beret (for the
period, a symbol of right-wing politics) and is at one point sold a *cas-
quette*, or worker's hat, which revolts him when he discovers the deception.

The next year, members of the group worked with director Claude
Autant-Lara on *Ciboulette* (1933, scenario by Jacques Prévert adapted
from an operetta set in a working class milieu). The film was a terrible
commercial and critical failure, though not because it reflected in any
meaningful way the political sympathies or the artistic strategies of
the October Group (no one stood up to tell the film's audience about
miners' strikes or Lenin's theories).[7] More political, but lacking the
group's satirical humor and spirit of play, was *Prix et Profits* (*Prices and
Profits*, 1933), directed by Yves Allégret (brother of Marc, and the
group's most notorious Trotskyite). This was a didactic docudrama
short made for a Communist educational group; it featured the Préverts and other group members as the various parties involved in the
growing and selling of potatoes (the capitalists get all the money).

These excursions into the cinema, however, were *divertissements*
compared to the group's primary concern, which was consciousness-
raising among the working masses. In 1934 political struggle in
France assumed a new, terrible urgency, and the group refocused its
energies on theatrical agit-prop. During the night of February 6,
1934, mass demonstrations by right-wing *ligues* seemed to threaten a
coup d'état; the National Guard had to be called out to protect the
Chamber of Deputies from the enraged mob. In the ensuing melée
fourteen demonstrators and one policeman were killed, and hundreds more on both sides were injured. Whether or not a coup had

been systematically plotted, the events profoundly frightened the French Left. Within a few months the P.C.F. had Moscow's blessing to abandon its previous policy of noncooperation with other political parties. An uneasy peace was quickly made with the Socialists, and even the centrist Radical Party was invited to join a Popular Front against fascism. In January 1936 the Front forged a common political platform, with the slogan "bread, peace, and liberty," for the national elections to be held in April of that year. Victory was virtually guaranteed, though when it came, the old quarrels within the Left inexorably reappeared, fatally weakening the new government and turning its once great promise into a source of new bitterness and suspicion.

In the last months of 1935, in the midst of the excitement and optimism generated by the Popular Front, members of the October Group returned to filmmaking for a project that was both more political than *L'Affaire est dans le sac* and *Ciboulette* and addressed to a wider public than was their theatre work: Jean Renoir's *Le Crime de Monsieur Lange* (*The Crime of Monsieur Lange,* 1936). Jacques Prévert wrote the film's screenplay after a story idea by Renoir and Jean Castanier (the set designer on several of the director's earlier films). Pierre Prévert was assistant director, and many October Group members, such as Jacques Brunius and Marcel Duhamel, were in the cast. The leading roles were played by mainstream, though left-leaning, cinema actors. The film was thus a kind of Popular Front in microcosm, bringing together in its conception and execution relatively apolitical antifascists and highly committed political activists. The next summer Renoir again worked with members of the October Group on the medium-length *Une Partie de campagne/A Day in the Country* (1936/46, after Maupassant). Ultimately, however, *Lange* and *Une Partie de campagne* were commercial projects in which the group's penchant for virulent satire and surreal juxtapositions had little room for expression. The fullest cinematic expression of their sensibility and methods may be found in the opening sections of the (justifiably) celebrated but (unjustly) little seen *La Vie est à nous* (*Life Is Ours,* aka *People of France,* 1936/69), the collectively made campaign film of the P.C.F. for the national elections of 1936.

A surprising number of commentators consider *La Vie est à nous* a Renoir film, a work dominated (as is, ultimately, *Le Crime de Monsieur Lange*) by the director's cinematic style and by his personal and political interests. Renoir himself, however, repeatedly asserted that he acted primarily as producer and coordinator for the project, though he did finally direct a few sequences. Stylistically, it is quite different from any of his other projects. As the anonymous nature of its original release indicates (original prints have no credits), *La Vie est à nous* is the very antithesis of an author's film. It is a collective project, a veritable anthology of themes and textual strategies espoused by the French Left, though its structure emphasizes orthodox P.C.F. positions and methods. Critics and historians have often neglected the importance of the October Group's influence on the film, probably because because neither Jacques nor Pierre Prévert worked on it. But Jean-Paul Le Chanois and Jacques Brunius both made major contributions to its planning, direction, and editing. Many other group members appear in the large cast—alongside such stalwarts of the Left as Jean Dasté (star of both of Vigo's fiction films) and Gaston Modot (star of Buñuel's *L'Age d'or*).

Determining exactly who did what is not, ultimately, the point in this kind of project. Besides the October Group, others heavily involved in the production included Renoir's assistant Jacques Becker, the still photographer Henri Cartier-Bresson, and the Communist writer and intellectual Paul Vaillant-Couturier. At any rate, the October Group's methods and its strong anti-bourgeois stance are much in evidence in the early portions of the film—most obviously in a sequence in which Brunius plays a dissolute and corrupt chairman of the board of a capitalist enterprise. At a board meeting, the bourgeois band chants rhythmically, *"Compression! Compression!"* ("Retrenchment! Retrenchment!"). The film abruptly cuts to workers in a courtyard chanting, to the same three-beat rhythm, *"Du travail! Et du pain!"* ("We want work! And some bread!"). Shock cuts such as this one abound in the first part of the film; it is lively, unsettling, and quite aggressive toward the audience, which is never allowed to relax and contemplate a seemingly objective window on the world. Through manipulations of newsreel footage, apparently of Brunius's devising, figures of the Right are mercilessly parodied: Hitler barks like a dog, and the French right-wing demagogue Colonel de la Rocque marches in a mincing, effeminate manner.

Later in the film, a slow, carefully modulated change of tone occurs. The October Group spirit of joyful aggression recedes, to be replaced by what seems to be a French attempt at socialist realism, at the time the dominant, "politically correct" fiction film style in the Soviet Union. This part of the work recounts (in self-effacing, almost Hollywood fashion) three supposedly typical stories of people whose lives are changed by the beneficent influence of the P.C.F. Viewers who enjoy the modernist fireworks of the film's earlier sequences often find the plodding, almost painfully earnest case studies an invitation to slumber. The film ends on a livelier note, with a rousing speech by Party leader Maurice Thorez and an odd but moving rendition of the "Internationale." Whether the work as a whole hangs together in tone and content, or remains an engaging smorgasbord, is a judgment for each viewer to make; there is little basis for such an evaluation because there is no other film quite like *La Vie est à nous*.[8] At no other moment did the militant French Left attempt so comprehensively to give expression to its various competing voices in a single work. For this reason no other film, not even *Le Crime de Monsieur Lange*, gives as full a cinematic expression of the spirit of the Popular Front.

La Vie est à nous is not the only example of filmmaking directly financed by a political party during the 1930s, though it is probably the most interesting to viewers of today. The year after its production, Jean-Paul Le Chanois directed *Le Temps des cerises* (*The Time of Cherries*, 1937), a propaganda work arguing for old age pensions, again with money from the P.C.F. The Socialist party (S.F.I.O.) and other Left organizations also financed film projects, but most of these have either been lost or are viewable today only in party archives.[9] With the exception of *La Vie est à nous*, for which commercial distribution was contemplated (though refused, probably as expected, by the censor), these films were generally meant to be adjuncts to party meetings and discussion groups, not self-sufficient works. Nonetheless, their loss or inaccessibility inevitably distorts our understanding of 1930s film culture, for they probably had some influence, however indirect, on the portion of mainstream commercial cinema which attempted to deal with the decade's many important social and political issues.

The most visible mainstream commercial filmmaker associated with left-wing politics—during the 1930s but not before or after—was Jean Renoir. If one includes *La Vie est à nous*, his major works of the decade intersect with most of the important social issues and creative artists of the Left. We must keep in mind, however, that Renoir's period of political commitment was suspiciously short-lived. After the demise of the Popular Front he ceased to believe in the efficacy of political struggle, though in his autobiography he declared that "If I were forced to [take a stand], with my back to the wall, I would opt for Communism": not exactly a ringing declaration of faith.[10] It seems likely that the very vagueness of Renoir's political commitment was what facilitated his remarkably good relations with the wide variety of activists—Stalinists, Trotskyites, Socialists, anarchists, *laissez-faire* anti-fascists—who collaborated with him on his films of the 1930s and profoundly influenced the works' political orientations. Had he been more deeply engaged in politics, the director inevitably would also have been more narrowly sectarian, forced by the period's bitter rivalries to choose one particular position and to oppose the others. Ironically, because he chose to maintain a degree of (polite) distance from political commitment, Renoir became the fiction filmmaker of the period whose works most completely expressed the fragile, contradictory spirit of the Popular Front.

Renoir's fascination with the social tensions of the 1930s began to surface in 1931 with *La Chienne*. That film's bitter, almost nihilistic tone comes in large measure from its source, a novel by the celebrated anarchist-pacifist, Georges de la Fourchardière. But beyond Fourchardière's influence, *La Chienne* was the film in which Renoir became fully aware of the social dimensions of speech. The range of vocal styles in the film makes its sound track not merely interesting in texture (as aural montage), but implicitly redolent of class conflict. *La Chienne* also features the first of a striking series of murders and other violent deaths that recur obsessively in the director's works of the 1930s. (The crime goes unpunished, as will the murders in *Le Crime de Monsieur Lange* and *La Règle du jeu*, though the implications of this fact are quite different for each of the three films.) Many critics tend to depict Jean Renoir as a genial, gentle humanist. But in most of his films of the 1930s people are, quite simply, out to kill one another sooner or later.[11] In mid-decade, if we are to judge by his films, Renoir came to believe for a while that some good could emerge from the violence which seems to have obsessed him. After the demise of the Popular Front, however, he returned to the view of life implicit in *La Chienne:* murder expresses a truth that most people do not wish to accept, that aggression and conflict are implicit in human relations—and most strongly between members of different classes. But the killing does not change anything; life goes on around it, in a kind of awful harmony with it.

Renoir's fascination with violence was again evident in his next project, an adaptation of his friend Georges Simenon's murder mystery *La Nuit du carrefour* (*Night of the Crossroads*, 1932). The director's approach to this relatively conventional subject matter was peculiar, to say the least. This odd, rarely screened film is the closest thing to an *hommage* to Luis Buñuel in Renoir's work (in one striking overhead shot, a woman plays languidly with a large tortoise). Simenon's detective Maigret (Pierre Renoir, Jean's brother) is as much a witness to violence and irrationality as he is an agent of their control. One wonders what the conservative Simenon—whose works were widely admired on the political Right—thought of Renoir's surreal, subtly anarchist adaptation of his novel. (Some of the film's odd atmosphere is apparently the result of several reels of footage having been lost just before final editing.)

For his next film, Renoir again strikingly transformed his source material. In *Boudu sauvé des eaux/Boudu Saved from Drowning* (1932) this process is directly and didactically sociopolitical. René Fauchois's original stage comedy concerned the successful education of a tramp in the gentle ways of the petty bourgeoisie. Renoir reversed the play's values and made the tramp (played with great brio by Michel Simon) the embodiment of liberty, and the middle class household he invades the citadel of mindless, if comic, repression. In *Boudu sauvé des eaux*, Renoir first fully elaborated the cinematic style of his great 1930s works. To the relatively lengthy, but also close and sometimes even claustrophobic shots of *La Chienne*, he added an exploration of image composition in depth and a sense of openness, spontaneity, and movement. Renoir's long take, depth-composed, and movement-oriented style—which did not abruptly appear, but rather was consolidated with *Boudu*—enabled him to balance and play off against each other the conflicting elements he was so fond of assembling in his early sound films (different accents, styles of behavior, moral points of view).

Renoir first touched upon a pressing social issue of the decade in *Toni* (1935), a work made very much under the influence of Marcel Pagnol. Pagnol did not, as is sometimes reported, act as the film's producer, but his guarantee of distribution through Les Films Marcel Pagnol probably enabled Renoir to get financing for what must have seemed an eccentric project. *Toni* is set among immigrant workers in the Midi and features extensive location shooting. Renoir used several actors from Pagnol's troupe; Charles Blavette, in the title role, had acted in both *Jofroi* and *Angèle*. Stylistically, the film also suggests Pagnol; despite some careful uses of composition in depth, its cinematography and editing are most often plain and functional. It is the story and the people that matter. Socially, *Toni* overtly takes the side of the earthy immigrants with their heavily accented speech, and criticizes the well-spoken, politely contemptuous agents of social control who rule their lives. This was a fairly courageous stand to take in the mid-1930s, when hysterical calls for suppression of immigration had become a major rallying point for the Right, and the slogan France for the French! had great popular appeal. Still, *Toni* mainly tells a story of love, jealousy, and murder, for which social and national tensions serve as background. It was in the *Le Crime de Monsieur Lange*, released just before the elections of 1936, that Renoir went beyond individuals and their passions and explored one of the Left's major themes, the building of working class solidarity via group action.

Lange is one of Renoir's most admired and critically examined works, a Left film that even cynical conservatives can admire. Just as he had insisted on using little-known Southerners to play in *Toni*, for his film about a workers' collective Renoir cast members of the collectively run October Group in many secondary roles. As scriptwriter Jacques Prévert probably had less impact on the work's emotional tone (the narrative was basically in place before he began the job) than he did as volatile center and focus of the performance group's freewheeling energies. The film's warm, zany atmosphere partially (and perhaps deliberately) obscures its cold-hearted endorsement of murder in the service of justifiable political ends: when mild-mannered Amédée Lange (René Lefèvre) kills the evil capitalist Batala (Jules Berry in one of his most appealingly wicked screen roles) in order to save the collective, an informal and extralegal jury of his peers acquits him and allows him to escape prosecution.

Le Crime de Monsieur Lange contains some of Renoir's most striking experiments in depth-composed images, often seen by a breathtakingly mobile camera. In *Les Bas-fonds* (*The Lower Depths*, 1936, after Maxim Gorky), he explored this aspect of his style even more daringly. Despite its cinematographic pyrotechnics, however, the film is generally considered the least satisfying of the director's Popular Front works. Renoir's anxiety to remain on good terms with the P.C.F., which insisted on overseeing his treatment of Gorky (whose writings were almost sacred writ for Communists of all nationalities), resulted in an odd compromise, a culturally vague fictional world that is neither Russian nor French. The film's insertion of measured doses of proletarian solidarity and mid-thirties Left optimism into a deeply despairing stage play created abrupt mood changes that have an almost manic-depressive aura. Although one can nonetheless enjoy the film for its very contradictions, most viewers prefer *La Grande Illu-sion* (*Grand Illusion*, 1937), in which Renoir was much more successful in mixing optimistic outbursts of group solidarity with a sense of the dangers that menace all attempts at forming meaningful social bonds in a context of national and class conflict.

An enormous amount has been written about *La Grande Illusion*, from a bewildering range of critical perspectives. Some commentators assert that the film's importance lies somehow beyond or above mere political questions, while others read it as making (quite diverse) state-ments about the society of its day. Critics and historians generally agree that the film is a landmark of cinema history, but one reason for this unanimity of judgment, clearly, is that the work lends itself so well to wildly different interpretations. Not everyone even agrees that Renoir (and scriptwriter Charles Spaak) made an unambiguously anti-war film. In the 1943 edition of their cinema history, Bardèche and Brasillach argued that "[Renoir] describes [war] just as it was, with an admirable honesty and sang-froid. It isn't his fault, nor ours, if some men were able to experience in war what they would never experience afterwards. This could come as a surprise if we didn't understand that Jean Renoir's war, by means of the standard para-dox, is the place of friendship, of youth, and perhaps of regret."[12] Perhaps Benito Mussolini and Hermann Goering, also great admirers of the work, found a similarly nostalgic love of conflict in it.

The work also elicited quite diverse reactions to its treatment of the so-called Jewish question. Before the war, most critics believed the film took a strong stand against anti-Semitism. Even its German fascist admirers presumably agreed, since the film was released to wide acclaim in Germany only after being stripped of all sequences show-ing the character played by the well-known Jewish actor Marcel Dalio in a sympathetic light. Sadly, most of these sequences were also cut for the work's general French release; they were only restored after the war, at which time they did not prevent the Left press from attack-ing the film as anti-Semitic. And perhaps in the postwar perspective it is. Dalio's character Rosenthal is sympathetic, but carefully shown as very different from the other French prisoners of war. That he is the only character from the *haute bourgeoisie* did nothing to dispel pop-ular myths about Jews stealing French wealth and controlling the country's economy. In a scene which the French public could see in 1937 (but not after the war, when Renoir cut it), Rosenthal offers chocolate to a German soldier while a French prisoner comments,

Tout est pourri ("Everything is rotten," the word *pourri* echoing the rhetoric of French anti-Semitism).[13]

These aspects of the film seem to speak for a sort of anti-Semitic unconscious in it, which partly undermines its courageous—and rare—employment of a sympathetic Jewish character. One can see a similar ambivalence in Renoir and Spaak's treatment of class conflict. Proletarian solidarity receives a solid endorsement, of course, but it is the aristocrats who get the grand gestures, and whose passing is mourned. Faced with such latent contradictions, one may choose to agree with Allen Thiher (and others) that Renoir deliberately structured his film with "systematic ambiguity," or with François Garçon, arguing that underneath the work's apparently progressive surface lurks an uncanny anticipation of the Vichy ideology of the Occupation years.[14] The film's clear endorsement of the wholesome country life depicted in its last third, as opposed to the conflict and debauchery of urban life, is either ironic (from Thiher's perspective) or ominously sincere, a precursor of Marshall Pétain's many diatribes on this theme (in Garçon's analysis).

Ideology is not the only interest of *La Grande Illusion*, of course. The film offers a superb example of Renoir's subtle direction of actors, with a cast fully capable of exploiting the extraordinary freedom and artistic responsibility given them. In terms of cinematography, it is less obviously and spectacularly concerned with camera movement and composition in depth than the director's two previous films, but its remarkable uses of such cinematic resources are more readily satisfying for being better integrated with the flow of narrative. However, this sense of stylistic rightness, which brings the film rather close in style and feel to classic Hollywood cinema, might make its political and ideological confusions all the more troublesome, because the fictional world and its representation seem so effortlessly coherent and natural.

It is possible that the *La Grande Illusion* Renoir unconsciously expressed his growing ambivalence about Left political themes, an ambivalence which was soon to approach outright rejection. But he conceived one last work in apparent harmony with the Popular Front, the historical epic *La Marseillaise* (1938). The most characteristically "frontist" aspect of this film was its initial method of financing—by popular subscription. By paying two francs in advance, future spectators (mainly members of Communist-dominated unions) became shareholders in the production and were to get a discount on the price of admission (though not, as sometimes reported, a portion of the profits). Unfortunately, the subscription did not raise enough capital, and the project was completed by conventional financing. *La Marseillaise* takes a curiously non-Communist, non-Socialist view of the French Revolution, which is seen alternately from the point of view of the court of Louis XVI and that of a batallion of revolutionary soldiers from Marseilles. The major Left idea in the film is that the court is fatally out of step with the progress of History, while the ragtag soldiers embody the rising force of the new Nation. But like *La Grande Illusion, La Marseillaise* treats the doomed reactionary group with great sympathy, finding implicit tragedy in the fact that members of the ruling class continue to play roles that have no meaning in the new historical context.

La Marseillaise examines a period in which French history made fundamental sense for Renoir. When he lost faith in his own day's historical process, after the fall of the first Popular Front government and with the growing threat of war, he also lost most of his sympathy for the contemporary descendants of both the Revolution's doomed aristocrats and their less privileged opponents. In *La Règle du jeu* (*Rules of the Game*, 1939), he would vehemently reject the studied optimism of his Popular Front films. But the cynical, nihilistic tone of his last, great prewar work, which in many ways brought him full circle back to the attitudes of *La Chienne,* did not manifest itself immediately after the demise of the unified Left. For a time Renoir still believed in political happy endings. He did, however, change course artistically, a move which must be read as his way of declaring provisional independence from his political allies. In 1938, he made his only contribution to a type of filmmaking reviled by 1930s Communists and fellow travelers (including himself just a few months earlier): poetic realism.

◼ Few labels in French film history are as vexing as *réalisme poétique.* It is arguably not a school, at least not to the extent that cinematic impressionism was. Nor is it a genre, yet it is something more than a style. Historians and critics do not even agree on a basic list of films to which it applies.[15] Some writers consider it an attribute of all French cinema of the 1930s, while others only use it in connection with certain films directed by Marcel Carné, Jean Grémillon, Julien Duvivier, Pierre Chenal, and perhaps Jacques Feyder (and written by

Jacques Prévert, Charles Spaak, Marcel Aymé, Marcel Achard, and a few others). One thing is certain: there would have been far less acrimonious debate about this trend in filmmaking had it not been for the enormous popular and (except on the extreme Left and Right) critical success of one work, Marcel Carné and Jacques Prévert's *Quai des brumes/Port of Shadows* (1938). That film, along with the same team's *Le Jour se lève (Daybreak*, 1939), would even be accused, during the Occupation, of contributing to the fall of France by their supposedly demoralizing themes and atmosphere. If Carné and Prévert did not create *réalisme poétique* (the label was first applied to cinema five years before *Quai des brumes*), their works nonetheless came to symbolize the trend, both for its detractors and admirers.

Marcel Carné was born in 1906 in the Batignolles neighborhood on the outer rim of Paris, where his father was a moderately prosperous cabinetmaker. His father's trade gave the family more money than many petty bourgeois households earned—André Antoine and Marcel Pagnol's families come to mind—but in this upper layer of the working class social advancement and education were not obsessions. Young Marcel received a primary school certificate and then was expected to learn woodworking and set up his own shop with money from the family. He thus had one of the shortest formal educations of all major French filmmakers, and it is clear from his memoirs that he always identified himself with the lower rather than middle classes. Carné's mother died when the boy was five, and he was raised by his grandmother and aunt; his father did not remarry but kept a series of mistresses. This unsettled family situation, and the fact that he was an only child, doubtless contributed to the boy's strong feelings of self-sufficiency and solitude. He was short, not particularly good-looking, and painfully aware of being different from other children, but he did not withdraw from human contact. He learned how to amuse and interest others, and like so many fundamentally lonely children he dreamed of becoming an entertainer. Cinema and music hall both fascinated him. Woodworking did not, and he abandoned it in his teens in favor of a series of menial jobs which gave him the means to attend films and spectacles, though he often had to return home across the capital on foot.

When Carné was twenty-one, some friends who knew of his love of cinema and his admiration for the work of Jacques Feyder introduced him to the director's wife, Françoise Rosay. Rosay was charmed by the young man and arranged an interview with Feyder, who engaged him as second assistant director on *Les Nouveaux Messieurs*. Carné learned as much as he could from the job, staying on as an unpaid participant in the film's editing and walking home across Paris late at night when work was done. (One thing Carné and Prévert had in common was a love of nocturnal excursions in the capital, often in disreputable neighborhoods.)[16] When Feyder left France to work for MGM, Carné found work as an assistant director, then as a film critic and journalist. With his modest income, he bought a newsreel camera and made a short documentary film which was well received in the art house and ciné-club circuit.

When the Feyders returned from the United States, Carné worked as assistant director on *Le Grand Jeu, Pension Mimosas,* and *La Kermesse héroïque.* These films made Françoise Rosay an important French movie star, and when she offered to act in a film under Carné's direction, he had little trouble interesting a small independent producer in the project on the basis of her participation alone. Like most inexperienced directors, however, he was obliged to accept subject matter which he found rather unpromising, in this case a sensationalistic pop novel called *Prison de velours (The Velour Prison)*. As a Communist sympathizer, Carné had attended many Party cultural events, and he had been much impressed by the October Group's play *La Bataille de Fontenoy.* He thought its author could help infuse some artistic life, and above all some striking dialogue, into his film's melodramatic story line. Jacques Prévert agreed to work on the project, apparently more to earn money and industry recognition than out of any hope of artistic achievement. The film *Jenny* (1936) did not entirely escape the pedestrian, slumming bourgeois voyeurism of the original novel, *Prison de velours,* but Carné and Prévert did succeed in creating some remarkable actors' set pieces (particularly among the secondary characters) and atmospheric effects (for example, nocturnal steam and smoke obscuring Rosay as she walks slowly above unseen railroad tracks).

Jenny was well enough received by the public and the critics that another independent producer (with extensive Left connections) agreed to back the two men in a second work. Prévert proposed an original story about a juvenile detention camp, but Carné, worried by the unfortunate precedent of Vigo's *Zéro de conduite,* took the then unusual step of submitting the treatment for advance examination by government censors. Told that any such film would face outright suppression, Carné and Prévert cast about for another project. Their producer already owned the rights to an obscure English detective novel, which the two men used as the slender pretext for one of the strangest (and funniest) French comedies of the 1930s. *Drôle de drame/Bizarre, Bizarre* (1937) is set in an imaginary England populated by upper-crust eccentrics speaking deadpan Prevértian non sequiturs. This surreal farce has nothing whatever to do with poetic realism, though it does strongly recall the humor and irreverence of *L'Affaire est dans le sac.* Barthélemy Amengual has argued that *Drôle de drame* marks the last appearance in cinema of Jacques Prévert's "brutal, sarcastic, destructive" spirit of his October Group period, and that his subsequent films became more somber and "realist."[17] Prévert was certainly as sensitive to the increasingly pessimistic spirit of the late 1930s as was Jean Renoir, and doubtless this was one reason for the shift in mood of his scripts. But the poet and his partner also had had a clear demonstration of what would sell and what would not: whereas *Jenny* made a reasonable profit, *Drôle de drame* was one of the true commercial disasters of the decade, despite a brilliant cast and witty script. When the team made their next film, it was very much a return to the spirit of *Jenny.*

After losing his backer's capital so completely, Carné had little hope of soon directing another film, but one important spectator had liked *Drôle de drame* very much. Raoul Ploquin, UFA's head of French-language productions, asked Carné for suggestions for a Jean Gabin vehicle to follow up on the success of Grémillon's *Gueule d'amour.* The director proposed Pierre Mac Orlan's novel *Quai des brumes.* Gabin liked the idea, and Ploquin bought the rights to the book and signed contracts with Carné and Prévert.[18] But the German studio rejected the scenario, quite prophetically, as "decadent" and "negative," and Ploquin was obliged to sell the package to an independent French producer. *Quai des brumes* was finally more faithful to Mac Orlan's novel in spirit than in its story or setting (the novel is set in Montmartre at the turn of the century, the film in Le Havre in a vaguely defined present). Its doomed, socially marginal characters move through a world of darkness and mist.

Simone de Beauvoir recalled this work as one of the few French films of the decade that she and Jean-Paul Sartre admired, and she praised its "fog of despair enveloping the entire film." Such despair was doubtless attractive to Beauvoir and Sartre because, like so many intellectuals of the period, they "were still not actively *for* anything. This struck us as quite reasonable, since in our opinion . . . the world

Jean Gabin, as an army deserter about to leave France on a dead man's pass-port, plays one of his all-but-obligatory (in the late 1930s) scenes of violent death in *Quai des brumes.*

and humanity were still to be created anew."[19] But the Communist party and its allies felt that the world was, in fact, *already* being created anew, by them. Thus they were violently opposed to a film like *Quai des brumes,* despite its careful identification with the aspirations of the downtrodden. Unlike the workers in *Le Crime de Monsieur Lange,* Jean Gabin's doomed deserter cannot assume control of his destiny, which follows him inexorably, like the little dog he befriends at the film's beginning.

When Jean Renoir chose to film *La Bête humaine* (*The Human Beast,* 1938) as his own essay in poetic realism, he was careful to convey a sense that some lower-class characters could take control of their des-tinies. In his very free adaptation of Emile Zola's novel, the director surrounded his tragic hero Jacques Lantier (Jean Gabin), a train engi-neer doomed to homicidal fits by his tainted heredity, with healthier friends and coworkers—a radical departure from the original work's vision of working-class frustration and violence. In one scene, Lantier and his fireman share their food and make a complete meal out of individually inadequate provisions, in an allegory of mutual support quite contrary to the spirit of the novel but wholly in keeping with the (rapidly fading) ideals of the Popular Front. Renoir shot much of the film in real locations (Carné preferred to work in the studio), giving large sections of *La Bête humaine* a documentary feel rather at odds with the film's stylized, darkly expressionist scenes of madness and murder. Perhaps Renoir, like many later commentators, found crippling artistic and political contradictions in his one exercise in poetic realism. In any event, he never again experimented with the film's curious but fascinating mixture of styles and ideas.

Marcel Carné, meanwhile, went from *Quai des brumes* to a rather similar project, *Hôtel du Nord* (1938, very freely after Eugène Dabit), a film about the mostly down-and-out residents of a hotel in a working-class Parisian neighborhood. Prévert was unavailable for the project, so the director worked first with Jean Aurenche and then with Henri Jeanson (both strong Left sympathizers) on the scenario. Originally the film was to have been a vehicle for Annabella, one of the decade's most popular stars, but the finished work gave most of its good lines and dramatic opportunities to a little-known actress the director had admired in a secondary role in Feyder's *Pension Mimosas*. Carné rarely succeeded in star-making, despite numerous attempts throughout his career, but Arletty is the major, brilliant exception. With her tinny, nasal voice, strong working-class accent, oddly attractive face, and great street-wise vitality, she could have only emerged as a star from a cinematic universe centered on the socially dispossessed. She was the last major addition to Carné's team of favorite collaborators, which aside from Prévert also included set designer Alexandre Trauner and composers Joseph Kosma and Maurice Jaubert. But though his films were very much the product of team effort, it is clear that Carné was always the guiding spirit. If Prévert's absence from *Hôtel du Nord* arguably leaves the film uneven in dialogue and dramatic progression, its fictional world is palpably related to the director's other serious films of the decade.

Prévert, who had been visiting the United States, returned to work on Carné's last prewar film, *Le Jour se lève*, based on an original story idea by Jacques Viot. Viot had conceived a tale told almost entirely in flashback; this structure gives visible, experiential form to the film's theme of implacable destiny. The opening sequence depicts the end of the story: a flashily dressed man dies of a gunshot wound on an apartment house staircase; his killer, played by Jean Gabin, retreats into his top-floor room where he is besieged by police and virtually certain to die—at least for the spectator aware of Gabin's previous roles. The rest of the film, narrated in flashback, tells how this came about. *Le Jour se lève* shows in the clearest manner the gist of Carné's endeavor in all of his poetic realist works: to create a proletarian tragedy, as contradictory a notion as this might seem at first glance (since tragedy traditionally strikes high-born characters). *Le Jour se lève* takes as its tragic hero an unschooled sandblaster who was raised in an orphanage. Allen Thiher argues that the protagonist's tragic flaw is "that he entertains the illusion that he might liberate himself from the daily oppression that binds him to his machine. His flaw would be quite simply his blindness to his true condition."[20] Another, less metaphysical reading would be that the Gabin character's flaw is jealousy, and that the filmmakers were already thinking about Shakespeare's *Othello*—which would be a major reference in their *Les Enfants du paradis* (*Children of Paradise*, 1943–44/45). In this reading, the murdered man (played by Jules Berry) is a vaudevillian Iago whose final scheme is to be killed by the man he hates, bringing down upon the hero the wrath of the avenging State.

The major works of poetic realism all sought in one way or another to find a tragic dimension in the lives of the socially marginal. In many of them, as Thiher argues for *Le Jour se lève*, the characters' tragic flaws may be seen as unwitting internalizations of their social conditions. In this light, "populist tragedy" might serve as a better label for the tendency, but *réalisme poétique* is not as inappropriate as some historians have argued. Realism, in one important (though now outdated) French meaning of the word, denotes a concern for the often violent lives of the lower classes (as witness the music hall *chanson réaliste*, in which a prostitute or kept woman laments her brutal lot in life). And poetic(s) can designate, as it did for Aristotle, tragic drama. But beyond the goal of finding the tragic dimension of lives limited by social and economic circumstances, the endeavor could be more or less overtly political in emphasis, and it did not always imply a left-wing perspective. Jacques Feyder, whose *Pension Mimosas* probably provided an important model for Carné's work, was anything but a leftist, and the moral destruction of his petty bourgeois heroine in that film is treated with subtle but corrosive irony.

The political vicissitudes and ambiguities of poetic realism emerge perhaps most strikingly in two works directed by Julien Duvivier. *Pépé le Moko* (1936, written by Henri Jeanson), while completely sympathetic to its socially alienated protagonist, displaces class conflict onto questions of race and sexuality. Jean Gabin plays a French gangster hiding from the police inside the Casbah in Algiers, much as his character in *Le Jour se lève* would be trapped in a room at the top of a suburban apartment building. In each case geography assumes symbolic weight, but in Carné's work Gabin is placed as a kind of terribly isolated, elevated ruler of the working class neighborhood he surveys (his "subjects" call up to him in pity and terror, but he does not listen). Duvivier and Jeanson's Casbah, on the other hand, implicitly makes the Arabs who shelter Pépé function as his jailors. As in so many other Duvivier films, the real danger for the virile, independent male is love, and Pépé dies in the end for a kept woman who remains unaware of his sacrifice. Sex, not social class, is the cause of his downfall.

Duvivier also directed the poetic realist film most overtly opposed to the ideals of the Popular Front: *La Belle Equipe/They Were Five* (1936). Often mischaracterized as "frontist" in spirit, *La Belle Equipe*, like *Le Crime de Monsieur Lange*, concerns a workers' cooperative, but there the resemblance ends. In Charles Spaak's original scenario, five friends win a large sum of money in the lottery and decide to build and operate a working-class dance hall and restaurant on the outskirts of Paris. But the dream quickly begins to go sour. One of the team is killed in a construction accident; another, an Italian, must leave the country because of new immigration laws. Soon there are only two men left, both in love with the same *femme fatale*. One of them (played, inevitably, by Jean Gabin) kills the other in a fit of jealous rage. This conclusion was quite badly received by nonbourgeois audiences, and a new ending was devised in which the two men reject the meddling, dangerous female and salvage the project. Even in this modified version, there is little of the joyous sense of proletarian solidarity that pervades *Le Crime de Monsieur Lange,* and the happy end rings hollow in comparison to the gloom and doom that precedes it, a sudden and arbitrary burst of light and animation in a world of darkness and stifled anger.

La Belle Equipe did not, however, become a truly scandalous film in the manner of *Quai des brumes* (which Jean Renoir and others renamed, in an obscene pun, *Cul des brèmes*, calling it a "fascist film"). The marked contrast in reactions to the two works almost certainly stemmed more from the argumentative, divisive mood on the Left in 1938 (year of *Quai des brumes*), as opposed to the heady optimism of

1936 (year of *La Belle Equipe*) than from Duvivier and Carné's politics or from the ideologies implicit in their films. It probably also mattered that Duvivier was a quintessential film industry insider by the late 1930s, while Carné was still a relative outsider. In raging against *Quai des brumes*, frustrated revolutionaries could vent their anger at the Left's increasingly apparent lack of unity without endangering their careers. That their discontents sounded in unison with those of the far Right was, apparently, an irony which they did not choose to notice.

Poetic realist films followed the lives of economically disadvantaged outsiders, and they were typically the work of other sorts of outsiders. One important reason for the contempt that many of these films inspired in some quarters was probably that their directors either did not come from the bourgeoisie, or were not born in France, or had unpopular Left politics or unconventional sexual orientations (and in some cases, two or more of the above). It is therefore perhaps surprising that only one of the major figures of the trend was a Jew, an outsider *par excellence* in the increasingly anti-Semitic atmosphere of prewar France. Pierre Chenal also had the dubious distinction of being the major filmmaker of the decade most thoroughly forgotten by the film community after World War II, for reasons from which prejudice may not, perhaps, be completely excluded. He saw his reputation and professional opportunities decline abruptly in the 1940s and 1950s, to the point that even his major works of the 1930s disappeared from many histories of French cinema. Today, however, his reputation is belatedly being reestablished, his films screened and discussed anew.

Chenal was born Philippe Cohen in 1904 in Brussels, Belgium, though he studied for his *baccalauréat* in Paris at the Lycée Buffon, where a classmate and good friend was the future cinema historian Jean Mitry. He studied chemistry at the Ecole Centrale des Arts et Métiers, and on graduation he seemed poised for the kind of respectable career that the school's students typically found at middle management levels in private industry. According to Mitry, Chenal soon left his job in a small chemical factory for health reasons, but one may speculate that consciously or unconsciously the young man effectively rejected the social and economic limitations of his situation. Certainly he fared far better in the cinema, at least until the war. He began by designing film posters and also made, at first collaborating with Mitry, a series of documentary short subjects.

Chenal's entry into fiction filmmaking came when he replaced, on short notice, the original director of a bizarre exploitation comedy, *Le Martyre de l'obèse* (*The Martyr of Obesity*, 1932). Having proved his competence at directing, he obtained financing for an adaptation of Marcel Aymé's populist novel *La Rue sans nom* (*Street without a Name*, 1933), the film which established his position as one of the industry's most promising newcomers. Michel Gorel, writing in *Cinémonde*, first applied the formula "poetic realism" to the cinema in reviewing *La Rue sans nom*, commenting that Chenal's most beautiful scenes "are perhaps those in which the characters, who are being worn down bit by bit, like the stones of the hovels in which they live, attempt to escape, some by love, others by wine, by adventure, or revolt, or finally, like the timid and pitiful Jouhanieu, in a long, ecstatic dream."[21]

Though in this film Chenal broke ground for the later works of Carné, Duvivier, and others, he did not remain wedded to poetic realism, or at least not to any single, static version of it. To judge by the stories he chose to film, he was as fascinated by violence and murder as was Jean Renoir, though his cinematic style had a much wider range than Renoir's, depending on his scripts. He followed in the impressionist footsteps of Marcel L'Herbier in adapting Pirandello's *The Late Mathias Pascal*, as *L'Homme de nulle part* (*The Man from Nowhere*, 1937, filmed in Italy). He made a German expressionist-style Dostoyevsky adaptation, *Crime et châtiment* (*Crime and Punishment*, 1935, dialogue by Marcel Aymé) in which he used set design, lighting, a breathtakingly mobile camera, and voice-over monologues to evoke a tormented consciousness at the breaking point. In adapting James M. Cain's *The Postman Always Rings Twice*, as *Le Dernier Tournant* (*The Last Turning*, 1939, dialogue by Charles Spaak), he shot extensively on location, in another French adumbration (along with Renoir's *Toni* and most of Pagnol's work) of postwar Neorealism. In *L'Alibi* (*The Alibi*, 1938, scenario by Marcel Achard), which stylistically and thematically is the closest of his films to the work of Carné and Prévert, he all but abandoned his habitual moving camera, while multiplying (studio shot) expressionistic effects of lighting and composition.

Chenal is hard to evaluate or classify because of his great versatility and because his work has, for the moment, received comparatively little serious study. His sudden loss of standing in the industry and in the eyes of postwar critics and historians is not unique, except in its extent: Carné and Duvivier suffered similarly negative reevaluations.

But Chenal appears to have become the principal sacrificial victim of the later period's rejection of the brooding, angry pessimism of *réalisme poetique* and its ultimately unpleasant, implicitly political message: that for the most wretched of the earth (those, precisely, with greatest need of a redeeming transcendence) nothing of any value can be done, no change effected at this time, in this world. They can only die, or come to accept their prisons.

IV

A New Kind of Cinema

❧ 10 ❧

War and Occupation

By mid-1939 the mood of even the most uninvolved and apolitical French citizens had turned morbidly pessimistic. After a brief flurry of optimism in the wake of the previous year's Munich Pact, men and women across the land, from the inner circles of government to the small farms and villages of the tranquil provinces, had concluded that war could probably not be avoided, as Germany simply ignored the Pact and continued its bellicose behavior. Little was left of the confident chauvinism that had characterized the public mood before the Great War—no talk of a conflict lasting only a few weeks, or months, nor any upbeat predictions of certain victory. The French were frightened, divided, and already arguing over who was to blame for their plight. Most films of the period resolutely ignored such sentiments, offering their audiences a refuge rather than a mirror of actuality.

But a few filmmakers tried to respond to and shape viewers' political sentiments. Raymond Bernard's *Les Otages* (*The Hostages*, 1939) tells the story of a group of French bourgeois in World War I who are to be executed in reprisal for the murder of a German officer. The men forget their many quarrels in the face of this danger, but when a French army advance liberates them, their conflicts reappear. Edmond T. Gréville's *Menaces* (*Threats*, 1939) is set in a kind of Hôtel du Nord for anti-fascist émigrés. Its residents pointedly agree that they must respect French hospitality and work for the country that has given them refuge. One of the refugees, an Austrian scientist (Erich von Stroheim), commits suicide when his request for French citizenship is refused; his body is discovered in the midst of frantic popular celebration of the Munich Pact, and its short-lived promise of peace.

Menaces bathes in the cinematic ambiance of *réalisme poetique* and the last remnants of the Popular Front's moral fervor. *Les Otages*, both stylistically and in its potential historical parallels (everyone knew that the German soldiers might come again), anticipates the more composed and ordered allegorical cinema of the Occupation. In both of these works solidarity in the face of danger can offer endangered groups at least some measure of hope. But the most notorious cinematic reaction to the situation of prewar French society, written and directed by Jean Renoir, offered no such comforting optimism. Many modern critics consider *La Règle du jeu* (*Rules of the Game*, 1939) to be the director's masterpiece, both stylistically—as the apotheosis of his 1930s film style—and morally. But in the year of its release the film was a terrible commercial and critical failure, despite the director's many attempts to salvage it.

La Règle du jeu is an often frantic sex comedy which culminates not in a marriage or remarriage, but in a murder. The film's mixture of genres (comedies don't normally end this way, even unhappy ones) was probably less disturbing to audiences than was its pointed social commentary. As in *La Grande Illusion*, Marcel Dalio again plays a privileged Jew, this time no different from the other characters except perhaps more polished and polite. The film is relentlessly anti-bourgeois, almost in the manner of early Prévert: a hypochondriacal woman continually babbles on about her husband's factory and believes that pre-Columbian art is "that stuff about black people" (*des histoires de nègres*). The military is represented by an old general, who at the film's end mistakenly concludes that his host has cold-bloodedly ordered the execution of his wife's lover and happily approves the deed. As in *Menaces*, displaced persons and outsiders are the most sympathetic characters. The least likeable figure is an Alsacian (read: German) gamekeeper who mouths fascist slogans.

It is difficult today not to see *La Règle du jeu* as a despairing, prophetic evaluation of French society in the last sad days of the Third Republic, and as a prediction of the debacle to come. In late August Germany and the U.S.S.R. announced the signing of a Nonaggression Pact, having secretly agreed to the partition of Poland. French military units were mobilized for the third time in less than a year. On September 1 the German army invaded Poland, and two days later France and Great Britain declared war. The allies, however, were ill prepared for the conflict and adopted a passive, defensive strategy.

French and British troops remained behind the supposedly impregnable Maginot Line, waiting to be attacked. The wait lasted just over six months, in what was called a *drôle de guerre,* or "phony war." Suddenly, on May 10, 1940, German forces simply bypassed the Maginot Line and began moving on France through the Low Countries. Little more than a month later, near the end of one of the great military routs of modern history, the Germans took control of the French capital, the government having fled in panic along with most of the city's population. In late June an armistice agreement was negotiated; France thereby undertook to cease all hostilities towards Germany but remained neutral in the continuing war with Great Britain.

Under the armistice terms France was partitioned by a line of demarcation which separated the occupied North and West from an Unoccupied Zone composed of roughly two-fifths of the country, economically and militarily its least significant region. The small southern resort town of Vichy became the political capital of what was, in effect, a new German satellite state. The legislature of the Third Republic had in effect voted itself and the constitution under which it operated out of existence, conferring almost absolute power on one man, Philippe Pétain, the last surviving Marshal of the victorious French army of the Great War. Though this choice had indisputable symbolic appeal, its consequences were to prove disastrous. Pétain was in his eighties, possibly senile, and definitely leaned to the extreme Right. He aspired to be the strong leader he and others thought France had lacked under the often chaotic republic, but in reality he was weak and easily influenced by others, and in retrospect shockingly willing to do the Nazis' bidding even before they formulated their desires. Much of the population had streamed South into the "free" zone, only to find that everything from civil liberties to economic activity was actually much freer in the occupied North. Pétain, following the advice of the home-grown fascist ideologues among the few notable citizens willing to join his puppet regime, called for collective sacrifice in the service of a purifying, authoritarian National Revolution. The new order's motto was *Travail, Famille, Patrie* ("Work, Family, Fatherland"), replacing the older, supposedly discredited *Liberté, Egalité, Fraternité.*

■ The outbreak of war, even a phony one, had brought French film production, along with all other nonessential industries, to a halt. But the government, divided and ineffectual as it was in the months before the debacle, had learned the lesson of the First World War's disastrous effect on the nation's cinema. Very soon filmmaking activity was allowed to resume; actors, directors, and technicians returned from the front to complete some films (such as Ophuls's *De Mayerling à Sarajevo*) and to start work on others. Producers were understandably reluctant to embark on complicated or costly projects, given the uncertainties of wartime production, but enough work was completed to supply, with the help of American and other imports, badly needed films to stock the newly reopened theatres and hastily improvised facilities at the front. The German army's brutal advance brought an abrupt end to this brief, tentative reestablishment of the industry. Few creative artists and technicians were killed in the brief conflict (the most important casualty was the composer Maurice Jaubert), though a number were among the many French prisoners of war. Most of the rest, both in and out of uniform, fled to the supposed safety of the Unoccupied Zone.

Thus at the beginning of the Occupation the French cinema was disastrously divided: production facilities and capital in the North, personnel in the South. Transporting people, equipment, and even bank credits across the line of demarcation in either direction was extremely difficult. Almost the only producer in a position to work on a film was Marcel Pagnol, who had his studio, actors, technicians, and bank accounts all in the Marseilles region. Production on his *La Fille du puisatier (The Well Digger's Daughter,* 1940) had begun during the German advance, was halted, and restarted less than a month after the armistice with only small changes in cast and crew. The film is vintage Pagnol, with a proud father (Raimu) who disowns his pregnant daughter until her lover, presumed lost in the fighting, returns and marries her. *La Fille du puisatier* was not entirely unaffected by its historical context, however. It is noticeably more somber and slow-paced than the director's earlier works, and he added to his original script a sequence (cut from many modern prints) in which the characters listen to Marshal Pétain's radio broadcast calling for an end to French participation in the war.

It was not merely geography that had made of Marcel Pagnol a happy exception among French filmmakers in late 1940. Even before the war, the industry was in such a sorry state that Pagnol's modest operation (which produced or coproduced only ten films during the 1930s) was one of the country's most stable and successful production companies. The once powerful Pathé and Gaumont organizations had been in receivership since the mid-1930s, and most films were produced by unstable ad-hoc companies, some of which did not survive even until their first project's release. One of the industry's greatest problems had been obtaining financing at a reasonable cost. One observer estimated that in the 1937–38 season 75 percent of French films were financed by English banks and insurance companies, whose interest rates were much higher than those charged by domestic lenders.[1] There had been heated debate throughout the decade (and two major government studies) about what could be done to stabilize the industry, but the film community was the victim both of parliamentary indecisiveness and of its own divisions, principally the rifts between foreign and domestic producers and between management and labor. All the talk produced little action, however.

By the end of the decade a rough consensus had emerged on how to revive the industry, spurred by a program formulated by Education Minister Jean Zay: the government would regulate and facilitate film financing arrangements, start a national cinema school, institute controls of box-office revenues, reduce the onerous taxes on cinema admissions, and work to exclude the many shady operators from the profession. Watered-down versions of some of these proposals were enacted into law just before the war, but much remained to be done. The cinema thus offered the new Vichy government a privileged arena in which to demonstrate the virtues of the National Revolution; quick, decisive action was possible thanks (ironically) to the careful work of Zay and other technocrats of the hated Third Republic. But Vichy was unremittingly hostile to direct government involvement, preferring corporatist arrangements that empowered the strongest elements in a given industry to regulate and organize matters ranging from pricing and allocation of scarce resources to labor relations and wages.

The vehicles for this oligarchical self-regulation were called *comités d'organisation;* their structure and powers were set by government decree, and their operations overseen by ministers who could veto their decisions and remove uncooperative officers if necessary. The Comité d'Organisation de l'Industrie Cinématographique (Organization Committee for the Cinema Industry), or C.O.I.C., was one of the first such entities created by Vichy, assuming its powers in December of 1940. The former UFA producer Raoul Ploquin, who had excellent contacts with German film interests (though he was no fascist) was appointed its first director. Governmental oversight was in the hands of a first-rate technocrat, Guy de Carmoy, author of an influential 1936 government report on the industry's problems.

Carmoy accepted the position as head of the Service du Cinéma, an office which predated the Vichy regime, despite his strong opposition to collaborating with the Germans. He played what proved to be a dangerous double game and was eventually arrested and deported to a prison camp for his work with the Resistance. His successor in the office, Louis-Emile Galey, held similar views and, like Carmoy, had worked for Léon Blum's 1936 Popular Front government. He too ended up being arrested, though only briefly, by the German authorities. Both men had excellent relations with the film community; their appointments by Pétain's government demonstrate the regime's occasional willingness to value organizational competence and harmony with the regulated industry over ideological purity, for there was no dearth of aspiring right-wing candidates for the post. Had a confrontational ideologue such as Robert Brasillach been appointed, French film history would have been very different indeed, and the great masterpieces of Occupation cinema would presumably not have been made, at least not in the rather surprising form and tone which they assumed. Filmmaking during the Occupation depended on a fragile, almost miraculous consensus within the film community, for which de Carmoy and Galey were in large measure ultimately responsible. Thus although the Third Republic was officially dead, its spirit seemed to live on in this one crucial area of government activity.

It is no exaggeration to say that C.O.I.C. (pronounced "co-eek," though its detractors called it "coo-ack," the sound a duck makes), with the support and direction of the Service du Cinéma, rescued the French film industry from near-collapse. The major problems of the previous decade were quickly and efficiently corrected. Perhaps the greatest difficulty had been that most films simply could not earn enough money to pay back their costs, much less turn a profit, because of ruinous competition in production (too many films for the small French market) and exhibition (double-feature presentations cut individual film revenues in half). C.O.I.C. established yearly quotas for feature films (set at roughly half the prewar rate of production); it prohibited double-feature exhibition and established other quotas to insure the correct number of short subjects necessary to complete the exhibitors' programs. (This policy also helped assure that enough film stock, which was in very short supply, could be had for each production.) Film revenues had also been low because of widespread cheating by exhibitors; a system of numbered tickets and unannounced audits and inspections of theatres assured that producers got the share of box office receipts to which they were entitled. The previous decade's problems of film financing were addressed by a new system: producers first had to prove that they possessed at least 35 percent of a work's projected budget; then, on C.O.I.C.'s approval, they could borrow the remainder from the Crédit National at the extremely reasonable rate (in an inflationary financial environment) of 5¼ percent interest.

As a result of these reforms, almost any project allowed to go into production (based on C.O.I.C.'s evaluation of its scenario, budget, and of the filmmakers' credentials) not only was certain be completed but was virtually guaranteed to make money. Though the system undoubtedly restricted French filmmakers' creative freedom and subtly contributed to the more uniform, controlled style that would mark the period, it is clear that the first priority of the entire film industry was financial survival, and that this goal was achieved to an extent that greatly surpassed most observers' expectations. Other reforms, however, had less to do with the industry's problems than with the Vichy ideological agenda. Most crucially, C.O.I.C. implemented a new law requiring that anyone working in the cinema had to obtain a "professional identity card." The regulators' notion of identity, however, was not exclusively professional: each applicant had to prove, among other qualifications, that he or she was not a Jew.

Immediately barred from the profession were hundreds of people, from carpenters and negative-cutters to major stars and influential producers such as Alexander Kamenka, Pierre Braunberger, and Jacques Natanson. Some of them had not waited for official measures of repression and were already bound for artistic exile and, typically, underemployment in Hollywood (Marcel Dalio, Max Ophuls, and many others) or elsewhere (Pierre Chenal went to South America, Jean Bénoît-Lévy to New York City, where he taught at the New School for Social Research). But many remained, sharing the shaky but real confidence of the French Jewish community that their country would not abandon them. This trust was misplaced, however. Vichy's anti-Semitic measures multiplied well before the German authorities requested such actions. Hiding in the Unoccupied Zone, the composer Joseph Kosma and the production designer Alexandre Trauner were lodged and supported by Jacques Prévert and his friends, an arrangement that was far from rare. Raymond Bernard, along with many others who had fled the capital, became an early member of the Resistance; his brother Jean-Jacques, who did not go into hiding, would later be in the first group of French Jews whose deportation to concentration camps was planned and carried out by their own government.

The application of Vichy's anti-Semitic laws to the cinema industry placed non-Jewish members of the film community in a difficult moral position, to say the least. There had previously been relatively little anti-Semitism within the industry; the few isolated examples of prejudice in the late 1930s had tended to single out nonassimilated, foreign-born Jews—more the expression of traditional French disdain for other cultures than any specific racial scapegoating. Suddenly, former friends, rivals, and coworkers were excluded from the film community by an externally imposed fiat. There were, for the moment, few hints of the terrible form that anti-Semitism would assume later in the Occupation, but from the very beginning working in the cinema industry meant accepting a privileged status (being of Aryan origins) grounded in a doctrine that few embraced and that many, particularly on the Left, vehemently rejected. Some filmmakers made their own pact with the devil by working in the industry while giving what help they could to their excluded former colleagues: money, shelter, even work on some film productions under pseudonyms.

Those who would not or could not resist the new laws, and they were presumably the majority (money and shelter were scarce, and helping Jews in any way was potentially dangerous), chose—virtually without exception—not to denounce those who did resist.[2] This collective refusal to inform is more remarkable than it might at first appear, for such denunciations, often anonymous and made for personal gain or to settle old scores, were widespread in other sectors of French society. Thus Jean-Paul Le Chanois, whose real surname of Dreyfus was common knowledge, worked undisturbed and in the open as scriptwriter on six films and codirector of another during the period.[3] A similar sort of collective, passive resistance to the Vichy and German campaign against Jews emerged in the area of film content. With a few, rare exceptions, and only one of them in a fiction feature production, the cinema of the Occupation studiously avoided the anti-Semitic stereotypes which were so abundant in other media of the period and which, as François Garçon has demonstrated, could sometimes be found in French films of the late 1930s.[4]

The moral question arises whether the film community's general refusal to encourage religious prejudice, or to inform on those who actively resisted the occupiers and their French agents, constituted a form of resistance in and of itself. One can argue, on the one hand, that these refusals were merely a form of compensatory behavior, a way of lessening the discomfort of having accepted and profited from measures against the Jews, whose absence from the industry made it easier for others to work and to advance in their profession. On the other hand, the most effective, and (elsewhere in French society) widespread way of justifying such privilege was to accept the Nazi definition of the Jew as an undesirable who did not *deserve* to work. And this is precisely what the overwhelming majority of fiction film-makers refused to do.

Within the film community, the wide range of responses to the moral dilemmas of the Occupation makes it difficult to draw any firm, unambiguous line of demarcation between heroes and villains (or dupes). The situation was very different for a Guy de Carmoy, an active supporter of the Resistance, than for a Marcel Carné, who at much less risk gave jobs to old friends in defiance of the ban on Jewish filmmakers. Many others did neither, but they also did not send anonymous letters to Gestapo headquarters in Paris nor include anti-Semitic propaganda in their films. Outside of the industry, particularly in radio and print journalism, standards of conduct were, sadly, much lower. If, after the Liberation, relatively few filmmakers could truthfully boast of heroic exploits during the Occupation, the industry as a whole could find a measure of justification—however limited it might seem in retrospect—in having collectively refused to embrace the madness which surrounded it.

▨ Pagnol's *La Fille du puisatier* was quickly followed by other French productions in the South, but not by any in the North, for the occupying military authorities at first refused to allow Parisian studios to be used for any activity except the French dubbing of German films. Furthermore, films made in the Unoccupied Zone were not allowed across the line of demarcation. The only option immediately open to French producers was to make films in the South in the hope that the Germans would later allow these works to be screened in the larger northern market—as they eventually did. Out of the approximately 220 French fiction feature films made during the Occupation, roughly 35 were made in the free zone before it ceased to exist in late 1942.[5] With the exception of Pagnol's film, these works are generally considered to be of little interest today, particularly compared to the great films made later from the industry's reestablished base in the capital. One reason for the general weakness of this Vichy cinema was the region's inadequate studio space and technical facilities. But a more important factor was the Vichy government itself, which considered the cinema to be of great importance in winning the hearts and minds of the French public.

The Pétain regime directly commissioned some films and exercised considerable control over the other works produced in the Unoccupied Zone by means of preproduction censorship. In large measure it managed to create a cinema in its own image, which emphasized favored Vichy themes such as the corruption of city life and the need to return to the land; respect for authority (which is to say, for patriarchy, with the Marshall as the ultimate father figure); and the sacred nature of the family, with divorce a kind of ultimate social evil. Because of the limited number of films available for exhibition, and thanks to the participation of established stars such as Fernandel and Viviane Romance, these works often made a great deal of money, though they found little favor with critics and industry observers outside the Vichy orbit. In November 1942, when the Germans occupied the free zone in response to Allied advances in North Africa and effectively put an end to the Pétain government, few French filmgoers mourned the death of the cinema of the National Revolution. The real French film industry had been reborn in Paris and was thriving under the unexpectedly benevolent tutelage of the occupying military authorities.

As Evelyn Ehrlich has forcefully argued, to understand German policy and attitudes with regard to French filmmaking it is necessary to remember that the Nazi power structure, like all authoritarian regimes, did not always speak with one voice, or have a single, coherent set of priorities.[6] The Germans' initial decision to flood the Occupied Zone with their own films, while refusing to allow exhibition of new French ones made in the south, was obviously beneficial to government-controlled film interests, but potentially disastrous for the military goal of keeping the captive French population reasonably content so that maximum available manpower could be employed in battle. Nazi censors had confiscated all the prewar French films they could find (many were conveniently "lost"), examined them for their racial and political pedigrees and ideological content, and then eithei destroyed them or returned them to distributors for approved showings.[7] French audiences in the winter of 1940–41 could therefore see only German films dubbed into French or revivals of earlier, uncontroversial and Aryan-produced domestic works. The German productions attracted large audiences at first, but audiences soon tired of them as a steady diet; box-office revenues started to decline in early 1941.

The German film industry, in any event, was no longer operating at full capacity because of wartime restrictions on manpower and resources. Of the smaller number of films it produced each year many were clearly ill suited to French audiences, who could not be expected to applaud Nazi armed service comedies about life at the front, or glorifications of German national genius. In order to assure exhibitors a supply of new, economically viable products, the German military authorities were obliged first to allow nationwide distribution of selected works from the Unoccupied Zone (beginning with Pagnol's *La Fille du puisatier*), and then to permit filmmaking activity to resume in Paris. The first new films to start production in the capital were not the work of French companies, however, but of a new German organization, Continental-Films.

Continental was an early, carefully crafted result of the process known as Aryanization, whereby businesses owned wholly or in part by Jews were seized and sold, at a fraction of their real value, to racially "pure" buyers. (Theoretically, the original owners got the meager proceeds; in practice, these monies often were consumed by "administrative expenses." After the Liberation, the companies were all returned to their rightful proprietors, or to their heirs.) The new firm was financed and assembled by the Cautio-Treuhandgesellschaft, a powerful holding company operated by the elusive financier Max Winkler with funds secretly provided by the German government through Joseph Goebbels's Ministry of Propaganda. Through Cautio, Goebbels covertly controlled the entire German film industry, and when Continental was added to the trust's extensive holdings the new company was completely, though indirectly, under the Propaganda Minister's control. Although Alfred Greven, the head of the new French enterprise, was officially an employee of Winkler's organization, he often dealt directly with Goebbels in Berlin.

Before becoming the most powerful film producer in occupied France, Greven was a respected though not particularly celebrated figure in the German cinema industry. He had served as head of production for the independent Terra film company before that firm was absorbed by UFA (with funding supplied by Goebbels, through the

Cautio trust) in 1937. Once a part of Max Winkler's empire, Greven rose quickly, soon joining the board of directors of the giant German studio. (In this covertly governmental milieu, his career was no doubt greatly facilitated by his close personal friendship with Hermann Goering, former head of the Gestapo and virtual dictator of the German economy from 1937 to 1943.) It is not surprising that such a relatively obscure figure was chosen to head the new French firm. From Goebbels's perspective, Greven's new position represented a professional as well as geographical exile from the center of true power. The Propaganda Minister clearly intended the new company to be a sort of reincarnation of French Paramount, turning out cheaply made, unambitious fare for a lucrative, quasi-colonial market. One of the most francophobic of all high-ranking Nazis, Goebbels considered France "a macabre nation, bent upon pleasure, which has rightfully suffered a catastrophe," its people "sick and worm eaten." For their cinema, "only light, frothy and, if possible, corny pictures are [to be] desired."[8]

But Greven had very different ideas, and he set about signing contracts with the best directors, writers, stars, and technicians he could convince to work with the company. One of the first to be approached, in late 1940, was Jean Renoir, who listened politely to Continental's offer of employment and then hastily (and with great difficulty) made arrangements to depart for the United States. For most other filmmakers, however, leaving the country was simply not an option, and few were willing to take the risk of offending one of the most influential Nazis in France. Continental soon became a kind of Occupation France answer to MGM, with Greven as its benevolently autocratic equivalent of Louis B. Mayer. This apparently odd comparison would probably not have offended the German studio head, who reportedly confided to Roger Richebé his opinion that "in the cinema, it's the Jews who are the most capable," and that "I have a Jew working for me, but he doesn't know that I know it."[9] Greven's surprising flexibility on this sensitive subject had a political parallel in his willingness to employ Communist party members and assorted Left sympathizers. Though some, such as Jacques Prévert, categorically refused, many from the Left agreed to work for the studio, among them Charles Spaak, Jean Aurenche, and Jean-Paul Le Chanois (who was probably the Jew Greven knew he had working for him—though the studio head *didn't* know that Le Chanois was also an important figure in the Resistance).

In general, Greven respected the Propaganda Ministry's wishes when he chose his film projects. "Light" and "frothy" subjects did in fact dominate the studio's output—though not entirely. In the summer of 1942, Goebbels screened two recent Continental productions and was disturbed by what he saw. "We will have to be careful about the French," he dictated for his diaries on May 13, "so that they won't build up a new moving-picture art under our leadership that will give us too serious competition in the European market."[10] Two days later he recorded his reactions to a third work, *La Symphonie fantastique* (*The Fantastic Symphony*, 1942, directed by Christian-Jacque and starring Jean-Louis Barrault as Hector Berlioz): "The film is of excellent quality and amounts to a first-class national fanfare. I shall unfortunately not be able to release it for public showing [in Germany]."[11] Greven was summoned from Paris to hear Goebbels's complaint that "our own offices in Paris are teaching the French how to represent nationalism in pictures," and on May 19 the two men had a "long argument" about the French film situation:

> Greven has an entirely wrong technique in that he has regarded it as his task to raise the level of the French movie. That is wrong. It isn't our job to supply the Frenchmen with good pictures and it is especially not our task to give them movies that are beyond reproach in their nationalistic tendency. If the French people on the whole are satisfied with light, corny stuff, we ought to make it our business to produce such cheap trash. It would be a case of lunacy for us to promote competition against ourselves. We must proceed in our movie policies as the Americans do in their policies toward the North and South American continents. We must become the dominating movie power on the European continent . . . After I talked to him for a long time Greven realized the wisdom of this course and will pursue it in the future.[12]

On one major point, Goebbels obviously won his argument with Greven: Continental made no more films like *La Symphonie fantastique*. (Other French producers, however, undoubtedly encouraged by the studio's example, continued to make such nationalistic works during the remaining years of the Occupation.) But Goebbels lost the dispute about aiming for "cheap trash"—probably because, as we will see, Greven was not the only German in a position of power to disagree with the Propaganda Minister's rigidly limited goals for French cinema. Although most of the studio's productions were relatively conventional exercises in established film genres, they were all carefully, stylishly constructed, and technically proficient. Drawing on the talents of cinema stars as diverse as Harry Baur, Fernandel, and Danielle Darrieux, benefiting from the energy and ambition of young directors such as Christian-Jacque and André Cayatte and the experience of veteran scriptwriters such as Charles Spaak, and—perhaps most important—having the luxury of significantly higher budgets per film than its competition, Continental set very high standards of commercial appeal and professional craftsmanship. Thirteen of the studio's films (almost half its total output) appear on the list published by the industry journal *Le Film* of the twenty-seven most commercially successful fiction features of the Occupation.[13] Several of these count among the most serious and controversial French films of the period.

In forcing the rest of the industry to compete with its always polished and sometimes artistically or politically adventurous films, the German company did indeed, as Goebbels feared, "raise the level of the French movie." The captive nation's cinema developed an emphasis on craftsmanship, production values, and technical competence that would later be extolled as a Tradition of Quality. (That this "tradition," spoken of so highly by most filmmakers in the years after the Liberation, came about to some extent as the result of the efforts of a self-serving Nazi producer is one of the great ironies of French film history.) Continental's influence on the larger industry also extended beyond the domain of production values. Because it was a German company, the studio was exempt both from Vichy oversight and from C.O.I.C.'s regulations and quotas, and its films were generally (though not always) untouched by military censorship. Ironically, directors and scriptwriters working for Greven had greater artistic and political freedom than any others in the industry. As a result, the studio often worked in the extreme vanguard of a more general, industry-wide effort to test and, where possible, to expand the social, political, and moral limits that had been imposed on French cinema.

It is hardly surprising that at the time such paradoxically beneficial effects of the German presence received little recognition, much less praise, from the larger film community. Those who did not work for Continental—as well as some who did—reviled Greven, his studio, and its films. The underground Resistance press launched virulent attacks against the company, and after the Liberation most of the profession's heaviest sanctions against collaborators were directed at filmmakers who had worked there (except for those who simultaneously were in the Resistance). Even Marcel Carné, who signed a contract with Greven but quickly found a slender pretext for refusing to continue beyond preproduction work on his first project, would be officially reprimanded. Three of the studio's films were completely banned from French movie screens after the Liberation, and those that were rereleased were given new credit sequences which gave no indication of their provenance.[14]

The Continental work which provoked the greatest vituperation both during the Occupation and afterwards was Henri-Georges Clouzot's very popular *Le Corbeau* (*The Raven*, 1943). Not only was the film banned after the Liberation, but almost everyone involved in its production received some sort of punishment for their participation; there were even some calls for the death penalty for its principal creators. The majority of postwar critics, historians, and political activists felt that most fiction films of the Occupation had served as an expression of the nation's political and moral independence from the occupiers. *Le Corbeau*, however, was not among them; like a horrible cancerous growth, it had to be removed from the cultural body politic. And yet in retrospect, the work's similarities to other Occupation fiction films are at least as striking as the ways in which it differs from them.

Le Corbeau tells the story of how a series of anonymous letters disrupts the life of a small town somewhere in the provinces, producing anger, suspicion and jealousy, a suicide, and eventually a murder. The setting and theme—a provincial community with violence, discord, and often madness hidden beneath an apparently tranquil surface— was anything but rare in Occupation cinema.[15] Beginning with Christian-Jacque's *L'Assassinat du Père Noël*/*Who Killed Santa Claus?* (1941, produced by Continental), set in a mountain village whose isolation is augmented by a heavy snowstorm, this type of closed setting for stories of violent social or familial conflict became a kind of stereotype during the period. Other notable examples include Carné and Prévert's *Les Visiteurs du soir* (*The Night Visitors*, 1943), which takes place in a medieval castle, and Jacques Becker's *Goupi-Mains Rouges*/*It Happened at the Inn* (1943), which not only restricts most of its action to a lonely roadside inn, but its characters to the members of an extended family. Modern critics and historians often suggest that these closed communities served as metaphors for France under the Occupation. This interpretation is certainly supported by the criticism of *Le Corbeau*, which was denounced as "anti-French" on the assumption that its small village represents the entire country (despite hints in the film that life is different, and perhaps better, elsewhere).

The work's mystery-story plot is also quite typical: French audiences and producers of the time showed a marked preference for this genre, though here *Le Corbeau* also differs to some extent from more conventional works of its period. Occupation mystery films generally treated their subject matter with a light, comic tone—as, for example, in Clouzot's earlier *L'Assassin habite au 21* (*The Murderer Lives at Number 21*, 1942). The pervasive sense of repressed violence that characterizes *Le Corbeau*, on the other hand, recalls the gloomy pessimism of 1930s works such as Chenal's *L'Alibi* and Duvivier's *La Belle Equipe*. The film is also related to these and other works of *réalisme poétique* in its expressionistic cinematographic style, and even to some extent in its implicit political stance. As Evelyn Ehrlich has convincingly demonstrated, the film is relentlessly anti-authoritarian and opposed to the moral and political values of the traditional French Right, though it does not—and this point is crucial—offer any positive alternative to the corrupt society which it depicts. The film shared these attitudes with most of the generally accepted canon of major Occupation cinema works, such as Claude Autant-Lara's *Douce/Love Story* (1943) and Carné and Prévert's *Les Enfants du paradis* (*Children of Paradise*, 1943–44/45). And yet, like Carné and Prévert's *Quai des brumes* and *Le Jour se lève* before the war, Clouzot's film was criticized as "decadent" and "demoralizing" by critics on the extreme Left.

What most clearly distinguishes *Le Corbeau* from other major works of the period, aside from its studio of origin, is the nihilistic tone of its denunciation of bourgeois values. In its relentless mockery of the leading citizens of a small town, the film recalls the ferocious social criticism of Jean Vigo's early work—an association which, though perhaps surprising in the light of the Left's dislike of the film, is far from arbitrary. The scriptwriter Louis Chavance wrote his first treatment of the scenario in 1933, when he was a friend and close professional associate of Vigo's (both men were working on *L'Atalante*, for which Chavance was film editor). Chavance had tried in vain to interest producers in the story throughout the 1930s, but it was repeatedly rejected as commercially and politically risky. Almost certainly the work also could not have been made during the Occupation had it not been for Continental's privileged position in the industry. French censors would undoubtedly have rejected it, given the opportunity, and C.O.I.C. was unlikely to have found it worthy of a place in its limited quota of films, so controversial was the subject matter. How could they not reject a film in which the doctor-hero is an accused

Decadence in *Le Corbeau*: the wanton heroine not only smokes and paints her nails but also has a slight deformity—of the foot she so lovingly adorns with color before receiving the man she desires.

abortionist (he freely admits saving women's lives at the expense of their unborn children); his new lover a promiscuous woman with a minor physical deformity (hence an offense both to Vichy moralism and to Nazi eugenics); and everyone else a fool, a knave, insane, or all three? Furthermore, German authorities could hardly have relished a film which denounced the sending of anonymous letters.

Despite its complex brew of anti-authoritarian, anti-Vichy, and anti-Nazi messages, *Le Corbeau* was released at precisely the wrong time to be received sympathetically by the one audience which would matter the most after the Liberation: the Communist-dominated Resistance. Clouzot's image of a France in which only a few outcasts and malcontents could behave with a semblance of morality and good will was completely unacceptable for those trying to promote a very different image of a nation capable of unity, collective heroism, and self-sacrifice in the face of a powerful enemy. *L'Ecran Francais,* the clandestinely published organ of the Committee for the Liberation of the French Cinema, denounced the film in an article entitled "The Raven

Has Its Feathers Plucked," contrasting it in very revealing terms with Jean Grémillon's *Le Ciel est à vous* (*The Sky is Yours*, 1944):

> The Germans can rub their hands with glee: after having repeatedly misjudged the professional worth of their French lackeys, they have finally unearthed two [Clouzot and Chavance] who are capable of turning out an impeccable, at times seductive merchandise; they will serve as excellent conduits for the enemy's cunning ideology . . . For this reason we must, first of all, contrast Monsieur Clouzot's work with another which, quite worthily this time, is triumphant on Parisian movie screens. With *Le Ciel est à vous*, the French cinema has dared to express itself in spite of the Nazi presence, and has perhaps saved its honor . . . For in opposition to the cripples, to the illicit lovers, to the corrupt ones who dishonor one of our provincial towns in *Le Corbeau*, *Le Ciel est à vous* gives us characters full of French vitality [*sève*], real courage, and moral health, in whom we may discover a national truth which will not and cannot die.[16]

That the clandestine Left press could condemn Clouzot's film using a vocabulary reminiscent of the diatribes of the Right—calling on the "real" France, full of national *sève* (literally, "sap") and moral health— is only one of the ironies of this episode. Equally important is the fact that, despite the authors' assertion that *Le Ciel est à vous* was "triumphant" in French cinemas, in reality it attracted much smaller audiences than the supposedly anti-French *Le Corbeau*. Compared to other films of the period, *Le Ciel est à vous* was a relative commercial failure, the beginning of the end of Grémillon's career in fiction feature films. In the 1950s, he would be forced to confine his activities to documentary short subjects, while Clouzot would continue, after two years of professional anathema imposed as punishment for his Occupation work, to make exceptionally popular suspense thrillers very much in the manner of his banned masterpiece.

◼ Although Continental-Films' productions were on the whole very well received by the French public (the firm's ownership of a large number of first-run cinemas may have had a lot to do with this), most of the studio's films go unmentioned in the many lists of major works of film art to emerge from the Occupation. These lists are often surprisingly long; the curious fact is that few, if any, periods of French film history have produced so many acknowledged masterpieces and near-masterpieces in so little time. For this reason, and because of the great historical interest of a successful national cinema under enemy occupation, few periods have been as intensively studied. One important point of contention among scholars is the extent to which to Occupation brought about a radical change, stylistically and in film content, from the previous decade.

Jean-Pierre Jeancolas, for example, titled his study of French cinema from 1929 to 1944 *Quinze ans d'années trente,* or "Fifteen Years of the 1930s," to indicate the essential continuity he sees in the films of these years.[17] Conversely, Evelyn Ehrlich, following the traditional, more generally accepted analysis, maintains that the Occupation years saw the birth of a "new movement" that "broke definitively with the styles of the 1930s."[18] To a large extent, these apparently conflicting arguments reflect differences in methodology and definitions of French cinema rather than fundamental disputes about historical processes. There was, as Ehrlich herself points out, great continuity in the ordinary program pictures which comprised most cinema presentations before and after the *débâcle* of 1941; the new approach to filmmaking was to be found only in a small number (perhaps thirty) of prestige productions from the Occupation years. And even these works, which contemporary critics such as Roger Régent hailed as a "new French school" of filmmaking, did not uniformly reject the works of the previous decade. The atmospheric, decor-dominated dramaturgy of poetic realism, and the ornate historical costume dramas directed in the 1930s by anti-fascist refugees such as Max Ophuls and Anatole Litvak and by natives such as Raymond Bernard arguably served as important precedents for the new tendency.

It is most obviously the freewheeling, heterogeneous approach to film form and content taken by Jean Renoir, Jean Vigo, and others before the war—the improvisational feel and the sense of openness to a world which extends beyond the boundaries of the cinema screen—which was conspicuously absent in the new approach to filmmaking. One striking manifestation of this shift may be seen in actors and acting styles. French films of the 1930s deliberately juxtaposed disparate playing styles, which could also symbolize differing class positions and moral points of view—a Julien Carette playing alongside a Pierre Fresnay, for example. The masterpieces of Occupation cinema tended to emphasize a more uniform, distanced, and homogeneous playing style based on that of the artistically advanced Parisian stage (as opposed to boulevard theatre and music hall).

Along with the more uniform and socially abstract playing styles appeared an emphasis, in many films, on overtly literary screenplays.

Film dialogue lost much of its previously close contact with everyday speech and often became poetic and declamatory. Many scripts sounded as if they had been written by such masters of poetic drama as Jean Giraudoux and Jean Anouilh—as in fact some were. After an absence from the medium of over a decade, Jean Cocteau contributed an idiosyncratic, poetic approach to feature film dialogue in several works. Jacques Prévert, who remained an important and influential scriptwriter, shifted ground substantially, virtually abandoning his interest in popular slang and different modes of speech in favor of a more uniform, Giraudoux-like *préciosité*. Many of the actors familiar from 1930s films sounded rather different speaking this new kind of dialogue. Even Arletty, formerly the very symbol of the lower-class *parisienne*, spoke her lines in a more restrained, neutral manner in films such as *Les Visiteurs du soir*, in which she plays a traveling medieval entertainer (and cunning, seductive agent of the devil). The popular cafe-concert and music hall melodies with which she and other vaudevillians had been associated in earlier films also receded in importance, completely disappearing from many of the new works in favor of lush, "high culture" symphonic scores.

Visually, the new films became more mannered and stylized, surpassing even the expressionistic vistas of *réalisme poétique* in their creation of visual fields removed both from everyday reality and from the characters who moved within them. Some works returned to the overt pictorialism of late silent film, perhaps most notably Grémillon and Prévert's *Lumière d'été* (*Summer Light*, 1942). Sets were often large and elaborate, despite the obvious financial difficulties that this entailed in a period of limited resources. Roger Régent, one of the period's most astute observers, spoke of the *décor-personnage* (the "set as character") as being an often abused cinematic cliché.[19] If decor could frequently function as a kind of (impersonal) character, fictional beings could by the same token lapse into relative, sometimes absolute stillness, assuming the function of decor in a larger, metaphysical drama.

In fact, most of the major Occupation films share a generalized trend toward relative stillness both of fictional characters—often seen in carefully composed, tableau-like formations—and frequently of the camera itself. This tendency stands in marked contrast to the explorations of cinematic movement in all its possible forms which characterized so many notable works of the 1930s and gave them their pervasive sense of fluidity, lively disorder, and transition (from one space to another, but also from one emotion or idea to another). The most obvious reasons for this striking change are easy to enumerate. The masters of cinematic mobility had left the country: Renoir, Clair, and Ophuls were in Hollywood, Pierre Chenal in South America. Expressive camera and character motion placed burdensome demands on capital, equipment, and technical expertise—all in very short supply. Despite these limitations, some big-budget films of the period do feature sweeping, if rather ponderous camera movements, but typically these serve only to reinforce a sense of fixity and sterile order in the fictional universes which they so carefully display.

Most of the stylistic trends of the Occupation's "new school" of filmmaking carried over with little change into the postwar Tradition of Quality, with the notable exception of this affinity for immobility. With the restoration of greater financial and technical resources after the Liberation, and later the return of leading prewar filmmakers who had been in exile, much—though not all—of the previous fascination with motion also reappeared. But clearly, material circumstances cannot entirely explain the Occupation cinema's cultivation of stillness. Immobility as a feature of the narrative, though not universal, is frequent in works of the period. Near the beginning of *Les Visiteurs du soir,* when an emissary of the devil sent to sow discord and disunity in a medieval kingdom begins his terrible work, he magically causes all motion to cease at a court dance; the attending lords and ladies are frozen cinematically and narratively in time and space. *Goupi-Mains Rouges,* in which a major character is immobilized for much of the film by a stroke, offers a possible meaning for such episodes of dangerous stillness. For the Goupi clan's patriarch is nicknamed Napoléon (meaning France, the revolutionary past), and he has a treasure to bequeath to his family, a legacy that his paralysis almost prevents him from passing on. If remote, closed spaces often symbolized France in microcosm, sudden immobility could signal the first stage of a dangerous possible dissolution of the body politic.

Such remarkable examples of narrative stasis often occur in notably large, open settings, such as the enormous white castle in *Les Visiteurs du soir,* the cavernous, empty inn of *Goupi-Mains Rouges,* or the void surrounding the stalled funicular car at the conclusion of *Lumière d'été.* In the place of the many examples of filmic claustrophobia so typical of *réalisme poétique* (Jean Gabin trapped in a small room in *Le Jour se lève,* for example), the major Occupation works often substituted agoraphobic renderings of threateningly unbounded space. The only

Before being turned to stone at the film's end, the young lovers of *Les Visiteurs du soir* (Marie Déa and Alain Cluny) hang in very decorative chains, in a striking example of the Occupation cinema's obsession with immobility.

important lines of demarcation, those defining the narrative microcosm, tend to remain off-screen; they are of no help in setting limits to human action within the fictional community. This often oppressive openness, threatened both by sudden immobility and by outbursts of uncontrolled violence, is a space not of tragedy or comedy, but of allegory. Occurring within a troublingly open, almost abstract space, narrative events call for explanations not contained within them, but dictated by their larger, historical context.

That the major works of Occupation cinema had an important allegorical dimension was widely recognized at the time by filmmakers, critics, and presumably by many spectators. The Resistance activists of *L'Ecran Français* interpreted *Le Corbeau* as a metaphorical attack on French society not because they saw the film as isolated and unique in this regard, but because they assumed that all important films would comment in one way or another on contemporary social reality, and would tend to do so indirectly. The most important unspoken subject matter was assumed to be the contemporary situation of France and her relations with Germany and with her own past. Evil characters were often assumed to represent the Nazis, and good characters the best elements of the suffering, occupied nation.

Evil could assume its most concentrated form with the appearance of the devil himself, as in *Les Visiteurs du soir* and Maurice Tourneur's *La Main du diable/Carnival of Sinners* (1943). In both cases many spectators apparently assumed that the evil one represented Germany. In Tourneur's film, an artist sells his soul in exchange for a magically dextrous (that is, free, not enslaved) hand, whose works will bring him fame and glory—a tale that invited reflection on the consequences of more contemporary instances of collusion with evil. (Ironically, after the Liberation Pierre Fresnay, who played the role, was briefly stigmatized as a collaborator, accused of having done the same thing as his character by selling his soul to Continental-Films, which—despite the film's widely recognized anti-Nazi resonances—had produced *La Main du diable*.) In *Les Visiteurs du soir*, one of the emissaries from hell falls in love with a beautiful princess and refuses to continue sowing hate and dissention. In revenge, the devil turns the couple to stone, but he hears their hearts still beating, signaling his final defeat by their love and goodness. For many spectators, the allegorical lesson was clear: though Germany might paralyze the French body politic, the nation's heart remained pure and alive.

La Main du diable and *Les Visiteurs du soir* were not alone in allowing—indeed, inviting—such political readings. Jean Delannoy's very popular *Pontcarral, colonel d'Empire* (*Pontcarral, Colonel of the Empire*, 1942), which Francis Courtade has called the only "authentic film of resistance" of the period, tells the story of an ex-officer from the Napoleonic era (played by Pierre Blanchar, a major organizer of

Resistance activities within the film community) who opposes, by small and large acts of rebellion, the authority of the restored monarchy. Despite this plot's obvious resonances with the situation of France under German rule, not all historians have been as convinced as Courtade of the film's Resistance message. If it is clear enough what and whom Pontcarral is fighting *against* (ultra-royalists, standing in for the Nazis), it is not nearly so clear what he is fighting *for:* the Napoleonic empire was glorified by Vichy ideologues as an example of a strong French state with a strong leader and great respect for authority—hardly values most Resistance members would have endorsed.[20]

But for all its troubling ambiguities, *Pontcarral's* covert analogy between French royalists and the German occupiers provides an important clue for understanding the allegorical resonances of class relations in many films of the period. The number of evil aristocrats in Occupation cinema is astonishing, given the fact that the aristocracy as a class had lost most of its influence (and, in general, its financial resources) several decades before. Conflicts between diabolical or mad aristocrats and good, sane members of the working class or the peasantry discreetly invited interpretation as the confrontation between Nazi or Vichy authoritarianism and republican civic virtue. The narrative weight and manichaean simplicity of class conflict in *Lumière d'été, Les Enfants du paradis, Douce,* and many other major Occupation films arguably represent a qualitative change from the previous decade's insistence on social position as an important aspect of character. Class positions in these works are extremely polarized, reduced to conflicts between aristocrats and lower-class characters with very little in between except for the occasional (generally comic) petty bourgeois figure. This absence of a viable middle ground between allegorically charged social extremes may be read as a historically charged rejection of ambiguity. For if aristocrats were typically mad or evil, and members of the lower orders good and sane, then intermediate positions could only represent an ambivalent, neither-good-nor-evil domain difficult to accept in a drama of moral absolutes.

The disappearance or de-emphasis of the bourgeoisie in the major films of the Occupation—with the crucial exceptions of *Le Corbeau* and *Le Ciel est à vous,* where the middle classes are, respectively, corrupt or potentially heroic—gives rise to one of the period's most striking historical ironies. For although the majority of the French population chose neither to collaborate with, nor actively to resist the Nazis, studies of the social composition of the Resistance and of the Vichy government's members and sympathizers show that the middle and upper bourgeoisie contributed disproportionately to both groups.[21] Thus the great social drama of collaborators versus active resisters was most prominently played out in the one social class that was studiously ignored by the period's serious fiction filmmaking. The devil did not have second thoughts, nor did the forces of light have ignoble fears, but French collaborators and Resistance members alike probably had both. In choosing to make allegorical dramas of Good versus Evil, the period's self-consciously artistic and committed filmmakers distanced themselves both literally and symbolically from the very personal political dilemmas all around them.

A few films did, however, evoke some of the pain and difficulty of making tough choices in a dangerous environment. As it happens, the two works which arguably did this most effectively were the scandalous *Le Corbeau* and the relative commercial failure *Le Ciel est à vous*. Near the end of Grémillon's film, in which a middle-class couple pursues an elusive dream of setting an aviation record, angry townspeople denounce the hapless garage owner who has apparently let his wife fly off to her death; mob violence seems a real possibility until the crowd learns that the aviatrix has achieved her goal. The film demonstrates that ordinary people can do extraordinary things, but it also shows that their efforts may meet incomprehension and even violent hostility from those who do not dare to dream. The isolation and torment of the "healthy," heroic French citizens in *Le Ciel est à vous* before the obligatory happy end is finally not very different from that of the "decadent" lovers in *Le Corbeau*. That the latter film provoked intense controversy, and the former had such limited commercial appeal, suggests that the industry's more typical pursuit of social commentary by indirection and allegory represented the path of least resistance, not with German military authorities (who seem to have raised few if any objections to either work), but with French public opinion.

■ Many leading filmmakers of the Occupation thought that by making their austerely beautiful, allusive films they had found a way of saying *merde* to the enemy. It was assumed at the time, and indeed until quite recently, that German government policy was consonant with Joseph Goebbels's well-known opinion that the conquered country was hopelessly corrupt and deserved only "light, frothy and, if possible, corny pictures." To make serious works of cinema art, often with important political subtexts, could therefore be interpreted as an act of defiance, a heroic demonstration that France still existed culturally if not politically and even thrived in this domain, despite its terrible burden. French filmmaking, like the beating hearts of the young lovers at the end of *Les Visiteurs du soir*, could be made a symbol of the power of good to resist evil. Alas, satisfying as this reading of wartime Franco-German relations may be to French nationalists and to francophiles throughout the world, it does not hold up under close scrutiny. If the German authorities had wanted only mindless trash from the French film industry, they had ample means at their disposal to ensure the production of such works. They could, for example, simply have refused to permit exhibition of undesired examples of quality cinema, or of political allegorizing. Not only did they not do this, they in many cases allowed the export of notable French productions to other Axis-controlled markets and in some cases even to Germany itself, where the films competed directly with their own (government controlled and financed) industry's products.

Furthermore, it strains credibility to argue that military censors could have been ignorant of the political resonances so easily found by others in the films submitted for examination. It seems more likely that they were aware of the works' many possible meanings, but that they were not, for whatever reasons, greatly concerned by such matters. At the very least, the Germans seem to have exercised a kind of benign neglect with regard to the captive cinema over which they had such extensive control. And it is quite possible that they actively promoted the the commercial and artistic development of French filmmaking. Evelyn Ehrlich has argued, on the basis on an analysis of the weekly reports to Berlin from the Paris Filmprüfstelle, or Film Control Board, that German policy consisted in making "special efforts to promote the quality of French films." One of the reports that she quotes discusses the need "to find talent, and to promote works that are worthy of French culture in the European [that is, fascist] frame."[22]

Several reasons may be found for this policy, which seems so surprising at first glance. The Germans needed to keep the French population reasonably satisfied with its condition, if they wished to avoid committing large numbers of troops to suppressing expressions of discontent; a successful national cinema was one obvious means of achieving this end. From the point of view of international propaganda, furthermore, if the French produced greater numbers of commercially successful and critically aclaimed films under the new order than they had under the supposedly discredited republic, this change could provide powerful evidence, in the court of world opinion, for the supposed benefits of fascism. But Ehrlich argues persuasively that the most important reason for German encouragement of the French industry was a coherent, long-term plan to break American hegemony in the world film market: "The French would supply the commercially appealing films that were necessary for the Germans to compete successfully with the Americans on the international market. This was, probably, a short term goal. Once the markets of Latin America and elsewhere had been penetrated by European (i.e., French) films, the Germans could use their market position to force purchase of their own films. The Germans thus saw that by encouraging French film production, they could use French films as an economic wedge to force the purchase of German films."[23]

This larger, ultimately unrealized project, which Ehrlich convincingly establishes from the Filmprüfstelle reports, casts a radical new light on the efforts of French filmmakers during the Occupation. Rather than resisting the enemy by making serious, high-quality works, they were, without knowing it, collaborating with the enemy in a devastatingly effective way. Had Germany's ambitious military and geopolitical goals been realized, the French cinematic efforts would have had a place of pride in the establishment of the New Order worldwide. Because Germany failed, but only because she failed, French film artists emerged not as collaborators, but as (apparently) heroes. This is not, perhaps, a very appealing moral lesson, but it is one which would have come as no surprise to Henri-Georges Clouzot and Louis Chavance. In their *Le Corbeau,* a seemingly respectable citizen who is eventually revealed to be the mad intelligence behind the anonymous letter campaign delivers a telling commentary on knowing the consequences of one's actions: "You are incredible. You think that people are all good or all evil. You think that good is light [he grasps a hanging lamp which casts a pool of light in the otherwise dark room] and darkness is evil. But where is darkness [he pushes the lamp and it begins to swing], where is light? Where is the border of evil? [The lamp illuminates different parts of the room as it moves.] Do you know which side you are on? Think about it and examine your conscience. You will perhaps be astonished."[24]

◼ 11 ◼

Liberation—Change and Continuity

Allied forces landed on the beaches of Normandy on D-day, June 6, 1944, and from the first hours of the nation's still tenuous liberation representatives of the Free French regime headed by General Charles de Gaulle began seizing control of the various strands of local, regional, and national government. As military operations advanced, so did the grasp of the new (theoretically the old, pre-Vichy) French state. The process had been carefully planned, in cooperation with leading Resistance groups, so as to prevent any significant power vacuum which could be filled by a provisional government of Anglo-American sponsorship. From its first moments, the reconstruction and, inevitably, the purification of the nation was entirely in French hands.

De Gaulle's government in exile had long been preoccupied with the problem of identifying and punishing French men and women who had actively collaborated with Germany. A major concern was to keep the process of *épuration* ("purification" or "purge") in the hands of duly constituted authority. In this the new government was largely successful. Despite some summary courts-martial and other less savory methods of dealing with accused collaborators in the first days of each region's liberation, most of the *épuration* was ultimately carried out by the state's hastily reconstituted judiciary system, aided by a variety of specially created, para-judicial bodies. Depending on the gravity of the accusations against them, most suspected collaborators were prosecuted in one of the regional Courts of Justice, by a Civic Chamber, or before a purification committee (*comité d'épuration*). The most serious cases went to the Courts of Justice, where sentences could include death, imprisonment, confiscation of property, and a specially created sanction, *indignité nationale,* or "disgrace in the eyes of the nation." *Indignité nationale* entailed loss of civil rights and exclusion from business and most professions, either for life or, more often, for a limited period of time. This was the principal punishment imposed by the specially created Civic Chambers, which dealt with less grave cases. At the lowest level of the process, the various purification committees could impose penalties such as barring offenders from exercising their professions.

Public sentiment was strongly in favor of dealing harshly with accused collaborators. Stars such as Sacha Guitry, Pierre Fresnay, and Arletty had been targets of the underground Resistance press during the Occupation. Some publications had already called for execution or prison terms for them, as well as for directors Henri-Georges Clouzot and Henri Decoin. In response, the government imprisoned certain highly visible suspects before any decision was taken whether to indict them, for what offense, and at which level of the system of judgment. Guitry was arrested and interned with other suspects in the Vélodrome d'Hiver—which had once served as a temporary prison for French Jews on their way to death camps—and then in the notorious prison at Fresnes. After almost two months of internment, he was indicted for collaboration with the enemy, but a month later the examining magistrate dismissed the charges and sent the case on to a Civic Chamber for a possible judgment of *indignité nationale.* The now unclandestine and very vocal Resistance press decried the government's supposed leniency. Three years later Guitry learned that the case against him had been dismissed. He had, in point of fact, profited handsomely and ostentatiously from his films and plays of the Occupation (while others could not or would not work), and he had flagrantly socialized with high German officials. But he had apparently done no more than this, which explains the decision of the prosecution only to ask for the sanction of *indignité nationale.* (Stronger sentences were generally reserved for those who had actively aided the Germans in crucial areas such as propaganda or the suppression of the Resistance.)

It seems a bit surprising that Guitry did not receive even a limited term of *indignité nationale,* given the penalties meted out to others. Perhaps his prosecutors were swayed by the strong nationalist themes of his Occupation works, or perhaps the Civic Chamber simply blundered. He did not rejoice in his narrow escape from official sanctions, however; embittered by the episode, he sought to explain his conduct to his beloved public. Probably his most successful plea for understanding and sympathy is embodied in his film *Le Diable boîteux* (*The Limping Devil*, 1948). In this (unusually for him) somber work he plays Talleyrand, the cunning statesman and crafty tactician who survived the *ancien régime*, the Revolution, the Empire, and the Restoration of the Bourbons, allying with each regime only later to embrace its successor. Guitry was certainly not the only accused Nazi sympathizer to invoke Talleyrand's example as a defense, but he was among the most witty and artful of them. His protagonist emerges as a clever man who adapts to new circumstances—always in good conscience and to good ends—in order to serve his nation. *Le Diable boîteux* was one of the director's best postwar films, and in it one notices a striking change. Before the Liberation, Guitry appeared on screen as a young dandy; playing Talleyrand he is suddenly old, conveying a touching sense of having passed from innocence to experience. His ultimate plea for sympathy was that he had now become an older and a wiser artist.

Other highly visible film artists who were arrested met fates similar to Guitry's. Pierre Fresnay was imprisoned on the basis of his work for Continental-Films but almost immediately released on the intervention of a high-ranking government official, who cited the actor's many recent charitable works in his defense. Arletty was first imprisoned, then placed under house arrest for many months before her case was heard by the National Purge Committee of Dramatic and Musical Performers and Performing Musicians. She received a reprimand for having engaged in "horizontal collaboration" with a handsome German officer and was released, though her long confinement had served as *de facto* punishment. But arrests, followed by trial or not, were comparatively rare in the film industry, and convictions on serious charges were even rarer. The director Jean Mamy was sentenced to death for having denounced members of a clandestine labor organization to the occupiers. The actor Robert Le Vigan received ten years hard labor, confiscation of his assets, and *indignité nationale* for his work on enemy radio propaganda broadcasts. (He was released on parole, like many other convicted collaborators, after four years.)

In general, the purification of the film industry was quite moderate both in the sanctions imposed and the level of its rhetoric. Most of the accused quietly waited their turn to answer the charges against them before various nonjudicial bodies. Radio and journalism, by contrast, generated some spectacular show trials and harsh punishments—as in the case of the editor, political commentator, and occasional cinema historian Robert Brasillach, who was sentenced to death by firing squad. The prosecutor at Brasillach's trial argued that even if the journalist had not actually committed the most serious of war crimes, he had been their "intellectual instigator."[1] Had such a standard of responsibility been applied to the film industry, a few directors and writers of Vichy propaganda short subjects would have risked a similar fate. But film propaganda was apparently low on the list of government priorities, and its creators mostly had their cases heard, along with almost everybody else in the industry, by the appropriate local purge committees.

The Committee for the Liberation of French Cinema (publisher of *L'Ecran Français*) had drawn up a list of persons it found particularly worthy of serious penalties. But rather than refer these controversial cases to the Courts of Justice (for possible prison sentences) or to Civic Chambers (which could impose *indignité nationale*), prosecutors turned over most of them to the Regional Interprofessional Committee for the Purification of Enterprises. The Committee for the Liberation of French Cinema's greatest quarrel was with Henri-Georges Clouzot, because of his scandalous *Le Corbeau*. The director had already been barred from working in his profession for almost a year by order of the Prefect of Paris, presumably in anticipation of a finding of *indignité nationale*. The Regional Interprofessional Committee heard a passionately argued case against Clouzot, but it also received a petition in his support organized by Jean-Paul Sartre and a letter from Jacques Prévert arguing that the notorious film was in no way "anti-French." The purge committee, in what seems a gesture meant to appease strong public opinion, extended the Prefect's ban for another two years.

Like Sacha Guitry, Clouzot was embittered by his treatment at the hands of the nation's liberators, and like Guitry he gave his own, oblique response to them in a film. In *Manon* (1949) he transformed the Abbé Prévost's celebrated eighteenth-century young lovers into lumpen refugees from a chaotic France in the midst of lawless "liberation." *Manon* is arguably one of Clouzot's least convincing and well-formed films, but it is also one of his most personal, deeply felt works, dripping with contempt for what the director saw as his critics' hypocritical refusal to admit that the evils of the Occupation years had not ceased when France was "free," because corruption has its roots in human nature itself and not in the actions of particular individuals.

But at the same time that he was making *Manon,* Clouzot was a prominent member, alongside of some of his former accusers, of the Committee for the Defense of French Cinema, an industry group lobbying for relief from American competition. Although old hatreds born of the Occupation and Liberation did not die, they were in most circumstances professionally and publicly muted, and were even beginning to fade by the end of the 1940s.

▧ Aside from the purification of the industry, another, equally important problem faced the divided and contentious film community in the first years after the Liberation. What was to be done with the various professional and governmental institutions created during the Occupation? About one Vichy creation there was little debate: after many years of fruitless proposals from industry and government in the prewar era, the Pétain regime had created a national film school, the Institut des Hautes Etudes Cinematographiques (or Institute for Advanced Study of Cinema). I.D.H.E.C. had evolved from modest beginnings as one of countless Vichy youth groups to the film school envisioned by industry reformers since the mid-1930s. After a brief occupation of its offices by Resistance groups and a short purification, the school reopened without any significant change of structure or personnel. During the Occupation, the government had also begun subsidizing a private institution, the Cinémathèque Française (still the most celebrated of French film archives); this relationship continued with little change after the Liberation. Creation of I.D.H.E.C. and support for the Cinémathèque were uncontroversial innovations, but the system of industry regulation embodied in C.O.I.C. was a more troubling legacy of the Vichy regime.

Early in the liberation of the capital, the Committee for the Liberation of French Cinema occupied the offices of C.O.I.C. and of Vichy's General Director for Cinema (who had supervised but not directly regulated the film industry). Under the control first of the Committee and then of new administrations, both offices continued to function—and to provide material for investigation of suspected collaborators—while debate continued about their restructuring and redefinition. There was no question of returning to the chaotic, unbridled free market of the 1930s, for the recent reforms, however tainted their origins, had been overwhelmingly beneficial to the industry. The major task, as most filmmakers saw it, was to make the regulatory system more consonant with the democratic values of the newly revived republic. This meant, above all, giving a voice to all levels of the industry, particularly labor and craft unions—for Vichy had created an oligarchical structure strongly biased in favor of producers. Another problem arose from Vichy's insistence on the privatization of regulatory activity, which had resulted in parallel, redundant structures and functions for C.O.I.C. and the government agency which oversaw it—a dual system which risked serious political and bureaucratic conflict between the industry and the state.

After much negotiation and lobbying, a law of October 25, 1946, finally created the Centre National de la Cinématographie, or National Cinema Center. The C.N.C. was a self-financing (via taxes on admissions) government agency with an administrative committee composed of members of the government and representatives of the various levels of industry. It continued to control French cinema very much as C.O.I.C. had, through essentially the same regulatory mechanisms. (As we will see, this continuity of the regulatory process goes a long way toward explaining the strong artistic continuity between the new French school of the Occupation and the postwar Tradition of Quality.) If the C.N.C. essentially continued C.O.I.C.'s role and means of stabilizing the industry, however, it changed policy in one crucial area. Although the C.N.C. continued the C.O.I.C. system of financial oversight to ensure completion of projects, it no longer sought to restrict the number of films made per year. The industry's main concern in the early postwar years was not to limit production but to expand it, to meet the new, daunting competition (and what today would be viewed as unfair trade practices) of the American cinema.

With the Liberation Hollywood films began to inundate the French market. Major U.S. studios had four years' worth of product, already amortized, which they could sell at bargain prices, and French audiences were eager to see it. Representatives of the industry pleaded for government protection, but France, with the rest of Europe, came under heavy pressure from the United States not to close its markets. A 1946 trade agreement negotiated by government representative Léon Blum with the U.S. Secretary of Commerce James Byrnes put in place a farcically weak protection of the French film industry. Individual theatres had to play domestic productions during sixteen weeks of each year; for the other thirty-six weeks they were free to choose films without regard to national origins. Thus "protected" by the Blum-Byrnes accord, the industry was left more or less on its own to fight for its existence, with the help of the C.N.C.

Because of the American menace, it was assumed that successful French films needed high budgets for popular stars, attractive costumes, elaborate sets, and so on. To increase production without sacrificing this sort of "quality" required large infusions of capital. One strategy to achieve this goal was international coproduction, in which studios from several countries (France, Italy, Spain, even Germany and Great Britain) pooled resources and produced multiple versions of expensive productions. From the late 1940s on, the French cinema was to generate a continuous stream of big films, often in color, with international casts and plots. Films featuring one or more major players from Italy, with sequences or occasionally entire narratives set in that country, were particularly abundant. Subsidies were another means of capitalizing films. (C.O.I.C. had already worked in this domain with its low-interest loans to favored productions.) In 1949 a C.N.C. committee composed of representatives of management, creative personnel, and labor began to select projects deemed worthy of *primes à la qualité,* or "bonuses for quality."

The kind of cinema which emerged largely as a result of these strategies is often called the Tradition of Quality—though it was a "tradition" at best only a few years old. "Quality" meant, first of all, that the films could not be inferior to the best American products, either technically (smoothness of editing, glitchless camera movement) or materially (eye-catching, expensive costumes and sets, appealing stars, "seeing the money on the screen"). Quality cinema attempted to meet the American threat in two ways: by beating it at its own game (making expensive movies with mass market appeal) and by emphasizing its home-court advantage, its Frenchness. But the American films had the appeal of exoticism, and therefore the Frenchness—or Europeanness, for coproductions—of domestically produced films had to be exaggerated, larger than life in order to compete. The Tradition of Quality continued to produce the same sort of nationalistic costume dramas that had flourished during the Occupation. Then, the unnamed enemy had been Germany; now it was America. Literary adaptation was a particularly prominent way of asserting national or European character. Stendhal, Zola, Maupassant, and other greats of the literary pantheon belonged to the national patrimony; films based on their works shared their relation to the national Spirit. But Frenchness alone could not guarantee mass market appeal. For that, the Tradition of Quality relied on production values, and above all on *stars.*

There had always been a French cinema star system, of course, since before the days of Max Linder. But mainstream postwar film-making depended upon stardom to an unprecedented degree. Stars were the most reliable means of attaining the high box-office revenues required to repay the large investments in quality works. All major films were, to some extent, star vehicles. Individual stars' bodies and personas became fetishes, in some cases to an outlandish extent, almost to the point of self-parody. The actress Martine Carol, whose body was one sort of 1950s French ideal, typically appeared in fitted, low-cut gowns often created by her own personal designer. In some of her work, one has the impression that the films have been planned and executed mainly in terms of her costumes, and the various ways that they display the Carolian figure. Gérard Philipe, who was certainly better at acting than Martine Carol, became a major cinema star thanks in large measure to his flattering costumes, his often gracefully athletic gestures *à la* Douglas Fairbanks, and variously revealed body parts, particularly his chest. Most major postwar stars had an exhibitionistic, narcissistic quality that often mixed curiously with the messages of the films they played in. Most, including even Martine Carol, had some talent for light comedy. But there were very few who could, like Gérard Philipe, strike a convincing note of honesty and force of conviction. If the Tradition of Quality was at its best in ironic, often frivolous works, it was largely because this was what its leading stars could do well.

One or two stars in an excellent vehicle could bring in very satisfactory revenues at the box office. A larger bill of stars in almost any film could also generally guarantee reasonable returns. International coproduction almost automatically raised the number of stars per picture, and the number of markets to which they appealed. Another way to do the same thing was to package together three or more short film narratives on a given theme, typically with different stars, directors, and designers. Such "sketch films" became reliable box-office workhorses, in much the same way that sequels and remakes are for today's American cinema—and with roughly the same levels of financial and artistic achievement. But all the stars in the industry could do little if there was no appropriate vehicle for them. With great amounts of money at stake, not the least of it in star salaries, producers insisted on careful preplanning, most of which revolved around the script. If onscreen the Tradition of Quality was most visibly about stardom, behind the scenes it depended principally on the craft of the scriptwriter. The cinema of the Occupation had effectively eliminated the

frequent (though by no means dominant) 1930s practices of impro-
visation on the set and script changes during shooting. (Two notable
examples had been *La Règle du jeu* and *La Grande Illusion*.) Mainstream postwar French cinema continued the implicit bans on these
practices, with the result that although the industry could make films
about spontaneity and openness, it could almost never make them *feel*
spontaneous or open. Most successful productions featured characters who had the same qualities as the films: irony, distance, control.
Some of the best works of the postwar era are about people who try
to be open and spontaneous but cannot manage, or who succeed just
once, with disastrous results (Ophuls' *Madame de . . .* , Clair's *Les
Grandes Manoeuvres*).

When one turns from the industry's structure and global predis-
positions to the films it produced and the filmmakers who prospered
or did not in the postwar period, one again notes more continuity
than change with respect to the cinema of the Occupation. There was
no longer any compelling reason to retreat from contemporary social
reality, and yet the cinema of quality never fully regained the strong
sense of contact with everyday life that had characterized many of the
best works of the 1930s. Life in contemporary France tended to come
to the foreground chiefly in the genre of the psychological thriller, or
French *film noir*.[2] This cycle of films itself is strong evidence for continuity between the Occupation and the Tradition of Quality, for these
works are the spiritual and stylistic descendants of Clouzot's *Le Corbeau*, with its bleak, paranoid vision of social relations. But the contemporary reality that serves as background and context for these
tales of deception and betrayal is inevitably associated with and
inflected by the extreme, neurotic emotion that they generate. As a
result, the settings do not give the impression of having an existence
independent of the films, despite, for example, the real location shots
of a Normandy beach town in *Une si jolie petite plage*/*Riptide* (1948)
directed by Yves Allégret (Marc's younger brother), or Julien Duvivier's carefully detailed rendering of a run-down Paris neighborhood
in *Panique* (*Panic*, 1947, after Simenon).

Most of the prestige productions of the Tradition of Quality
avoided contemporary social reality altogether by escaping, as had so
many films of the Occupation, into the past. Often that past could be
quite recent: Sacha Guitry and Henri-Georges Clouzot were far from

the only French filmmakers to depict and comment upon the events of the Occupation. Raymond Bernard's *Un Ami viendra ce soir* (*A Friend Will Arrive Tonight*, 1946) and René Clément's *Le Père tranquille*/*Mr. Orchid* (1946, scripted by and starring Noël-Noël), for example, both presented ironically amusing vignettes of life in and around the Resistance, when things were never as they seemed, and anti-Nazis could masquerade as collaborators or political innocents, and all would turn out happily in the end. But most big-budget quality productions escaped to a more distant and less sordid past. The Revolution and the Empire starred, respectively, in Richard Pottier's *Caroline chérie* (*Dearest Caroline*, 1951, with Martine Carol and her wardrobe) and his Carol-less sequel *Le Fils de Caroline chérie* (*Son of Dearest Caroline*, 1954). Then came the Restoration, in Claude Autant-Lara's vivid adaptation of Stendhal's *Le Rouge et le noir* (*The Red and the Black*, 1954). Christian-Jacque directed his wife Martine Carol as Zola's *Nana* (1955), the *femme fatale* who symbolically brings down the Second Empire. Jean Renoir, in his most conventional quality work of the period, featured returned fellow expatriate Jean Gabin in a musical comedy set in turn-of-the-century Paris, *French Cancan*/*Only the French Can* (1955). And Autant-Lara, with his favorite writing team of Jean Aurenche and Pierre Bost, adapted Raymond Radiguet's short novel of illicit young love in World War I, *Le Diable au corps* (*Devil in the Flesh*, 1947), a film highly admired in its day though arguably less impressive in retrospect when compared with works like *French Cancan* or *Madame de*. . . .

The young François Truffaut and his fellow critics at *Les Cahiers du Cinéma* contemptuously labeled the mainstream quality productions *le cinéma de papa*, a blanket condemnation that later critics and historians have often cited approvingly. Nonetheless, there was both good and bad in the Tradition of Quality; *papa* sometimes had things to say that remain of interest to modern viewers. (And Truffaut and many of his comrades-in-arms eventually made some films that looked a lot like papa's, by midpoint in their careers.) But the virulence of the young Turks' anger at the old men who ran the industry does underline a curious cultural disjunction. The Tradition of Quality continued the political, moral, and artistic concerns of Occupation filmmaking, while more and more of its audience was living in a greatly transformed postwar France. Quality productions routinely took traditional Left potshots at the clergy, at a time when the old conflict between clericalism and anti-clericalism finally had begun to seem

Star power in *Le Rouge et le noir*: it may have been difficult to forget Gérard Philipe and Danielle Darrieux as themselves and to accept them as Stendhal's Julien Sorel and Madame de Reynal.

outdated, at least to younger French citizens. And social analysis in the tradition of 1930s Marxism, such as informs *Le Rouge et le noir* and many other works, seemed equally a thing of the past for young people finding their way in the increasingly Americanized postwar European culture. In not yet fully confronting the postwar ethos, French cinema provided an odd parallel to the nation's progress on the political front. The Fourth Republic was largely a revival of the Third, with cosmetic changes, because nothing else could be agreed upon. And so France limped into the postwar world with a prewar system of government. Similarly, its cinema, though purified, was not yet fully liberated.

Continuity between Occupation and postwar cinema, though great, was far from absolute. At the level of film genre, the most notable change was the rapid decline of one of the Occupation's favored subjects: the fantastic. Stories of ghosts, prophetic dreams, devils and demons, love potions, and the like had greatly appealed to French filmmakers and audiences in the spiritual half-light of the occupied country. Not only did Pierre Fresnay sell his soul to the devil in exchange for a magical hand (in *La Main du diable*) and a handsome demon bewitch a court dance (in *Les Visiteurs du soir*). There was also a ghostly aristocrat in Serge de Poligny's charming romantic comedy *Le Baron fantôme* (*The Phantom Baron*, 1943), and a set of dreams that became reality in Marcel L'Herbier's award-winning *La Nuit fantastique* (*The Fantastic Night*, 1942). In the years immediately after the war fantastic tales continued to appear, but most were projects that had been conceived during the Occupation or in its immediate aftermath. Claude Autant-Lara's *Sylvie et le fantôme* (*Sylvia and the Phantom*, 1946) featured Jacques Tati as ghostly comic relief in a romantic comedy in the manner of *Le Baron fantôme*. Jean-Paul Sartre contributed an original story about a dead man and woman in a bureaucratic purgatory for Delannoy's *Les Jeux sont faits* (*The Chips Are Down*, 1947). L'Herbier's *La Nuit fantastique* unleashed a whole fantastic subgenre, the dream-and-reality film. Gérard Philipe had his first starring film role in one notable example, Georges Lacombe's *Pays sans étoiles* (*Country without Stars*, 1946), playing a young man with a very bad case of dreamed *déja vu*. The last major film of this trend, and of the period's strong penchant for the fantastic, was Carné's *Juliette ou la clé des songes* (*Juliette, or the Key to Dreams*, 1951), a work which would certainly have had a better reception had the director been able to make it when he first wanted to, in 1942. In 1951 it was a terrible anachronism, received with great hostility at the Cannes film festival and closing after a few weeks of mediocre box office returns, despite having Gérard Philipe (by then a big star) in the male lead. Life was no longer a dream, for most critics and film spectators, or at least not so self-proclaimedly one. The Tradition of Quality continued with cinema fantasy—stars turned into fetishes acting in wish-fulfilling decors and stories—but abandoned the fantastic.

It is arguably this shift in audience attitudes which explains the sudden decline of the filmmaking team of Marcel Carné and Jacques Prévert. Carné and Prévert had collaborated on only two films during the Occupation, but both works were extremely popular and acclaimed by critics as landmarks in cinema history. They were two historical dramas: the medieval fantasy *Les Visiteurs du soir* (1943) and the epic, two-part chronicle of the nineteenth century stage, *Les Enfants du paradis* (*Children of Paradise*, 1943–44/45). *Les Enfants du paradis* is one of the best-loved works of all French cinema, and for good reason; it is also very much a film of its time, thematically as well as stylistically.[3] The central character, the mime Baptiste (Jean-Louis Barrault), has fled the harsh reality of his early life and become a waking dreamer; his fantasy stage spectacles expand the work's inevitable life-is-art-is-life structure to include dreamscapes. The film seems to be mainly about mental projections, specifically the way each of the four men, in love with the beautiful courtesan Garance (Arletty), projects onto her the image he desires. She says, "I'm so simple," but they cannot see her as she is, only as they want her to be. Only Baptiste, in the end, can see her clearly, in his mind's eye as she leaves him forever.

In *Les Visiteurs du soir* and *Les Enfants du paradis*, Carné and Prévert had left realism, poetic and otherwise, far behind, and had explored metaphysical questions (What is reality? What is love?) that eclipsed their former sociopolitical concerns (How do class roles function? Can workers control their own lives?). This shift, popular at first, eventually left them fatally out of touch with their audience. Their first and only postwar collaboration was *Les Portes de la nuit* (*The Gates of the Night*, 1946), a dreamscape view of a contemporary France peopled by childlike young lovers and infantile, neurotic ex-collaborators. Many critics found in the work's mythically unreal atmosphere an offensive way of treating recent, morally charged events; commercially, the film was an unmitigated disaster. Both Carné and Prévert continued to work in films into the New Wave period, but never again together, and never as successfully as in the years between 1938 and 1945. Prévert wrote his last major commercial screenplay for André Cayatte's metacinematic variations on Shakespeare's *Romeo and Juliet, Les Amants de Vérone* (*The Lovers of Verona*, 1949, original story by Cayatte), a film which stylistically and thematically owes more to the oniric, metaphysical cinema of the Occupation than to the distanced, generally ironic Tradition of Quality. Four years after the disastrous *Les Portes de la nuit*, Carné made his long-delayed dream film *Juliette ou la clé des songes.*[4] *Juliette* was based on a neosymbolist play by Georges Neveux—not very promising material in light of the high-stakes box-office requirements of the 1950s. After the film met with commercial disaster equaling that of *Les Portes de la nuit*, Carné continued to work in films, but only on more routine commercial projects which gave him little occasion to exercise more than honest craftsmanship.

Carné and Prévert were not the only important figures of Occupation cinema whose careers went into relative decline with the Liberation. Jean Grémillon's wartime films earned less money than Carné and Prévert's, but they were very well received by most critics, even on the extreme Right, and their director became something of a culture hero of the Resistance press as a counterexample to the hated Henri-Georges Clouzot. Grémillon's first film of the War years was *Remorques/Stormy Waters* (1939–41), a poetic realist love story set among maritime rescue workers (speaking dialogues by Jacques Prévert). The film had a solid success with the public, in large measure because it was the last appearance on French screens until the Liberation of stars Jean Gabin and Michèle Morgan. Grémillon again worked with Prévert on *Lumière d'été* (*Light of Summer*, 1943), a stylistically hyperactive love story with melodramatic flourishes (the film ends with a climactic confrontation between Good and Evil on and around a huge, mountaintop tramway). Grémillon was a master at adopting the cinematographic style most appropriate to the screenplays he filmed, and he took the fevered, emotionally overstimulated tone of Prévert's dialogues as the occasion for some striking formal play with images and sound—particularly a sonic montage sequence in which a faded beauty, played by Madeleine Renaud, displays her collection of personal artifacts, and noises associated with each object successively overwhelm the sound track.

Le Ciel est à vous (*The Sky is Yours*, 1944) took Grémillon in a very different direction, at least stylistically.[5] Albert Valentin and Charles

Spaak's script portrayed an ordinary petty bourgeois husband and wife who suddenly find a heroic dimension in their lives when they attempt to break an aviation record. Grémillon developed and situated these characters with cinematic means that were economical and self-effacing, compared with the aural and visual fireworks of *Lumière d'été*. Although greatly praised by critics and political activists, *Le Ciel est à vous* was the first in a crippling series of commercial failures that curtailed the director's career in fiction filmmaking even before the end of the Occupation. In 1945 he completed a medium-length poetic documentary on the invasion of Normandy, *Le Six juin à l'aube* (*June Sixth at Dawn*), one of his very best nonfiction works. He began but was forced to abandon several projects before he finally made *Pattes blanches* (*White Paws*, 1949, original scenario by Jean Anouilh), a work which strongly recalls *Lumière d'été* in style, story, and atmosphere (Anouilh and Prévert had similar interests in this period). *Pattes blanches* also failed at the box office, probably because of its anachronistic style and subject. Grémillon made only two more fiction features in the decade which remained of his career, neither one widely esteemed, though he won praise for several short documentaries.

▨ If Grémillon faded quickly, the man *L'Ecran Français* considered his evil nemesis had a much easier time mastering the new cinema of quality. Henri-Georges Clouzot had helped spark the rise of French *film noir* with *Le Corbeau*, and he continued to make notable contributions to the genre with *Quai des Orfèvres/Jenny L'Amour* (1947), *Le Salaire de la peur* (*The Wages of Fear*, 1953), and *Les Diaboliques/Diabolique* (1954). Though a highly visible presence in the Tradition of Quality, Clouzot remained an isolated figure—the victim of bad health, a controversial past, and his own misanthropy. He made only eight feature works and one contribution to a sketch film between his return to the profession in 1947 and his last commercial success, *La Vérité* (*The Truth*, 1960).

Many critics and industry insiders seemed to regard French *film noir* as a kind of commercial art cinema, a prestigious supplement to the period's money-making historical dramas, comedies, and sketch films. Generalized mistrust and facile pessimism seem to make these films tick. A trio of *films noirs* directed by Yves Allégret from scripts by Jacques Sigurd—*Dédée d'Anvers* (*Dédée from Antwerp*, 1948), *Une si jolie petite plage/Riptide* (1949), and *Manèges/The Cheat* (1950)—are among the most resolutely despairing and misogynist works of all French cinema. Such films presented the supposed lessons of the Occupation in brutally stereotyped form: everyone is corrupt, unless they are only stupid, and anyone who thinks otherwise will become a hapless victim of the evil inherent in the human condition. Of course, postwar French producers did not ask audiences to accept such unvarnished (and, critics might say, simpleminded) pessimism as daily fare. But even happier or less obviously ambivalent quality works typically had an undercurrent of *film noir* nihilism, a mildly paranoid doubting of any apparent innocence or sincerity.

Clouzot was the unofficial film community spokesman for the fear that trusting someone—anyone—can be a very dangerous thing to do. He played most gleefully with this theme in *Les Diaboliques* (by the end, it turns out that the spectator should not have trusted the film itself), but for many commentators this work also marks the beginning of its director's artistic decline. It seems likely that by the mid-1950s Clouzot continued to find his despairing view of human existence to be accurate, but he ceased to find it interesting or compelling as material for film narative. His best film of the 1950s, in a very different emotional register, is probably *Le Mystère Picasso* (*The Picasso Mystery*, 1956), a feature-length documentation of a great artist painting. Nonfiction films about the visual arts were fairly common after the war but other directors such as Jean Grémillon and Alain Resnais made these works when they were unable to get backing for fiction features. Clouzot made his film with Picasso as a luxury which his commercial success permitted him, and because he was an avid Sunday painter. But his choice of subject also implicitly reflected his continuing alienation from the film community. Now look here, he was saying to his peers, *this* is true art making (and we, by contrast, are mere entertainers).

Both in the kind of films he made and in his slow rhythm of production, Clouzot was atypical among the major filmmakers of the Tradition of Quality. In one respect, however, he was absolutely representative: he was forty years old when he made *Quai des Orfèvres* in 1947. Yves Allégret was the same age, Christian-Jacque and Claude Autant-Lara a few years older, Marcel Carné a little younger. If they were not yet old men, they were no longer young. When Clouzot made *La Vérité* in 1960, almost two years after the arrival of a new wave of young filmmakers, he offered his own portrait of contemporary French youth culture. Despite its obvious sympathy for the young, the film gives the impression of being a calculatedly commercial assembly of clichés: jazz clubs, all-night cafés, and cheap hotels; pop music, mopeds, and casual promiscuity; impatience with adult hypocrisy; and the entire Latin Quarter, symbolized by Brigitte Bardot, on trial before bourgeois "justice." Clouzot's youth culture is viewed very much from the outside, in a film whose slow cutting and careful compositions exude control and order. Though *La Vérité* is about the search for freedom, little in it, cinematically, is free.

Clouzot was not alone in making an old man's film about youth culture in the early years of the New Wave: Marcel Carné's *Les Tricheurs* (*The Cheaters*, 1958) and Claude Autant-Lara's *En cas de malheur/ Love is my Profession*, 1958) were among the many works in which the masters of the *cinéma de papa* studied the situation of young people across a quite perceptible moral and aesthetic divide. Carné was widely seen as pandering uncritically—and unsuccessfully—to the young, while Autant-Lara's world view had much in common with Clouzot's: *En cas de malheur* attempts to demonstrate that in a world where hypocrisy reigns, youth's attempts at honesty and rejection of authority are touching but doomed. Autant-Lara had been attracted to such subject matter for some time, probably because he saw himself as the eternally rebellious adolescent who refused to grow up. Like most of his generation, Autant-Lara was hurt and confused when his works were denounced by the young critics of *Cahiers du Cinéma*, and deeply disturbed when his tormentors began to make films which had greater apeal than his own for young audiences. This sort of pain and rejection, however, was exactly what Autant-Lara expected (and probably unconsciously sought) out of life. To judge from his lengthy and vituperative memoirs, he spent most of his days spoiling for a fight:

> My birth [he wrote in the aptly titled *La Rage dans le coeur*] had not helped matters any [in his family].
> I was destined, in any case, never to help matters.
> I am pepper on a wound.
> Oil on the fire.
> Rope in the household of a hanged man.
> Roast meat during Lent.[6]

Claude Autant-Lara was born in 1901, the son of Edouard Autant, a young Parisian architect from a family of Parisian architects, and his actress wife, who acted at the Comédie Française using the stage name of Louise Lara. As his choice of last name indicates, their son was at great pains to emphasize his bond with his mother and with the performing arts.[7] Autant-Lara saw his heritage as starkly divided between staid bourgeois respectability on his father's side and antisocial revolt, an artistic vocation, and high spirits on his mother's. Educated at first in the world of his father (at a first-rank *lycée*, and an English public school during the Great War) he showed little aptitude for schooling until he decided—arbitrarily, he maintained—to become a sculptor.[8] He studied at the Ecole des Arts Décoratifs and then won entrance to the more prestigious Ecole des Beaux-Arts. When he was sixteen, his mother obtained for him the position of assistant costume and set designer for a play in which she was to act written by an up-and-coming poet-dramatist: Marcel L'Herbier. Two years later, L'Herbier engaged Autant-Lara as codesigner on *Le Carnaval des vérités*, and the two men continued to work together throughout the 1920s. The young artist also designed sets and costumes for Jean Renoir's *Nana* and worked extensively on the commercial development of Henri Chrétien's "Hypergonar" widescreen process, the direct ancestor of Cinemascope.

With the coming of recorded sound to the film industry, Autant-Lara, eager to direct fiction features (he had made three short works during the 1920s, one in Chrétien's widescreen process), journeyed to the United States to work for Metro-Goldwyn-Mayer, where he directed and adapted films for the French market. At the end of his contract he returned home, disgusted with the studio system and with American culture in general. When he later decided to remain in France and to work there during the Occupation, his choice was undoubtedly influenced by his extreme dislike of his one viable alternative—Hollywood—which he saw as a major threat to European artistic life. On his return to France, Autant-Lara's first feature was *Ciboulette* (1935), co-adapted with Jacques Prévert from a *belle époque* operetta and featuring members of the Groupe Octobre. The production became one of the decade's most notable cinema disasters, disliked by its first industry audiences, recut by the producer, and finally disavowed by its director. For the remainder of the 1930s he had little work, and even less artistic freedom and responsibility.

The scarcity of experienced filmmakers during the Occupation, and the new, more composed and distant cinematographic style which emerged at that time favored Autant-Lara's belated rise to prominence in his profession. He established himself as an adept exponent of the historical romance in *Le Mariage de Chiffon* (*Chiffon's Wedding*,

1942, after Gyp) and *Lettres d'amour* (*Love Letters*, 1942). Writing just after the war's end, Roger Régent found *Le Mariage de Chiffon* significant as "the first really conclusive example of the 'French style' which was to crystallize, then to flower, during these four years of misery."[9] In the view of most observers, the director's final work of the Occupation, *Douce/Love Story* (1943) was not merely an example, but one of the true high watermarks of the new French cinema style. A major ingredient in Autant-Lara's success with the historical film, which was to remain his speciality for the rest of his career, was his extensive experience in costume and set design. Another, decisive factor was his continuing collaboration, first with scriptwriter Jean Aurenche, then with the team of Aurenche and Pierre Bost (beginning with *Douce*). With their able and highly professional collaboration, he directed and coscripted an impressive series of historical dramas and comedies, many adapted from celebrated literary works.

The case against Autant-Lara and his collaborators, made most violently by François Truffaut in his 1954 polemic, "A Certain Tendency of the French Cinema,"[10] is compelling. Autant-Lara and company reduced often great, always highly individual works of literature to the lowest common denominator of the quality historical picture. Stendhal in *Le Rouge et le noir* (*The Red and the Black*, 1954), Radiguet in *Le Diable au corps/Devil in the Flesh* (1946), as well as Colette, Feydeau, and others, serve as grist for this very efficient mill, which seems ever ready to alter and abridge the original works to make them serve up its favored topics of anti-clericalism, bourgeoisie-bashing, and the corruption brought by social and political power. Autant-Lara, Aurenche, and Bost can be seen as embodying one variety of knee-jerk leftism prevalent in postwar French society, particularly among Communists and fellow travelers disappointed with the quick return to republican normalcy and the end of hope for any significant redistribution of political power. There is a strong sense in all of the team's films of a social universe that is dissected and criticized, rather than followed, observed, and made to give up its deeper secrets. The films and the worlds they depict are calculating, precise, and always at least a bit cruel—sometimes very cruel.

Yet at his best Autant-Lara could evoke a stylized poetry of the socialized human gesture. Even in the mutilated prints generally screened today,[11] the Paris sequences of *Le Rouge et le noir* have wonderful moments of balletic social ritual and chess-like interplay of conflicting, class-differentiated behaviors. Autant-Lara's films are distanced, ironic, aspiring to an impersonality which is, paradoxically, the expression of a very personal world view, in which the films serve as "character armor" or defense mechanisms. When he adapted relatively minor literary works, or (occasionally) original screen stories, the director's strong beliefs and almost compulsive reaching for detachment became less obtrusive. He was arguably at his best in comedy, either romantic—*Sylvie et le fantôme* (*Sylvia and the Phantom*, 1945, after Alfred Adam)—or violent and corrosive, as in *L'Auberge rouge* (*The Red Inn*, 1951, original story by Aurenche) and *La Traversée de Paris/Four Bags Full* (1956, after Marcel Aymé's tale of the Occupation). The cinematographic style of Autant-Lara's films always seems somewhat stiff and conventional; for example, he generally favored rather mechanical shot-reverse shot configurations for the depiction of intimate dialogue. But to give the films a feeling of spontaneity and artistic individuality would have suggested that life itself could be spontaneous and expressive—a utopian pretension which the director took great pains to avoid, perhaps because it secretly tempted him.

The other leading exponent of the costume film during the postwar period was of a more cheery disposition than Autant-Lara, though in almost all other ways Christian-Jacque was, if not his twin, at least a very close relation. Christian Maudet had intended to become an architect when he entered the Ecole des Beaux-Arts at roughly the same time Autant-Lara studied there. He and a fellow architecture student moonlighted first as film poster artists, then as set and costume designers, signing their work with an amalgam of their first names. When his friend quit working in films, Maudet continued to use their pseudonym. He had the immense good fortune to become the regular set designer for the director André Hugon just before the coming of sound. Christian-Jacque designed the sets for Hugon's *Les Trois Masques*, the extravagantly profitable first French talkie, and continued to design for its director until 1932. By that time he had had more experience with the talkies than most of the country's more established filmmakers. Hugon, now also a successful independent producer, hired him to direct a low-budget feature. From then on he worked steadily, though rarely on distinguished projects, through the rest of the 1930s.[12] His career lacked the violent ups and downs of Autant-Lara's, but it also got the final push it needed from the German Occupation.

Christian-Jacque directed the first Continental-Films work to begin production in 1941, *L'Assassinat du Père Noël/Who Killed Santa Claus*, and it was also for the German studio that he made his other major work of the period, *La Symphonie fantastique* (*The Fantastic Symphony*,

1942). After the Liberation he had no difficulty being "purified," unlike most others who had worked directly for the enemy, probably because he, like Autant-Lara, had excellent Left connections. In 1946, in fact, the Communist-dominated *L'Ecran Français* named him one of the top five French directors of the day, a judgment which most modern commentators must find rather strange. But this was before the days of *auteur* criticism, and few writers at the journal or elsewhere felt that great directors had to leave their personalities indelibly imprinted on their works. Christian-Jacque is perhaps the ultimate French non-*auteur* director, the continental equivalent of a Michael Curtiz in the American cinema. Like Curtiz, Christian-Jacque had a recognizable cinematic style and was enormously proficient technically, but he rarely left his mark as an artistic temperament. Like Curtiz, he could give a bracing, kinetic feel to the historical swashbuckler, perhaps most notably with Gérard Philipe as star in *La Chartreuse de Parme* (*The Charterhouse of Parma*, 1947, after Stendhal) and *Fanfan-La-Tulipe* (1951). Like Claude Autant-Lara, he made films with a decorator's eye for detail and composition, from carefully crafted, politically Left scripts ofen adapted from literary works.

In Christian-Jacque's career, the counterpart of Autant-Lara's scriptwriting team of Aurenche and Bost was the truculent but celebrated Henri Jeanson, who wrote most of the director's notable films of the postwar period. Their *Nana* (1955), with Martine Carol playing Zola's famous courtesan, was a kind of apotheosis of the historical costume drama, 1950s-style. Jeanson's script transformed Zola's rather dull and vicious character (to whom Jean Renoir had been more faithful in the 1920s) into a fun-loving hooker with a heart of gold, creating a very effective vehicle for Carol's limited but real talent as a comedienne. A similar sea change characterizes the work as a whole, even in its somber conclusion: the film is ironic and self-conscious where Zola is brutally direct. *Nana* is at once subtle and solidly constructed, virtues of "quality" cinema which perhaps compensate for the loss of the original novel's raw energy. In this film one can see the Tradition of Quality doing what it knew how to do best, unapologetically, with a knowing leer at the audience: making decorative, sexy, ironic, class-conscious, bourgeois entertainment.

◼ Postwar cinema was, from the point of view of aspiring entrants to the profession, virtually a closed shop. After the Liberation, some of C.O.I.C.'s former powers, most notably certification of professional status, devolved upon the various unions and professional organizations. These understandably favored their members at the expense of outsiders. For example, the Technician's Union demanded that anyone hired to direct a film have worked as an assistant director on at least three previous productions, a daunting requirement at a time of widespread underemployment. The Occupation had brought a rough equilibrium of supply and demand for labor at all levels, but the postwar industry received an influx of personnel who had not recently worked in the industry. The most celebrated of these were (Christian) anti-Nazi refugees, such as Julien Duvivier and René Clair, who had eschewed working for the New Europe. French Jews, who had either remained in the country in hiding (such as Raymond Bernard) or gone into exile (Pierre Chenal, Max Ophuls), returned in numbers— though not in strength; most would never have the same confidence in their country that they had had before the war. At all levels of the industry resources were scarce, the market uncertain thanks to the Blum-Byrnes accords, and the pool of qualified personnel very large. For those who had been away, the challenge was not so much to move up in status and responsibilities, but to avoid sliding down into forced semi-retirement. The formerly brilliant careers of many respected filmmakers went into genteel decline, at least in the eyes of their peers: Duvivier is a notable example. Critics and historians who today argue strongly for the postwar works of, for example, Jean Renoir or Max Ophuls, do so with twenty-twenty hindsight. In postwar France, the only returnee widely thought to have equalled, or indeed surpassed, the level of his prewar work was René Clair.

In 1960, when his kind of cinema was all but officially dead and gone, Clair became the first filmmaker elected to the Académie Française for his work in the medium. (Marcel Pagnol had joined the venerable body already in 1946, in recognition of his work in diverse genres and media, including fiction film.) By that point Clair represented cinematic conservatism, the "traditional" values of the well-made film. He consciously recognized his role as symbol and spokesman for the old school of cinema in a 1962 tirade against the New Wave worthy of an Autant-Lara:

> It seems that the most important thing [for the cinema's young rebels] is
> to "express oneself" with the help of a camera the way one used to
> "express oneself" in the past by means of the essay, the poem, or the

novel . . . In filmmaking, this desire to "express oneself" is stamped all over with perfectly frank conceit . . . Stylistic weirdness or obscurity is most often used for nothing better than covering up weakness of thought. Those who have nothing to say try to give an original appearance to their ordinary ideas, while a good author's job is to make his originality look ordinary. Nothing becomes conventional more quickly than anti-conventionalism. And Condillac was right to think that "the mania for making oneself stand out denatures the best minds."[13]

Following in the great French tradition, Clair's election to the Academy signaled the virtual end of his creative powers. But during the postwar period he had directed four films which were among the greatest critical and commercial successes of their day—*Le Silence est d'or* (*Silence Is Golden*, 1947),[14] *Les Belles-de-nuit* (*Beauties of the Night*, 1952), *Les Grandes Manoeuvres*/*The Grand Maneuver* (1955), and *Porte des Lilas*/*Gates of Paris* (1957)—as well as one respectable failure, *La Beauté du diable*/*Beauty and the Devil* (1950, a Franco-Italian coproduction filmed in Rome). All but *Porte des Lilas* were set in the past, where Clair now had to retreat to find the carefree, simpler world of his earlier films. (The present day of *Porte des Lilas* was a grim one indeed.) He worked deliberately, though far from slavishly, within well-established film genres. *La Beauté du diable* had a fantastic subject (the Faust legend) worthy of the Occupation. *Les Belles-de-nuit* was a joyful parody of a dream film. *Le Silence est d'or* and *Les Grandes Manoeuvres* were period love stories with bittersweet overtones. This was an old man's cinema in the best possible sense: reflective, tenderly ironic, with the strong sense of the absurd that Clair had always brought to his work.

René Clair had the enormous advantage of not having made a film in France in the second half of the 1930s, though he had returned from England to begin work on a new project just before the *drôle de guerre*. He had no associations with the bad old days, only with the relatively good ones that had come before. French critics congratulated him, and with good reason, for having managed to make personal, European-style films (often very profitable ones) even in Hollywood. Few other returning filmmakers started their new careers from such a position of strength, and few were so well suited to the new sorts of films which the French industry would demand. A major theme in postwar French film culture was the widespread rejection of prewar filmmaking, still thought by many to have contributed to the country's disastrous defeat. As in most commercial cinema at most times, a filmmaker was only as good as his last picture, and if that last work was a controversial one from the late 1930s, finding good jobs could be difficult indeed. Furthermore, production practices had changed dramatically during the four years of misery, and returnees had to learn quickly the rules of a largely new game, already in progress. Having worked in American films was an excellent alternative credential to recent French industry employment, not only because of Hollywood's great (though generally unavowed) prestige, but also because the new French practices were organized to a large extent on the American model.

The difficulties of reentry were perhaps most stark for the film community's many Jews, though there were great variations depending on individual circumstances. Well-placed Resistance members, such as Raymond Bernard and Pierre Braunberger, were able to resume their former standing and responsibilities with little trouble. Often the government nominated such people to administrative positions in various organizations. But the ones who were less esteemed, or were not French, or had no Resistance connections, sometimes encountered what they saw as industry anti-Semitism.[15] And, in fact, Jews would never again be as visible or influential in the industry as they had been before the war. The different fortunes of Max Ophuls and Pierre Chenal demonstrate some of the variables which could come into play in the postwar context. Both men were Jewish and both had had secure positions in prewar French cinema, though Chenal had been more celebrated and successful at the box office. Ophuls had worked, albeit belatedly, in Hollywood, making medium-budget films there between 1947 and 1949 after years of inactivity and failed projects. Chenal had gone to South America, where he had immediately become a leading director of major projects. Yet it was Chenal who almost failed altogether to reestablish himself in France.

Chenal returned quickly—too quickly, one may say with the benefit of hindsight. His first postwar film was *La Foire aux chimères/The Devil and the Angel* (1946), a star vehicle designed to relaunch the French acting career of Eric von Stroheim, an archetypal figure of many supposedly demoralizing films from the late 1930s. Stroheim was paired with Madeleine Sologne, one of the most popular new stars of the Occupation, who played a role that had recently become something of a stereotype: the young blind woman. Most critics compared the work unfavorably with the season's other big film featuring a blind blonde, Jean Delannoy's *La Symphonie pastorale* (*The Pastoral Symphony*,

1946, script by Aurenche and Bost after André Gide), which had all the virtues and defects of a major quality production. *La Foire aux chimères*, perceived as old-fashioned and clumsy, quickly faded from view, while *La Symphonie pastorale* won major awards and had great commercial success. Today, however, it is Chenal's work that many critics and historians find the better film.

Bad luck continued to pursue Chenal. His next work, *Clochemerle* (1948), a frankly commercial, safe project, was mutilated at the demand of government censors, who found it to contain anti-republican sentiments. Though the film did respectably at the box office, Chenal had become firmly established as a problem director. He was obliged to return to South America, where he made a ferocious, English-language *Native Son* (1951, after Richard Wright, who also starred) and two Spanish-language films before an international coproduction, filmed in Buenos Aires with French actors, gave him renewed entrée to the industry of his former homeland. This time he was able to stay, becoming a respected craftsman of crime films, such as *Rafles sur la ville* (*Raids in the City*, 1958), though he never regained his prewar eminence or creative freedom.

More than a year after Pierre Chenal returned to France to make his first postwar film there, Max Ophuls finally got to direct one in Hollywood. Three other American projects quickly followed, made (like the first) for independent producers, and having modest but solid commercial careers. *Letter from an Unknown Woman* (1948), after Stephan Zweig, produced by John Houseman) is widely considered one of his masterworks, and one of the best films made by a European director in studio-era Hollywood. Three of Ophuls's American works were released in France, all to tepid critical and popular response, but the director had sufficiently established his American credentials to be able to return and work in his adopted country, By then the industry had stabilized after the disruptions of the Liberation and the unpredictable audiences of the first postwar years. It was quite clear which sorts of films would sell, properly executed and packaged, and which would not.

Ophuls's *La Ronde* (*Rondelay*, 1950, after Arthur Schnitzler) was an eccentric but eminently commercial project, simultaneously a costume film, a sex comedy, an integrated sketch film using multiple stars, and an adaptation of a scandalous literary classic. That it also managed to be one of the director's most personal works is one of the occasional small miracles of cinema history. Critical reaction was on the whole quite hostile: Ophuls was accused of pandering to the lowest sort of

The ten sketches of Max Ophuls's *La Ronde* give a whirlwind tour of the class system of turn-of-the-century Vienna. In this scene, a soldier (Serge Reggiani) has seduced a chambermaid (Simone Simon) and now wishes to be rid of her.

audience interests. Despite bad reviews, the film did excellent box office. Its good fortunes allowed Ophuls to make his three next (and last) French works, all of them to varying extents commercial and critical failures: *Le Plaisir/House of Pleasure* (1952, a sketch film after three stories by Maupassant),[16] *Madame de . . .* (1953, after Louise de Vilmorin), and *Lola Montès* (1955, a French-German-Italian coproduction in color and CinemaScope, starring Martine Carol). These four works arguably mark the summit not only of his artistic career but of the Tradition of Quality as well—though this is a judgment made very much in retrospect. During the 1950s Ophuls was if anything an even less central figure in the industry than he had been before the war: respected for his visual pyrotechnics and incredibly sure direction of actors (and for his heroic anti-Nazi past), but not a name to contend with, either financially or in terms of critical esteem. Like Chenal, he was a 1930s-style artisan in the midst of an Americanized, capital-intensive and efficiency oriented industry. He supervised and collaborated on all aspects of his films with rare intensity, particularly on costumes, sets, scenarios, and cinematography.

Ophuls was no avant-garde rebel—though his last film gave him the appearance of one—nor, like Chenal, a stubborn individualist. His costumes, scenarios, and so on, were entirely in keeping with mainstream quality standards. His originality lay in the way he adapted these to his own personal obsessions (the difficultly of sexual control, money, class relations, performance) and artistic vision (continuity in space and time, visual and aural excess, symmetry, synesthesia). He was a subtle ironist in a period which prized irony but generally found it difficult to employ subtly. *Lola Montès* became the most notorious commercial failure of the 1950s not because it defied the Tradition of Quality, but because it embodied it too intensely, too self-consciously, and perhaps too well. It caused the almost immediate bankruptcy of its principal producer, Gamma Films. When Pierre Braunberger went to the public auction of the company's holdings, he found himself the only bidder for Max Ophuls's last, great work, which by then existed only in radically cut, reordered copies. It took over a year to reestablish a version close to the original release, by which time the director was dead and generally forgotten within the industry, though not by young outsiders, such as the critics at *Cahiers du Cinéma*, who found him one of the few real artists in a kind of filmmaking which they generally despised.

❧ 12 ❧

An Alternative Film Culture

If, immediately after the Liberation, most of the French film community took pride in the industry's recent accomplishments and voiced guarded optimism about its future, a few important figures expressed caution and dissatisfaction. The young critic André Bazin, while acknowledging that "three years of wartime production today reveal themselves [in late 1944] as not only honorable but of an exceptional richness," was worried about the future. The great works of the Occupation, he wrote, had been produced in response to very particular circumstances:

> A captive nation that refused to exalt its slavery and yet could not proclaim its desire for freedom naturally had to develop an escapist cinema . . . The public wanted the screen to be its window and not its mirror. The result was this paradoxical phenomenon: the social art par excellence—the one that drew together the greatest number of people, the most realistic art in terms of its means of expression—is the one to least express contemporary French society . . .
> Despite its very important qualities, for the last four years our cinema has been marked by a social exile that has diluted its sap. If the incontestable artistic value, the suppleness and exactitude of our cinema's style, are to survive under the new circumstances, they must adapt to the new climate. We cannot stand up against the gust of grandeur, violence, hate, tenderness, and hope that will sweep over us with the American cinema unless we too set down the deepest roots in the soul of our time—in its angers and its sorrows as well as in its dreams. French cinema will only save itself if it learns how to become even greater by rediscovering an authentic expression of French society.[1]

Bazin's hopes for a French cinema that would be more attuned to everyday life did not spring from a simpleminded, moralistic ideal of artistic realism in the service of the greater social good. Cinema would not come to the aid of reality, but vice versa. He assumed that close contact with contemporary life would strengthen French films as works of art; the crucial issues were aesthetic, not sociological. Like the partisans of quality cinema, he worried about the flood of American works on French screens. But whereas industry insiders saw the threat of this formidable competition in its technical perfection and dramaturgical craftsmanship, Bazin saw Hollywood cinema as more organically linked to the society for which it was made, and thus more compelling and well formed.

The Tradition of Quality typically commented on modern life through the deforming optics of historical allegory (the costume film) and psychopathology (*film noir*). The closest that mainstream filmmaking got to cinematic realism was in occasional works in the Soviet socialist realist tradition such as Le Chanois's *L'Ecole buissonnière/Passion for Life* (1948) and in "thesis films" like Clouzot's *Si tous les gars du monde* (*If All the Guys in the World*, 1955) and André Cayatte's *Nous sommes tous des assassins* (*We Are All Murderers*, 1952). In Paris and other large cities, however, some postwar filmgoers did have the opportunity to see a series of alternative, less formulaic visions of the possible relations between film and contemporary reality. The activist social cinema of the 1930s, though widely thought to be both politically and artistically discredited, remained visible for a time in major revivals (*Le Jour se lève* in 1945, *La Grande Illusion* in 1946) and in two first releases of films previously banned by government censors: André Malraux's *Espoir/Man's Hope* (1938–39/45, after his novel), and Jean Vigo's *Zéro de conduite* (1933/45, quickly joined by the restored *L'Atalante*). The same period also saw the much delayed assembly and release of Jean Renoir's *Une Partie de campagne* (1936/46). These works were debated, discussed, and generally admired by the young patrons of ciné-clubs, art cinemas, and the public screenings at the Cinémathèque Française, though the general public remained unresponsive.

Espoir, one of the most original works of 1930s world cinema, attracted a great deal of attention thanks to the political prestige and newsworthiness of its writer-director. But despite a showcase presentation at a major Paris cinema and widespread critical acclaim, commercially Malraux's film was a respectable failure, in large measure because of his refusal to allow its Spanish dialogue track to be dubbed into French. His story of a badly equipped unit of Spanish republican pilots and their heroic attack on a fascist-controlled air strip was acted by actual participants in the struggle, and filmed largely in real locations—though with very professional, polished lighting and composition by cinematographer Louis Page. Malraux supposedly knew little of the specific techniques of the cinema, but he had obviously seen and analyzed some powerful filmic models, among them doubtless Sergei Eisenstein's celebrated explorations of montage, and probably also Renoir's *Toni* and the works of Marcel Pagnol. His film combined montage and cinematic metaphor (birds suddenly flying off figure a fatal collision) with extreme realism of speech, gesture, and social ritual.

The Eisensteinian side of Malraux's only film linked it to the cinema's past. The extreme social realism of its fictional world pointed to the future, foreshadowing (as had *Toni* and Pagnol's works) one of the most important currents in postwar filmmaking: Neorealism. The periodic, much discussed presentations at festivals and first-run cinemas of works by Rossellini, De Sica, and other members of the Neorealist movement gave French audiences another vision of the striking cinematic possibilities offered by everyday social reality. Though politically committed to a materialist, class-based analysis of contemporary life, the innovative Italian directors constructed their films around the lived experiences of typical individuals. Their realism was direct, emotional, and generally unironic. The implicit storytellers in their works did not withdraw from their characters, either to criticize or to extol them. The Italian films' frequent use of nonprofessional actors, and their general practice of shooting in real locations strengthened the sense that they portrayed a reality independent of the narration, a world which had its own distinct claim on the viewer's attention.

Postwar French cinema only produced a few films that can be termed realist in comparison with works like Rossellini's *Roma Città aperta/Open City* (1945) or De Sica's *Ladri di Biciclette* (*Bicycle Thieves,* 1948). Why no French Neorealist movement developed at the same time that one flourished in Italy is a question still open to debate. Material differences, such as the condition of studios and technical facilities (both somewhat—but only somewhat—worse in Italy) were probably less important than the two industries' different strengths and structures. Production in France was oriented to big budget works that necessitated large audiences, and (as generally happens in commercial cinema at all times and in all countries) maintaining large audiences meant providing escapist fare. Even though small films required only limited audiences to be profitable, they could but rarely break the economic blockade effectively created by large French distributors and theatre circuits, which could generate easy, predictable profits from quality films and from the plentiful, low-cost American works which flooded the market. Italian production and exhibition, by contrast, was economically weaker, much like the uncontrolled, open French industry of the 1930s. In the absence of a strong regulatory system, film budgets were small, as were expectations of success at the box office, and many independent producers with a wide range of financial resources and artistic ambitions vied for a share of the chaotic market. As a result, innovation in film form and subject matter met less resistance there than in France.

Furthermore, the aesthetics of quality cinema conflicted sharply with Neorealist practices, and filmmakers and critics committed to the former sometimes violently attacked the latter. The most divisive debate of the 1945–46 film season concerned Georges Rouquier's *Farrebique* (1946), a semi-fictionalized chronicle of a year in the life of a peasant family. Greatly admired by many in the film community, particularly on the Left, the work also had powerful and vocal detractors who managed to prevent its selection as a French entry in the Cannes film festival.[2] In addition to being denied the helpful publicity of a Cannes screening, the film probably reached a limited audience for reasons of aesthetics. Compared with the more fictionalized, yet also more straightforward Italian works, it must have seemed anachronistic in its intrusive, extra-narrative metaphors (worthy of late silent cinema, and considerably less subtle than Malraux's similar effects in *Espoir*)[3] and painterly pictorialism à la André Antoine. Today one may savor, or at the very least accept, these qualities, but in 1946 they worked to Rouquier's disadvantage. There was no clamor for a sequel. The director only returned to his setting and characters three and a half decades later, when the farm was being sold, in *Biquefarre* (1982).

After 1946 Rouquier turned to more conventional, less poetic and less fictionalized documentaries. His career continued and prospered, but it never achieved the impact on mainstream commercial cinema that *Farrebique* had briefly suggested was possible. One reason the film fell into oblivion, however, was that it had been eclipsed by another innovative work which also briefly suggested that a realist impulse could sustain itself in the new French cinema. This was René Clément's *La Bataille du rail* (*Battle of the Rail*, 1946), which won two awards at the Cannes festival and became one of the most financially success-ful French films of its day. After this remarkable début in commercial narrative cinema, Clément went on to become the French filmmaker most often honored at Cannes, and the mainstream director most widely praised as an innovator during the years of the Fourth Repub-lic.[4] Yet his undeniable commercial and critical successes remained admired exceptions to mainstream norms, with almost as little impact on the industry as *Farrebique*. Clément became the token intellectual maverick, the official semi-rebel of postwar French cinema, his works a series of attempts to break new artistic ground within a "tradition" hostile to change.

René Clément had been a successful cameraman and director of short documentaries in the 1930s, though like many other nonfiction filmmakers he aspired to work in fiction features. In a profession overwhelmingly dominated by older people, he was thirty-one years old when he began work on *La Bataille du rail* in late 1944, becoming one of the relatively few directors of his age to make a first feature film between the Liberation and the late 1950s. He joined this select if largely undistinguished group almost by accident, when his short semi-documentary about the resistance activities of railroad workers was expanded to feature length, because of strong audience interest in films about recent events. Had *La Bataille du rail* begun life as a feature project, it is unlikely that its producer would have approved Clément's casting, for he employed actual train workers in most major roles. Perhaps because of its players' limited acting abilities, the film almost always directs the spectators' interest toward overall situations rather than to the lived experiences of people in them, and provides little individualization or development of characters (or even simple background information about them). In this regard, the work is less allied to Italian Neorealism than critics and historians generally claim, and closer in spirit to traditional documentary (specifically, to ethno-graphic film, in which Clément had been a specialist). The trains, almost by way of compensation for the underdevelopment of char-acters, are occasionally personified, as when they seem to protest, by their whistles, the execution of a group of workers in reprisal for acts of sabotage. In the film's most spectacular sequence, explosive charges set beneath the tracks demolish an entire train; the viewer's attention is almost entirely focused on what happens to the machinery, whose fate assumes a kind of tragic grandeur.

La Bataille du rail left open to doubt the question of how its director would fare with less political—and mechanical—subjects. And so, despite the work's good critical reception and massive popular success, Clément was unable to find a producer who would allow him to develop his own projects. He worked as a kind of glorified technician on projects of Jean Cocteau and the actor Noël-Noël before being able to direct, in the fullest, European sense of the word, another feature work. *Les Maudits* (*The Damned*, 1947), was set aboard a German submarine in the last days of the war. Its melodramatic scenario (about disparate individuals in physical and moral crisis, in the manner of Hitchcock's *Lifeboat*) was filmed in a decor which exactly reproduced the space of an actual submarine. This allowed bravura, *cinéma vérité*-style visual effects such as an extended tracking shot following characters from one end of the ship to the other, and a constant, Stroheim-like sense of physical, if not psychological, realism. This time Clément used professional actors, though he took the (commercially) radical step of having each player in the international cast speak his own native language. Although today the film's mixture of physical realism and stylized psychodrama seems unsatisfying to most observers, it won Clément his second grand prize at Cannes, and its good box office returns established him once and for all as a "bankable" commercial director.

Clément had retreated from the stark, functional realism of his first feature; *Les Maudits*, if not exactly ordinary commercial cinema, was recognizably a fiction film constructed with traditional, perhaps even clichéd, dramaturgy. Its experiments in cinematic realism were highly controlled and integrated into mainstream practices. The film marks the beginning of his series of efforts to explore the limits of realist filmmaking practices within the commercial mainstream. Many of these works seem quite self-consciously to address specific formal and generic issues, and have the quality of one-time experiments. In *Au-delà des grilles*/*The Walls of Malapaga* (1949, an Italian-French co-production), for example, he consciously made a link between 1930s poetic realism (incarnated by Jean Gabin in his traditional prewar role of the doomed proletarian hero) and Italian Neorealism (shots of the streets and people of Genoa, associated with costar Isa Miranda)—a mixture of style and ethos not easily transferable to other subjects. His best-known work (for modern audiences) also played with cinematic traditions, though in a less eccentric manner: *Jeux interdits* (*Forbidden Games*, 1952) is both an historical picture set in the days of the German *blitzkreig* and an offbeat *film noir* about children's reactions to

Whereas the masterpieces of Italian Neorealism concern the social and moral experiences of ordinary people, René Clément's *La Bataille du rail* often directs our attention more toward machinery and milieu than toward human drama.

death and mourning. Perhaps more remarkable than this canny mixture of genres (though who else would have thought of it?) were the film's use of untrained young actors in leading roles and its deliberately unromantic portrait of the French peasantry.

Ten years after he made his first fiction film, Clément seems to have lost most of his will to experiment with film genres, styles, and subject matter. Although *Gervaise* (1956, script by Aurenche and Bost after Zola's *L'Assommoir*) is one of the period's better historical costume dramas, there is little in it that another, equally competent filmmaker of the day would not have done. Possibly he had become discouraged by the hostile reviews of his work in that official organ of youthful rebellion, *Cahiers du Cinéma*. At any rate, just a few years before the arrival of the New Wave, Clément abandoned his role as the industry mainstream's in-house innovator and became a simple artisan of the *cinéma de papa*.

▨ With Clément's progress from *La Bataille du rail* to his experiments in testing the boundaries of mainstream cinema, and finally to straightforward quality filmmaking, the last remnants of the postwar interest in cinematic realism had largely vanished. An alternative film culture could not crystallize around a cinema of reality, as it had in Italy. Indeed, it was difficult to see how any meaningful alternative to the commercial mainstream could exist at all, given the industry's closed, tightly controlled structure. Nonetheless, a few other unconventional filmmakers still challenged mainstream practices, some of them in more radical ways than Clément ever did. By themselves, these individualistic, often eccentric artists could not have amounted to an alternative French film culture without the glue that was provided by a new variety of film criticism—an activist, often theoretical discourse aimed at a new kind of cinema as yet rarely realized in images and sounds. Its critical ideal was not a cinema of reality but a cinema of *authors,* of creators who "wrote" in images with, in Alexandre Astruc's celebrated formulation, the *caméra-stylo,* or "camera-pen."

Astruc composed his famous essay "The Birth of a New Avant-Garde" in frustrated reaction to the many obstacles to entry into the industry. "One had to have one's card—like prostitutes do," he later recalled, "to make, in order to be a second assistant director, three films as an apprentice; to be a first assistant, three films as a second; to be a director, three films as a first assistant . . . In other words, life in prison."[5] Since one could not make cinema, he felt, one had to begin by describing what one would do if one could. This he did in 1948:

> The cinema is quite simply becoming a means of expression, just as all the other arts have been before it, and in particular painting and the novel. After having been successively a fairground attraction, an amusement analogous to boulevard theatre, or a means of preserving the images of an era, it is gradually becoming a language. By language, I mean a form in which and by which an artist can express his thoughts, however abstract they may be, or translate his obsessions exactly as he does in the contemporary essay or novel. That is why I would like to call this new age of cinema the age of the *caméra-stylo* . . .
>
> The fundamental problem of the cinema is how to express thought . . . All thought, like all feeling, is a relationship between one human being and another human being or certain objects which form part of his universe. It is by clarifying these relationships, by making a tangible allusion, that the cinema can really make itself the vehicle of thought.

From today onwards, it will be possible for the cinema to produce works which are equivalent, in their profundity and meaning, to the novels of Faulkner and Malraux, to the essays of Sartre and Camus.

So there we are. This has nothing to do with a school, or even a movement. Perhaps it could simply be called a tendency: a new awareness, a desire to transform the cinema and hasten the advent of an exciting future. Of course, no tendency can be so called unless it has something concrete to show for itself. The films will come, they will see the light of day—make no mistake about it. The economic and material difficulties of the cinema create the strange paradox whereby one can talk about something which does not yet exist; for although we know what we want, we do not know whether, when, and how we will be able to do it.[6]

Astruc eventually managed to put his ideas about cinema into practice in a subtle and eerie medium-length film, *Le Rideau cramoisi* (*The Crimson Curtain*, 1953, after Barbey d'Aurévilly), and in a first feature, *Les Mauvaises Rencontres* (*Bad Encounters*, 1955). Unfortunately, the release of his next work, which he considered "the only truly successful film [in artistic terms] I believe I have made,"[7] coincided with the first, striking impact of a new generation on the film community. *Une Vie* (*A Life*, 1958, after Maupassant) failed commercially and even today is seldom screened despite its remarkable qualities. Its potential impact was eclipsed, even for those in search of alternatives to mainstream filmmaking, by Louis Malle's *Les Amants*, Claude Chabrol's *Les Cousins*, and praise of a new wave that would quickly pass Astruc by. His films mattered far less in the creation of the climate for this change than did his celebrated polemical essay. Its themes and standards of judgment became widely shared by others who were dissatisfied with commercial cinema.

The formula of the *caméra-stylo* resonated profoundly in an alternative film culture largely thanks to André Bazin: its central figure and the most influential French film critic since Louis Delluc. Bazin's position as conspicuous critical and intellectual outsider of the film community had its origins in his early life. Born in 1918, he was the only son of a provincial, petit-bourgeois family (his father was a bank clerk). He was educated first in a Catholic school in his home town just north of Bordeaux, then in the municipal high school of Courbevoie, near the capital, where the family moved for a time to give him better schooling, and finally at a departmental Ecole Normale (teachers' college). Talented young students of Bazin's modest background could advance socially and professionally by pursuing a career in teaching at the Ecole Normale Supérieure at Saint-Cloud, near Paris. (Their more privileged peers interested in the same profession generally attended the Ecole Normale Supérieure in the capital, rue d'Ulm.) Bazin easily won admission to Saint-Cloud, which included a government fellowship, and began to study literature, philosophy, and the arts. But at the beginning of his second year his military regiment was mobilized; it was late 1939 and thoughts of career had to be set aside. Bazin spent the *drôle de guerre* far from the front. With little to do, he and a friend haunted the cinemas of Bordeaux, and for the first time he became passionately interested in films. When the Ecole Normale of Saint-Cloud reopened in the fall of 1940 he returned to his studies, but the school had changed. Politically suspect professors had been dismissed; German soldiers were everywhere; the atmosphere was tense.

Bazin had already felt somewhat alienated from his school even before it was pressed into the service of the New Europe. Intellectually, it was ferociously devoted to the tradition of materialist, anticlerical thought that had dominated bourgeois education since the late nineteenth century (and which would find its cinematic embodiment in many of the works of the Tradition of Quality). Bazin, however, was drawn to the newer, radical Catholic counter-currents centered on the magazine *Esprit*, which emphasized intuition, personal commitment to felt ideals, and the existential dimensions of human life. He had organized an *Esprit* study group during his first year at Saint-Cloud, but such meetings were forbidden during the Occupation, for radical Catholics were almost invariably anti-Nazi and anti-Vichy. His school's complicity with this repression probably added to his sense of estrangement from the institution, and when he took his examination for certification (success would have enabled him to teach in a *lycée*), he stammered badly during his oral *explication de texte*, and failed. He did not take the exam a second time, as he could have done, preferring to avoid the likelihood of another humiliation. It is difficult not to read his failure as unconsciously willed, a rejection of the hypocrisy implied by success in what he considered a corrupt, soul-destroying system. His speech impediment allowed him to renounce the career for which he had so assiduously prepared (and on which the ambitions of his family had depended, probably to a crippling degree) and to begin a new life as a journalist and critic.

Bazin organized a ciné-club in occupied Paris, one of the first notable revivals of an institution which had been moribund since the early 1930s. He began to write film reviews. With the Liberation, he continued to organize and administer film societies of various sorts and to write about cinema, often for *Esprit*. He contributed to the Communist-dominated *L'Ecran Français* (as did other, similarly inclined activists, including Astruc) until growing discord between Communists and non-Communists made this impossible. He dreamed of an *Esprit* for the cinema, a journal which would examine the medium in terms of the largest moral, intellectual, and aesthetic problems it raised, and which would continually ask: What is cinema? What can it be? What should it be? In collaboration with fellow critics Jacques Doniol-Valcroze and Lo Duca, he created this magazine in 1951: *Les Cahiers du Cinéma*.[8] He would be its dominant critical personality, leading a team of young writers such as François Truffaut, Jean-Luc Godard, Jacques Rivette, Claude Chabrol, and many others, until his death in 1958 at the age of forty, the victim of the ill health that dogged him all his life.

If Bazin became an even more important figure for the evolution of French cinema than Louis Delluc (whose life and career resembles his in some striking ways) it is probably because he had a much broader—almost messianic—idea of what film criticism should do. His best works grew out of a philosophical and religious quest for totality; he eschewed atomistic analyses such as the exam *explication de texte* that had made him stammer. As a result his essays have led, as it were, two lives. When he wrote them, they were meant not as objective theorizing, but as actively engaged criticism with a definite polemical bent. After his death, however, they were widely seen as the ideal of realist cinema theory, a current more systematically (if less richly) embodied in works such as Siegfried Kracauer's *Theory of the Film*. But one neglects Bazin the critic at one's peril. He was and remains the cinema commentator who could best elucidate coherent theoretical support for his ongoing engagement with the history of the medium. The critical force which he achieved may be seen in the way his evaluations of films (for example, Bresson's *Le Journal d'un curé de campagne*) seem accepted verities today; most modern film criticism is still profoundly Bazinian.

Much of contemporary film theory, on the other hand, is profoundly ambivalent toward Bazin as theorist (to the extent that he can be construed as such). He serves for many writers as a kind of idealist whipping boy, the exemplary demonstration of what not to do. This has had the ironic effect of making recent cinema theory almost as Bazinian (by this systematic rejection) as is contemporary film criticism. Modern film theory tries to purge itself of Bazinian idealism, and in so doing it rejects what was most original and productive in the critic's thinking, the inextricable mingling of idealist and realist impulses. The notion of cinematic realism was the major point of departure for all of his thinking, but he did not assume it as a neutral, scientific fact. For Bazin, the photographic image did not merely reproduce reality but transformed it, radically altering its nature for the spectator by the very fact of reproducing it as literally as possible. The result was surprisingly close to the Russian Formalist critical ideal of *ostraneniye*, or "making strange."[9] But for Bazin the end product had a specifically spiritual, even religious, dimension: "The aesthetic possibilities of photography reside in the revelation [*révélation*] of the real. This reflection in a wet sidewalk, that gesture of a child, did not depend on me to be distinguished within the fabric [*tissu*, also organic tissue] of the external world; only the impassive lens, stripping the object of the habits and prejudices, the spiritual dust and grime with which my perception has covered it, could present it in its virginal purity to my attention, and consequently to my love."[10] Had Bazin confined his analysis of the medium to its most basic level, as "the completion in time of the objectivity of photography,"[11] he might have approved of the aleatory, unstructured experiments of Andy Warhol (*Empire, Sleep*) and other later experimentalists. But his thinking led in a more aesthetically conservative direction because he believed that at the level of the whole film another sort of reality had to make itself felt. One way this could take place was through interactions between the cinema and other media. Bazin viewed literary and theatrical adaptation, as well as other varieties of what he called "impure" cinema, as fundamentally positive to the extent that they brought into the medium the structured, intended reality of the cultural artifact. Faithful adaptations, for example Jean Cocteau's *Les Parents terribles/ The Storm Within* (1948, after his play), could offer the revelation of the original work in much the same way that photography could offer a child's gesture, or a reflection, to our attention and our love. They could also, crucially, enrich the living tradition of cinema with new possibilities of artistic creation, to be used in what he saw as the ultimate goal of the cinema medium: the expression of *style*.

Bazin's sense of "style" was closely related to Astruc's notion of the *caméra-stylo*'s "language": a means of expressing thought—first and foremost, the thought of an artist. At this level, too, the cinema *needed* reality—but a spiritual, personal one imposed through the lens of the camera. The greatest moral and aesthetic danger lay in spurious attempts at objectivity, which would invariably result in bad film-making. Despite his emphasis on personal vision, however, Bazin was not categorically opposed to cinematic formulas; to be artistically viable these had to arise organically from their social context, as he thought happened with American film genres such as the Western. In this case, the ideal reality needed by good cinema was not that of the individual artist, but of the audience as functioning social entity. Mainstream French cinema, on the other hand, was caught in a no-man's-land between these two possible sources of artistic truth—the isolated, creative individual and the connected, consensual society. When it adapted great works of literature or theatre, it too often squandered the artistic riches it mined, reducing complex, highly individual art works to a nonorganic "tradition" of the lowest common denominator.[12]

Though Bazin sought to engage in dialogue with quality film-making, distinguishing the good from the bad and encouraging what he saw as progressive tendencies, he reserved his highest praise and his most serious essays for a group of independent figures on the fringes of the French industry, such as Robert Bresson and Jacques Tati. Largely thanks to his efforts, these artists gained coherence as an alternative artistic/moral/political current in postwar cinema, its opposition party, so to speak. Bazin passed on this vision to the younger generation of critics and future filmmakers at *Cahiers du Cinéma:* radical, but still completely recognizable Bazinians. However, they had little of his tolerance and will to encourage reformist tendencies in the industry. In their manichaean view of the film community, one was either on the right side of things—and hence either not making films at all or making them with difficulty and outside current norms and practices—or one was an imbecile. Bazin often gave qualified praise to many of René Clément's and Claude Autant-Lara's works, but the younger writers at *Cahiers* grouped them with Richard Pottier and Christian-Jacque as styleless hacks.

But what Bazin's disciples lacked in critical subtlety and moral disinterestedness (for they were criticizing the works of people they hoped to replace), they made up in intensity, focus, and sincerity. Many critics and historians would later see the young men's intemperate blasts of protest as validated, in retrospect, by the brilliance and innovation of their first films, which they began to make in the same season that marked the death of their mentor and, for some, surrogate father. François Truffaut, for whom Bazin was a virtual adoptive father, wrote the magazine's most celebrated attack on quality filmmaking. In "A Certain Tendency of French Cinema" (1954), Truffaut drew up his own list of *Cahiers*-approved living French filmmakers. He found a stark contrast between these exemplary figures and the artisans (above all, the scriptwriters) of psychological realism, which he saw as the industry's dominant moral-aesthetic trend:

> In the films of "psychological realism" there are nothing but vile beings, but so inordinate is the authors' desire to be superior to their characters that those who, perchance, are not infamous are, at best, infinitely grotesque.
>
> Well, as for these abject characters, who deliver these abject lines—I know a handful of men in France who would be INCAPABLE of conceiving them, several cinéastes whose world-view is at least as valuable as that of Aurenche and Bost, Sigurd and Jeanson. I mean Jean Renoir, Robert Bresson, Jean Cocteau, Jacques Becker, Abel Gance, Max Ophuls, Jacques Tati, Roger Leenhardt; these are, nevertheless, French cinéastes and it happens—curious coincidence—that they are *auteurs* who often write their dialogue and some of them invent the stories they direct.[13]

In a penetrating, bracingly hostile analysis of Truffaut's essay, John Hess has argued that the young critic's quarrel with mainstream filmmaking was more moralistic and implicitly political than it was artistic: "The most important determinant of an *auteur* was not so much the director's ability to express his personality, as usually has been claimed, but rather his desire and ability to express a certain world view. An *auteur* was a film director who expressed an optimistic image of human potentialities within an utterly corrupt society. By reaching out both emotionally and spiritually to other human beings and/or to God, one could transcend the isolation imposed on one by a corrupt world."[14] While this is a valid reading of Truffaut's essay, and of other early *Cahiers* articles by Rohmer, Rivette, and Godard as well as Truffaut, it does rather serious violence to many of the films they liked. One has trouble regarding Jean Cocteau as "optimistic" in any obvious sense, or believing that Max Ophuls's characters are innocents tortured by a corrupt society; many of the films most highly regarded within the alternative film culture were more radically, if subtly, despairing than anything penned by Jean Aurenche and Pierre Bost. It is true that the young *Cahiers* critics had, like their mentor, a penchant for Catholics and mystics of all sorts: Renoir had returned to the Church and also embraced Eastern religions; Bresson was often regarded as a quasi-Jansenist; Cocteau's religion was Art. But the underlying, Bazinian unity in the list of Cahiers-approved film *auteurs* was their opposition to the old positivist, anti-spiritual French intellectual tradition.

The postwar film industry was dominated by the contemporary Marxist variant of this orientation, however, which is probably one reason why these filmmakers often found it difficult to work in the Tradition of Quality. Truffaut's list is largely an honor roll of semi-failures: Gance, in 1954, had not made a fiction feature in over a decade; Leenhardt, primarily a critic and director of documentaries, had made only one at that point in his career; the others (except for Renoir and Ophuls) worked very slowly. Aside from this, they shared above all a stubborn commitment to their highly individual artistic temperaments, their very diversity adumbrating that of the new wave which was to follow. A film aesthetic which favors individual expression will seek out highly individualistic creators as models. And so the affection of Truffaut, Godard, and the other young heterosexual admirers of American genre film for the aging, homosexual aesthete Jean Cocteau is not so strange as it might at first appear, and it is not the expression of some secret *nostalgie de la perversion.* Jean-Luc Godard, for example, dedicated his early fiction short *Charlotte et son jules* (*Charlotte and Her Boyfriend,* 1958), a most un-Cocteaulike film, to the older artist, and François Truffaut gave him the financial backing to make his last film, *Le Testament d'Orphée* (*The Testament of Orpheus,* 1960).

Most of Truffaut's great directors were significantly older than the leading exponents of quality filmmaking; some, like Cocteau, were near the ends of their careers. The *Cahiers'* reverence for grandfather-figures probably had at least some underpinning of self-interest: older men will die or retire soon, the better to open a place for their heirs. More significantly, though, it illustrates the young critics' profound respect for the past, which also found expression in their love of traditional film genres and in their anger at the many liberties quality literary adaptations took with their sources. The quarrel between *Cahiers* and the industry mainstream was in large measure a quarrel over traditions—the recently elaborated Tradition of Quality versus the legacy of the 1930s and before. The great living representative of prewar French cinema was Jean Renoir, though he was soon to represent something rather different in French film culture, as he abandoned the political orientation of his prewar work to express his new sense of the world and what it meant to live in it. Because he was Renoir, he was a "tradition" all to himself, and although the exponents of quality filmmaking took little interest in his new work, it continued to inspire respect and in many cases love among the French film community's young rebels.

When *Cahiers du cinéma* was founded, Renoir had only recently returned to Europe and had not yet worked in France again. In fact it would be more accurate to say that in the early 1950s he began his first lengthy *visits* to the Continent, since he was now an American citizen with a rose- and vine-surrounded home in Beverly Hills. His cousin Gabrielle, who had raised him as a child, lived next door with her American husband. His son, after having fought in the American army in the Pacific and gone to college on the G.I. Bill, was pursuing doctoral studies in literature at Harvard. "For me," Renoir had written to a friend, "exile was not a little promenade as it is for many. It was a very serious thing which profoundly changed me."[15] His affective life now lay primarily in California, though after *The River* (1950, after Rumer Godden, made in English in India) his professional life was entirely European. Probably the main reason Renoir ceased making films in the United States was that his American projects had all failed to give him the broad responsibilities he felt he needed to be effective. As he argued to his American agents, in 1941: "I am much more an author of films than a director. The successes that I have managed are due above all to my work on their scenarios .... My work as a director will certainly be better if I participate in the scriptwriting."[16]

Renoir's inability to shape the scripts he filmed in Hollywood probably explains why his American works often have a curiously muffled quality, and why they lack the sharp, well-delineated outlines of character and environment seen in his prewar French films. He also had little control in America over editing and scene construction. He was often forced to make sequences out of many disparate shots, when he would have preferred to shoot them in relatively long takes, with camera movement and composition in depth. In leaving Hollywood, he regained control over the writing and visual constructions of his films. *The River* is a stunning return to Renoir the visual stylist of the 1930s, with the added element of Technicolor cinematography, but Renoir the writer now had rather different things to say. Although death intruded now and again in his films, he had lost his earlier fascination with violence. He noticeably shifted his emphasis away from socially defined groups, toward individuals and their families. His films were now far more likely to end happily, and to offer positive views of humanity. In his own old age, he had rediscovered the energy and optimism of his youth, which had been muted during the 1930s by his fear of violence. Now the violence had come and gone, and the fear was lifted.

Critical opinion is sharply divided on the merit of Renoir's post-Hollywood films. Those who see his value in the 1930s as mainly that of a social commentator dismiss his later work as a moral and political cop-out. Those who value his late films, on the other hand, reinterpret his political subjects of the 1930s as pretexts for a deeper, more personal set of meditations which find their fullest expression in his works of the 1950s. It is indeed true that the later films refer in many ways to the early ones: *Eléna et les hommes/Elena and Her Men* (1956) reorders and examines scenes (a comic chase through a country *château*) and themes (a woman who inspires a man to heroic ambition) from *La Règle du jeu; Le Caporal épinglé/The Elusive Corporal* (1962) has the same basic plot as *La Grande Illusion*. But it is most fruitful to see the two periods as fundamentally discontinuous, almost the work of two different men, in which similar themes and interests play themselves out in very different contexts. For example, Renoir remained fascinated by speech in his films. But whereas in the 1930s he emphasized its function as social marker (through confrontations of different accents and word patterns), in his postwar French films voices seem to express more directly the emotional lives of his characters; vocal variety has become affective rather than (socially) objective.

Renoir's work has often been examined in terms of the opposition it frequently sets up between nature and theatre. This persistent dichotomy, too, changed profoundly. In his prewar work theatrical performance had mainly represented and commented upon social situations. Though nature could be beautiful, it was indifferent to and independent of men, even when they behaved violently towards it. After the war, Renoir de-socialized theatre: *The Golden Coach* (1952, made in English in Italy with Italian, British, and French actors) transports a *commedia dell'arte* company to an eighteenth-century Peru where no one talks of imperialism, and all the natives are happy. But *The Golden Coach* isn't about Peru, and in a way it isn't about the theatre either. It concerns, rather, the psychology of the individual performing artist. *French Cancan/Only the French Can* (1955) similarly examines the affective situation of a wily, blunt-spoken theatrical impresario, played by Jean Gabin in a role that seems to suggest an idealized Jean Renoir of the 1930s—minus politics. If the director desocialized the theatre in his last works, he increasingly personalized nature, almost to the point of sentimentalizing it, as in *Le Déjeuner sur l'herbe/Picnic on the Grass* (1959), while identifying it with human sexuality.

Exile had indeed profoundly changed Jean Renoir. Many of his former supporters heatedly denounced his work after *La Règle du jeu.* Where, they lamented, was the old Renoir, the real one of the 1930s? Though he rarely acknowledged them, the criticisms probably stung, making his residence in the United States seem doubly desirable. He derived much consolation, however, from the admiration and support of the alternative film culture. *Cahiers du Cinéma* devoted its first issue of 1952 to his work, including an interview in which he gave a profession of faith that probably inspired the terms of François Truffaut's later attack on "psychological realism": "Today, the new being who I am realizes that the time for sarcasm is passed, and that the only thing which I can bring to this illogical, irresponsible, and cruel world is my 'love.'"[17]

Although in the 1950s Renoir was no longer the Renoir of the 1930s, his place had been filled by another member of Truffaut's list of *Cahiers*-approved directors: Jacques Becker. If Becker's films beginning with his first mature work, *Goupi-Mains Rouges/It Happened at the Inn* (1943), and ending with the unjustly neglected masterpiece *Le Trou* (*The Hole*, 1960), seemed to keep alive the prewar Renoir spirit which Renoir himself had abandoned, it was for good reason. Becker had learned his craft as Renoir's assistant director on eight films between 1932 and 1937. He was one of the Left activists most influential in Renoir's involvement with the Popular Front and the P.C.F.; *Le Crime de Monsieur Lange*, for example, was originally his project. Becker was born in 1906, his life a slightly eccentric version of the classic French director's progress: a bourgeois family (Protestant, with a Scottish mother), a business he was slated to take over (manufacturing batteries), and rejection of this destiny and of his social position. He met Renoir in the 1920s, when the two men shared their period's love affair with American jazz (as they would later share a strong stand against fascism). Their professional relationship was severely strained when Renoir took over *Le Crime de Monsieur Lange,* which Becker wanted to direct. They soon ceased to work together, though Becker was to be one of Renoir's few former Left associates who did not reject and denounce him in the postwar period—in itself a very Renoirian attitude.

The Occupation finally brought Becker his chance to direct fiction features. After an essay in the crime film genre, he made *Goupi-Mains Rouges,* one of the period's only films that can be even remotely described as realist. It was an adroit compromise between Occupation fantasy (an isolated provincial microcosm peopled by lovable eccentrics) and 1930s-style social observation (hierarchical relations within the Goupi family, money worship, images of colonialism), and by any standard one of the greatest works of Occupation cinema. For the rest of his career Becker pursued two guiding principles he follows in the film, both recognizably (1930s) Renoiresque: an interest in the group rather than the individual, and a focus on the influence of the group's social *milieu.* Becker's fine sense of social differentiation, however, led him to avoid repeating himself: different groups and *milieux* found different sorts of expression, both socially and filmically. His *Antoine et Antoinette* (1946) and *Edouard et Caroline* (1950), despite their similarities of title and narrative premise (strains on a young couple's relationship), are quite different in structure and ethos. The working class characters of the earlier film live in a culture full of solidarity and group process, whereas the second film's bourgeois couple inhabits a sort of emotional void, which finds filmic expression in a frantic, farcical comedy of morals.

Becker also shared with prewar Renoir a discreet but almost palpable sense of polite detachment from his characters. This common ground is particularly evident in *Casque d'or* (*Golden Headpiece,* 1952), probably his most thoroughly Renoiresque film. In another way, though, this is one of his least typical works, because of its period setting. He generally was at his best with contemporary subjects, where he could be more certain of the social truth of his stories. His *Rendez-vous de juillet* (*July Reunion,* 1949), sometimes cited as the first film about postwar youth culture, is perhaps more accurately about the intersection of that subculture with the traditional bourgeoisie. Becker felt he had to situate his characters, to show where they came from before they could go to the jazz club or the Left Bank café. It was no fellow traveler's sense of political duty which made him do this, however. He was, like Renoir, profoundly interested in the affective lives of his characters, which he saw as shaped (and limited) by their social positions.

Becker continued a vital if widely rejected tradition of pre-quality filmmaking. Jacques Tati, otherwise very different from Becker in style and social orientation, was another cinematic traditionalist whose fidelity to the past made him stand out from mainstream filmmaking. Tati was born Jacques Tatischeff in 1907, in a quiet Paris suburb. His father, the son of a Russian diplomat and a French mother, worked in the capital as a picture framer. The family's relative affluence (skilled artisans could earn a very good income) allowed the boy enough leisure time to take a passionate interest in sports. He played rugby and tennis, and he boxed. He was a keen observer of human behavior, and soon he began to give pantomime impressions of various sports, first for his friends and later, beginning in the early 1930s, in amateur theatrical performances and then for music hall audiences. Out of his music hall earnings he financed a number of short films which he wrote and starred in, of which the most accomplished is probably *Soigne ton gauche* (*Watch Your Left*, 1936, directed by René Clément). By the end of the decade, he was on the brink of international theatrical stardom.

Tati was a sergeant in the French army, and like many soldiers he did little during the brief war and the briefer *débâcle*, though he did meet and carefully observe a distracted soldier who would become the basis of his famous character, Monsieur Hulot. His return to the music hall was interrupted by a lengthy stay in a small village in the Berry region, where he went to avoid conscription into forced labor in Germany (the hated Service du Travail Obligatoire), and where he got the idea for his first postwar film. In 1947 he returned to the village to star in and (for the first time) direct the short *L'Ecole des facteurs* (*The School for Postmen*, 1947), with a cast which included many local residents. This tale of a mail carrier obsessed with speed and efficiency was so successful that he obtained backing to remake it as a feature, *Jour de fête* (*Festival Day*, 1949), which won widespread critical praise and returned several times its production costs. Most producers, however, hesitated to back silent-style films more than two decades after the coming of sound, and problems with financing repeatedly interrupted production of Tati's next work, *Les Vacances de Monsieur Hulot* (*Mr. Hulot's Holiday*, 1953). These difficulties seem to have had no impact on the carefree spirit and breathtaking grace of the film, one of the best-loved postwar French comedies and arguably one of the best works of comic cinema from any time or place.

Shot on location in a very untrendy Normandy resort, *Les Vacances de Monsieur Hulot* shows middle-class people doing funny but generally plausible things. Tati's humor typically emerges from timing and from the formal development of his gags.

Tati made his first two features in black and white, on location, with severely limited budgets, but the enormous earnings of *Les Vacances de Monsieur Hulot* (particularly in the coveted American market) finally gained him the respectful attention of French producers. He made his next two films in color, with elaborate sets and big budgets. *Mon Oncle* (*My Uncle*, 1958), in which the distracted Monsieur Hulot is revealed to live in Paris and have a pompous, Americanized brother-in-law, was another hit. But Hulot's adventure in a dehumanized Paris in *Playtime* (1967) was a terrible commercial and critical failure, in part because Tati refused to release it except to theatres equipped to show the original seventy-millimeter, stereophonic version. He made his last two films, *Trafic* (1971) and *Parade* (1973, for Swedish television), in reduced circumstances which recalled those of his first two features, but without duplicating their great popular and critical success.

Visually, Tati's direct artistic ancestors were the great, unsentimental silent clowns, particularly Linder and Keaton. Aurally, he owed much to Chaplin's pioneering work in sound cinema. Thematically, at least up until *Playtime*, he carried on the populist tradition of prewar René Clair, celebrating the honest *petits gens* (shopkeepers, peasants, and workers) and ridiculing their "betters." His respect for ordinary people extended to his film audiences, and he deliberately filmed his scenes in long shots, often quite lengthy ones, leaving to the spectator the task of picking out and ordering important details. In *Playtime*, he finally seems to have asked too much of his audiences, both in terms of the attention required to follow the multiple jokes hidden away in his high-definition widescreen images, and in his subject matter. The film belongs in the illustrious company of the cinema's most noble failures, from *Intolerance* to *Lola Montès*, doomed by formal daring and by messages that most spectators did not wish to hear. Tati's unpleasant message was that France's creeping Americanization had rendered moot the comfortable opposition in *Mon Oncle* between nice, unambitious *petits gens* and the gadget-obsessed bourgeoisie. In *Playtime*, Monsieur Hulot and all the other characters of all classes work, play, and even occasionally triumph in the brave new, environmentally egalitarian world of gadgetry and mechanical regimentation. There is no comfortable *vieux Paris* to escape to as there was in *Mon Oncle*, nor do people seem to yearn for one, accepting instead its mass-marketed simulacra.

Like Max Ophuls, Jacques Tati saw himself primarily as an entertainer, but what entertained him in his last major film was confusing and repellent to others. *Playtime* recalls Ophuls's *Lola Montès* both in the dimensions of its financial and critical disaster and in its unintended evolution into what many viewers and critics saw as an avantgarde film. However, Tati (like Ophuls) drifted away from commercial norms not to make a radical statement about the nature of art, but to express his own personality and world view. In this he was typical of the oppositional film artists promoted by *Cahiers du Cinéma:* when they innovated, it was in the interest of self-expression, and not primarily for the sake of aesthetic experiment. Like most of the *Cahiers* critics who would become New Wave directors and who took them as examples, their goals were personalist rather than formalist. This was even the case with Jean Cocteau, the most obviously avantgarde artist on Truffaut's list of model filmmakers.

After an absence of over a decade Cocteau had returned to the cinema during the Occupation to help his lover, the actor Jean Marais, become a film star. This goal he achieved spectacularly well in his first original commercial screenplay, for Jean Delannoy's *L'Eternel Retour* (*The Eternal Return*, 1943). Marais became an early prototype of the postwar film star as sex symbol, playing a contemporary Tristan to Madeleine Soulogne's similarly updated Isolde. The aesthetic problem of having two very modern, glamorous young players in an "eternal" story is compounded in the film by their disturbingly Aryan appearance, but Cocteau thought himself beyond politics. If his visions seemed to overlap with Nazi fantasies of the ideal hero, that was not his problem. For him, the mission of the work of art was personal, not social. This view of his art, along with his literary prestige, enabled him to become a noteworthy presence in the commercial cinema of the Occupation despite his scandalous personal life. He wrote the dialogues for two of the greatest works of the period, Serge de Poligny's *Le Baron fantôme* (*The Phantom Baron*, 1943)—in which he had a suitably bizarre cameo role—and for Robert Bresson's *Les Dames du Bois de Boulogne* (*The Ladies of the Bois de Boulogne*, 1944/5).

Although afterwards he continued occasionally to work on other filmmakers' projects, Cocteau directed his most striking and personal films himself. Some of them were adaptations of literary works; others had original scenarios. He retained the linear, narratively motivated style he had mastered in his early commercial projects as he slowly retreated from mainstream filmmaking (perhaps because he was no longer intimately involved in Jean Marais's career). His Occupation-style fantastic retelling of *La Belle et la Bête* (*Beauty and the Beast*, 1946, codirected with René Clément) is a striking blend of Coctelian themes and the visual style of the silent film fantasies of René Clair. By the time of his masterpiece, *Orphée* (*Orpheus*, 1950), Cocteau had almost completely returned to the directly poetic vein of *Le Sang d'un poète*, though without that film's density of cinematic effects or strong sense of narrative arbitrariness. One can only regret that so few artists of his stature have been able to write, in Alexandre Astruc's sense of the word, directly in images and sounds. But Cocteau's films are arguably more significant as expressions of his personality and artistic vision than as contributions to film history. Though *in* the cinema's evolution, they are not *of* it.

In his best work Jean Cocteau was a *visionary* filmmaker. Unlike Renoir, Becker, or Tati, who typically gave their own view of a world which spectators could recognize as overlapping with their own, Cocteau presented a universe only he could see, a zone between the recognizable, everyday world and whatever might lie beyond it. Commercial French cinema, like commercial cinema everywhere, has nurtured few such visionaries: Gance and Dreyer before Cocteau, Raoul Ruiz after him, and—at first contemporary with Cocteau but continuing on long after the poet's death—Robert Bresson. Bresson was born in 1907 in a town in the Auvergne region, where he was raised and first educated, and he directed his first feature film in 1943, after a series of unsuccessful attempts to establish himself in the industry before the war. Frustratingly little information is available about this highly personal filmmaker's life. For example, one would like to know at what age he first read Dostoyevsky; whether there were any tragedies in his family during his childhood; what sort of a painter he tried to be when he studied art; and exactly why he abandoned painting in favor of cinema. But Bresson seems to have exercised extraordinary control over what information about him is available from the public record, a control almost as impressive as that which he typically managed to achieve over the players in his films.[18]

Perhaps one day a biographer will ferret out the facts of his life, as Roger Icart did with Abel Gance's, but for the moment Bresson has had his way, and we must deal with the films alone in attempting to understand his work, along with his brief, cryptic, but often revealing *Notes on Cinematography*.[19] Artistically, Bresson's career breaks into two highly unequal parts. His *Les Anges du péché* (*Angels of Sin*, 1943) and *Les Dames du Bois de Boulogne/Ladies of the Park* (1944/45) were both landmarks of high Occupation cinema. They were very much of their time stylistically (with distanced, obviously composed images and highly worked sounds) and thematically (rejection of the everyday, a sense of spiritual isolation, stories of sin and redemption). But after the Liberation the director abandoned the filmmaking practices he had employed so brilliantly. For the polished and stylized dialogues of his first two films (written by Jean Giraudoux and Jean Cocteau, respectively), he substituted plain, functional language. He purged his images of their former pictorialist bent, giving them a pseudo-documentary quality. Above all, he ceased entirely to use professional actors, preferring untrained players whom he called models (rather than actors—a painterly as opposed to theatrical reference).

This new, austere orientation at first made it difficult for Bresson to interest producers in his projects. *Le Journal d'un curé de campagne* (*Diary of a Country Priest*, 1950, after Bernanos) appeared six years after the Liberation, and *Un Condamné à mort s'est échappé/A Man*

Escaped (1956) six years after that. The great critical acclaim and reasonable commercial careers of his first two postwar works, and the
loosening of constraints on film production in the early days of the
New Wave subsequently allowed him to work at the more reasonable
rate of a film every two or three years, beginning with *Pickpocket*
(1959). Later, the director was able to revive two of the many projects
he had conceived during the difficult days of the Tradition of Quality:
Au Hasard Balthazar (*Balthazar Here and There*, 1966) and *Lancelot du
Lac* (*Lancelot of the Lake*, 1974).

Although a true visionary, Bresson in his post-Liberation works
became—unlike Gance or Ruiz—a cinematic minimalist. In his notes
on the *cinématographe* (in the literal sense of "cinema writing") he
described mainstream commercial filmmaking as a hopeless morass
of self-delusion and bad faith. His own task was "To rid myself of
accumulated errors and untruths," by using resources which he
understood profoundly and over which he had the greatest possible
control. "The faculty of using my resources well diminishes when
their number grows," however, or put more positively: the fewer artistic means one uses, the better.[20] The most important single resource
which Bresson insisted on doing without was the extra level of meaning introduced by the presence of the professional actor. The actor
plays *someone else,* his psychology is double, whereas Bresson's
"models" do not play, they *are.* He thought it necessary to "Reduce to
the minimum the share [which the models'] consciousness has,"
because "Models who have become automatic (everything weighed,
measured, timed, repeated ten, twenty times) and then are dropped
in the middle of the events of your film—their relations with the
objects and persons will be *right,* because they will not be *thought.*"[21]
One wonders whether Bresson himself aspired to such a state of non-
conscious automatism (as release from suffering?) or if it was something he feared—or both. The distress of his fictional characters, and
much of the evil they do, seem to arise from their tormented self-
awareness. (One of the most "human" characters in his work is the
donkey Balthazar, which is persistently equated with Jesus Christ.)

Bresson's spiritual issues seem, curiously, to overlap with Gance's:
Why do humans suffer so much? Can they escape their torment?
What is Good, and what is Evil? Has God abandoned the world?
These concerns are fundamental to the stories into which he dropped
his models, but while he was always ready to discuss the models and
other basic elements of his art, he said little or nothing about the tales

they were meant to illustrate and illuminate. The recurring, central problem in his works is finding *grace*, defined as release from suffering—as the young priest finally does at the mystical end of *Le Journal d'un curé de campagne*, or as the very Dostoyevskian pickpocket achieves through love of another being. But one may see a turning toward pessimism and despair in his later works: beginning with *Au Hasard Balthazar* redemption, for humans at least, is no longer possible. God is nowhere, grace is unattainable; how can one live in such a world?

This shift may have been Bresson's response to his changing social and artistic environment rather than an indication of inner personal evolution. Replying to the Tradition of Quality's general pessimism, he showed that release and redemption were possible. Conversely, in the midst of the New Wave's generally resolute optimism and self-confidence, he told stories of horrible limitations and spiritual dead ends. He may well have judged the exuberant energy and self-conscious search for authenticity of his younger colleagues to be just as dangerous and delusional as the self-congratulatory cynicism of their predecessors. If in the 1950s he felt he had to convince audiences that grace was possible, later on he apparently felt obliged to insist on how profoundly it was lacking in everyday human experience. The most important thing was to break down his audiences' preconceptions, to make them see the world in a new way—to help them, perhaps, to find release from their pain and loneliness through acceptance, understanding, and love.

The Nouvelle Vague
and After

◪13◪

Fourth Wave

In the late 1950s the French film industry was, for the fourth time in its history, in deep trouble. The hard-won financial stability of the Occupation and postwar years had all but disappeared in a shockingly short period of time. The French attended the cinema less often with each passing year; this trend, moving in tandem with the steady rise in the number of the nation's television sets, continues to the present day. With their market contracting in France and in the rest of Europe, big budget quality productions were less and less likely to turn a profit. And audiences had become unpredictable. Old formulas, like the multi-star costume drama, were no longer as reliable as they had once been.

The transformation of French cinema that came about as a response to this new set of problems coincided with a sociopolitical crisis in the nation at large: the crucial 1958–59 film season took place during the creation of the Fifth Republic under the leadership of Charles De Gaulle. After a political exile of a decade and a half, De Gaulle was called back to power to deal with the intractable social rift produced by the bloody colonial war in Algeria, but he refused to govern without a new, American-style constitution of the sort which he had unsuccessfully promoted in the early postwar years. The Fifth Republic thus broke definitively with the unstable structure of its predecessors; its chief executive was popularly elected (for a fixed term of office) and thus independent of shifting parliamentary majorities. At last the leader of the French nation could act decisively in times of crisis—and President De Gaulle did (to the consternation of many of his supporters) in ending the Algerian War and giving the former colony its independence.

Together with the financial crisis in the cinema industry, this troubled social context helped bring about (or at the very least, amplified) a marked shift in film content and a less substantive but widely discussed change in cinematic style. This change was initially the work of a highly visible group of new film artists, from directors and producers to scriptwriters and stars, many of whom entered the industry in the late 1950s and early 1960s. The nation's press, seizing on this aspect of the transformation, spoke enthusiastically of a *nouvelle vague*, or new wave. Although useful as such labels go, the metaphor of a New Wave has had a complicated and confusing history, assuming a variety of meanings in the hands of different historians and critics. For some writers, for example, *nouvelle vague* designates only the work of the young ex-critics from *Cahiers du Cinéma* who made their first feature films in the late 1950s and early 1960s. While this usage at least has the virtue of precision, it is ultimately misleading, separating out these filmmakers from the context which assured their success, and from the many other figures who, like them, participated in the industry's reconstitution and restructuring.

In addition, to limit the New Wave to a small group of film artists subtly implies that it was a variety of cinema art movement, on a par with Italian Neorealism or German cinematic expressionism. But this it was not, not only because of the industry-wide dimensions of the transformation (cinema art movements are small, marginal, and focused) but also because of the highly diverse temperaments and goals within the ranks of the *Cahiers* activists themselves. A broader, though chronologically more limited, sense of the label takes it to designate a brief period of upheaval and innovation in the late 1950s and early 1960s. (From this perspective, which will be adopted here, French filmmaking after roughly 1962 should be called post-New Wave cinema.) Aside from being closer in spirit to how the notion was ultimately elaborated in the French press of the period, this usage has the advantage of following up, and extending, the label's founding metaphor. Waves, after all, crest and break, retreating back into the sea from whence they came.

The catch phrase *nouvelle vague* had initially applied to the generation that had been formed culturally and politically after the Liberation. This was the sense given to it by the weekly *L'Express* in a cover story in October 1957. The magazine's "new wave" was the group that would soon shape the France of the second half of the twentieth century. What, the magazine asked, did these young people want? Who were they? Who would lead them, and would these leaders finally change the way the nation was governed? In the second half of 1958, *L'Express* awarded itself the title of "journal of the *nouvelle vague*," obviously hoping that whatever else the new generation would do, it would buy publications that catered to it. But the magazine's commercially motivated boosterism reflected a real, wholly justified sense that profound transformations had occurred in the nation since the end of World War II. Population growth, long a national obsession, had turned positive and was accelerating. The country's Gross National Product, which at the Liberation was almost exactly what it had been at the end of World War I, had more than doubled in just over a decade.

The recent prosperity and demographic transformation were inextricably linked with profound social change, which many citizens found unsettling. The nation's rural population was in decline, and with it the towns which had been a mainstay of traditional French culture. The traditional bourgeoisie, both *grande* and *petite,* was weakened by the rise of American-style big business, big banking, and mass merchandising. Many formerly prosperous bourgeois families were, in social position and often also financially, downwardly mobile, in the process of slipping into the salaried middle classes. Small shopkeepers appeared to be an endangered species. Huge, seemingly faceless and interchangeable suburbs were developing in major urban areas. The people who lived in them were on the whole better off materially than they or their parents had been before the war, but many felt a sense of rootlessness in the emerging mass society. (Their children, on the other hand, would know nothing else. They would express their own misgivings, briefly but forcefully, in May of 1968.)

The phrase *nouvelle vague* may have been new in the late 1950s, but the idea was not. *L'Express*'s campaign was only the latest manifestation of a growing national interest of the media in youth culture. Ironically, this was in a decade when the actual numbers of adolescents and young adults were low, a result of the declining birth rates of the Depression and war years. If *la jeunesse* became a popular Fourth Republic theme, it was not because of demographics, but in large measure thanks to the widespread notion that the old French social structure was under siege, even in its most solid political points of reference. One can argue that the postwar period in politics began to end with the 1954 French defeat in Viet Nam. The decline of France's standing as a colonial power shook the country on the political Right, beginning a process of polarization that would culminate in the military rebellion of the Algerian crisis. The publication in 1956 of the Khrushchev report on the crimes of the Stalin era and the Soviet Union's invasion of Hungary in the same year shook the Left, causing many to leave the P.C.F. The last years of the Fourth Republic recalled the paralysis and division of the end of the Third. Eerily, both regimes ended in the same manner, through the French legislature's abdication of its powers in favor of a Strong (military) Leader who could assume responsibility in the face of a national crisis.

But De Gaulle was not Pétain. Though the General was by that time an old man (if not as old as Pétain had been), many observers fervently hoped that his Fifth Republic would finally enfranchise, both socially and politically, the nation's younger generation; they could then perhaps begin to build a France better adapted to its new circumstances. The *nouvelle vague* was promoted, in *L'Express* and elsewhere, as both the cultural *raison d'être* of the Fifth Republic and, later, as the proof of its vitality. This connection continued when the label became more and more exclusively attached to filmmaking. Though today this may seem curious, the independent-minded, often anarchic New Wave was, for many of its initial publicizers, the cinema of Charles De Gaulle.

The *nouvelle vague* seemed to many observers—particularly to willfully naive journalists in search of a good story—almost to materialize out of thin air. In fact, many of the new filmmakers who came to symbolize the upheaval in the film industry were in place before the 1958–59 season, waiting for a chance to make their mark. Some had actually become established a year or two before the official beginning of the new era. Although much of the publicity (and most subsequent film histories) singled out directors, it should be remembered that the crisis of the late 1950s also brought to prominence previously unknown scriptwriters, cinematographers, composers, producers, and stars. This group of new or newly prominent personnel came to fiction film production via three routes. The largest number had followed the traditional course of apprenticeship within the commercial mainstream: directors had begun as various sorts of assistants and moved up slowly through the system, as had cinematographers and others; future producers had worked as publicists; many stars of the early 1960s had started out as extras in the 1950s. Major directors among this group included Marcel Camus, Michel Deville, and Pierre Kast. A second, smaller faction—which could overlap with the first, as in the case of Kast—had followed the equally traditional path of working in documentary before moving on to fiction features. Following thus in the footsteps of Jean Grémillon and René Clément were, most prominently, Alain Resnais, Georges Franju, and Jacques Demy.

The third typical path to New Wave prominence, however, by-passed these time-tested methods. A small number of filmmakers, many of them associated with *Cahiers du Cinéma,* moved directly into production with little or no previous practical experience with the medium. They made their first feature films on small budgets with unconventionally small technical crews, location shooting to cut costs, and unknown or even nonprofessional actors. The success of Claude Chabrol, François Truffaut, and Jean-Luc Godard's first features seemed for a time to indicate that this was as sure a route to pleasing the public (and the critics) as the more traditional forms of appren-ticeship. After 1960, however, when producers and the public became more discriminating and harder to please, an increasing number of "first films" never reached French movie screens, or did so only briefly.[1] But for about two years, the filmmakers who began their commercial careers in this apparently more spontaneous and authen-tic manner appeared to many enthusiasts to represent the greatest hope for renewal of the industry. There had been only a few prece-dents for this method of entry into the profession—the most notable examples probably being Jean Renoir and Dmitri Kirsanov—and very few indeed since the coming of synchronized sound. One highly unorthodox entry had been effected by the man who once claimed, with some justification, to have invented the *nouvelle vague:* Jean-Pierre Melville.

Melville was born Jean-Pierre Grumbach in 1917. Culturally sepa-rated from the majority of New Wave directors by having reached maturity before World War II, he shared with many of them, and with their generation, a love of things American. For most of his adult life he wore a Stetson hat and dark glasses, and smoked large cigars. He took the name Melville in the late 1930s, out of admiration for the American author of *Moby-Dick* (and also, perhaps, to shed an "unde-sirable"-sounding name). His family was of the middle Parisian bourgeoisie, his father a wholesale merchant, his uncle an antique dealer. When Melville was six years old he was given a 7.5 millimeter Pathé Baby camera and projector; when he was twelve, he graduated to 16 millimeter. But he initially preferred watching films to making them, and he shared with the future filmmakers of *Cahiers du Cinéma* the way of learning cinema by *watching* films—watching them attentively, analytically, and repeatedly. Because of his date of birth (he was mobilized in 1937, at the age of twenty), he spent a large part of his early adult life in uniform, first in the French army and then (after Dunkirk), the British, and finally the Free French forces. This experience probably accounts for his lifelong interest in war, violence, and relationships within all-male groups.

Demobilized in 1945, Melville tried to enter the French film industry, only to encounter the same draconian barriers to newcomers that frustrated so many aspiring filmmakers, such as Alexandre Astruc. Astruc, like most of his peers, accepted provisional defeat. He wrote his celebrated essay on the *caméra-stylo*, eventually managed to work as an assistant director and script doctor, and finally got to make his first feature after almost a decade of apprenticeship. Melville, however, rejected the system outright and became his own producer. After one documentary short subject, he embarked on an ambitious project, an adaptation of Vercors's celebrated short narrative of provincial life under the Occupation, *Le Silence de la mer* (*The Silence of the Sea*, 1947/49). This project was a gamble in several ways. Melville did not obtain the theoretically obligatory authorization from the C.N.C. to make his film, nor did he work with a standard-sized crew (in defiance of union regulations). He shot his script in twenty-seven days, entirely on location. Vercors, moreover, had been wary of offers to adapt his celebrated work for the screen and only agreed to let Melville film it when the director proposed to submit the finished adaptation to a jury of former Resistance members; if they did not find it worthy, the negative would be destroyed. Endorsed by the jury, the film had its premiere at a gala benefit for the Comité d'Action de la Résistance. Melville had gambled with his own money, and with almost two years of intensive labor (he wrote the adaptation, produced, directed, and was co-editor), and he had won.

Le Silence de la mer is today widely accepted as one of the few truly powerful and authentic films about the Resistance, but it is not a melodrama about Good versus Evil. It is, rather, a study of small, everyday acts of defiance, and the price that must be paid for them. The "silence" of the title is the refusal of a provincial household to speak with a German officer—a "good" German who likes the French—for whom they are forced to provide a home. In adapting the work faithfully, Melville (as André Bazin would have predicted) expanded the formal range of fiction cinema. The film employs an extensive, essayistic voice-over narration that would have given a quality scriptwriter nightmares; there are scenes in which the characters' blocked communication becomes almost palpably frustrating. Melville later said that he wanted to make an "anti-cinematographic" film, "from which movement and action would be more or less vanished."[2] It would be more accurate to say that in being faithful to Vercors, he made an anti-mainstream work (though one which was commercially and critically successful) which redefined and expanded the domain of the cinematographic.

Within the French film community, reaction to *Le Silence de la mer* was divided. Industry insiders, particularly Communists and fellow travelers, could not forgive Melville for having violated union and governmental regulations. The director had to pay a stiff fine to the C.N.C. for shooting without its authorization. But those unhappy with the status quo embraced the work enthusiastically. Jean Cocteau, who had by this time become both patron and symbol of the alternative film culture, asked Melville to film his celebrated novel *Les Enfants terribles*. Cocteau was presumably impressed by the director's fidelity to Vercors's work, but ironically the two men later quarreled because the poet wanted to tinker with his original narrative while the director insisted on fidelity to the original work (except for modernizing costumes and leaving the time of the story undefined).

Les Enfants terribles/The Strange Ones (1950) was financed and shot in a more orthodox manner than Melville's first feature, though by acting as producer he retained close to absolute control over it, and he continued to work with a small, tightly knit team of collaborators. Often regarded as a "Cocteau film" that happens to have been directed by someone else, the work is more accurately to be viewed as a stunning demonstration of the cinematic possibilities of faithful literary adaptation in the hands of a gifted director. The novel's author had little to do with the film's script or shooting, except for reading the voice-over narration and insisting (making this a contractual obligation) that Edouard Dhermitte, the successor in his affections to Jean Marais, play the role of Paul.

Although *Les Enfants terribles* was greatly admired, particularly by future *nouvelle vague* filmmakers such as Truffaut and Chabrol, it was the last time Melville adapted a landmark work of French literature.

After this production, he changed artistic course. Perhaps the major problem in filming literary works, from the director's point of view, was that his own intensively creative work in solving the daunting aesthetic problems of faithful literary adaptation went widely unappreciated. Once he had established himself as a film artist, Melville apparently wanted to express his own sensibility more directly, and to more widespread acclaim. After a purely commercial work to establish himself with those in the industry who still saw him as a curious eccentric, he made the first film in which he became the mature Melville: *Bob le flambeur*/*Bob the Gambler* (1955).

Unlike *Le Silence de la mer* and *Les Enfants terribles*, *Bob le flambeur* features characters and situations instantly recognizable from popular (American, or American-influenced) fiction and film: tired professional criminals and callow young ones, and the policemen who know them all too well; young amoral women out for thrills who betray the men without thinking, and older, jaded ones who can predict the deceptions to come; a perfect crime that will go wrong. Like the American studio system directors so admired by *Cahiers du Cinéma*, Melville made of these generic materials a highly personal film, which displays most of the themes and narrative developments to which he would return again and again. In the context of 1950s French cinema, there was much that was new and innovative in *Bob*. Henri Decaë, who became one of the New Wave's most influential cinematographers (initially thanks to the notice taken of his work on Melville's first three features), contributed evocative, location-shot images of a contemporary Paris in which a street-cleaning machine or the play of light from neon signs produces a kind of desolate visual poetry. These serve as counterpoint for the wanderings of the film's lumpen leisure-class characters, who seem light years away from the bourgeois, workers, and peasants of mainstream Fourth Republic cinema. Unlike the Tradition of Quality but like so much of New Wave and post-New Wave cinema, Melville featured prominently a pop, jazz-influenced music score. Like the first *nouvelle vague* directors, he employed little-known actors, in a film shot on a budget small enough that its financial viability did not require huge audiences.

Until his loft apartment/studio was destroyed in a fire in the late 1960s, Melville was a small-scale Parisian equivalent of Marcel Pagnol. He had his own, virtually self-sufficient facilities in the capital, where he wrote and edited his films and shot many of their interior sequences; his favorite sites for location work were close at hand. Like

Pagnol, Melville developed a highly personal fictional universe—one which became a major element of the cinema of his time. And like so many of the younger filmmakers who would follow in his footsteps, he slowly gained public recognition, working with the new generation of stars created in the first years of the New Wave—such as Jean-Paul Belmondo, the star of Godard's rather Melvillian *A bout de souffle*— and eventually becoming one of the most consistently successful directors of the 1960s and 1970s. By the mid 1960s his cinematic world of wary loners (gangsters, spies, investigative journalists, Resistance heroes) was a significant component of the commercial mainstream, the springboard for one major star image (Alain Delon) and the artistic center of one of post-New Wave cinema's most reliably popular genres, the *film policier* or cops-and-robbers film.

Still, despite the great strengths of his best later works, such as the Resistance melodrama *L'Armée des ombres* (*Army of the Shadows*, 1969), Melville may be seen as paying an artistic price for his retreat from the more austere, directly poetic vein of his first two films. He addressed a larger public beginning with *Bob le flambeur*, but one may argue that he eventually began to exhaust the aesthetic possibilities of his favorite commercial formulas, however personally meaningful they remained for him and for the many admirers of his later work. Beginning his career as a radical innovator, he had by its end become a beloved *petit maître* of genre filmmaking. In this way his later work, like his beginnings on the fringes of the industry, makes him a precursor, if not of the entire *nouvelle vague* generation, at least of a major strand in its evolution.

🖎 It is only in retrospect that the great significance of *Bob le flambeur* for New Wave and later French cinema has become apparent; in the alternative film culture of the mid-1950s it was completely overshadowed by films that displayed other signs of change. In the year of its release, Alexandre Astruc's first feature, *Les Mauvaises Rencontres* (*Bad Encounters*, 1955) received much more notice from *Cahiers du Cinéma* if not from most spectators—the public was still unreceptive to the sort of stylistically eccentric, youth-centered film that would become almost a cliché only three years later. Cinema audiences (though not the majority of critics) were much more impressed by another manifestation of youthful exuberance: Roger Vadim's first feature, *Et Dieu créa la femme* (*And God Created Woman*, 1956). Vadim was a virtual charter member of the Parisian youth culture chronicled by Astruc the year before, though he had also been a good apprentice in French commercial cinema of the early 1950s. (It was presumably from Marc Allégret, for whom he worked as an assistant, that he learned to glorify the bodies of his players, and like Allégret, he was to become adept at star-making.) *Et Dieu créa la femme* was at once a clever piece of commercial filmmaking and a highly personal exploration of the relations between men and women, as the director constructed them through a character modeled on, and played by, his young bride Brigitte Bardot.[3] The film was a *succès de scandale* in France, launching Bardot as a major sex symbol. It was also a big hit in the American market, a first indication that a youth-oriented cinema could be highly exportable, and thus a possible remedy to the film industry's growing financial crisis. But Vadim soon became something of an embarrassment both to the new French government—his *Les Liaisons dangereuses* (*Dangerous Affairs*, 1959) was the object of a censorship campaign by local government bodies—and to proponents of the new cinema, who generally found his films distasteful. In its unremittingly adolescent sensibility, its unsubtle, self-proclaiming modernity, and its frank exploitation of sex, Vadim's work represented, for many observers, the new cinema's worst tendencies writ large.

The year after Vadim's scandalous first film, two other features by new directors challenged the commercial mainstream in another way. Marcel Camus's *Mort en fraude*/*Fugitive in Saigon* (1957) and Claude-Bernard Aubert's *Patrouille de choc* (*Shock Patrol*, 1957) both treated the until then taboo subject of France's disastrous experience in Viet Nam. Camus's film was relatively conventional, the prelude to a career which, after his widely admired *Orfeu Negro* (*Black Orpheus*, 1958, filmed in Portugese in Brazil), rapidly faded into respectable obscurity. *Patrouille de choc* was a more radical venture, shot on location with nonprofessional actors and directly raising questions of racism and imperialism. It was the first of a series of now largely forgotten features which attempted to shed new light on France's troubled relations with the Third World.[4] This trend, perhaps most widely known through Jean Rouch's *Moi un noir* (*Me, a Black*, 1958) and Michel Drach's *On n'enterre pas le dimanche* (*They Don't Have Funerals on Sundays*, 1959), soon all but disappeared from commercial movie screens in the wake of retrenchment and consolidation in the film industry in the early 1960s. Post-*nouvelle vague* cinema would be in somewhat closer contact with French social reality than the Tradition of Quality had been, but there would still be clearly defined limits.

In 1958 and 1959 the new wave of filmmaking hit mainstream French cinema with its full force. Because of their striking independence of normal channels of production, Louis Malle, Claude Chabrol, and François Truffaut were the most visible exemplars of the upheaval. Malle's *L'Ascenseur à l'échafaud/Frantic* won the Prix Louis Delluc in 1957 and went into general release in early 1958. His *Les Amants* (*The Lovers*, 1958) became a scandalous success in the manner of *Et Dieu créa la femme* for its steamy love scenes, though it won more critical respect than Vadim's first film. Chabrol's *Le Beau Serge/Bitter Reunion* (1958) and *Les Cousins* (*The Cousins*, 1959), more conventionally moralistic but at the same time more adventurous in cinematic style, were also great successes both critically and with audiences. Truffaut's semi-autobiographical *Les Quatre Cents Coups* (*The Four Hundred Blows*, 1959) won the Cannes festival prize for Best Direction and became one of the most profitable French films of the decade. All five works were financed by the directors themselves, or their families. But mainstream French producers had also begun to encourage new talent in the same years, probably inspired by the example of Roger Vadim.

Understandably, even the most adventurous of experienced producers chose at first to back new directors with more conventional industry track records than those of Malle, Chabrol, or Truffaut. So it was that two seasoned apprentices, Pierre Kast and Michel Deville, made their first fiction features in 1957 and 1958. After years of working on documentary short subjects, Georges Franju filmed the nightmarish tale of alienated youth, *La Tête contre les murs* (*Head against the Walls*, 1959). Alain Resnais, from a similar professional background, turned a proposed documentary on the atomic bomb into the innovative *Hiroshima mon amour* (*Hiroshima, My Love*, 1959), inspired by the literary "new novel" trend. When Franju and Resnais's films first appeared on French screens, the rush to discover and exploit new filmmaking talent was on. Some producers became more daring, willing to back such eccentric *protégés* as *Cahiers du Cinéma* critic Jean-Luc Godard, who was at work on *A bout de souffle/Breathless* (1960). The profits and government subsidies from the first *nouvelle vague* hits had meanwhile begun to flow into new projects. Two of the most resolutely independent figures of the new generation, Eric Rohmer and Jacques Rivette, began work on features for Claude Chabrol's production company, thanks to the profits and government subsidies generated by *Le Beau Serge* and *Les Cousins*. By the time that Rohmer's *Le Signe du lion* (*The Sign of Leo*, 1959/62) and Rivette's *Paris nous appartient* (*Paris Belongs to Us*, 1958–61) were released, however, Chabrol's enterprise was all but bankrupt. Its failure was only one of many manifestations of the commercial hangover that followed—as the few outspoken critics of the new filmmaking had predicted it would—the heady intoxication of the *nouvelle vague*.

By the mid 1960s the industry had reconsolidated. The French filmgoing public, and most producers, had lost their sympathy for formal experiment and unbridled self-expression. But it would be an exaggeration to argue that French cinema was essentially unchanged, and that most films of the late 1960s resembled those of the previous decade. Much had, in fact, been irretrievably altered. The film community was no longer closed to new talent. New directors (for example, Constantin Costa-Gavras, in 1965) and other personnel entered the industry with much greater ease than during the Tradition of Quality, though most of them worked on unadventurous, if occasionally stylish, commercial projects. Historical costume pictures, many of them international coproductions such as Malle's *Viva Maria* (1965), continued to appear, but they were now only one kind of film among many. The industry's structure quickly ceased to resemble the Tradition of Quality and began to take on the look of the disorganized 1930s, with many independent companies competing for the shrinking audience—though the C.N.C. still exerted a strong, stabilizing influence. "Small" genres such as romantic comedy, domestic drama, and *films policiers* signaled signs of the shape of things to come.

Most works now told stories set in a sanitized present, generally ignoring contentious issues such as racism, international politics, or birth control and abortion. The *nouvelle vague* bequeathed to later French cinema a fascination with the details and small rituals of everyday life: lighting cigarettes, shopping, conversing in cafés, walking in the streets. The theatricalized, socially neutral speech which dominated the Tradition of Quality disappeared. Now characters spoke again with the accents, vocabulary, and rhythms of the world in which most film spectators lived. Location shooting, though it quickly ceased to characterize entire films, became a standard accent even for otherwise routine stories of young love or criminal activities. The deliberately unpolished and often chaotic images of many early *nouvelle vague* works found their continuation in a generally anti-pictorialist visual style offering what Roland Barthes would call *effets de réel*, or "reality effects."[5] Soundtracks of post-New Wave films likewise introduced measured doses of "real" noises of traffic, the din of conversation in a café, or birds and animals in the country. Their music scores showed much greater variety of inspiration than had works of the 1950s. Many films explored jazz and pop idioms, and even the more traditional symphonic scores typically used smaller musical ensembles and emphasized diverse instrumental colors over massed orchestral effects. The new generation of directors often chose to work with new composers, such as Michel Legrand, Georges Delerue, and Maurice Jarre, who had distinctive and recognizable musical styles.

But perhaps the most important change was making more room for diversity: a necessary correlate of the partial return to the fragmented structure of film production that had characterized the industry in the 1930s. Although mainstream commercial production reconsolidated, evolving its own (only partly new) set of generic formulas, stylistic conventions, and "bankable" stars which, cleverly combined, could generally assure the financial viability of a project, a sector now remained viable for productions that targeted smaller audiences. The economic blockade against nonconformity in style and subject matter which had characterized the Tradition of Quality was at least partly lifted; resourceful producers and directors could work much more easily in the margins of the system. The French film industry of the 1950s had had little room for committed individualists such as Robert Bresson. But after 1959 Bresson was able almost to double the rate at which he made films, and he was not alone. A number of filmmakers who first made their mark during the *nouvelle vague* or immediately afterwards would choose to join him on the fringes of the commercial mainstream, not challenging it so much as working alongside it, doing things which it had no interest in doing.

How the new filmmakers had arrived at their positions in the industry had a great deal to do with how they responded to the freedom to choose between marginality and the commercial mainstream. The more extensive their experience in the industry, the more likely they were to adapt to its demands without much apparent discomfort, making the sorts of works which most producers (and apparently most of the filmgoing public) required. And so Philippe de Broca, despite being a favorite of the *Cahiers* critics and having made his first film for Claude Chabrol's production company, became a clever confectioner of safe star vehicles, particularly after the commercial failure of his bittersweet historical fable, *Le Roi de coeur* (*King of Hearts*, 1965).[6] On the other hand, many former outsiders such as Jacques

Rivette and Eric Rohmer remained on the margins of the industry, making "uncommercial" films with some difficulty, of course, but with the assurance that their works could be made and exhibited, at least to the small audiences of specialized urban cinemas.

Rivette and Rohmer both came to filmmaking from *Cahiers du Cinéma,* but most of their former colleagues at the magazine (and others closely associated with its positions) did not join them on the fringes of commercial filmmaking. For there was a third possible position with regard to the industry mainstream—a less stable one than deliberate marginality but, for many veterans of the *nouvelle vague,* more rewarding. Some of the most visible of the new filmmakers attempted a compromise, either by oscillating between securely commercial and relatively marginal projects, or by attempting to inflect popular formulas with expressions of their own sensibilities, or by doing a little of both. These were the members of what one might term the reformist tendency in New Wave and post-New Wave cinema, those who attempted to test and reshape the limits of the commercial mainstream from a position within its by now rather fluid boundaries.

■ The first highly visible "reformist" filmmaker of the new generation never wrote for *Cahiers du Cinéma,* nor were his works generally well regarded by the magazine. Yet the eclectic and mercurial Louis Malle was at the very heart of the *nouvelle vague* and its subsequent impact on French commercial cinema. Malle's early fiction films helped launch the new era by their commercial and critical success; his work in the 1960s and early 1970s reflected divided loyalties, alternating between innovation and personal expression in some works and a willingness, in others, to resort to familiar formulas and commercial strategies. One reason for a sense of estrangement between Malle and many of his contemporaries was probably social. Whereas the young critics of *Cahiers du Cinéma* and the filmmakers whom they championed came mainly from the middle and lower bourgeoisie, Malle was born into one of the wealthiest families in France, his mother an heiress to an immense fortune amassed in the sugar trade.

Louis Malle was born in 1925 in Thumières, in the north of France, and received a highly traditional Catholic education which would subtly influence all of his works, even (perhaps particularly) those which rejected religion and traditional values. During the Occupation he witnessed the arrest of some Jewish children who had been hidden in the Jesuit *collège* of Fountainbleau where he was in school. This incident must have profoundly impressed him; he would return to the situation of Jewish children under the Occupation and the people who hid or denounced them in two of his most personal works, *Lacombe, Lucien* (1974) and *Au revoir les enfants* (*Goodbye, Children*, 1987). After receiving his *baccalauréat*, Malle studied political science before deciding to pursue a career in filmmaking. He first learned his craft at I.D.H.E.C., and then joined celebrated oceanographer Jacques-Yves Cousteau as filmmaker on a voyage of the ship *Calypso*. Malle and Cousteau's *Le Monde du silence* (*The Silent World*, 1956) was the first of a series of travel and ethnographic documentaries which the director made in alternation with his fiction projects, and which would take him to Thailand, India, the American Midwest, and many other (for him, and for most of his audience) exotic places. These films seem to express Malle's sense of rootlessness and his unease with his own culture. Like Jean Renoir, he eventually became a French filmmaker with a home, family, and part of his professional career in the United States.

After his work with Cousteau, Malle used some of his family fortune to create his own production company and make his first fiction feature. *L'Ascenseur à l'échafaud/Frantic* (1958) was a carefully conceived project whose small budget was the mark of fiscal prudence rather than limited resources. Generically a *film noir* in the commercially reliable tradition of Henri-Georges Clouzot, it was innovative in its extensive Paris location shooting and in its music score by the American jazz trumpeter Miles Davis. Jeanne Moreau and Maurice Ronet, playing the film's doomed lovers, became the New Wave's first ideal couple, and two of its most striking and characteristic stars. Though the film was quite successful, it was Malle's next fiction feature that established him as a leader of the *nouvelle vague*. *Les Amants* (*The Lovers*, also 1958) depicts a bourgeois world choking on its own conventions, and sex as the only sure remedy for its mindless repression. Its underlying moral stance differs little from the Tradition of Quality's denunciations of middle class morality, except—crucially— in its neoromantic optimism. There *is* a way out: youthful rebellion finds expression in sexual liberation. In addition to its frank exploitation of sex, the film is emblematic of much of the new cinema for its use of consumerist icons, particularly automobiles, as signs of character. The corrupt, moneyed pillars of society drive Jaguars and Rolls Royces; the honest young lover has a citroen *deux chevaux*. When the

Jeanne Moreau character leaves her incapacitated car at the side of the road to ride with the noble hero, it's with the top down and with both doors open, a symbol of her coming rejection of her class and marital situation.

It is characteristic that Malle did not immediately follow up the sex-based, Vadimesque success of *Les Amants* with another similar work. In *Zazie dans le métro* (*Zazie in the Subway*, 1960) he adapted one of Raymond Queneau's novels, attempting to find cinematic equivalents (pixillated images, speeded up motion, etc.) of the author's inimitable wordplay. Most critics have found the results unsatisfactory, but the film remains at the very least a striking, humorous, and perhaps noble experiment. After *Vie privée/A Very Private Affair* (1962), a more calculatedly commercial work starring Brigitte Bardot, he again turned to literature, though of a very different sort, with *Le Feu follet/The Fire Within* (1963). Widely regarded as his most accomplished and moving film, *Le Feu follet* is Malle's one excursion into the deliberately unpolished cinematic style which many historians take to be the epitome of the *nouvelle vague:* hand-held camera, jagged editing, real locations (most, like the Café de Flore, associated with youthful rebellion). But Malle employed this style in the service of a bitter critique of the youthful quest for purely individual authenticity—as befits the film's source, a novel by the proto-fascist Drieu La Rochelle. New Wave cinematic fireworks do not celebrate freedom from constraint, but rather indicate the disordered, unhealthy nature of a world in which real community has been lost. In his last, despairing message, the film's anti-hero (Maurice Ronet, in one of his greatest performances) says that he will kill himself because there is too great a distance between himself and others, that through his suicide he can finally reach them—if only to *leave a stain* on them.

After *Le Feu follet*, Malle again veered towards mainstream formula with *Viva Maria* (1965), a period farce set in nineteenth century South America and starring Brigitte Bardot and Jeanne Moreau as revolutionary agitators (!). The simple need to make money cannot wholly explain Malle's artistic split personality, which in his American career would lead him to follow up the relatively straightforward, elegant commercial productions *Pretty Baby* (1978) and *Atlantic City* (1980) with the small, eccentric talk comedy *My Dinner With André* (1981). He seems to have been perpetually torn between pleasing the larger film-going public and making serious cinema art for smaller audiences.

Occasionally, as in the brooding costume drama *Le Voleur/The Thief of Paris* (1966) and in his two films about the Occupation, he managed the sort of compromise between these goals that someone like François Truffaut could achieve more frequently and easily. But the dilemma, if not his uneasy, perpetually shifting response to it, was characteristic of his generation. If in refusing to choose definitively between the various possibilities open to him as a filmmaker Malle became a difficult figure indeed for *auteur* criticism, by this very refusal he also became a sort of icon for French cinema of the New Wave and after.

Few cinema careers begun during the *nouvelle vague* have been as varied and as artistically contradictory as Louis Malle's. Directors with a temperament better suited to compromise could find more stable intermediate positions between the commercial mainstream and artistic self-expression. Soon after Malle's début, Claude Chabrol was the second highly visible young outsider to enter the film industry by means of a fiction feature made with his own money. However, the petty bourgeois Chabrol lacked Malle's (high bourgeois) fiscal and artistic prudence. After his failure as a producer he was obliged to undergo the period of commercial apprenticeship he had initially avoided, before achieving the stability in position and attitute toward the commercial mainstream that Malle never found.

Chabrol was born in 1930 in Paris, where his father (himself the son of a provincial druggist) owned and operated a modest pharmacy. An only child like so many born between the wars, young Claude was an avid moviegoer. In his autobiography he lists some of the films which impressed him at an early age: all are American, most of them classic genre pictures like Michael Curtiz's *Captain Blood* (1935) and Curtiz and Keighley's *The Adventures of Robin Hood* (1938). Chabrol also recalls sitting motionless in a window for hours on end and imagines that his parents must have worried about having an idiot son. "What they didn't know, and what would have reassured them," he wrote in his autobiography, "was that behind my dull face a spirit was active: I was interested in the people passing in the street. I watched them, from my high position, as one contemplates an anthill . . . But my subjects were more appealing than insects thanks to their great diversity—different behaviors, faces, bodies, clothes, which indicated an age, a social class, a certain sort of character."[7] When he finally achieved commercial and artistic stability in the late 1960s, Chabrol's originality consisted in combining these two childhood impulses: distanced observation of human behavior, and a love of the repetitive framework of popular film genres.

Except for a period of private study far from Paris during the Occupation years, Chabrol was educated in solid Parisian institutions such as the Lycée Louis-le-Grand. He received his *baccalauréat* with high honors, and after a brief period of pharmacy studies he became a "professional student" of political science, literature (in which he obtained a *maîtrise*), and law. He seems to have led a life much like that of his character Paul in *Les Cousins*. He was more interested in student culture than in his studies, and for a while—despite his socialist leanings—he frequented a group of right-wing anarchists whose leader was Jean-Marie Le Pen, much later to become a notorious racist agitator. He became an assiduous *cinéphile,* attending screenings at the Latin Quarter Ciné-Club and the Cinémathèque Française, and he began writing for *Cahiers du Cinéma.*

Chabrol's first wife's grandmother had left her a legacy of 32 million (old) francs, about one-third of the budget of an ordinary fiction feature. This was at the time when the young critics began seriously to think of making films. Chabrol used his wife's money to found Films Ajym, whose first project (coproduced with the perspicacious Pierre Braunberger) was Jacques Rivette's narrative short subject *Le Coup du berger* (*The Shepherd's Gambit,* 1956, screenplay by Chabrol). *Le Coup du berger* is quite unlike Rivette's subsequent work in its economical storytelling and lightly ironic tone. In contrast, Chabrol's screenplay anticipated very clearly his commercially successful work of over a decade later, in its main subject—adultery—and in its detached observation of subtly comic social rituals. Encouraged by the film's modest success, and by similar short subjects for other producers by Truffaut and Godard, Chabrol sank virtually his entire capital into the production of a scenario he had written a few years before. Unlike *Le Coup du berger, Le Beau Serge/Bitter Reunion* (1958) was a slow-paced, somber work rich in details of life in a provincial village (most of which Chabrol was obliged to delete in order to reduce the film to a commercially viable ninety minutes). Chabrol was still a Catholic (albeit a Left one, who associated with Right anarchists), and his first feature was a reworking of themes and situations from Robert Bresson's adaptation of Bernanos's *Le Journal d'un curé de campagne.* The role corresponding to that film's young priest is taken in *Le Beau Serge* by a visitor from the capital who attempts to save—in the religious sense of the word—an old friend from the vices of life in the countryside (particularly alcoholism), and from despair (Pascal's "misery of man without God").

Le Beau Serge received a *prime à la qualité* from the C.N.C. and was presented out of competition at the 1958 Cannes festival. It was well enough received to obtain several foreign distribution contracts and a run at a small Paris cinema. With the C.N.C.'s award for "quality" (an ironic distinction for this small, rough-hewn film) and the advances on distribution, Chabrol was able to embark on production of his second film before his first had even begun its modestly successful commercial career. The script for *Les Cousins* (*The Cousins*, 1959) dated from the same period as that of *Le Beau Serge*. Though Chabrol reports that he lost his religious faith between the two productions, intending the second as a "blasphemous" work, it was still profoundly marked by his youthful Catholicism. The two films are symmetrical in plot: in *Les Cousins* it is a young idealist from the provinces who strays into the youth culture of the capital. Parisian decadence is not presented as particularly attractive, but rather as the moral equivalent of *Le Beau Serge*'s despair and alcoholism among the peasantry. Ironically, the cynical and lazy urban cousin succeeds in law school, while the sincere, hard-working country bumpkin fails. The film concludes not with an uplifting affirmation (as *Le Beau Serge* does), but with an ironic, unmerited death—though in this work, as elsewhere, such "blasphemy" accords great importance to faith, by opposing it so strongly.

With *Les Cousins* Chabrol's career reached a premature climax: the film opened at a major Parisian cinema and earned many times the income of *Le Beau Serge*. Ajym Films initiated several projects by other youthful directors, while Chabrol found mainstream financing for his first two films entirely conceived and executed after his loss of religious conviction, on which he worked for the first time with his friend and frequent collaborator, the scriptwriter Paul Gégauff. Both works attempted to infuse the tradition of French *film noir* with the *nouvelle vague*'s stylistic energy and emphasis on the texture of everyday life. *A double tour/Web of Passion* (1959) failed commercially and critically; *Les Bonnes Femmes* (*The Good Women*, 1960) was an outright disaster. Thus began a series of crippling failures which cost Chabrol his independence and forced him to become a simple contract director until

Party time for Parisian law students and their friends in *Les Cousins*. It may not look like much fun (it isn't meant to), but the scene has a disorderly spontaneity unlike anything the Tradition of Quality could summon up.

the success of *Les Biches/Bad Girls* (1968) and *La Femme infidèle* (*The Unfaithful Wife*, 1969) reestablished him both commercially and in the eyes of most critics.

Yet Chabrol reclaimed a leading position in French commercial cinema not by making films of a radically different nature from *A double tour* and *Les Bonnes Femmes,* but by being more "professional" in treating his subjects. He learned his craft well; the (often compelling) rough edges of his early work disappeared in favor of an apparently effortless, slick cinematographic style. He was careful to rely on measured doses of Hitchcock-like suspense, and not to stray too far from generic conventions. "These dark years," he wrote in his autobiography, "taught me that a filmmaker must carefully keep track of his box office grosses in order to obtain a correct level. It's a study of marketing, like any other."[8] However necessary these lessons may have been in commercial terms, the director's progress nonetheless entailed the loss of something important. *Les Bonnes Femmes* is one of the least well-known and most perverse masterpieces of the *nouvelle vague.* It shuns narratively based suspense in favor of a freefloating anxiety that seems to emanate not from story but from milieu. The brutal strangulation murder that concludes the film does not come as a surprise, but its careful preparation is on the level of spectator desire: one waits and waits for something—anything—to happen, and the longer the deed is delayed, the more extreme is the need for it.

Chabrol's compromise with mainstream filmmaking enabled him to continue to explore *Les Bonnes Femmes'* troubling, realistically portrayed world of universal guilt in ways more acceptable to large audiences, though inevitably his films became less original in narrative form and more dependent on the "thriller" tradition pioneered by Henri-Georges Clouzot. Aside from his debts to Clouzot and other French masters of *film noir,* Chabrol's cinematic universe after the late 1960s shows the clear influence of the American suspense films of Alfred Hitchcock and the 1950s domestic dramas of Douglas Sirk. (These two European masters of Hollywood filmmaking were particularly admired by the critics at *Cahiers du Cinéma.* In 1957 Chabrol and Rohmer had published a book-length critical study of Hitchcock's films.) To these models Chabrol added a careful and precise observation of the details of everyday life, using abundant location shooting and deliberately unstylized decor and costumes. The implements of bourgeois ease assume a kind of awful weight in many of his films, serving as ironic counterpoint to the brutal passions that lurk beneath the surface of ordinary relationships of family, romance, and friendship. When the protagonist of *Que la bête meure/This Man Must Die* (1969) discusses his murderous plans with his lover, it is in an intimate, comfortable restaurant, with a waiter carving a beautifully browned duck in front of them.

Many critics have accused Chabrol of having a debilitating fondness for satiric stereotypes (the bullying, cowardly bourgeois father in *Que la bête meure,* for example). But as Robin Wood and Michael Walker have pointed out, the worst examples of such easy caricature are to be found in the films scripted by Paul Gégauff.[9] In Chabrol's other works, one generally finds a more subtle approach to character and social type. He is obviously fond of satire, perhaps as a defense against the violence that he probably finds both frightening and seductive. Yet in *Le Boucher (The Butcher,* 1970, story and script by Chabrol), for example, he works *against* stereotypes: the film's serial murderer is a curiously appealing, vulnerable character, while the normal people are uncaring and more unsettling than he is. It seems that Chabrol must either work with caricatures or against them, but he cannot ignore them.

Chabrol provides a kind of litmus test for critics and historians of recent French cinema. He probably never ceased wanting to make blasphemous films, which is to say that he never fully disengaged from his Catholicism. For this reason it is tempting to view him as a covertly religious filmmaker, much in the manner that he and Rohmer interpreted the work of Alfred Hitchcock. Those who dislike Chabrol, considering him a pretentious, facile cynic, often decry his lack of humanism. Indeed, his later work may be viewed as a subtle, post-New Wave variant on the psychological realism denounced by the young François Truffaut. Significantly, those who reject Chabrol generally embrace Truffaut—who, unlike Chabrol and Malle, never seems to have taken religion seriously. Of the most commercially inclined serious filmmakers of the *nouvelle vague* generation, it is Truffaut who best merits the label of secular humanist. Perhaps this is one reason his works have found so many admirers among the liberal intelligentsias of France and the United States. In their career trajectories and in the way they related to mainstream filmmaking after the demise of the New Wave, Truffaut and Chabrol are brothers. In the ethical, philosophical aspects of their cinema work, however, they are only distantly related.

Truffaut was born in Paris in 1932. His father was an architect, his mother a secretary. His early life was painful and he rarely spoke of it with interviewers, though he gave a semi-fictional account in *Les Quatre Cents Coups*. One must be wary of taking this work too literally, however: like many autobiographical works, Truffaut's film is not solely self-revelation but also a settling of old scores. He moves his family several notches down on the social scale, for example, and makes his protagonist a bastard child. Like the film's Antoine Doinel, young François was first raised by his grandmother. When he went to live with his parents at age eight, his troubled family life found expression in his erratic behavior at school. He eventually ran away from home and lived with a friend's family, but his father found him and had him committed to an institution for juvenile delinquents. But unlike Antoine Doinel, Truffaut had discovered a father surrogate before his incarceration, through his passionate love of the movies. André Bazin had met young François through ciné-club meetings, and when he was incarcerated Bazin obtained his release, taking responsibility for the boy's conduct.

Bazin enabled Truffaut to channel his energies into the one area of his life which had become a sort of religion for him: cinema. In his early twenties, after a disastrous experience in the French army from which Bazin again had to rescue him, he began writing criticism for *Cahiers du Cinéma*. Soon his savage attacks on mainstream French productions gave the magazine's editors pause. They fretted over "A Certain Tendency of French Cinema" for several months, finally publishing it with other material that qualified his extreme positions, and partly disassociated the journal from them. Truffaut had not been made part of the journal's team merely for sentimental reasons, however. He had become the aggressive "point man" in *Cahiers*' campaign to reform French cinema—very much in the way that political parties often encourage their radical fringe elements to attack enemies and ignore social norms, while preserving the organizations' "deniability." But the young critic's anti-social behavior concealed a profound ambivalence about the French filmmaking establishment. After denouncing the Cannes festival throughout the 1950s, for example, he became a member of its jury in 1962.

Perhaps the most interesting sign of this ambivalence, one which would directly lead to his becoming a part of the establishment he apparently hated, was his marriage in 1957 to Madeleine Morgenstern, daughter of a well-known French producer and distributor. With his wife's dowry Truffaut established his own film company, Les Films du Carosse (named in honor of Renoir's *The Golden Coach*), and immediately embarked on production of a narrative short subject, *Les Mistons* (*The Brats*, 1957, after Maurice Pons).[10] His father-in-law, angry over Truffaut's continuing attacks on mainstream French cinema, challenged him to make his own feature and prove that he could do better. And so it happened that Ignace Morgenstern, relishing what he saw as his son-in-law's inevitable comeuppance, provided the crucial seed capital for one of the most profitable and highly regarded French films of all time, *Les Quatre Cents Coups* (*The Four Hundred Blows*, 1959). The film was awarded a *prime à la qualité* (which Truffaut immediately used to bankroll Jean Cocteau's last film), was chosen to represent French cinema at Cannes (winning the festival's prize for best direction), and became a smash hit both domestically and in foreign markets.

The enormous success of *Les Quatre Cents Coups* placed Truffaut in an oddly difficult position, though one which less successful directors could only envy. The industry, and the French filmgoing public, was waiting to see how he would follow this stunning *coup de cinéma*. His second feature would inevitably be submitted to the test of comparison with his first. He chose—wisely, in artistic if not commercial terms—to make an entirely different sort of film. *Les Quatre Cents Coups* tells the simple, angry tale of a neglected child at the mercy of uncomprehending adults (often seen as more "childish" than the children themselves). Its major cinematic point of reference is Jean Vigo's similarly autobiographical *Zéro de conduite*, which a number of images deliberately recall, without directly quoting; the film's final sequence, of Antoine gazing expressionlessly at the sea, reworks a similar scene from Vigo's *L'Atalante*. He chose a different source of inspiration for *Tirez sur le pianiste* (*Shoot the Piano Player*, 1960), adapting an American crime novel of the sort that was soon also to interest Claude Chabrol, though with very different results. Truffaut deliberately created a hybrid cultural landscape (somewhat reminiscent of Renoir's *Les Basfonds*), a France peopled with bumbling American-style gangsters and characters with names like Charlie, Fido, and Chico.

Whereas *Les Quatre Cents Coups* is realist, even perhaps Neorealist in style and ethos, *Tirez sur le pianiste* is playful, contradictory, and ironic.[11] It is the first of the director's many works in recognizable cinema genres, and like so many of them it is at least as much *about* a genre as *in* one. Critics have often praised—or condemned—Truffaut for his simple, unmannered way of telling a story, yet this characterization does not apply to his second feature, or to his other early genre pictures such as his one essay in science-fiction, *Fahrenheit 451* (Britain, 1966).[12] In *Tirez sur le pianiste*, an absurdly caricatured gangster declares that if he is not telling the truth his mother should drop dead. The film abruptly cuts to a shot of an old lady in a rocking chair, seen through a D. W. Griffith-style elliptical mask, who obligingly has a fit and dies. The film is studded with such exhilarating narrational interventions (perhaps most notably a jarring change of narrator within a long flashback), and with abrupt mood swings which continually remind the spectator of the storyteller's presence.

Though greatly admired by some critics at the time, and by many more today, Truffaut's second feature received mixed notices in the press and a poor reception from French audiences. His response was not, however, to return to his original, and more profitable, autobiographical inspiration. He chose instead to make another genre picture, this time muting, though not eliminating, the mood swings and authorial markers of *Tirez sur le pianiste*. *Jules et Jim* (*Jules and Jim*, 1961) was the first of his many essays in that reliable staple of the Tradition of Quality, the historical costume picture adapted from a literary source. That Truffaut would work in this well-trodden

Jules et Jim recasts the postwar literary adaptation/costume drama, but transformation of the genre is less extreme than appears on first viewing. This is arguably the most tradition-bound and conservative of Truffaut's early features.

domain demonstrates the extent to which he saw himself as a reformer of commercial cinema, not a revolutionary. *Jules et Jim* reformulates the traditional costume drama in New Wave terms: more sex (and less courtship), no sociopolitical analysis, characters more sympathetic than those in similar works of the 1950s, and a sensibility which might perhaps best be described as appealingly adolescent. Now *this* is how it should be done, he might have said. Audiences and most critics agreed, and the film remains one of his best-loved works. Lovers of cinematic excess, however, can only regret Truffaut's retreat from the wild, anti-social abandon of his second feature, which was to reappear, with small exceptions, only in his parodic examination of female criminality, *Une Belle Fille comme moi* (*Such a Gorgeous Kid Like Me*, 1972). Though as a critic he had violently denounced the industry's stiffling of personal expression, as a filmmaker he found, ironically, that he had to reshape his own cinematic personality to conform to the demands of the commercial mainstream.

Truffaut's first three features largely define the dominant impulses in his cinema career. On the one hand, he often told simple, contemporary stories centered on themes of loneliness, friendship, and love, the necessity of knowing and following one's desires, and the danger of having them turn into obsessions. These works include the cycle of Antoine Doinel films—begun with *Les Quatre Cents Coups* and continued in *Baisers volés* (*Stolen Kisses*, 1968) and in two other features and one contribution to a sketch film—as well as tales of frustrated passion such as *La Peau douce* (*Soft Skin*, 1964) and *La Femme d'à côté* (*The Woman Next Door*, 1981) and the more lighthearted *L'Homme qui aimait les femmes* (*The Man Who Loved Women*, 1977). These films do not rely on recognizable formulas of commercial cinema; they are, to use an unwieldy but accurate label, "nongenre pictures."

The majority of Truffaut's films do consciously place themselves in generic traditions, though in two somewhat different ways. Like *Tirez sur le pianiste* (though without its spirit of wild abandon), works such as *La Mariée était en noir* (*The Bride Wore Black*, 1968) and his last film *Vivement dimanche*/*Confidentially Yours* (1983) playfully explore the legacy of the classic Hollywood cinema of the 1940s and 1950s. But the genre that dominated his work was the traditional French historical costume drama, which he generally treated with less playfulness and irony. Aside from *Jules et Jim*, his most highly regarded explorations of this area are probably *Les Deux Anglaises et le Continent*/*Two English Girls* (1971) and *L'Histoire d'Adèle H.* (*The Story of Adele H.*, 1975). (*L'Enfant sauvage* [*The Wild Child*, 1970] and the remarkable *La Chambre verte* [*The Green Room*, 1978] are generically historical films but in style and themes have more in common with his contemporary narratives.)

These three dominant strands in Truffaut's work continually demonstrate his sense of indebtedness to his cinema masters: Rossellini (for whom he had worked, briefly, as an assistant) in the linear narratives; Hitchcock, Hawks, and other masters of American formula filmmaking for his contemporary genre films; and Max Ophuls in the historical costume pictures.[13] And many other filmmakers as diverse as Griffith, Vigo, and Fellini also received his loving *hommages.* Jean Renoir's influence, though generally less obvious in any given film, is nonetheless consistently strong in their conception of character and direction of actors. The striking diversity of Truffaut's cinematic models is one important key to his wide popularity both with the general public and with cinema aficionados. His work offers something for almost everyone, with the notable exception of those who insist on cinema as a form of political action.

Although he became a central figure in the filmmaking establishment which he had once so bitterly criticized, and though he loved to created complicated webs of references to others' works, Truffaut succeeded at being a personal filmmaker who addressed broad audiences in a period when this was becoming increasingly difficult goal to attain. Perhaps the most important reason for this success (and for his wish to achieve it) lay in the personality which he was able to express. Shy, truly at ease only with old friends or with children, Truffaut probably never ceased feeling the wounds of his childhood. It is not necessarily a condemnation of his work to characterize most of it as profoundly adolescent in nature: it speaks to the adolescent dreams and frustrations buried more or less deeply in every spectator, and does so in reasonably sophisticated and varied ways. In filmmaking Truffaut found a perfect way to remain invisible and yet reveal himself, to express his inner child's playfulness, but also melancholy, and his fascination with an adult world of which he never fully felt a part.

◪14◪

Filmmaking at the Margins

The excitement generated by the *nouvelle vague*, though widespread, was far from universal. Those with an important stake in the status quo (for example union leaders, particularly Communists, and major producers and distributors) looked with distaste on the new upstart filmmakers and their allies. These malcontents had ample reason to be disturbed, for the New Wave did in fact break their grip on the industry. While the cinema market grew smaller, competition increased at all levels for the slowly diminishing box-office take. Like the industry itself, film audiences also became fragmented, and this changed the ground rules of competition. Even such a major benefi-ciary of the new situation as the independent producer-director Fran-çois Truffaut could look back with a certain nostalgia on the bad old days:

> André Bazin could not write today that "All films are born free and equal." Film production, like book publishing, has become diversified and specialized. During the war, Clouzot, Carné, Delannoy, Christian-Jacque, Henri Decoin, Cocteau and Bresson addressed the same public. This is no longer true . . . .
>
> When I was a critic, films were often more alive though less "intelli-gent" and "personal" than today. I put the words in quotes precisely because I hold that there was no lack of intelligent directors at that time, but that they were induced to mask their personalities so as to preserve a universality in their films . . . .
>
> All that is changed; not only has cinema caught up with life in the past fifteen years [since 1960], sometimes it seems to have gone beyond it. Films have become more intelligent—or rather, intellectual—than those who look at them. Often we need instructions to tell whether the images

on the screen are intended as reality or fantasy, past or future; whether it is a question of real action or imagination.[1]

Truffaut did not name names in this lament, and for good reason: many of his former colleagues and allies, such as Alain Resnais, were making precisely the sort of film he found frustrating. And it is not by chance that he spoke of Robert Bresson in the context of World War II, for after the war Bresson was one of the first filmmakers deliberately to address a smaller segment of the filmgoing public.

Truffaut, Chabrol, Malle, and a few other leading directors of their generation strove to make films that addressed broad audiences and at the same time expressed their particular views of life and of cinema. In this they followed the examples of older, popular film artists such as Jean Renoir or Max Ophuls. However, one of the results of the new structure of the industry was to give viability to the more commercially limited ambitions of Bresson and others like him. By keeping budgets low and by managing to interest a sector of the cinema public in their works, *nouvelle vague* filmmakers less interested in capturing mass audiences could express themselves with considerable liberty. This freedom from all but the most minimal commercial demands was perhaps the most striking effect of the breakdown of the postwar system of production. But during the heyday of the Tradition of Quality, making a commercially marginal feature film was a daring, even foolhardy act, one which required the steely determination and singlemindedness of a Robert Bresson—or the freespirited willingness to experiment of the first of the new generation's resolutely independent filmmakers: Agnès Varda.

Varda, of French and Greek ancestry, was born in 1928 in Brussels. She was raised and educated in France, studying at the Sorbonne and the Ecole du Louvre to be a museum curator. The life of a cultural bureaucrat did not appeal to her, however, and she chose to become a professional photographer. In the 1950s she worked for the Théâtre National Populaire; this experience aroused her interest first in theatre and then, logically enough given her profession, in cinema. By her own account, she had seen very few films when, at the age of twenty-seven, she wrote and directed her first feature in the summer of 1955. *La Pointe-Courte* (1956)—named after the fishing village where it was shot, and where she had spent much of her childhood— was made for less than ten million (old) francs, a small fraction even of the tiny budgets for *Les Cousins* and other early *nouvelle vague* classics. Most of the actors and technicians worked for a share of the film's revenues, which were meagre indeed. The C.N.C. classified the work as an "amateur" production, since Varda had not asked for the organization's authorization to begin filming (nor would she have received it, given the modesty of her financing and her small, "unprofessional" team). Regular commercial distribution was therefore impossible, though the film did have a short run at a Parisian art cinema.

La Pointe-Courte has much the same status in the lore of the *nouvelle vague* as Jean-Pierre Melville's contemporary *Bob le flambeur:* little noted at the time, in retrospect it has come to be seen as a highly significant precedent for later developments. But if Melville's film was generally unappreciated because it seemed deceptively familiar and predictable, Varda's work was, on the other hand, bewilderingly innovative and original. Released two to five years later, it would certainly have benefited from the greater critical and commercial tolerance of the peak of the New Wave. But even then, it might have had a difficult reception. The director's willful ignorance of both the commercial mainstream and of the classic works of the art house circuit—in stark contrast to the compulsive cinephilia of the young *Cahiers du Cinéma* critics and their allies—led her to conceive a work based on avant-garde literary and theatrical models.

La Pointe-Courte is two very different films in one, combined in a structure of strict alternation. Half of the film is devoted to the problems of fishermen and their families, played by real inhabitants of the village. Alternating (in ten-minute units) with this realistic study of contemporary political and social issues is the story of a young man from the village and his wife, who have come to discuss their failing marriage and perhaps to decide on separation and divorce. These characters are played by professional theatre actors (Sylvia Montfort and a very young Philippe Noiret, who much later would become a reliable star of commercial features) speaking a dreamy, vaguely neo-Symbolist dialogue. Just when one has become involved in one strand of the film, the other appears, in a jarring change of tone and themes. Spectator identification with the characters is periodically brought to the surface, and undermined. Though the film borrows this technique from literature (Varda cites Faulkner's *Wild Palms* as a model), its effects resemble those of Brechtian "distanciation" techniques in the theatre. The viewer must consciously decide how to relate the film's two strands of discourse, a problem for which there is no easy, narratively mediated solution.

The young couple of *La Pointe-Courte* talk inside the open shell of a boat. Agnès Varda began her artistic career as a photographer, which perhaps accounts for the pictorialist bent of many of her fiction features.

After this impressive debut, Varda alternated—like Louis Malle, but with very different methods and goals—between nonfiction films (generally short subjects) and fiction features. Most of her later interests in feature filmmaking are to be found in *La Pointe-Courte:* a strong sense of place, expressed in striking cinematic landscapes; the mixing but not blending of reality and artifice (typically expressed in the presence of both professional and nonprofessional actors in a single work); and formal structures which do not seem to flow naturally from the fiction but rather are a mark of authorial intervention. These concerns have expressed themselves in a highly diverse body of work. Varda's films, documentary and fiction alike, have been a form of intellectual autobiography. In them one can follow both her personal and political issues—in particular, the development of her feminism—and her formal and aesthetic interests (generally derived not from mainstream cinema but from literature, theatre, photography, and painting).

A question of widespread interest about Varda's work is whether she should be considered a feminist filmmaker. Certainly she has demonstrated her continuing interest in women's issues, beginning with her second feature, *Cléo de 5 à 7* (*Cleo From 5 to 7*, 1961). In that film the title character, a pop vocalist whose professional activities may be seen as creating an exemplary sexual stereotype, must rethink her life while awaiting the results of a test which will reveal whether or not she has cancer. Normally a public object of spectacle, Cleo must learn to reappropriate and redirect the act of seeing (and hearing), as a private individual who must be for herself, not for others. The film's story is demarcated by title cards which tick off the passing minutes and announce, in Brechtian fashion, some of the content of each scene. By foregrounding the objective aspects of narrative (time, characters), these interventions throw into relief the completely subjective focus of the drama. At the end of a journey from the center of Paris to a park on its southern edge, Cleo meets a young soldier and has a pleasant, healingly banal conversation which may or may not enable her to find a new sense of herself in the world. But will she change? Should she? Varda deliberately leaves these questions posed, but unresolved.

For Varda is not a feminist or a Left activist (she has made documentaries about the Black Panthers, Cuba, and Hispanic graffiti artists in Los Angeles) in the sense of making polemical *films à thèse*. She is <u>interested in raising questions but not in answering them.</u> Sandy Flitterman-Lewis applauds Varda's "profound comprehension of the radical possibilities of a feminist politics of form."[2] But some observers, less concerned with formal issues, have been uneasy with much of the director's work, because of its openness to varied and contradictory responses. Many viewers, men and women alike, are particularly disturbed by her third feature, *Le Bonheur* (*Happiness*, 1965). A stunning exploration of the painterly use of color in cinema (sequences end with fades, not to black, but to blue, yellow, and other vivid hues), *Le Bonheur* depicts a completely, unthinkingly male-dominated family constellation (the man, the wife and children, and his lover). When the dutiful wife dies, she is effortlessly replaced (to a joyful Mozart piece on the soundtrack) by the compliant mistress. Life and patriarchy go on, unexamined. "If this is happiness," the spectator sympathetic to feminism may well say, "then I want none of it." Since there are no overt markers of authorial irony in the film, any anger one directs at its characters can easily extend to their creator. Why doesn't she *tell* us this is "bad"? Has she no *feelings* about the dead woman?

This is, presumably, exactly the sort of response Varda wants to evoke, even though it is probably dangerous to antagonize one's audiences to this extent with unmarked irony. When she made her next overtly feminist feature, *L'Une chante, l'autre pas* (*One Sings, The Other Doesn't*, 1977), Varda was more circumspect and encountered the opposite response. That story of two women's lives and loves in a period of growing feminist consciousness was widely viewed as simplemindedly thesis-oriented in its exploration of charged issues such as divorce and abortion. This, too, is arguably a valuable sort of reaction to evoke, posing the crucial question of how to deal with women's issues in narrative cinema. In both *Le Bonheur* and *L'Une chante, l'autre pas*, Varda (perhaps courageously) did not seek to be admired as exemplary, idealized film artist. It is the spectator who must become the center of judgment and attempt to solve the nagging problems that these films pose.

As if to demonstrate, however, that she is not categorically opposed to films that are less aggressive and difficult, Varda has recently made what many regard as her masterpiece, *Sans toit ni loi/Vagabond* (1985), which represents a return of sorts to the basically contemplative, though politically situated world of *La Pointe-Courte*. *Sans toit ni loi* is Varda's least aesthetically fragmented film, though it continues her interests in locale as organizing principle, in mixing different acting styles, and in obliging the spectator to make undirected judgments about the psychology, indeed the ultimate human value, of its characters. Its protagonist, a homeless adolescent whose story is told in flashback by those who met her before her death, lives on the very margins of French society. Her problems are by definition less personally compelling to most spectators than those of Varda's other characters—though one imagines that an audience of homeless people would have very strong and not necessarily supportive reactions to the film. *Sans toit ni loi* is an easy film to like, at least for viewers accustomed to "art cinema" and with no direct knowlege of homelessness, but for that very reason it does not pack the disturbing moral and political punch of the director's less well-known and less widely admired works.

Throughout her career, Agnès Varda has been one of the most unclassifiable figures of recent Fench cinema. One thing, however, is clear: she had almost nothing to do with *Cahiers du Cinéma* in the 1950s, or with the filmmakers associated with it. On the other hand, she was initially linked by friendship, by marriage (to Jacques Demy), and by professional collaboration (for example, with Alain Resnais) to the documentary production sector of the *nouvelle vague* generation. These filmmakers are often called the Left Bank School of French cinema, as a way of distinguishing them from the ex-*Cahiers* critics. However, Varda's relation even to this strand of the New Wave was limited and circumstantial. It is true that she lived and worked on the left (south) side of the Seine, where she knew Resnais, Georges Franju, Chris Marker and other *rive gauche* filmmakers, and that Resnais edited *La Pointe-Courte* and later reported that he learned much from that film's innovative structure. If Varda may be considered a Left Bank film artist, she is nonetheless atypical of this group in some important ways. She has made documentary films, but this was not the path by which she came to make features. Nor do any of her works since *La Pointe-Courte* strongly reflect the influence of contemporary experimental fiction, as seen in so many of Resnais's films, or in the cinema work of "new novel" exponents Alain Robbe-Grillet and Marguerite Duras.

As Varda's case suggests, the notion of a Left Bank School, and any generalizations about the influence of documentary on French fiction filmmaking since 1958 often have only limited value. There was as much variety of professional experience, artistic goals, and career trajectories within the ranks of the documentarians and their associates as there was in the *Cahiers* group—if not more. Most of those who began their careers in nonfiction film never returned to that area once they had "graduated" to fiction features, and many seem to have worked in documentary only as a convenient form of apprenticeship. Edouard Molinaro, for example, became one of the most commercially successful artisans of post-New Wave cinema, making films— such as *La Cage aux folles* (*The Coop for Queens,* 1979)—many times more remunerative than those of more critically respected ex-documentarians such as Alain Resnais and Georges Franju. And some filmmakers often cited as members of the Left Bank School, such as Varda's husband Jacques Demy, attempted much the same kind of compromises with mainstream commercial filmmaking as did Claude Chabrol and François Truffaut.

Demy, born in 1931, had studied graphic arts and filmmaking and was for a time an assistant to the celebrated French animator Paul Grimault. In the early 1950s he continued his apprenticeship with the documentarian Georges Rouquier, before directing several nonfiction short subjects and an adaptation of a one-act play by Jean Cocteau at the end of the decade. Demy's overriding ambition was to be a director and writer of film musicals, though his first chance to direct a feature entailed a typically small *nouvelle vague* budget. *Lola* (1961)— dedicated to Max Ophuls, with whom Demy shared a great fondness for ornamentation and complicated tracking shots—is sometimes said to have the structure of a musical by critics who want to see more unity in the director's work than may actually be there. This first feature and his second, *La Baie des Anges* (*Bay of the Angels*, 1963) arguably have more in common in both style and theme with other low-budget features of the period than with his later works.

Many critics characterize *La Baie des Anges* as Demy's finest film, though his third feature, *Les Parapluies de Cherbourg* (*The Umbrellas of Cherbourg*, 1964, music by Michel Legrand) has many admirers and is much more widely known. This big-budget film "opera," in which even expository dialogue is sung rather than spoken, won wide admiration (and the Best Film award at the Cannes festival) for its attempt to radicalize and transform the traditional genre of the musical, which by the mid-1960s had lost most of its artistic and commercial viability. Unfortunately, Demy was unable to repeat its great critical and commercial success in his subsequent work. *Les Demoiselles de Rochefort* (*The Young Girls of Rochefort*, 1967) was widely considered a pale imitation of *Les Parapluies de Cherbourg*. His attempts to extend the generic boundaries of the musical to encompass fairy tale—*Peau d'ane* (*Donkey Skin*, 1971)—and political commentary—*Une Chambre en ville* (*A Room in Town*, 1982)—met with tepid critical and popular response.

Demy's career might well have been better served had he heeded *Cahiers du Cinéma*'s recommendation in the late 1950s that aspiring directors take a "vow of poverty" and remain independent of the commercial mainstream, rather than try to renew one of its most fragile, and costly, genres. Of course, *Cahiers* critics such as Truffaut and Chabrol ultimately chose not to take their magazine's advice. If Demy's own attempts to work within the system have been less successful than theirs, his quixotic efforts have in some ways been more daring and— as in *Les Parapluies de Cherbourg* and *Une Chambre en ville*—manage to provide odd, curiously affecting experiences not to be found anywhere else in French cinema.

N Both Demy and Varda profited from, but were not deeply influenced by, their early work in documentary film. Others of their generation, however, were more directly marked by their first nonfiction projects, and it is among them that one must look for the core of the Left Bank School of French cinema. Documentary filmmaking has always been a fragile endeavor and almost inevitably dependent for its survival, as Paul Rotha has cogently argued, on some form of institutional or governmental sponsorship.[3] The remarkable flowering of nonfiction French cinema in the 1940s and 1950s, from which so much of the notable alternative fiction filmmaking of the New Wave period would flow, was anything but accidental. Those who, following the lead of the young *Cahiers* critics, denounce the postwar *cinéma de papa* as repetitive, repressive, and stereotyped, too easily forget that quality cinema deliberately nurtured within itself its own alternative film culture, in the area of the short subject. Here officially sanctioned experiment and innovation was not only tolerated but encouraged.

Like most aspects of postwar filmmaking, this one dates back to the German Occupation. When C.O.I.C. banned double-feature presentations as a way of reducing harmful competition among exhibitors, it required all cinemas to show at least one short subject (along with the obligatory propaganda newsreel) per program. These works, which had their own quotas, low-interest loans, and guaranteed allotments of film stock, were to be prominently publicized as well: all posters advertising a feature film had to carry the title and the director's name for each short subject.[4] The majority of these *films de complément* were documentaries; although their number included a few notorious exercises in Vichy propaganda, most of them were honorable exercises in nonfiction cinema—and sometimes distinguished ones such as Georges Rouquier's *Le Tonnelier* (*The Barrelmaker,* 1942). Their producers received a small, unvarying share (3 percent) of the box-office receipts of each feature film which they accompanied.

This system remained essentially unchanged, minus the quotas and allotments of film stock, until 1955, when it was replaced by a system of *primes à la qualité,* "bonuses for quality" awarded by a jury, which supplemented whatever income the films could earn on the now deregulated exhibition market.[5] Though nonfiction filmmakers protested the new system (fearing politically motivated jury judgments), it did not materially change the economic and artistic situation of most short-subject production, because the amount of money any work could earn from rentals and quality bonuses remained quite small—in most cases enough to pay for basic costs but not to assure any substantial profit. To be economically viable, short subjects generally had to have additional funding. For documentary works, this was typically found in institutional sponsorship: museums, government agencies, industrial councils, tourist boards, and the like underwrote practically all of the notable works of the period. The necessity of such sponsorship explains the rarity of fiction short subjects in the period: they could rarely hope for such supplementary funding.[6]

In its virtually total dependence on sponsorship, documentary film production in postwar France differed little from its counterpart in Great Britain and in the United States before the war, except that the French system of state regulation and virtually guaranteed commercial exhibition resulted in a much larger number of works. This sheer volume of production created a community of filmmakers who were all very much aware of each other's activities and made common cause when they felt menaced—by the governmental initiative to reward "quality," for example. In addition, the regular exhibition of their works encouraged an awareness of nonfiction film among critics and presumably among a certain number of film spectators. Documentary film was not merely a means to serve the interests of a sponsor; it was also an object of ongoing aesthetic and political evaluation—as good or bad art, as progressive or reactionary. Sponsors were pleased when works they initiated received critical attention in the pages of *Cahiers du Cinéma* and other publications, and when—on rare occasions—spectators went to a cinema to see the short subject as much as for the feature presentation. As a result, successful nonfiction filmmakers enjoyed a remarkable degree of freedom in the elaboration of their projects, a liberty which they occasionally used to undermine or modify the sponsor's expectations for a given project.

Outright subversion of a film's official intent—as in Franju's *Hôtel des Invalides* (1951), for example, a film about a war museum that subtly suggests the horror of all warfare—was rare. But in the best postwar documentaries there is always a strong sense of the filmmaker's attitude toward his or her subject matter: playful—Resnais's *Le Chant du styrène* (*The Styrene's Song*, 1958); melancholy—Franju's *Le Grand Méliès* (*The Great Méliès*, 1952); invocatory—Jean Rouch's *Mamy Water* (1955); dryly ironic—Varda's *Du côté de la côte* (*The Riviera Way*, 1959). This strong emotional tone emerges in large measure from carefully crafted voice-over narrations, many of which were written by noted authors: Raymond Queneau (*Le Chant du styrène*),[7] Jacques Prévert

(Franju's *Mon Chien* [*My Dog,* 1955]), Paul Eluard (Resnais's *Guernica* [1950]), Jean Cocteau (a number of regrettably minor works), and many others.

The crucial importance of the films' often highly literary verbal tracks underlines another aspect of pre-*nouvelle vague* documentaries that had important artistic consequences: they were almost all shot as silent works, with music, commentary, and sound effects added during postproduction. This was because lightweight, easily portable tape recorders and synchronous 16-millimeter cameras were simply not available until the early 1960s. When this equipment came into widespread use it radically changed documentary film production throughout the world, and perhaps nowhere more profoundly than in France. The *cinéma vérité* movement, developed largely under the leadership of the ethnographic filmmaker Jean Rouch, used the new technology in an active, often confrontational way. French audiences saw the new approach directed at their own culture in Rouch's *Chronique d'un été* (*Chronicle of a Summer,* 1961) and in Chris Marker's *Le Joli Mai* (*The Lovely Month of May,* 1963), films in which ordinary Parisians were asked open-ended questions such as "Are you happy?" and "What does money mean to you?" In *Chronique d'un été,* some of the interviewees were invited to view the footage in which they had been interrogated, and their responses were incorporated into the finished film.

Jean Rouch's use of such direct interactive techniques in French documentary after 1960 marked his dissatisfaction with his earlier and more traditional ethnographic films, such as *Les Maîtres fous* (*The Mad Priests,* 1955). But if Rouch and other leading documentarians rejected the pre-1960 French nonfiction tradition, it nonetheless had a continuing impact on those of his peers who took advantage of the opening provided by the *nouvelle vague* to move into the production of fiction works. By their production methods, earlier nonfiction films had an almost inevitable tendency to continue, and to develop, the aesthetic traditions of the silent era. Individual shots were composed to be striking and effective in and of themselves. The editing of these typically pictorialist images was characterized by a freedom and expressivity that most other sound cinema had lost in the early 1930s. The montage theories of Sergei Eisenstein, outmoded in the context of commercial narrative productions, were still highly relevant to documentary filmmakers working at the margins of the Tradition of Quality. It is hardly surprising, then, that many filmmakers who worked extensively in documentary film production during the post-war period—for example Alain Resnais and Georges Franju—would make fiction features quite different from the ones conceived by ex-assistant directors of fiction features, or by the former critics from *Cahiers du Cinéma.*

The fiction films of the most celebrated ex-documentarians were also highly literary, often employing voice-over narrations. Music and sound effects played a crucial role in the development of the works' emotional tone. The films typically deployed images of obvious physical authenticity yet of a highly pictorialist character, often characterized by camera movements which underlined their relative autonomy. Editing, frequently proceeding by Eisensteinian "shocks" provoked by the collision of two radically different images, was evident and expressive, not merely a way of stitching shots together seamlessly. These formal characteristics, of course, offer only the beginnings of an analysis of the specificity of Left Bank cinema. It should be noted that some of the ex-*Cahiers* critics also occasionally indulged in shock editing, stylized images of very real objects and landscapes, and expressive music and effects tracks—for they, too, had seen and been influenced by the Tradition of Quality's official alternative cinema. If the notion of a *rive gauche* group of filmmakers is to have historical validity, it must also include the extra-cinematic artistic and political influences which combined, for a time, to produce something very much like a school or cinema art movement which first entered fiction filmmaking in the early days of the New Wave.

Like cinematic impressionism, *réalisme poétique,* or foreign movements or tendencies such as Soviet montage filmmaking, the Left Bank School of French cinema can only be defined in relation to a small number of films, by a limited number of creative artists. The names most frequently cited in commentaries on this movement include not only industry professionals formed in documentary production—Alain Resnais, Georges Franju, Henri Colpi—but also a number of individuals who came to filmmaking after having established themselves as writers of poetry, plays, and experimental fiction. This group—for example Jean Cayrol, Alain Robbe-Grillet, and Marguerite Duras—entered the film community first as scriptwriters, either for documentaries or fiction features. One *rive gauche* filmmaker combined the two backgrounds: Chris Marker had written fiction, poetry, and literary criticism when he began directing documentary short subjects in the early 1950s; at that point in his career he was in his early thirties and little known in either literary or filmmaking circles. The second great source of the Left Bank School, then, was contemporary French literature—not the best-selling novels which contended for the *Prix Goncourt* and were sometimes adapted as mainstream films, but avant-garde works read largely by urban intellectuals. The greatest single literary influence was undoubtedly experimental fiction, the "new novel" which developed at roughly the same time as the great flowering of French documentary cinema. Another, older but still vital source of inspiration was the Surrealist movement, whose influence could be felt in much contemporary poetry. (Recall, also, the 1950s nonfiction scripts written by Eluard, Queneau, Prévert, and Cocteau.)

Much of *rive gauche* filmmaking shows its debt to Surrealism in its persistent interest in dream-like mental states—the free floating, hallucinatory nature of narrative in Robbe-Grillet's work, for example— and often also in clear and stark but disturbing images which recall the cinema of Luis Buñuel. But the Surrealist strain in this area of French filmmaking is probably most evident in the work of one of its less-known figures, a director whom most observers (perhaps unjustly) consider a *petit maître,* or "minor master" of postwar cinema: Georges Franju. Like many of his peers who had worked extensively on short subjects Franju was essentially formed, both as artistic temperament and as cinematic technician, by the time he was able to make his first feature, *La Tête contre les murs/The Keepers* (1959), the grueling story of a young man unjustly committed to an insane asylum. Indeed, many critics consider the director's earlier documentary work—particularly his study of Parisian slaughterhouses, *Le Sang des bêtes* (*Blood of the Beasts,* 1949)—superior to his fiction features.[8] Whether one agrees with this judgment or not, it is clear that Franju's career is all of one piece. In emotional tone and its oneiric yet shockingly authentic images, *Le Sang des bêtes* serves as fitting prelude to his celebrated exercise in the horror film, *Les Yeux sans visage* (*Eyes Without a Face,* aka *The Horror Chamber of Dr. Faustus,* 1960).

Franju quite consciously situated his work in the Surrealist tradition, in which "the object, disoriented, *anxious,* has a living, meticulous realism . . . [but] never have *relations* [between objects] been more unpredictable—from which are born these new resonances, these dynamisms, this 'shudder' ['*frisson*'] which is an art."[9] Franju often sought these new resonances in cinematic versions of literary works, such as Mauriac's *Thérèse Desqueyroux* (1962) and Cocteau's *Thomas l'imposteur* (*Thomas the Imposter,* 1965). In these he crafted wholly personal adaptations of much the same caliber and faithfulness to their sources as those produced by Jean-Pierre Melville before the latter's entry into genre filmmaking with *Bob le flambeur.* Franju was not exclusively committed to high literary art, however. He had his own favorite cinematic and literary genre: the *fantastique,* or "fantastic tale," which he explored in collaborations with thriller writers Boileau and Narcejac (particularly *Les Yeux sans visage*) and in a remake of the classic Louis Feuillade serial, *Judex* (1964).

Franju regarded all of his cinema work as a kind of self-therapy, a way of dealing with the anxiety and chronic depression which he constantly had to fight. He made films about anxiety, depression, torture, and mental breakdown as a way of magically warding off the threat of these experiences. By his own account such concerns date from his earliest childhood, and yet he is far from being the only member of the Left Bank School to manifest them. This kind of subject matter would perhaps have been less widely attractive to audiences and to filmmakers of his generation, had it not been for an overarching, less personal experience which they all shared later in life. Along with postwar nonfiction filmmaking and contemporary literary trends, the crystallization of *rive gauche* filmmaking was stamped with the indelible experience of modern warfare, social disintegration, and political repression in the war years. If one compares the Left Bank filmmakers with those who got their start writing for *Cahiers du Cinéma,* the one striking difference is age. Resnais and Robbe-Grillet were born in 1922, Marker and Colpi in 1921, Duras in 1914, and Franju in 1912. For most of World War II, they were in their twenties, while the future *Cahiers* critics, on average a decade or so younger, were in their mid teens.[10] That this chronological gap marks a crucial developmental and cultural difference between the two groups may be seen in the older filmmakers' obsessional interest not only in warfare, but more generally in violence and torture, and in the lasting effects of various sorts of physical and psychological trauma.

Despite the convergence of all these determinants, this complex brew of influences would certainly have assumed another form in French fiction film, or indeed might never have become the basis for a cinema art movement at all, had it not been for the central role played by Alain Resnais. Resnais was born in the small city of Vannes, in Brittany, where his father was a reasonably prosperous pharmacist. Beginning at an early age, the boy suffered from attacks of asthma;

this condition contributed to his erratic, eclectic education, much of it acquired in home study, and doubtless also to his intense sensitivity and omnivorous receptiveness to the world around him. He read and admired the work of Marcel Proust and other great authors, as well as comic books of all sorts, and dime novels such as the adventures of master detective Harry Dickson, which he would later try, unsuccessfully, to adapt to the cinema. His parents indulged his enthusiasms; they gave him an 8-millimeter home movie camera with which, at the age of twelve, he made his first films, one of them a version of the adventures of master criminal Fantômas (twenty years after Feuillade's great serial melodrama on the same subject).

Despite his irregular schooling, Resnais obtained his *baccalauréat* when he was only seventeen years old. Just before the beginning of the *drôle de guerre* he moved to Paris to study acting and begin a career in the theatre. Like many aspiring performers, he was anything but extroverted in everyday life; the reclusive, meditative temperament encouraged by his childhood illness would continue to mark his personality even when he was a celebrated film director. Near the end of the Occupation he enrolled in the newly created national film school, I.D.H.E.C., though he only studied there for a little over a year, at a time when the curriculum was still rather disorganized. Probably his film school experience confirmed, rather than developed, the extensive knowlege of cinema born of his almost compulsive cinephilia, though his courses did give him the beginnings of his working knowledge of 16 and 35 millimeter production methods.

After the war's end Resnais found work in the film industry on various marginal projects as a cinematographer, film editor, and assistant director, while also directing a series of independently financed 16-millimeter shorts, both fiction and documentary. His entry into the industry mainstream came with the last of these, a study of impressionist painting entitled *Van Gogh* (16 mm. 1947, 35 mm. 1948). This work so impressed Pierre Braunberger and others at Les Films du Panthéon that they commissioned a remake in the larger, theatrical format.[11] Films about painting were a staple of the postwar documentary, both because of their high-culture cachet (which dovetailed beautifully with the cultural politics of the industry in general and the C.N.C. in particular) and their relatively low production costs. Resnais followed up on his first success in the sub-genre with *Gauguin* (1950) and *Guernica* (1950), both also produced for Braunberger.

As the subject matter of the latter film—Picasso's celebrated painting about a Spanish Civil War massacre—indicates, Resnais did not view himself solely as a cinematic aesthete. For his next project, he collaborated with his friend Chris Marker on *Les Statues meurent aussi* (*Statues Also Die*, 1953), about the destruction of African art under the pressure of French colonialism. The film was sufficiently effective to be banned outright by the government after one public showing. His next film was also daring and controversial. *Nuit et Brouillard* (*Night and Fog*, 1955) is not only Resnais's best-known documentary; it is also probably the most frequently screened and discussed of all films about the Holocaust. Yet the film's political engagement took a form little recognized either at the time or since. Perhaps the most curious aspect of this widely admired study of the Nazi death camps is that a historically naive spectator could watch it virtually unaware of the fact that the overwhelming majority of the victims it depicts were Jews. The work studiously avoids such historical specificity; as has often been remarked, it is not so much about the camps as about the *memory* of them—a theme which has obvious resonances with the director's later work in fiction features.

Nuit et Brouillard is a film about past and present, its central, anguished question only posed at the very end: could this happen again? When, almost three decades after its release, Charles Krantz asked Resnais about the film's political intent, the director replied, "The whole point was Algeria," where French forces had already committed, and were continuing to commit, their own racially motivated atrocities. Probably sobered by the suppression of *Les Statues meurent aussi*, however, Resnais and scriptwriter Jean Cayrol kept this contemporary political parallel completely implicit. *Nuit et Brouillard* thus remains a film which subtly dehistoricizes genocide, turning the viewer's attention, to a great extent, away from specific victims and specific criminals.[12] This universalizing tendency gives the spectator a great deal of freedom in reading the film, and it becomes a kind of historical Rorschach test. Most viewers don't even notice its curious reluctance to explain that the German death industry was devised to "solve" the so-called Jewish problem.

By the mid 1950s Resnais had become a major figure in the eyes of those who advocated an alternative French film culture. He was one of the few of the nation's younger filmmakers regularly cited as a model in the pages of *Cahiers du Cinéma*. Resnais had already met, and in many cases developed lasting friendships with, the young critics who would later emerge as leaders of the film community. He first encountered André Bazin during the Occupation, when he attended the future critic's ciné-club and brought his own prints of German expressionist masterpieces for screening and discussion. Through Bazin, and through the screenings of classic films at the Cinémathèque Française, he met Truffaut, Chabrol, Godard, and other future *nouvelle vague* filmmakers. (When Truffaut deserted from the French army, Resnais and Chris Marker helped hide him until Bazin managed to persuade the military authorities not to sentence him to prison.)

It thus seems significant that Resnais never worked on film projects with members of the *Cahiers* group, doubly so since few filmmakers in the history of French cinema had been more interested in collaboration with others. Resnais, however, always had a very clear idea of the exact sort of assistance he needed to make his films, and he consistently sought the aid not of film critics but of literary figures—many well known, some relatively obscure—whose concerns meshed well with his own. He has always taken great pleasure in involving other strong artistic temperaments in his work, with the result that to generalize from his films to a "cinema of Alain Resnais" is an enterprise fraught with peril. In many cases—Duras, Robbe-Grillet, Cayrol—the authors whom he first introduced to filmmaking have gone on to cinema work on their own. Because of the consistency of favored themes and formal interests which they share—time, memory, suffering; montage, ellipsis, shifting or indeterminate point of view—these writers' cinema works typically have a kind of family resemblance with Resnais's own films. (Of course, they have been to some extent influenced by his works, and by each other.) Resnais's temperament, so elusive in his own cinema, clearly lingers *somewhere* behind almost all of the Left Bank School: if he did not exactly *create* this filmmaking tendency, he nonetheless may be said to have been its *chef de cuisine*, choosing and subtly influencing the mixing of its ingredients.

The cinema of Alain Resnais is often said to be a cinema of time and memory, though these themes do not always dominate his films. More generally, one could say that he elaborated a cinema of comparisons and juxtapositions, which have often played themselves out in the arenas of memory and history. The implicit comparison of the Holocaust with French colonial activities in Algeria in *Nuit et Brouillard* is not an isolated case. In his first fiction feature, *Hiroshima mon amour* (*Hiroshima, My Love*, 1959, script by Duras), the experience of a French woman who had a German lover during the Occupation is systematically juxtaposed with a meditation on the impact of the atomic bomb on the city of Hiroshima. This daring, potentially taste-

In *Toute la mémoire du monde* (*All the Memory in the World,* short subject 1956), Alain Resnais examines the Bibliothèque Nationale in ways that eerily recall *Nuit et Brouillard.* Note the rails laid for one of the director's celebrated tracking shots.

less metaphor is given surprising force and clarity by the development of a common theme of memory: what does it mean to remember a traumatic event, and does the telling of a story neutralize, fatally, its impact? *Hiroshima mon amour* is first and foremost a film about remembrance and loss; it is even less about the atomic bomb, or the Occupation, than *Nuit et Brouillard* is about the Holocaust.

But the juxtapositions that seem so central to Resnais's works need not involve memory per se. His second film, *L'Année dernière à Marienbad* (*Last Year at Marienbad,* 1961, script by Robbe-Grillet) is a kind of narrative puzzle. Different possible versions of events—perhaps from the past, perhaps fantasies—are elliptically presented to the spectator. But who is the source of these images and sounds? The male character who seems to be the film's narrator? The female character, who might conceivably be hallucinating the presence of a storyteller? An unseen dreamer/author? Are the events which may or may not have taken place allegorical? (The woman's husband or protector may or may not represent Death, in which case the film would be a retelling of the Orpheus myth.) Are they illustrative of the workings of a troubled psyche? Or explications of the process of fiction making and its roots in human desire? *L'Année dernière à Marienbad* seems to be not about any of these possibilities, but about the necessity of grappling with them. Spectators must decide for themselves what to make of this fascinating, never soluble set of problems within problems. Simply to let the film be, to accept its splendid ambiguity, is doubtless the theoretically correct solution, though this is all but impossible for most viewers.

L'Année dernière à Marienbad takes place in a psychic no-man's-land, a dystopia of suffering and repetition. *Muriel, ou le temps d'un retour* (*Muriel, or the Time of a Return*, 1963, script by Cayrol) has a very specific, historically charged context. The film juxtaposes two distinct, war-related "returns": the stepson of an antiques dealer has come back from the Algerian War in the early 1960s, brooding about his experiences there; the antiques dealer's former lover, whom she has not seen since World War II, arrives to visit her, and to confront their shared (but is it really shared?) past. The two men bring their histories with them like the return of the repressed. Though the entire story takes place in a (disjointed) present, the devastation of the war of two decades before is all around the characters, in the bombed-out buildings of the city. (One minor character owns a wrecking company: he demolishes the past for a living. The others destroy it, only somewhat less effectively, by talking about it. The thematic links with *Hiroshima mon amour,* and its connection of narration with forgetting, are evident.) Many critics consider *Muriel* to be Resnais's greatest film, though audiences often find it hard to follow because of its jagged, Eisensteinian editing and highly elliptical screenplay.

Resnais's first three features, conceived in the heyday of the *nouvelle vague,* are his most difficult, uncompromising fiction works. As his career progressed, he clearly decided to moderate his taste for the formal experiment of avant-garde literature, in order to continue to interest audiences in his works. He has probably never lost the actor's overwhelming need to engage the public—though he certainly has never carried this to the extremes of one of his avowed masters, Sacha Guitry. His films since *Muriel* have placed more emphasis on narrative motivations for their juxtapositions of historical moment and psychological point of view. *Stavisky* (1974, script by Jorge Semprun), for example, displays alternate versions of events in many ways worthy of

L'Année dernière à Marienbad, but they are justified by the film's *Rash-omon*-like structure of historical enquiry. Like *Hiroshima mon amour* and *Muriel,* the work juxtaposes two distinct series of historical events, the Stavisky affair and a brief visit to France by Leon Trotsky. At the film's end, however, a link between the two stories is given: the domestic scandal contributes to the ex-Soviet revolutionary's expulsion from the country. *Je t'aime, je t'aime (I Love You, I Love You,* 1968, script by Jacques Sternberg) is even more *Marienbad*-like in its (often hard to follow) montage editing and narrative leaps in time and space, but these are justified by its science-fiction plot of a man who relives his past in fits and starts while in an experimental time machine.[13]

Whereas Resnais has been unwilling to cut himself off from the large public which once applauded *Hiroshima mon amour,* some of his former collaborators have had less hesitation to do so. Alain Robbe-Grillet's first film as a writer-director, *L'Immortelle (The Immortal One,* 1963), extended the formal concerns and psycho-sexual issues he had explored as writer in *L'Année dernière à Marienbad,* though in a somewhat less florid cinematographic style. Robbe-Grillet has made one attempt to make his work more accessible to mainstream audiences, in the rather heavily playful *Trans-Europ Express* (1967), but in general his cinema has served as a kind of exploration and refinement of his literary practice: dense, narratively elusive, based on fragments of experience repeated and successively juxtaposed in new combinations, so that the outlines of a possible story (or stories) emerge. *L'Homme qui ment (The Man Who Lies,* 1968), for example, seems entirely determined by the various possible combinations of repeated, cryptic bits of action. Violence and sado-masochism—sometimes disturbingly literal, as in *Glissements progressifs du plaisir (Successive Slidings of Pleasure,* 1973)—haunt Robbe-Grillet's work, often making it difficult to appreciate, even for spectators willing to confront the films' many levels of ambiguity.

Marguerite Duras's cinema work has been more varied and typically more difficult to understand than Robbe-Grillet's. Rather than simply working in the margins of commercial filmmaking, Duras virulently rejects it, striving to create a kind of anti-cinema which has assumed a variety of forms. As a committed Marxist, she sees mainstream cinema first and foremost as an instrument of social control. "The type of perfection to which commercial filmmaking aspires (the use of its technical capabilities solely to maintain the established order)," she has argued, "mirrors precisely its subservience to dominant social codes. One shows an act of incest, but cut up and rear-ranged, so that everyone recognizes it but no one participates; only a pornographic film will show it directly. Commercial filmmaking can be very clever, but rarely intelligent."[14] Duras, on the other hand, is passionately interested in a cinema which can be intelligent, though this goal is certainly not the only wellspring of her work. The example she cites, incest, is symptomatic of the fascination with violence, pain, and sexuality which surfaces in almost all of her work. But her films so deliberately reject the intelligibility of well-made cinema that often the viewer has little direct sense of what they are about, as in *India Song* (1975), cited by many admirers as her best film. Even in the relatively straightforward *Nathalie Granger* (1973), one suspects that the events depicted are incidental to an unnarrated, more tragic story which the film refuses to tell. Duras's characteristic use of indirec-tion and suggestion may indeed represent a dispassionate working through of her theoretical orientation, but it may also serve as a way by which she can distance herself from aspects of her experience too painful to be confronted directly.

The new French cinema's Left Bank School was not the only niche opened up within the *nouvelle vague* by self-consciously mar-ginal filmmakers. Even among the staff of *Cahiers du Cinéma* there were aspiring directors who did not wish to follow in the paths of Jean Renoir, Alfred Hitchcock, or the magazine's many other revered *auteurs,* making films for mass audiences which nonetheless carried a subtle personal touch. Jacques Rivette and Eric Rohmer, for example, were to make works for small audiences willing to follow these direc-tors' imaginations into territories previously unexplored by fiction cinema. Rivette, by most reports, carried his filmmaking generation's compulsive cinephilia to its greatest extreme. He was also the most anxious among them to begin work on a fiction feature, for he began shooting *Paris nous appartient* (*Paris Belongs to Us,* 1961) in 1958 with a small sum of money borrowed from the magazine, not knowing where the rest of his budget would come from. (His more fiscally con-servative colleagues Truffaut and Chabrol funded the work's comple-tion, through their own production companies.)

Yet for all Rivette's compulsive need to view and to make films, *Paris nous appartient* and his later works such as the masterful *L'Amour fou* (*Mad Love,* 1968) have little in common with the commercial narrative works by directors whom he and the other critics at *Cahiers du Cinéma* had so lavishly praised. His works do have many points of similarity, however, with the films of Alain Resnais and others of the Left Bank School, perhaps most obviously in their subject matter. Rivette has said that "the cinema is necessarily fascination and rape, that is how it acts on people; it is something unclear, something one sees shrouded in darkness, where you project the same things as in dreams."[15] Rivette's cinema centers on themes of madness, paranoia, conspiracy, and the dissolution of human bonds. His cinematic dreams, with the only partial exception being the apparently light-hearted *Céline et Julie vont en bateau* (*Céline and Julie Go Boating*, 1974), are really waking nightmares. At the beginning of his story outline for *L'Amour fou*, he put a quotation from Pirandello: "I have thought about it and we are all mad."

However, two crucial formal and strategic concerns set Rivette apart from the *rive gauche* filmmakers. Whereas Alain Resnais and his colleagues emphasized montage, the power of film editing to move the spectator through an abstract, purely mental space of often brutal contrasts, Rivette is clearly obsessed by duration, by the cinema's capacity to give a sense of lived time, the *durée* of Bergsonian theory.[16] Also, while the Left Bank School seems primarily an encounter between *writers* and the cinema, Rivette's films have almost all sprung from collaborations with specific *actors*. His films typically have the feel of improvised, open works, even when they have been carefully scripted. What makes Rivette a difficult filmmaker for many spectators is his slow, deliberate, and sometimes maddening fidelity to the process of cinema storytelling. His films can seem at the same time too inclusive and yet deliberately unfinished. On occasion, as in *L'Amour fou* and *Céline et Julie vont en bateau,* a miraculous balance obtains between cinematic process and overall structure, an accomplishment similar to that of Renoir's *La Règle du jeu:* perfectly equilibrated, yet palpably the result of an openness to the present moment and to the workings of group creation. In other works Rivette has not hesitated to allow his shooting methods to produce what they will, which often results in gaps, dull stretches, and incoherencies. These, too, are life—and cinema. But most spectators demand more polish, and perhaps less honesty.

Even Rivette's most satisfying works can seem frustratingly uneven and unpolished to the spectator who values consistency and coherence in the narrative cinema. His colleague, and—after the death of

André Bazin—editor at *Cahiers du Cinéma,* Eric Rohmer has, in contrast, produced a body of work of almost stunning uniformity of subject matter and formal precision. Yet the striking consistency of Rohmer's best-known works is as much the result of his particular situation in post-New Wave French cinema as it is the product of a singleminded creative intelligence. Though in many ways as obsessed with a highly personal vision of what can be done in the film medium as is Rivette, Rohmer has also been much more careful to accommodate his audiences and his producers. In so doing he has produced a body of work of more limited range than he probably would have liked. After the commercial failure of his first feature *Le Signe du lion* (*The Sign of Leo,* 1959/62), and a temporary retreat to the production of 16-millimeter short subjects, Rohmer established himself as a viable fiction filmmaker with *La Collectionneuse* (*The Collector,* 1967) and *Ma Nuit chez Maud* (*My Night at Maud's,* 1969). These works, the third and fourth of his series of *contes moraux* ("moral," meaning "psychological" tales), took as their primary subject matter the ever popular cinema theme of sex—or, rather, more typically in Rohmer's work, talk *about* sex.[17]

This was apparently the missing ingredient necessary to please audiences, for otherwise these films show great continuity with the methods and themes of *Le Signe du lion:* a strong sense of locale and season of the year; strikingly authentic, unobtrusive location shooting; large stretches of dialogue, most of it idle conversation often used as a kind of social weapon; and an almost oppressive sense of restraint, both on the part of the characters and the films' storytelling agents. After completing the *contes moraux* with *Le Genou de Claire* (*Claire's Knee,* 1970) and *L'Amour l'après-midi/Chloe in the Afternoon* (1972), Rohmer shifted ground radically, with two historical costume dramas adapted from literary works, *Die Marquise von O . . .* (*The Marquise of O . . .,* Germany 1976, after Heinrich von Kleist) and *Perceval le Gallois* (1979, after Chrétien de Troyes). The crushing financial failure of the latter film, however, forced the director to return to the contemporary, sexually oriented subjects of his *contes moraux,* with a new series which he called *comédies et proverbes.* Such were his limited resources that he shot the first of these, *La Femme de l'aviateur* (*The Aviator's Wife,* 1981) in 16 millimeter. Whereas Rohmer's "psychological tales" center on men and their attitudes toward sex, love, and social life, the "comedies and proverbs" feature women protagonists. Perhaps because of this shift of gender identification, and also perhaps because Rohmer had finally distanced himself from his earlier career as a teacher, the second series is generally lighter in tone, with fewer literary and philosophical references.

In choosing the word *moraux* to characterize his first series of successful fiction films (and it applies equally well to the *comédies et proverbes*), Rohmer placed himself quite consciously in the great French tradition of *moralistes* such as Pascal and La Rochefoucauld. Like these writers, the director is interested in the analysis of thought and emotion, in their hidden patterns and their often ironic function in human life. But Rohmer's "moral" viewpoint is complicated, and becomes implicitly reflexive, in that his characters are typically also interested in the same sorts of problems. In an early sequence of *La Collectionneuse*, three characters debate the question: can one have real affection for someone one finds physically ugly? In *Ma Nuit chez Maud*, a very different trio discusses the problem of rebelling against one's parents' religious beliefs, and whether one can revolt in the same way against a lack of faith. These topics could easily have been subjects of pithy maxims in the style of La Rochefoucauld; in discussing such ideas, however, Rohmer's characters reveal not so much the intellectual possibilities of the questions, but their own prejudices, limitations, and hidden agendas. These people typically use conversation to play an ongoing social game, the stakes of which are not always completely clear. Sex is quite often a goal of the game, but so is finding one's preferred position of dominance or submission. The assertion of one's social position, and the discovery of the interlocutor's as well—for few directors are as acutely aware of class issues as is Rohmer—are also constant concerns.

Rohmer's characters are often so neurotically caught up in strategies and counterstrategies that they lose contact with their own feelings. Social and sexual innocents, such as the title character in *Pauline à la plage* (*Pauline at the Beach*, 1983), are quickly and cruelly initiated into this polite but ultimately almost Sadean world. In this way, the Rohmer's cinema can seem as bleak as that of Rivette or the *rive gauche* filmmakers. Yet occasionally in his films a character experiences a kind of direct self-knowledge or fulfillment, an escape from neurosis, as when Delphine finally sees the "green ray" of the setting sun in *Le Rayon vert/Summer* (1986). Such events—or the sense of their possibility—have assumed greater salience in his more recent works. In these small, curious moments one can glimpse, if not happiness, at least the temporary absence of pain—a "time out" in the game. The director seems to have progressed from a dispassionate, often almost despairing analysis of neurosis to the more optimistic project of suggesting ways to effect a sort of cure.

Rohmer clearly would have preferred to make films like his adaptations of Kleist and Chretien de Troyes. Indeed, after *Die Marquise von O . . .* he stated flatly that he intended to concentrate his efforts exclusively in this area. However, he has made a virtue of necessity, embracing the "vow of poverty" recommended by *Cahiers du Cinéma* in the days of the Tradition of Quality. (Of his generation, no one has worked more frequently in 16 millimeter—even as recently as *Le Rayon vert.*) Literature-based costume dramas of the sort that he would like to make cost too much money, but cannot attract large audiences because he is unwilling to employ the proven elements of commercial success in the genre: well-known stars, with roles carefully crafted to satisfy audience expectations; heavy doses of spectacle and sexual display; and so on. Rohmer's failure to create a viable alternative for historical literary adaptations demonstrates how little the *nouvelle vague* really changed the traditional commercial core of French cinema. And so he remains a filmmaker on the margins of an industry which, although it does not persecute him or ignore his works altogether, finally is little affected by what he does.

◾15◾

Winds of Change

The filmmakers who worked at the margins of their industry in the wake of the *nouvelle vague* did not court commercial success, though few of them would have rejected it had it come easily. They were simply unwilling to make the necessary compromises with popular taste to insure it. Most of them made the "study of marketing" recommended by Claude Chabrol—though with more modest goals—and found various ways to remain active, as Rohmer did with his series of comedies and chamber dramas. Meanwhile the industry, and most of the new filmmakers, had settled down to the traditional work of churning out slick literary adaptations, crime thrillers, comedies featuring popular stars in predictable roles, and so on. The most ambitious of these works often had a strikingly familiar look and feel to them. Thus François Truffaut made glossy costume dramas in the Ophulsian manner such as *L'Histoire d'Adèle H.;* Louis Malle produced the frantic, cynical sex farce *Viva Maria,* carefully crafted to the star images of Jeanne Moreau and Brigitte Bardot; and Philippe de Broca's *Le Roi de coeur* had the fragile, bittersweet irony of so many of the best films of the 1950s.

For most of the New Wave generation, working within established genres was the only way of addressing relatively large audiences, once public interest in cinematic innovation had declined. But one prominent filmmaker did not recycle established formulas; when he did employ them it was to subvert and call them into question. Jean-Luc Godard was the one *enfant terrible* of the New Wave who remained *terrible* even when the industry slouched back to commercial normalcy in the mid 1960s. Although only his first feature film was a genuine smash hit, and though many viewers paid to see his works only to denounce them as puerile and self-indulgent, Godard attracted good-sized audiences throughout his remarkably prolific first decade as a fiction filmmaker. Until his voluntary exile from commercial cinema in response to the events of May 1968, he continued to serve as the symbol of the *nouvelle vague*'s anarchic energy and experiment, neither compromising with the commercial mainstream nor retreating from it. *Auteur* critics might argue that Godard could do this because of the sheer force of his personality, so clearly and insistently expressed in all of his work. Sociologically inclined historians would add, however, that his unusual success shows that his films must have touched an exposed nerve, or perhaps several of them, in postwar French culture.

Jean-Luc Godard was born in Paris in 1930, the second child of a classic upper-bourgeois household. His father was a prominent physician, his mother an heiress from a family of Swiss bankers. These social origins would make him something of an anachronism in the context of the New Wave, most of whose leading figures came from the *petite bourgeoisie* or slightly higher.[1] The young Jean-Luc received an education worthy of his class; he studied at the Lycée Buffon, one of Paris' strongest classical preparatory schools, though he does not seem to have internalized the strong self-discipline which normally characterizes such a formation. François Truffaut recalled him in the 1950s as "always very nervous and impatient," a man "capable of going to see fifteen minutes each of five different films in the same afternoon." He had a similar attitude toward print: "If we were at a friend's house, during one evening he would open easily forty books, and he always read the first and last pages."[2] This omnivorous but cavalier attitude toward cultural artifacts would also characterize his films, in which he liked to quote or reproduce all manner of written texts, pieces of music, paintings, book covers, radio broadcasts, and the like, often in quite arbitrary ways. When he uttered his celebrated dictum that a film must have a beginning, middle, and end, but not necessarily in that order, he simply admitted that he made cinema in much the same manner that he watched it.

Godard obtained his *baccalauréat* and briefly studied ethnology at the Sorbonne. But he spent more time attending ciné-clubs and screenings at the Cinémathèque Française than he did on his studies. He abandoned his academic career to become a wandering itinerant laborer, a journalist, and an aspiring filmmaker. During the 1950s he made four short films (and completed a fifth that had been begun by Truffaut) and became one of *Cahiers du Cinéma*'s most eccentric and penetrating critics. Along with Chabrol, Truffaut, and other young men of his age, he frequented the Cinéma MacMahon, a haven for film cultists who worshipped American action pictures, and he absorbed for a time the MacMahonist taste for stereotypically masculine stars such as John Wayne, Charlton Heston, and Humphrey Bogart.[3] In his first feature, *A bout de souffle/Breathless* (1960), he crafted for the rather diffident Jean-Paul Belmondo a Bogart-inflected, "macho" star image that would make the young actor's fortune.

A bout de souffle was widely greeted as a truly revolutionary film, the culmination of the *nouvelle vague* generation's rejection of the *cinéma de papa*. Yet the most obviously radical aspect of Godard's first feature, its celebrated "jump cuts," came about as an inspired afterthought. The director had filmed a simple story originally written by Truffaut about a young criminal on the run from the police. The rough cut ran about two hours; in the opinion of most who saw it, it needed to shed about thirty minutes of footage to be commercially exploitable. Rather than dropping entire sequences or parts of them, as would normally be done, Godard went through the film chopping out whatever he found boring, without regard to the normal rules of continuity cutting. The film that emerged truly lives up to its title: it seems "out of breath," gasping along in fits and starts that are wonderfully suggestive of the spiritually fragmented, alienated world of its protagonists. Thus launched, the jump cut became something of a cinematic cliché in the 1960s, though mainly in the hands of other directors; Godard himself used it only sparingly in later works. The more linear, straightforward *Le Petit Soldat* (*The Little Soldier*, 1960/63) probably gives a reasonably good idea of what *A bout de souffle* was like before he cut it. Audiences did not get to see this second feature for several years, however, because government censors found its cloak-and-dagger plot, about secret organizations and the Algerian crisis, a threat to public order.

Although many critics and historians have viewed *A bout de souffle* as a deliberate call to cinematic revolution, Godard himself saw it quite differently. In a 1962 interview he recalled that the film was "not at all what I thought [while making it]. I thought I had made a realistic film like Richard Quine's *Pushover* [1954], but it wasn't that at all. In the first place I didn't have enough technical skill, so I made mistakes; then I discovered I wasn't made for this kind of film. There were also a lot of things I wanted to do but which I can't bring off." And in *Le Petit Soldat*, he tells us, "I wanted to discover the realism I had missed in *A bout de souffle*, the concreteness."[4] But one must ask what sort of realism Godard aspired to. Clearly he meant more than mere technique—location shooting with natural light sources and portable cameras—because in these terms his first feature is as realistic as his second. Probably he meant both an "impression of reality" (the product, inevitably, of technical mastery) and a coherence and deliberate limitation of subject matter (he called *A bout de souffle* a film "where anything goes").[5]

Godard soon discovered what he did well, and it had little to do with traditional realist film style. Although a commitment to authenticity of sight and sound (location shooting, direct sound recording) characterized most of his work, it would always, after *Le Petit Soldat*, be accompanied by a strong interest in the formal manipulations of the basic elements of cinema. He was, perhaps most strikingly, the most adventurous French filmmaker of the 1960s in the exploration of the many possible uses of film sound. Although he largely abandoned the jump cut as a *visual* principle after *A bout de souffle*, it did not vanish from his work but migrated to his sound tracks, particularly in their treatment of music. Compared with conventional fiction films and with the other aural elements in his films, many of his location-recorded sounds (such as café pinball machines, and street noises) seem, even today, curiously stylized and arbitrary.[6] Visually, Godard explored long takes and also bursts of rapid montage, extravagant camera movements and claustrophobically fixed points of view. He developed a particular fondness for (often cryptic, or punning) title cards, and isolated shots of written materials—advertising, book covers, and so on.

Contemporary film theorists have elaborated a critique of mainstream commercial filmmaking which provides a powerful justification for Godard's apparently eccentric practices. Films based on classical narration and scene construction achieve a convincing coherence of their fictions by creating a unified place to which the events depicted all refer: the position of an ideal, disembodied spectator. The unity of realistic films is not to be sought in their fictional worlds, but in the systematic way in which they create this "position of the subject." Continuity editing creates, first and foremost, a continuity of the implied viewer, which then seems to guarantee the veracity and coherence of what is represented. Theorists such as Jean-Louis Baudry and Stephen Heath, following the French psychoanalyst Jacques Lacan, argue that the unity of the viewing subject is such a powerful illusion because it has its origins in the strong need of the child to impose unity on fragmented, dispersed sensations. The infant first comes to construct him- or herself as a unity through the image of his or her body in a mirror; for the spectator, the cinema screen functions as another sort of mirror, recreating a sense of unity and mastery which, because illusory, is always in danger of dissolution.[7]

The reinforcing of the viewer's potentially fragile coherence of self and sense of mastery of the world is, from this point of view, the major product sold by narrative cinema. Mainstream commercial films strengthen each spectator's sense of him- or herself as an isolated and unified subject, a process which has profound, ultimately political consequences. The (constructed) unity of the self purveyed by classic cinema narrative may be seen as reinforcing an individualism which forecloses the possibility of authentic solidarity with others. For this reason, many theorists argue that narrative cinema is the ideal vehicle of "bourgeois ideology", helping to maintain the boundaries which separate individuals from other individuals, classes from classes, nations from nations—regardless of a given work's subject matter.

Godard's films are often cited as examples of an attempt at creating a countercinema, a nonbourgeois filmmaking which refuses to provide the misleading coherence of mainstream commercial narrative, but which instead relentlessly critiques dominant cinema practices. And it is indeed true that the jump cuts of *A bout de souffle*, the Brechtian title cards of *Vivre sa vie/My Life to Live* (1962), the asides by fictional characters in many of his films uttered directly to the camera/spectator, and other similar departures from "classical" narrative conventions serve to break the works' illusion of reality and the untroubled coherence of the implied spectator. One can rarely forget, watching a Godard film, that in it the spectator is responsible for constructing the work's meaning for him- or herself, and that this process is anything but simple, logical, or natural.

In this context, however, it is somewhat surprising that, before he knew his own technical and temperamental limitations, Godard set out to make realistic films. It seems significant that in 1962, when he had just completed the stylistically unconventional *Vivre sa vie*, the first work on his *Cahiers du Cinéma* list of the year's best films was Howard Hawks' *Hatari*, a classical bourgeois piece of filmmaking if ever there was one. And the *characters* in his early works also often aspire to be in this kind of film: Michel and Patricia in *A bout de souffle* imitate Humphrey Bogart's screen persona; Angéla and Alfred, in *Une Femme est une femme* (*A Woman Is a Woman*, 1961), proudly announce their desire to be in a Stanley Donen musical. The director often cast well-known figures from classic bourgeois cinema in his films: directors Jean-Pierre Melville (the novelist in *A bout de souffle*) and Fritz Lang (playing himself in *Le Mépris* [*Contempt*, 1963]), as well as actors Jack Palance (*Le Mépris*) and Eddie Constantine (*Alphaville* [1965]), among others. These references to traditional commercial cinema seem to stand for an unattainable ideal: Michel Poiccard can never become Humphrey Bogart.

At least until the late 1960s, Godard does not seem to *criticize* traditional cinema so much as to assume that its time has passed. He made *Une Femme est une femme* not as a critique of the musical comedy, but as a kind of autopsy: "the musical is dead," he said bluntly; his film "is nostalgia for the musical."[8] Why did Godard regard traditional film formulas and conventions with such nostalgia? His characters typically seek precisely the coherent selfhood and sense of mastery which contemporary film theory imputes to traditional narrative cinema, but they do not find it; the fix does not work. They remain rootless drifters in a world where culture has lost its power to provide them a stable place, a unified identity. Their search for meaning and coherence leads them not only to the cinema, but into many other domains of high and low culture. Angéla, in *Une Femme est une femme*, looks at a Paul Klee reproduction and cries, explaining that "I want to be these two little yellow creatures, both at the same time." Ferdinand, in *Pierrot le fou* (1965), devours books on art history as well as children's comic strips in the course of this road movie about a disaffected bourgeois. Nana, in *Vivre sa vie*, talks with the philosopher (in real life) Brice Parrain about the liberating power of language (but at the end of the film she is kidnapped, sold, and senselessly murdered—philosophy has done her no good).

Another (less frequent) source of meaning and coherence for the characters of Godard's early films is politics, from the confused anti-terrorism of *Le Petit Soldat* to the shadowy revolutionary group of *Pierrot le fou*. For the hero of *Le Petit Soldat*, being a member of a secret, right-wing paramilitary group is an attempt at self-definition on the same level as Michel's wish to be a Bogart character in *A bout de souffle*. Until 1967, political action—which, from the very beginning of Godard's career, is inseparable from *violence*—offers merely one possible kind of meaning among many in a world of fragmentation and anomie. But in that year something changes. *Made in U.S.A.* (1967) is his last work of nostalgia for American mass culture: set in an Atlantic City which is visibly Paris, the film affectionately reworks the classic tough-guy detective formula with reversed sex roles (featuring Anna Karina as the trenchcoated protagonist). But already while making this film, Godard was at work on *Deux ou trois choses que je sais d'elle* (*Two or Three Things I Know About Her*, 1967). This was to be the first of the director's works to seek coherence and meaning in *its own* political positions (and not merely to feature characters who attempt this), and to reject the American mass culture which had once so fascinated him. What had happened? Most obviously, for Godard (as for so many French artists and intellectuals) the war in Viet Nam had shed new light on the United States' role in world politics and culture: American imperialism had ceased to be an abstract concept.

But although *Deux ou trois choses* contains many allusions to the Viet Nam war, it focuses principally on the Americanization of French economic and cultural life, from the growing consumerism of the middle and working classes to the relentless, housing-project suburbanization of the *région parisienne* (the *elle* of the film's title). The film can be criticized, from a Left perspective, as manifesting a reactionary nostalgia for the good old days of bourgeois life (and architecture); it shows the Americanization of French life as a process which produces only victims, and no organized opposition. In the face of the inhuman order which he depicts, Godard seems to retreat into metaphysical speculation, as when his whispered voice-over commentary questions the work's possible relations to its subject matter. Defenders of the film would argue, however, that precisely this sort of questioning of the cinema itself is a necessary prerequisite to its use for political purposes. In the film's perhaps most spectacular sequence, a cup of coffee becomes the obsessive center of an implicit meditation on subjectivity and objecthood, a kind of cinematic poem about the thingness of things and the role of consciousness in a world which is irreducibly *other*.

Deux ou trois choses que je sais d'elle arguably represents a moment of moral and intellectual crisis in Godard's career. His next two features, the last major works of the first phase of his career, both feature groups of young revolutionaries who refuse to submit to a hostile, inhuman world and who, with the films' apparent endorsement, attempt to work for radical change. But the remedy, like the disease, is extreme. The young Maoists of *La Chinoise, ou plutôt à la chinoise* (*The Chinese, or rather, In the Chinese Manner,* 1967) are apprentice terrorists. The Liberation Front of Seine et Oise in *Weekend* (1967) responds to the "horror of the bourgeoisie" with its own counterhorror: cannibalism. In both works Godard pointedly does not make his young revolutionaries into easy objects of identification as traditional film heroes. *La Chinoise* and *Weekend* are difficult films to watch, and not just because of Godard's typically unconventional form and style. One can never be certain just how far their savage irony extends. Perhaps the revolutionary groups are not exempt: does eating a few German tourists, or bungling an assassination attempt and killing the wrong person, really qualify one to build a new society? Or are these merely the first, admittedly comic, signs of a will to transform modern life? *La Chinoise* is peppered with political commentaries given in title cards, the last of which reads: "End of a Beginning." But what comes next?

■ Aside from Jean-Luc Godard, few observers of contemporary French society took much notice of the increasing radicalization of large numbers of the nation's young people, even after the first manifestations of revolt in the universities during 1967. In retrospect, however, it is easy enough to see how potentially explosive the situation was. By the late 1960s one in three French citizens was under the age of twenty—a demographic imbalance brought about by the troublingly low birth rates during the 1930s and the Occupation, followed by much higher ones shortly after the Liberation. The Fifth Republic had brought significant change to the nation's political system, but not to the social and administrative institutions which underpinned it. The continuing transformation of French life had barely touched the educational system, which still formed the country's future rulers in a few prestige institutions, the *grandes écoles* which few young people had any reasonable chance of entering. Large numbers of students were automatically segregated into dead-end degree programs which served, socially, the same function that a piano had in a traditional bourgeois household—as a (generally unused) marker of respectability.

The Marxist-Leninists of Godard's *La Chinoise* live in a world of quotations and slogans. The slogan on the wall of their apartment says: "A Minority with the Correct Revolutionary Line Is No Longer a Minority."

At the same time that they saw their future constrained by the still remarkably efficient French class system, the nation's young men and women were the first generation to come to maturity in a society that had lost the ideological underpinnings of the old order: traditional values were rapidly dissolving in a new mass society which offered the promise of the good life to all who could find the money to pay for it. The student rebellion which sparked the "events of May 1968" was directed not only against the social stratification which the majority of young people saw as oppressive, but also against the new consumerism which had heightened consciousness of the old order while promising so little of any real value to replace it.

The 1968 protests began in March at the University of Nanterre and spread quickly to the Sorbonne and to other educational institutions throughout the country. But the rebellion did not remain confined to the campuses. As the government reacted with increasing severity against the demonstrations, young workers, many of them barely older than the students, joined in, and they in turn brought older coworkers and sympathizers into the revolt. By late May, the strikers numbered roughly ten million. The large labor unions and the Parti Communiste belatedly joined the protests, though they would soon be urging the protesters to accept the concessions and reforms offered by a desperate government. With surprising rapidity, the crisis passed. Little real change came about as a result of it—particularly in the universities where the failed revolution had begun; the most radical and unrepentant of the protesters were unable ever again to mobilize the massive, society-wide discontent which the events of May had brought, however briefly, to the surface of French society.

The film community also had its own May of 1968, and as elsewhere the initial impetus came from students.[9] Strikes and occupations closed the Institut des Hautes Etudes Cinématographiques and the Ecole Nationale de Photographie et de Cinématographie. Leaflets circulated with calls to action and mass organization:

> Given that in present conditions, a free Cinema and Television do not exist, given that a tiny minority of film-makers and technicians have access to the means of production and expression,
> Given that for all professional categories decisive changes are called for at all levels,
> Given that the cinema has a major mission to fulfill today and that it is gagged at all levels in the present system,
> Film-makers, technicians, actors, producers, distributors and critics in film and television, resolved to bring an end to the present state of affairs, have decided to convene the Estates General of French Cinema.
> We invite you all to take part in the Estates General, the date of which will be announced later. Revolutionary Committee of Cinema-Television.[10]

A mass meeting—attended, according to some reports, by a thousand people—was held on May 17 in the student-occupied school of photography and cinematography. At this first session, the Estates General passed motions calling for a strike by all cinema personnel, and for immediate cessation of the Cannes film festival. At Cannes, even relatively apolitical figures such as François Truffaut and Claude Chabrol joined in the successful effort to disrupt the screenings.

Four days later, the Estates General attempted to move from mass organization to specific proposals for reform. After heated debate, in the carefully chosen words of *Cahiers du Cinéma:* "The following motion is passed and signed by a certain number of those participating in the Estates General: 'The Estates General considers the reactionary structures of the C.N.C. abolished. Consequently, they affirm that its existence, its representativity, and its regulations are no longer recognized by the profession.'"[11]

"A certain number of those participating" meant that the consensus on "decisive changes are called for at all levels" had already begun to come apart. It was one thing to speak in seductive generalities; it was quite another to seek to liquidate the Centre National du Cinéma, the source of so much film financing and of the regulatory activity which kept the industry running smoothly. Although the Estates General continued to proclaim their mission "to denounce and destroy the reactionary structures of a cinema which has become a commodity," the organization was unable to agree on any specific proposals for the restructuring of French filmmaking.[12] Its final, inconclusive meeting was held on June 5, and by the end of the summer the cinema industry, like most of French society, had returned to business as usual.

Although they brought about no significant change in the structure of the industry, the events of May 1968 had lasting effects for the film community in the areas of film journalism and in the teaching and academic study of cinema. The radical Marxist review *Cinéthique* published its first issue in 1969. After a power struggle within its board of directors and a brief publishing hiatus, *Cahiers du Cinéma* became an avowedly Marxist-Leninist (that is, Maoist) journal in 1970. Both magazines provided forums for the initial development of post-1968 French film theory, a heady and sometimes unstable blend of semiotics, psychoanalysis, and various schools of Marxism (particularly the work of the Communist philosopher Louis Althusser). In universities, first in France and later in the United Kingdom, the United States, and elsewhere, this body of theoretical work became widely accepted, for more than a decade, as the very epitome of serious, politically committed study of cinema, though today its influence appears to be waning. (To some extent, this decline of what was once known simply as contemporary film theory is as much a result of the widespread acceptance of its basic assumptions as a sign of decadence or dispersion.)

Although the production system in general remained unchanged, a number of individual filmmakers responded in various ways to the failed May revolution. Louis Malle temporarily abandoned both France and fiction film projects, journeying to India to make *Calcutta*

(1969) and *L'Inde fantôme* (*Phantom India*, six-hour TV series, 1969), his first nonfiction works since the mid 1950s. Perhaps more profoundly and certainly more lastingly affected was Jean-Luc Godard, who abandoned fiction features in favor of small-scale, directly political film essays, most of them difficult to understand for spectators unversed in the arcana of *gauchisme* and in the director's increasingly flamboyant and aggressive cinematographic style. In these, for the first time, he consciously criticized mainstream commercial filmmaking on political and ideological grounds, posing his own work—though not always explicitly—as a radical alternative. A few younger, less celebrated filmmakers also changed direction in response to the great upheaval. Marin Karmitz was an I.D.H.E.C.-trained director and independent producer (with a strong commitment to avant-garde projects) before 1968. After the events of May, he came to view the cinema as a means of political agitation, and became deeply committed to Left issues such as women's and prisoners' rights, freedom of the press, and protest against totalitarian governments in the Third World.

In 1972 Karmitz, Malle, and Godard (working with Jean-Pierre Gorin) each completed feature-length projects which demonstrated the range of possible cinematic treatments of a crucial issue raised by the events of May: the sociopolitical situation of factory workers. Malle's *Humain, trop humain* (*Human, Too Human*) is a sober documentary which examines the psychological dimensions of work on an assembly line. Karmitz's *Coup pour coup* (*Blow for Blow*) and Godard and Gorin's *Tout va bien* (*Everything's OK*), on the other hand, are fiction films, though both are based on real events. Malle's film received polite attention and some mild praise, but it was quickly forgotten, by the Left in any case, in the wake of the extended controversy over the two fiction works.

Coup pour coup is a cinematic reconstruction of a strike by women employees in a textile factory. Aside from employing deliberately unpolished, *cinéma vérité*-style camera work, the film does not emphasize its own work of representation, but rather tells its story in a relatively conventional fashion. It takes the side of the strikers and encourages spectator identification with them using the strategies by which commercial cinema has always distinguished heroes from villains. *Tout va bien* takes a very different approach to similar subject matter, a wildcat strike in a meat processing plant. The film constantly calls attention to its own storytelling techniques: sound and image are often used contrapuntally; camera movements (slow, sweeping lateral tracking shots) are frequently independent of fictional events; characters often speak directly to the camera. Where Karmitz's film is stylistically self-effacing and traditional, Godard and Gorin's work is baroque, extravagant, and flagrantly experimental in its use of the cinema's resources.

Coup pour coup quickly became a favorite target for the new extreme-left cinema journalism and film theory. Karmitz was denounced as perpetuating bourgeois cinema, an enemy of the Left all the more dangerous because his politics seemed, on the surface, to be "correct."[13] *Tout va bien* was invoked by the same commentators as a salutary counterexample, a work which attempted to explore new structures of film viewing to correspond to the new consciousness necessary for a truly new sort of society. Karmitz's defenders replied that Godard and Gorin's work was decadent formalism, inaccessible to the very members of society who ought to be at the very center of any new order. But although they succeeded in provoking heated debate in the Left press, both films failed to reach the large audiences which they attempted to address and to influence. Godard returned to his hermetic explorations of radical politics, which were seen only by a small number of spectators. Marin Karmitz was obliged to scale back his cinema activities for several years, until hē had rebuilt a financial and organizational base and reemerged in the late 1970s as one of France's leading independent producers. Unrepentant of his interest in bourgeois film practices, he would eventually produce one of the smash hits of the late 1980s, Etienne Chatiliez's *La Vie est une longue fleuve tranquille* (*Life Is a Long Quiet River,* 1987), a film which in the view of some observers reduces important issues of social class to the level of television sitcom humor.[14]

Ironically, Karmitz' MK2 productions coproduced the film with which Jean-Luc Godard returned to fiction features, eight years after *Tout va bien. Sauve qui peut (la vie)/Every Man for Himself* (1980, made in collaboration with Anne-Marie Miéville) is the first work of Godard's third distinct period as a filmmaker. The now middle-aged *enfant terrible* has turned from politics and social issues to myth and autobiography, and from a focus on groups to a study of individuals, much as Jean Renoir did in his later years. Like Renoir, Godard is stylistically very much the same filmmaker he was as a younger, more politically engaged artist, and also like Renoir he has in his last films perplexed and alienated many of his earlier admirers, particularly on the Left. After the overtly autobiographical *Sauve qui peut*, he has made his own inimitable reworkings of Prosper Mérimée (in *Prénom: Carmen* [*First Name: Carmen*, 1983]), the New Testament (*Je vous salue, Marie* [*Hail Mary*, 1985]), and even Shakespeare (*King Lear*, 1988). Critical reactions to these works have been mixed, to say the least. Unlike Renoir, who had the strong admiration and support of the young rebels at *Cahiers du Cinéma*, Godard grew increasingly isolated in the French film community of the 1980s; his most vocal admirers are of his own age. He remains one of the most resolutely individualistic, personal filmmakers in all of contemporary French cinema, but he is widely viewed as a respected culture hero from the glorious past, rather than a role model for the present. Younger filmmakers and cinéphiles have other, competing demands on their attention; a new generation is already at work in the industry, not waiting on the fringes of the film community as did their counterparts in the 1950s.

▧ Unlike the *nouvelle vague* generation, the latest newcomers to the French cinema did not arrive in a sudden, well-publicized wave. Bertrand Blier (born in 1939), the creator of bitter, anarchic, and misogynistic comedies such as *Les Valseuses/Going Places* (1974) and *Préparez vos mouchoirs* (*Get Out Your Handkerchiefs*, 1978), wrote and directed his first feature in 1962. Jean Eustache (1938–1981), whose brief, difficult career and tragic death made him the Jean Vigo of his generation, began working as a feature director in 1969. Bertrand Tavernier (born in 1941) has been a careful craftsman of historical and family dramas since 1974. The first post-*nouvelle vague* filmmakers were, in general, roughly a decade younger than the youngest of the New Wave directors (with a few important exceptions such as Maurice Pialat, who was born in 1925 but made his first feature in 1968). The critic and historian René Prédal considers most of them to be members of a relatively distinct generation of the 1970s. Prédal sees a potent allegory for the renewal of French filmmaking in the nation's very different official entries in the Cannes festivals of 1972 and 1973:

> Of course, the reality of film production was less clearly differentiated [than was the festival], because the change in selection criteria produced an emphasis on disappointing professionalism in 1972 and on very original creations in 1973. But the break was nonetheless real. It is indeed during this period that appear the first fruits of 1968. All this time was necessary to understand the meaning of May 1968, to digest its lessons,

to conceive, produce, and present films which were different—in order that the cinema, in short, no longer reflected recent events, but corresponded to new mentalities.[15]

Prédal makes a strong case for his generation of the 1970s, but one may wonder if the change seen at Cannes was as qualitatively significant as he argues. The 1973 festival's *succès de scandale,* and winner of a special jury prize, was Eustache's *La Maman et la Putain (The Mother and the Whore,* 1973), a deeply felt tale of alienated youth and, in the view of many critics, one of the truly great films of the decade. But this work seems as much a throwback to the height of the *nouvelle vague* as the sign of any radically new approach to filmmaking. Its rootless characters seem to come straight out of an early Godard film and to have been transplanted into the relentlessly slow, deliberate *mise-en-scène* of Rivette works such as *Paris nous appartient* or *L'Amour fou.* Starring the archetypal New Wave player Jean-Pierre Léaud, shot on location in Paris streets, cafés, and apartments, laced with cinephilic references, *La Maman et la Putain* may be taken as the symbol of the end of an era, rather than of a new beginning.

For the film industry as a whole, the Cannes festival of 1973 was a less significant sign of lasting change than was the sudden death of President of the Republic Georges Pompidou in 1974, and the election of Valéry Giscard d'Estaing to replace him. Pompidou's brief presidency represented the last gasp of the old Gaullist coalition (the general himself having retired in 1969); Giscard brought with him a new, more technocratic and business-oriented approach to government. One immediate effect of the new government on cinema production was in the area of censorship, which Giscard's administration all but abolished. With shocking rapidity, a new network of producers and exhibitors of X-rated pornographic films came into being. More mainstream productions also profited from the removal of restrictions on the representation of sexuality. Just Jaeckin's soft-core hit *Emmanuelle* (1974) became one of the top-grossing French films of all time. Relatively graphic lovemaking scenes, such as the opening sequence of Jean-Jacques Beineix's *37,2 le matin/Betty Blue* (1986), have by now become almost commonplace, even in some films coproduced for television.

The virtual abolition of censorship consolidated and developed a trend which was already well under way in the industry: since Louis Malle's *Les Amants* in 1958, French fiction films had been slowly becoming more sexually explicit. In a similar fashion the Giscard government's dramatic gesture also affected, though somewhat less radically, the evolving political content of French cinema. No longer fearful of offending government ministries with tales of conspiracy, incompetence, and wrongdoing in high places, contemporary filmmakers (almost exclusively of the Left) made such narratives a staple of big budget, mainstream productions. The great popular appeal of political melodramas had became apparent, well before the election of Giscard, with works such as Constantin Costa-Gavras's *Z* (1969), a deft thriller (set in Greece and based on actual events) starring Jean-Louis Trintignant as a courageous magistrate who unravels a right-wing assassination plot. The great popular and critical success of *Z* encouraged the production of similar films set in France, and after 1974 French screens were flooded with stories of dirty tricks, assassinations, and conspiracies on home soil. Aside from Costa-Gavras, the best-known specialist in this area has been Yves Boisset, in works such as *Le Juge Fayard* (*Judge Fayard*, 1976). These films exploit—one might even say, pander to—the public's traditional paranoia about politics and government. Unless one wishes to believe that heinous crimes in high places are the exclusive province of the extreme Right, they teach few lessons, and have mainly served as profitable, effective star vehicles for Trintignant, Michel Piccoli, and other well-known actors, even including one of contemporary French cinema's archetypal sex symbols, Miou-Miou (in Boisset's *La Femme-flic* [*The Woman Cop*, 1980]).

Though it produced immediately visible results on the nation's movie screens, the new government's initiative in the area of film censorship was ultimately less significant for the future of French cinema than its other grand gesture of 1974: the reorganization of the national radio and television. The Giscard administration broke the old O.R.T.F. into smaller units, splitting the nation's three television channels into separate competing entities and reorganizing the old Service de la Recherche as the Institut National de l'Audiovisuel (I.N.A.). As with the abolition of censorship, this sudden structural change had the effect of consolidating and accelerating a transformation which had begun several years earlier. In 1966 the O.R.T.F. had first acted as coproducer of a film made to be screened in cinemas before playing on television, Robert Bresson's *Mouchette*. Other similar works, all by established directors, had followed at a relatively slow pace. After 1974, the breakup of the old organization greatly increased the number of such coproductions, and opened them up to less well-known filmmakers. Almost immediately, television became a major source of funding for quite varied types of production; although the three new networks generally emphasized middle-of-the-road, commercial fare, the I.N.A. became the major support of funding for noncommercial, experimental works.

At the same time that television assumed a growing importance in French filmmaking, international coproductions with foreign producers declined in number, with the crucial exception of coproductions with foreign *television* producers. By the late 1980s it was widely felt that most films simply could not be made without first obtaining, if not direct coproduction financing, at least a firm agreement for television presentation.[16] The election in 1981 of France's first Socialist government since 1936 had little influence on this trend, except to accelerate it and to give it, from the point of view of the film and television community, a threatening new direction. The creation of additional, privately owned networks, a pay television service (Canal Plus), and the privatization of one of the older, formerly state-owned channels have been accompanied by an increasing quantity of dubbed American television fare on the nation's home screens. Though for the moment there are still trade barriers which limit the sale of American audiovisual products in the French marketplace, the United States government continues to press for free trade. French producers worry that the complete deregulation of international media competition would substantially diminish the revenues of domestic productions, and fatally undermine the nation's film and television industry.

The situation of contemporary audiovisual media is much more complicated and fluid than that of the cinema industry before the rise of television. The feature film remains the preferred, prestigious form of production, but how long this will remain the case is far from clear. The development of high-definition television and direct satellite broadcasts, the coming integration of the European community, the possibility of further privatization of government-controlled networks, all promise dramatic, unpredictable change in the near future. Though such uncertainty gives nightmares to media producers and to government cultural bureaucrats, the filmmakers of the generation of the 1970s have had, on the whole, little difficulty in adapting to the industry's new circumstances. Most of them did not learn their craft in cinema but in television production, which has in this regard become the contemporary equivalent of the documentary short subjects of the 1950s. For this reason, and because their works must inevitably be conceived to some extent with the small screen in mind, this group might most appropriately be called the television generation rather than the generation of the 1970s.

One of the most striking and genuinely new aspects of the television generation is the dramatic increase in the number of women writers and directors of feature films. Before 1968 French women filmmakers were isolated exceptions in a basically masculine environment. From Alice Guy to Germaine Dulac, to Marie Epstein, to Agnès Varda and Marguerite Duras, no more than a handful of women at any given time (other than actresses) participated meaningfully in the creation of films. In the 1970s this situation changed with striking suddenness. Women filmmakers, and works about so-called women's issues (sexual exploitation, rape, abortion, and so on) have become a highly visible presence in contemporary French cinema, though one must not overstate the trend: most films are still made by men.

The new women filmmakers have had a wide range of commercial and artistic recognition, from obscurity to celebrity. Diane Kurys's first film, *Diablo Menthe* (*Peppermint Soda*, 1977), the semi-autobiographical story of a rebellious adolescent, won the Prix Louis Delluc and became the highest grossing French film of its season. Among other, generally quite successful works, Kurys has since made *Cocktail Molotov* (1979), a sequel to *Diablo Menthe* set in May of 1968, and *Entre nous* (*Between Us*, 1983), the story of two women in the 1950s who feel trapped in middle class marriages. She is one of the most commercially savvy writer-directors of her generation, but she has been studiously ignored both by academic feminists and by art cinema-oriented historians such as René Prédal and Marcel Martin, neither of whom even mention her in their surveys of contemporary French filmmaking.[17] Such reticence is easy enough to understand: Kurys makes technically proficient, cinematographically self-effacing films that tug at the heartstrings in generally unsurprising, but effective, ways. Radical feminists and proponents of art cinema may find such stylistic conservatism and emotional manipulation reprehensible, but Kurys's success is nonetheless an important sign of the French cinema's new openness to women: mass culture's ultimate mark of acceptance of a social trend is to package it as an attractive commodity and put it up for sale.

Diane Kurys is probably best described as a talented director of women's pictures rather than as a committed feminist: she is more of an observer than a revolutionary, or even a reformer. The same may be said, to varying extents, of most of her contemporaries such as Yannick Bellon and Coline Serreau.[18] Perhaps the most radical temperament among the women filmmakers of the television generation is Nelly Kaplan, whose works have nonetheless sparked some debate among feminist critics. Kaplan's first feature, *La Fiancée du pirate/A Very Curious Girl* (1969), tells the story of a young gypsy, once the sexual slave of the inhabitants of a small village, who takes a carefully calculated and hilarious revenge on her former persecutors. Using makeup, perfume, sexy clothing, and a hilarious assortment of tacky consumer goods, she enslaves her oppressors, making them pay for what they once enjoyed for free and setting them up against one another. In this very funny but troubling film, Kaplan seems to imply that women should not reject sexual objectification but rather use it to their advantage. Feminism should be like judo, using the energy and strategy of one's opponent against him; rather than positing a better, less exploitative world, she considers what can be done with the tools within one's grasp in the world we live in. In *Néa* (1982), the adolescent daughter of a repressive bourgeois household achieves personal liberation by writing pornography. Clearly, such films are not designed to please utopian militants.

Kaplan's works, like those of Kurys and most other recent women filmmakers, are stylistically polished and conventional, making essentially no effort to challenge the norms of mainstream cinema. In cinematographic style and subject matter, the most innovative of French women filmmakers remains—even in the late 1980s—Marguerite Duras. The intellectual and aesthetic distance between Duras's continuing, radical experiments in film form and the artistic conservatism of most other women writers and directors is a phenomenon far from unique to "women's cinema"; it is, rather, typical of recent French cinema in general. Filmmakers of the television generation have not, on the whole, explored the middle ground between radical experiment and the commercial mainstream—the commercially marginal art cinema made by New Wave independents such as Jacques Rivette and Alain Resnais. The most commercially and critically successful "new" director of art cinema in the 1960s and 1970s was Luis Buñuel, who returned to France after an absence of over three decades to make masterful, subtly surreal features such as *Belle de jour* (*Beauty of the Daytime,* 1967) and *Le Charme discret de la bourgeoisie* (*The Discreet Charm of the Bourgeoisie,* 1972). The other major newcomer to this type of filmmaking was not French either: Alain Tanner (born in Geneva in 1929) has made enigmatic, deliberately stylized and distanced narratives in Switzerland, beginning with *Charles mort ou vif* (*Charles, Dead or Alive,* 1969).

For better or for worse, French art cinema seems to have begun a slow withering away—the victim, perhaps, of the influence of television, or of the breakdown of bourgeois values and the rise of consumer culture. In the past two decades, most of the nation's best narrative filmmaking by younger filmmakers has been close in style and subject matter to the commercial mainstream. Most of the artistically ambitious narrative filmmakers of the television generation followed the examples of Truffaut, Malle, and Chabrol, attempting to make films at once widely accessible and personally meaningful, generally working with reliable formulas and established stars. In some cases their careers strikingly recapitulate the evolution of the commercially oriented part of the New Wave, moving from low-budget, informally structured works to carefully crafted exercises in popular genres.

The career of Maurice Pialat offers a good example of this pattern. After a decade of work in television, Pialat made his directorial debut with *L'Enfance nue* (*Naked Childhood,* 1968), a New Wave-style drama of adolescence featuring a cast of nonprofessional players. Such films, ten years after the arrival of the *nouvelle vague,* had become a kind of recognized genre unto themselves rather than a striking gesture of independence from established norms, and it is therefore not surprising that Pialat's subsequent work often led him in other directions. Although in the last decade he has experimented, in *Loulou* (1980), with a higher-budget version of New Wave naturalism (hand-held camera, emphasis on atmosphere over narrative, and on the small details of everyday life), he has also made *Police* (1985), a slick crime drama, and a sober, meditative adaptation of Georges Bernanos's novel *Sous le soleil de Satan* (*Under Satan's Sun,* 1989). That film won the Palme d'Or, the grand prize at Cannes, but the announcement of the award was greeted with jeers from many festival patrons. This reaction is understandable: with its carefully composed cinematography and its highly literary dialogue and linear narrative construction, *Sous le soleil de Satan* takes a giant, unashamed step backward in film history, to the days of the Tradition of Quality.[19]

Pialat is not the only contemporary French filmmaker to explore the once-discredited cinema aesthetic of the 1950s. In this context, the most striking development of recent years has been the rehabilitation (a kind of return of the cinematic repressed) of the old style, big-budget historical drama, perhaps best exemplified by the films of Bertrand Tavernier. In early explorations of this genre, such as *Le Juge et l'Assassin* (*The Judge and the Assassin*, 1976) and *Coup de torchon/ Clean Slate* (1981), Tavernier even enlisted the collaboration of Jean Aurenche, whose 1950s scripts written with Pierre Bost had been cited by François Truffaut in *Cahiers du Cinéma* as the very epitome of the corrupt *cinéma de papa*. Tavernier's collaborations with Aurenche take historical subjects as a pretext, more as a means of commenting on contemporary society and on human relations in general than as serious vehicles for an examination of the meanings of the past. *Coup de torchon*, for example, is more about racism, colonialism, and the terrible fragility of liberal ideals in a context of systematic oppression than it is about French Africa in the 1920s.

In more recent works Tavernier has continued to use historical narratives as a means of examining other, less political issues. The professional and historical situation of the minor impressionist painter in *Un Dimanche à la campagne* (*A Sunday in the Country*, 1985) is less important than his difficult position as *père de famille;* the medieval setting of *La Passion Béatrice* (*The Passion of Beatrice*, 1988) seems almost incidental to the film's violent drama of incest. In such works Tavernier has updated the old Tradition of Quality approach to the historical film, substituting a new extra-historical theme of wider contemporary appeal—family relations—for the older films' emphasis on class relations and ideology. Other recent works in the genre, however, have featured a new emphasis on the highly specific, particular character of past eras. Although the television generation has not rediscovered or reinvented the historical film, it has sometimes brought to it a renewed emphasis on carefully documented fidelity to the historical record, in works as diverse as René Allio's *Les Camisards* (1971) and Daniel Vigne's *Le Retour de Martin Guerre* (*The Return of Martin Guerre*, 1983).

Although Tavernier's revitalization of the Tradition of Quality historical film seems somewhat anachronistic in comparison with works such as *Le Retour de Martin Guerre*, in another way the director is highly representative of a major, relatively new trend in French filmmaking. *La Passion Béatrice* and *Un Dimanche à la campagne* share with more modern narratives such as Kurys's *Diablo Menthe* and Pialat's *À nos amours* (*To Our Loves*, 1983) the central subject of disturbed intergenerational family relations. The recent cycle of contemporary French family dramas probably has its cinematic origins in the great financial and critical success of Truffaut's *Les Quatre Cents Coups*, and its sociological roots in the postwar baby boom. The influence of television is probably also important in the genre's prominence since the mid-1970s, for intimate stories of human relationships play well on the small screen. Many filmmakers of the television generation, such as Pialat and Kurys, have worked extensively in this area. One of the most interesting specialists in the genre has been Jacques Doillon, in films such as *La Vie de famille* (*Family Life*, 1985), the story of a young girl's troubled relationship with her divorced father. One of the many strengths of Doillon's work is his consistent refusal to sensationalize his material; other films about adolescence, such as Catherine Breillat's *36 fillette* (*Girl's 36*, 1988), take difficult family relations as the point of departure for somewhat lurid tales of sexual initiation.

When characters such as Breillat's heroine go in search of love outside the family unit, they meet other victims of dysfunctional family relationships among whom meaningful communication, even about such fundamental matters as what one wants to do in bed, is all but impossible. The pessimistic view of life conveyed in recent film dramas of living in—and leaving—the family is perhaps merely the most visible symptom of a profound nihilism that lurks beneath the surface of much serious French narrative filmmaking of recent years (and which also characterizes more commercial genres such as the crime drama). The possibility of a transcendence, be it through love, religion, or political commitment, is rarely evoked, except in deliberately "retro" works such as *Sous le soleil de Satan*. The new nihilism is probably most visible in a recent tendency or genre as yet without a commonly accepted name, which one might call punk hyperrealism: "hyperrealism" because of the hard-edged, hallucinatory clarity of the films' industrial landscapes (subway stations, high-rise apartments, almost empty loft apartments); "punk" because of their aggressive rejection of contemporary consumer culture.

These works, such as Peter Del Monte's *Invitation au voyage* (*Invitation to the Voyage*, 1982), Luc Besson's *Subway* (1985), and Bertrand Blier's *Buffet froid* (*Cold Cuts*, 1980), are futuristic "road movies" which take alienation, dysfunctional relationships, and random violence as givens. They ask: in an ugly world, what are the uses of ugliness? (One

may laugh at it, or aestheticize it, but never reject it, for there is nothing else.) In an inhuman world, what may one enjoy if not the small
pleasures of inhumanity? (For example: eating dinner with your
wife's murderer, in *Buffet froid*.) The most commercially successful
exponent of this genre—or tendency, or style—is probably Jean-
Jacques Beineix, who has infused films such as *Diva* (1982) with a
glossy romanticism that makes them palatable to general audiences.
Nonetheless, Beineix's world is certainly not, for example, Truffaut's.
No one asks "are women magic?" or says *les gens sont formidables*. These
films sound, or try to sound, the death knell of humanism; in this
they perhaps attempt to speak for an entire generation, that of the
young students and workers of May 1968 who tried to change the
world and failed.

"Punk hyperrealism" is probably the closest that French cinema
has come to a relatively coherent "narrative avant-garde" like that of
the 1920s. Whether or not these films are one day accorded a significant place in the history of the medium, they are strikingly different
from the works of earlier cinema art movements or tendencies in
being part of a larger, international trend—which includes works such
as David Lynch's *Eraserhead* (1977), Slava Tsukerman's *Liquid Sky*
(1983), and more commercial efforts like Ridley Scott's *Blade Runner*
(1982). World media culture has become increasingly international in
the past two decades. Although it has always been somewhat arbitrary
to speak of French filmmaking as a distinct entity (because the cinema
from its earliest days has depended on international markets), in
recent years the very notion of a national cinema has become less and
less tenable.

The area of filmmaking most strikingly characterized by the internationalization of audiovisual production has been the so-called
experimental cinema, which in the past few decades has had remarkable and sustained development thanks to financial support from
state-run television networks throughout Europe and from other governmental institutions such as, in France, the Institut National de
l'Audiovisuel. Perhaps because of the international nature of such
funding—which frequently results in coproductions combining, for
example, the I.N.A. and Britain's Channel Four—contemporary
European experimental filmmaking has tended to be cosmopolitan
and culturally eccentric. Aside from Marguerite Duras, the best

known "French" woman experimental filmmaker is Chantal Acker-man, who is Belgian. The *enfant terrible* of the television generation, the ecclectic fabulist and neosurrealist Raoul Ruiz, is an expatriate Chilean. Jean-Marie Straub and Danièle Huillet, creators of an uncompromisingly literary and political cinema in the tradition of the Left Bank school, have worked more frequently in Germany than in France. And Philippe Garrel, who has not chosen or been obliged to work outside his native land, has nonetheless produced a body of elliptical, poetic films based on myth and ritual which have more in common with the work of American independent cinema artists such as Maya Deren and Stan Brakhage than with contemporary French filmmaking.[20]

Although the cinema avant-garde has been, appropriately, in the forefront of the recent international trend, the rest of the French film community may soon surpass the experimentalists in this regard. The nation's commercial mainstream has always defined itself in terms of its greatest rival, the United States. However, in recent years the nature of this competition has begun to change. Until the mid 1960s French filmmaking sought to distinguish and market itself as specifi-cally *French*—or, during the years of the Tradition of Quality, *Euro-pean*. But the European cinema market, weakened by the rise of tele-vision, is no longer large enough to permit amortization of the elevated production costs of major film projects. And with American media threatening to invade the domestic market to a greater degree than ever before, via television, French producers have been forced to attempt to compete in a new, more direct way. One clear sign of the new Franco-American media relationship is the increasing num-ber of works filmed in English by French directors, such as Taver-nier's *Round Midnight* (1986) and Besson's *The Big Blue* (1988). Such films, which represent the latest permutation of the great tradition of international coproduction, aim at enlarging their potential markets in quite traditional ways; what is new about them is the direct attempt to reach not merely Continental but American spectators as well.

Another sign of the same trend is the growing number of recent films made in French but featuring popular American stars in leading roles: thus the curious pairing of Sigourney Weaver and Gérard Départieu in Daniel Vigne's *hommage* to classic screwball comedy, *Une Femme ou deux* (*One Woman or Two*, 1985). But the pressure for greater international competitiveness has been felt also on the other side of the Atlantic. American film producers have experienced the same shrinking of revenues due to competition from television; it is now widely estimated that 50 percent of the income of U.S. media companies comes from abroad. Paramount, Universal, and Twentieth Century-Fox have recently expanded their European production operations; the Walt Disney Company has created a small production facility as part of its Euro-Disneyland theme park in suburban Paris. Stars, directors and producers, even subject matter now cross the Atlantic with relative ease. The major remaining obstacle to a complete merging of French and American media markets is linguistic; spoken language may soon become virtually the only truly distinctive trait of the French commercial mainstream. For the larger, worldwide English-speaking market, American producers have recently taken to remaking popular French films with American casts: Coline Serreau's *Trois Hommes et un couffin* (*Three Men and a Cradle*, 1985), for example, has been "covered" in English by Leonard Nimoy's *Three Men and a Baby* (1987).

The pace, and indeed the very character, of the internationalization of audiovisual media will be profoundly influenced by technological and political developments such as direct satellite broadcasting and the economic and political integration of Europe. It is entirely possible that in the not too distant future, the story of French cinema will have effectively come to an end, dissolved into that of a larger entity whose nature is still difficult to conceive. Conversely, a resurgence of global nationalism or some as yet unforseen consequences of the new technologies of satellite and cable transmission may significantly defer, or perhaps even prevent, this outcome. At the very least, the advent of high-definition video systems will soon render film (as we know it today: images and sounds fixed on a celluloid base) obsolete, and French cinema history will have become the primitive prelude to the evolution of French television.

Distinctions other than those of cultural and technological form, however, seem more likely to resist change. As Jean Renoir and Charles Spaak suggested half a century ago in *La Grande Illusion,* class boundaries may be more significant than national ones. The stratification of audiovisual media into elite and mass cultures may well remain long after the "grand illusion" of French nationhood has passed into history, and the only film projectors still in use are in museums. In this brave new media culture, one can only hope that personal expression and aesthetic exploration will not be restricted to works made by and for an intellectual and artistic elite. And if the audiovisual media of the future do maintain some space for a more or less popular art of storytelling in images and sounds, this will represent, to a significant degree, the heritage of French filmmaking and the future of its "republic of images."

Notes
Bibliography
Index

Notes

1. The Cinema Before Cinema

1. The first manifestations of this shift, which may be found in the Enlightenment, are not—purely for reasons of space—considered in this brief introduction to the cultural context of the so-called "birth" of cinema.

2. Quoted by Georg Lukacs in *Studies in European Realism* (New York: Grosset and Dunlap, 1964), p. 67. (This citation is intended as a reference not only to Balzac but also to Lukacs—and to debates about the origins and nature of literary "realism.")

3. Quoted in Beaumont Newhall, *History of Photography* (New York: Museum of Modern Art, 1964), pp. 14, 16.

4. Georges Sadoul, *Histoire générale du cinéma*, 3rd ed., revised with Bernard Eisenschitz (Paris: Denoël, 1977), I, 122. As often happens, Sadoul's specific details are unreliable, as even cursory research into the history of the bicycle will reveal, but his general thesis is extremely useful.

5. This explains how a band like *Poor Pierrot* could contain 500 images and yet last ten or twelve minutes, which works out to an average of less than one image per second. Images could remain on the screen for any length of time thanks to the constant illumination afforded by the machine's mirrors.

6. This fascinating bit of cinema prehistory was unearthed by Beaumont Newhall. See his "The Horse in Gallop," in Marshall Deutelbaum, ed., *"IMAGE" on the Art and Evolution of the Film* (New York: Dover, 1979), p. 3.

7. The fascinating and still in places unclear story of Muybridge's work for Stanford is outside the purview of this book. See Gordon Hendricks, *Eadweard Muybridge: The Father of the Motion Picture* (New York: Viking, 1975), and Thom Andersen's 1975 film *Eadward Muybridge, Zoopraxographer*.

8. Gordon Hendricks has established Edison's borrowing from Marey, as well as most of the rest of this story, in *The Edison Motion Picture Myth* (Berkeley: University of California Press, 1961, reprinted in *Origins of the American Film* [New York: Arno, 1972]).

9. Quoted in Jacques Deslandes, *Histoire comparée du cinéma* (Tournai, Belgium: Casterman, 1966), I, 219.
10. The house may be seen in Ghilain Cloquet's documentary film *Lumière*.
11. Cited in Sadoul, *Histoire générale du cinéma* I, 210.
12. See the complaints by Albert Londe cited by Deslandes, *Histoire comparée du cinéma*, I, 232–233.
13. Quotes and description of the Lyon *congrès* from ibid., pp. 224–227.

2. An Industry Begins

1. For the sake of consistency, Lumière titles are given throughout as they appear in the company's catalogs. On different programs they could vary: this work was called *La Sortie des usines Lumière à Lyon* at the Grand Café. The film screened there (and seen in most compilations) was actually the second version of that work, the first having been screened at a few of the tryout presentations in 1895. Perhaps the first negative was worn out by repeated printing in the original Cinématographe, or (more likely) Louis Lumière thought he could improve on his first effort.
2. Also known in the United States as *The Gardener and the Bad Boy*, and the origin of the early "bad boy" series by American producers. This film was never listed in the company's catalogs, which offered instead Louis Lumière's remake of the subject, *Arroseur et Arrosé* (1896, often mistakenly named *L'Arroseur arrosé*). Remakes of the early Lumière subjects were frequent.
3. Marshall Deutelbaum, "Structural Patterning in the Lumière Films," in John Fell, ed., *Film Before Griffith* (Berkeley: University of California Press, 1983), pp. 299–310.
4. Donald Crafton, *Emile Cohl, Caricature, and Film* (Princeton, N.J.: Princeton University Press, 1990), pp. 252–253.
5. Alexandre Astruc, "Fire and Ice," cited (from *Cahiers du Cinéma in English*, no. 1) in Brian Henderson, "The Long Take," in *A Critique of Film Theory* (New York: Dutton, 1980), pp. 51–52. The film restaurations recently completed by the Munich Film Archive reveal Murnau to have been, on the whole, an early master of classical editing.
6. Roger Shattuck, *The Banquet Years* (New York: Vintage, 1968), p. 6.
7. According to Michelle Perrot, the living standard of French workers actually declined in the period or at best remained stable. See her contribution to Fernand Braudel and Ernest Larousse (series eds.), *Histoire économique et sociale de la France*, vol. IV part 1: *Panoramas de l'ère industrielle (années 1880–années 1970)* (Paris: Presses Universitaires de France, 1979–80), p. 495.
8. Quoted in Jacques Deslandes, *Le Boulevard du cinéma à l'époque de Georges Méliès* (Paris: Cerf, 1963), p. 21.
9. This description follows the summary given by Deslandes, ibid., pp. 38–40. The hyperactive, pretentious head scientist of *Le Voyage dans la lune* will also, according to the Star Film catalogues, be named Barbenfouillis.
10. Quoted from the *Warwick Film Catalog* of 1901 by Paul Hammond in *Mar-*

velous Méliès (New York: Saint Martin's, 1974), pp. 30–31. The film, once thought lost, survives in a print now owned by Les Amis de Georges Méliès.

11. Our knowlege of Méliès's sophisticated editing is due to John Frazer (*Artificially Arranged Scenes: The Films of Georges Méliès* [Boston: G. K. Hall, 1979]) and especially Jacques Malthête ("Méliès technicien du collage," in Madeleine Malthête-Méliès, ed., *Méliès et la naissance du spectacle cinématographique* [Paris: Klienksieck, 1984]). The term "substitution splicing" has been proposed by Tom Gunning; see his "'Primitive' Cinema—A Frame-up? or The Trick's on Us," *Cinema Journal* 28, 2 (Winter 1989): 3–12.

12. For the original Méliès story, and Deslandes's proposed correction of it, see Jacques Deslandes and Jacques Richard, *Histoire comparée du cinéma*, II (Tournai, Belgium: Casterman, 1968), p. 419.

13. See Katherine Singer Kovacs, "Georges Méliès and the Féerie," in Fell, ed., *Film Before Griffith*, pp. 244–257.

14. See Fernand Braudel's monumental trilogy, *Civilization and Capitalism: 15th–18th Century* (New York: Harper and Row, 1981–1984), particularly Vol. II, *The Wheels of Commerce*, Chap. 4.

15. Georges Sadoul, *Histoire générale du cinéma*, 3rd ed. (Paris: Denoël, 1977–78), II, 337.

16. Presumably Jacques Pathé put his money into something less chancy—perhaps meat processing. Théophile, on the other hand, remained in the industry; his Société Théophile Pathé is sometimes mistakenly identified as a Pathé Frères affiliate, but in fact the latter company once unsuccessfully brought suit against the former for using the family name.

17. Cited in Deslandes and Richard, *Histoire comparée du cinéma*, II, 313–314.

18. Enumeration of scenes from the Pathé catalog, cited in Sadoul, *Histoire générale*, II, 187.

19. Ibid., pp. 310–311. Zecca eliminated one of the museum's seven *tableaux*, the trial scene, from his film, presumably as a cost-cutting measure.

3. Growth and Diversification

1. Pathé's assertion, as well as his flatly contradictory income figures, may be found in *De Pathé Frères à Pathé Cinéma* (reprinted in a special edition of *Premier Plan*, No. 55), pp. 38 and 51.

2. In this assertion I follow the careful argument of Jacques Deslandes in his *Le Boulevard du cinéma à l'époque de Georges Méliès* (Paris: Cerf, 1963), pp. 51–57.

3. For example, Georges Sadoul, in his *Histoire générale du cinéma*, 3rd ed. (Paris: Denoël, 1977) asserts that the company bought up a number of traveling cinemas and provided direct competition to the fairground operators (II, pp. 231, 339). Though this assertion makes good sense, it was flatly denied by Charles Pathé's son (cited by Sadoul at n. 3, p. 231).

4. Recently, there have been attempts to rehabilitate Guy's reputation through screenings of her work made in the United States after 1910. Such efforts, however well intentioned, arguably do the filmmaker a dis-

service. Works like *The Beasts of the Jungle* (1913) do not, to say the least, show off her talents to great advantage.

5. Quoted in Sadoul, *Histoire générale,* II, p. 316. Like most such publicity claims, this one is not wholly accurate.

6. This film is available in the United States in a very useful compilation from the Museum of Modern Art, *Ferdinand Zecca Program.* A selection of comparable, somewhat later films from Gaumont may be found in the Museum's *Cohl, Feuillade, and Durand Program.*

7. It is dangerous to make such generalizations, however, because very few pre-1906 Gaumont productions survive.

8. Alice Guy Blaché, *The Memoirs of Alice Guy Blaché* ed. Anthony Slide, trans. Roberta and Simone Blaché (Metuchen, N.J.: Scarecrow, 1986), p. 28 (translation slightly amended).

9. However, much of the allegedly English approach to comedy seems to have developed through reworkings of diverse material from French sources. As late as 1904, for example, William Paul made an elaborate remake of *Le Jardinier et le petit espiègle,* set in a (studio) kitchen and called *Drat That Boy.*

10. Prince made his films for the Société Cinématographique des Auteurs et Gens de Lettres, a Pathé front designed to compete with the Film d'Art. The comic's claims may be found reprinted in Marcel Lapierre, ed., *Anthologie du cinéma* (Paris: La Nouvelle Edition, 1946), p. 70.

11. Some historians, including Linder's daughter Maude in her film *L'Homme au chapeau de soie* (*The Man in the Silk Hat,* 1983), give an estimate of the total number of his films based on the prevalent rate of production of one such work per week. But Jean Mitry (though he is not normally noted for his meticulous treatment of data) has established the rate of production cited here based on the Pathé catalogs. See his "Max Linder," *Anthologie du cinéma,* 2 (Paris: L'Avant-Scène, 1969): 293, 343–347.

12. Charles Musser, however, argues convincingly that the widespread view of Chaplin as apolitical, sentimental humanist is inaccurate, at least in his early work. See "Work, Ideology, and Chaplin's Tramp," *Radical History Review,* 41 (1988): 37–66.

13. Quoted in Sadoul, *Histoire générale,* II, p. 499.

14. Most of Pouctal's film, including this scene, is available in the Museum of Modern Art compilation, *Great Actresses of the Past,* along with a somewhat confusing print of the company's *Madame Sans-Gêne* (also 1911, after Victorien Sardou and directed by André Calmettes)

15. "Scènes de la vie telle qu'elle est," in Richard Abel, *French Film Theory and Criticism: A History/Anthology, 1907–1939,* Vol. I: *1907–1929* (Princeton, N.J.: Princeton University Press, 1988), p. 54 (translation slightly modified). Abel and other historians attribute this text to Louis Feuillade, though it originally appeared (in *Ciné-Journal,* 1911) unsigned.

16. Richard Abel, "Before *Fantômas:* Louis Feuillade and the Development of Early French Cinema," *Post Script,* 7, 1 (Fall 1987): 4–26.

17. It would continue dominating certain French institutions for some time, for example the Ecole Normale Supérieure of Saint Cloud, where two

decades later the future cinema critic and theorist André Bazin would rebel against it.

18. "Pictorialist melodrama" is a somewhat idiosyncratic label employed here (among other reasons) to suggest that Perret's work may be seen as an important precedent for the postwar work of André Antoine and his followers, a tendency which in this book (in Chapter 5) will be called "pictorialist Naturalism."

19. Feuillade's style could vary enormously depending on the genre he worked in. Comments in this section are based only on his serial melodramas. See Richard Abel's careful, detailed analysis of the director's work, "Before *Fantômas*."

20. Feuillade and Perret must here serve as symbols of an entire group of gifted early French film artists, including Victorin Jasset, Henri Pouctal, and others, whose work—alas—is rarely shown even at major film archives.

4. Decline and Mutation

1. Francis Lacassin, ed., "Le Cinéma selon Léon Gaumont, à travers ses lettres à Feuillade," in Lacassin, *Pour une contre histoire du cinéma* (Paris: Union Générale d'Editions, 1972), p. 67.

2. This all too brief account of the rise of the feature film owes much to Eileen Bowser, *The Transformation of Cinema, 1907–1915* (New York: Scribners, 1990), pp. 191–215.

3. The figures, from Bachlin's *Histoire économique du cinéma* (Paris: La Nouvelle Edition, 1947), are cited by Paul Léglise in his *Histoire de la politique du cinéma français: Le Cinéma et la IIIe République* (Paris: Librairie Générale de Droit et de Jurisprudence, 1970), p. 8. Such numbers are difficult to evaluate and often appear contradictory, though the general trends are clear enough. Much fascinating data may be found in Kristin Thompson, *Exporting Entertainment: America in the World Film Market 1907–1934* (London: British Film Institute, 1985), for example the disparate but suggestive information about Pathé Frères' share of the U.S. market in 1908, 1910, and 1911 (pp. 12 and 18–19)—though again this is tricky stuff.

4. Alain and Odette Virmaux, eds., *Colette at the Movies* (New York: Ungar, 1980), p. 19. Punctuation slightly modified.

5. Ibid., pp. 44–45. The translation is by Sarah W. R. Smith.

6. Fernand Braudel, *Civilization and Capitalism: 15th–18th Century*, Vol. II, *The Wheels of Commerce* (New York: Harper and Row, 1982), Chap. 3 ("Production, or Capitalism Away from Home").

7. The true story of Gance's birth and childhood was told publicly for the first time in Roger Icart's extensively documented *Abel Gance ou le Prométhée foudroyé* (Paris: L'Age d'Homme, 1983), a work which may serve as a model of responsible, primary source research in the life and work of a major filmmaker.

8. This plot summary is based not on extant versions of the film, which in some places radically change the story, but on Roger Icart's summary of

the original published version of the scenario. For the reasons to prefer this written record to Gance's later reorderings of the film, see Icart, *Abel Gance*, pp. 106–111.

9. The most complete version of *La Roue* is probably Marie Epstein's restoration for the Cinémathèque Française (1985). A long-promised American restoration project has apparently been stalled by lack of funding.

10. Review excerpted in René Clair, *Cinema Yesterday and Today* (New York: Dover, 1972), p. 55.

11. See Richard Abel, *French Cinema: The First Wave 1915–1929* (Princeton, N.J.: Princeton University Press, 1984), pp. 326–329.

12. But let the American viewer beware. Brownlow's definitive reconstruction has roughly 9 percent more footage than the American release version—in which, for example, one important character, Tristan Fleuri's daughter Violine, has been effectively eliminated from the story, though one still sees her, unnamed, in some images.

13. Léon Moussinac, "A French film: *Napoléon*," reprinted and translated in Norman King, *Abel Gance: A Politics of Spectacle* (London: British Film Institute, 1984), pp. 36–37. Translation slightly modified.

14. Some authors claim that Gance's experiments in rapid editing served as an important example (along with Griffith's *Intolerance* [1916]) for the Soviet montage school. This argument seems rather dubious. One source (cited in Richard Abel, *French Cinema*, p. 581, n. 6) gives the film's release date in the U.S.S.R. as 1926, too late to have had much impact.

15. Victorin Jasset and Colette (whose style was obviously a model for his own) are but two of Delluc's many predecessors. He was not the first French critic to be widely known mainly for cinema criticism in a major Parisian newspaper: his contemporary Emile Vuillermoz began a weekly film column in *Le Temps* in late 1916. Nor was he the first to collect his cinema essays in an anthology. For an extremely helpful overview of these and other related issues, see Richard Abel, "On the Threshold of French Film Theory and Criticism, 1915–1919," *Cinema Journal* 25, 1 (Fall 1985): 12–33. Texts by and information about Jasset, Colette, and Vuillermoz may be found in Richard Abel, *French Film Theory and Criticism: A History/Anthology 1907–1939*, Vol. I: *1907–1929* (Princeton, N.J.: Princeton University Press, 1988).

16. For extensive information on the postwar alternative film culture, which eventually included the world's first specialized art cinemas, see Richard Abel, *French Cinema*, part III ("The Alternate Cinema Network").

17. Louis Delluc, "Photogénie," in *Ecrits cinématographiques I* (Paris: Cinémathèque Française, 1985), p. 34.

18. Ibid., pp. 41, 56.

5. The Mental and the Physical

1. Germaine Dulac (trans. Stuart Liebman), "Aesthetics, Obstacles, Integral Cinégraphie," in Richard Abel, *French Film Theory and Criticism: A History/Anthology 1907–1939*, Vol. I: *1907–1929* (Princeton, N.J.: Princeton Uni-

versity Press, 1988), pp. 393–394. Dulac's expression *état moral* has been translated as "mental condition."

2. David Bordwell, *French Impressionist Cinema: Film Culture, Film Theory, and Film Style* (New York: Arno, 1980), pp. 146, 271–292. Bordwell's model is extremely detailed and precise. In this partial summary it has been simplified and reordered to emphasize the parallelism between the renderings of a filmmaker's "impressions" and those of fictional characters.

3. L'Herbier's birthdate is sometimes given as 1890. He probably lied about his age until rather late in life. This account of his career is largely based, with reservations, on his memoir *La Tête qui tourne* (Paris: Belfond, 1979). We desperately need someone like Roger Icart to investigate his life and work, for it is possible that he lied about more than just his age. This would have been completely in the French tradition of *blague*, of which Jacque Catelan's wholly unreliable early biography of the director—cited approvingly in his memoirs—is a prime example.

4. Ibid., p. 115.

5. Noël Burch, "Marcel L'Herbier," in Richard Roud, ed., *Cinema: A Critical Dictionary* (New York: Viking, 1980), pp. 621–628.

6. Eugène Lourié, *My Work in Films* (New York: Harcourt, Brace, Jovanovich, 1985), pp. 2–3.

7. Jay Leyda, *Kino: A History of the Russian and Soviet Film* (New York: Collier, 1973), p. 115. Most of this section is based on Leyda's book. But see Jean Mitry, "Ivan Mosjoukine," in *Anthologie du cinéma*, 5 (Paris: L'Avant-Scène, 1969): 424–425, for a flatly contradictory account of the Russians' departure from their homeland.

8. The titleless, much reduced version of *Le Brasier ardent* currently available from some sources gives a hopelessly muddled, incoherent idea of this very interesting film. Good prints exist; it is to be hoped that eventually one will be made available for American audiences.

9. Théophile Gautier is cited in Jerrold Seigel, *Bohemian Paris: Culture, Politics, and the Boundaries of Bourgeois Life, 1830–1930* (New York: Viking, 1986), p. 308.

10. This brief commentary on the *culte du moi* is based on Jerrold Seigel's *Bohemian Paris*, which contains a great deal of interesting material contributing toward an analysis of French cinema's earliest "bohemian" subcommunity, the cinematic impressionists.

11. Jorge Luis Borges, "The Lottery in Babylon," in *Labyrinths* (New York: New Directions, 1964), pp. 30–35.

12. Raymond Chirat and Roger Icart, *Catalogue des films français de long métrage: Films de fiction 1919–1929* (Toulouse: Cinémathèque de Toulouse, 1984).

13. The exception is Richard Abel's *French Cinema: The First Wave 1915–1929* (Princeton, N.J.: Princeton University Press, 1984), where these works are called "provincial realist films."

14. Richard Abel (ibid.) is the major exception. A later parallel to this situation may be found in the continuing neglect of the post-World War II Tradition of Quality by so many recent critics and historians, who base

their arguments on the 1950s writings of the "young Turks" of *Cahiers du Cinéma*—whose opinions were anything but disinterested.

15. André Antoine, "The Future of Cinema" (originally in *Lectures Pour Tous*, December 1919), *Framework*, 24 (Spring 1984): 50. Translator Stuart Liebman's very useful introduction to Antoine's theories appears on pp. 33–44.

16. Jean Epstein, "Mémoires inachevés," in *Ecrits sur le cinéma*, (Paris: Seghers, 1974), I, 29. Most of the information given here on Epstein's career comes from these unfinished memoirs, the accuracy of which is always open to doubt.

17. Epstein's lecture was incorporated into his *Le Cinématographe vu de l'Etna* (1926), reprinted in *Ecrits sur le cinéma*, I. The quote is from pp. 148–149 of that edition.

18. Richard Abel, *French Cinema*, p. 471. *La Chute de la Maison Usher* and *La Glace à trois faces* are far too complex to be treated adequately in a brief commentary. Interested readers are referred to the films themselves—both readily available—and to Abel's intelligent and subtle close readings of them (pp. 456–471).

19. This is the thrust of Jacques Brunius's commentary in *En marge du cinéma français* (Paris: Arcanes, 1954), pp. 75–78. It is worth pointing out that Brunius's comments on Epstein are tinged with overt homophobia, and worth remembering that several of the cinematic impressionists were homosexual or bisexual, or interested—to judge by their films—in homoerotic themes. The Surrealists and their associates, of whom Brunius was one, were surprisingly prudish in their attitudes toward sexuality, and a great deal of the sometimes virulent hostility between them and the impressionist filmmakers probably has its origin in this area.

20. Did Flaherty ever see *Finis terrae?* His *Man of Aran*, made five years later, has images that sometimes strongly recall Epstein's film.

6. The Commercial and the Esoteric

1. English-language theorists and historians sometimes label this orientation "invisible editing," because it is so difficult for most spectators to notice. A more useful label—because it emphasizes the crucial, overriding function of this set of techniques—is "continuity editing," or perhaps even better, the "continuity *system*" (since more is involved than just types of cuts).

2. My debt to Bazin's "L'Evolution du langage cinématographique" will be evident to all who have studied that seminal text. I quarrel with almost all of the essay's "facts" (for example, Murnau and Stroheim were, Bazin to the contrary, masters of *découpage classique*) but find its argument compelling and useful. See André Bazin, *Qu'est-ce que le cinéma?* 2nd ed. (Paris: Cerf, 1981), pp. 63–80. Hugh Gray's rather free translation may be found in Bazin, *What Is Cinema?* (Berkeley: University of California Press, 1967), pp. 23–40.

3. "Genre" is a tricky word applied to cinema, but we seem to be stuck with it. Film genres have a different level of specificity than do literary ones, which are defined by form and social function as much as by content. To reconcile this disparity, most commercial cinema would have to be considered a single genre (analogous to the novel, or the epic). Cinematic genres such as the domestic drama or the gangster film would then be *sub-genres* (if the word were used consistently with its origins).

4. The treatment of film genres in the 1920s in this chapter is greatly indebted to Richard Abel's *French Cinema: The First Wave, 1915–1929* (Princeton, N.J.: Princeton University Press, 1984), pp. 69–238.

5. Both men had been born illegitimate and appear to have spent most of their lives and their creative energies trying to grapple with this situation. For Dreyer's background and its possible effects on his work, see Maurice Drouzy, *Carl Th. Dreyer né Nilsson* (Paris: Cerf, 1982).

6. Paul Monoco nonetheless lists Dreyer's film, along with *Napoléon* and *La Merveilleuse Vie de Jeanne d'Arc*, as one of the most commercially successful works of the period in his *Cinema and Society: France and Germany During the Twenties* (Amsterdam: Elsevier, 1976), pp. 161–164. The problem seems to be that even rough box-office figures were rarely published during the period, and reports of "success" meant different things for different films. *La Passion de Jeanne d'Arc* probably did do better business than is generally reported, but how much better is for the moment impossible to determine.

7. René Clair, review [from *Théâtre et Comoedia illustré*, 1924] of Epstein's *Coeur fidèle*, reprinted in *Cinema Yesterday and Today* (New York: Dover, 1972), p. 72.

8. Although Renoir was not, like Clair and so many others, obviously traumatized by his war experiences, his leg wound was to plague him all his life, eventually contributing to the series of illnesses that caused his death. Nonetheless, his Great War was a relatively happy one, to judge by his depiction of it in *La Grande Illusion* and the image of warfare in general in his other works.

9. Alexander Sesonske, *Jean Renoir: The French Films, 1924–1939* (Cambridge, Mass.: Harvard University Press, 1980), p. 43.

10. See Richard Abel's critique of the label "impressionism" in his *French Cinema*, pp. 279–281.

11. Jacques B. Brunius, *En Marge du cinéma français* (Paris: Arcanes, 1954), p. 15.

12. Robert Desnos, "Cinéma d'avant-garde" (1929), reprinted in his *Cinéma* (Paris: Gallimard, 1966), pp. 189–190.

13. For some of the ways in which early American independents used the French work of the 1920s as models, see P. Adams Sitney, *Visionary Film: The American Avant-Garde* (New York: Oxford University Press, 1974 and later editions), chapters 1–3. The program notes and references for an early, important effort to give the American avant-garde a historical tradition, mainly French, may be found in Frank Stauffacher, ed., *Art in Cin-*

ema (San Francisco Museum of Art, 1947; reprinted New York: Arno Press, 1968).

14. Quoted in Charles Ford, "Germaine Dulac," in *Anthologie du cinéma*, 4 (Paris: L'Avant-Scène, 1968): 7.

15. Unpublished, unspecified text by Dulac cited in René Jeanne and Charles Ford, *Histoire encyclopédique du cinéma* (Paris: Laffont, 1947), I, 142. The text quoted also appears in Ford, "Germaine Dulac," p. 8.

16. For a comprehensive treatment of the curious and complex relations between Dulac and Artaud, see Sandy Flitterman-Lewis, "The Image and the Spark: Dulac and Artaud Reviewed," in Rudolf E. Kuenzli, ed., *Dada and Surrealist Film* (New York: Willis Locker and Owens, 1987), pp. 110–127. The original scenario may be found in Artaud, *Collected Works* (London: Calder and Boyars, 1972), III, 19–25.

17. Roland Barthes (trans. Richard Howard), *Camera Lucida* (New York: Hill and Wang, 1981), p. 49.

7. An Unexpected Upheaval

1. The principle of periodization which governs this book's division into five parts is well illustrated here. A genuine "new period" is defined by a radical change—whether causally related or, as here, not—within the film industry, and a simultaneous transformation in the larger society (a war, depression, significant change of government, and so on).

2. But the only "proof" that filmgoers were "ready for change" is, precisely, that they embraced the talkies so enthusiastically. There had been no decline in film revenues, nor significant expressions of discontent in the press or elsewhere, and so this interpretation is eminently debatable. Yet how else to explain the sudden change of allegiance by audiences throughout the world, from the subtle art of the silent film to the technically and artistically crude first talkies?

3. Alexandre Arnoux, cited [from "L'Expression de la peur," *Pour Vous*, 2 May 1929, p. 8] in René Clair, *Cinema Yesterday and Today* (New York: Dover, 1972), pp. 128–129.

4. Ibid., pp. 138–139.

5. The film's inappropriately correct language was doubtless the inspiration for a *Cinémagazine* reviewer's celebrated dictum that "Il fallait que *Les Trois Masques* fussent faits pour qu'on ne les refît pas" (cited in René Jeanne and Charles Ford, *Histoire encyclopédique du cinéma* [Paris: S.E.D.E., 1958], IV, 27).

6. Raymond Chirat, *Catalogue des films français de longue métrage: Films sonores de fiction 1929–1939*, 2nd ed. (Brussels: Cinémathèque Royale, 1981). Unfortunately this catalog, despite the second edition's *additions et précisions*, omits a number of important works—presumably because of its rigid definition of *long métrage*, which allows *L'Age d'or*, for example, but excludes *Le Sang d'un poète*. Many early talkie "features" were of comparatively short duration.

7. See Roger Icart, *Abel Gance ou le Prométhée foudroyé* (Paris: L'Age d'Homme, 1983), pp. 212–213.
8. Cited in Francis Courtade, *Les Malédictions du cinéma français* (Paris: Alain Moreau, 1978), p. 51.
9. Cited and translated in Alexander Sesonske, *Jean Renoir: The French Films 1924–1939* (Cambridge, Mass.: Harvard University Press, 1980), p. 123.
10. Claudia Gorbman has provided a useful analysis of the film's many departures from aural plausibility in *Unheard Melodies: Narrative Film Music* (Bloomington: Indiana University Press, 1987), pp. 140–150.
11. In the United States the film had many admirers. Charles Chaplin liked *A Nous la liberté* enough to borrow extensively from it in his *Modern Times* (1936). Tobis wanted to sue for copyright infringement, but Clair refused to participate, saying that he had learned much from Chaplin and was delighted that the master had paid his work this great compliment.
12. Just before World War II Clair returned to France and began work on a film called *Air pur* (*Fresh Air*), which was abandoned after a few days of shooting. For a description of this highly interesting project, see R. C. Dale, *The Films of René Clair* (Metuchen, N.J.: Scarecrow, 1986), pp. 273–274.
13. French Paramount has been described by many who worked there, or who reported on it as journalists. One must be more wary of most of these accounts than many historians have been. René Jeanne and Charles Ford (*Histoire encyclopédique*, IV, 30), for example, cite approvingly Ilya Ehrenburg's description in *Usine de rêves* (Paris: Gallimard, 1939), but do not mention that Ehrenburg was the Paris correspondent for *Izvestia* and one of the Soviet Union's most effective political agents in France. The company was too tempting a target for Communists or fellow travelers for their accounts to have much credibility. A less political—or at least less obviously so—description (and, in its own way, scathing critique) is offered by Marcel Pagnol in his *Oeuvres complètes*, (Paris: Editions de Provence, 1967), III, 25–64.
14. The word "generation" to describe a new group of film artists in a given period has a long tradition in French histories of the cinema. It must be remembered, however, that although there is a rough age center for each of these groups, some of their members could be very youthful, others very old. The common factor is when their artistic careers first began, or first stabilized.

8. Art and Entertainment in the Sound Film

1. Henri Fescourt, *La Foi et les montagnes, ou le septième art au passé* (Paris: Paul Montel, 1959, reprinted Plan de la Tour: Editions d'Aujourd'hui, 1980).
2. Through most of the history of the French film industry, Jews and Protestants have played prominent roles—more than one would expect from their numbers in the general population. Though there is almost certainly no "Jewish sensibility" to be found anywhere in French cinema, there may

well be a Protestant one, perhaps growing out of responses to the work of writers associated with the *Nouvelle Revue Française* in the first half of this century. Aside from Feyder, notable Protestants in the French film community have included (to name only directors): Jacques Becker, Jean Delannoy, André Gide's nephews Marc and Yves Allegret, Roger Leenhardt, and Jean-Luc Godard. Some interesting commentary on this issue may be found in Leenhardt's *Les Yeux ouverts* (Paris: Seuil, 1979), particularly pp. 36–40.

3. Most of Feyder's original story ideas and many of the works he adapted feature a Good Parent and a Bad Parent, whether these be biological mother and father (*Les Gens du voyage*, *La Kermesse héroïque*), a foster parent versus a biological one (*Pension Mimosas*, *Gribiche*), or more symbolic configurations (Crainquebille versus his judges). In Feyder's own family romance, his mother clearly had the more sympathetic role. In later life, he himself often played the Bad Parent to others, if one believes his protégé Marcel Carné's recollections. See Carné, *La Vie à belles dents* (Paris: Olliver, 1975), particularly pp. 43–45.

4. Pierre Leprohon, "Julien Duvivier," in *Anthologie du Cinéma*, 4 (Paris: L'Avant-Scène, 1968): 230–236.

5. *Nuits de feu* is another good example (with *La Kermesse héroïque*) of a striking 1930s anticipation of the much later Tradition of Quality.

6. Interview with Sandy Flitterman-Lewis, excerpted in her *To Desire Differently: Feminism and the French Cinema* (Urbana: University of Illinois Press, 1990), p. 150.

7. Ibid., p. 151.

8. Lovers of exploitation film might think of Gréville as an intellectual, consciously avant-garde version of the American master of the B picture, Edward D. Wood, Jr., with Erich von Stroheim as his Bela Lugosi.

9. Marcel Pagnol, "Cinematurgy of Paris," in Richard Abel, *French Film Theory and Criticism: A History/Anthology*, Vol. II: *1929–1939* (Princeton, N.J.: Princeton University Press, 1988), p. 135. Translation slightly modified.

10. René Clair, *Cinema Yesterday and Today* (New York: Dover, 1972), p. 178.

11. Marcel Pagnol, *Oeuvres complètes* (Paris: Editions de Provence, 1967), p. 41.

12. André Bazin, "Theatre and Cinema," in *What is Cinema?* (Berkeley: University of California Press, 1967), pp. 76–124.

13. *Jofroi* was covered by a separate agreement, in which script collaboration was not specified. For an account of the Pagnol-Giono dispute, see C. E. J. Caldicott, *Marcel Pagnol* (Boston: Twayne, 1977), pp. 108–110.

14. Sacha Guitry, *Le Cinema et moi*, 2nd ed. (Paris: Ramsaye, 1984), pp. 50–51.

15. Ibid., p. 73.

9. Politics, Poetics, and the Cinema

1. Alice Yeager Kaplan, *Reproductions of Banality: Fascism, Literature, and French Intellectual Life* (Minneapolis: University of Minnesota Press, 1986), p. 155.

2. Rebatet wrote film criticism during the 1930s under the name of François Vinneuil. Six of his articles are collected in Richard Abel, *French Film Theory and Criticism: A History/Anthology, 1907–1939*, Vol. II: *1929–1939:* (Princeton, N.J.: Princeton University Press, 1988); see, for example, his denunciation of Renoir's *Les Bas-fonds* (pp. 228–229).

3. Jean Renoir, *Ecrits 1926–1971* (Paris: Belfond, 1974), p. 114.

4. P. E. Salles-Gomes, *Jean Vigo* (Berkeley: University of California Press, 1971), pp. 52–69.

5. Raymond Bussières quoted in Michel Fauré, *Le Groupe Octobre* (Paris: Christian Bourgois, 1977), p. 82.

6. Ibid., p. 137.

7. For an amusing, highly polemical, and possibly even largely accurate account of the film's production and why it failed commercially, see Claude Autant-Lara's *Les Fourgons du malheur: Mes années avec Jacques Prévert* (Paris: Carrère, 1987).

8. One film—probably a conscious, though free *hommage* to the 1936 work—comes close: Chris Marker's *La Bataille des dix millions/Cuba: Battle of the Ten Million* (1970).

9. Jonathan Buchsbaum provides careful, illuminating descriptions and analyses of many of these works in *Cinema Engagé: Film in the Popular Front* (Urbana: University of Illinois Press, 1988).

10. Jean Renoir, *My Life and My Films* (London: Collins, 1974), p. 124.

11. Renoir's attraction to violent material may be seen in the following 1938 commentary on what he had to leave out of his adaptation of Zola's *La Bête humaine:* "From each of these secondary plot-lines, one could draw the scenario for a feature film. I think, for example, that Pierre Chenal, who did such beautiful work with *L'Affaire Lafarge* [1938], could have done at least as well with the story of Misard, who, in his crossing guard's cottage, slowly but surely poisons his wife" (*Ecrits*, p. 260).

12. Cited in Alice Yeager Kaplan, *Reproductions of Banality*, p. 145.

13. The scene and the reactions of the Left press to the film are described in Marc Ferro, "*La Grande Illusion* and Its Receptions," in *Cinema and History* (Detroit, Mich.: Wayne State University Press, 1988), pp. 132–136.

14. Allen Thiher, *The Cinematic Muse: Critical Studies in the History of French Cinema* (Columbia: University of Missouri Press, 1979), p. 98; François Garçon, *De Blum à Pétain: Cinéma et société française (1936–1944)* (Paris: Cerf, 1984), pp. 10, 148, 158, 174, 179.

15. For the record, here is the present author's tentative list (writers cited are not always the only ones on each film): *La Rue sans nom* (Chenal/Aymé, 1933), *Le Grand Jeu* (Feyder/Spaak, 1934), *Crime et Châtiment* (Chenal/Aymé, 1935), *Pension Mimosas* (Feyder/Spaak, 1935), *Jenny* (Carné/Prévert, 1936), *Pépé le Moko* (Duvivier/Jeanson, 1936), *La Belle Equipe* (Duvivier/Spaak, 1936), *Gueule d'amour* (Grémillon/Spaak, 1937), *L'Alibi* (Chenal/Achard, 1937), *Hôtel du Nord* (Carné/Aurenche & Jeanson, 1938), *Quai des brumes* (Carné/Prévert, 1938), *La Bête humaine* (Renoir, 1938), *Le Jour se lève* (Carné/Prévert, 1939), *Le Dernier Tournant* (Chenal/Spaak, 1939), *Menaces* (Gréville, 1939), *Remorques* (Grémillon/Prévert, 1939/41).

16. Prévert probably took his most artistically fruitful walks through the capital at night in the company of the photographer Brassaï, whose images of "secret Paris" suggest strong visual and thematic affinities with the films of Carné and Prévert.

17. Barthélemy Amengual, *Prévert, du cinema* (Montreal: La Cinémathèque Québecoise, 1978), p. 5.

18. The case of *Quai des brumes* is not the only German link with poetic realism; Ploquin also produced Grémillon's *Gueule d'amour* for UFA. This Franco-German connection makes sense at the stylistic level: the films often suggest, in their lighting and set design, the visual texture of late German cinematic expressionism. Politically, however, the link is rather ironic, because the Nazis anathematized Expressionism in all the arts as "decadent" and "unhealthy."

19. Simone de Beauvoir, *The Prime of Life* (New York: Harper Colophon, 1976), pp. 279, 116. Note that the second part of the citation is taken from a commentary on an earlier part of the decade, though the attitudes Beauvoir describes seem to have changed little by the late 1930s; see, for example, her comparison of American and French films on pp. 257–258.

20. Allen Thiher, *The Cinematic Muse*, p. 117.

21. Quoted in Jean Mitry, *Histoire du cinéma* (Paris: Jean-Pierre Delarge, 1980), IV, 326–327.

10. War and Occupation

1. Alexandre de Rougemont, quoted from *Kinematograph Weekly* in Paul Léglise, *Histoire de la politique du cinéma français: Le Cinéma et la IIIᵉ République* (Paris: Librarie Générale de Droit et de Jurisprudence, 1970), p. 184. Léglise asserts that Lloyds of London financed a large number of French productions during the 1930s, which means that interest rates were very high indeed.

2. Leaks to the Gestapo from the film community were sufficiently rare that when the scriptwriter Charles Spaak spent a few days in jail in late 1943 some cynics accused him of having anonymously denounced himself to the authorities on a groundless charge, in order to appear more anti-German than he had actually been up to that point.

3. For those fortunate enough to have been overlooked by the extreme Right press in years past, it was possible to obtain forged documents to establish the proper "professional identity." At least one German, Continental-Films head Alfred Greven, apparently did know that Le Chanois was a Jew. But the point is that the Gestapo never found out, nor did Vichy.

4. Francois Garçon, *De Blum à Pétain: Cinéma et société française (1936–1944)* (Paris: Cerf, 1984). The one anti-Semitic exception among feature films was *Les Inconnus dans la maison* (*Strangers in the House*, 1943, produced by Continental-Films), directed by Henri Decoin, script by Henri-Georges Clouzot after a novel by Simenon. The film, a courtroom mystery drama in which the criminal is clearly meant to be taken as Jewish, also contains

a Pétainesque diatribe on the necessity of setting a wholesome example for the moral development of French youth.

5. The number depends on how one defines terms and dates. Evelyn Ehrlich lists 219 works in her authoritative *Cinema of Paradox: French Filmmaking under the German Occupation* (New York: Columbia University Press, 1985), pp. 193–201—of which she counts 35 as "Vichy" films (p. 36).

6. Ibid., pp. 39–46, 139–153.

7. According to Henri Langlois, this is how the last known copy of Feyder's silent *Thérèse Raquin* was seized and burned in Lille (notes to Feyder retrospective, Cannes Film Festival, 1973), probably more on account of the work's Jewish producer than because of the director's known hostility to the Nazis. Langlois and Georges Franju apparently saved a large number of films in Paris (for example, Renoir's *Une Partie de campagne,* made for Pierre Braunberger), many with the help of a cinephilic German officer. See Richard Roud, *A Passion for Films: Henri Langlois and the Cinémathèque Française* (New York: Viking, 1983), pp. 47–54.

8. Joseph Goebbels (ed. and trans. Louis P. Lochner), *The Goebbels Diaries, 1942–1943* (Garden City: Doubleday, 1948), pp. 85, 159, 215.

9. Roger Richebé, *Au-delà de l'écran: 70 ans de la vie d'un cinéaste* (Monte Carlo: Pastorelly, 1977), pp. 151–152.

10. Goebbels, *The Goebbels Diaries,* p. 213.

11. Ibid., p. 215. The film had opened in Paris six weeks before Goebbels saw it.

12. Ibid., p. 221.

13. For a complete list of the twenty seven films, see Ehrlich, *Cinema of Paradox,* pp. 193–201, where they are indicated by the notation "P."

14. The banned films were *Les Inconnus dans la maison* (see n. 3), *Le Corbeau* (see below), and a minor comedy directed by Albert Valentin, *La Vie de plaisir* (*Life of Pleasure,* 1944), which apparently offended the rather prudish Liberation censors by its images of Parisian "immorality."

15. One explanation for Occupation cinema's apparently obsessive interest in the provinces may lie in a C.O.I.C. directive summarized by Roger Régent in *Cinéma de France: De "La Fille du puisatier" aux "Enfants du paradis"* (Paris: Bellefaye, 1948; reprinted Plan de la Tour: Editions d'Aujourd'hui, 1976), pp. 42–43: the organization strongly recommended the development of subjects capable of appealing to the provincial market where, it asserted, most people never went to the cinema (!?).

16. Olivier Barrot, *L'Ecran Français 1943–1953: Histoire d'un journal et d'une époque* (Paris: Les Editeurs Français Réunis, 1979), pp. 14–15. This text (later known to have been written by Georges Adam and Pierre Blanchar) suggests that socialist realist ideas were still quite important to the Communist-dominated French Left: the denunciation of *Le Corbeau* recalls many orthodox Communist critics' denunciations of "sick" modern art.

17. Jean-Pierre Jeancolas, *Quinze ans d'années trente: Le Cinéma des français 1929–1944* (Paris: Stock, 1983).

18. Ehrlich, *Cinema of Paradox,* p. 94.

19. Roger Régent, *Cinéma de France,* p. 229.

20. Francis Courtade, *Les Malédictions du cinéma français* (Paris: Alain Moureau, 1978). For one commentary on the political ambiguities which undermine Courtade's characterization, see Ehrlich, *Cinema of Paradox*, pp. 109–112.

21. See Adeline Daumard, "La Bourgeoisie française au temps des épreuves (1914–1950)," in Fernand Braudel and Ernest Labrousse, eds., *Histoire économique et sociale de la France*, vol. IV part 2: *Le Temps des guerres mondiales et de la grande crise* (Paris: Presses Universitaires de France, 1980), pp. 808–809.

22. Ehrlich, *Cinema of Paradox*, pp. 147, 146.

23. Ibid., p. 150.

24. Ibid., p. 185 (translated from *L'Avant-scène du Cinéma*, no. 186 [April 1977]); I have slightly modified and expanded the description of the scene's action. Ehrlich's commentary on *Le Corbeau* is an extremely useful study of this great, troubling film.

11. Liberation

1. For a brief summary of Brasillach's trial based on primary sources, see Herbert R. Lottman, *The Purge: The Purification of French Collaborators After World War II* (New York: Morrow, 1986), pp. 137–140. The radio commentator and film critic Lucien Rebatet (François Vinneuil) served a prison sentence of about eight years for collaboration.

2. *Film noir* was a genre category in France before being applied to *le film noir américain*, a label which crossed over into English as simply *film noir*, so that now one must say French *film noir* to recover the original meaning. French *film noir* is very different from the now more celebrated American works. It is less markedly expressionistic in visual style, more attuned to social differentiation, and more given to literary and psychological pretensions, sometimes justified.

3. Visually, the film was marred by the extreme shortage of film stock that characterized the period. This very talky work resorts, quite uncharacteristically for Carné before the mid 1950s, to continuous, monotonous shot-reverse shot scene construction for practically all of its dialogue. As a result, much of the film looks like a modern made-for-television movie.

4. The film had not been made during the Occupation, according to Carné, because Alfred Greven was incensed that Carné had evaded his contract with Continental-Films. Greven threatened to block exhibition of any film by Carné based on the original Neveux play, which was his first proposed post-Continental project.

5. In a carefully detailed reading of *Le Ciel est à vous*, Henri Agel argues that the film carries on the metaphysical interests of *Lumière d'été* in a more covert fashion. See his *Jean Grémillon*, 2nd ed. (Paris: L'Herminier, 1984), pp. 65–76.

6. Claude Autant-Lara, *La Rage dans le coeur* (Paris: Veyrier, 1984), p. 35.

7. A tempting, if simplistic, interpretation of Autant-Lara's comments in the first volume of his memoirs (ibid., p. 16)—and his inflammatory prose

cries out for such crude readings—would be that, feeling rejected by his mother in favor of the theatre, he strove to ally himself to that which she preferred to him.

8. But was it so arbitrary? And did he so entirely reject his father's values? See the revealing anecdote of Edouard Autant's scandalous Rodin sculpture (ibid., pp. 39–45).

9. Roger Régent, *Cinéma de France: De "La Fille du puisatier" aux "Enfants du paradis"* (Paris: Bellefaye, 1948, reprinted Plan de la Tour: Editions d'Aujourd'hui, 1976), p. 83.

10. François Truffaut, "A Certain Tendency of the French Cinema" (originally in *Cahiers du Cinéma*, 31 [January 1954]), in Bill Nichols, ed., *Movies and Methods* (Berkeley: University of California Press, 1976), pp. 224–237.

11. Autant-Lara's final cut was about three and a half hours long. Thirty minutes were cut by the film's producers, with an additional forty-five (!) deleted from most English subtitled prints, which often end scenes with abrupt fades to black and do not manage to hide the fact that they originally went on quite a bit longer.

12. One of his best films of the 1930s, *Les Disparus de Saint-Agil/Boy's School* (1938), is a clear precursor of the controlled, subtly expressionistic French school of cinema of the Occupation.

13. René Clair, preface to the published screenplay of *Tout l'or du monde* (1961), excerpted in R.C. Dale, *The Films of René Clair* (Metuchen, N.J.: Scarecrow, 1986), II, 425, 426.

14. Though not perhaps the most interesting of Clair's postwar films, *Le Silence est d'or* has many appealing moments, most of which are utterly ruined in the appalling English-language version entitled *Man about Town*.

15. Pierre Chenal: "I had the bad taste to come back. I was not cremated, I didn't disappear into thin air, which the [former] collaborators didn't forgive me" (radio interview with Leonard Lopate, WNYC [New York], November 18, 1987). Marcel Dalio: "The Germans were gone, but the Resistance continued. Against me . . . Did [producers] see me as a living reproach for their work with Continental during the war?" (*Mes Folles Années*, rpt. Paris: Ramsay [1986], p. 219. Feelings were often intense: see Pierre Braunberger's story of his revenge on Claude Autant-Lara in *Cinémamémoire* (Paris: Centre National de la Cinématographie, 1987), pp. 128–130.

16. English-language prints of *Le Plaisir,* and a few French ones as well, change the order of the sketches. The original sequence—"The Mask," "Madame Tellier's Establishment," and finally "The Model"—produces a much more Ophulsian work in terms of overall structure and emotional tone.

12. An Alternative Film Culture

1. André Bazin, "Reflections for a Vigil of Arms," in his *French Cinema of the Occupation and Resistance: The Birth of a Critical Esthetic* (New York: Ungar, 1981), pp. 95, 97–98, 99–100. Bazin's thinking, here as later in his career,

was strongly influenced by the arguments of Valéry Jahier's essays for *Esprit* in the 1930s. For information on Jahier and three of his articles, see Richard Abel, *French Film Theory and Criticism: A History/Anthology*, Vol. II: *1929–1939* (Princeton, N.J.: Princeton University Press, 1988), pp. 147, 157–158, 182–188.

2. Much of this polarization may have been political in origin: the film was coproduced by the Communist-dominated magazine *L'Ecran Français*.

3. The film which *Farrebique* most ressembles in its lavish use of metaphors and in their content is Marie Epstein and Jean Benoît-Lévy's *Maternité* (1929).

4. He won *grands prix* (Best Film) for *La Bataille du rail* and *Les Maudits*, as well as *prix de la mise en scène* (Best Direction) for *La Bataille du rail*, *Au-delà des grilles*, and *Monsieur Ripois/Knave of Hearts* (1954, a French-English coproduction and one of his most unjustly neglected works).

5. Alexandre Astruc, *La Tête la première* (Paris: Olivier Orban, 1975), p. 70.

6. Alexandre Astruc, "The Birth of a New Avant-Garde: La Caméra-Stylo," in Peter Graham, ed., *The New Wave* (Garden City: Doubleday, 1968), pp. 17–18, 20, 22.

7. Astruc, *La Tête la première* p. 138.

8. The magazine emerged, phoenix-like, from the ashes of *La Revue du Cinéma*. For its early history and for more information about Bazin's life and work, see Dudley Andrew, *André Bazin* (New York: Oxford University Press, 1978).

9. On *ostraneniye*, see Victor Shklovsky, "Art as Technique" (1917), in Lee Lemon and Marion Reis, eds., *Russian Formalist Criticism: Four Essays* (Lincoln, Neb.: University of Nebraska Press, 1965), pp. 3–24.

10. André Bazin, "L'Ontologie de l'image photographique," in his *Qu'est-ce que le cinéma?* 2nd ed. (Paris: Cerf, 1981), p. 16. Compare with Hugh Gray's very free translation, from which I have borrowed where I could, in Bazin, *What is Cinema?* (Berkeley: University of California Press, 1967), I, p. 15.

11. Bazin, "L'Ontologie de l'image photographique," p. 14.

12. Furthermore, adaptations of great noncinematic works served to validate the inferior films which were purveyed as their equals, a point Bazin made in one of his most incisive critiques of quality filmmaking, "De la Carolinisation de la France," *Esprit*, 22 (1954): 298–304.

13. François Truffaut, "A Certain Tendency of French Cinema," in Bill Nichols, ed., *Movies and Methods* (Berkeley: University of California Press, 1976), p. 233. It should be noted that Claude Autant-Lara, Henri-Georges Clouzot, and other leading directors of the Tradition of Quality also wrote their own dialogue and sometimes devised the stories which they filmed.

14. John Hess, "La Politique des Auteurs, Part Two: Truffaut's Manifesto," *Jump Cut*, 2 (July-Aug. 1974): 20.

15. Quoted in Célia Bertin, *Jean Renoir* (Paris: Librairie Académique Perrin, 1986), pp. 301–302.

16. Ibid., p. 249. Bertin's French rendering of an unpublished letter has been retranslated into English.
17. Ibid., p. 337.
18. The reason Bresson gave for his reticence is that his films should speak for him, saying things that he could not say (except through cinema). But one may also suspect that this careful policy reflects a psychic orientation profoundly grounded in a need for control.
19. Robert Bresson, *Notes on Cinematography* (New York: Urizen, 1977). Readers unable to consult the French text (Paris: Gallimard, 1975) should keep in mind that translator Jonathan Griffin has uniformly rendered Bresson's term *cinématographe* as "cinematography," which often causes problems of clarity but is probably the best that one can do.
20. Ibid., p. 1. Translation slightly modified.
21. Ibid., pp. 26, 12.

13. Fourth Wave

1. One example, among many: in 1960, with money from his family, Claude Lelouch made *Le Propre de l'homme* (*The Right of Man*). Though Lelouch had had much more experience at filmmaking than Chabrol or Truffaut, his first feature proved to be unexploitable, and was abandoned after a series of disastrous previews. This story, unlike many similar ones, has a happy end. Six years later, after several less disastrous failures, Lelouch triumphed with the extraordinarily popular *Un homme et une femme* (*A Man and a Woman*, 1966)
2. Rui Nogueira, ed., *Melville on Melville* (New York: Viking, 1972), p. 27. Alexandre Astruc was probably inspired by the film when he made *Le Rideau Cramoisi*, another work in which the characters' lack of speech—in this case complete, radical, again balanced by a voice-over narration—becomes an overriding, fascinating yet oppressive formal principle. Melville claimed, and the idea has some merit, that Robert Bresson was also inspired by the form and several of the images of *Le Silence de la mer* in adapting *Le Journal d'un curé de campagne* (ibid., pp. 26–27).
3. It does not take much imagination to read Vadim's *Memoirs of the Devil* (New York: Harcourt, Brace, Jovanovich, 1977) as the key to *Et Dieu créa la femme*, with the Jean-Louis Trintignant character standing in for the director in his difficult relations with the beautiful, sexually active women he knew how to woo, but not to keep. From this point of view, the film's distasteful conclusion (the way to keep a potentially "loose" woman faithful is to slap her around) would represent what Vadim wanted to do, but couldn't. Ironically, Bardot fell in love with Trintignant during shooting, and Vadim's marriage soon ended.
4. These films are very difficult to see today. For an overview of this activity, see Jacques Siclier, *Nouvelle vague?* (Paris: Cerf, 1961), pp. 78–86.
5. Generalizations such as this one are always by definition rather rash. Many post-New Wave historical costume pictures continued the pictori-

alist impulse of the Occupation and the Tradition of Quality. *L'Histoire d'Adèle H.* (1975) is one good example: Truffaut appears to have asked cinematographer Nestor Almendros for a visual style modeled on Christian Matras's work for Max Ophuls in the 1950s.

6. *Le Roi de coeur* was both an intensely personal film for De Broca and a striking throwback to the Tradition of Quality, both in its subject matter (ironic costume comedy *à la Caroline chérie*) and in its international coproduction format. Despite its failure in France, the film became a staple of the American art house circuit, and in the 1970s it was one of the few films that specialty cinemas could program when they needed a sure hit.

7. Claude Chabrol (ed. René Marchand), *Et pourtant je tourne . . .* (Paris: Laffont, 1976), pp. 20–21 (films) and 25 (quotation).

8. Ibid., p. 170.

9. Robin Wood and Michael Walker, *Claude Chabrol* (New York: Praeger, 1970), p. 113.

10. The film was not distributed by his father-in-law but by Pierre Braunberger. Prints currently in distribution are of the later, abridged version, which omit nine minutes from the twenty-seven minute original.

11. *Ne tirez pas sur le pianiste* is a French idiom meaning, roughly, "Please be patient!" Thus an alternate rendering of the title in English, more in keeping with the film's anarchic spirit, might be: *Get Agitated* or *Don't Put up with This.*

12. *Fahrenheit 451* has a rigorously imposed system of shooting and editing in which the world of the "book people" is portrayed in extremely long takes, and that of the firemen (agents of the Television State) in montages of short, discontinuous shots. Truffaut probably got the idea for this opposition from *Citizen Kane,* where it serves much the same thematic purpose of opposing impersonal, public life with the realm of private experience and memory.

13. The many circles and arch-forms in *Jules et Jim* are remarkably Ophulsian, as are the color cinematography and the portrayal of the main character in *L'Histoire d'Adèle H.* Ophuls's importance for Truffaut's work also extends beyond the costume pictures. He often receives small *hommages,* such as the musical watch in *Tirez sur le pianiste* which plays the theme to *Lola Montès.* The suicide attempt of "The Model" which ends *Le Plaisir,* most completely evoked in *L'Homme qui aimait les femmes,* seems to be the most frequent Ophulsian reference point in Truffaut's work.

14. Filmmaking at the Margins

1. François Truffaut, *The Films in My Life* (New York: Simon and Schuster, 1978 [French publication 1975]), pp. 6–7.

2. Sandy Flitterman-Lewis, *To Desire Differently: Feminism and the French Cinema* (Urbana: University of Illinois Press, 1990), p. 222.

3. Governments and extragovernmental institutions of course seek to fur-

ther their own agendas when they sponsor works of nonfiction cinema. Rotha boldly employs, almost as a synonym for "documentary film," the label "propaganda film," and not in a pejorative manner. See his *Documentary Film* (New York: Norton, 1939), pp. 47–68.

4. Paul Léglise, *Histoire de la politique du cinéma français*. Vol. II: *Le Cinéma entre deux républiques (1940–1946)* (Paris: Lherminier, 1977), pp. 56–57, 76.

5. Actually, this system was first promulgated in 1953, but its implementation was delayed by a noisy quarrel between the government and a lobbying group of nonfiction filmmakers. For the full story, see François Porcile, *Défense du court métrage français* (Paris: Cerf, 1965), pp. 19–28.

6. Fiction shorts were not completely neglected, often being produced either on a shoestring budget—for instance, Godard's *Charlotte et son jules* (*Charlotte and her Boyfriend*, 1958)—or with family money, as Truffaut's *Les Mistons* (*The Brats*, 1958). Franju's *La Première Nuit* (*The First Night*, 1958) is a rare example of an institutionally sponsored fiction short subject, though exactly why the R.A.T.P., the Parisian mass transit authority, thought that this surreal narrative would encourage ridership in the *métro* is not clear.

7. *Le Chant du styrène* exists in an alternative version, sometimes screened in the United States and elsewhere as simply *Styrène;* it does not have the original Queneau text. Apparently in this work Resnais went too far for his sponsors: the poet's highly playful verses have been replaced by the most banal of "voice of God" commentaries.

8. For French cinema history, Franju's role as cofounder of the Cinémathèque Française is perhaps as important as either phase of his career as a filmmaker.

9. Franju, in Marie-Magdeleine Brumagne, ed., *Georges Franju: Impressions et Aveux* (Geneva: L'Age d'Homme, 1977), p. 13.

10. Such distinctions are never as neat as one would like, of course: Varda was born in 1928 and Demy in 1931—though perhaps this is part of the explanation for their peripheral involvement with the Left Bank School. Eric Rohmer, the oldest of the *Cahiers* critics, was born in 1920.

11. Braunberger played a crucial role in the early development of New Wave filmmaking. For a brief overview of his influence, see the partial filmographies and commentary in William F. Van Wert, *The Theory and Practice of the Ciné-Roman* (New York, Arno, 1978), pp. 315–321.

12. See Charles Krantz, "Teaching *Night and Fog:* History and Historiography," *Film History* 15, 1 (February 1985): 2–15.

13. Only in *La Vie est un roman/Life is a Bed of Roses* (1983) has Resnais recently abandoned such narrative motivations for his juxtapositions and comparisons. Made immediately after his surprisingly popular *Mon Oncle d'Amérique* (*My American Uncle*, 1980)—and probably as a result of the director's (and the producers') euphoria at this success—this unfortunately neglected, if perhaps minor, film tells three rigorously independent stories, one of them a fantasy musical. It is, for the moment at least, the swan song of the director's playful formalism.

14. Marguerite Duras, et al., *Marguerite Duras* (Paris: Albatros, 1979), p. 129. For an idea of how completely political ideas have influenced Duras's work, see the 1977 interview (from *Le Monde*) reprinted on pp. 111–117.

15. Jacques Rivette, interview with *Cahiers du Cinéma* (1968), in Jonathan Rosenbaum, ed., *Rivette: Texts and Interviews* (London: British Film Institute, 1977), p. 37 (translation slightly modified).

16. Montage and an emphasis on cinematic duration, however, are not so mutually exclusive and contradictory as one might think. When Sergei Eisenstein was unable to continue his montage experiments in the era of Soviet socialist realism, he began making films very much in the tradition of *mise-en-scène*, with long takes, composition in depth, and expressive relations within shots. And there *is* expressive editing in Rivette's work, on a very slow scale at the level of the sequence.

17. The first two *contes moraux* were filmed as 16-millimeter short subjects. For a useful annotated filmography of the director's works, which includes descriptions of his early short subjects and his nonfiction television works of the early 1960s, see Joël Magny, *Eric Rohmer* (Paris: Rivages, 1986), pp. 100–198.

15. Winds of Change

1. The other filmmaker of his generation from the *grande bourgeoisie* was Louis Malle. Rivette, Resnais, and Chabrol, to name a few more typical figures, were all the sons of pharmacists. Communists and others on the traditional Left who denounced the *nouvelle vague* sometimes called it "petit bourgeois cinema."

2. Godard's peculiar film viewing habits extended to works for which he had great admiration. Truffaut also recalled that "during the entire first-run showing of [Bresson's] *Pickpocket,* I think he went to see it quite often, but always in twenty minute slices." All quotes from Jean Collet, *Jean-Luc Godard* (New York: Crown, 1970), p. 168.

3. For a brief commentary on MacMahonism, see J. Hoberman and Jonathan Rosenbaum, *Midnight Movies* (New York: Harper and Row, 1983), pp. 25–28.

4. Jean-Luc Godard, *Godard on Godard* (New York: Viking, 1972), pp. 175, 177.

5. Ibid., p. 173.

6. Godard began using direct sound recording in 1961. For an overview of his sound practices, see Alan Williams, "Godard's Use of Sound," in Elisabeth Weiss and John Belton, eds., *Film Sound: Theory and Practice* (New York: Columbia University Press, 1985), pp. 332–345.

7. An excellent though quite dense and difficult synthesis of this position may be found in Jean-Louis Baudry, "Ideological Effects of the Basic Cinematographic Apparatus," in Phil Rosen, ed., *Narrative, Apparatus, Ideology: A Film Theory Reader* (New York: Columbia University Press, 1986), pp. 286–298.

8. *Godard on Godard,* p. 182.

9. It is sometimes asserted that the film community's involvement in the May 1968 rebellion began several months earlier, with the protests by leading filmmakers and others against the government's dismissal of Henri Langlois as the head of the Cinémathèque Française. Though there is some merit to the argument, the *affaire Langlois* differs significantly from later events: it was led from the top of the film community; it was highly specific in purpose; and it was successful.

10. Leaflet quoted in a history of the May events published by *Cahiers du Cinéma*, no. 203 (August 1968), translated in Sylvia Harvey, *May '68 and Film Culture* (London: British Film Institute, 1978), pp. 121–122 (translation slightly modified).

11. Ibid., p. 124.

12. Motion of the Estates General in ibid., p. 123.

13. See, for example, the comments of *Cinéthique*'s Gérard Leblanc in *Ecran 72*, 4 (April 1972), translated in Harvey, *May '68*, pp. 131–133.

14. Karmitz has, however, also coproduced some of the most widely acclaimed works of commercial French cinema in the last decade, such as Louis Malle's *Au revoir les enfants (Goodbye, Children*, 1987), Claire Denis's *Chocolat (Chocolate*, 1988), and Claude Chabrol's *Une Affaire de femmes/Story of Women* (1988).

15. René Prédal, *Le Cinéma français contemporain* (Paris: Cerf, 1984), p. 113.

16. In 1987, Claude Durand estimated that one-third of the production funding of French films came directly or indirectly from television, not including videocassette and cable revenues which, though difficult to calculate, may well have the effect of making this proportion closer to one-half. See Durand, "Les Données économiques du problème," in Guy Hennebelle and René Prédal, eds., *L'Influence de la télévision sur le cinéma*, *CinémAction* no. 44 (1987).

17. Prédal and Martin both offer lists of notable women filmmakers, concentrating on commercially less successful figures. See René Prédal, *Le Cinéma français contemporain*, pp. 121–126, and Marcel Martin, *Le Cinéma français depuis la guerre* (Paris: Edilig, 1984), p. 104.

18. One can make a case, however, for Serreau's strong feminist sensibility in *Romuald et Juliette/Mama, There's a Man in Your Bed* (1989), a remarkable comedy that puts a black immigrant scrubwoman on an equal footing with a powerful, established white male executive.

19. But not entirely: during the 1950s Bernanos's novel would never have been so sympathetically adapted by anticlerical filmmakers such as Claude Autant-Lara or his scriptwriting team of Aurenche and Bost.

20. It should be remembered that in the 1920s most of the notable artists of modernist avant-garde cinema were foreigners. This abbreviated commentary on contemporary experimental filmmaking is, obviously, far from exhaustive.

Bibliography

The bibliography that follows should not be taken as a comprehensive guide to the scholarly literature on French cinema; it is, quite simply, a list of the works consulted while I composed the book. It has been dictated by my own recurring themes and interests and my prejudices and preferences for authors and types of source material, not by any pretense of objectivity or comprehensiveness. The reader interested in analysis and criticism of particular films or filmmakers' *oeuvres* will have to look elsewhere for guidance. Although a few such works appear on this list, they have mainly been consulted for historical information rather than for critical commentaries. I have, however briefly, studied almost all of the films about which I have written more than a short phrase. The films are my "primary texts," and I have generally sought to give my own reactions to them rather than paraphrase and dilute the insights of others.

Works which have served as my principal sources for particular topics are indicated in the bibliography by an asterisk. In three instances, however, this system cannot begin to suggest the full extent of my debts to particular scholars. Most of Chapter 1, on the "pre-history" of the cinema, is a series of meditations on the information and insights of Jacques Deslandes in his first volume of the *Histoire comparée du cinéma*. It is regrettable that Deslandes will apparently never take this seminal work of film history beyond its almost equally brilliant second volume, written with Jacques Richard—which I have consulted almost as extensively for much of Chapter 2. Chapters 5 and 6, on the 1920s, owe an enormous debt to the research and historical syntheses of Richard Abel in *French Cinema: The First Wave 1915–*

1929. Abel's book should serve as a model for works on other periods (we desparately need a study of similar scope and erudition, for example, of the 1930s). Finally, Evelyn Ehrlich's *Cinema of Paradox: French Filmmaking under the German Occupation* provides a remarkable, eye-opening reinterpretation of the German role in the creation of the "new French school" of filmmaking during that troubled period and has served as the basis for much of my discussion in Chapter 10.

For the general history of the film industry in other periods I have generally based my account on various sources. Significant portions of Chapter 3 and the beginning of Chapter 4 lean heavily on Georges Sadoul's *Histoire générale du cinéma.* More important, Sadoul provided much inspiration for the overall form of this book, with its mixture of commentaries on general conditions in the industry, on particular schools or tendencies, and on selected individual filmmakers. (This pioneering work, despite its age and its occasional inaccuracies, remains a standard account. I have not found Jean Mitry's *Histoire du cinéma* nearly as helpful nor, unfortunately, as reliable.) For dates and other production information on particular films, I have gratefully consulted the three volumes published so far of the *Catalogue des films français de long métrage: 1919–1929* (ed. Raymond Chirat and Roger Icart), *1929–1939* (ed. Raymond Chirat), and *1940–1950* (ed. Raymond Chirat). The usefulness of this publication goes well beyond detail, covering generic trends in the industry, the careers of individuals who will probably never have books or monographs devoted to them, the general relations between cinema, theatre, and prose fiction in French filmmaking, and a host of other topics.

For the careers of particular filmmakers I have generally relied on one or two sources per individual. Roger Icart's *Abel Gance, ou le Prométhée foudroyé* provides an exemplary illustration of what primary source-based research (*real* primary sources, not just journalistic accounts and interviews) can do to illuminate the personality and professional life of an important creative artist. Equally serious, credible research on a less monumental scale underlies Vincent Pinel's monograph "Louis Lumière." Unfortunately, the available material on Julien Duvivier, Robert Bresson, and a few others is fragmentary and thinly documented. Most of the studies consulted fall in a continuum between these two extremes. Autobiographical accounts by Jean Epstein and Claude Chabrol, for example, are useful but, inevitably, always a bit suspect. (Anthony Slide's English-language edition of

Alice Guy's memoirs can serve as a model of what a good editor can do to provide helpful supporting material for such works.)

A few recently published works bring new information and perspectives to topics covered in this book. I have consulted them while revising the manuscript, but would certainly have made more and better use of them had I read them earlier. These are Jonathan Buchsbaum's *Cinema Engagé: Film in the Popular Front;* R. C. Dale's *The Films of René Clair;* Richard Abel's *French Film Theory and Criticism: A History/Anthology 1907–1939;* and Edward Turk's *Child of Paradise: Marcel Carné and the Golden Age of French Cinema.* The bibliography which follows will serve to place this book in its own historical moment in the writing and rewriting of the history of French filmmaking. For the convenience of those who do not read French, wherever a satisfactory English-language edition of a work exists it is cited here (and quoted, sometimes with modifications, in the main text).

*Abel, Richard. "Before *Fantômas:* Louis Feuillade and the Development of Early French Cinema." *Post Script* 7, 1 (Fall 1987): 4–26.

———— *French Cinema: The First Wave 1915–1929.* Princeton, N.J.: Princeton University Press, 1984.

———— *French Film Theory and Criticism: A History/Anthology 1907–1939.* 2 vols. Princeton, N.J.: Princeton University Press, 1988.

———— "On the Threshold of French Film Theory and Criticism, 1915–1919." *Cinema Journal* 25, 1 (Fall 1985): 12–33.

*Agel, Henri. *Jean Grémillon.* 2nd ed., Paris: Lherminier, 1984.

Allen, Don. *Finally Truffaut.* New York: Beaufort, 1985.

*Andrew, Dudley. *André Bazin.* New York: Oxford University Press, 1978.

Antoine, André (trans. Stuart Liebman). "The Future of Cinema." *Framework,* 24 (Spring 1984): 45–51.

*Aranda, Francisco (trans. and ed. David Robinson). *Luis Buñuel: A Critical Biography.* New York: Da Capo, 1976.

Armengual, Barthélemy. *Prévert, du cinéma.* Montreal: Cinémathèque Québecoise, 1978.

Armes, Roy. *French Cinema.* New York: Oxford University Press, 1985.

Artaud, Antonin (trans. Alastair Hamilton). *Collected Works,* vol. 3. London: Calder and Boyars, 1972.

Astruc, Alexandre, *La Tête la première.* Paris: Olivier Orban, 1975.

Autant-Lara, Claude. *Les Fourgons du malheur: Mes années avec Jacques Prévert.* Paris: Carrère, 1987.

———— *La Rage dans le coeur.* Paris: Veyrier, 1984.

*Bachy, Victor. *Jacques Feyder: Artisan du cinéma, 1885–1948.* Louvain, Belgium: Librairie Universitaire de Louvain, 1968.

Barrot, Olivier, ed. *L'Ecran Français 1943–53: Histoire d'un journal et d'une époque.* Paris: Editeurs Français Réunis, 1979.

Baudry, Jean-Louis (trans. Alan Williams). "Ideological Effects of the Basic Cinematographic Apparatus." In Phil Rosen, ed., *Narrative, Apparatus, Ideology: A Film Theory Reader*, pp. 286–298. New York: Columbia University Press, 1986. (Other published versions of this translation omit small portions of the original French text.)

Bazin, André (ed. Jean Narboni). *Le Cinéma français de la libération à la nouvelle vague (1945–1958).* Paris: Etoile/Cahiers du Cinéma, 1983.

—————— (ed. François Truffaut, trans. Stanley Hochman). *French Cinema of the Occupation and Resistance: The Birth of a Critical Esthetic.* New York: Ungar, 1981.

—————— "De la Carolinisation de la France." *Esprit*, 22 (1954): 298–304.

—————— *Qu'est-ce que le cinéma?* 2nd ed. (in one volume). Paris: Cerf, 1981. Part of text trans. and ed. by Hugh Gray as *What Is Cinema?* Berkeley: University of California Press, 1967.

Beauvoir, Simone de (trans. Peter Green). *The Prime of Life.* New York: Harper Colophon, 1976.

Becker, Wolfgang. *Film und Herrschaft: Organisationsprinzipien und Organisationsstrukturen der nationalsozialistischen Filmpropaganda.* Berlin: Volker Spiess, 1973.

*Bertin, Célia. *Jean Renoir.* Paris: Librairie Académique Perrin, 1986.

*Beylie, Claude. *Max Ophuls.* 2nd ed. Paris: Lherminier, 1984.

Beylie, Claude, ed. *Cinémagazine 1930.* Paris: L'Avant-Scène, 1983.

Billard, Pierre. "Jean Grémillon." In *Anthologie du cinéma*, 2 (Paris: L'Avant-Scène, 1967): 521–568.

*Bordwell, David. *French Impressionist Cinema: Film Culture, Film Theory, and Film Style.* New York: Arno, 1980.

*Bowser, Eileen. *The Transformation of Cinema, 1907–1915*, vol. II of Charles Harpole, series ed., *History of the American Cinema.* New York: Scribners, 1990).

Braudel, Fernand, and Ernest Larousse, series eds., *Histoire économique et sociale de la France*, vol. IV: *L'Ere industrielle et la société d'aujourd'hui (siècle 1880–1980)*, parts 1 and 2. Paris: Presses Universitaires de France, 1979–1980.

*Braudel, Fernand (trans. Siân Reynolds). *Civilization and Capitalism: 15th-18th Century*, vols. I–III. New York: Harper and Row, 1981–84.

Braunberger, Pierre (ed. Jacques Gerber). *Cinémamémoire.* Paris: Centre National de la Cinématographie, 1987.

*Bresson, Robert (trans. Jonathan Griffin). *Notes on Cinematography.* New York: Urizen, 1975.

Brownlow, Kevin. *Napoleon: Abel Gance's Classic Film.* New York: Knopf, 1983.

*Brumagne, Marie-Magdeleine, ed. *Georges Franju: Impressions et Aveux.* Geneva: L'Age d'Homme, 1977.

Brunius, Jacques. *En marge du cinéma français.* Paris: Arcanes, 1954.

Buache, Freddy. *Claude Autant-Lara.* Paris: L'Age d'Homme, 1982.

Buchsbaum, Jonathan. *Cinema Engagé: Film in the Popular Front*. Urbana: University of Illinois Press, 1988.

Burch, Noël. "Marcel L'Herbier." In Richard Roud, ed., *Cinema: A Critical Dictionary*, vol. II, pp. 621–628. New York: Viking, 1980.

*Caldicott, C. E. J. *Marcel Pagnol*. Boston: Twayne, 1977.

*Carné, Marcel. *La Vie à belles dents*. Paris: Jean-Pierre Olivier, 1975.

*Chabrol, Claude (ed. René Marchand). *Et pourtant je tourne . . .* Paris: Laffont, 1976.

*Chenal, Pierre (ed. Pierrette Matalon, Claude Guiguet, and Jacques Pinturault). *Pierre Chenal: Souvenirs du cinéaste—Filmographie—Témoignages—Documents*. Paris: Dujarric, 1987.

Chirat, Raymond, and Roger Icart. *Catalogue des film français de long métrage: Films de fiction 1919–1929*. Toulouse: Cinémathèque de Toulouse, 1984.

Chirat, Raymond. *Catalogue des films français de long métrage: Films sonores de fiction 1929–1939*. 2nd ed. Brussels: Cinémathèque Royale de Belgique, 1981.

——— *Catalogue des films français de long métrage: Films de fiction 1940–1950*. Luxembourg: Imprimerie Saint-Paul, 1981.

Chirat, Raymond, and Olivier Barrot. *Christian-Jacque*. Travelling, 47/Documents Cinémathèque Suisse, 8 (Fall 1976).

*Clair, René (ed. R. C. Dale, trans. Stanley Appelbaum). *Cinema Yesterday and Today*. New York: Dover, 1972.

Colette (ed. Alain and Odette Virmaux, trans. Sarah W. R. Smith). *Colette at the Movies*. New York: Ungar, 1980.

*Collet, Jean. *Jean-Luc Godard*. New York: Crown, 1970.

Comes, Philippe de, and Michel Marmin, eds. *Le Cinéma français: 1960–1985*. Paris: Atlas, 1985.

——— *Le Cinéma français: 1930–1960*. Paris: Atlas, 1984.

Courtade, Francis. *Les Malédictions du cinéma français*. Paris: Alain Moreau, 1978.

Crafton, Donald. *Emile Cohl: From Caricature to Film*. Princeton, N.J.: Princeton University Press, 1990.

Dale, R. C. *The Films of René Clair*. 2 vols. Metuchen, N.J.: Scarecrow, 1986.

Dalio, Marcel. *Mes Années folles*. Paris: Ramsaye, 1986.

*Delluc, Louis. *Ecrits cinématographiques*, vol. I. Paris: Cinémathèque Française, 1985.

*Deslandes, Jacques. *Le Boulevard du cinéma à l'époque de Georges Méliès*. Paris: Cerf, 1963.

——— *Histoire comparée du cinéma*, vol. I. Tournai, Belgium: Casterman, 1966.

*Deslandes, Jacques, and Jacques Richard *Histoire comparée du cinéma*, vol. II. Tournai, Belgium: Casterman, 1968.

Desnos, Robert. *Cinéma*. Paris: Gallimard, 1966.

Deutelbaum, Marshall. "Structural Patterning in the Lumière Films." In John Fell, ed., *Film Before Griffith*, pp. 299–310. Berkeley: University of California Press, 1983.

Douin, Jean-Luc, ed. *La Nouvelle Vague 25 ans après*. Paris: Cerf, 1983.

Drouzy, Maurice. *Carl Th. Dreyer né Nilsson*. Paris: Cerf, 1982.

Duras, Marguerite, et al. *Marguerite Duras*. Paris: Albatros, 1979.

Durgnat, Raymond. *Jean Renoir*. Berkeley: University of California Press, 1974.

*Ehrlich, Evelyn. *Cinema of Paradox: French Filmmaking Under the German Occupation*. New York: Columbia University Press, 1985.

*Elmas, Cindy. "La Technique formelle de Luis Buñuel dans *Un Chien andalou* et *L'Age d'or* et son contexte surréaliste dans le cinéma avant-garde." Undergraduate honors thesis. New Brunswick: Rutgers University, 1986.

*Epstein, Jean. *Ecrits sur le cinéma*, vol. I. Paris: Seghers, 1974.

Estève, Michel. *Robert Bresson*. Paris: Seghers, 1974.

Faulkner, Christopher. *The Social Cinema of Jean Renoir*. Princeton, N.J.: Princeton University Press, 1986.

*Fauré, Michel. *Le Groupe Octobre*. Paris: Christian Bourgois, 1977.

Ferro, Marc (trans. Naomi Green). "*La Grande Illusion* and Its Receptions." In Ferro, *Cinema and History*, pp. 132–136. Detroit: Wayne State University Press, 1988.

*Fescourt, Henri. *La Foi et les montagnes, ou le septième art au passé*. Paris: Paul Montel, 1959. Reprinted Plan de la Tour: Editions d'Aujourd'hui, 1980.

Flitterman-Lewis, Sandy. "The Image and the Spark: Dulac and Artaud Reviewed." In Rudolf E. Kuenzli, ed., *Dada and Surrealist Film*. New York: Willis Locker and Owens, 1987.

———— *To Desire Differently: Feminism and the French Cinema*. Urbana: University of Illinois Press, 1990.

*Ford, Charles. "Germaine Dulac." In *Anthologie du cinéma*, 4: 1–48. Paris: L'Avant-Scène, 1968.

Frazer, John. *Artificially Arranged Scenes: The Films of Georges Méliès*. Boston: G. K. Hall, 1979.

Garçon, François. *De Blum à Pétain: Cinéma et Société française (1936–1944)*. Paris: Cerf, 1984.

Gilson, René. "Jacques Becker." In *Anthologie du Cinéma*, 2: 169–216. Paris: L'Avant-Scène, 1967.

*Godard, Jean-Luc (ed. Jean Narboni and Tom Milne). *Godard on Godard*. New York: Viking, 1972.

Goebbels, Joseph (ed. and trans. Louis P. Lochner). *The Goebbels Diaries, 1942–1943*. Garden City: Doubleday, 1948.

*Gorbman, Claudia. "Film Music: Narrative Function in French Films." Ph.D. diss. Seattle: University of Washington, 1978.

———— *Unheard Melodies: Narrative Film Music*. Bloomington, Ind.: University of Indiana Press, 1987.

Graham, Peter, ed. *The New Wave*. Garden City: Doubleday, 1968.

Grindon, Leger. "The Politics of History in *La Marseillaise*." In "The Representation of History in the Fiction Film", pp. 39–100. Ph.D. diss. New York: New York University, 1986.

Guillot, Gérard. *Les Préverts*. 2nd ed. Paris: Seghers, 1966.

*Guitry, Sacha. *Le Cinéma et moi*. 2nd ed. Paris: Ramsaye, 1984.

Gunning, Tom. "'Primitive' Cinema: A Frame-up? or The Trick's on Us." *Cinema Journal,* 28, 2 (Winter 1989): 3–12.

*Guy Blaché, Alice (ed. Anthony Slide, trans. Roberta and Simone Blaché). *The Memoirs of Alice Guy Blaché.* Metuchen, N.J.: Scarecrow, 1986.

*Hammond, Paul. *Marvelous Méliès.* New York: Saint Martin's, 1974.

*Harding, James. *Jacques Tati: Frame by Frame.* London: Secker and Warburg, 1984.

Harlan, Veit (trans. Albert Cologny). *Souvenirs, or le cinéma allemand selon Goebbels.* Paris: France-Empire, 1974.

*Harvey, Silvia. *May '68 and Film Culture.* London: British Film Institute, 1978.

*Haudiquet, Philippe. "Jean Epstein." In *Anthologie du Cinéma,* 2: 465–520. Paris: L'Avant-Scène, 1967.

Henderson, Brian. "The Long Take." In Henderson, *A Critique of Film Theory,* pp. 48–61. New York: Dutton, 1980.

Hendricks, Gordon. *Eadweard Muybridge: The Father of the Motion Picture.* New York: Viking, 1975.

————— *The Edison Motion Picture Myth.* Berkeley: University of California Press, 1961.

*Hennebelle, Guy, and René Prédal, eds. *L'Influence de la télévision sur le cinéma.* Special issue (no. 44) of *Cinémaction* (1987).

Hess, John. "La Politique des auteurs, Part Two: Truffaut's Manifesto." *Jump Cut,* 2 (July-Aug. 1974): 20–22.

Hoberman, J., and Jonathan Rosenbaum. *Midnight Movies.* New York: Harper and Row, 1983.

*Hughes, Philippe de, and Dominique Muller, eds. *Gaumont: 90 ans de cinéma.* Paris: Ramsaye, 1986.

*Icart, Roger. *Abel Gance ou le Prométhée foudroyé.* Paris: L'Age d'Homme, 1983.

*Insdorf, Annette. *François Truffaut.* Boston: Twayne, 1978.

*Jeancolas, Jean-Pierre. *Le Cinéma des français: La Ve République (1958–1978).* Paris: Stock, 1979.

————— *Quinze ans d'années trente: Le Cinéma des français 1929–1944.* Paris: Stock, 1983.

Jeanne, René, and Charles Ford. *Histoire encyclopédique du cinéma.* Vol. I: *Le Cinéma français, 1895–1929.* Paris: Laffont, 1947. Vol. IV: *Le Cinéma parlant (1929–1945, sauf U.S.A.).* Paris: S.E.D.E., 1958.

*Kaplan, Alice Yeager. *Reproductions of Banality: Fascism, Literature, and French Intellectual Life.* Minneapolis: University of Minnesota Press, 1986.

Katz, Ephraim. *The Film Encyclopedia.* New York: G. P. Putnam's Sons, 1982.

King, Norman. *Abel Gance: A Politics of Spectacle.* London: British Film Institute, 1984.

Kovacs, Katherine Singer, "Georges Méliès and the *Féerie.*" In John Fell, ed., *Film Before Griffith,* pp. 244–247. (Berkeley: University of California Press, 1983).

*Kováks, Steven. *From Enchantment to Rage: The Story of Surrealist Cinema.* Cranbury, N.J.: Associated University Presses, 1980.

*Krantz, "Teaching *Night and Fog:* History and Historiography." *Film History* 15, 1 (February 1985): 2–15.

*L'Herbier, Marcel. *La Tête qui tourne.* Paris: Belfond, 1979.

Lacassin, Francis. *Pour une contre histoire du cinéma.* Paris: Union Générale d'Editions, 1972.

————* "Louis Feuillade." In *Anthologie du Cinéma,* 2: 217–288. Paris: L'Avant-Scène, 1967.

Langlois, Henri. Program notes for Jacques Feyder retrospective, Cannes Film Festival, 1973.

Lapierre, Marcel, ed. *Anthologie du cinéma: Rétrospective par les textes de l'art muet qui devint parlant.* Paris: La Nouvelle Edition, 1946.

Leenhardt, Roger (ed. Jean Lacouture). *Les Yeux ouverts: Entretiens avec Jean Lacouture.* Paris: Seuil, 1979.

*Léglise, Paul. *Histoire de la politique du cinéma français: Le Cinéma et la IIIe République.* Paris: Librairie Générale de Droit et de Jurisprudence, 1970.

———— *Histoire de la politique du cinéma français 2: Le Cinéma entre deux républiques (1940–1946).* Paris: Lherminier, 1977.

*Leprohon, Pierre. *Présences contemporaines: Cinéma.* Paris: Nouvelles Editions Debresse, 1957.

*Leprohon, Pierre. "Julien Duvivier." *Anthologie du cinéma,* 4: 201–264. Paris: L'Avant-Scène, 1968.

*Leyda, Jay. *Kino: A History of the Russian and Soviet Film.* New York: Collier, 1973.

*Lottman, Herbert R. *The Purge: The Purification of French Collaborators After World War II.* New York: Morrow, 1986.

———— *The Left Bank: Writers, Artists, and Politics from the Popular Front to the Cold War.* Boston: Houghton Mifflin, 1982.

Lourié, Eugène. *My Work in Films.* New York: Harcourt, Brace, Jovanovich, 1986.

*Magny, Joël. *Eric Rohmer.* Paris: Rivages, 1986.

Malthête-Méliès, Madeleine, ed. *Méliès et la naissance du spectacle cinématographique.* Paris: Klincksieck, 1984.

Marrus, Michael R., and Robert O. Paxton. *Vichy France and the Jews.* New York: Basic, 1981.

*Martin, Marcel. *Le Cinéma français depuis la guerre.* Paris: Edilig, 1984.

Michaelson, Annette. "Books" [on Bazin's *Qu'est-ce que le cinéma?*]. *Artforum,* 6, 10 (Summer 1968): 67–71.

Mitry, Jean. *Histoire du cinéma.* Vols. I–III, Paris: Editions Universitaires, 1967–73. Vols. IV–V, Paris: Jean-Pierre Delarge, 1975–80.

———— "Ivan Mosjoukine." *Anthologie du cinéma,* 5: 393–440. Paris: L'Avant-Scène, 1969.

———— *"Max Linder." *Anthologie du Cinéma,* 2: 289–348. Paris: L'Avant-Scène, 1967.

Monoco, Paul. *Cinema and Society: France and Germany During the Twenties.* New York: Elsevier, 1976.

*Monoco, James. *The New Wave: Truffaut, Godard, Chabrol, Rohmer, Rivette.* New York: Oxford University Press, 1976.

Museum of Modern Art, New York (various authors). Film notes for "Rediscovering French Film" (1981–83) and other exhibitions.

Musser, Charles. *The Emergence of Cinema: The American Screen to 1907*, vol. 1 of Charles Harpole, general ed., *History of the American Cinema*. New York: Scribners, 1990.

*Newhall, Beaumont. *History of Photography*. 4th ed. New York: Museum of Modern Art, 1964.

—— "The Horse in Gallop," in Marshall Deutelbaum, ed., *"IMAGE" on the Art and Evolution of the Film*, p. 3. New York: Dover, 1979.

*Noëll, René. *Histoire du spectacle cinématographique à Perpignan de 1896 à 1944*. *Cahiers de la Cinémathèque*, numéro spécial (1973).

*Nogueira, Rui, ed. *Melville on Melville*. New York: Viking, 1972.

Nori, Claude (trans. Lydia Davis) *French Photography from Its Origins to the Present*. New York: Pantheon, 1979.

Ophuls, Marcel. Interview with James Blue, Rice University Media Center, March 7, 1973. Unpublished (author's collection).

Ophuls, Max (trans. Max Roth). *Max Ophüls par Max Ophüls*. Paris: Robert Laffont, 1963.

*Pagnol, Marcel. "Cinématurgie de Paris." In *Oeuvres complètes*, vol. III, pp. 9–158. Paris: Editions de Provence, 1967.

*Pathé, Charles (ed. Bernard Chardère). *De Pathé Frères à Pathé Cinéma*. Abridged reprint, *Premier Plan*, 55 (1970).

Petley, Julian. *Capital and Culture: German Cinema 1933–45*. London: British Film Institute, 1979.

*Pinel, Vincent. "Louis Lumière." *Anthologie du Cinéma*, 8: 395–474. Paris: L'Avant-Scène, 1974.

*Porcile, François. *Défense du court métrage français*. Paris: Cerf, 1965.

*Prédal, René. *Le Cinéma français contemporain*. Paris: Cerf, 1984.

—— *80 ans de cinéma: Nice et le 7ᵉ art*. Nice: Serre, 1979.

Régent, Roger. *Cinéma de France de "La Fille du puisatier" aux "Enfants du paradis"*. Paris: Bellefaye, 1948. Reprint edition, Plan de la Tour: Editions d'Aujourd'hui, 1976.

*Renoir, Jean (trans. Norman Denny). *My Life and My Films*. London: Collins, 1974.

—— (ed. Claude Gauteur). *Ecrits 1926–1971*. Paris: Belfond, 1974.

Richebé, Roger. *Au-delà de l'écran: 70 ans de la vie d'un cinéaste*. Monte Carlo: Pastorelly, 1977.

*Rosenbaum, Jonathan, ed. *Rivette: Texts and Interviews*. London: British Film Institute, 1977.

Roud, Richard. *A Passion for Films: Henri Langlois and the Cinémathèque Française*. New York: Viking, 1983.

*Roussou, Mateï. *André Antoine*. Paris: L'Arche, 1954.

Sadoul, Georges. *Louis Lumière*. Paris: Seghers, 1964.

—— *Histoire générale du cinéma*, vols. I–VI. 3rd ed. Ed. Bernard Eisenschitz. Paris: Denoël, 1977.

*Salles Gomes, P. E. *Jean Vigo*. Berkeley: University of California Press, 1971.

Seigel, Jerrold. *Bohemian Paris: Culture, Politics, and the Boundaries of Bourgeois Life, 1830–1930.* New York: Viking, 1986.

*Sesonske, Alexander. *Jean Renoir: The French Films, 1924–1939.* Cambridge, Mass.: Harvard University Press, 1980.

Shattuck, Roger. *The Banquet Years.* Rev. ed. New York: Vintage, 1968.

*Siclier, Jacques. *Nouvelle vague?* Paris: Cerf, 1961.

———* "Sacha Guitry." *Anthologie du Cinéma,* 2: 113–168. Paris: L'Avant-Scène, 1967.

Sitney, P. Adams. *Visionary Film: The American Avant-garde.* New York: Oxford University Press, 1974.

Spehr, Paul C. *The Movies Begin: Making Movies in New Jersey 1887–1920.* Newark, N.J.: Newark Museum, 1977.

Steegmuller, Francis. *Cocteau: A Biography.* 2nd ed. Boston: Godine, 1986.

Strebel, Elizabeth Grottle. *French Social Cinema of the Nineteen Thirties: A Cinematographic Expression of Popular Front Consciousness.* New York: Arno, 1980.

Thiher, Allen. *The Cinematic Muse: Critical Studies in the History of French Cinema.* Columbia: University of Missouri Press, 1979.

Thompson, Kristin. *Exporting Entertainment: America in the World FilmMarket 1907–34.* London: British Film Institute, 1985.

Tiersky, Ronald. *French Communism 1920–1972.* New York: Columbia University Press, 1974.

Truffaut, François (trans. Leonard Mayhew). *The Films in My Life.* New York: Simon and Schuster, 1978.

———* "A Certain Tendency of the French Cinema," in Bill Nichols, ed., *Movies and Methods,* pp. 224–237. Berkeley: University of California Press, 1976.

Turk, Edward Baron. *Child of Paradise: Marcel Carné and the Golden Age of French Cinema.* Cambridge, Mass.: Harvard University Press, 1989.

Vadim, Roger (trans. Peter Beglau). *Memoirs of the Devil.* New York: Harcourt, Brace, Jovanovich, 1977.

Van Wert, William F. *The Theory and Practice of the Ciné-Roman.* New York: Arno, 1978.

Vialle, Gabriel. "Jean-Pierre Melville." *Anthologie du Cinéma,* 8: 541–593. Paris: L'Avant-Scène, 1974.

Vincendeau, Ginette. "Community, Nostalgia, and the Spectacle of Masculinity—Jean Gabin." *Screen,* 26 (November-December 1989): 18–39.

Vincendeau, Ginette, and Keith Reader, eds. *La Vie est à nous: French Cinema of the Popular Front.* London: British Film Institute, 1986.

Williams, Alan. "Godard's Use of Sound." In Elisabeth Weiss and John Belton, eds., *Film Sound: Theory and Practice,* pp. 332–345. New York: Columbia University Press, 1986.

——— "The Lumière Organization and 'Documentary Realism'." In John Fell, ed., *Film Before Griffith,* pp. 153–161. (Berkeley: University of California Press, 1983.

Wood, Robin, and Michael Walker. *Claude Chabrol.* New York: Praeger, 1970.

Index

Page numbers in italics indicate illustrations.

Abel, Richard, 68, 90, 124
A bout de souffle/Breathless, 335, 337, 381–385 passim
Achard, Marcel, 177, 199, 206, 233, 241
Ackerman, Chantal, 402
Action Française, 172
Adam, Alfred, 291
A double tour/Web of Passion, 345
Adventures of Robin Hood, The, 343
Aerogynes (flying women), 40, 52
Affaire Dreyfus, L'/Dreyfus Court Martial, 38
Affaire est dans le sac, L' (The Deal Is in the Bag), 223, 224, 235
Affiche, L' (The Poster), 123
Age d'or, L' (The Age of Gold), 153–154, 178
Albert-Dulac, Louis, 146
Alerme, André, 191
Alexander, Curt, 211, 212
Alibi, L' (The Alibi), 206, 241, 260
Allégret, Marc, 151, 199, 200, 202, 336
Allégret, Yves, 223, 280, 286, 287
Allio, René, 399
Almereyda, 216
Alphaville, 384
Althusser, Louis, 389
Amants, Les (The Lovers), 337, 341–342, 393
Amants de Vérone, Les (The Lovers of Verona), 285

Amengual, Barthélemy, 235
"American shot," 72, 137
Ames de fous, 146
Ames d'enfants (Children's Souls), 196
Ami viendra ce soir, Un (A Friend Will Arrive Tonight), 281
Amour fou, L' (Mad Love), 374, 375, 393
Amour l'après-midi, L'/Chloe in the Afternoon, 376
Anderson, "Bronco Billy," 78
Anemic Cinéma, 151
Angèle, 203, 228
Angelo, Jean, *139*
Anger, Kenneth, 149
Anges du péché (Angels of Sin), 322
Annabella, 174, 237
Année dernière à Marienbad, L' (Last Year at Marienbad), 371–373
A nos amours (To Our Loves), 400
Anouilh, Jean, 264, 286
A nous la liberté (Give Us Liberty), 171–172
Anti-Semitism, 230–231, 240, 251–252, 295
Antoine, André, 99, 201, 204, 302; profile of, *113–118*; and Grémillon, 125; approach of, 135
Antoine, André-Paul, 206, 210, 211
Antoine et Antoinette, 317
Apollinaire, Guillaume, 68
A propos de Nice (On the Subject of Nice), 217

Argent, L' (Money), 107
Aristotle, 238
Arletty, 185, 190, 237, 264, 273, 284
Armée des ombres, L' (Army of the Shadows), 335
Arnoux, Alexandre, 160
Arrivée des congressistes à Neuville-sur-Saone/Debarkation of Photographic Congress Members at Lyon, 27, 28
Arrivée d'un train en gare/Arrival of a Train at La Ciotat, 28
Arroseur et Arrosé (Waterer and Watered), 29
Artaud, Antonin, 148
Art cinema, 2, 124, 131, 397, 398
Arzner, Dorothy, 176
Ascenseur à l'échafaud/Frantic, 337, *341*
Assassinat du Père Noël, L'/Who Killed Santa Claus, 259, 291
Assassin habite au 21, L' (The Murderer Lives at Number 21), 260
Assommoir, L' (Zola), 305
Atalante, L', 218–*219*, 220, 260, 300, 350
Atlantide, L', 128–129, 186, 188
Astruc, Alexandre, 30, 306–307, 321, 332, 335
Atlantic City, 342
Au bagne/Scenes of Convict Life, 56
Auberge rouge, L' (The Red Inn), 124, 291
Aubert, Claude-Bernard, 336
Au-delà des grilles/The Walls of Malapaga, 304
Au hasard Balthasar (Balthasar Here and There), 323, 324
Au pays de George Sand (In the Country of George Sand), 124
Aurenche, Jean, 191, 237, 256, 281, 290, 296, 305, 312, 399
Au revoir les enfants (Goodbye, Children), 341
Autant, Edouard, 288
Autant-Lara, Claude, 105, 174, 191, 200, 216, 217, 223, 260, 281, 283, 287, 292, 311; profile of, 288–291
Auteur, 312
Auteurs Associés, Les, 202
Aux jardins de Murcie (In the Gardens of Murcia), 117
Aventures de Robert Macaire, Les (The Adventures of Robert Macaire), 124
Aymé, Marcel, 233, 241, 290

Bachlin, Pierre, 81
Baie des Anges, La (Bay of the Angels), 361
Baignade en mer/The Sea, 27
Baisers volés (Stolen Kisses), 352
Balin, Mireille, 198
Ballet mécanique, 106, 142–144, *145,* 152
Ballon-Cinérama, 48
Balzac, Honoré de, 8, 124
Barbey d'Aurévilly, Jules-Amédée, 307
Bardèche, Maurice, 214, 230
Bardot, Brigitte, 288, 336, 342, 379
Baroncelli, Jacques de, 118
Baron fantôme, Le (The Phantom Baron), 283, 321
Barque sortant du port (Boat Leaving the Port), 28
Barrault, Jean-Louis, 257, 284
Barrès, Maurice, 112
Barrymore, Lionel, 174
Barthes, Roland, 151, 338
Bas-fonds, Les (The Lower Depths), 229, 350
Bassin aux Tuileries/Boat-Sailing in the Tuileries, 30
Bataille de Fontenoy, La, 222, 234
Bataille du rail, La (Battle of the Rail), 303–304, *305*
Batcheff, Pierre, 222–223
Baudelaire, Charles, 13, 149
Baudry, Jean-Louis, 383
Baur, Harry, 185, 195, 258
Bayard, Hippolyte, 11
Bazin, André, 127, 202, 299, 300, 333, 348, 376; profile of, 307–312, 369–370
Beau Serge, Le/Bitter Reunion, 337, 344–345
Beaute du diable, La (Beauty and the Devil), 294
Beauvoir, Simone de, 235
Becker, Jacques, 225, 269, 312, 316, 318
Beineix, Jean-Jacques, 393, 401
Bell, Marie, 174, 189
Belle de jour (Beauty of the Daytime), 398
Belle époque, La, 31–32
Belle Equipe, La/They Were Five, 239, 260
Belle et la Bête, La (Beauty and the Beast), 321

Belle Fille comme moi, Une (Such a Gorgeous Kid Like Me), 351
Belle Nivernaise, La, 122–123
Belles-de-nuit, Les (Beauties of the Night), 294
Bellon, Yannick, 397
Belmondo, Jean-Paul, 335, 381
Benjamin, Walter, 8
Benoît-Levy, Jean, 122, 195, 251
Berlioz, Hector, 257
Bernanos, Georges, 322, 344, 398
Bernard, Jean-Jacques, 252
Bernard, Raymond, 130, 131, 185, 186, 245, 251, 263, 281, 293, 295
Bernard, Tristan, 131
Bernhardt, Sarah, 65, 80
Bernstein, Henry, 116
Berry, Jules, 174, 229, 238
Berthelot, M., 68
Besson, Luc, 400, 402
Bête humaine, La (The Human Beast), 236
Biches, Les/Bad Girls, 346
Big Blue, The, 402
Biquefarre, 302
Birth of a Nation, The, 86
Black Crows, 1–8
Blade Runner, 401
Blanchar, Pierre, 267
Blanchette (Brieux), 116
Blavette, Charles, 228
Blier, Bertrand, 392, 400
Blum, Léon, 250, 277–278
Blum-Byrnes accord, 277–278
Bob le flambeur/Bob the Gambler, 334, 356, 367
Bogart, Humphrey, 381, 384
Boileau, N., 367
Boireau. *See* Deed, André
Boisset, Yves, 394
Bonheur, Le (Happiness), 195, 358, 359
Bonjour Cinéma (Epstein), 121–122
Bonne Chance (Good Luck), 207
Bonnes Femmes, Les (The Good Women), 345, 346–347
Bordwell, David, 102, 105, 111, 113
Borges, Jorge Luis, 112
Borlin, Jean, 143
Bost, Pierre, 191, 281, 290, 296, 305, 312, 399
Boucher, Le (The Butcher), 347
Boudu sauvé des eaux/Boudu Saved from Drowning, 228

Brakhage, Stan, 402
Brasier ardent, Le (The Fiery Furnace), 110, 136
Brasillach, Robert, 214, 230, 250, 275
Brasseur, Pierre, 174
Braudel, Fernand, 40, 83
Braunberger, Pierre, 162, 166, 251, 295, 298, 344, 368
Braunberger-Richebé, 202
Brecht, Bertolt, 170
Breillat, Catherine, 400
Bresson, Robert, 309, 311, 312, 313, 339, 344, 355, 394; profile of, 322–324
Breton, André, 151
Bricolage, 9, 18, 19, 23
Brière, La, 117–118
Brieux, Eugène, 116
Broadway Melody of 1929, 160–161, 169
Broca, Philippe de, 339, 379
Brooks, Louise, 168–169
Brownlow, Kevin, 91
Brumes d'automne (Autumn Mists), 151
Brunius, Jacques, 140, 223, 224, 225
Buffet froid (Cold Cuts), 400, 401
Buñuel, Luis, 100, 134, 139, 140, 149, 151, 178, 228, 366; profile of, 152–154, 397–398
Burch, Noël, 107

Cage aux folles, La (The Coop for Queens), 360
Cahiers du Cinéma, Les, 2, 281, 288, 298, 305, 313, 314, 316, 320, 328, 331, 332, 334, 335, 337, 339, 340, 344, 347, 349; group, 356, 359–363 passim, 365, 367, 369, 370, 374, 375, 378, 381, 388, 389, 392, 399
Cain, James M., 241
Calcutta, 389
Call of the Flesh, 174
Calmettes, André, 64
Calypso, 341
Caméra-stylo, 306, 307, 310, 332
Camisards, Les, 399
Camus, Marcel, 331, 336
Cannes film festival, 302, 304, 337, 345, 349, 361, 388, 392–393, 398
Capellani, Albert, 114
Caporal épinglé, Le/The Elusive Corporal, 315
Captain Blood, 343

Carette, Julien, 185
Carmen, 186
Carmoy, Guy de, 250, 253
Carnaval des vérités, Le, 289
Carné, Marcel, 164, 191, 232, 233, 237,
    240, 253, 260, 283, 287, 288; profile
    of, 258–259, 284–285
Carnet de bal, Un (A Dance Program), 194
Carol, Martine, 1, 279, 281, 292, 298
Caroline chérie (Dearest Caroline), 281
Carpentier, Jules, 24, 54
Cartier-Bresson, Henri, 225
Casque d'or (Golden Headpiece), 317
Castanier, Jean, 224
Catelan, Jacque, 111, 140, 184
Catherine, 136
Cautio-Treuhandgesellschaft, 255–256
Cavalcanti, Alberto, 105, 176
Cayatte, André, 258, 285, 300
Cayrol, Jean, 365, 369, 370, 372
Céline, Louis Ferdinand, 215
Céline et Julie vont en bateau (Celine and
    Julie Go Boating), 375
Cendrars, Blaise, 121
Censorship, 393–394
Centre National de la Cinématographie
    (C. N. C.), 277, 278, 338, 345, 356,
    368, 389
Cercle Gaulois, 115
César, 202
Chabrol, Claude, 307, 309, 331, 333,
    337, 339, 350, 355, 360, 361, 370,
    374, 379, 381, 388, 398; profile of,
    343–348
Chambre en ville, Une (A Room in Town),
    361
Chambre verte, La (The Green Room), 352
Chant du styrène, Le (The Styrene's Song),
    363
Chanteur de Seville, Le, 174
Chapais, André de, 59
Chapeau de paille d'Italie, Un (An Italian
    Straw Hat), 134
Chaplin, Charlie, 61, 98, 121
Charity Bazaar, fire at, 51
Charleston, 137
Charlotte et son jules (Charlotte and Her
    Boyfriend), 313
Charme discret de la bourgeoisie, Le (The
    Discreet Charm of the Bourgeoisie), 398
Chartres, 119

Chartreuse de Parme, La (The Charterhouse
    of Parma), 292
Chatiliez, Etienne, 391
Chavance, Louis, 260, 271
Cheat, The, 81, 86, 95, 97, 160–161
Chenal, Pierre, 181–182, 206, 232, 251,
    293; profile of, 240–242, 295–296
Chevroton, Mlle., 58
Chien andalou, Un (An Andalusian Dog),
    153, 223
Chienne, La (The Bitch), 166, 167, 168,
    227, 228, 232
Chinoise, ou plutôt à la Chinoise, La (The
    Chinese, or rather, In the Chinese
    Manner), 386, 387
Chirat, Raymond, 113, 162
Chrétien, Henri, 289
Christian-Jacque, 257, 258, 259, 281,
    287, 311; profile of, 291–292
Chronique d'un été (Chronicle of a
    Summer), 364
Chute de la maison Usher, La (The Fall of
    the House of Usher), 124, 153
Ciboulette, 223, 224, 289
Ciel est à vous, Le (The Sky Is Yours), 262,
    268, 269, 285, 286
Cinéa, 122
Cinéaste, 97
Ciné-clubs, 124, 213
Ciné-Journal, 175
Cinéma et Cie (Cinema and Company;
    Delluc), 96
Cinémagazine, 175
Cinema Jungle, The (Delluc), 122
Cinéma MacMahon, 381
Cinéma-Monopole, 53
Cinémathèque Française, 91, 98, 118,
    276, 344, 370, 380
Cinematic impressionism, see
    Impressionism
Cinematic rhythm, 98, 102–103
Cinématographe, 23–26, 54
Cinématographie Française, 175
Cinéma vérité, 304, 364, 390
Cinémonde, 241
Cinerama, 93
Cinéromans, 82
Cinéthique, 389
Citizen Kane, 172
Clair, René, 3, 88–89, 90, 92, 100, 154,
    161, 165, 185, 186, 293, 320, 321;

profile of, 131–135, 168–173; devices of, 134; and *Entr'acte,* 143–144; and Pagnol, 200; "visual" cinema of, 204; social themes of, 220

Clément, René, 281, *305,* 311, 318, 321, 331; profile of, 302–306

Cléo de 5 à 7 (Cleo from 5 to 7), 358

Clochemerle, 296

Clouzot, Henri-Georges, 174, *261,* 271, 280, 285, 300, 341, 347; profile of, 259–262, 275–276, 286–288

Clown and His Dogs, The, 15

Cluny, Alain, *266*

C. N. C. *See* Centre National de la Cinématographe

Cocoanuts, The, 176

Cocktail Molotov, 396

Cocteau, Jean, 88, 93, 178, 179, 264, 304, 310, 312, 313, 333, 349, 360, 364, 366; profile of, 320–322

Coeur fidèle (Faithful Heart), 122, 129, 134, 142, 184

Coeurs farouches, 192

C. O. I. C. *See* Comité d'Organisation de l'Industrie Cinématographique (Organization Committee for the Cinema Industry)

Colette, 81, 86, 199, 211, 290

Collectionneuse, La (The Collector), 376, 377

Collier de la Reine, Le (The Queen's Necklace), 161, 162

Collins, Alf, 58

Colpi, Henri, 365, 367

Comandon, Jean, 58·

Comédie Française, 63

Comédies et proverbes, 376, 377

Comic films, 58–61, 66, 68

Comité d'Action de la Resistance, 332

Comité d'Organisation de l'Industrie Cinématographique, 249–250, 260, 362; under Vichy, 276–277

Committee for the Defense of French Cinema, 276

Committee for the Liberation of the French Cinema, 261, 275

Communist party, 213, 221, 388

Comoedia Illustré, 95, 201

Compagnie Générale des Cinématographes, Phonographes, et Pellicules, 43

Comptoir Général de Photographie Léon Gaumont et Cie, 54

Condamné à mort s'est échappé, Un/A Man Escaped, 322–323

Constantine, Eddie, 384

Contes moraux, 376–377

Continental-Films, 255, 258, 262

Coquille et le Clergyman, La (The Seashell and the Clergyman), 148, 152

Corbeau, Le (The Raven), 259–262, *261,* 267, 268, 269, 271, 275, 280, 286

Costa-Gavras, Constantin, 338, 394

Coup de torchon/Clean Slate, 399

Coup du berger, Le (The Shepherd's Gambit), 344

Coup pour coup (Blow for Blow), 390–391

Course en sacs (Sack Race), 29

Courtade, Francis, 267

Cousins, Les (The Cousins), 307, 337, 344, 345, *346,* 355

Cousteau, Jacques-Yves, 341

Crafton, Donald, 29

Crainquebille/Old Bill of Paris, 186

Credo, ou la tragédie de Lourdes, 192

Crime de Monsieur Lange, Le (The Crime of Monsieur Lange), 66, 217, 224, 226, 227, 229, 236, 316, 317

Crime et Châtiment (Crime and Punishment), 241

Curtiz, Michael, 185, 292, 343

Dabit, Eugène, 237

Dada movement, 142, 143, 151–154, 172

Daguerre, Louis-Jacques-Mandé, 8–11

Dali, Salvador, 78, 153

Dalio, Marcel, 230, 246, 251

Dame aux camélias, La/Camille, 65

Dames du Bois de Boulogne, Les/Ladies of the Park, 321, 322

Dame vraiment bien, Une (A Really Swell Lady), 58

Darrieux, Danielle, 174, *282*

Dasté, Jean, 225

Daudet, Alphonse, 116, 123

David Golder, 193

Davis, Miles, 341

Déa, Marie, *266*

Debuts d'un patineur, Les/Max Learns to Skate, 60

Decaë, Henri, 334

Decoin, Henri, 273
Décor-personnage, 264
Découpage classique, 127, 181
Dédée d'Anvers (Dedee from
    Antwerp), 286
Deed, André, 59
De Forest, Lee, 158
Déjeuner sur l'herbe, Le/Picnic on the
    Grass, 316
Delac, Charles, 65
Delannoy, Jean, 267, 283, 295, 296, 321
Delerue, Georges, 339
Delluc, Louis, 88, 101, 104, 109, 112,
    113, 176, 307, 309; profile of, 94–
    100; and Antoine, 116; and Epstein,
    122; and Dulac, 146
Del Monte, Peter, 400
Delon, Alain, 335
De Mayerling à Sarajevo (From Mayerling
    to Sarajevo), 211, 212, 248
Demazis, Orane, 202
Demenÿ, Georges, 21, 54
De Mille, Cecil B., 81, 86, 98
Demoiselles de Rochefort, Les (The Young
    Girls of Rochefort), 361
Démolition d'un mur (Destruction of a
    Wall), 28
Demy, Jacques, 331, 359, 361
Dépardieu, Gérard, 402
Deren, Maya, 149, 402
Dernier Milliardaire, Le (The Last
    Billionaire), 173
Dernier Tournant, Le (The Last Turning),
    241
De Sica, V., 301
Deslandes, Jacques, 36
Desnos, Robert, 140, 152
Deutelbaum, Marshall, 28
Deux Anglaises et le Continent, Les/Two
    English Girls, 352
Deux ou trois choses que je sais d'elle (Two
    or Three Things I Know About Her), 385
Deval, Jacques, 206
Deville, Michel, 331, 337
Dhermitte, Edouard, 333
Diable au corps, Le (Devil in the Flesh),
    281, 290
Diable boîteux, Le (The Limping Devil),
    274
Diable dans la ville, Le (Devil in the City),
    148

Diablo Menthe (Peppermint Soda), 396,
    400
Diaboliques, Les/Diabolique, 286, 287
Dickson, W. K. L., 20, 22
Dieudonné, Albert, 136
Dimanche à la campagne, Un (A Sunday in
    the Country), 399
D'Indy, Vincent, 119
Disque 927, 149
Diva, 401
Divine, 211
Dix Femmes pour un mari/Ten Women for
    One Husband, 58
Dixième Symphonie, La (The Tenth
    Symphony), 86, 91
Documentary films and nouvelle vague,
    361–365
Doillon, Jacques, 400
Donen, Stanley, 384
Doniol-Valcroze, Jacques, 309
Douce (Love Story), 268, 290
Drach, Michel, 336
Drame au château d'Acre, Un (Drama at
    the Acre Chateau), 86
Drames du cinéma (Delluc), 96
Dreyer, Carl, 130, 131
Dreyfus, Jean-Paul, 221. See also Le
    Chanois, Jean-Paul
Drôle de drame (Bizarre, Bizarre), 235
Duchamp, Marcel, 141, 143, 151
Du côté de la côte (The Riviera Way), 363
Duhamel, Marcel, 224
Dulaar, Abraham, 52
Dulaar, Jérome, 52
Dulaar family, 41
Dulac, Germaine, 96, 101, 217, 396;
    profile of, 108–112, 144–149
Dullin, Charles, 119–120, 184
Dumas, Alexandre fils, 65, 110
Dumas, Alexandre père, 116, 161
Duras, Marguerite, 360, 365, 367, 370,
    396, 397, 401; profile of, 373–374
Duvivier, Julien, 135, 186, 198, 232,
    238, 239, 240, 280, 293; profile of,
    191–194

Eastman, George, 19
Eclair studios, 60, 66, 78, 79
Eclipse company, 67
Ecole buissonière, L'/Passion for Life, 300

Ecole des facteurs, L' (The School for Postmen), 318

Ecran Français, L', 261–262, 267

Edison, Thomas Alva, 19–23, 31, 79, 158

Editing, classical, *see découpage classique*

Edouard et Caroline, 317

Ehrlich, Evelyn, 254, 260, 263, 270–271

Eisenstein, Sergei, 221, 301, 364

El Dorado, 104, 105

Eléna et les hommes/Elena and Her Men, 315

Eluard, Paul, 361, 366

Emak Bakia, 151–152

Emanuelle, 393

Empire, 310

En cas de malheur/Love is my Profession, 288

Enfance nue, L' (Naked Childhood), 398

Enfant de l'amour, L' (Child of Love), 195

Enfant de Paris, L' (Child of Paris), 71

Enfant sauvage, L' (The Wild Child), 352

Enfants du paradis, Les (Children of Paradise), 238, 260, 268, 284

Enfants terribles, Les/The Strange Ones, 333

Entr'acte (Intermission), 133, 143–144, *145*, 152, 172

Entre nous (Between Us), 396

Epstein, Jean, 108, 110, 129, 140, 152–153, 195; profile of, 120–125

Epstein, Marie, 121, 123, 124, 396; profile of, 195–198

Epuration, 272–276

Eraserhead, 401

Ermoliev, Joseph, 109, 110

Eruption volcanique à la Martinique/ Eruption of Mount Pelée, 35

Escamotage d'une dame chez Robert-Houdin/The Vanishing Lady, 36

Espoir/Man's Hope, 300–301, 302

Esprit, 308

Et Dieu créa la femme (And God Created Woman), 335, 337

Eternel Retour, L' (The Eternal Return), 321

Etoile de mer, L' (Starfish), 152

Etrange Monsieur Victor, L' (The Strange Monsieur Victor), 198–199

Eustache, Jean, 392, 393

Events of May 1968, 387–388

Execution of Mary Queen of Scots, The, 36

Express, L', 328–329

Fahrenheit 451, 350

Fairground entertainers, 40–41, 49, 52–53

Fanfan-La-Tulipe, 292

Fanny, 202–203

Fantômas, 67, 68, 69, 368

Fantôme de Moulin-Rouge, Le (The Ghost of the Moulin-Rouge), 133–134

Faraday, Michael, 11

Farrebique, 302, 303

Fauchois, René, 228

Féerie (fairy play), 37

Fellini, F., 352

Femme d'à côté, La (The Woman Next Door), 352

Femme de l'aviateur, La (The Aviator's Wife), 376

Femme de nulle part, La (The Woman from Nowhere), 95, *99*

Femme du boulanger, La (The Baker's Wife), 203, 204

Femme est une femme, Une (A Woman Is a Woman), 384

Femme-flic, La (The Woman Cop), 394

Femme infidèle, La (The Unfaithful Wife), 346

Fernandel, 254, 258

Fescourt, Henri, 71, 83, 127, 185

Fête espagnole, La (Spanish Festival), 96, 146

Feu follet, Le/The Fire Within, 342

Feuillade, Louis, 56, 72–73; 77–78; 82, 83, 128, 129, 133, 187, 192, 367, 368; profile of, 67–71

Feuillère, Edwige, 174, 202

Feu Mathias Pascal (The Late Mathias Pascal), 107

Feyder, Jacques, 108, 118, 128, 135, 174, 193, 204, 232, 238; profile of, *186–191*

Fiancée du pirate, La/A Very Curious Girl, 397

Fièvre (Fever), 96, 98–99, 101

Fille de l'eau, La/Whirlpool of Fate, 136

Fille du puisatier, La, 255

Film, Le, 95

Film criticism: Delluc and, 94; new variety of, 306. *See also* Bazin, André
Film d'art, 60, 63–66, 192
Film exhibition (fixed), 49–51, 53
Filmic narration, 103, 105, 107
Film noir, 280, 286, 300, 304–305, 341, 345, 347
Filmprüfstelle, 270
Films Ajym, 344, 345
Films Albatros, 110, 123, 124, 134
Films du Carosse, Les, 349
Films Marcel Pagnol, Les, 228
Fils de Caroline chérie, Le (Son of Dearest Caroline), 281
Fils improvisé, Le (The Improvised Son), 166
Fin du jour, La (Day's End), 193, 194
Fin du monde, La (The End of the World), 163, 194
Finis terrae (Land's End), 125
Flaherty, Robert, 125
Flitterman-Lewis, Sandy, 196, 358
Florelle, 184
Florey, Robert, 162
Foire aux chimères, La/The Devil and the Angel, 295, 296
Folie du docteur Tube, La (The Insanity of Doctor Tube), 86
Foolish Wives, 136
Forfaiture, 81
Forgerons (The Blacksmiths), 27
Forster, E. M., 61
Fouchardière, Georges de la, 166, 227
Française, La, 146
France, Anatole, 186
France-Actualités-Gaumont, 149
Francis, Eve, 95, *99*, 105, 109, 146
Franco-Film, 216
Franju, Georges, 331, 337, 360, 363–367
Frederix, Jacques, 187. *See also* Feyder, Jacques
French Cancan/Only the French Can, 281, 316
Frères corses, Les (The Corsican Broth..., 116
Fresnay, Pierre, 202, 267, 273,
Freud, S., 178
Froelich, Carl, 162
Fusil photographique, 18

Gabin, Jean, 164, 185, 193, 198, *236*, 237, 239, 265, 281, 285, 304, 316
Gabrio, Gabriel, *205*
Galey, Louis-Emile, 250
Gamma Films, 298
Gance, Abel, 101, 102, 121, 122, 135, 140, 163–164, 165, 194–195, 312, 313, 322, 323; profile of, 84–94
Garbo, Greta, 188
Garçon, François, 231, 252
Gardiens de phare (The Lighthouse Keepers), 120, 125
Garrel, Philippe, 402
Gasnier, Louis, 59
Gastyne, Marco de, 130, 131
Gauguin, 368
Gaumont, Léon, 21, 67, 77–78, 104, 105; profile of, 53–57
Gaumont Company, 56, 82–83, 158, 180, 248–249
Gaumont-Peterson-Poulsen process, 161, 163
Gautier, Théophile, 111–112
Gégauff, Paul, 345, 347
Genina, Augusto, 169
Genou de Claire, Le (Claire's Knee), 376
Gens du voyage, Les (People of the Road), 191
Gervaise, 305
Geule d'amour (Love Face), 198, 235
Gide, André, 199, 296
Giono, Jean, 203
Giraudoux, Jean, 264, 322
Girl from Arizona, The, 78
Giscard d'Estaing, Valéry, 393, 394
Glace à trois faces, La (The Three-Paneled Mirror), 124
Glissements progressifs du plaisir, Les (Successive Slidings of Pleasure), 373
Godard, Jean-Luc, 3, 309, 312, 313, 331, 335, 337, 344, 370, *387*, 390, 391–392; profile of, 379–386
Godden, Rumer, 314
..., 290, 290
...oethe, W. F., 211
Golden Coach, The, 315–316, 349
Golem, The, 148
Gorel, Michel, 241
Gorin, Jean-Pierre, 390, 391

Gorky, Maxim, 229
Goupi-Mains Rouges/It Happened at the Inn, 259, 265, 316, 317
Grand Amour de Beethoven, Un/Beethoven, 195, 206
Grande Illusion, La (Grand Illusion), 136, 230–232, 280, 300, 315, 403
Grandes Manoeuvres, Les/The Grand Maneuver, 280, 294
Grand Jeu, Le (The Great Game), 189, 234
Great Waltz, The, 194
Greed, 88
Gréhan, 59, 60
Grémillon, Jean, 232, 262, 264, 285–286, 287, 331; profile of, 119–120, 198–199; style of, 164–165
Greven, Alfred, 255–259
Gréville, Edmond T., 200, 245
Gribiche, 186
Gribouille, 199, 206
Grierson, John, 176
Griffith, D. W., 60, 86, 98, 103, 126, 352
Grimault, Paul, 360
Grimoin-Samson, Raoul, 48
Grivolas, Claude-Agricol-Louis, 43
Grumback, Jean-Pierre. See Melville, Jean-Pierre
Guernica, 364, 368
Guitry, Lucien, 64, 206–207
Guitry, Sacha, 64, 200, 280, 372; profile of, 205–209, 273–274
Guy, Alice, 54–57, 67, 396
Gyp, 290

Hammon, Joe, 78
Hart, William S., 111, 121
Hatari, 384
Hawks, Howard, 127, 185, 352, 384
Hayakawa, Sessue, 97, 111
Heath, Stephen, 383
Hervil, René, 116
Hessling, Catherine, 136, 137, 139, 166, 176
Heston, Charlton, 381
Hillel-Erlanger, Irene, 146
Hirondelle et la Mésange, L', 118
Hiroshima mon amour (Hiroshima, My Love), 337, 370, 372, 373
His Glorious Night, 174

Histoire d'Adèle H., L' (The Story of Adele H.), 352, 379
Histoire du cinéma (Bardèche/Brasillach), 214
Histoire d'un crime, L' (Story of a Crime), 46
Historical (costume) film, 68, 129–131, 300, 352
Hitchcock, Alfred, 304, 347, 348, 352
Homme aimanté, L' (The Magnetized Man), 58
Homme à la tête de caoutchouc, L' (The Man with the Rubber Head), 38
Homme de nulle part, L' (The Man from Nowhere), 241
Homme du large, L' (Man of the Sea), 104–105
Homme qui aimait les femmes, L' (The Man Who Loved Women), 352
Homme qui ment, L' (The Man Who Lies), 373
Hôtel des Invalides, 363
Hôtel du Nord, 164, 237
Houseman, John, 296
Hugo, Victor, 116, 117
Hugon, André, 161, 291
Huillet, Danièle, 402
Humain, Trop humain (Human, Too Human), 390
Humanité, L', 91–92
Hypergonar (process), 289

Icart, Roger, 113, 322
I. D. H. E. C. See Institut des Hautes Etudes Cinématographiques (Institute for Advanced Study of Cinema)
Immobility, cinematic, 265, 266
Immortelle, L' (The Immortal One), 373
Impressionism, cinematic, 84, 101–102, 107–113, 120, 124
I. N. A. See Institut National de l'Audiovisuel
Ince, Thomas, 98
Inde fantôme, L' (Phantom India), 390
India Song, 374
Indignité nationale, 273–275
Inhumaine, L'/The New Enchantment, 105, 106, 142
Inondation, L' (The Flood), 96, 99

Institut des Hautes Etudes
Cinématographiques (I.D.H.E.C.;
Institute for Advanced Study of
Cinema), 276, 341, 368, 388, 390
Institut National de l'Audiovisuel
(I. N. A.), 394–395, 401
Integrity of the shot, 30, 61–62, 72,
126, 181–182
Intolerance, 320
Intransigent, L', 132
Invitation au voyage, L' (Invitation to the
Voyage), 149, 400
Ironie du destin, L' (The Irony of Fate),
150
Isola brothers, 35

J'Accuse (I Accuse), 86–88, 91, 194
Jaecken, Just, 393
Janssen, Pierre-Jules-César, 18, 26
Jardinier et le petit espiègle, Le/A Little
Trick on the Gardener, 27, 29, 35, 58
Jarre, Maurice, 339
Jasset, Victorin, 66, 67, 187
Jaubert, Maurice, 219, 237, 248
Jazz Singer, The, 159, 166, 169, 201
Jeancolas, Jean-Pierre, 263
Jeanson, Henri, 175, 206, 237, 238,
239, 292, 312
Jenny, 234
Je t'aime, je t'aime (I Love You, I Love
You), 373
Jeux interdits (Forbidden Games), 304
Jeux sont faits, Les (The Chips Are Down),
283
Je vous salue, Marie (Hail Mary), 392
Jocelyn, 118
Jofroi, 203, 228
Joli Mai, Le (The Lovely Month of May),
364
Jolson, Al, 159
Joly, Henri Joseph, 42
Jour de fête (Festival Day), 318
Journal d'un curé de campagne (Diary
of a Country Priest), 322, 324
Jour se lève, Le (Daybreak), 164, 233,
———, 191, 193, 202
———, 69, 367
Juge et l'Assassin, Le (The Judge and the
Assassin), 399
Juge Fayard, Le (Judge Fayard), 394

Jules et Jim (Jules and Jim), 350–351,
352
Juliette ou la clé des songes (Juliette, or the
Key to Dreams), 283–284, 285

Kamenka, Alexandre, 110, 251
Kane, Robert T., 175, 201
Kaplan, Alice Yeager, 214
Kaplan, Nelly, 397
Karina, Anna, 385
Karmitz, Marin, 390, 391
Kast, Pierre, 331, 337
Kaufman, Boris, 217
Kean, 110–111, 142
Keaton, Buster, 174
Kermesse héroique, La/Carnival in
Flanders, 189–190, 191, 234
Kinetoscope, 20–22
King Lear, 392
Kirsanov, Dimitri, 149–151, 331
Kiss, The, 188
Klee, Paul, 384
Kleine, George, 79
Kleist, Heinrich von, 210, 376, 378
Kobelkoff, Nicholas, 41
Korda, Alexander, 202
Kosma, Joseph, 237, 251
Kracauer, Siegfried, 309
Krantz, Charles, 369
Kurys, Diane, 396–397

Lacan, Jacques, 383
Lac aux dames (Lake of Ladies), 199
Lacombe, Gérard, 283
Lacombe, Lucien, 341
Ladri di Biciclette (Bicycle Thieves), 301
Lafitte, Paul, 63, 114, 121–122
Lamartine, Alphonse-Marie, 118
Lancelot du Lac (Lancelot of the Lake), 323
Lang, Fritz, 209, 211, 212, 384
Lara, Louise, 288
La Rochelle, Drieu, 342
Late Mathias Pascal, The (Pirandello),
107, 241
Lavedan, Henri, 64, 116
Léaud, Jean-Pierre, 393
Le Bargy, Charles, 63, 64, 114
Le Chanois, Jean-Paul, 222, 225, 226,
252, 256, 300
Leenhardt, Roger, 312, 313
Lefèvre, René, 217, 229

Left Bank School, 360, 362, 365–367, 370, 374, 375
Léger, Fernand, 88, 105, 139, 142–144
Legrand, Michel, 339, 361
Leprohon, Pierre, 193
Les Misérables (Hugo), 185, 186
Letter from an Unknown Woman, 296
Lettres d'amour (Love Letters), 290
Le Vigan, Robert, 274
Lévi-Strauss, Claude, 9
Leyda, Jay, 109
L'Herbier, Marcel, 94, 110, 122, 140, 176, 182, 195, 241, 283, 289; profile of, 103–107
Liaisons dangereuses, Les (Dangerous Affairs), 336
Liebelei (Flirtation), 210
Lifeboat, 304
Liliom, 211
Linder, Max, 59–61, 62, 66, 84
Lion des Mogols, Le (Lion of the Mogols), 111, 123
Liquid Sky, 401
Lissenko, Natalie, 109, 110, 123
Litvak, Anatole, 209, 210, 212, 263
Location shooting, 56–57, 117, 338
"Loïe Fuller number," 40
Lola, 361
Lola Montès, 1–2, 219, 298, 320
Loulou, 398
Lourié, Eugène, 108, 109
Lozinska, Elisabeth ("Lydou"), 216
Lumière, Antoine, 21, 26
Lumière, Auguste, 21, 28
Lumière, Louis, 21, 58, 117; profile of, 22–26; films of, 28–30; as producer, 30–31
Lumière Cinématographe, 18
Lumière d'été (Summer Light), 264, 265, 268, 285, 286
Lune à un mètre, La/The Astronomer's Dream, 38
Lynch, David, 401

Mac Orlan, Pierre, 235
Madame Bovary, 189
Madame de . . . , 280, 297
Made in U. S. A., 385
Main du diable, La/Carnival of Sinners, 267, 287
Maîtres fous, Les (The Mad Priests), 364

Maldone, 119–120, 184
Mallarmé, Stéphane, 152
Malle, Louis, 307, 337, 338, 355, 357, 379, 389, 390, 393, 398; profile of, 340–343
Mallet-Stevens, Robert, 105
Malraux, André, 300, 302
Maman et la Putain, La (The Mother and the Whore), 393
Mamy, Jean, 274
Mamy Water, 363
Mam'zelle Nitouche, 199
Manèges/The Cheat, 286
Manès, Gina, 184
Mankiewicz, Joseph, 172
Manoir du diable, Le/The Haunted Castle, 35
Manon, 275
Ma Nuit chez Maud (My Night at Maud's), 376, 377
Marais, Jean, 320–321
March, Frederic, 175
Marey, Etienne-Jules, 17–18, 20
Maria Chapdelaine, 193
Mariage de Chiffon, Le (Chiffon's Wedding), 289–290
Mariée était en noir, La (The Bride Wore Black), 352
Marius, 49, 201, 202
Marèze, Janie, 166, 167
Marker, Chris, 360, 364, 365–366, 367, 369, 370
Marquise von O . . . , Die (The Marquise of O . . .), 376, 378
Marseillaise, La, 231–232
Martin, Marcel, 396
Martyre de l'obèse, Le (The Martyr of Obesity), 241
Mater Dolorosa/The Torture of Silence, 86, 91, 128, 194
Maternelle, La (Nursery School), 196–197
Maudet, Christian. See Christian-Jacque
Maudits, Les (The Damned), 304
Maupassant, Guy de, 224, 278, 297, 307
Mauprat, 124, 152
Mauriac, François, 366
Mauvaise Graine (Bad Seed), 211
Mauvaises Herbes/Burning Weeds, 28
Mauvaises Rencontres, Les (Bad Encounters), 307, 335

Max et son chien (Max and his Dog), 61
Max jongleur par amour/A Tantalizing Young Lady, 61
Max joue le drame (Max Plays at Drama), 61
Max victime du quinquina (Max and the Quinquina), 61
May, Joe, 211
Mayerling, 212
Méliès, Gaston, 33, 78
Méliès, Georges, 30, 54, 58; profile of, 32–40
Méliès, Henri, 33
Méliès, Louis, 32–33
Melodramas, 66–71, 128
Mélomane, Le (The Melomaniac), 38
Melville, Jean-Pierre, 356, 367, 384; profile of, 331–335
Menaces (Threats), 245–246
Ménilmontant, 150
Mépris, Le (Contempt), 384
Mercanton, Louis, 117
Méré, Charles, 161
Merimée, Prosper, 186, 392
Merveilleuse Vie de Jeanne d'Arc, La (The Wondrous Life of Joan of Arc), 130, 131
Metro-Goldwyn-Mayer, 160, 188, 194, 289
Miarka, 117
Miéville, Anne-Marie, 391
Million, Le (The Million), 170, *171*
Miou-Miou, 394
Miracle des loups, Le (Miracle of the Wolves), 130
Miranda, Isa, 304
Mirande, Yves, 176, 177
Misérables, Les (Hugo), 185, 186
Mistons, Les (The Brats), 349
Mitry, Jean, 240
Modernists and modernism, 139–154, 177–179
Modot, Gaston, 174, 178, 225
Moins de Trente Ans, Les ("The Under Thirties"), 204–206
Moisson, Auguste, 30
Moisson, Eugène, 22, 24
Moi un noir (Me, a Black), 336
Molinaro, Edouard, 360
Molnàr, Ferenc, 211
Mon Chien, 364
Monde du silence, Le (The Silent World), 341

Moniteur de la Photographie, Le, 25
Mon Oncle (My Uncle), 319, 320
Montage, 126, 301, 364, 365, 375
Montfort, Sylvia, 356
Morand, Paul, 124
Moreau, Jeanne, 341–342, 379
Morgan, Michèle, 285
Morgenstern, Ignace, 349
Morgenstern, Madeleine, 349
Mort du duc de Guise, La/Assassination of the Duc de Guise, 64, 66, 116
Mort du soleil, La (Death of the Sun), 101
Mort en fraude/Fugitive in Saigon, 336
Mouchette, 394
Mosjoukine, Ivan, 107, 110, 111, 123, 184
Motion Picture Patents Company (M. P. P. C.), 53, 79
Moussinac, Léon, 91–92, 122, 217, 221
Movement: analysis of, 9; optical synthesis of, 9, 11–16; phenomenon of, 16–18
Moyens métrages, 182, 217
Mozhukhin, Ivan, 109. *See also* Mosjoukine, Ivan
Muriel, ou le temps d'un retour (Muriel, or the Time of a Return), 372, 373
Murnau, F. W., 30
Murphy, Dudley, 142
Mussolini, Benito, 173, 230
Muybridge, Eadweard, 17–18, 20
My Dinner with André, 342
Mystère du chateau de dés (Mystery of the Chateau of Dice), 152
Mystère Picasso (The Picasso Mystery), 287

Nalpas, Louis, 86, 96
Nana, 136–137, *139*, 281, 289, 292
Napierkowska, Stacia de, 146
Napoléon vu par Abel Gance (Napoleon, as seen by Abel Gance), 87, 91–93, 130, 153, 182, 195
Natan, Bernard, 165
Natanson, Jacques, 206, 210, 251
Nathalie Granger, 374
Native Son, 296
Naturalism, 46–47, 68–69, 116. *See also* Pictorialist naturalism
Néa, 397
Neorealism, 301–302; Italian, 303, 304, *305*
Neveux, Georges, 285

New Wave, see *Nouvelle vague*
Nick Carter, 66
Nickelodeon, 78, 80
Niepce, Isidore, 10–11
Niepce, Joseph-Nicéphore, 10
Nimirowsky, Irène, 193
Nimoy, Leonard, 403
1940, 189
Noailles, Vicomte de, 152, 153, 178
Noé, Yvan, 174
Noël-Noël, 281, 304
Noiret, Philippe, 356
Notes on Cinematography (Bresson), 322
Nounez, J.-L., 218
*Nous sommes tous des assassins (We Are All
Murderers)*, 300
*Nouveaux Messieurs, Les (The New
Gentlemen)*, 188, 234
*Nouvelle Mission de Judex, La (Judex's
New Mission)*, 70
Nouvelle vague (new wave), 328–330,
337–338, 342, 345, 354–355, 356,
360, 372, 380, 393, 398
Novarro, Ramon, 174, 188
*Nuit du carrefour, La (Night of the
Crossroads)*, 227
Nuit est à nous, La (The Night Is Ours),
162
Nuit et Brouillard (Night and Fog), 369,
370
Nuit fantastique, La (The Fantastic Night),
283
Nuits de feu/The Living Corpse, 195

Occupation cinema, 250, 262–271, 299
October Group, 222–225, 229, 289
*On a volé un homme (A Man Has Been
Stolen)*, 211
*On n'enterre pas le dimanche (They Don't
Have Funerals on Sunday)*, 336
On purge bébé (Baby Gets a Laxative), 166,
176
Ophuls, Marcel, 1
Ophuls, Max, 1–2, 206, 248, 251, 263,
293, 295, *297*, 312, 313, 352, 355,
361; profile of, 209–212, 296–298
Or des Mers, L' (Gold of the Seas), 195
Orfeu Negro (Black Orpheus), 336
Orphée (Orpheus), 321
O. R. T. F., 394
Ostraneniye, 310
Otages, Les (The Hostages), 245, 246

Othello (Shakespeare), 238
"Oval Portrait, The" (Poe), 124

Pabst, G. W., 168, 170, 209, 212
Page, Louis, 301
Pagnol, Marcel, 49, 210, 228, 241, 248,
255, 293, 301, 334; profile of, 200–
206
Palance, Jack, 384
Panique (Panic), 280
Parade, 319
Paramount Pictures, 80, 175, 177, 201–
202, 403
*Parapluies de Cherbourg, Les (The
Umbrellas of Cherbourg)*, 361
Parents terribles, Les/The Storm Within,
310
Paris, 8, 32, 138
*Paris nous appartient (Paris Belongs to
Us)*, 337–338, 374, 393
Paris qui dort/The Crazy Ray, 133, 134
Parlor, Bedroom, and Bath, 174
Parrain, Brice, 384
Parti Communiste Français (P. C. F.),
220–226, 229
*Partie de campagne, Une/A Day in the
Country*, 224, 300
*Partie d'écarté/Friendly Party in the Garden
of Lumière*, 28
Passeur, Steve, 206
*Passion Béatrice, La (The Passion of
Beatrice)*, 399
*Passion de Jeanne d'Arc, La (The Passion
of Joan of Arc)*, 130, 131
Pasteur, 122, 207
Pathé, Charles, 41–44, 52–54, 64–65
Pathé, Emile, 43
Pathé, Jacques, 43
Pathé, Théophile, 43
Pathé Consortium, 82, 122–124, 195
Pathé Frères, 43–46, 53, 58, 67, 78–80,
82, 158
Pathé-Natan company, 165, 166, 173,
180, 223
Pattes blanches (White Paws), 286
Patrouille de choc (Shock Patrol), 336
Paul, Robert W., 21, 35, 44
Paulin, Gaston, 15
Pauline à la plage (Pauline at the Beach),
377
Pays sans étoiles (Country without Stars),
283

Peau d'âne (Donkey Skin), 361
Peau douce, La (Soft Skin), 352
Pêche aux poissons rouges (Fishing for Goldfish), 27
Penseur, Le (The Thinker), 117
Pension Mimosas (Hotel Mimosa), 189–190, 234, 237, 238
Pépé le Moko, 193, 198, 206
Perceval le Gallois, 376
Père tranquille, Le/Mr. Orchid, 281
Périnal, Georges, 119
Perles de la couronne, Les (The Pearls of the Crown), 208
Perret, Léonce, 71–73, 84, 117, 126
Personal, 58
Petain, Philippe, 231, 247, 254, 330
Petit Café, Le (The Little Cafe), 131
Petite Lise, La (Little Lisa), 164–165, 166, 167, 198
Petite Marchande d'allumettes, La/The Little Match Girl, 137
Petit Soldat, Le (The Little Soldier), 381–382, 384–385
Phèdre (Racine), 7
Phénakistoscope, 12, 13–14
Philipe, Gérard, 279, 282, 283, 284, 292
Photogénie (Delluc), 96
Photogénie, 142
Photogénie Mécanique, 142
Photography, development of, 9–11
Pialat, Maurice, 392, 398, 400
Picabia, Francis, 133, 143, 144
Picasso, Pablo, 368
Piccoli, Michel, 394
Pickpocket, 323
Pictorialist naturalism, 113–120, 129.
   See also Naturalism
Pierrot le fou, 384
Pirandello, Luigi, 107, 375
Place des Cordeliers à Lyon, La (The Place des Cordeliers at Lyon), 27
Plaisir, Le/House of Pleasure, 297
Planer, Franz (Frank), 212
Plateau, Joseph, 11–13
Playtime, 319, 320
Ploquin, Raoul, 174, 198, 235, 249
Poe, Edgar Allen, 124
Poil de Carotte (Carrot Head), 192
Pointe-Courte, La, 355–357, 359, 360
Poirier, Léon, 117, 195
Police, 398

Poligny, Serge de, 174, 283, 321
Pommer, Erich, 211
Pompidou, Georges, 393
Pons, Maurice, 349
Pontcarral, colonel d'Empire (Pontcarral, Colonel of the Empire), 267–268
Poor Pierrot, 15
Porte des Lilas/Gates of Paris, 294
Portes de la nuit, Les (The Gates of the Night), 284, 285
Postman Always Rings Twice, The (Cain), 241
Pottier, Richard, 281, 311
Pouctal, Henri, 65, 83, 114, 118
Prédal, René, 392–393, 396
Préjean, Albert, 174, 184
Première Sortie d'un collegien, La (The School Boy's First Outing), 59
Prénom: Carmen (First Name: Carmen), 392
Preparez vos mouchoirs (Get Out Your Handkerchiefs), 392
Pretty Baby, 342
Prévert, Jacques, 66, 164, 191, 229, 233, 251, 256, 259, 260, 264, 275, 289, 366; profile of, 221–225, 284–285, 363–364
Prince, 60
Princesse de Clèves, La, 8
Prix de beauté/Miss Europe, 169
Prix et Profits (Prices and Profits), 223
Protozanov, Yakov, 109, 133
Puits fantastique, Le/The Enchanted Well, 38
Punk hyperrealism, 400, 401
Pushover, 381

Quai des brumes/Port of Shadows, 233, 235–236, 239, 260
Quai des Orfèvres/Jenny L'Amour, 286, 287
Quatorze Juillet (Bastille Day), 173
Quatre Cents Coups, Les (The Four Hundred Blows), 337, 348, 349–350, 400
Que la bête meure/This Man Must Die, 347
Queneau, Raymond, 342, 363, 366
Quine, Richard, 381

Racine, Jean, 7
Radiguet, Raymond, 281, 290
Rafles sur la ville (Raids in the City), 296

Raimu, 199, 202
Ravel, Gaston, 187
Ray, Man, 134, 139, 141, 143, 151–152
Rayon vert, Le/Summer, 377, 378
Réalisme poétique, 233, 238–240, 241, 242, 260, 264, 365
Rebatet, Lucien, 215
Red and the Black, The (Stendhal), 21
Reflet de Claude Mercour, Le, 192
Regain/Harvest, 203–205
Régent, Roger, 263, 264
Reggiani, Serge, 297
Règle du jeu, La (Rules of the Game), 220, 227, 232, 246, 280, 315, 316, 375
Reine Elizabeth, La (Queen Elizabeth), 80
Réjane, 117
Remorques/Stormy Waters, 285
Renard, Gabrielle, 135, 136
Renard, Jules, 192
Renaud, Madelaine, *197*, 285
Rendez-vous le juillet (July Reunion), 317
Renoir, Jean, 3, 66, 84, 100, 108, 154, *139*, 161, 176, 185, 186, 189, 215, 224, 236, 241, 246, 256, 263, 281, 289, 292, 293, 300, 301, 312, 313, 331, 341, 349, 350, 352, 355, 374, 375, 391, 392, 403; profile of, 135– 138, 165–169, 226–232, 314–317; style of, 181, 182; social themes of, 220
Renoir, Pierre-Auguste, 135, 136
Repas de bébé (Feeding the Baby), 27, *29*
Requin, Le (The Swindler), 162, 169
Resnais, Alain, 208–209, 287, 331, 337, 355, 360, 364, 365, *371*, 375, 397; profile of, 367–373
Retour à la raison, Le (The Return to Reason), 141, 151
Retour de Martin Guerre, Le (The Return of Martin Guerre), 399
Revenant, Le/The Ghost and the Candle, aka *The Apparition*, 37–38
Reynaud, Emile, 9, 14–16
Richard-Willm, Pierre, 189
Richebé, Mme. Léon, 49
Richebé, Roger, 49, 166, 256
Rideau cramoisi, Le/The Crimson Curtain, 307
Riefenstahl, Leni, 214
Rien que des mensonges (Nothing But Lies), 177
Rien que les heures (Only the Hours), 176

Rigadin, 60
River, The, 314
Rivette, Jacques, 309, 312, 337, 344, 397; profile of, 339–340, 374–376
Robbe-Grillet, Alain, 360, 365, 366, 367, 370, 371, 373
Robert-Houdin, Jean-Eugène, 33, 34
Rodin, Auguste, 117
Roget, Peter Mark, 11
Rohmer, Eric, 312, 337, 347, 374, 379; profile of, 339–340, 376–378
Roi de coeur, Le (King of Hearts), 339, 379
Roma Città aperta/Open City, 301
Romance, Viviane, 254
Roman d'un mousse, Le (Story of a Cabin Boy), 71–72
Roman d'un tricheur, Le/The Story of a Cheat, 207–208, 209
Ronde, La (Rondelay), 296–297
Ronet, Maurice, 341, 342
Rosay, Françoise, 185, 187–188, 189, 190, 233, 234
Rose-France, 104
Rossellini, Roberto, 301, 352
Rotha, Paul, 362
Rouch, Jean, 336, 363, 364
Roue, La (The Wheel), 87, 88–91, 103, 121, 122, 142
Rouge et le Noir, Le (The Red and the Black), 281, *282*, 283, 290
Round Midnight, 402
Rouquier, Georges, 302, 360, 362
Roussou, Mateï, 115
Route est belle, La (The Road Is Beautiful), 162, 166
Royaume des fées, Le (In the Kingdom of the Fairies), 37
Rue sans nom, La (Street without a Name), 241
Ruiz, Raoul, 323, 402

Sacré d'Edouard VII, Le (The Coronation of Edward VII), 35–36
Sadoul, Georges, 14, 41
Saint-Saëns, Camille, 64
Salaire de la peur, Le/The Wages of Fear, 286
Sallès-Gomes, P. E., 217
Sand, George, 124
Sang des bêtes, Le (Blood of the Beasts), 366

Sang d'un poete, Le (Blood of a Poet), 93, 178, 179, 321
Sans lendemain (No Tomorrow), 206, 211
Sans toit ni loi/Vagabond, 359
Sarah and Son, 175–176
Sartre, Jean-Paul, 235, 275, 283
Satie, Eric, 143
Saut à la couverture (Blanket Toss), 27
Sauve qui peut (la vie)/Every Man for Himself, 391, 392
Sauvetage en rivière (Rescue on the River), 35
Schnitzler, Arthur, 210
Schufftan, Eugen, 212
Scott, Ridley, 401
Scribe, Eugène, 115
Semprun, Jorge, 372
Serreau, Coline, 397, 403
Sesonske, Alexander, 137
Séverin-Mars, 192
Shakespeare, William, 210, 285, 392
Shattuck, Roger, 32
Short subjects, 362–363
Shot-reverse shot, 127, 137
Sibirskaia, Nadia, 150, 151
Signe du lion, Le (The Sign of Leo), 337, 376
Signora di tutti, La (Everybody's Lady), 211
Sigurd, Jacques, 286, 312
Si l'empereur savait ça, 174
Silence de la mer, Le (The Silence of the Sea), 332–333
Silence est d'or, Le (Silence Is Golden), 294
Simenon, Georges, 227
Simon, Michel, 167, 168, 184, 193, 218, 228
Simon, Simone, 297
Siodmak, Robert, 209, 212
Sirk, Douglas, 347
Si tous les gars du monde (If All the Guys in the World), 300
6 1/2 × 11, 124
Six juin à l'aube, Le (June Sixth at Dawn), 286
Sleep, 310
Smith, George Albert, 44, 58
Socialist party (S. F. I. O.), 226
Société Cinématographique de Auteurs et Gens de Lettres, 65, 114, 116
Société des Films Marcel Pagnol, La, 202

Soigne ton gauche (Watch Your Left), 318
Sologne, Madeleine, 295, 321
Sortie d'usine/Workers Leaving the Lumière Factory, 27, 28
Sound, effect of, 179–181
Soupault, Philippe, 151
Souriante Madame Beudet, La (The Smiling Madame Beudet), 147–148, 182
Sous le soleil de Satan (Under Satan's Sun), 398, 400
Sous les toits de Paris (Under the Roofs of Paris), 132, 169–170, 171, 173
Spaak, Charles, 164, 198, 230, 233, 256, 258, 286, 403; profile of, 189–191
Spectre vert, Le, 174
Stampfer, Simon, 12
Stanford, Leland, 17–18
Stasis, illusion of, 11, 12, 13
Statues meurent aussi, Les (Statues Also Die), 369
Stavisky, 372–373
Stendhal, 21, 278, 281, 282, 290, 292
Sternberg, Jacques, 373
Straub, Jean-Marie, 402
Stroheim, Erich von, 88, 136, 245, 295
Subway, 400
Surrealists and Surrealism, 148, 150–151, 218, 366
Sylvie et le fantôme (Sylvia and the Phantom), 283, 291
Symphonie fantastique, La (The Fantastic Symphony), 257, 291
Symphonie pastorale, La (The Pastoral Symphony), 295, 296

Taine, H. A., 68
Talbot, William Henry Fox, 11
Taris, 217
Tati, Jacques, 283, 311, 312, 318–322
Tavernier, Bertrand, 392, 399, 402
Tedesco, Jean, 137, 142, 150
Television, 395–396, 403
Temps des cerises, Le (The Time of Cherries), 226
Tendre ennemie, La (The Sweet Enemy), 206, 211
Testament d'Orphée, Le (The Testament of Orpheus), 313
Tête contre les murs, La/The Keepers, 337, 366
Thalberg, Irving, 88

Thèmes et variations, 149
Theory of the Film (Kracauer), 309
Thérèse Desqueyroux, 366
Thérèse Raquin, 186
Thiher, Allen, 231, 238
37, 2 le matin/Betty Blue, 393
36 Fillette (Girl's 36), 400
Thomas l'imposteur (Thomas the Imposter), 367
Thorez, Maurice, 226
Three Men and a Baby, 403
Threepenny Opera, 170
Tire au flanc, 137–138
Tirez sur le pianiste (Shoot the Piano Player), 350, 352
Tobis Klangfilm, 161, 169, 189, 190, 191
Tolstoy, Leo, 195
Toni, 228, 241, 301
Tonnelier, Le (The Barrelmaker), 362
Tonnerre, Le (Thunder), 122
Topaze, 201, 202
Tour au large, Un (A Sea Journey), 119
Tourneur, Maurice, 267
Toute Sa Vie (All Her Life), 175, 176
Tout va bien (Everything's OK), 390, 391
Tradition of Quality, 258, 277, 278–284, 286, 287, 292, 298, 300, 313, 324, 364, 365, 398, 399, 402
Trafic, 319
Trans-Europe Express, 373
Trauner, Alexandre, 237, 251
Travailleurs de la mer, Les (Those Who Work at Sea), 117
Traversée de Paris, La/Four Bags Full, 291
Tricheurs, Les (The Cheaters), 288
Trintignant, Jean-Louis, 394
Triumph des Willens, Der (Triumph of the Will), 214
Trois Hommes et un couffin (Three Men and a cradle), 403
Trois Masques, Les (The Three Masks), 161–162, 291
Trou, Le (The Hole), 316
Trou dans le mur, Un (A Hole in the Wall), 176
Troyes, Chrétien de, 376, 378
Truffaut, François, 98, 281, 290, 309, 312, 313, 316, 331, 333, 337, 343, 344, 360, 361, 370, 374, 379, 381, 388, 398, 399, 400; profile of, 348–355

Tsukerman, Slava, 401
Twentieth-Century Fox, 175, 211, 403
Tzara, Tristan, 141

Une chante, l'autre pas, L' (One Sings, the Other Doesn't), 359
Une Femme ou deux (One Woman or Two), 402
Unholy Night, The, 174
United Artists, 175
Universal (studio), 403
Universum Film Atkien Gesellschaft (UFA), 173–174, 255

Vacances de Monsieur Hulot, Les (Mr. Hulot's Holiday), 318, 319
Vadim, Roger, 335–337
Vaillant-Couturier, Paul, 225
Valentin, Albert, 285
Valseuses, Les/Going Places, 392
Vampires, Les, 69
Vanel, Charles, 184
Van Gogh, 368
Varda, Agnès, 355–360, 363, 396
Vercors, 332
Verdun, visions d'histoire (Verdun, Visions of History), 118, 119
Verité, La (The Truth), 286, 287–288
Verkaufte Braut, Die (The Bartered Bride), 210
Vichy government, 247, 251–254
Vie, Une (A Life), 307
Vie de famille, La (Family Life), 400
Vie est à nous, La (Life Is Ours aka People of France), 224–225, 226
Vie est une longue fleuve tranquille, La/ Life Is a Long Quiet River, 391
Vie privée/A Very Private Affair, 342
Vie sans joie, Une (A Life without Joy), 136
Vie telle qu'elle est, La ("Life as It Really Is"), 68, 114, 129
Vigne, Daniel, 399, 402
Vigo, Eugène Bonaventure de, 215–216
Vigo, Jean, 93, 260, 263, 300, 350, 352, 392; profile of, 215–220
Vilmorin, Louise de, 297–298
Viot, Jacques, 237
Visiteurs du soir, Les (The Night Visitors), 259, 264, 265, 267, 270, 283, 284
Viva Maria, 338, 342, 379

Vivement dimanche/Confidentially Yours, 352
Vivre sa vie/My Life to Live, 383, 384
Voleur, Le/The Thief of Paris, 343
Volkov, Alexander, 108, 109, 110
Voltige (Horseback Jumping), 27
Voyage à travers l'impossible/An Impossible Voyage, 38
Voyage au Congo, 199
Voyage dans la lune, Le (A Trip to the Moon), 38
Voyage imaginaire, Le (The Imaginary Voyage), 134

Wachter, Lt. L., 16–17
Wagner, Richard, 144
Walker, Michael, 347
Walt Disney Company, 403
Warhol, Andy, 310
Warner Brothers, 159, 175, 201
Wayne, John, 381
Weaver, Sigourney, 402
Weekend, 386
Wegener, Paul, 148
Weill, Kurt, 170
Welles, Orson, 126, 172
Werther, 211
Western Electric Company, 158–159, 161
Western films, 78

Wilde, Oscar, 112
Wilder, Billy, 209, 211
Wild Palms (Faulkner), 356
Williamson, James, 58
William Tell, 16
Winkler, Max, 255
Wood, Robin, 347
World's Fair (Paris): (1900), 48, 157–158; (1937), 214
Wright, Richard, 296

Yermoliev. *See* Ermoliev
Yeux sans visage, Les (Eyes without a Face aka *The Horror Chamber of Dr. Faustus),* 366
Yoshiwara, 211

Z, 394
Zay, Jean, 249
Zazie dans le métro (Zazie in the Subway), 342
Zecca, Ferdinand, 44–46, 67
Zéro de conduite, 93, 216, 217–218, *219,* 350
Zoëtrope, 12–*13*
Zola, Emile, 107, 115, 116, 136, 186, 236, 278, 281, 292, 305
Zukor, Adolph, 80
Zweig, Stephan, 296